THE WALL AND THE GATE

THE
WALL
AND
THE
GATE

Israel,   Palestine,
and the Legal Battle
for Human Rights

MICHAEL
SFARD

TRANSLATED BY
MAYA JOHNSTON

Metropolitan Books
Henry Holt and Company   New York

Metropolitan Books
Henry Holt and Company
Publishers since 1866
175 Fifth Avenue
New York, New York 10010
www.henryholt.com

Metropolitan Books® and m® are registered trademarks of
Macmillan Publishing Group, LLC.

Library of Congress Cataloging-in-Publication data

Names: Sefarad, Mikha'el, author. | Johnston, Maya, translator.
Title: The wall and the gate : Israel, Palestine, and the legal battle for human rights /
    Michael Sfard ; translated by Maya Johnston.
Description: New York : Metropolitan Books, Henry Holt and Company, 2017. | Includes
    bibliographical references and index.
Identifiers: LCCN 2017000822| ISBN 9781250122704 (hardcover : alk. paper) |
    ISBN 9781250122711 (electronic book : alk. paper)
Subjects: LCSH: Palestinian Arabs—Civil rights—West Bank. | Palestinian Arabs—Civil
    rights—Gaza Strip. | Human rights—West Bank. | Human rights—Gaza Strip. | Law
    and geography—West Bank. | Law and geography—Gaza Strip.
Classification: LCC KMM746 .S44 2017 | DDC 342.569408/50899274—dc23
LC record available at https://lccn.loc.gov/2017000822

Research for this book was supported in part by the Open Society Fellowship, which is funded and
administered by the Open Society Foundations. The opinions expressed herein are the author's own
and do not necessarily express the views of the Open Society Foundations.

Our books may be purchased in bulk for promotional, educational, or business use. Please contact
your local bookseller or the Macmillan Corporate and Premium Sales Department at (800) 221-7945,
extension 5442, or by e-mail at MacmillanSpecialMarkets@macmillan.com.

First Edition 2018

Designed by Kelly S. Too

Printed in the United States of America

1 3 5 7 9 10 8 6 4 2

For my parents, Anna and Leon, who raised me to be critical
of the centers of power and respect all human beings,
For my clients, who allow me the privilege of
taking part in a just struggle,
and for my opponents, thanks to whom
my work has become my mission.

For Romi and Roee, who are discovering that
the world is full of walls and learning that the
meaning of life is dismantling them,
And for Nirith, my partner in everything,
who means more to me than language can say.

CONTENTS

The snow has stopped and the streets are basking in the pleasant New York winter sun, which is calling me to leave the apartment we have rented in a beautiful Brooklyn neighborhood and come outside. But at this moment my heart is in the East. As I write, thousands of police are evacuating the settler outpost of Amona, east of Ramallah in the West Bank. Israeli security forces and Jewish settlers are in combat on land belonging to my clients, Palestinians from nearby villages. The settlers invaded the land about twenty years ago and have forcibly controlled and lived on it ever since. The government and the military, officially charged with protecting Palestinians from the theft of their land, not only failed to lift a finger but did whatever they could to help the offenders.

In long and complicated legal proceedings that began nine years earlier, in 2008, I represented the victims of this landgrab on behalf of Yesh Din, an Israeli human rights organization. In late 2014 we won our case and the High Court of Justice ordered the evacuation of the intruders. The government tried everything in its power to get around the judgment, but thanks to Yesh Din's determination, its efforts failed. And so the day of the return of my clients' land had arrived.

It should be a day of joy and hope, but with the gratification comes deep concern. I know that after the evacuation there will be a long Sisyphean battle to make the victory a reality, to secure for the landowners free access to their land. The fear that the army will find a way to deny or restrict their access is based on the long experience of the lawyers and

NGOs who defend the rights of Palestinians. There is also the fear of hate crimes by settler extremists, a grave threat that has grown increasingly widespread and to which the authorities have responded with shameful indifference. And more: the government is likely to approve the construction of a great many housing units, perhaps a whole new community, for the evacuees. A new settlement means another thrust of the colonial knife into the heart of the West Bank. Israel's taxpayers will pick up the tab for this new settlement—that is, my family and I will put up the money for the gifts the government will shower on the settlers, all to appease them for the rare occurrence of the law having actually been enforced.

This is why my satisfaction that the invasion of my clients' land is finally ending is tempered by unease about the long-term outcome of the achievement.

THIS BOOK WAS conceived on the Tel Aviv–Jerusalem highway. The questions it covers and the insights it explores absorbed me during the hundreds of hours I clocked in commuting to my home or office in Tel Aviv after hearings in Jerusalem's High Court of Justice. On the way there I would be immersed in the details of the case, the arguments I was planning to make. But coming back, traveling the twists and turns of the Jerusalem hills, unwinding after the tension before and during the hearing, I would find myself engaged in professional soul-searching.

As a human rights lawyer representing people living under occupation whose civil rights have been suspended for fifty years, does my work make any difference? Does it in some cases even cause harm? Is it possible, in this sort of context, to bring real and significant social change through legal advocacy? Or does the fundamental nature of the judiciary prevent it from serving as an engine for change in certain situations? Can such change only happen outside the courtroom? And worse: Am I a pawn in the greatest swindle of the Israeli occupation, just passing its half-century mark, by helping to prop up the illusion of a regime that has mechanisms and laws in place to prevent arbitrary acts, contain state violence, and thwart injustice?

Usually, somewhere near Ben Gurion International Airport, after about half an hour of back-and-forth between contradictory but equally convincing arguments, I would give up on my internal debate. I would tell myself that I have no definitive answers and beating myself up over it will accomplish nothing. One day, I promised myself, I'll take some time off and devote myself to exploring these issues.

The Wall and the Gate is the result of that exploration, made possible by a grant from the Open Society Foundations. Dozens of Israeli lawyers, veteran and young, as well as peace and human rights activists helped by sharing their memories and insights with me. I interviewed many of them and corresponded with others. I relied heavily on books and reporting from the relevant period and of course on decisions and judgments given by the High Court of Justice. Using all of these, I have tried to tell the story—or at least part—of the legal struggle against the occupation.

The chapters that follow recount eight major legal battles against practices that entail widespread violations of Palestinian human rights in the Occupied Territories. Those practices have shaped the lived reality of millions of victims: deporting Palestinian militants, creating Jewish settlements, using torture in interrogations, building the separation barrier, constructing unauthorized outposts, imposing administrative detention, demolishing the homes of families of suspected terrorists, and assassinations (also known as "targeted killings"). Each of these struggles involved dozens and sometimes hundreds of court proceedings. I hoped that the cumulative experience of these campaigns would yield some practical insights into the possibilities and limitations of using litigation as a tool for protecting human rights, primarily in the context of military occupation but also in other settings.

A few cautionary remarks: First, many occupation-related challenges that were brought to the High Court were left out of this book, including the fight against land seizures and confiscation, revocation of Palestinian residency, prevention of family unification, lack of accountability for perpetrators of attacks on Palestinians, restrictions on Palestinian movement within the territories, use of prohibited methods of warfare, and violation of due process rights in the military court system.

Second, I am not an impartial observer and my book makes no claim to detachment. These struggles are described from the point of view of the human rights community and particularly of human rights lawyers, some of whom are my friends. I have been personally involved in some of the battles included here, and I have a view on those in which I did not take part—a view not spared the reader.

Finally, since this book focuses on the Israeli legal struggle, it naturally refers to the work of Israeli lawyers, both Jewish and Palestinian. Regretfully, the invaluable work of West Bank and Gazan Palestinian lawyers and human rights organizations is largely absent, although they have applied their devotion and dedication to fighting the occupation with legal tools for decades. Their story warrants its own book.

As I was writing, Israel was changing. The antidemocratic, nationalist, even racist currents that have always been present grew significantly stronger. Not a day went by without a new and more heinous attack on the basic freedoms that are the foundation of any democracy. Not a week passed without the government and its allies spewing incitement against human rights and peace activists and civil society organizations simply because they are critical of its policies. Israel's democratic space has shrunk and the discrimination against its Palestinian citizens has expanded.

At the same time, the world was also changing. Syrian refugees were knocking on Europe's doors, and xenophobia and nationalism flourished in many parts of the continent; a majority of British citizens chose to leave the European Union; American voters elected Donald Trump president after a campaign filled with nativist, misogynist, and racist rhetoric and attacks on humanism in the shape of support for torture and compiling a registry of Muslims. The most basic values of the Enlightenment, values we never imagined would need defending in our lifetime, are under assault. The world looks poised to turn its back on global liberalism and return to conservative, nationalist tribalism.

One of the main arenas for the struggle over any society's character—and therefore that of humanity—is the court. It is no wonder, then, that only a week after Trump's inauguration, American human rights lawyers were flooding federal courts all over the country with applications to quash executive orders the new president had signed. These days bring great challenges to human rights activists in general and human rights lawyers in particular. The role of lawyers in the struggles ahead requires familiarity with the tools that they have. I hope this book will contribute to the understanding of litigation as a tool for social change.

THE WALL AND THE GATE

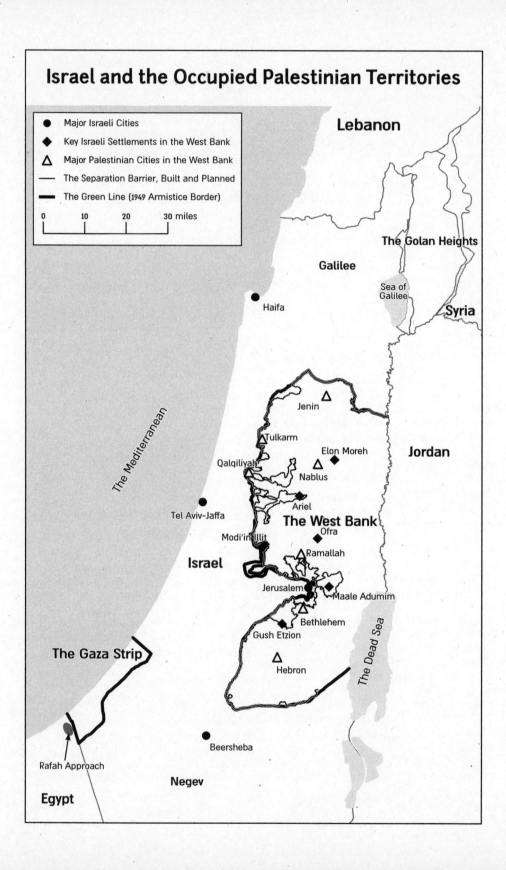

Israel and the Occupied Palestinian Territories

Legend:
- ● Major Israeli Cities
- ◆ Key Israeli Settlements in the West Bank
- △ Major Palestinian Cities in the West Bank
- — The Separation Barrier, Built and Planned
- ▬ The Green Line (1949 Armistice Border)

0   10   20   30 miles

Lebanon

The Golan Heights

Galilee

Sea of Galilee

● Haifa

Syria

△ Jenin

△ Tulkarm

Elon Moreh ◆

Jordan

Qalqiliyah

△ Nablus

◆ Ariel

The West Bank

● Tel Aviv-Jaffa

Ofra ◆

Modi'in Illit

△ Ramallah

Israel

Jerusalem ●

◆ Maale Adumim

△ Bethlehem

◆ Gush Etzion

The Mediterranean

△ Hebron

The Dead Sea

The Gaza Strip

↑ Rafah Approach

● Beersheba

Egypt

Negev

The Zufin Gate

The thick olive orchard was breathtakingly beautiful—twelve hundred dunams of fertile land, covered in a blanket of that special green hue of mature olive trees. We were standing on a slightly higher hill, behind the gas station that overlooks these vast orchards. A researcher from the Israeli human rights organization HaMoked translated what I said into Arabic for our two hosts and then their responses back into Hebrew for me. There is something very soothing about the sight of sturdy olive trees gleaming in the September sun, even if deep down you know the sight is illusory. The trees look strong, firmly rooted in the land. Some have been there for dozens of years. Others, we were earnestly told, for hundreds. But the experience of recent months had shown that an olive tree that had stood in place for centuries, providing income for generations of people, could be uprooted in the space of five minutes. Seven minutes if its roots stubbornly held on to the rock.

At the foot of the gas station, between the station itself and the first row of olive trees below, stood the separation fence. It is Israel's largest national project since the national water carrier, an ambitious waterworks system that brings water from the Sea of Galilee in the north all the way to the arid Negev desert in the south. Once, we rerouted water for hundreds of miles across the country to make diverse farming in the desert possible. Now, we put up hundreds of miles of fencing that keeps farmers from their land. On the excuse that the fence—in fact a barrier system consisting of fences, walls, ducts, patrol roads, and watchtowers—is a security measure, meant to block would-be attackers from the West Bank from reaching Israeli city centers, Prime Minister Ariel Sharon chose an intrusive, invasive route.

Most of the fence is not located on the Green Line, the boundary demarcating the 1949 armistice between Israel and Jordan, but penetrates deep into the occupied territory of the West Bank, effectively annexing huge areas to the "Israeli side." Tracing the route (approved by the Israeli government) reveals a pattern that exposes the true objective of the fence: whenever it nears a Jewish settlement or a cluster of settlements, the fence balloons, encircling the area and creating an enclave. But these enclaves do not just swallow the built-up parts of the settlements, they also gobble up a massive amount of surrounding land. The map that emerges is the fulfillment of Israel's colonial fantasy: maximum land, minimum Palestinians.

Eretz Israel–Palestine, which was split into two geopolitical units in the 1949 armistice—one stretching from the Jordan River to the Green Line (the West Bank) and the other from the Green Line to the Mediterranean Sea (the State of Israel)—and then reunited in 1967, has been divided again: today, the two units run from the Jordan River to the fence, and from the fence to the Mediterranean. The area that is locked between the Green Line and the fence, which has come to be called "the seam zone," is governed by a shameful permit system that allows Jews to travel freely while Palestinians need special permission to remain there or just pass through. The permit system is painfully reminiscent of South Africa's pass laws that policed travel by black people through "white" areas during the country's apartheid years. Israeli human rights organizations, like HaMoked and the Association for Civil Rights in Israel, which hired me to represent communities harmed by the fence, consider it a crime, both legally and morally. The International Court of Justice ruled in a 2004 advisory opinion that the fence is unlawful and a violation of many prohibitions under international law.

Given these features and the interests the fence was meant to serve, it was small wonder that along with their communities, my hosts on that September day in 2004, the council heads of two villages in the Qalqiliyah district, Azzun and a-Nabi Elyas, found themselves on one side of the fence, while their farmlands, their groves, were on the other. Unfortunately for them, in 1989, Israel built the settlement of Zufin to the west of their villages, and the fence, which sought to separate the villages from the settlement, also swallowed their farmland. The part of the fence in that particular spot was built two years before my visit there. According to the information we were given by the village council heads, fifteen families had lost their livelihoods entirely after the fence was built. The remaining families in both villages had lost between 50 and 80 percent of their annual income.

I spread out a map of the area on the hood of the car that had brought us to the spot, ignoring the fact that this stance was a particular favorite with the fence's builder, then prime minister Ariel Sharon. "Look," I said, "the distance between the separation fence and the farthest houses in the settlement is about two and a half kilometers. It goes against everything the army and the Ministry of Defense say about how much they need. In all the legal hearings, they've been talking about an area that's only as far as a light weapon's shooting range—four hundred meters at most."

The two council heads listened to the translation, eyeing the young Israeli lawyer in front of them with suspicion, and waited for my conclusion.

"So I think we have a pretty strong case and not a bad chance of convincing the Israeli court, too," I said.

Silence. I went on enthusiastically. "I propose we petition the High Court and argue that the route is not legal, even under Israel's own criteria. We'll demand that they dismantle the fence, get it out of here. If they want the fence, they can build it right next to the houses in the settlement."

The council heads exchanged glances. They looked at the map, and then gazed at their orchards, which they had not been able to access in some two years.

"How long will it take?" one of them asked.

"I estimate two to three years," I said, somewhat uncomfortably.

The two men exchanged glances again.

"Maybe, sir, you could ask them to put a gate here in the fence for us?" one of them asked.

I wasn't sure I'd heard right.

"If there's a gate here, where the gas station is, and they open it for us so we can pass through, we can harvest the olives," the other said.

WHAT DOES A human rights lawyer want in his professional life? To defend the good guys and fight the bad. To do good. To help the disempowered, the marginalized, the victims. To stop human rights abuses. Any sort of complexity that intrudes into the dichotomy between advancing good and serving evil is an unpleasant dissonance that ruins the harmony of legal human rights activism.

But life is complicated. A human rights lawyer often has to choose between two bad options. I reasoned, back then, that a gate for the village residents where they wanted it was feasible; the army, which had failed to place agricultural gates in the fence where they were needed, gates that were meant to allow farmers to reach their land, would be happy to create another gate. Lack of understanding and apathy served the unofficial objective of gradually eliminating Palestinian life from the seam zone. The two gates that had been installed in the section of the fence running near Azzun and a-Nabi Elyas were so far from the farmers' land that the farmers were unable to reach their orchards with their agricultural vehicles. Israel had taken a lot of heat from the international community for the fence, especially at that time, soon after the ICJ's ruling, and it was desperately looking for ways to show the world that the fence was reasonable, that farmers could actually work their land. We knew, from experience, that the gates were mostly a publicity stunt. They would initially open every day. Then they would be closed from time to time based on various excuses, and then passage would be limited to the harvest. We also knew that even when the gates were open, the permit system made it difficult to cross and involved never-ending red tape. Palestinian and Israeli NGOs constantly received reports about farmers and workers being humiliated at the gates and of mishaps in their operation. Palestinians would need a tremendous amount of tenacity and perseverance in order to stick with farming land trapped on the other side of the fence.

My position and that of HaMoked, which had enlisted me to represent the village residents, was that the fence, inasmuch as it is not located on the Green Line or inside Israel, is illegal. Period. It is a violation of the international laws of war and international human rights law. We saw the permit system specifically as a particularly serious crime that entrenches discrimination based on national or ethnic origin.

Asking the army to put in a gate to give the farmers better access to their land would mean putting ourselves exactly in the position the army would like human rights activists to be: collaborators in the management of a human rights violation—in this case, the fence. We would show the army what it could not or would not find out for itself, and while we're at it, we would extend the fence's shelf life, because adding a gate would temporarily alleviate some of the difficulties it has created for Palestinians living nearby and give some credence to Israel's claims that things are not as bad as they seem.

On the other hand, how could we ask the village residents, who had been suffering for two years as the fence destroyed their livelihoods, to sacrifice a few more years of income for the larger fight? What is the correct "human rights" approach: opting to fight for comprehensive change of an injurious policy, or protecting the rights and needs of an individual victim? The two interests do not always collide, but sometimes they do, and then things get complicated. Even if, say, we ask for a gate and simultaneously petition the High Court to remove the fence in that area, adding the gate would weaken the legal argument, given the (temporary, partial) improvement in the farmers' situation.

Some things just aren't taught in law school, not even in human rights programs. This was one of them.

DR. KING AND RABBI HESCHEL

A few years ago in New York I met Clarence Jones, Martin Luther King Jr.'s legendary lawyer. We sat in his office in a mid-Manhattan consulting firm, a huge portrait of the Reverend Dr. King hanging above us, and talked about the relationship between the black and Jewish communities. "I have to tell you a story," he said, when I proudly mentioned American Jews' deep involvement in the fight for racial equality in the United States. Jones looked at the portrait of his late leader and sailed back more than four and a half decades.

It was in 1967. Jewish community leaders had organized an event in a New York synagogue to mark the sixtieth birthday of one of the most important American-Jewish thinkers of the twentieth century, Rabbi Abraham Joshua Heschel. He had been a staunch supporter of the fight for equality, and he and King had become good friends. King decided to honor Heschel and attend the event. Heschel, for his part, decided to repay his friend's act with his own show of respect. He entered the synagogue arm in arm with the reverend. "As soon as they walked in," Jones told me, visibly moved, "the crowd, which included hundreds of rabbis, stood up and broke into song." They were singing the black liberation anthem "We Shall Overcome."

I stepped out of Jones's office into the busy, rainy New York street, my heart sinking.

The Jewish people have founders' stock in the notion of the sanctity of human life. Jewish morality promoted and entrenched the recognition that every person, no matter who they are, has fundamental, natural rights. The concept harks back to the Jewish myth of creation, where it is said that man was made in the image of God. This is taken to mean that there is something special about humans that makes them worthy, simply by virtue of being human. Jewish spiritual leaders believed their small, persecuted, discriminated nation, which was spread all over the world (and became, to use a term coined by the sociologist Zygmunt Bauman,[1] the first "inter-national nation" or "non-national" nation), had a mission to "mend the world," or in Hebrew *tikkun olam*.

A moral concept evolved in Judaism that imposed a responsibility for the welfare of all of humanity and (therefore) a duty to better the world. These principles, hailing from the categorical edict "Love thy neighbor as yourself," have been and remain the bedrock of the belief in human dignity, the yearning for liberty, the longing for equality among all people created "in the image of God." Being a perpetual minority, forever different, victims of racism, hate, and discrimination throughout the centuries, gave the Jewish people a unique collective perspective on the relationship between ruler and subject, majority and minority. In light of this moral, historical background, it is no surprise that Jews everywhere have been the allies of the oppressed, the victims of discrimination, and the disempowered. They were there in the struggle against apartheid in South Africa, in the creation of the Universal Declaration of Human Rights, and in the American civil rights movement.

Five decades have gone by since King and Heschel joined hands—bad, sad, shameful years. Years in which separatist undercurrents in the Jewish national movement have dragged us all away from the universal view that sees everyone as having been created in the image of God, and have forced on us the superior, racist approach of "a kingdom of priests, and a holy nation." We have become the only democracy in the world that has held another nation under occupation for half a century and has settled in their territory, brutishly taking over their land. Who would have believed it? Millions of people, all created in the image of God, suffering, for the fifth decade, under the yoke of military rule by a nation that knows better than any other the pain of losing freedom, property, and human dignity.

The longer it goes on, the more our rule over the occupied resembles the regimes our parents, and their parents before them, fought to defeat. This is our current national project: Our army controls the lives of the occupied, who need its permission and the permits it issues for every daily action. Our soldiers protect, and often help, thieves from among our people who invade the territory we have captured and, at gunpoint, do there as they please. Our jurists design a two-tiered legal system: one (modern, generous, respectful) for our brethren living in occupied land, and another (military, brutal, cruel) for their neighbors, the people we occupy. Our business entrepreneurs send their greedy hands into the occupied land, sucking up its riches, pillaging its natural resources, emptying its soul. All of us, each and every one, every day and every hour, dispossess millions of people, who, like us, were born in the image of God, of their right to shape their own future, pursue their happiness, and determine their own fate. Five decades of the antithesis of the Jews who stood up and sang "We Shall Overcome" in a New York synagogue.

THE STRUGGLE OF OUR GENERATION

When I studied law at the Hebrew University in Jerusalem, I knew I wanted to be involved in human rights, but the image I had of the work had been shaped by American courtroom dramas. I envisioned highbrow discussions about the meaning of freedom of expression in some sort of avant-garde niche, or the right to privacy in the age of the information super-highway. I pictured myself plunging into the current human rights debates, splitting hairs in an argument between schools of thought that to an outsider appear to be exactly the same.

I grew up in Jerusalem, on the border between its east and west, right next to three hundred thousand Palestinians living under occupation, but the foreign languages I was taught at school were English and French. Like most young people my age, I didn't see the hundreds of thousands of Palestinian residents of the city in which I was born. They came in and out of my line of vision but never left a mark on my brain or heart. Their brothers and sisters in the remaining parts of the occupied West Bank were even less present for me than the Palestinians of East Jerusalem. This absent presence of Palestinians under occupation in the minds of Israelis continued only until the First Intifada, the uprising of rocks and burning tires that erupted in late 1987 and pushed the conflict, which was always in the background, front and center, making it visible and palpable. So palpable, in fact, one night it reached our very doorstep, when a young Palestinian from East Jerusalem torched our car in the parking lot. (Later, when that Palestinian was not so young anymore, I represented him in the release proceedings, but that's a story for another book.)

When I finished law school I got an internship with one of the most prominent human rights lawyers in Israel, Avigdor Feldman. He had become a member of the bar in the early 1970s and quickly made a name for himself as a trailblazer when it came to representing Palestinians in cases against the occupation. Feldman later took his representation of victims of human rights abuses beyond the occupation, and was known for his extraordinary debating prowess. Working with him, I quickly understood what I must have subconsciously known all along: the most important, the most critical human rights battle of our generation in Israel is the fight against the occupation.

Human rights legal activism in Israel means going back to basics, to the most fundamental principles, because in a reality of long-term colonial occupation there are no underlying assumptions about essential rights. Human rights lawyering in this kind of situation means fighting for recognition of what we were told in law school was self-explanatory: a person's right to take part in deciding his or her fate as an element of human autonomy and dignity; a person's right to property; a person's freedom of movement; a person's right to equality. Human rights lawyering in the context of the Israeli occupation makes for legal discussions in which the discourse is primal and raw. The fight is for the very core of the right being contested. The myriad books and articles written about the intricacies of specific human rights stay on the library shelf. The occupation debate has yet to internalize the works of John Locke and Jeremy Bentham, thus legal advocacy stays focused on the very basics of human rights philosophy.

In Feldman's office I had a chance to work on legal cases fighting landgrabs, settlements, torture, and assassinations. I discovered the possibility of legal activism for human rights in the context of the Israeli occupation.

But the occupation is not the only context in which human rights must be defended in Israel. The State of Israel offers lawyers interested in litigation for social change a wide array of possibilities: LGBTQ rights, where discrimination has been the subject of litigation for some three decades, with some impressive success stories; deep discrimination, partly institutional-historical and partly socio-cultural, against Mizrahi Jews; institutionalized, systemic discrimination against Palestinian citizens of Israel in every aspect of life; various social justice battles for social and economic rights in a country that has privatized itself in almost every facet over the last thirty years and lowered its social safety nets to a point that made it one of the leaders in income inequality among OECD (Organisation for Economic Co-operation and Development) countries; battles for religious equality among the different streams of Judaism in light of the monopoly of Orthodoxy in the country; feminist struggles, some of which stem from the fact that Israeli society, like most in the world, is patriarchal; the ongoing conflict between the state and the Bedouin, the most disempowered community in Israel, whose sons and daughters were dispossessed of their traditional land and have mostly ended up living in abject poverty.*

It's a truly impressive assortment, a veritable smorgasbord of human rights battles, each of them noble and worthy. But still, there is a fundamental difference among these struggles, which carry on at various intensities, and the fight against the occupation. The victims in all these examples are citizens of Israel. Many suffer discrimination and some have sustained painful, humiliating abuses, but they are all citizens, whose civil rights are recognized, at least formally, by the state: the right to protest, express themselves, organize, travel, participate in social decisions, have their say. It is not so for subjects of the occupation,† and this difference is crucial.

---

* I did not mention environmental protection or animal rights, which are classified by some as human rights issues. While this classification may be contested, they certainly are causes for social change lawyering.

† In this regard, the fight for the rights of asylum seekers is also a fight for non-citizens, and everything said here about the unique features of the fight against the occupation applies to it as well. The collective responsibility discussed here is certainly evoked with respect to the unseemly xenophobia with which asylum seekers arriving in Israel from war-torn countries in Africa, at various intensities over the last twenty years, have been received, particularly by a nation that has experienced firsthand what it is like to be denied asylum.

Millions of people have no right to influence their own fate. Millions of people are prohibited by law from politically organizing or staging protests. Their rallies are often quashed by military and legal might—in Bil'in, Ni'lin, Budrus, a-Nabi Saleh, and everywhere else in the occupied space. In terms of human rights, the occupation is a mass casualty with multiple victims, each of whom suffers from multiple injuries—an all-systems fail.

What is special about this fight is that it does not concern a violation of a specific right of an individual or even a community. It is that the whole gamut of civil rights (the right to elect and be elected, to take part in public life) has been suspended, and when that happens, nearly all the human rights people have simply by virtue of being human lose their protection, almost as a matter of course. When Palestinians want to build a home on land they own, throughout most of the West Bank, applications are decided by planning committees on which their communities—by definition and by law—have no representation, and whose track record indicates that their role is in fact to curb Palestinian development. When Israeli settlers invade their land, build on it, or sow crops, Palestinians must rely on police officers—some of them settlers themselves and all of them Israeli—to fight against criminals who are their compatriots. When Palestinians want to protest their predicament, they are prevented by draconian laws forbidding demonstrations, laws that neither they nor their people enacted. Add to all of this the persistence of the occupation—five decades with no end in sight—and we have the most rancid, noxious offering in Israel's human rights smorgasbord.

Recognition of the unique nature of the fight against the occupation as a human rights cause is what brought me, first as a legal intern and then as a lawyer, to understand that this is *the* struggle of our generation in Israel, the most important battle of them all; that putting time and effort into domestic human rights causes (all of them important), while ignoring the millions of people who have no civil rights and only the faintest shadow of human rights, is like opening a gourmet restaurant on a street where people are starving.*

---

* I have one reservation about this distinction between internal Israeli struggles and the fight against the occupation, and that is the fight for equality for Palestinian citizens of Israel. It is true that members of this group are citizens, with rights that allow them to take

So the fight against the occupation is important even if only for the sheer magnitude of abuses it generates. But there is another reason why it is the critical struggle for activists of our generation, and that is our collective responsibility as Israelis for everything that happens in the Occupied Territories. Abraham Joshua Heschel was the most prominent Jewish leader to participate in the civil rights movement. There is a famous photograph of him, arm in arm with other protesters in the first row of the march for voting rights from Selma to Montgomery, Alabama. But the civil rights movement was not the cause for which Heschel raised his clear moral voice. In the late 1960s, he joined the fight against the Vietnam War. In a television interview in 1972, a few weeks before his death, he explained his need to protest the war: he, too, he said, was "co-responsible for the death of innocent people in Vietnam." He told the somewhat bemused interviewer, "In a free society, some are guilty, all are responsible."[2] The distinction Heschel drew between guilt and responsibility is the foundation of the Jewish notion of *tikkun olam*. It is the understanding that a person's moral obligation toward another is as broad as the commandment to love your neighbor as yourself, and it clearly goes beyond the legal responsibility that defines guilt.

As Israelis, we are all responsible for the realm of occupation, even if we do not man the checkpoints, live in settlements, or hand out permits, because our society, its institutions, and its governing bodies make their discriminatory decisions in partnership with us and implement their discriminatory policies in our name; and, inasmuch as this injustice yields profits (financial profits, for instance), Israeli society benefits as a whole. The occupation is an Israeli project, not only the project of those who support it. The Israeli government draws the resources to sustain the occupation from all the country's citizens, not just those who support its continuation, and the benefits of the occupation to the country's economy are enjoyed by all its citizens, whether directly or indirectly. Our responsibility, even for decisions and actions we oppose, comes from

part in the political process, and so their struggle should be classified as internal. But given the severity of the discrimination against them and the multiplicity of mechanisms that negate their political power, this struggle has the characteristics of one between a collective and an external actor. It is a hybrid of the two types of causes I have mentioned.

our belonging to a collective, being part and parcel of its behavior toward outside parties; the fact that the majority of the collective takes decisions in opposition to the minority, with which we might identify, does not free the minority from responsibility for the actions of the collective to which they belong.

In this sense, external injustice is very different from injustice that occurs within a society. In that case, the opposition's responsibility is light. They are not a part of the collective act against an external element. They have tried to prevent harm to themselves or to others at the hands of forces in the same collective. These internal victims were not harmed by society as a single body (they themselves are members of the society and have participated in the process that produced the decision that has wronged them), but by one section of the society to which they belong, a section that initiated and supported the injurious practice or policy. In most cases, that section is the majority, but it can also be a minority that has managed to leverage political power. For this reason, the occupation is an Israeli act, whereas discrimination against the LGBTQ community, for example, is an act of homophobes and their political allies. For this reason, local environmental activists hold only local polluters and their allies responsible for environmentally unsound policies rather than society at large, whereas a whole country that suffers from the pollution of a neighboring country holds its neighbor—including the domestic opposition to the polluters—responsible for the damage and compensation.

Collective responsibility is the moral responsibility society bears for external actions carried out by the collective. It derives from belonging and also from partnership. Being part of a collective enriches both the whole and its members. Each individual supplies the collective with energy and power. A citizen gives his or her country political, economic, and social wealth, and in turn feeds off what others bring in. Other than the family, it is hard to imagine a more nurturing relationship between an individual and a collective than citizenship. For the individual, it permeates almost every area of life; for the state, it provides resources and power. Partnership comes with individual responsibility for the actions of the society in which people live and to which they contribute every day and every hour.

That is our situation as Israelis, even for those who oppose the occupation. We are responsible. To take Heschel's words, some are guilty of the occupation but all are responsible for it, and this responsibility cannot be erased. It is with us wherever we go as Israelis. But our responsibility is not guilt. Guilt is personal. It stems from a wrongful act committed by an individual, and the acts of others cannot be attributed to that individual. Nonetheless, responsibility creates a moral duty that is incumbent on members of the collective, even if they themselves carry no guilt. And the primary moral duty is to fight to end the injustice. It is the duty to resist.

THE LAWYERS ARE COMING

Veteran residents of Jerusalem will tell you that the winter of 1968 was particularly harsh and snowy. And they know that when it snows in Jerusalem, Hebron is usually also covered in white. In the winter of 1968 both of these biblical cities and the road between them were blanketed in snow.

But neither snow nor impassable roads could stop Felicia Langer. With her famous determination, she decided to take to the slippery road and drive from her office in downtown Jerusalem to the Hebron police station. A Palestinian sheikh from East Jerusalem had come to her office in the middle of the storm and told her that his son, who had just returned from studying in Turkey, had been arrested and taken to the Hebron station. When the parents sent their son clean clothes through the authorities in the detention facility, they received, in return, a dirty bundle that contained a bloody shirt. They had no idea what had happened to their son and they were very worried. Having been retained by the father to represent the son and visit him, Langer took a file folder and marked it with the number 1, the first case involving a subject of the occupation.[3] Client number 1, the son of an East Jerusalem sheikh, would be the first of hundreds, maybe thousands, of Palestinians Langer would represent before the Israeli authorities over the next twenty-two years.

The Hebron police and the jail were housed in an old building in the center of the city, the Taggart Building, named after a British police officer who had gained expertise suppressing insurgencies in India and who designed fortified police stations all over Mandatory Palestine for His Majesty's forces. The Israeli army was the third regime to use the structure, following the British themselves and the Jordanians.

When Langer arrived, she looked not just for the sheikh's son, but also for two other clients, 'Abd al-'Aziz Sharif and Na'im 'Odeh, both members of Palestinian Communist movements in the Hebron area. Unlike the sheikh's son, who, Langer found out during her visit, was suspected of membership in Fatah and infiltration into the country, the two Communists were suspected of nothing. They had been arrested under special powers stipulated in the Defense (Emergency) Regulations that were enacted by the British Mandate and had survived long after it ended. The regulations permit "preventive" (or administrative) detention, which is designed not to respond to an act already committed but to stop the potential danger posed by the detainee. Administrative detainees are neither accused nor suspected of anything and may be held without trial or charges being brought.

The logic behind the draconian power to arrest people without accusing them of anything and to prevent them from mounting a defense is roughly this: the authorities have information that is based on evidence, which is either inadmissible or cannot be revealed, indicating that the detainee will harm security in the future if he or she is not held in custody. Theoretically, this power should be used extremely rarely and judiciously as it violates the two fundamental principles underlying the governmental power to deny liberty: first, a person may be denied liberty based on actions rather than intentions; second, that liberty is denied through due process, including the opportunity to mount a defense against the allegations.

Langer's clients, Sharif and 'Odeh, were to be the first raindrops in a monsoon of administrative detentions that would flood the West Bank and the Gaza Strip. Thousands of Palestinians have been put in administrative detention over the course of the occupation, some for stints amounting to years. Like all extreme powers, this one has been widely abused. Many people have been placed under administrative detention for myriad reasons, not necessarily based on evidence, albeit inadmissible, of posing any danger. Denying Palestinians' liberty without due process began in the earliest days of the occupation and has continued until today.

Langer was born in Poland in the early 1930s. Nearly all her relatives were murdered in the Holocaust. She and her parents managed to escape the Nazis to the USSR, but her father fell victim to Stalin's regime. He died a short while after being released, in very poor health, from a Soviet gulag where he was held in dreadful conditions. Langer nevertheless became a devout communist. After immigrating to Israel, she joined the local Communist Party and became a pivotal activist. She began practicing law in 1965 and for a while worked in a Tel Aviv law office as an associate litigating all sorts of cases, but immediately after the 1967 war, Langer decided to devote her practice to representing Palestinians living under the occupation and opened her own office on Jaffa Street in Jerusalem.

In the late 1960s, she was one of just a handful of lawyers representing West Bank residents. Most of these lawyers were Palestinian citizens of Israel, almost all of whom had ties to the Communist Party of Israel (known as Maki). At the time, communist factions were deeply entrenched in Palestinian urban centers and the connections between the Israeli and West Bank and Gaza Communist movements paved the way for lawyers from Israel to represent Palestinian residents under occupation. Following Langer's lead, these lawyers laid the groundwork for the extensive legal activism that continues today, activism marked by partnership, Sisyphean legal battles, and trust, given daily by Palestinians to Israeli lawyers, some of them Jewish, to represent them before Israeli institutions, primarily the High Court of Justice. This trust and partnership was maintained through five decades of occupation: even in the hardest times, when it seemed as though all the bridges between Palestinians and Israelis had been burned or bombed, solidarity in the fight against human rights violations did not wane.

What began as a project dominated exclusively by lawyers with ties to the Communist Party expanded during the 1970s. Antiestablishment activists such as Leah Tsemel, a member of the Revolutionary-Marxist movement Matzpen, made their own connections with young Palestinian leaders, and staunchly liberal human rights activists such as Israeli-Palestinian lawyer Elias Khoury, Israeli-Jewish lawyer Avigdor Feldman, and Palestinian lawyer and author Raja Shehadeh developed the use of petitions to the court as a key tool for legal battles on issues of principle. This legal activism spared no policy or practice inflicted on the Palestinians, whether it was the deportation of leaders, punitive house demolitions, administrative detention, denial of family unification, land seizures and settlement building, revocation of residency for people who traveled abroad, or the countless restrictions on freedom of movement and expression. Israeli lawyers represented Palestinian petitioners, defendants, and plaintiffs on a huge number of issues, always having to keep up with an occupation that constantly reinvented itself, introducing new means of oppression and control to enhance, compound, or replace the previous methods.

Through the 1980s, with the proliferation of civil society organizations in Israel and the increasing influence of human rights groups as leaders in the legal fight, other areas of advocacy were added: challenging assassinations, torture during interrogations, and the creation of the separation fence; seeking law enforcement against Israeli civilians and security forces for harm to Palestinians and their property; and contesting certain methods of urban warfare. Thus the relationship between the Israeli military government and the Palestinian subject suffered a constant intrusion—by the human rights lawyer, a third wheel in what was supposed to be an exclusive, if miserable, relationship.

In 1990, after a long career of public and dramatic battles with the authorities, Felicia Langer closed her Jerusalem office and left Israel to take up a teaching position in Germany. In an interview in the *Washington Post* Langer said, "I couldn't be a fig leaf for this system anymore."[4]

GIVING UP ON THE HIGH COURT

The Israeli occupation has equipped itself with a full suit of legal armor from the very beginning. The military government made sure that every draconian authority and injurious power is codified in orders, procedures, and protocols, maintaining the appearance of a system that operates in an orderly, rational fashion. The architects of the occupation's legal system knew that the law has a normalizing, legitimizing effect. They knew even though some of the worst crimes in history were perpetrated with the help of the law and in accordance with it, a regime predicated on laws that define general norms and seem to ensure that people are not left to the whims of officials will acquire an air of decency.

And so military legislation blossomed throughout the Occupied Territories. Young recruits, fresh out of law school, were snatched up by the Civil Administration to draft, on behalf of the military commander, orders to regulate the procedures for administrative detention, the punishment of protesters, the criminalization of political associations, and the prohibition on storing rainwater, as well as to facilitate land seizures and settlement building. Legal permit systems sprang up like mushrooms after the rain to help occupation authorities control and construct life under occupation. Each permit system, with its restrictions on a certain free-dom, making it contingent on permission granted by the authorities, was enshrined in orders, protocols, guidelines, and forms. This created a huge bureaucracy to police travel through the Occupied Territories, a bureau-cracy designed by legal fledglings who, as deemed necessary and using orders they drafted, closed areas, sealed borders, and restricted movement on the main roads, but also invented exemptions for permits from the mil-itary commander. The guidelines they came up with determined what type of permits would be available and instructed those with the power to grant them how to use their discretion. The permit system flourished. Over the years, Palestinians needed more and more permits to get through their day: for certain kinds of business transactions, for travel abroad, or even just to gather with people on the street or in a shopping area if more than ten were in attendance.

The occupation's legislative system, though it relied on one per-son's authority to enact primary laws—the IDF (Israel Defense Forces) commander—became a massive apparatus, operated by many lawyers, that produces primary legislation, secondary regulations, and legislative amendments on a daily basis. All this effort just to give the forced, brutal intervention into every aspect of Palestinian life an air of legality. Instead of the emperor's thumbs up or down, which decides who should live and who should die, the occupation's pen legislates what to withhold and what to prohibit, what to deny and what to permit.

This particular feature of the occupation—enshrining every power and authority in legislation—opened up the possibility of litigating against almost every occupation-related issue. The extensive legisla-tive activity and intense litigation made Israel's occupation a candidate for the most legalistic regime in history. Thousands of military ordinances, a sea of administrative orders, tens of thousands of petitions and crim-inal trials, and countless judgments and judicial decisions have been greasing the wheels of the occupation for fifty years. Human rights lawyers have pushed their way into this well-oiled machine, first by force, then with the blessing of the authorities. If the regime uses the law as a basis for its actions, lawyers have the professional tools to engage with it on behalf of its subjects.

The idea of lawyers, especially Israeli lawyers, representing Palestin-ians and pleading for them against the military government was initially received with hostility by the authorities, but over the years they have learned not just to accept the lawyers' presence but to reserve a place for them in the decision-making and implementation process. In retrospect, the authorities seem to have learned that in some respect, the work of human rights lawyers helps and supports them. As long as the civil rights movement is not too successful in court, the regime is better off with it than without it. The reason for this is the image of fairness that the regime is able to project when its opponents fight their battles in the regime's own arena. This image directly contradicts the opponents' explicit characterization of the regime.

When lawyers representing subjects of the occupation bang their fists on the podium in righteous anger and passionately accuse Israel of outrageous violations of their clients' basic rights, or when they make statements in the courthouse lobby to journalists from all over the world—as they do all this—they seem to send a certain message. It is not the message they want to send, but it's there nonetheless. Their court submissions, interviews, and oral arguments tell one story, but it is always trailed by a shadow, a secondary story. The shadow says yes, we have an undemocratic regime of occupation, but it still allows those living under it to obtain excellent legal representation and gain access to the highest legal forums of the occupying country. This regime speaks the language of the rule of law and human rights and is committed to them, at least officially.

When a human rights lawyer asks for a permit to allow her client access to his land, which is in an area sealed off by military order to protect an Israeli settlement, that lawyer becomes an agent of the access-blocking apparatus. When she files a petition to the High Court of Justice, arguing against the need to close off the area to protect the settlement, claiming that other solutions are available, the shadow is saying that the area really *was* closed to protect the settlement, that the settlement's illegality is not relevant, and that the Israeli court has legitimate business ruling in a dispute between Palestinians and Israelis over Palestinian land.

The lawyer often has to set aside more radical arguments, such as the international prohibition on building settlements, or the fact that a Palestinian's right to work his land trumps an Israeli's desire to live in the occupied territory, because Israeli jurisprudence has shut out these lines of argument. And by doing so, by availing herself of the limited avenues offered by the occupation, the human rights lawyer becomes part of it. When she goes to the occupier's court, she is forced to accept the limits of the discourse unilaterally determined by the occupation. She does this because she simply cannot resist the prize waiting at the end of the process—the possibility of concrete relief, full or partial, for her client, alleviating his suffering and mitigating the harm. But on the way to this reward, which the court dangles before the lawyer like a dog trainer with a tasty treat, she strengthens the shadow that undermines her most basic beliefs about the occupation.

Fighting a regime that massively and systematically produces abuse of human rights can take two forms: the first involves turning to outside institutions; the second is using the regime's own. Israeli legal activism against the abuses inflicted by the occupation has been pursued almost exclusively as an internal struggle. The danger of internal struggles is that they help create a sort of symbiotic relationship between the regime and the movements that oppose it. This danger is particularly acute when the struggle is legal rather than public, and when the domestic institutions enjoy prestige and trust as professional, independent bodies. (There is also an attendant danger of crippling other forms of advocacy and focusing too much on the courts.)

The regime can use the opposition to best evaluate the stability and strength of its policies, and to moderate practices that may prompt too much backlash. It needs human rights lawyers as part of the process by which it drafts and evaluates its injurious policies. It needs them for public relations, too. The lawyers and organizations who oppose the regime and work to end it find themselves sucked into its process of quality control and used to promote its image as a decent, legitimate system. This is a rather unnerving realization: the opposition, if it uses internal tools only, becomes part of the policy it fights; its resistance is neatly contained and given a permanent role in the mechanism that creates the very policies it opposes.

In June of 2007, Israeli NGOs engaged in defending human rights in the Occupied Territories gathered in the Arab-Jewish community of Neve Shalom to take stock and evaluate their activity on the fortieth anniversary of the occupation. It was near the end of the Second Intifada, which had taken the lives of some one thousand Israelis and almost five thousand Palestinians. Permit systems, fences, and closed military zones had been distributed all over the West Bank.* Restrictions on Palestinian access to Palestinian land had reached new heights, serving an unprecedented expansion of Jewish settlements. Millions of rightless Palestinians were being pounded by all sorts of new methods to control them and suppress resistance. Civilian life was choked by the grip of restrictions and prohibitions. Above all, Israeli policies worked to entrench Israel's civilian presence in the West Bank, accelerate long-term spatial changes, and send a clear message that not only was there no intention of ending the occupation, the goal is the opposite: to perpetuate it for generations to come—at least in the West Bank.

The conference was meant to be the beginning of a process of soul searching. The participants felt that over the preceding decades the number of organizations and lawyers fighting human rights abuses under the occupation had significantly increased, as had the resources they had at their disposal, and that their knowledge and expertise were constantly improving, and yet the situation only got worse. Human rights abuses against civilians living under the occupation worsened and intensified. So where did we go wrong, the organizations asked themselves. Are we using the wrong methods? Are we pursuing the wrong channels?

The question was somewhat misleading: clearly, there were a great many external factors that made matters worse. Measuring human rights activism against human rights abuses as a method of assessing the effectiveness of activism is an error in logic. At worst, it creates the illusion that one is a result of the other; the most optimistic interpretation is that the activism has no influence on the abuse. Neither of these is the necessary conclusion, and both are most likely incorrect. What the participants failed to take into account was the possibility that without their work, the measure of abuse would show a surge; the fact that a car is racing toward an abyss does not mean that the foot pressing hard on the brakes has no impact.

The main event at this gathering was a three-guest panel including a journalist and a former head of the civil administration, who tried to give

---

* The Gaza Strip, which had been cleared of Israeli settlements as part of the 2005 disengagement, was free of roadblocks and checkpoints, but now subjected to a closure by Israel and Egypt. Its 1.5 million residents would eventually be trapped by a harsh siege, and both sides entered periodic rounds of violence, each peaking with a savage full-scale indiscriminate military assault on Gaza by the strongest army in the Middle East.

an outside perspective on the organizations' work. The officer, Ilan Paz, who, upon his retirement from the military at the rank of brigadier general, publicly cautioned against the complete subjugation of government policy to settler pressure, threw a grenade into the room.

"Without you, without human rights organizations, there is no occupation," he said, causing an uproar. "The system can't function a single day without you," he went on. "The army and the mechanisms that control life in the area rely on what human rights organizations do, on the fact that you represent Palestinians and bring their requests, needs, and demands to its people. Thanks to you, the most acute issues are resolved and major incidents are avoided, both locally and in terms of how the world sees things. To a great extent, your actions allow the occupation to go on."

Paz was referring to the kinds of humanitarian work the organizations do—accompanying Palestinians to register complaints with the authorities, helping them to submit permit applications, coordinating with the army during the olive harvest to keep farmers free of harassment by settlers or soldiers. He might not have been referring to legal activity; nor was it clear whether he meant to criticize the organizations or commend them. There is no doubt, however, that the audience was shocked and dismayed. The last thing the dedicated doctors of Physicians for Human Rights—Israel, B'Tselem's researchers, the volunteers for Machsom Watch, the field workers of Yesh Din, and the lawyers for ACRI and the Public Committee Against Torture wanted to hear was that the occupation exists thanks to them or even with their help.

After the conference, I received an e-mail from Limor Yehuda, director of the Occupied Territories department in ACRI and a lawyer. The subject line read: "Forty years of occupation and the High Court of Justice—do we just carry on?" She suggested we put together a team of lawyers from Israeli human rights organizations who deal with the occupation and continue the discussion that began at the conference with a focus on legal activity, in other words, deep introspection and a reevaluation of the effectiveness of our legal battles in court. At first only the two of us met. Others joined later and soon the group met once a month for a year.

We wanted to reassess the fundamental assumptions underlying our legal work, not just whether human rights litigation in the context of an occupation can achieve its immediate goals, but also the long-term impact of our work. We wanted to be able to answer the accusation that we heard, that filing petitions in the court of the occupier not only fails to help but in fact harms the fight against occupation. The group included legal activists from eight human rights organizations. We analyzed the achievements of legal action over the years, identified the failures, and assessed the price of legal activity. Everyone in the group felt a strong underlying sense of discomfort and frustration. Discomfort because of the price that comes with fighting this battle as an *internal* battle, which, for any success, requires no small amount of conformity with the narrative of the establishment, which, in turn, makes us supporting actors in the farce of the enlightened occupier with a liberal justice system. Frustration because of what looked like a frighteningly pitiful record of effecting policy changes.

After all, the Supreme Court had gone ahead and approved almost every harmful policy and practice pursued by the military in the Occupied Territories. The High Court might sometimes tone down a military practice. We sometimes managed to get justices to put pressure on the military, resulting in the prevention or mitigation of the harm in the specific case before the court, which, it has to be said, is no small matter. While the group was engaged in this evaluation, ACRI (Israel's oldest and largest human rights organization) took on an empirical study to look at the results of its own occupation litigation from 1985, when it began working on the issue, up to 2004, a period of almost twenty years. The study showed that in a very high proportion of the cases, the specific remedy sought was obtained to some degree, and that the proceedings did have a mitigating effect on policy making.[5]

Still, ACRI's empirical study focused on different issues than those of the group, looking at whether the specific remedy sought had been obtained, and only examining ACRI cases, which were a sample size and involved a limited range of violations (for example, half the cases the organization took on during this period related to the rights of prisoners and suspects). Our group, on the other hand, sought to understand the impact of litigation on the occupation itself and its core abusive policies. Our conclusion was that as a rule, there were very few cases in which the judicial system granted relief that blocked a significant policy (such as administrative detention, deportation of activists, house demolitions, land seizures, and settlement building). In fact, we sadly concluded that in its judgments, the High Court of Justice had helped deepen and strengthen the hold of the occupation and its core enterprise, Israel's settlements.

We reached the conclusion that in many cases not only had the High Court failed to provide relief against abusive policies, but seeking legal relief from them had caused real damage to the fight against the occupation. The court's seal of approval had helped assuage the fears of many Israelis who worried about the corrupting effect of the occupation but counted on the court's justices, who shared their elite social-cultural background, to stand guard and ensure that government and military's actions in the Occupied Territories remain within the realm of "reasonableness." The effect was similar in various influential international circles, where Israel's highest court (still) enjoys a reputation for its bold activism and commitment to basic humanistic values, an image we believed that even if warranted in terms of jurisprudence on domestic issues (although this too is a matter of contention) was completely misguided when it came to the Occupied Territories.

The discussions among the group, which we referred to as the High Court Assessment Team, increasingly focused on the toughest question of all: Given our disturbing experience, was it right to continue to petition the High Court on behalf of the occupied? And if not, what alternative avenues of legal activism could we pursue to continue the fight to end human rights violations and the occupation itself?

It is interesting to note that the participants were all Israeli. There were no representatives of the occupied population, no members of Palestinian organizations or lawyers. There was no small degree of arrogance in our view of ourselves as sovereign to make decisions on questions that are so vital to contesting the occupation. But in the eleventh hour, before we drafted our recommendations, we met with Palestinian human rights organizations in Ramallah to discuss the dilemma. Some of the Palestinian representatives opposed ceasing legal action, emphasizing the measure of protection our High Court petitions had given to individual victims. One speaker noted that this was one of the only tools Palestinians could use against the military regime and that relinquishing it would be irresponsible. Others focused on the larger fight to end the occupation, and thought, as we did, that High Court petitions actually got in the way.

In August 2008, a year after the Neve Shalom conference, after thorough research and many discussions, we drafted a document with our recommendations:

> The occupation is a serious, daily violation of the human rights of millions of people. This is true of occupation in general and of the Israeli occupation in particular, which, from its inception, has been marked by violations of the fundamental tenets of international humanitarian law, which was designed to protect the civilian population in the occupied territory: prohibiting annexation, the transfer of civilians into the occupied territory, the transfer of sovereignty to the occupying power (the occupier may not act as owner . . .), imposing a duty of trusteeship toward protected persons, specifying the temporary nature of the occupation.
>
> We, Israeli organizations who for years focused on submitting petitions to the High Court of Justice in an attempt to improve matters, have, after forty years of occupation, come to the conclusion that although the gains made by appealing to the High Court are important, they are, nevertheless, negligible, a mere drop in the bucket compared to the ongoing abuses. The experience we have gained through close contact with these abuses and their victims and as seasoned applicants to all Israeli authorities, primarily the High Court of Justice, in an attempt to remedy the violations, has led us to this two-fold conclusion:
>
>> On one hand, the High Court of Justice is not the right tool and cannot achieve what we aim to do. There is real concern that litigation has, in fact, buttressed human rights abuses, particularly thanks to the public legitimacy it generates, which leads us to estimate that it is actually harmful. Our use of High Court petitions has been misguided.
>>
>> On the other hand, only intensive international intervention can bring an end to the occupation.
>
> This evaluation compels all organizations to do and say the following: We will not submit High Court petitions against policies that violate human rights in the Occupied Territories over the next year, and redirect our efforts toward other courses of action.

The document was distributed to the directors of the various organizations and discussions on whether or not to adopt it took place in the following months.

A CONVERSATION THAT NEVER TOOK PLACE

LAWYER: So what can I do for you?

CLIENT: I'm a resident of Nablus. I was born there. My father is a doctor. My grandfather was a doctor. He was a doctor back during the British Mandate. Anyway, until two years ago, I was studying in Amman, medicine of course. That's where I met my wife. She was also a medical student, and she was also born in Nablus, but her parents decided to move to Jordan when she was a baby, so she grew up there. We got married in Amman and we have two kids, a four-year-old boy and a two-year-old girl. Here, look . . .

L: Beautiful children. Cute. Where are they?

C: In Amman, with their mother.

L: I'm guessing you want your wife and children to join you in Nablus.

C: Yes. We finished med school two years ago. I have a job in Nablus, and the family built an apartment for us.

L: Have you filed a family unification application?

C: Yes, right after I came back to Palestine, almost two years ago. I got no answer until two weeks ago, when they said the application was rejected.

L: Did they say why?

C: No. They never even sent me a response. I went to the Coordination Office every few weeks to see what was going on, and the last time, they gave me a piece of paper saying that the application had been rejected.

L: Does your wife work?

C: No. She and the children are waiting for permits to join me. If she comes, I'll probably be able to get her a job at a clinic in our area.

L: I see.

C: Can anything can be done?

L: Look, in principle, since your application was rejected, it's possible to petition the High Court of Justice. This court can intervene in the authorities' decisions, including the army's. The military government treats family unification as a privilege, not a right. They used to approve family unification for minors and their parents, or for couples, like in your case. Then the policy changed, and marriage was no longer a sufficient criterion. If you file a petition, the state has to submit a response explaining why they object to letting your wife come. They might just say that current policy is not to approve applications beyond a certain quota. They might say that your wife, specifically, is denied for security reasons.

C: What security reason could there be? She's a 25-year-old doctor. Who is she, Bin Laden?

L: What can I tell you? They find security reasons everywhere. Maybe her father was a Fatah activist in the seventies. Maybe she joined a Palestinian student union in Jordan—the Shin Bet doesn't like that. You weren't born yesterday, you know how it works. There's no point speculating.

C: And the fact that my wife was born in Nablus? She's supposed to be a Palestinian resident. How can they deny her entry? They must have her registered, no?

L: The military government defines Palestinians in the Occupied Territories as residents, not citizens. Residency depends on presence. Unlike citizens, residents who are absent for a time lose their residency status, and with it the right to reenter the country and stay there. They become foreigners. It sounds crazy when it comes to civilians under occupation, but that's the way it is. Tens of thousands of Palestinians who left the West Bank or Gaza for different reasons have lost their residency. How long were you at medical school in Jordan? Seven years? Be thankful they didn't revoke your residency as well.

C: So what do we do?

L: What you already did: apply for family unification, as if your wife's a complete stranger in Palestine and is asking to enter by virtue of your marriage, because you're a resident. But since your application was rejected, the only chance is a High Court petition.

C: Okay, so what are the odds?

L: It's hard to say, but . . . you and your wife are doctors, well educated, you look secular, middle class, you might get some sympathy. The justices may push the lawyers for the state to accept your application. It happens sometimes.

C: And if the justices push the army capitulates?

L: It often happens, but sometimes not. It's a sort of game between the justices and the army, like bartering in secret code. In cases where something about the story touches them, or when the justices feel the army has gone too far, they push the state to find a solution, to stand down, compromise with the petitioners. Then the state checks whether it can "concede" the case to the justices, and if the army doesn't strongly object, they give in. It's a sort of ongoing dialogue that continues from one case to the next, where the justices ask the army to give them as much as possible. This way, the army and the justices work together to give the court a certain record of granting petitioners relief. But there's this tacit agreement that when the army puts its foot down, the justices don't object.

C: So there's a chance?

L: There's always a chance.

C: Okay. If you petition the court, how much does it cost?

L: I work for an Israeli human rights organization. We don't take money. The organization pays my fees and covers the court expenses.

C: Wow, really? That's great. So will you file the petition?

L: No.

Silence.

C: No?

L: No.

C: Why not?

L: It's a little complicated, and I'm really sorry, but here's the thing: Human rights organizations and lawyers have decided that High Court petitions do more harm than good for the fight to end human rights violations in the West Bank and Gaza and the occupation, which is the source of most of the violations. These petitions legitimize the occupation and very few of them actually help.

C: But you said there's a chance in my case.

L: Yes, but it could damage the larger fight against the occupation. Look, if I file this petition, and the state bases its refusal on security grounds, I have to agree to let the justices look at classified material about your wife with only state lawyers present. This is a violation of due process. The justices will decide whether or not there really is a security risk, without us knowing anything about the allegations against your wife, and we won't be able to respond to them. But I'll have to give consent, otherwise the petition will be dismissed. This way, the Shin Bet can feed the justices whatever they like because there's no danger of us calling their bluff. Besides, I'll be forced to accept the underlying presumption in this sort of proceeding, which is that Israel has the right to revoke the residency of Palestinians who left the West Bank for several years, and it has the right to deny Palestinians family unification, even between first-degree relatives. These presumptions defy international law, which requires Israel to honor residency status and allow family unification.

C: So why can't you make that argument to the court? That international law requires recognition of the right to family unification?

L: Because then I open the door to a judgment that would further obscure the cruelty of Israel's policies. See, many Israelis don't like the situation, they think that not allowing a man to reunite with his wife is cruel. If we file that kind of principled petition, chances are one of the following happens: the court ends up saying that all unification requests should be subject to security considerations, which will be measured according to secret evidence that neither you nor I will ever see. Or the court will (re)affirm the policy that doesn't recognize the right of family unification. Or it might put pressure on the state to find a specific solution in your wife's case. Any one of these scenarios will soothe the concerns of the public, who generally instinctively object to such a denial of rights, because they trust the Supreme Court justices.

C: But you said that they might put pressure on the army to let my wife join me in Nablus.

L: Yes, but then we're collaborators in the justice system's greatest lie, which is that Palestinians can exercise their rights and have access to justice and legal relief. Don't forget, for every person who gets what they ask from the court, ten others are denied based on secret evidence. But Israel would cite your case in its reports to the UN, and the papers will report it, and the court secretariat might even translate the judgment into English. If your case is successful, it becomes another slide in Israel's PR presentation of the occupation. And anyway, chances are that we won't succeed. The vast majority of Palestinian petitioners leave the court without any remedy. Hundreds and thousands of cases like yours end up reinforcing and legitimating the system, but mostly get nothing in return.

C: I don't get it, if there's a chance . . . even a remote one?

L: Look, I don't expect you to agree. I understand your family's predicament, but think about it this way: It may be that the kind of petition you want me to file on your family's behalf will facilitate the refusal of other family unification applications and give the army confidence to go even harder on these permit requests. It may be that if we stop filing these petitions, the army would be more cautious in refusing reunification because the responsibility would be with its officers, not the justices. Maybe the domestic and international criticism of forced separation of spouses and parents and children would be stronger. There's a chance that these petitions make the policy more prevalent rather than less, and that they indirectly victimize others.

C: But you don't represent the others. You represent me and my wife.

L: Yes, but cause lawyering requires considering the broader impact of legal activism. Unlike regular lawyers, we can't just look at things at the level of the specific case, because we're trying to advance a more principled goal. If a human rights organization believes that fighting for a specific person might increase the harm to others, maybe even delay the goal of fundamental change, it cannot ignore that. It has to weigh whether to continue the fight. In our case, petitions like the one you want me to file will harm the larger fight.

C: What larger fight? I want my wife and children to live with me in our house in Nablus! I've spent two years without them. I hardly know my little girl. I only see her once a year. My big boy . . .

L: I understand, and again, I really am sorry, but you have to see the bigger picture.

COULD WE POSSIBLY have such a conversation? For human rights lawyers working in a context of massive rights violations and a justice system that offers very little relief, is this a plausible response to their dilemma? Or must those lawyers, who fight for a worldview in which the individual is revered and may never be sacrificed for the greater good, ignore the impact of the individual battle on the larger struggle?

The dilemma is doubly difficult because human rights attorneys are both activists and lawyers. They are committed to both the ethics of human rights and the ethics of the legal profession.

WHAT HAS BEEN WILL BE AGAIN

DRAFT

For all the reasons stated in the High Court Team statement of principles, the Board of Directors of this organization hereby decides on the following changes to the strategy for legal activism with respect to human rights violations in the Occupied Territories:

1. The organization will not file public interest, or principled, petitions to the High Court of Justice, unless so decided in the inter-organizational Exceptions Committee. For this purpose, a public-interest petition is defined as a petition aiming at the revocation, cessation, or amendment of legislation, policy, or practice related to an unspecified number of cases.

2. The organization will continue to file individual petitions on behalf of civilians who seek its assistance on a specific legal issue, all subject to strictly professional considerations. The organization will not be named as petitioner in such petitions.

3. The organization empowers the High Court Team to plan a joint foreign legal activism strategy for Israeli human rights organizations to address human rights violations in the Occupied Territories. To clarify,

the organization will not undertake legal action abroad without specific approval from the organization's board.

This draft resolution, which we wrote for the boards of the organizations, was an attempt to square the circle. No to public-interest petitions but yes to individual petitions. No petitions aimed at changing a policy or a general practice, except for those authorized by an inter-organizational committee, like a major union's strike committee that makes special allowances for workers to break a strike. The premise for the distinction between public-interest and individual petitions was that the damage that could result from petitions directed at a general issue is potentially worse, and that the direct humanitarian imperative in individual cases is stronger. The idea was to proceed on behalf of individual petitioners in cases of humanitarian necessity and a reasonable chance at getting the relief sought, and to pursue public-interest, or principled, petitions in very rare cases, but that as a rule, we would hold back.

But it is not that simple. The truth is that it is very difficult, if not impossible, to distinguish clearly between the two types of legal proceedings. The difference might seem self-evident at first: a public-interest petition targets and challenges a policy or practice that applies to a group of cases with common features, whereas an individual petition does not challenge the legality of the policy or the practice but only its application to the specific individual. For example, a petition arguing that the imposition of a certain permit is unlawful would be categorized as a public-interest petition, while one claiming the authorities had erred in denying a permit to a specific applicant (who, in fact, meets the necessary conditions and is therefore entitled to the permit) would be an individual petition. However, cases that start off as individual petitions, in the sense that they do not purport to change legislation or policy, might become general if the court, either on its own initiative or with the encouragement of the respondents, decides to put the whole policy under scrutiny, rather than just the specific application. The arguments made against the specific implementation of the policy could extend logically to impugn it in its entirety. And since precedent requires that an individual decision be applied to similar cases, that "individual" petition could result in a broader judicial discussion. This is exactly what we hoped to avoid because of the impact a broad ruling on principle might have on the larger fight against the occupation.

Our resolution—which we hoped would help settle the ethical conundrum posed by giving up on legal proceedings to fight human rights violations—relied on making a distinction between types of cases that does not always hold up. And even when it does, we might still be left with the ethical dilemma. Moreover, our premise that the harm we were seeking to prevent is exclusively, or nearly exclusively, the result of public-interest petitions was incorrect. Realizing that, we also suggested restricting filing individual petitions to "humanitarian" cases only, where the expected injury to the petitioner is particularly grave. Ultimately, we had gotten caught in the tangle of our lofty ethical principles and the interests we wanted to advance.

ACRI's board of directors untangled the web for us. In December 2008, they made the following unequivocal decision:

> The Board of Directors supports the use of timely discretion with respect to the petitions we file to the High Court of Justice, with a future emphasis on petitions designed to expose the unacceptable fundamental assumptions that provide the basis for the occupation and the substantial human rights abuses that characterize it. To remove any doubt, ACRI's Board of Directors *does not* accept the recommendations made by the inter-organizational team ("The High Court Assessment Team") to stop petitioning the High Court of Justice with respect to human rights violations in the Occupied Palestinian Territories, with the exception of individual petitions on behalf of residents seeking legal aid on a specific issue, with the approval of an inter-organizational committee ("the exceptions committee").

Plain and simple. Emphasis in the original. A flat-out rejection.

ACRI's board did not mince words with regard to pursuing legal action abroad either: "ACRI's Board of Directors does not accept the recommendation of the inter-organizational team regarding legal action abroad."

The adults put an end to what they probably saw as a children's tantrum. Abandoning litigation in the High Court of Justice could only have worked if all the relevant organizations had come on board. Once ACRI said no, there was no point in the other organizations considering the idea. The most radical initiative proposed in fifty years of occupation—to

boycott the court, the judicial body that oversees the occupation's institutions, openly and publicly—was buried before it drew its first breath.

OPEN SESAME

Four years before ACRI's decision, I had faced a similar dilemma and I
made a similar decision. "I write to you seeking an immediate response to
the urgent problem facing residents of Azzun and a-Nabi Elyas in the fast-
approaching olive harvest season," I wrote in September 2004 in a letter
addressed to the prime minister, Ariel Sharon, and the attorney general at
the time, Menachem (Meni) Mazuz. Then I added (emphasis in original):

> As you are certainly well aware, the olive harvest is upon us and we expect
> it to begin in the coming weeks. *I, therefore, request that you instruct your
> staff to install an additional gate in the southern side of the Zufin enclave,
> near the Tahsin Mansur gas station, located near Izbat al-Tabib.* A gate in
> this location would provide a shorter route to the land (I estimate it will
> save some eight kilometers, half the distance on footpaths), and allow the
> residents to reach their farmland with agricultural vehicles, using a dirt
> road located in the area. I also request that this gate be staffed continu-
> ously throughout the olive harvest, to ensure that farmers from Azzun
> and a-Nabi Elyas are able to work as required during this time. Installing
> the gate also requires granting permits that would allow residents to access
> their land *with agricultural vehicles (tractors, trailers, pick-up trucks, etc.).*
>
> Failure to install the gate as requested may result in the loss of the entire
> annual olive crop.

On behalf of my clients, I asked for a gate to be installed in the separation fence.

On behalf of my clients, I asked that the gate be continuously staffed
during the olive harvest, echoing the army's position that the farmers have
no inherent right to access their land at other times.

On behalf of my clients, I asked for the appropriate permits to allow
them to cross the gate and enter the seam zone, which, according to a closed
military zone order, is off limits to Palestinians (and only Palestinians)
unless they obtain permission from the military commander.

I was trading in legitimacy.

I will serve the permit system. I will help you "improve" the separation fence by providing you with information critical for its management; in this case, information about the most appropriate placement of an agricultural gate and the schedule for opening it. In return, you will let my clients reach their land and make a living. Building and operating the separation fence had become a joint project of the army and human rights lawyers.

For history's sake, and for the sake of the petition I was planning to submit against the fence that cut off my clients from their land, my letter to the prime minister and the attorney general also said: "Clearly, my request herein in no way indicates agreement that the fence or the route chosen for it are lawful." Like any good lawyer, I added fine print. I could never have predicted, not in a million years, the course this case would take after I sent the letter, a drama that would result in the removal of both this segment of the fence and the man who headed the authority in charge of building it, and the reunification of the residents with their farmland. It is a story I shall tell in due course.

ALMOST FIVE DECADES have gone by since Felicia Langer visited the sheikh's son and the two administrative detainees in their cells in the Taggart Building in Hebron. Dozens of Israeli and Palestinian lawyers have submitted tens of thousands of petitions, participated in thousands of trials, and represented countless subjects of the occupation, yet they still puzzle over the right way to fight the extensive, large-scale violation of human rights Israel is committing against millions of people.

It is tempting to think that there is something to be learned from the huge arsenal of experience gained through the legal fight against the occupation, that there is a refrain hiding in the epic poem of the struggle waged in the Supreme Court over the years, and that if we can only find it we'll be able to write the next verse perfectly.

Even if this were true, finding the insight is no easy task. It takes an open mind and a recognition of the limitations of social change theories when trying to apply them. It also requires awareness of how hard it is to design a blueprint for action based on immutable principles. So many variables come into play in each battle and in each strategy that we devise. This is true for every social shift, especially in a world where political realities, public engagement—both local and international— and the nature of media and its power are constantly changing.

Perhaps the hardest nut to crack in terms of drawing conclusions from past experience is the question of its relevance to the present (and therefore to the future). The notion that past experience can help improve future performance is based on assumptions from hard science, that two similar situations will be similarly affected by the application of the same process. Therefore, if we can eliminate previous errors, we can improve outcomes. If the notion is applicable to legal cases—that our outcomes should improve based on correcting our past strategies—then Israeli human rights lawyers are the very embodiment of the lay definition of insanity: repeating the same action time after time in the hope of getting a different result. The lawyers have challenged hundreds of demolition orders to destroy the family homes of suspected terrorists, claiming that the orders are collective punishment and therefore prohibited, and have almost never won. They have filed scores of petitions against deporting Palestinian activists, claiming this is a clear violation of an explicit prohibition under the international law of occupation, and never won. They have challenged restrictions on Palestinian travel countless times, with little success that achieved no significant change. The list goes on, but the point is clear. So why do they keep hitting their heads against a wall and refuse to accept that the physics of head-meets-brick is not going to change?

There are many reasons. One reason, perhaps the most important, is that the notion of success in the context of social change is much wider than an individual court victory. The effect that litigation has on politics, on the media, and on social perceptions means that the judicial rulings—the wins and the losses—are only one element in the matrix of litigation's outcomes. This complicated question of how to measure success (and failure) in the legal struggle for social change is explored throughout this book.

Another reason for the lawyers' stubbornness has to do with the question of what exactly "sameness" or "similarity" means in terms of a legal-social-political situation. The scientific principle is not necessarily useful for predicting the outcome of social-political initiatives, including legal battles for social change. This type of action is so complex and there are so many variables that the odds of actually duplicating a particular situation are zero.

A third reason is that it is difficult to predict the outcome of a proceeding based on past outcomes in similar proceedings due to the complexity of identifying which of the similarities in two cases are relevant and which are not. Legal petitions that look alike always involve many differences, and it is never clear which of them matter. The context of each case is different, as is the focus of the legal argument or the style of the litigator. Above all, two cases might seem to address identical issues, but our social and political reality is ever-shifting. That reality is the single most influential factor on the chance of winning a politically sensitive case. The smallest change in our reality will shape the possibility of different outcomes in two similar cases. Lawyers are programmed to find the disparities between the case that failed and the one they are litigating, which is why they do not despair in the face of past failures.

So you can relax. Human rights lawyers in Israel are not crazy, just obsessive. And though past experience might teach us some things, history does not really repeat itself, it just reflects itself, each time from a slightly different angle. Although the river might look the same, each time we step in it the water has changed a little.

With all this, and despite the reservations, one thing is clear: even if it is hard to learn from the past, knowing it enriches us if only because it introduces the spectrum of outcomes of the type of battles we want to engage. Even if this knowledge cannot give us a predictive system and hence a tool for planning our battles, it does somewhat reduce the uncertainty. For anyone fighting the occupation in the legal arena, familiarity with the history of the battle so far is like using exams from previous years to study for this year's final. The questions will probably be different, but at least we have some idea of what we are up against.

Still, the value of lessons from the past only takes us so far: the fact is, human rights lawyers will never ask themselves *whether* to fight for victims of abuse. Shutting their mouths, shelving the legal books, burying their pens deep in their pockets—this is not an option, no matter what the context, the abuse, the legal arena. Because they cannot stay silent in the face of evil; because passivity is moral complicity; because their particular role in the struggle—wording its manifesto—is crucial. Although they might sometimes ask themselves *how* best to use their skills, they will never question whether there's a place for the law in this fight. For human rights lawyers, enlisting the law to combat oppression is not a choice. It is an existential act.

1

The Battleground

THE LAW AND THE COURT

The legal struggle for human rights, like any legal dispute, takes place mostly (though not only) in the courtroom. The swords wielded in this battle are the legal norms—that is, the rules—of any given legal system; these determine what is permitted, what is prohibited, and what powers, rights, and obligations are allowed to people, corporations, and public authorities. Without these two conditions—a law and a court—there is no legal battle.

The West Bank and Gaza Strip are not part of the State of Israel. Other territories occupied in 1967, the Golan Heights and East Jerusalem, were put under Israeli law and administration by the legislature (an act that is not recognized by the international community as it defies international law that prohibits the annexation of a territory seized by force).[1] Therefore, from Israel's perspective, its courts have jurisdiction to hear any dispute that arises in the Golan Heights and East Jerusalem and must make decisions according to Israeli law.

The West Bank and the Gaza Strip have, at least thus far, not been annexed by Israel, and so, even from Israel's own perspective, its laws and administration do not apply there.

So in which theater can the legal battle against human rights violations in the West Bank and Gaza Strip take place? Which law applies? Which court has jurisdiction to oversee its implementation? The Israeli authorities have devised various answers to these questions, which define the field in which the internal legal battles affecting the Occupied Territories are fought.

THE HIGH COURT OF JUSTICE

On August 5, 1971, in response to a labor dispute between the Christian Society for Holy Places, an association that ran a hospital and an orphanage in Bethlehem, and its employees, the military commander of the West Bank decided to introduce an amendment to the Jordanian labor law. The domestic pre-occupation laws that were in force in the West Bank were a mixture of Jordanian laws, British Mandatory ordinances, and Ottoman laws. The amendment concerned the appointment of members of the mediation council that helps resolve labor disputes. However, the Christian association, through its Israeli lawyer, Shlomo Tusya-Cohen, filed a petition with Israel's High Court of Justice to annul the amendment. Tusya-Cohen argued that the military commander had no power to change labor laws. The High Court dismissed the argument by a majority of two, who believed the exception that allows the occupying power to amend local laws applied in the case.[2] Thus the High Court heard and ruled on an argument regarding the legality of an act that—from start to finish—took place outside the state and was not governed by Israeli law.

The courts are one of the foremost expressions of a country's sovereignty. They are the official institutions that interpret law enacted by the country's legislature and oversee its implementation. Just as the territorial application of state laws has geographical boundaries (for the most part, the country's borders), so does the jurisdiction of its courts. Just as the imposition of one country's laws on another is a violation of the other country's sovereignty, it is also a violation for one country's courts to adjudicate events that have occurred in foreign territory.

When it comes to an occupation, matters are obviously more complicated. The sovereign has been defeated and no longer exerts effective control over the territory, which is now controlled by the occupation authorities. Do they bring their judicial institutions with them? In the case of the Christian Society, this question never even arose. The court made its decision on the merits of the case without first addressing its jurisdiction. Israel's government, for its part, decided not to object, even consenting to the High Court's jurisdiction de facto, without ever defining it as a matter of law.[3]

The military advocate general at the time, Meir Shamgar, who would go on to become president of the Supreme Court, has written that this was a deliberate decision of the authorities. Shamgar claims legal advisers sought judicial review of the military administration's actions as a way of preventing arbitrary conduct and ensuring the rule of law.[4] A more skeptical explanation is that the government wanted judicial review for political reasons, perhaps even for public relations, to provide a sense that the occupation is not a naked use of blunt force, but rather a series of acts that are subject to serious judicial review.*[5] In any event, the state agreed to the litigation and did not deny the court's jurisdiction. The justices, for reasons that remain unclear, never questioned their power to rule on an issue that relates to matters outside Israel's borders. And so, quietly, without hesitation or doubt, Israel's judiciary took upon itself the power to hold judicial review over the acts of the state's authorities in occupied, non-annexed territories.

This might seem self-evident in the present day, but for a jurist in the early 1970s it was an exceptional decision and far from obvious. In the early 1950s, for instance, a case was brought before the American court by five German soldiers who had been convicted of war crimes during World War II, and were being held in prison in an American-occupied part of Germany. The petitioners sought an order to compel their release. The US Supreme Court held that American courts have no jurisdiction to hold judicial review over acts of the authorities that take place outside the country's sovereign territory.[6] That approach has been mitigated over the years, mainly through petitions relating to prisoners held in Guantánamo Bay in Cuba after the 9/11 terrorist attacks,[7] but at the time the Israeli High Court of Justice ruled in the Christian Society case, its decision was highly unusual.

But it seemed quite natural for the High Court and Israel's government to take this approach, to expand its jurisdiction as Israel expanded the territory under its control. To understand why, we need to become better acquainted with the character of this particular judicial body. The High Court of Justice was founded in 1922 by the British Mandate

---

*   In *The Occupation of Justice: The Supreme Court of Israel and the Occupied Territories*, David Kretzmer raises the hypothesis that the government considered opening the avenue of High Court petitions to the Palestinians as a means of legitimizing Israeli control.

authorities. The structure of the Mandate's judicial system contained three main instances—the Magistrates Courts, the District Courts, and the Supreme Court, which was the final appellate address.[8] The High Court—distinct from the other three instances—was established following a model that existed in England since 1875[9] to concentrate in one court all powers to issue orders to state authorities and government officials. The procedure in the High Court begins with a lawyer's petition to the court for an order nisi (a conditional order) directed at the authorities. The court then decides whether there are grounds to compel the state officials to mount a defense. Only after the order nisi has been issued and the relevant authority has responded does the court hold an oral hearing, followed by a decision.

However, in contrast to the United Kingdom, where the High Court of Justice[10] is a court of first instance, with appellate courts above it, Mandate rule instated the High Court of Justice of Palestine–Eretz Israel as a bench within the top instance, the Supreme Court. This means that in Israel the final appeals court in civil and criminal matters, with its justices, also serves as the first administrative instance. It is not clear why the British entrusted judicial review over state authorities to the final instance, but the leading explanation among scholars is that they wanted to avoid a situation where local justices, who were not British and who served in the lower courts, would have the power to issue orders directed at Mandate authorities.[11] While there were non-British justices serving in the Mandatory Supreme Court, the chief justice, who held many administrative powers, including the power to appoint panels, was necessarily British. In addition, an order signed by the British high commissioner in 1924 stipulated that all High Court panels had to include at least one British justice.[12]

This special construct, which sends civilians to file petitions against state authorities directly with the top court, was passed down to Israel with very few changes made to it. Israel's High Court of Justice, also serving as the administrative bench of the Supreme Court, has the power to issue injunctions, mandamus (or mandatory) orders, and other orders "to State authorities, to local authorities, to their officials, and to other bodies and persons holding public office under the law, to act or refrain from acting while lawfully exercising their office."[13] In addition, the High Court has general powers, framed very broadly, to hear matters regarding which "it deems it necessary to provide relief for the sake of justice."[14] This is, without a doubt, an odd power for a judicial instance that exists to grant remedies according to the law, rather than according to justice. Historical research indicates that the phrase "for the sake of justice" likely originated in a mistranslation of the Mandatory definition for the High Court's power to issue orders required "for the administration of justice."[15] This mistranslation penetrated Israeli law and has had great influence in shaping the notion of the High Court as one vested with the power to deliberate and make decisions when "justice," not only formal law, so requires.[16]

This constitutional construct, which defines the power of the judicial instance according to its objects—state authorities and officials—might explain why the High Court easily considered that its jurisdiction extends to wherever those authorities exercise control. And indeed, in the Christian Society case—the first reported case in which the court ruled on a petition against the Israeli military commander in the Occupied Territories,[17] the justices exercised their ordinary power over "State authorities, . . . local authorities, . . . their officials, and . . . other bodies and persons holding public office under the law." The military, even when acting as an occupying power, is part of Israel's executive branch. Its powers are determined by Israeli law and it fulfills a public function.

A few years later, rather than simply relying on the state's voluntary consent to its intervention the High Court explained why its territorial jurisdiction does not end at the Green Line: its justices determined that the court's power follows "persons holding public office under the law" personally.[18]

All this means that the legal battle for the human rights of the occupied has its court, the Supreme Court of the State of Israel sitting as the High Court of Justice. Still, a legal battle also needs law, a normative framework, a set of rules by which the court decides whether the actions of the military regime are legal or not. What is the law of the occupation?

THE LAWS OF OCCUPATION

When the IDF took control of the Gaza Strip and the West Bank, the commanders of the two areas issued proclamations stating that the law in force prior to the occupation would remain in place so long as it did not conflict with any future orders. The law applicable in Gaza for the next four decades and in the West Bank to the present day[19] is founded on these proclamations and on thousands of orders signed over the years by a succession of military commanders. In addition, the Israeli legislature (the Knesset) has applied some laws extraterritorially to Israelis living in the Occupied Territories, and the military commander has adopted some Israeli laws and applied them to the settlements by military decree. This way, "enclaves" of Israeli law were created that encompass the settlers. The outcome is a partial dual legal system, one for Palestinians and one for (Jewish) Israelis who reside in the same territory.[20]

But where do the military commanders derive the power to declare which laws apply and which do not? Since when is a military commander a legislator? One could, of course, argue that the power comes from their guns, and this would make sense as a political response, but the legal answer is different.

Conflicts between states, or between states and external entities, are regulated by international law. Like domestic law, international law is a system of norms that determines what is permitted and what is prohibited, as well as the powers, rights, and obligations of those to whom it applies. International law regulates various areas of international relations, such as trade, diplomatic relations, the work of international institutions like the United Nations and its agencies, and mechanisms for peaceful resolution of conflicts. One of the oldest and most important branches of international law is the *laws of war* (or *Laws of Armed Conflict*). These laws, which some say date back to antiquity and whose modern version has been under accelerated development since the nineteenth century, have two branches: *jus ad bellum*, the laws that govern when it is permissible to use force in international relations; and *jus in bello*, which governs how force is used and determines what may and may not be done on the battlefield (also known as *international humanitarian law*, since its core aim is to protect people not taking part in hostilities from the effects of war and to mitigate human suffering). These laws apply regardless of the legality of the decision to use force or its justification.[21]

One of the situations the laws of war seek to regulate is the eventuality of a military gaining effective control over a territory outside its own country, that is, a situation of occupation. International humanitarian law accordingly includes a set of regulations and principles intended to determine what powers an occupier has in the occupied land and what restrictions and prohibitions apply to it. These are the laws of occupation, and they govern not only the relationship between the occupying power (the term used in international law for the occupying country) and the occupied land, but also between the occupying power and the civilians who find themselves under occupation. These laws have been codified in two major international conventions: The Fourth Hague Convention Respecting the Laws and Customs of War on Land from 1907 and the Fourth Geneva Convention Relative to the Protection of Civilian Persons in Time of War from 1949. Israel signed and ratified the Geneva Convention. The Hague Convention was signed before Israel was established, but is still applicable as it reflects binding international custom.[22] Today, the Geneva Convention is also considered customary.

The laws of occupation are based on three principles aside from the prohibition on annexation: occupation is not sovereignty; occupation is temporary; occupation is a trusteeship by the occupier for the occupied.[23] A thorough explanation of what these principles mean exceeds the scope of this book, but for our purposes, we can say that these laws aim to prevent anarchy in the occupied territory and restore security and civil life to the extent possible under occupation. To do so, they allow for the institution of a new, temporary regime and give the occupier the powers required to fulfill its duty—powers that would have been held by all branches of the previous regime. Thus the military commander, under powers vested in him through international law, has legislative authority in the occupied territory, and the orders he issues constitute primary and secondary legislation. He also serves as the head of the executive branch in the occupied territories, and the officers under his command have all the powers previously held by the defeated government. The military commander may also set up military courts with jurisdiction over security matters.

The laws of occupation do offer important, if few, checks and balances for what is expected to be an authoritarian regime ("authoritarian" in the sense that its subjects are not involved in the process of determining the norms that govern them). First, the military commander is expected to preserve the existing situation as much as possible. He may not amend local legislation unless such amendment is absolutely necessary for the fulfillment of his obligation. He is also expected to make no long-term changes in the occupied territory, as such changes are an expression of sovereignty, and the military commander is not a sovereign but a temporary administrator. Second, managing the territory, the military commander must serve the interests of the occupied population,[24] an expression of the fact that he holds the territory in trust. Third, he must avoid violating the fundamental rights of the occupied population and protect it from harm by others.

Most of the rights of the occupied population are not absolute, and security considerations could justify their proportional violation. There are, however, a few rights bestowed on the occupied without exception, and these may not be violated, no matter the circumstances. One such inviolable right is the prohibition on confiscating the property of the occupied.[25] Another is the prohibition on expelling members of the occupied population outside the occupied territory.[26] A third is the prohibition on transferring the population of the occupying power into the occupied territory and creating a community of occupiers alongside the occupied.[27]

AND SO THE answer to the question of which law applies in an occupied territory has four layers. The first is the law that was in effect prior to the occupation, insofar as the military commander has not issued orders to change it. In the West Bank, this is Jordanian law. In Gaza, it is the military law imposed by Egypt during its occupation of the Strip.[28] The second layer comprises military law, or the orders issued over the years by the military commanders. Thousands of such orders have changed the laws predating the occupation beyond recognition, and in every possible sphere. The third layer is Israeli administrative law. This applies to the actions of the Israeli rulers in the occupied territory and regulates how authorities may exercise their powers and discretion. The topmost legal layer is the international laws of occupation. These make up the highest normative order, and they trump any contradictory provisions in the lower layers. If what remains of Jordanian law or a military order permits something that is explicitly prohibited under the laws of occupation, those provisions are legally null and void. The laws of occupation function somewhat as a constitution of the occupied territory and they govern the fundamental principles of the relationship between the regime of occupation and its subjects.*

For this reason the High Court of Justice, when it was asked in the case of the Christian Society whether the military commander had exceeded his powers by giving an order to change Jordanian labor law, examined the question through the lens of the branch of international law that addresses belligerent occupation. The judges disagreed over whether, in that particular case, the military needed to amend local law to uphold its obligation to restore civil life, but they all concurred that the legality of the order was governed by the norms of the laws of occupation.

Israel's government, which, for political and ideological reasons, wanted to avoid defining the territories as "occupied" and maintain its claim internationally that they are "disputed," adopted a rather strange position on the applicability of the laws of occupation to the territories it was occupying. According to its position, the territories were not "occupied" in the legal sense and therefore the laws of occupation did not apply. However, the government "voluntarily" undertook to uphold the humanitarian provisions of these laws.[29] The strangeness of this stance is that when it comes to legal norms one cannot pick and choose. Either the norms apply or they do not. And if the laws of occupation do not apply, what is the law that governs Israel's military rule in the Occupied Territories?

In keeping with the government's position, the state advised the court in the Christian Society case that it was not being asked to rule on the applicability of the laws of occupation, since the military commander was in any case "doing as the conventions command."[30] And during the first decade of the occupation, cases continued to be ruled according to those conventions on the shaky grounds that the state agreed to their application while preserving its argument that they do not, in fact, apply. However, in the years that followed, the High Court stopped viewing the state's

---

* At least, this is the international legal perspective. However, Israel's High Court has ruled that the primary commitment of judges in domestic courts is to the laws of their country. If a domestic law contradicts international law, Israel's courts are bound to uphold the act of Israel's parliament. In the context of the occupation, this approach governed the annexation of East Jerusalem and the Golan Heights, which is illegal under international law (hence the international community's refusal to acknowledge it), but is recognized by Israel's courts. But unlike acts of the Knesset, military orders in the Occupied Territories do not override international law.

consent as a condition for applying the laws of occupation. Fierce disputes arose between petitioners and respondents and among the justices themselves over what exactly the laws of occupation say and which parts are binding on Israel. However, the jurisprudence of the High Court gradually and carefully came to accept that the international laws of occupation are the legal field governing Israel's control of the Occupied Territories.[31]

With that, the way those laws have been applied and their interpretation by the High Court have not infrequently gutted their core humanitarian purpose, prompting fierce criticism. What follows are the pivotal events, cases, and decisions that ultimately shaped the reality in the Occupied Territories.

2

Deportation: Raising the Stakes

ABU AWAD

At 3:00 p.m., a guard walked up to Riad Abed Rashid Abu Awad's cell.

Abu Awad, a student at Birzeit University near Ramallah and an activist in the Popular Front for the Liberation of Palestine, had been held under administrative detention for some time. It was not his first stint in jail. Two years after Israel took control of the West Bank, he was arrested, tried, and convicted of membership in an illegal organization and sentenced to two years' imprisonment. After his release, he resumed activity in Palestinian left-wing organizations and continued taking part in protests against the occupation. In the late 1970s, Birzeit University was a hotbed of political action and hence a target for the Israeli security forces, who often shut it down using force.

At the time, a group of left-wing activists from Jerusalem, including Jewish intellectuals, Arab students, and Hebrew University professors, joined together to support Birzeit, and they met with people from Ramallah, including Abu Awad. The two groups were united by opposition to the occupation, concern for Birzeit, and revolutionary socialist ideology. Leah Tsemel, one of the Israeli activists and a young lawyer, was a member of the Socialist Organization in Israel, more commonly known by the title of its journal, *Matzpen* (Hebrew for "compass"). Matzpen was founded as a response to the expulsion of several members of Maki, the Communist Party of Israel (which had itself splintered, creating the New Communist

List, or Rakah). Members of Matzpen espoused revolutionary socialism, recognition of Palestinian national rights, and the creation of a shared socialist entity in the Middle East; to the Israeli public, the organization was synonymous with sedition. Leah Tsemel's legal work made her one of Matzpen's most recognizable members, and through the Jerusalem-Birzeit group, she came to know Abu Awad.

In the 1970s, a general travel permit issued by Defense Minister Moshe Dayan immediately after the occupation allowed Palestinians from the West Bank and Gaza Strip to enter Israel freely, and Israelis could also freely visit the Occupied Territories. Thus Birzeit activists and the joint group in Jerusalem frequently attended each other's meetings. The members had fervent ideological discussions, authored articles, and put out political pamphlets. The activism that had begun as solidarity with a Palestinian university sowed the seeds for strong political and social bonds. Israelis and Palestinians, all left-wing activists, spoke a common socialist language, envisioned identical political solutions, and dreamed of their societies coming together. One of the connections that grew out of this group was that of Tsemel and Abu Awad.

The group's joint activity did not go unnoticed by Israeli security officials, and they soon began following its actions, setting their sights on a new, short-lived organization that sprang up at the Hebrew University, apparently as a result of the connections between Jerusalem and Birzeit, the Progressive National Movement. The movement did little beyond putting out a pamphlet or two, but one of the pathos-filled publications soon became a topic of discussion at the High Court of Justice, or rather Abu Awad's part in drafting it. The pamphlet called for an end to the "Zionist entity" and rebuked attempts made by Rakah, which was accused of recognizing this entity, to represent Palestinian interests. The Israeli authorities thought the text expressed the positions of the Palestinian Liberation Organization, which had been outlawed as a terrorist group, and the pamphlet caused an uproar when right-wingers demanded that the full weight of the law be brought to bear on its authors.

On January 29, 1979, at 3:00 p.m., a guard came to Abu Awad's cell and told him that the same morning, the military commander of the West Bank had signed an order for his deportation to Lebanon. Abu Awad knew what the issue was. He had been interrogated at length about his part in drafting the pamphlet. "The advisory committee"—a review panel—"will hold a hearing at 7:00 p.m.," the guard said. Abu Awad asked to make a telephone call.

The Defense (Emergency) Regulations are the brainchild of the British Mandate. They were enacted by the high commissioner for Palestine by virtue of the supreme normative document of Mandatory law, the King's Order in Council. The British monarch, the head of the world power to which the League of Nations gave a mandate to prepare Palestine for independence, was the country's supreme legislative authority. In 1937, at the height of the Arab Revolt (a violent protest against colonial rule and increasing Jewish immigration), the king empowered the high commissioner to enact emergency regulations.[1] The King's Order was read and signed by King George VI with much British pomp and ceremony on March 20, 1937, at Buckingham Palace and in the presence of his council. It is doubtful that the four-man council could have imagined that the legal document enacted, which was intended to contain a brewing colonial insurgency, would outlive not only the Mandate but also the regime that followed it. Who could have guessed that the King's Order in Council would serve in future decades as the legal basis for draconian sanctions and human rights violations by another people in Mandatory Palestine, who were also fighting to throw off British rule?

Ultimately, the King's Order and the Emergency Regulations would fare quite differently from the country to which they originally applied. While Palestine was divided only eleven years later among several different regimes, each with a distinct legal and political tradition, the King's Order and the Emergency Regulations would continue to apply to the entire territory. As far as the order and the regulations go, the country was never partitioned. Not one of the regimes that replaced His Majesty's Government relinquished the far-reaching powers the British king had bestowed upon his officials, although there is, as we shall see, a question whether the Jordanians repealed the power to deport.

The King's Order gave the high commissioner tremendous latitude to adopt regulations to counter security threats, public disturbances, and insurgencies. In the relevant section, the king defined the commissioner's powers thus:

> The High Commissioner may make such regulations . . . as appear to him in his unfettered discretion to be necessary or expedient for securing the

public safety, the defense of Palestine, the maintenance of public order
and the suppression of mutiny, rebellion and riot, and for maintaining
supplies and services essential to the life of the community.

Elsewhere in the order, the king provided a non-exhaustive list of security measures the high commissioner may put in place, powers that allowed
for broad administratively sanctioned violations of many fundamental
freedoms: freedom of speech, freedom of movement, and property rights.
In fact, the regulations gave the regime the legal tools to control and restrict
every aspect of civilian life. Also, the fact that some of the powers were
designated as "administrative" meant that the regime was held to an
extremely low standard of justification for using them, much lower than
the standard used for a criminal sanction, for example. The regime was
only required to demonstrate the suspicion—based on evidence that would
be inadmissible in a criminal court, such as hearsay—that a target was a
threat to public safety for the sanction to be permissible.

Many of the powers the king allowed the high commissioner to enact
would become the topic of much deliberation in Israel's High Court of
Justice, because the military regime in the Occupied Territories went on
to use them on a wholesale scale. These include house demolitions, administrative detention, and military censorship, but the measure that appeared
in the first section of the king's list related to deportation. The king determined that the high commissioner would be allowed to provide for "the
deportation and exclusion of persons from Palestine."

The most recent version of the high commissioner's Defense (Emergency) Regulations dates back to 1945.[2] Two of the regulations—108 and
112—formalize the power to deport individuals from Mandatory Palestine.[3] They stipulate that the high commissioner may issue a deportation
order against a person whose removal is deemed necessary for "securing
the public safety, the maintenance of public order, or the suppression of
mutiny, rebellion or riot." In the final year of the Mandate, in 1947, the
high commissioner added a subsection that allowed candidates for deportation to ask for an advisory committee, whose members were also
appointed by the high commissioner, to review the legality and justification for the deportation order and advise the government whether or not
to execute it.[4]

After the occupation of the West Bank and the Gaza Strip, the Israeli government's legal advisers claimed that the Mandatory Defense Regulations had remained in force in those parts of Mandatory Palestine that had been governed, since 1949, by Egypt (the Gaza Strip) and Jordan (the West Bank)—not a single one of the regulations had been repealed (and in fact they had stayed in force in Israel, too). They argued that the Egyptian military commander and the Jordanian government had inherited the powers given to the high commissioner, and thus these same powers had been bequeathed to Israel's military commanders. The wonders of contiguous law and government.

Forty-two years after the British king empowered his high commissioner to deport people from Mandatory Palestine, the IDF commander of the West Bank, an officer with the rank of brigadier general, put himself in the British ruler's shoes and signed an order for Abu Awad's removal from his home and native land. Abu Awad was taken to a prison room with a telephone. He had one wish: before the advisory committee convened in several hours and perfunctorily recommended the order's execution and he found himself on Lebanese soil, he wanted to get hold of his friend and lawyer, Leah Tsemel.

SO THAT THEY HAVE NO LEADERSHIP

The deportation power is one of the harshest and most far-reaching of the regulations. Before 1948, the British used it to deport hundreds of Jewish residents suspected of membership in underground Zionist organizations. The Jewish community in Mandatory Palestine strongly objected to the use of the regulation, and some of the most scathing objections to the Defense Regulations in general and deportation in particular came from its top jurists. A number of these jurists went on to lead independent Israel's legal system, but by then their burning disdain for the Defense Regulations had evidently cooled down, since they made no effort to revoke them.[5]

The forcible removal of people from their country is a fatal blow on two counts. The first is the direct impact that uprooting someone from their society has on their very being. As we know, humans are intensely social creatures. Their identities, their essence, are formed by their families, communities, and nations, and their relationships with the social circles in which they live write the stories of their lives. Removing people from their social structures cuts them off from the very roots that nurture who they are and form a central component of their identity. It might be harder to grasp what physical expulsion means to a deportee in our current digital age, but imagine a much less fluid world, the world as it was in the previous century, with no Internet, no mobile phones, and with the very solid borders of a world split into two blocks locked in a Cold War. In this world, a person who was deported to an enemy state might not have seen their relatives and friends for decades, and long-distance communication was scarce.

Additionally, deportation severs people from their life's setting—the landscapes, sites, nature, and climate that shaped them. If the term "human dignity" has any meaning, and by human dignity we mean the notion that every person's life has metaphysical value separate and apart from their biological existence, and that this value is the ultimate, most exalted thing society must protect, then the basic condition for ensuring human dignity is to allow people to exercise their right to live in the social and geographical frameworks that have formed who they are and have given meaning to their identity. More than a violation of a specific fundamental right, deportation is a full-frontal assault on the deportees' human dignity, on the notion that they are entitled to live under the basic conditions without which they would find it difficult to realize their value as human beings. This is the philosophical foundation that guided the human rights movement and inspired international human rights law—to recognize the prohibition on deporting people from their country and to protect a group of fundamental rights that, together, express this notion, such as the right to family life, the right to enter one's country, and the right to citizenship.

This is the first blow inflicted by deportation: it cuts people off from their human and geographic environment.

Deportation has another dimension, one that is just as bad as, if not worse than, the first. Deportees who have no other citizenship to rely on become stateless refugees. Legal status (mostly citizenship, but, to a large extent, also permanent residency) is a prerequisite for exercising a large proportion of human rights, civil, political, and socioeconomic rights. A state's duty to grant or respect fundamental rights often applies only to its subjects. The right to work is one example: countries do not generally have an obligation to give foreign nationals work permits, but their own citizens and residents clearly have that right. The same holds true for freedom of movement in and out of the country, as well as within it, and for many socioeconomic rights. With few exceptions, these rights can only be exercised in a country where the person has status. The state is nothing if not a social association through which people are able to exercise their rights as human beings, and the state, as a collective, is charged with protecting the rights of its members from harm by others. Stateless deportees lose the main channel for exercising their human rights and the main tool that is meant to protect them from violations of their rights. They are like animals without a pack or herd, wandering the world without the benefits a pack provides in securing food and basic living conditions. The international conventions that deal with refugees and stateless people are meant to provide some basic protections, but they clearly do not cover anything like the array of rights that citizens and permanent residents enjoy.

Such is the deportee's predicament today. And such was the case when Abu Awad was handed his deportation order in the late 1970s. Even if a deportee faces no immediate mortal danger—one thinks of Cain, "a fugitive and a vagabond in the earth; and it shall come to pass, that every one that findeth me shall slay me"[6]—even if the deportee's destination is a decent place, free of arbitrary abuse from thieves and thugs, deportation still spells real risk for a life that cannot transcend physical subsistence.

DEPORTATION IS ONE of the gravest sanctions and there is no doubt that a regime equipped with deportation powers can use them to terrorize its opponents. The use of deportation against a regime's adversaries is a powerful deterrent. But a regime confronting insurgency might find deportation attractive for its political impact, which is often more important than the deterrence it creates. A person's removal has an impact not only on the individual deportee but also on the environment he has left behind. The trauma of displacement also affects the country from where the deportee's roots have been torn up; all that is left is an empty hole in the ground.

The political strategy served by deportation was articulated, in his direct, no-holds-barred style, by Rafael Eitan, the IDF chief of staff in the early 1980s. In a security discussion with Prime Minister Menachem Begin the morning after the attempted assassination of several West Bank mayors by an extremist Jewish underground, deportation was discussed as a tool for tightening control over the West Bank. Two mayors who had been deported about a month earlier (Fahed Qawasmeh of Hebron and Muhammad Milhem of Halhul) had petitioned the High Court against their deportation. During Begin's meeting, some participants voiced the concern that the High Court would order their return to attend an advisory committee hearing, which had been denied them. Eitan argued for a military crackdown to prevent public disturbances and curtail Palestinian political activity. He believed this goal could be achieved by deporting leading public figures within Palestinian society. The transcripts of this discussion[7] immortalize Eitan's words, which leave no doubt about the purpose of deportation: "So that they have no leadership to encourage action against us in all spheres, politically and violently, the leadership must be removed each time. 'Removed' means sent away, imprisoned, or outlawed. . . . In a situation where some have been injured, some have fled, some are abroad, and some are outlawed, there's chaos, confusion, no one knows what to do, and the result is that on the ground there's less violence."[8]

The conversation, which took place after a brutal attack on Palestinian leaders by Jewish extremists, focused on the type of force to be used against Palestinians in an effort to quell the outraged response. The deputy defense minister, Mordechai Tzipori, explained how deportation eliminates the deportee's leadership, making it effective: "As Avraham explained [Avraham Ahituv, head of the Shin Bet, who was also at the meeting], when a leader is deported from the country, after two weeks of gallivanting around the world, the party's over. Fatah in Beirut doesn't need any extra leaders and they reject him, and the man, depressed, is reduced to ashes, maybe even becomes a laughingstock to his family. This is why deportation is a good tool that needs to be used."[9]

There you have it, the whole concept in a nutshell. Deportation turns deportees into a laughingstock and erases their social presence and political clout. These injurious consequences of deportation, which is why it is considered a frontal assault on the deportees' human dignity, are exactly what makes this violation so attractive to those doing the deporting. Once expelled, the deportee will diminish until there is nothing left. And the home he or she has left behind is left without a leader. The resulting vacuum, so the authorities hope, will be hard to fill and the ensuing chaos will make it difficult for the resistance to function and easier for the military to control the population.

Over the decades, this oppressive logic motivated successive Israeli governments to make extensive use of the deportation powers originally granted by King George VI to the Mandatory government. Whenever Palestinian leadership emerged, either locally or nationally, deportation orders served to cut it down, making sure that the occupied had no shepherd. Deportation became one of the major means the occupation used to suppress the people under its rule.

FELICIA LANGER

The history of Palestinian deportations from the West Bank and Gaza by Israel divides into three periods: the earliest covers the first decade of the occupation, the second spans from the late 1970s to the early 1990s, and the third continues to the present. In the years after 1967, Israel deported Palestinians on a massive scale, not always based on the Defense Regulations. In fact, it's possible that some people were deported with no legal basis at all. According to official figures, during that time, there were 989 deportation orders for Palestinians from the Occupied Territories.[10] The use of deportation powers changed according to the security situation. During relative calm, they were deployed less widely, but when security officials sensed a buildup of tension, approaching boiling point, and when Palestinians were resorting to violence, deportation, along with house demolitions and administrative detention, was one of the main tools used by the military to subdue unrest. Key figures were deported, people perceived as leaders, and there were collective deportations, usually of Palestinian prisoners who fit certain criteria. Recently revealed documents describe one such collective deportation from Gaza in 1970–1971.

Deteriorating security led IDF commanders to deport groups of detainees, usually under administrative detention, over the Jordan River, in groups of ten to twenty. These deportations were called "patient operations" and the criterion for expulsion was detainees who were relatively old and had been in administrative detention for at least two years.[11] When Gaza became even more volatile, the deportations were expanded to include families of suspects who were sent to the Sinai Peninsula. Hundreds of people were deported in the "patient operations," which apparently stopped in late 1971.[12] These were carried out without proper legal proceedings; indeed, no one even imagined at the time that they could be challenged in Israeli court. In the early days of the occupation, no petitions were filed in the High Court of Justice challenging the administration's actions in the Occupied Territories, and the notion that this institution has jurisdiction over government acts conducted outside Israel's sovereign borders was not at all clear.[13]

The authorities often plucked political activists under administrative detention out of their cells and deported them for one reason or another. The destination was Jordan, but since the Jordanian authorities refused to play along and would not allow the deportees passage over the Allenby Bridge, the Israeli military would transport them to the Araba desert, where the Jordanian border was not fenced off, and force them eastward. In 1975, due to growing Jordanian resistance and concern over possible diplomatic pressure, the IDF began deporting Palestinians to southern Lebanon.[14]

Because deportations were always sudden, and because Israel ignored the provision in the Defense Regulations that allowed deportees a hearing before an advisory committee, their families would find out about the expulsions only after the fact, and, as it turns out, so did their lawyers. "In 1970 and 1971, my clients would disappear one by one," Felicia Langer recounts in her book.[15] "My office was crowded with family members of administrative detainees who were still in jail. The fear of deportation brought them to me."[16] This is a classic case in which lack of information thwarts any possibility of initiating legal action. On the one hand, it is impossible to ask for a remedy against a sanction that is, at that point, speculation. On the other, once the action moves from theory to practice, it is too late.

Langer knew it would be hard to file a petition for her clients against a deportation order that had not yet been signed and perhaps never would be, but she was not put off by possible futility. It would be neither her first nor her last petition that seemed hopeless. The risk is a given for someone devoting their professional life to representing the oppressed and the disempowered. A lawyer who represents the strong and well connected has timely access, via their clients' status, to vast amounts of reliable information from sources in positions of power. A lawyer representing rightless civilians living under occupation has to guess at the authorities' intentions. She often follows her clients' gut feelings. The defense minister does not share his decisions with her. The risk of being thrown out of court or even reprimanded by the justices was present, but Langer was unperturbed. For her, any legal act, no matter how desperate, was legitimate, and preferable to waiting for the phone call with the news that her client was already across the border. The source of Langer's toughness and her ability to withstand the derision of her colleagues is rooted in her biography.

Langer arrived in Israel in 1950, after living through the rough years of the war in the USSR, where, as we know, her family had fled from Poland. Her father had been sent to the gulag for refusing to become a Soviet citizen (he feared being unable to return to Poland after the war). After he died in late 1944, Langer and her mother struggled to provide for themselves in extremely harsh conditions, selling their few possessions to survive. When the war ended, Langer returned to Poland, where she met her future spouse. Her mother, who had remarried, emigrated to Palestine; Langer and her husband answered her pleas and eventually followed her.

In the early 1960s, Langer realized a dream, and, unusual at the time for a woman who had a child, she enrolled in the Hebrew University Law School branch in Tel Aviv. Her past compelled her to represent the disempowered, to fight for people who, like her family and herself, were victims of government malice. She studied law to put her worldview, which had crystallized during the war, into action and challenge discrimination and injustice. By the mid-1960s, Langer had become a qualified lawyer, but her attempts to find work in the public sector were unsuccessful. Langer claims she was written off because of her Marxist convictions and her membership in Maki, Israel's Communist Party, at the time.[17] She had no choice but to turn to the private sector. But there she faced a different obstacle—her own conscience. After refusing to represent a man who was a pimp and was trying to evade paying alimony, she realized she had to set up her own practice if she wanted to pick her cases according to her many principles.

In her practice Langer represented clients who aligned with her ideological commitments: detained protesters, women whose rights had been violated, and Arab citizens of Israel in conflict with the authorities. This continued until 1967, when, in the space of six days, 1.5 million Palestinians came under Israeli occupation. At a time when Israeli society, with its many Holocaust survivors, was dedicated to the notion that the moral of the rise of the Nazis, their conquest of Europe, and the Final Solution was that the remnants of the Jewish people were obliged to build an invincible country that would protect Jews from victimhood, Langer drew a different lesson: any discrimination or occupation was fraught with danger, not just by the Germans and not just against Jews.

Representing Palestinians who had suddenly come under Israeli military rule, a regime of all-powerful army generals, was the very fulfillment of the goal for which she had studied law. The only lawyers representing the occupied at the time were a handful of Palestinian Israelis. Langer was a far cry from the typical defender of Palestinians: a woman, a Communist, and a European Jew. With her Polish accent and command of Latin, her partnership with West Bank and Gaza Palestinians may have been the strangest sight in the Middle East. To provide access to West Bank residents, Langer rented a small office on Koresh Street in Jerusalem, which would be her home base for the next twenty-three years. She soon became synonymous with the fight for Palestinian rights. To others she was a traitor and an enemy sympathizer.

Let them attack her, let them say she was wasting their time. Langer had a thick skin when it came to justices who were unwilling to help her clients. Though there was no signed deportation order that anyone knew of, she prepared a High Court petition in the name of twenty-eight clients who were under administrative detention and demanded an injunction against the defense minister to prohibit him from deporting them. Legally a preemptive petition is extremely problematic. It is entirely speculative, seeking remedy for an act that has not yet occurred and might never happen. And yet Langer managed to get an order nisi out of Justice Haim Cohn, prohibiting her clients' deportation (if there were a plan to deport them) pending a hearing.

In the hearing, however, unsurprisingly Supreme Court president Yoel Zussman scolded Langer. If the court were to allow such a petition, when there was no specific indication of plans to deport the petitioners, then every one of Israel's three million citizens could file the same petition. There was no way Langer could get what she was asking for so long as no deportation order had been signed and the defense minister had not confirmed any plan to deport her clients. Langer asked the court for time to contact the defense minister to ask him to inform the court whether there were plans to deport any of her clients, and to allow an advisory committee hearing, as required by the Defense Regulations. Langer also asked that the order nisi remain in effect until the minister responded. After some discussion, the panel granted her request.

In his response, the minister kept his cards close to his chest: "There are no plans, at the present time, to deport the Petitioners." At the present time. The minister would not guarantee that the petitioners would not be deported, say, three minutes after the petition was dismissed. With regard to any advisory committee hearing, the minister used evasive language: "Any past or present action taken by the competent authorities with respect to these detainees has and will be taken pursuant and according to the law."[18] As far as the justices were concerned, Langer had gotten more than she had asked for. The minister had said there was no plan to deport, even if only "at the present time." They certainly could not go on hearing the case given that response. But Langer wanted even more. She asked the court to note, in its judgment dismissing the petition, that the law requires a hearing by the advisory committee. Langer knew that a statement to that effect would make it hard to avoid holding a hearing in the future because that's how bureaucracy works. A comment by a justice, no matter how technical or procedural, is received by the legal advisors working for the government or the military, who are part of the legal community and therefore agents of the court in state institutions. The justices dismissed the petition but gave in to Langer's pestering and quoted the section that requires a hearing by the advisory committee.

This judgment did not end the fight for the right to a hearing. In fact, it had only just begun. The relevant section of the law states that the advisory committee will convene "if so requested to do by any person in respect of whom a deportation order has been made." Aha! Only if the deportee asks—and how will a deportee ask if he or she does not know they have the right to and cannot meet with their lawyer before the deportation occurs? From that point on, deportations proceeded on the assumption that deportees had a right to a hearing, but there was no obligation to inform them of this right. As long as deportees did not ask for a hearing, the deportation could go ahead. Langer had tried to insert a procedural hoop through which the authorities would have to jump, making summary deportations difficult, but the security establishment and its legal advisers had their own plans, and they too knew how to work the law.

There was no choice but to find a case that would allow a challenge to a deportation order as it was issued. A prisoner would not do, because they would not be able to inform family or a lawyer in advance. It would have to be someone who was taken from his home and who knew of his right to demand a hearing. Langer landed such a case in 1976.

At the time, local and city council elections were taking place in the Occupied Territories. Israel had decided to allow the elections, partly to burnish its image as an enlightened occupier who permits local democracy, even if only for the sake of appearances. But the military and the government quickly realized that the elections might have been a terrible mistake: PLO-affiliated candidates were poised for a landslide victory over the old guard, some of whom had been council members since Jordanian rule and were much more accommodating to the Israeli authorities. One of the leading candidates set to win against a sitting mayor was Ahmad Hamzi Natsheh, a physician who challenged Hebron mayor Muhammad Ali Ja'abari, a henchman of the Jordanian king. The last person Israel's government wanted as mayor in a complex city such as Hebron was Ahmad Hamzi Natsheh, who had been part of a group that forged a local leadership organization, the Palestinian National Front, and was considered radical. The solution was to deport him.[19]

The plan testifies to the value of the power to deport for Israel. Without it, the authorities would have had to fake the election result, oust an elected mayor, and lose the publicity boost to the enlightened occupation, or, alternately, live with an oppositional mayor in one of the West Bank's most significant cities. The military and the government were spared this mess because, instead, they could simply remove the candidate from the map, using some security pretext, and make him disappear. It did not even have to be forever. Keeping him away for a few years would suffice—he still wouldn't get to be mayor. But for deportation to work as a magic solution, the process could not turn into a fiasco. It could not take a heavy public or international toll. To reduce the political cost, deportation had to be done quickly. It couldn't turn into a lasting affair, going on for weeks or even months. A dragged-out process could draw fire that was liable to combust. Deportation had to be like ripping off a Band-Aid: rip and forget.

And so on Friday night, March 26, 1976, two weeks before the local Palestinian elections, Natsheh was arrested at home. His family contacted Langer and she quickly wrote a petition asking the High Court to order his release, expressing concern that his deportation might be in the works.

Since it was the weekend, Langer tracked down the court secretary on Saturday morning and he spoke to the justice on duty, Moshe Etzioni. After reading the petition, in which Langer argued that the arrest and deportation—if indeed that was the purpose of the arrest—were unlawful and motivated for political rather than security reasons, Etzioni urgently summoned a lawyer from the State Attorney's Office for a hearing to be held that day at 4:00 p.m.

At 2:00 p.m., Langer found out that a deportation order had, in fact, been issued against Natsheh. She also learned that Natsheh had asked to come before an advisory committee and be represented by Langer (which would have delayed the committee convening). Natsheh's request for representation was denied and he appeared before a quickly appointed committee. Two hours later, when Langer appeared in Etzioni's courtroom, state counsel notified the court that Natsheh had been deported fifteen minutes earlier. And so, he said, there was nothing to discuss. Etzioni steamed. "I cannot understand why there was a need to execute the deportation order fifteen minutes before I was going to review the petition," he wrote in the decision he gave that day, in which he had no choice but to dismiss the petition. "It appears that, quite unfortunately, what took place here was an attempt to prevent a hearing before this Court, which has no place in a law-abiding country."[20] Etzioni did not stop there. He ordered the attorney general to investigate what had happened.

Whether or not the investigation ever took place remains unclear. If it did, it appears to have left no mark. But those who wanted to carry on with quick and easy deportations now had a new headache. Getting away with summary deportations and preventing judicial review had gradually become more difficult. Natsheh's deportation signaled a new phase in the history of the practice, in which the security establishment was gradually and begrudgingly cornered into engaging with the deportees in court. Etzioni's outrage at the state's manipulations, which had prevented the hearing he had called for, reminded lawyers working on deportations that if justices dislike human rights violations, they truly hate being bypassed, their prestige and authority undermined. The Natsheh case implied that perhaps justices would agree to implement procedures and protocols that would make deportations much more difficult, raising the political stakes for Israel. But again, to win such rulings, lawyers had to find at least one case in which the state would be unable to carry out the deportation quickly enough to prevent a hearing. December 1979 brought that case, that of Abu Awad.

LEAH TSEMEL

By sheer coincidence, Leah Tsemel called the office in the middle of the workday. She could just as easily have not called, and Abu Awad would have likely found himself in Lebanon later that day, like Natsheh before him.

The day had begun like any other, with a calendar of court-martial hearings. By the late 1970s, Leah Tsemel had become known as a lawyer representing Palestinian detainees and defendants. She spent days upon days in the military courts scattered all over the West Bank and Gaza. This time it was the military court in Nablus. Another day of arguing with Israeli military judges and prosecutors who were also IDF officers. Another day of fighting for Palestinian detainees who came to court a shadow of their former selves, disheveled, eyes dead with despair, after being held in one of the IDF's or Shin Bet's foul facilities.

For any ordinary lawyer, a visit to the IDF's military courts in the West Bank and Gaza's major cities was a journey into the worst nightmare of their lawyerly imagination. Detainees in chains, minors and adults together, were brought into the courtroom as if on a conveyor belt, many of them having suffered humiliation and torture by Shin Bet agents or just by plain soldiers going above and beyond the call of duty. They would stand before a single Israeli judge, a Jewish military officer, or a panel of three, only one of whom would be a jurist, the others officers with no legal training who volunteered to take part sealing the fate of Palestinian defendants.[21] The defendants were expected to mount a defense under impossible conditions of military justice procedures, against charges that could send them to prison for years in the occupiers' jail.

Still today, trials take place in a foreign language—even the charge sheet is in Hebrew only. The judges, prosecutors, interpreters, and court clerks are all officers and soldiers of the occupation army. Evidence and legal procedures involve few of the rights granted to defendants in modern legal systems. The detainee may be denied a meeting with counsel for weeks, for example, and military judges have the power to hold suspects in pre-charge detention for many months. But over and above all this, most judges in this system see themselves first as emissaries of the occupying power, and their fundamental hostility, which is keenly felt by the defendants appearing before them, creates the sense that the trial is just a show and its conclusion is already fixed. Courts-martial are places where hope has been chewed up and spat out, congealing in stinking detention facilities and fetid prison vans. And so for an ordinary lawyer, a day in military court is a legal and human horror show.

But Leah Tsemel had never been an ordinary lawyer. Her years with Matzpen had accustomed her to being denounced and hated by almost everyone. She had overcome the need to be liked by the public and approved by the establishment at a relatively young age. Her life was one of scrapping and fighting with the regime and with the majority of the country. At the same time, her life was filled with a sense of mission and deep faith in her chosen path. When she started out as a lawyer, her Matzpen activism and her political associations made it very difficult to find work. After her studies, she was accepted to intern with a Magistrates Court judge in Jerusalem, but after an interview to determine her security clearance, in which she happily talked about her ideological Matzpen anti-Zionist convictions, she was made to understand that she would have to look for an internship elsewhere. Her attempt to intern with Felicia Langer also ended in failure. According to Tsemel's account, as a Rakah member and an honorary Knesset candidate in the party's parliamentary list, Langer refused to accept an activist from Matzpen. And so Tsemel found herself rejected by both Zionist and anti-Zionist establishments in Israel and, after completing an alternative small-practice internship and joining the bar, she struggled to find cases.

Dejected, Tsemel returned to her parents' town, Haifa, a rookie lawyer with lots of ambition but no job. Within a few months, something happened that would spell the breakthrough in her legal career. In December 1972, the Shin Bet and the police raided the homes of Red Front activists, arresting sixty. In a caricature of left-wing movements, the Red Front was an offshoot of an offshoot of Matzpen. If Rakah was not socialist enough for Matzpen, Matzpen was not revolutionary enough for a few activists who broke away. The offshoot was soon accused of some kind of ideological transgression and a splinter group set up as the Red Front, comprising revolutionary Marxists, Leninists, Jews, and Palestinian Israelis working together (but not for long). Back to December 1972: many Front members were imprisoned and the Shin Bet alleged that it had unearthed a network of terrorist cells that were poised to launch attacks across the country. The most serious allegation concerned a trip some of the activists, including Jewish members Udi Adiv and Dan Vered, had made to Syria. The indictment served against them stated that they had received weapons training in Syria and had made contact there with intelligence agents. The arrests caused an uproar. Jews, Israel's own sons, had joined with Arabs in violent struggle against the Zionist state! That had never happened before. The Jewish public's hate and loathing for the group and what it stood for was bottomless.

Though Tsemel belonged to Matzpen, the organization the detainees had rejected, she was still their natural go-to person. Immediately after the arrest, she was asked to represent one of them. In the courtroom she ran into Langer, who was representing Rami Livneh, a leader and founder of the Front. The woman she did not want in her practice was now her colleague, sitting with her on the lawyers' bench. The Red Front trial took several months, produced many headlines, and put Tsemel in the spotlight, this time as a lawyer. The main defendants were convicted and sentenced to long prison terms. At the appeal stage, Tsemel was asked to represent a number of clients. Security prisoners in jail started to pass her name around and she gained a reputation as a prominent lawyer willing to take on security cases. Her visits to jail became more and more frequent, and often a visit to one client would end up with a retainer from another.

Judges and prosecutors could not believe that a nice Jewish girl from Haifa, the daughter of a family of Holocaust survivors, would serve the enemy faithfully and passionately; they abhorred her and what she stood for. But her assertiveness and the moral force of her convictions deflected any effort to belittle her. In fact, the stronger the revulsion for her positions, the greater the respect she earned; and the more the respect grew, the more the anger toward her intensified. The respect for Tsemel came in response for her daring to break with the consensus and question the national ethos. The anger toward her was the cost of holding up a mirror to Israel's unpleasant face, especially from one of its own.

Their anger sometimes drove the judges over the edge, prompting them to abandon the reserve and civility of their position. One paragraph included in a judgment written by Moshe Landau, deputy president of the

Supreme Court, is no doubt one of the most blatant examples of abuse of the liberty judges have in what they write. In 1977, a panel over which Landau presided dismissed a petition filed by Tsemel after she had been denied the right to represent a Palestinian defendant in a case involving security offenses. The grounds for the denial were that Tsemel would be privy to classified material, putting national security at risk. The panel was provided with classified information that purported to explain the risks of revealing secret material to Tsemel, but as it was not disclosed to her, she could not respond. The reasoning behind the petition's dismissal included the following remarkable statements:

> We were provided with a copy of a letter written by the head of Military Intelligence dated May 5, 1977, listing the grounds for the objection to have Ms. Tsemel appear in the court-martial. With her consent, we admitted this document without revealing its content to her. According to the content of this document, there is no doubt that national security would be severely compromised should a person who has been disqualified from serving as a military defense lawyer participate in the judicial hearing and hear the testimonies—and as known—among these people there are those, like Ms. Tsemel herself, who sympathize with the enemies of the country who seek its destruction.[22]

Of course Tsemel was not the only lawyer to be rebuked by the establishment and the public. Her senior colleague Felicia Langer was the object of far worse hatred and incitement, prompting death threats and graffiti on her office door. But Langer was a key member of Rakah and enjoyed the party's support, including speeches about her cases given in the Knesset by her party's representatives and coverage of her work in the party newspaper *Zo Haderekh*. Tsemel had no backing from any sort of significant political camp at the time—no party, no paper. She was on the farthest margins of Israel's left wing.

Having weathered disapproval and equipped with a worldview that sees even the smallest progress, the Sisyphean rolling of the rock to the top of the mountain, as a worthy part of the fight, Tsemel has charged at the military courts since the beginning of her legal career and has not stopped. Over the years, her office has represented thousands of detainees and defendants in impossible legal circumstances, and the real wonder is that none of this seems to have worn her down or left the faintest mark of despair. I have often called her for one thing or another, only to find that even on a Friday afternoon, as most of the country had shut down for Shabbat, she would be on her way to the Hebron detention facility or to an arrest hearing at Ofer Camp, enraged over a political arrest or a rude prosecutor, as if it was her first case. In a place like the Occupied Territories' military court system, a graveyard for legal passion, a place where lawyers the age of Tsemel's children hang up their robes, unable to stomach the distress and the burnout, Tsemel continues to plead with the same energy and conviction she has had for forty-five years. And judges, also young enough to be her children, continue to be angry at her—and to give her respect.

THE END OF FLASH DEPORTATIONS

Abu Awad was handed a deportation order two and half hours ago, Tsemel's secretary told her. The IDF commander who had signed the order had also signed for the appointment of several officers to serve as the advisory committee. With this head-spinning efficiency, the committee was ready to convene to discuss Abu Awad's case at 7:00 p.m. Tsemel glanced at her watch. It was 5:30. She was in Nablus. She could make it. She got into her car and raced south to Ramallah on West Bank roads. When she arrived, she was able to have a short meeting with Abu Awad, and they decided to tell the committee they were not interested in having the hearing after all; they were going to file a petition against the deportation the next day. They also decided to demand undertaking a commitment that the deportation would not take place before the petition had been filed. The Natsheh case and Justice Etzioni's wrath had left their mark. The powers in the security establishment were fearful of the court's ire, and Tsemel received assurance that nothing would happen before the petition's filing.

Tsemel returned to her Jerusalem office and worked on the High Court petition well into the night. This was a pivotal moment in the fight against deportation: the first petition against a signed order, one that had not yet been executed. This was not a theoretical situation or speculation about a possible future deportation, and the petitioner was still in the country. In her petition, Tsemel raised every argument against the practice, objections that had never been considered on their merits in the decade and more of deporting Palestinian political activists.

The first argument was that the Defense Regulations granting the power to deport had in fact been revoked by Jordan. In 1952, during Jordan's rule over the West Bank, the Hashemite Kingdom had enacted a constitution, which included a clause that forbade, without exception, deportation of subjects from its territory.[23] A constitution is a statute of a higher normative order than the Defense Regulations, and it therefore trumps them. Thus the constitutional provision against deportation implicitly revokes the Regulations' power to carry it out. Since Israel inherited the law in the West Bank as it was when it occupied the territory, Jordan's revocation of the Regulations meant they remained invalid. Second, Tsemel offered the argument that would become the focus of many principled deliberations by the High Court in years to come: even if we assume that the regulation allowing deportation had stayed in effect, it contradicts an explicit prohibition in the Fourth Geneva Convention against the deportation or forcible transfer of residents of an occupied territory outside that territory.[24] In fact, under the Geneva Convention, such deportation or forcible transfer is considered a war crime that requires investigation and prosecution.[25] Tsemel claimed that since Israel's power in the territories it occupied derive from international law and, more specifically, from the laws of occupation (which are partly formalized in the Geneva Convention), it cannot breach an explicit Convention prohibition. The third line of argument had to do with Abu Awad himself and the justification for his deportation, assuming it was permissible to deport persons who put public safety at risk. Tsemel insisted that Abu Awad was being deported for political reasons, that the accusation of his being a danger was a joke, his actions were legitimate, and his contacts with Israeli students were no cause for deportation.

The petition was filed along with a motion for an interim injunction that would prevent the deportation pending a decision. The case landed on the desk of Duty Justice Shlomo Asher, who immediately issued the interim injunction and ordered the State Attorney's Office to submit its response to the petition. The next day, *Davar*, a left-leaning daily, published a story about the unusual injunction. Under the heading "High Court Issues Interim Injunction Against Deportation of Birzeit College Student," the paper reported that the order had been issued because of

Abu Awad's involvement in drafting the "PLO Support Letter," that is, the Progressive National Movement's pamphlet calling for dismantling the Zionist entity that was distributed at Hebrew University. Two days later, a panel headed by President Zussman and Justices Meir Shamgar and Shlomo Asher convened to hear the petition. The justices wondered why Tsemel and Abu Awad had waived the advisory committee hearing. Tsemel told them that when she is notified of a hearing an hour and a half ahead of time, during which she has to make her way from Nablus to Ramallah, she has no time to meet with her client, let alone prepare arguments. The justices accepted Tsemel's explanations. In fact, they scoffed at the military's lawyers:

> At the very opening of the hearing in the aforesaid petition, the Deputy State Attorney provided us with the affidavit of Col. Moshe Feldman, which he made before her on January 31, 1979, in support of Respondent's position. When we remarked to the Deputy State Attorney that the affidavit should have been filed earlier, she replied that she had only one and a half days to prepare the material. We find this explanation acceptable, but it greatly increases our puzzlement over the fact that the Petitioner, a person held in detention, was expected to prepare a defense and present such to the advisory committee when he was given only several hours to do so.[26]

It was agreed that Tsemel would seek a new hearing by the committee and that she would be given enough time to prepare. The lawyer for the army, Dorit Beinisch, who went on to become state attorney, a justice, and then president of the Supreme Court, had to provide assurances not only that the deportation would not take place pending the committee hearing but that should the order be approved, Abu Awad would be given forty-eight more hours to file another petition. The High Court of Justice was done, for the time being, and Abu Awad's removal was transferred to the newly created slow track for deportation.

The advisory committee convened a few days later and, predictably, recommended the execution of the deportation order (which had been signed by the same person who appointed its members). Tsemel filed a new High Court petition against the order—now backed by the advisory committee—which was heard at the end of February. Now Beinisch claimed, in response to Tsemel's argument that the Jordanian constitution revoked the power to deport, that Jordan had not intended to revoke the Defense Regulations, and, even if it had, a military order issued early on in the occupation stated, "to remove any doubt," that the Defense Regulations may not be considered repealed "unless a later statute so determines explicitly rather than implicitly."[27] Tsemel retorted that any such military order could not trump the restrictions set forth in the international law of occupation regarding laws passed by the occupying power: the occupying power must uphold existing law "unless absolutely prevented" from doing so.[28]

An argument ensued as to whether Jordanian law itself saw the Regulations as obsolete, or whether this was Tsemel's private interpretation. The deliberation in Israel's Supreme Court left Israeli law and turned to Jordanian law. And so, three Israeli justices, an Israeli lawyer, and an Israeli state attorney cited Jordanian law and quarreled over the content and meaning of various Jordanian judgments. But everyone knew Israel would not subject its powers to the laws of an enemy state. The fight was over whether Israel could or could not rely on existing law to deport Palestinians. If not, Israel would have to either give up the idea of deportation or change existing legislation to grant itself the power to carry on, a move that would inevitably draw criticism at home and abroad. Even if it could be done, the cost was best avoided.

Since none of those present was an expert on Jordanian law, Tsemel asked for leave to submit the expert opinion of Wasfi al-Masri, a lawyer in the West Bank who had served as a Jordanian district court judge. The justices gave Tsemel just one week, which was not enough time to get an affidavit from al-Masri. Instead, Tsemel submitted an affidavit from another Palestinian lawyer, who claimed that the common understanding among Jordanian jurists was that the deportation regulation had, in fact, been revoked, due to the constitutional prohibition on exiling subjects. Beinisch countered with an expert opinion from Ya'akov Meron, a Hebrew University professor specializing in law in Arab countries.

The judgment was not delivered until May 1979, three months after Abu Awad's deportation order had been issued. The justices dismissed Tsemel's arguments one by one. They found that Jordanian law had not revoked the deportation regulation and expressed their regret at the fact that the affidavit from al-Masri had not been submitted, which meant, "We did not have the benefit of hearing the opinion of a high-ranking jurist in the Hashemite Kingdom regarding Jordanian law."[29] The subtext of the remark was that the justices believed that al-Masri's opinion did not suit the petitioner, that he disagreed that the Jordanian constitution had revoked deportation powers.

The justices also rejected Tsemel's claim that military powers were subordinate to the prohibitions set forth in the Geneva Convention. "I have found no merit in the argument that use of the aforesaid Regulation 112 contradicts Article 49 of the Fourth Geneva Convention," wrote Justice Zussman. "Indeed . . . the Convention is meant to protect civilians from arbitrary action by the administering military and the purpose of said Article 49 is to prevent acts such as the heinous acts committed by the Germans during World War II, during which millions of civilians were expelled from their homes for various purposes, usually to Germany to perform forced labor for the enemy, and Jews and others were taken to concentration camps to be tortured and exterminated." Zussman quoted the Defense Regulations, which stipulate that deportation should be used only against persons whose deportation is necessary for securing public safety or suppressing mutiny, rebellion, or riot, a legitimate purpose, in his view, and one quite different from the mass population transfers of the Nazis. Zussman concluded that the Geneva Convention prohibition is not breached by the deportation powers granted by the Defense Regulations.

But in his finding, Zussman simply ignored the unequivocal language used in Article 49, firmly asserting that "individual or mass" deportation or forcible transfers were prohibited "*regardless of their motive*." A slave to the thesis that Article 49 only prohibits deportation for the purpose of forced labor, extermination, and other such crimes, Zussman held that "clearly, the aforesaid convention does not detract from the duty of the administering power to ensure public order and safety in the administered territory, imposed upon it in Article 43 of the Hague Convention of 1907, or from its right to take the necessary measures to ensure its own security."[30] This bears repeating: Zussman believed that deportations motivated by security considerations of the type permitted by the Defense Regulations are a completely different beast from the deportations referred to in the Geneva Convention. The fact that the text says outright that the motive for deportation is irrelevant to the question of its legality did not sway him.

The question that remained was the threat posed by Abu Awad and whether it justified his deportation from his homeland. Tsemel submitted a letter signed by Israeli and Palestinian professors who stated that the positions expressed in the Progressive National Movement's pamphlet against Zionism and against Rakah were not unusual and were often heard among both Arabs and Jews. Putting it mildly, the justices were not too impressed by the professors' letter: "Each of these professors is probably a great expert in his profession, as per the affidavit, such as topology, physics, sociology, and others," Zussman said mockingly. "But not one of them carries the burden of ensuring security and public safety in the administered territories, and they are not the ones to shoulder the responsibility for quelling the riots that erupt there. The responsibility for this lies with the military."

The petition was denied. Abu Awad was deported to Lebanon several days later.

This was an unusual case for Tsemel, not just because it was the first time the High Court of Justice discussed the power to deport but also because the client was not a stranger but a political ally and a friend. Tsemel and Abu Awad stayed in touch after the deportation. He married a woman from Lebanon and with her received legal status first in Cyprus and then in Egypt. He worked as a journalist in both countries. After Abu Awad left Lebanon, he and Tsemel met a few times in Egypt, where he still lives.

THE LEGAL FIGHT against Abu Awad's deportation created a new format for the process. Flash deportations by night, carried out by the stroke of the military commander's pen and a truck to drive the deportee to the border, were over. Henceforth, the process involved a hearing by the advisory committee, including the right to counsel, which required time, and then more time to bring the order to the High Court. Deportation became a time-consuming process of weeks or even months, which meant the press had the ability to report on it, diplomatic circles were able to take action, and the public had an opportunity to discuss it.

In the years that followed, the format was further refined. Lawyers representing candidates for deportation devoted a great deal of time to arguing before the advisory committee. Tsemel came up with a method and tried to convince every lawyer representing deportation cases to follow it. The system worked as follows: Waive nothing. Take advantage of every procedural right and even try to create new ones. Make all possible arguments. Demand all possible demands. Petition against any obstacle encountered along the way. You want to deport? Work for it! And indeed, after the Abu Awad case, the small group of lawyers who fought deportations did use every possible argument and demand to put spokes in the wheels of the process. They demanded to question the military commander about his motives, which resulted in a practice of submitting a questionnaire and receiving answers in writing. They demanded to bring witnesses and won a ruling to allow this in special circumstances.[31] They fought to compel the army to open the advisory committee hearings to the public and won a High Court directive to open parts of the hearing that do not involve classified material.[32] Deportation became a labor-intensive task for the military commanders, their legal advisers, and the State Attorney's Office.

Abu Awad might have lost his case, but his deportation marked the beginning of the long path toward shifting the cost-benefit to the state when it came to deporting Palestinian leaders and activists.

THE SHAKA DEBACLE

This was the headline the security establishment had been waiting for. "I Fully Sympathize with the Murder of the Bus Passengers on the Coastal Road." The statement, attributed to Nablus mayor Bassam Shaka, was at the top of a news item by the military correspondent for *Haaretz* in November 1979,[33] and it caused a public and political uproar. The coastal road bus attack was one of the worst acts of Palestinian terror in Israel's history. A Fatah cell arrived by sea from Lebanon in March 1978, hijacked an Israeli bus, and, after a killing spree, blew up the bus with the passengers still inside. Thirty-four people were killed and more than seventy injured. For Israelis, the attack came to symbolize the cruelty of the Palestinian struggle. And the fact that public figures in the West Bank did not condemn the attack (nor did they support it), instead charging that it was the result of "continued occupation and oppression," prompted outrage. The story in *Haaretz*, purporting to describe Shaka's comments made the previous day in a meeting with the Coordinator of Government Activities in the Territories, Danny Matt, struck a raw nerve.

Rewind three and a half years, back to April 1976. Israel allowed elections to local councils in the West Bank and Shaka was one of a slew of young local leaders who challenged the old mayors and council heads who were quite accommodating of the Israeli authorities, loyal to the Hashemite regime, and open to a settlement of the conflict involving Jordan. Shaka easily beat the Nablus incumbent, Ma'azuz al-Masri. It did not take Shaka long to turn from a local leader into a national one. Together with his colleagues, the newly elected mayors and council heads,* he established the National Guidance Committee in October 1978. The NGC sought to represent residents of Gaza and the West Bank collectively.

Though its members were all considered PLO supporters, the NGC was also an expression of dissatisfaction with the fact that the interests of the Palestinians under occupation were represented only by the leadership in the diaspora. It was also a response to the Camp David agreements, in which Israel and Egypt had committed to start talks on Palestinian autonomy, a notion the NGC vehemently opposed as it fell far short of full Israeli withdrawal from the Occupied Territories and Palestinian independence. The NGC set up local guidance committees and for several years stood at the helm of the fight against the occupation. The first NGC conference produced a declaration asserting that autonomy was a nonstarter: "There shall be no peace without full withdrawal from occupied Arab land and so long as the Palestinian people cannot return to its homeland, determine its future, and establish an independent state in its land and patrimony, with Jerusalem as its capital."[34] And so, unlike the previous generation of compliant mayors, Israel was now up against a local leadership with national awareness who demanded self-determination uncoupled from Jordan, and considered its role to be leaders in the fight to end the occupation.[35]

In June 1979, Shaka led the struggle against the confiscation of land from the village of Rujeib for the purpose of building Elon Moreh, a settlement. He led a widely covered protest march from Nablus to the village site. This fight, which culminated in a rare victory that prevented the

---

* The most prominent of whom were Ramallah mayor Karim Khalaf, Hebron mayor Fahed Qawasmeh, and Tulkarm mayor Hilmi Hanoun.

confiscation,[36] propelled Shaka to the forefront of the NGC as chief spokes-person—an authentic, elected leader with an agenda that was perceived as radical, who caused the authorities more than a minor headache.

This was the backdrop for Shaka's meeting with Danny Matt. Visiting Nablus in his capacity as government coordinator, Matt met with Shaka to discuss municipal matters. Shaka, however, did not want just to talk about the water supply and waste disposal. Seeing himself as more than a local leader, he raised some topics that were troubling his constituents, such as the holding conditions of Palestinian inmates and the treatment they received. He also condemned the use of torture in investigations. In response, Matt asked him to condemn the coastal road attack, though it had happened some eighteen months earlier. After the meeting, one of Matt's staffers leaked a few quotes from the meeting to the *Haaretz* reporter. The source alleged that Shaka "said . . . he fully sympathized with the murder of the bus passengers on the coastal road and that until there is a solution to the Palestinian problem, such actions are justified, effective, and self-evident."

When the news ran, several MKs asked Defense Minister Ezer Weizman to take measures against Shaka and he assured them he would do so. Prime Minister Begin told reporters he had requested that the defense minister "investigate the affair and draw his conclusions."[37] The issue was put on the Knesset's agenda.

The next day, it turned out there was some disagreement over what Shaka had actually said to Matt. *Al HaMishmar* reporter Amnon Kapeliouk published Shaka's response to the *Haaretz* report, in which he staunchly denied expressing sympathy for the murder of the coastal road bus passengers. He explained that in his conversation with Matt, he had expressed understanding for the motivation for the act but not for the act itself. He said he had simply repeated a phrase that had been heard in the past from Palestinian leaders, which was that so long as there is occupation, oppression, and settlements, there is no way to prevent such acts. Shaka charged that the *Haaretz* news item was a smear tactic against the mayors who were proving a nuisance to Israel, intended to assist the move to have them removed.[38]

Langer immediately saw grounds for concern about deportation. Many of her clients had been deported for far less than the statements attributed to Shaka, and so she warned him that a deportation order might soon

be forthcoming. Although the Abu Awad affair had changed the procedures, Langer did not trust the military to fulfill its duty to hold a hearing, and she recommended filing a petition even before a possible
deportation order was signed. Shaka heard her and agreed.

Langer, who was at the Lod military court when she spoke to Shaka,[39]
started working on the petition in the taxi on the way back to her office
in Jerusalem. It was quickly typed up and hurried over to the Supreme
Court. Though there was no certainty that the security authorities were
about to use the sanction for which the petition sought remedy, given the
situation and the public climate, Duty Justice Shlomo Asher accepted that
deportation was plausible and immediately signed an interim injunction
prohibiting Shaka's removal prior to a hearing.

Shaka's case had become a big deal. The NGC held a meeting the same
afternoon, and television crews came to hear Shaka's version of his conversation with Matt and what else he had to say. In the evening, it turned
out that the head of the Israel Broadcasting Authority, Tommy Lapid,
refused to let the interview air, claiming that Israel's public broadcasting
authority should not be a platform for PLO supporters.[40]

The next morning, the media reported that the IDF commander in the
West Bank had, in fact, signed a deportation order against Shaka. He had
not yet received notice of it, but military correspondents were rather reliable when it came to these things. The State Attorney's Office asked Justice Asher for a clarification that the interim injunction forbade only the
deportation itself but did not preclude any of the preliminary procedures,
such as the advisory committee hearing. Justice Asher provided the clarification, which meant that the hearing could go ahead.[41] It also meant
that Shaka could be arrested ahead of deportation. And so four days after
the initial report in *Haaretz*, Shaka was summoned to the military governor's Nablus office, where he was presented with the deportation order
and told that the plan was to deport him to Lebanon. Until then, the governor said, he would be taken into custody and held at Ramla Prison. The
governor allowed Shaka to call his wife, and she told Langer.[42]

Coming after Abu Awad's deportation, this one would proceed according to the court's timetable, not a schedule that was convenient for the
security or political establishments, both of which no doubt wanted to see
Shaka at the foot of Mount Lebanon, erased from local consciousness,
the moment the order was signed. But given the legal constraints, they

were facing a process that could drag on for weeks. All the ills the authorities would have preferred to avoid with a quick deportation materialized
in their attempt to get rid of Shaka. Palestinians had a leader behind
bars, not yet deported, and hence a very good reason to mount a huge
public campaign to reverse the order. The press had a story to run with,
complete with a feeble excuse for the deportation that was based from the
start on a Rashomon tale. Diplomatic circles had the time that suited their
habitually slow pace, and the honor fell to the judicial system to control
the entire circus. Only the army and the politicians had nothing to gain
from this protracted process.

A commercial and school strike was declared the day after Shaka's
arrest. A few dozen women staged a sit-in at the municipality building, and
in a special council session, council members decided to submit a collective letter of resignation to the military governor, which they did the next
day. At the same time, other Palestinian cities held gatherings to show
solidarity with Shaka. The mayors, most of them members of the NGC,
demanded a meeting with the defense minister and a revocation of the
deportation order. The strikes spread from Nablus to other West Bank cities. Langer, who managed to visit Shaka at Ramla, passed on a quote to
the media: "I'm innocent." The press published his denial: "I did not preach
violence or bloodshed. I am for peaceful coexistence. I was simply serving my people as I see fit and that is my only crime."[43] That was not all.
News of Shaka's arrest and the plan to deport him made headlines in major
American newspapers like the *New York Times*[44] and the *Washington
Post*,[45] which forced the American administration to address the issue. In
response to a question from Israeli journalists, a "senior U.S. official" cautiously noted that the administration believed that measures of this type
had a negative impact on the efforts to advance peace talks.

In the meantime, the transcripts of Shaka and Matt's meeting were
leaked. The contents were very different from the *Haaretz* story that had
set the ball rolling. According to the record, Matt had asked Shaka several times for his thoughts about the coastal road attack and was told, each
time, that the occupation and the settlements will lead to such acts. Matt
was not able to extract a clear denunciation of the attack (except for a very
clear and unequivocal condemnation of the murder of children), but Shaka's statement did not amount to sympathy or support for the attack either.

The public campaign to free Shaka continued at full speed over the next few days. Protests were held in almost every Palestinian city. A rally at Birzeit University included other mayors and Shaka's wife, Inaya. Hundreds of students showed up. More mayors announced that they were joining Nablus city council members and resigning. The resignations accumulated and there was a real danger that the West Bank would be left with no mayors, whose democratic election had been a source of pride for Israel. Three days after his arrest, Shaka announced that he would go on a hunger strike until his release. Langer periodically released quotes from Shaka in prison. Delegations from Israel's left wing came to Ramallah to show support for the council members stepping down. Major papers all over the world reported on the developments on a daily basis, usually on the front page.

At that point, Shaka's impending deportation had become a burning diplomatic issue. It was discussed in an unofficial UN Security Council meeting, and its president at the time, the Bolivian delegate, issued a unanimous condemnation. The American administration was also ready to condemn the plan to deport Shaka, which it did via a State Department communiqué.[46] The communiqué was particularly painful as it raised doubts about the legality of the move. Naturally, the Shaka affair was covered extensively in Israel. The national broadcasting authority's radio and television news shows opened with the topic, and the developments were front-page news every day. West Bank leaders decided to keep up the commercial and school strikes, and many people took up hunger strikes in solidarity with Shaka.

What had begun as a conversation about municipal affairs between a mayor of an occupied city and an officer of the occupying army, one that was enlisted and distorted in the effort to wipe out the new West Bank Palestinian leadership, had grown into a diplomatic crisis and nightmare of a headache.

THE HEARING ON Shaka's petition was set for November 22 and was sure to attract a lot of attention. State Attorney Dorit Beinisch hoped it would be a short hearing. Her plan was to repeat her tactic in the Abu Awad case and refer Langer to the advisory committee, rendering the hearing moot. Beinisch knew that Shaka objected to appearing before the military advisory committee since he thought the entire proceeding was rigged, so she threw in a complication. In her written response to the petition, Beinisch clarified that if Shaka wanted a hearing, he had to first ask for the advisory committee to convene, as per the language in the Regulation, which allowed the committee to meet "if so requested to do by any person in respect of whom a deportation order has been made." Forcing Shaka to request a military procedure in which he had no faith was, as Beinisch well knew, a challenge to his honor.

But Langer had other plans for the High Court hearing. She fully grasped the public and media importance of the events and had no intention of passing on the opportunity to argue that deportation, any deportation, was unlawful and contrary to international law. She could not be sure the justices would let her use that line of argument, given that one of the fundamental rules for a High Court hearing is that the petitioner must exhaust all possible legal remedies to counter the authority's action before turning to the highest judicial instance. Shaka's petition, as recalled, was filed even before there had been a deportation order, let alone a legal proceeding of any kind.

As expected, long before the hearing was due to start the courtroom was packed with people who had come to show solidarity with Shaka. His family was there. His NGC colleagues and other West Bank mayors were there (Israel prevented Gaza mayor Rashad al-Shawa from arriving), Israeli MKs, friends, and lawyers, and many foreign human rights lawyers had shown up as observers. When Shaka was brought into the courtroom, he was received with enthusiastic applause and hands raised in the victory sign.[47]

Although the panel, headed by Deputy President Moshe Landau, appeared to agree with Beinisch, who spoke first and briefly argued that Shaka must exhaust proceedings before the advisory committee, they did allow Langer to assert that there was no point in doing that. Langer argued that deporting a resident of an occupied territory was unlawful because the laws of occupation, that is, the Geneva Convention, prohibit it. Thus it made no difference if the advisory committee gave its approval. This was the second attempt, after the Abu Awad case, to challenge the actual power to deport. In her unapologetic way, Langer even cited a judgment given by the Nuremberg military tribunal, which convened to try Nazi war criminals, and held that deportation from an occupied territory was a war crime. Mentioning the Nuremberg trials in the context of Israel's military administration in the Occupied Territories is something few lawyers would dare to do, but for Langer, comparisons to World War II were not a rarity, which often outraged state attorneys and justices alike.

Nor did Langer spare the advisory committee, arguing that turning to it was pointless since the committee members were appointed by the officer who signed the deportation order and could hardly be expected to recommend revoking an order issued by senior military and political figures. Langer accused the committee members of being nothing more than rubber stamps and yes-men to their superiors, who were in turn rubber stamps for their own superiors.

The court's decision was to give Shaka three days to decide whether to use his right to a hearing before the advisory committee. Should he decide to do so, the justices instructed the state that if the committee approved the deportation, it should be stayed for three days. This would allow Shaka to return to the High Court and raise arguments of principle against deportation itself once more. If he waived his right to an advisory committee hearing, the justices would go ahead and rule on the arguments of principle that had just been made. Langer's motion for Shaka's release pending a final ruling in the case was rejected, and he was returned to the prison in Ramla.

After the hearing, Shaka, with a heavy heart, decided to go before the advisory committee. However, in the few days before it convened, several perfectly timed developments took place internationally. First, the UN General Assembly discussed Shaka's impending deportation and passed a resolution denouncing it, with 132 countries in favor.[48] UN General Assembly resolutions may not have binding legal power, but no one in Jerusalem was happy to see Bassam Shaka, the mayor of a small city in the Middle East, becoming an iconic victim of Israeli harassment in the eyes of delegates from almost every country in the world. And it was not just the UN General Assembly. The *Washington Post* reported that President Carter's administration, whose displeasure with the Shaka affair had been voiced in increasingly clear and harsh tones, had asked Prime Minister Begin to reconsider the deportation.[49]

The Shaka deportation was becoming an ever bigger burden on Israel. It was suddenly keeping the government busy around the clock. The military was facing unrest all over the Occupied Territories and spokespeople were having to deflect questions from journalists, communications from foreign governments, and condemnations from all kinds of international bodies. The cost-benefit balance of the deportation was running away from the people who had initiated it in the first place.

Defense Minister Weizman looked for a way out. The Palestinian mayors' request to release Shaka was lying on his desk, and he used it to try to reach a compromise. Maybe Shaka could resign; maybe he could state publicly that he had not expressed support for the coastal road attack. But Shaka was not in a conciliatory mood. He had decided to go all the way. Due to his deteriorating health, he agreed to a request from his colleagues to stop his hunger strike but said there would be no deals over his deportation or release.

On November 28, three weeks after the affair blew up, the advisory committee convened for a hearing that lasted ten hours. The lengthy session surprised correspondents, who were used to these hearings being brief and mechanical: "*Davar* correspondent notes that in previous deportations of Palestinian public figures from the West Bank, the committee was extremely quick, and there were cases where in the space of just a few hours, the person was arrested, the committee convened, deportation recommended and executed," the daily *Davar* told its readers in astonishment, adding: "This time the committee collected a great deal of material during its lengthy session and judicial proceedings may last two more weeks."[50] It took five more days.

The pressure on the government was mounting, and it clearly needed a way to step back from the ledge. The public was being prepped for the deportation's cancellation with media commentary and predictions. *Davar* quoted "very senior security officials" who expressed hope that the military committee would recommend not deporting Shaka.[51] Miraculously, their hopes were realized, and the committee accepted Shaka's position that his comments had been distorted. "We believe," the committee members wrote in their decision, "that the military commander would be wise to accept our recommendation to reconsider his initial decision, as justice must also be seen."[52] The commander of the West Bank, Binyamin Ben Eliezer, concurred, though not before receiving approval from the defense minister.

In the early afternoon of December 5, 1979, just under a month after his arrest, Shaka was released to his home in Nablus and received a hero's welcome by thousands of Palestinians and his colleagues, the mayors.

This was the first—and last—time a decision to deport was not implemented, but Israel learned an important lesson about the limits of the power to expel people and about the price it cost. The Shaka affair recalibrated the balance of power in cases of deportation. Israel's military and national governments of course still had the final word, but both realized that the days of risk-free and cost-free deportation were over. The price Israel pays is not in legal currency but in political, public, and international capital. However, it is the legal proceedings that allow the debt to accrue, with the delays they create, the media attention they attract, the drama they build, and the fact that a good legal argument gives opponents to deportation a moral rallying point.

After nearly four weeks in prison, Shaka resumed his place as the militant mayor of Nablus, affiliated with the PLO, and a national leader for the occupied Palestinian population. Six months later, on June 2, 1980, a Jewish underground cell booby-trapped his car. It blew up when Shaka got inside and he lost both legs in the explosion.

ONE LAST STAB AT DEPORTATION WITHOUT A HEARING (AND WITHOUT THE HIGH COURT)

When Israeli leaders tried to deport Palestinian leaders again, the Shaka affair hung over their heads like a menacing shadow. In May 1980, six Jewish worshippers, students at the Hebron Yeshiva, were murdered. The government searched for a strong response to the attack, and one of the shiniest objects in its toolbox was, as usual, the power to deport. Within one day of the murder, Binyamin Ben Eliezer signed deportation orders for the mayors of Hebron and Halhul and the imam at the Ibrahimi Mosque, who was also chief *qadi*. The two mayors—Fahed Qawasmeh, who had been elected in Hebron after replacing Ahmad Hamzi Natsheh, who was deported shortly before the 1976 election, and Muhammad Milhem from Halhul—were prominent members of the NGC. The government had wanted for some time to stem the NGC's power, and the worshippers' murder presented a good opportunity for deportation, which had failed in Shaka's case. The *qadi*, Sheikh Rajib al-Tamimi, was an important and well-connected religious leader in Hebron who had often spoken out, sharply, against Jewish settlement in the city, and it was a good opportunity to get rid of him, too.

But neither the government nor the military commanders wanted a repeat of the Shaka fiasco. How would they avoid the quagmire of a lengthy deportation process that would slowly leach the reputation of Israel's regime in the Occupied Territories? The decision makers in Jerusalem came to the conclusion: swift deportation was the key; legal proceedings were the problem.

The three were arrested at home on the evening of June 3, without being told that deportation orders had been signed. Instead, they were told that the IDF commander wanted to speak to them in light of the escalating security situation. Under this false pretense, they were brought to the IDF headquarters near Beit El. There they heard that the commander was busy, but the defense minister wanted to see them, and they would be flown to Tel Aviv to meet him. They were transported by helicopter, with bags over their heads to prevent them from seeing their location, but not to Tel Aviv. They were taken to the Lebanese border, where they learned, for the first time, that they were being deported and forced across the border. This time Langer's early planning was of no help. With her keen instincts, she had sensed the coming deportation just hours after the murder of the yeshiva students and had been in touch with Qawasmeh to arrange to represent him if an order was issued.[53] But the three were expelled without having a chance to tell their families or lawyer.

It is hard to imagine a more brazen move to thwart a court hearing. All the rules for deportation set in place after the Abu Awad and Shaka cases, after Justice Etzioni's wrath at the speedy removal of Natsheh just fifteen minutes before his hearing, had been broken. The deportees had no opportunity to get legal representation, appear before the advisory committee, or challenge the order before the High Court. Someone in Jerusalem thought they should, and could, go back to the days of flash deportations. But whoever came up with the idea of summary action had failed to calculate the havoc this would cause between the executive branch and the judiciary.

Since the deportees—who were now in enemy country—could not sign retainers, Langer filed a petition to revoke the deportation orders on behalf of the mayors' wives and the *qadi*'s cousin. In the petition, which she filed with her colleague, Abed al-Asali, she made the usual arguments: deportation of residents of an occupied territory outside that territory violated the prohibition stipulated in Article 49 of the Geneva Convention, and it was a breach of international human rights law. Only this time, the petition included arguments about miscarriage of justice in the deportation procedure itself: denying the right to a hearing before the advisory committee stipulated in the Defense Regulations.

Langer even argued that the way the deportation had been carried out was intended to prevent the High Court from considering the matter and to establish the act as a fait accompli. She claimed there was no justification for the trio's deportation, as there were no allegations that they were involved in any way in the murder of the Hebron Yeshiva students, and therefore the deportation was purely political, motivated by the government's desire to get rid of key local leaders who oversaw legitimate opposition to the occupation. Langer enclosed affidavits from Victor Shem-Tov, the general secretary of Mapam, a Zionist socialist party, and from Matti Peled, a reserve major general, both of whom declared, based on their personal acquaintance with the two mayors, that they were peaceful moderates.

Because it was no longer possible to ask for an interim injunction against the deportation, the hearing, which took place two and a half weeks after the fact, focused on its legality. Ahead of the hearing, the state submitted its response, in which it argued that the deportation order had been signed due to inflammatory statements made by the deportees against Israel and against the authorities, and that therefore their removal from the West Bank was meant to serve a security purpose. The trouble was that the panel selected for the case, headed by deputy president Justice Haim Cohn, along with young Justice Aharon Barak and Justice Hadassah Ben-Ito, saw clearly what had been left out of the state's response. At the start of the hearing, Justice Cohn turned to State Attorney Gabriel Bach, who, because of the case's high profile, decided to appear in person, and said, "We have not found one word in the State Attorney's Response about the manner in which the three were arrested or the manner in which they were deported."[54]

Cohn was a key figure in Israel's legal system following the country's establishment and had served both as the executive director of the Justice Ministry and as attorney general. Once appointed to the Supreme Court, he was known as the institution's liberal standard-bearer. He was willing to go head-to-head with the executive to protect human rights, and, more than any other justice, he gave the judicial instance in which he served the image of the lone citizen's bastion of protection against the authorities. With his vast experience, Cohn understood exactly what was going on, and he did not like it one bit.

Bach explained that security officials, aware of the traumatic impact of the yeshiva students' murders, felt that the deportation had to take place immediately; there was no time to wait. Cohn, annoyed, quoted the part of the petition describing how the military administration had tricked the deportees, leading them to the border under a false pretext. "The murder was traumatic," Cohn agreed, "but why did the deportation order have to be traumatic?"[55] Uncomfortable, Bach hinted that the military and state legal advisers had not known about the plan to evade a hearing, and he repeated the claim that the deportation was justified because of the deportees' statements in favor of war and jihad against Israel. The justices did not even bother to ask for Langer's response, issuing an order nisi then and there compelling the defense minister to explain why he should not revoke the deportation.

The deportation of the "trio," as the Israeli press came to call them, was heading down the same path as the Shaka affair, with deportation carried out for dubious reasons and executed using deceit; an abundance of international attention and local criticism; and a long legal proceeding that would keep it in the headlines for some time to come.

The deportees did everything in their power to wage a public campaign. When they arrived in Beirut, they held a press conference where they decried having been punished without having been charged or tried. Around the world the media quoted their claim that the deportation was intended to weaken Palestinian resistance to the occupation. From Beirut the trio went to Amman, where they declared they would try to reenter the West Bank via the Allenby Bridge, and, if unsuccessful, take their widely covered campaign to the United States and Europe. Meanwhile, the UN Security Council passed a resolution against the deportation, with fourteen members voting in favor and one abstaining—the United States. Since the legal proceeding was under way, the media saw it as a developing story to be followed that would probably generate more headlines.

In Israel, the press tried to get to the bottom of the three leaders' deportation. The military provided quotes attributed to the deportees that had led to the conclusion that their presence in the West Bank caused unrest and threatened security. Danny Matt, still serving as Coordinator of Government Activities in the Territories, despite his questionable conduct in the Shaka affair, called in the press. He claimed that two months before the murder of the yeshiva students, Hebron mayor Qawasmeh had declared an "end to talking," and that with his colleagues he would do whatever it took to topple "the Zionist empire, which will fall as the British Empire fell, and as the Nazis fell." Sheikh Tamimi was alleged to have said of the Jews, "We will fight them until they are gone." He purportedly went on, "This land has an owner, and it is Muslim. Not just Hebron, but Haifa and Jaffa as well." Halhul mayor Milhem was accused of saying, "We talk, and Israel is Judaizing Hebron and the Tomb of the Patriarchs. What was taken by force shall be taken back by force."[56]

After the trio unsuccessfully tried to return to the West Bank, an effort that was more of a protest and a media stunt than an actual attempt to breach an IDF checkpoint, they went to New York, where they spoke to members of the Security Council. Throughout their campaign, they gave interviews and made militant statements against Israel. These were collected by the Shin Bet and IDF intelligence and provided to the Ministry of Justice as a way of retroactively bolstering the justification for the deportation. With the fear that the High Court would order the trio's return, humiliating the Israeli government and elevating the deportees to the status of heroes, the deportation was quickly spiraling into another fiasco.

A month after the deportation, on the morning of June 2, cars belonging to three Palestinian mayors exploded. Shaka, the mayor of Nablus, lost both his legs. Karim Khalaf, the mayor of Ramallah, lost his foot and suffered an injury to his other leg. Ibrahim Tawil, the mayor of al-Birah, was saved after the military administration gave him advance warning, following the attack on the other two mayors, but a Druze IDF sapper working on disarming the explosive device in Tawil's car was seriously injured and lost his eyesight. The cars were booby-trapped by members of a Jewish cell, mostly residents of settlements, whom it would take four years to arrest. They were known as the Jewish Underground, and aside from the assassination attempts against the mayors, they committed a long list of bloody attacks on Palestinians for quite some time. Though some were eventually sentenced to lengthy prison terms, they were pardoned by Israel's president and released early. Ironically, it may be that Qawasmeh and Milhem, the deported mayors, were saved from a similar fate thanks to the deportation.

In any event, the day after the attack on the mayors, Prime Minister Begin held a meeting with Israel's top security figures to discuss the situation. Defense Minister Weizman had resigned for political reasons a week earlier, so Begin was serving as defense minister as well. Others present at the discussion were IDF chief of staff Rafael Eitan, Shin Bet head Avraham Ahituv, newly appointed deputy defense minister Mordechai Tzipori, commander of the IDF's Central Command Moshe Levy, and Danny Matt, in charge of government activities in the territories. The subject discussed, according to recently uncovered transcripts,[57] was prevention of mass protests in the West Bank and Gaza Strip after the attempted assassinations, and the issue of the deported mayors also came up. The participants were very concerned that the High Court would order the mayors' return for a hearing before the advisory committee.

"I fear there will be serious trouble in the territories," said Matt, "should the High Court take that action." Begin replied, "We've already agreed that as soon as the High Court case is over, we will change the law and propose a bill to amend the existing law in the Knesset." Begin was talking about removing the requirement to allow a hearing prior to the deportation, only he was wrong about needing the Knesset to change legislation in the territories. The commander of the occupying military forces, Moshe Levy, who was sitting at the table, could make the amendment with a stroke of his pen. However, Begin went on. "Once this law, that I intend to propose to the Knesset, is passed, we will have no trouble using deportation. After that, if they go to the High Court, they go to the High Court." The justices have shown, he noted, "that they are sensitive to the failure to let people go before the advisory committee. I was advised to wait until this case is over, and then submit the bill to the Knesset . . . not retroactively. If we file before the High Court case [ends], since the justices are human, it might make them angry and have an impact." Begin estimated that the High Court would make its ruling in five weeks.

For some reason, Levy did not correct the prime minister. Instead, like Matt, he was concerned that the High Court would order the mayors' return. "Are we making preparations for this eventuality?" he asked. Begin preferred to believe this would not happen. He spoke indignantly about the prospect of the court intervening in decisions made by an elected government. "It would be disastrous, in my opinion, but the truth is that as far as the state is concerned, the honorable justices will decide. The government must obey the decree of the court. The court is above the government. But it would be very grave. At the end of the day, there is an elected authority and there are institutions that are trusted with security matters, and this repeated interference with security matters cannot be tolerated. In other words, we have to start arguing that certain things are nonjusticiable, and if that doesn't help, there will be no choice but to change the law."

Begin's attitude was typical of the anger of successive Israeli governments at court intervention in their decisions. It is commonly said in Israel that intervention by an unelected judiciary in an elected government's decisions is undemocratic and that the court's rulings can be circumvented by legislation. This expresses a technical approach to democracy—majority rule—which exposes a failure to understand the essence of constitutionalism.

The idea of amending the Defense Regulations to provide for a retroactive hearing was very attractive to those present at the meeting. Levy made it clear that as far as he was concerned, the law is a tool to serve the security establishment, not limit it. The military, he said, needs powers, "within the law, and if need be, by changing the law."

However, the proposed amendment was forward-looking and would not solve the problem on the table. The chief of staff, though, had an idea for how to deal with a possible court order to return the deportees. "If they come back, we could jail them right at the bridge for incitement against the state." Begin was skeptical. "We could, but this might be perceived as refusal to obey the will of the court. We could deport them again after the law changes, but to jail them on their return? I'm not sure." Chief of Staff Eitan insisted. "If the three deportees are returned by the High Court, we need to prepare indictments right now for what they've said abroad and jail them as soon as they cross the bridge. They can sit here in jail, or sit in Mitzpe Ramon, and no one will know where they are. A little disrespect to the honorable justices is the lesser of the evils compared to what could happen if we allow them to go back to their positions. I think it would mean Israel losing control over Judea and Samaria." No more and no less.

IN LATE JUNE, following the court's order, State Attorney Bach submitted a response to the petition filed by the mayors' wives, on behalf of the defense minister. The affidavit was signed by the IDF commander of the West

Bank. The High Court's anger had had an effect. The chosen tactic was to admit that an error had been made but insist that the deportation was completely justified and therefore must not be reversed. The response cited statements attributed to the deportees, both before the deportation and after, which had appeared in the media in Europe and the United States. The state argued that the trio incited the public to violence and that the restraint shown by the military administration had ended with the murder of the yeshiva students, which necessitated immediate deportation to prevent further escalation. Bringing the deportees back would reward people who really did not deserve such a reward. Legally, Bach had to face up to the fact that the deportees' rights had been violated, and he did so with a creative, novel approach: the Defense Regulations indeed allow for a hearing, but they do not specify that it has to take place prior to the deportation. The deportees, the affidavit noted, could request a hearing now and their counsel, Langer, could appear before the advisory committee.

What Bach was asking for, in fact, was an interpretation that would obviate the need for the legislative change the prime minister had proposed. Such an interpretation, unlike Begin's amendment, could apply to this case, too, not just to future cases. But it is a complete perversion of the notion of a hearing. A hearing, any hearing, is intended to allow someone who is about to be harmed by an act of the authorities to try to dissuade the authorities from carrying out said act, to show that the act is unjustified or illegal, or that there are good reasons not to go through with it. A retroactive hearing asks the authorities to turn back the clock, perhaps after the damage has already been done. Moreover, the state attorney's position exploited the fact that these deportees had legal counsel to argue that the hearing could be carried out without them. In the absence of legal counsel, the deportees would have to be brought back even for a retroactive hearing, which Israel wanted to avoid at all costs. Bach's proposition also ignored the fact that legal representation is a right, not a duty. A person may choose to appear at a hearing without counsel, and even if they choose representation, it would be crippled if the client were not a full and present partner in their defense.

Finally, the affidavit of response included an argument that the security establishment makes whenever it fears a painful court loss: a veiled threat directed at the justices that accepting the petition would result in bloodshed. Returning the deportees, it was claimed, would destabilize security and could seriously threaten public safety. A show of force for justices who exhibit a tendency toward intervening with security decisions. A justice would have to be particularly brave to ignore the risk of the "threat" materializing and to find somewhere down the line that blood had been shed because of their judgment.

A hearing was scheduled for early July, and in the meantime the trio continued their parade unabated. There were rallies, meetings with foreign officials, even a joint speech with Israeli peace activists at Temple Sinai Reform Synagogue in Washington, D.C., after which Langer added an affidavit from Israeli left-wing activist Haim Baram, who had taken part in the event, which detailed the deportees' moderate views.

APPARENTLY, BECAUSE OF the case's importance, the president of the Supreme Court had decided a more senior panel was in order, with him at the helm. Now President Moshe Landau and Justice Isaac Cohen joined Haim Cohn. Just as in the Shaka hearing, the courtroom was packed with public figures, lawyers from abroad observing the proceedings, and members of the local and international press. The justices' comments indicated that they thought the manner in which the deportation had been executed was unacceptable. They had trouble accepting the argument for a retroactive hearing, and even greater difficulty with the notion of holding a hearing in the absence of those being heard.

On the other hand, at least Landau and Isaac Cohen seemed to think that the statements attributed to the deportees justified their deportation. When Langer criticized the fact that the deportees had not been given the chance to counter the allegations against them, Justice Haim Cohn asked why she had not submitted an affidavit on their behalf. Langer countered that they were abroad, which made it hard to get an affidavit. Cohn scornfully replied, "Then you have one week. You can do it through Cyprus."[58] In the time she had been given, Langer managed to provide an affidavit from the trio, in which they clarified that they supported peace and opposed bloodshed and generally denied any statements attributed to them that implied a call for violence.[59] The week's delay necessitated another hearing, in which Landau was tough on Langer. He believed the deportees' affidavit did not refute the allegation that they support the PLO. To this Langer replied that all West Bank mayors shared this flaw and asked whether that was a reason to deport them all.

The High Court delivered its judgment more than a month later, in mid-August. Justices Landau and Cohn agreed that the deportation had been carried out in a manner that breached the Defense Regulations. Neither of them accepted the state attorney's reading of the Regulations as allowing a retroactive hearing; nor did they accept that a hearing may be held without the deportees present. Landau added that if the military commander wished to do so, he could amend the Defense Regulations such that the requirement to hold a hearing prior to the deportation is removed, but so long as this has not been done, the hearing must be held before the deportation is executed. This was a formalistic approach to fundamental rights and due process. Still, Landau rebuked what he perceived as an attempt to prevent a High Court hearing and recalled the deportation of Dr. Ahmad Hamzi Natsheh:

> The Respondents' conduct is graver still as this is not the first time they have attempted to outsmart this Court. There has been a previous occurrence, in the Dr. Natsheh case. . . . Indeed, times have changed, and this time the action was carried out . . . on a day of special sensitivity and tension following a horrendous act perpetrated by haters of Israel. However, the heavy task with which those charged with maintaining security are burdened notwithstanding, it must be reiterated that they too are subject to the law and that assiduousness in upholding the law is not a nuisance but a duty that must be respected under all circumstances. This is the duty of anyone exercising powers in the state or on its behalf, not just for the sake of upholding the rights of individual citizens and residents, whatever their sins, but also, and perhaps mainly, for the sake of preserving the nature of this country as one that abides by the law for all its citizens.[60]

Unlike his colleagues, Justice Isaac Cohen believed that the Regulation as phrased already allowed for deportation prior to a hearing. In his judgment, he wrote that even if the hearing should be held before the deportation, it is not an absolute rule and circumstances might justify departing from it. In his view, the case at hand was an exception and therefore there was no impediment to holding the hearing retroactively.

While Landau and Haim Cohn agreed that the military commander had violated the Regulations, their views differed on the remedy to which the mayors were entitled. Cohn ruled to accept the petition and called for an order to revoke the deportation; Landau, however, was quite struck by the alleged security threat that would follow the trio's return to the West Bank. His legal position was that the violation of a deportation candidate's right to a hearing did not necessarily negate the deportation order, since the Regulations do not stipulate a hearing as a condition for signing the order, and, in any case, they provide for a hearing only if the deportee asks for it. Therefore, Landau ruled that the violation was to be remedied by holding a hearing, not by revoking the deportation order. And since there was no alternative, the hearing would be held retroactively. Haim Cohn differed from Landau both with regard to the level of security threat of the trio's return and on the legal significance of the violation of their right to a hearing. Cohn addressed the assessment of the security establishment with a skepticism that is rare among judges in general and Israeli judges in particular:

> Had we been presented with evidence, and were I satisfied that there truly is a real danger that upon the Petitioners' return to their homes, public safety in the Judea and Samaria Area would come to real harm, I would have seriously considered whether the law did not require to abstain from granting the Petitioners remedy, in order to prevent said harm. We have been presented with no evidence, and I am far from being persuaded. In his affidavit of response, the Commander of the Area says he has "certain knowledge" that the return of the Petitioners at present "could seriously jeopardize peace and safety in the Area"; but we do not know the source of this "certain knowledge." The fact that the Petitioners have made the statements they have made in the past proves nothing about their future conduct. It may be that upon their return, they would take great care to avoid any clashes with security authorities, if only just to prevent another deportation.[61]

With regard to the violation of the right to a hearing, Justice Cohn ruled that even if the deportation order was legal at the time it was signed, the order became illegal once the deportees' rights had been violated: "The ongoing validity of the deportation orders . . . depends on whether the stipulated right [to a hearing] is upheld: if the right is denied, the order is null and void."

Three justices, three opinions. Since the majority (Landau and Isaac Cohen) did not agree that the orders were null and void, the only question remaining was the retroactive hearing. The state's fear of humiliation if the deportees returned to the West Bank led State Attorney Bach to argue that there was no point in holding a retroactive hearing because no possible argument could trump the abhorrent statements the deportees had, he alleged, spread all over the media (mostly in Arabic) while they were outside the West Bank. Landau accepted this claim with respect to Sheikh Tamimi, whose alleged statements against the Jewish presence in Palestinian cities, not only in the Occupied Territories but also inside the sovereign territory of the State of Israel, had been harsher than those attributed to the mayors.

This left only the mayors. In their case, Landau did a double maneuver to help the state avoid the eventuality of their return. First, he ruled that a retroactive hearing would be held only if the deportees asked for such, and only if the request "includes a clear statement from the Petitioners that they intend to obey the laws of the administration in their public role, and refers clearly to the incendiary speech" attributed to them. Second, they could be arrested once they crossed the Allenby Bridge pursuant to the regulation that allows detaining deportation candidates.[62] This would make sure the deportees did not return to their cities as heroic victors.

What the judgment never addressed was whether the basic power to deport was lawful. The justices left that for a second petition that might be filed after the retroactive hearing, if one was held. In fact, in the trio's case, the court only addressed its own standing. Everyone involved knew that the way the deportation had been carried out was aimed at preventing a petition from being filed and to avoid court intervention. On this, Justice Cohn was firm and sharp, as always. President Landau tried to walk on the razor's edge: he rejected the state's position that there was no duty to hold a hearing prior to a deportation, which, if accepted, would have severely undermined the court's power to perform judicial review of deportations; at the same time, he did not agree that the violation should be remedied by revoking the orders, and he allowed for the deportees' arrest on their return. Thus Landau drastically diluted the judicial sanction of the attempt to circumvent the court by breaking the law. In this, Landau made the stick the court holds up to the executive rather a soft one.

Still, the judgment did help the fight against deportations in two ways: First, it established the legal obligation to hold a hearing before the deportation and to give the deportee a chance to petition the High Court of Justice, also before the order is executed. Second, in this specific case, the judgment significantly extended the life of the affair, with an option to file for and hold another hearing, the mayors' return via the Allenby Bridge, and filing another petition after the deportation order was approved. All these steps meant that anyone hoping for a quick deportation, forgotten in a few days and bringing Israel nothing but gain, could now expect the burden of a great many procedures.

And so Langer and al-Asali immediately started preparing for a hearing. Langer met with Qawasmeh and Milhem in Sofia, Bulgaria, and had them sign an affidavit that met the terms for a hearing stipulated in Landau's judgment. The military had no choice but to convene the advisory committee. But to minimize any sort of media frenzy or flood of attention, the hearing would take place behind closed doors, in a booth at the Allenby Bridge border crossing. Thus the mayors' return to the West Bank would not exceed the minimum requirements. Still, for all the state's efforts to avoid attention, the public debate continued throughout the developments that followed the trio's return. Qawasmeh and Milhem resumed their hunger strike and in Israel voices called for the deportation order to be revoked.

The hearings were held over the course of two days in October and ended with the committee's recommendation to implement the deportation order, although it also recommended that the two mayors might be allowed to return to the West Bank in the future, if they changed their attitude and proved their commitment to peace. Prime Minister Begin approved the deportation and within forty-eight hours the lawyers filed a second High Court petition.

Now Langer and al-Asali brought every possible argument against the lawfulness of deportation, including the prohibition on deporting residents of an occupied territory in the Geneva Convention. They even repeated the argument made in the Abu Awad case, that the Jordanian constitution had implicitly revoked the Defense Regulations that allowed for deportation. They submitted an expert opinion from four lawyers who were experts on Jordanian law: Palestinian human rights activist Raja Shehadeh, Juda Shahawan, Aziz Shehadeh, and, in a coup de grâce, former

Jordanian district court judge Wasfi al-Masri, whose opinion Tsemel was unable to get in time for the Abu Awad case, the same al-Masri who, the justices had hinted, did not think the Jordanian constitution had revoked deportation powers. With this expert opinion, Langer and al-Asali asked the justices to reconsider the judicial finding in the Abu Awad judgment that the Jordanian constitution had not revoked the power to deport. State Attorney Dorit Beinisch agreed that the mayors could not be deported while the petition was being heard, and an interim injunction to that effect was given.

FOR THE FIRST time a panel of the High Court of Justice* would deliberate seriously on the core legal argument that deporting civilians from occupied territory is illegal, as stated in the explicit and absolute prohibition stipulated in Article 49 of the Geneva Convention. Although the prohibition had come up in the Abu Awad case—where Tsemel had argued, to no avail, that Article 49 prohibits the deportation of a specific person on security grounds, and President Zussman had held that the prohibition concerned only mass deportations for the purpose of forced labor and the like—the issue was dealt with in a single paragraph, and the discussion was hardly exhaustive.

The judgment issued by the panel now would set Israel's legal stance on deportations, and was therefore dramatic. It included a discussion of whether the deportation regulations remained in effect after the enactment of the Jordanian constitution; the meaning of Article 49 of the Geneva Convention; and the question of whether the deportation of the mayors, given their statements against Israel, had been justified. In light of the affidavits of four experts on Jordanian law, including a former judge, which determined that the deportation regulations had indeed been revoked by the 1952 constitution, Landau had to resort to the 1968 military-issued Order Regarding Interpretation.[63] Section 3 of the order stipulates that the emergency legislation to be considered valid in the Occupied Territories is the version in effect before Israeli independence on May 14, 1948, unless explicitly revoked.

---

*   The hearing took place in early November 1980, and the judgment was given in early December. Supreme Court president Landau decided that the same panel that heard the previous petition would hear this one, too.

The military order got around all the problems: it determined that valid law in the territories was the law in force not when the IDF entered the West Bank but the law that was in force at the time Israel was established, which was four years before the Jordanian constitution. It also thwarted any possibility of relying on the constitution's revocation of the Mandatory Defense Regulations, since any revocation of existing law had to be done explicitly. In other words, the revocation had to specifically list the law being revoked. Deputy President Cohn agreed with Landau's legal analysis, but he clarified that "in the administered territories, the power to deport is merely the fruit of laws made by the Commander of the Area."[64] As such, Cohn essentially accepted Langer and al-Asali's argument that a military order from 1968 could not revive a law that had died before the order was issued (if we accept that the deportation regulations were revoked in 1952 by the constitution). Hence the order was not a revival of a Mandatory power but rather a military law enacting a new power to deport.

The major issue in the judgment was Article 49 of the Geneva Convention, which, for the first time since the occupation of the West Bank, was being fully addressed. The opening paragraph of Article 49 stipulates:

> Individual or mass forcible transfers, as well as deportations of protected persons from occupied territory to the territory of the Occupying Power or to that of any other country, occupied or not, are prohibited, regardless of their motive.[65]

It is hard to imagine more categorical, absolute language. Justices Landau and Isaac Cohen dismissed the argument that this article prevents Israel from deporting Palestinians from the West Bank on the grounds that Israel is not bound by it. How is it that an article in an international convention Israel signed and ratified is not binding? To understand these justices' legal position, we should pause to review the important distinction in international law between *treaty* law (norms put in place through treaties and conventions) and *customary* law (norms that have become binding because they are in practice universally respected out of a belief that they are to be adhered to). Israel is one of the countries in which domestic law automatically incorporates the customary principles of international law. This is not, however, the case with treaty law, which, to become part of domestic law, must be incorporated through domestic legislation. The High Court of Justice ruled in the early 1950s that customary law forms part of Israel's law of the land and hence the law the court uses to reach its judgments. However, international treaty law is not part of the law of the land and therefore provides no basis for claiming a remedy for its breach by individuals in the domestic court.[66]

Landau and Cohen ruled that Article 49 of the Geneva Convention had not reached the level of customary law and that the principle forbidding the exile of residents of occupied territory had not yet become a custom accepted by most nations as binding. This position spared Landau the need to rule on whether the deportation of Palestinians was a breach of Article 49.[67]

Deputy President Cohn again found himself dissenting. In one of the most courageous judgments given in the High Court of Justice, he demonstrated how a liberal judge seeking to strengthen human rights may use the discretion he has, drawing on profound legal knowledge, to serve the fundamental principles he believes to be the basis for the law. Cohn agreed that the Geneva Convention, which was opened for signing in 1949, had not yet attained the status of international customary law. But, he ruled, this did not mean that the convention does not contain permissions and prohibitions that *reflect* customary international law in effect even before it was drafted.

Cohn analyzed the principle that prohibits deportation and reached the conclusion that for the most part, the first paragraph of Article 49 reflects "a nucleus of customary international law that has been in effect, for all intents and purposes, since ancient times all over the world."[68] Cohn analyzed states' practices with regard to deporting people from their territories and reached the conclusion that while states do reserve the power to deport foreign nationals, a parallel legal practice had developed that forbids the deportation of citizens. "State practice, in upholding legal duties, in forbidding the deportation of their own citizens from their soil, is universal and prevalent, and amounts to customary international law. This is written in books, repeated in judgments, and repeated again in practice, but still it is not yet common knowledge of the sort that requires no evidence," Cohn wrote, citing a great many examples from books, judgments, and state practice.[69]

Therefore, while the prohibition on deporting foreign nationals is a new concept introduced in Article 49 of the Geneva Convention and does not constitute customary law, the prohibition in the same article on the deportation of citizens expresses an ancient practice that has reached the level of customary law and is, therefore, binding under domestic law. Moreover, given Cohn's determination that the deportation regulations were, in fact, military legislation created out of thin air (through the Order Regarding Interpretation), the rules of international law trump military law, even if they do not trump law made by parliament. All this led to the conclusion that the prohibition on deporting citizens from their own country, which is enshrined in international law, and a nucleus of which is embedded in Article 49 of the Geneva Convention, to which Israel is party, nullified the deportation power bestowed by the Defense Regulations. "Thus, the commander's power under Regulation 112 is reduced to a power to deport foreign nationals only," Cohn concluded.[70] The mayors' deportation, in fact the deportation of any Palestinian from the Occupied Territories, was unlawful.

The judgment on the mayors' deportation was decided by the majority opinion, and Qawasmeh and Milhem were deported two days later. While the Shaka affair lasted a month, the proceedings in the trio's case dragged on for seven months: seven months of protest, international attention, local as well as international media, and political debate. The judgment, which for the first time thoroughly addressed the legality of the deportation power, did ultimately rule it lawful, but Cohn's strong dissenting opinion gave the principled argument against the practice a tailwind, leaving an opening for more legal deliberation on the issue in the future. Additionally, the argument that Israel was allowed to deport, since the prohibition against it was not customary law and therefore not binding in domestic courts, caused difficulties for Israel: in terms of international relations, treaty law is binding and countries are expected to uphold it (even if it is not possible to obtain an order rooted in this law in local courts); and, of course, the prohibition on deportation is perceived as an expression of moral principles, while the argument presented by Landau and Isaac Cohen was mostly technical.

It was clearly only a matter of time until the question of whether Israel was violating the prohibition on deportation—and committing a war crime—would reappear on the High Court's docket.

SO IS DEPORTATION ALLOWED OR NOT?

In the years that followed the mayors' deportation, the military government continued sporadically to expel Palestinian activists suspected of subversive action against the occupation. Their lawyers, like lawyers, tried to use every possible argument to reopen questions that had been decided in previous judgments or to come up with new arguments that had not been heard before. In one case, Langer tried to convince the court to rule that the power to deport defies international human rights law, referring to the prohibition on deportation in the Universal Declaration of Human Rights. The court ruled that the UDHR may apply to the relations between a person and his or her country but not between a person and a military government established as a result of hostilities, and not while the hostilities were still ongoing.[71] In another case, the court fended off Langer and Tsemel's joint attempt to revisit the application of Article 49 and the revocation of the Defense Regulations by the Jordanian constitution.[72] In a third case, Langer submitted an opinion by Oxford University professor Ian Brownlie, a renowned expert on international law, stating that the prohibition on deportation in the Geneva Convention is customary and therefore should be binding under Israeli domestic law. The idea was to bolster Justice Cohn's dissenting opinion and reopen the issue. When the presiding justice, Justice Dov Levin, announced at the start of the hearing that the petitioners could not pursue this line of argument, they withdrew their petition in protest.[73] This unusual incident, which suggested that the court was not interested in hearing the deportees' arguments, was widely reported in Israel and around the world.

At the same time, lawyers defending deportees honed the use of advisory committee hearings. The authorities no longer dared try to evade their obligation to hold a hearing, and hearings were carried out in such a way that allowed the lawyers to argue, submit questions to the military commander, receive nonclassified material, demand a court review of the classification of certain materials as confidential, and petition the High Court of Justice once the committee made its recommendations. Each deportation was a lengthy process that came with headlines and public debate.

In 1983, Justice Meir Shamgar was appointed president of the Supreme Court. He replaced Isaac Cohen, who served for a short time after Landau's retirement. His appointment signaled a changing of the guard.

Shamgar had been military advocate general in 1967, playing a key role in shaping the military law applied in the territories occupied during the war. He subsequently served as attorney general until his court appointment in 1975. In his youth, Shamgar had been a member of the Irgun, a pre-state Zionist paramilitary organization. Arrested by British Mandate forces, he was exiled to a detention camp in Africa, yet his personal experience did not make him an opponent of deportation. In fact, as a founder of the military government and a former attorney general who gave the executive branch legal advice on its powers, he had made major contributions to shaping the power to deport and had legitimized it for the government and the military. He had been one of the panel presided over by President Zussman that had rejected Abu Awad's petition, and he had served as justice and president on several panels that rejected attempts to relitigate the legality of deportations.

However, the pressure applied by lawyers, the many expert opinions, and the international debate over the prohibition set down in Article 49 of the Geneva Convention ultimately had had an effect. The question of whether Israel was in violation of the Geneva Convention remained unanswered, given the court's approach that the prohibition in the convention does not apply to Israel's domestic law. Justice Cohn's dissenting opinion, which hovered above Israel's entire jurisprudence, also had yet to be addressed. Shamgar was looking for a case that would allow the court to rule on the substantive question: Does deportation of Palestinians breach the prohibition set down in Article 49 of the Geneva Convention, even if the article is treaty law and not binding in a domestic court? Normally the court would have no reason to address a question it considers theoretical, which it was, since the court had taken the position that violation or not, the article could not lead to revocation of the power to deport because it is treaty law. But who knew better than Shamgar that the question was not only legal but also societal, moral, and political? And in those spheres, the claim that Israel is violating a convention signed after World War II whose purpose is to prevent humanity from committing war crimes against civilians could not be more troubling.

In 1987, Shamgar decided to combine three petitions challenging the deportation of three members of illegal Palestinian organizations, and expand the panel to five justices to allow the court to hold a definitive discussion of whether the Defense Regulations contradicted Article 49 of the

Fourth Geneva Convention on the issue of deportation. The first Palestinian was Abd al-Aziz al-Affo, a member of the Popular Front for the Liberation of Palestine from Jenin, who was about to finish serving his third prison term for organizing protests, membership in an illegal organization, and soliciting others to join. (Security officials said al-Affo's subversive activities began back in his high school days, when he stole a stencil machine to print political flyers.) The second deportee was Abd al-Aziz Rafia, a Gaza resident, who, according to the authorities, was a spiritual leader of the Islamic Jihad movement in the Gaza Strip, was a member of the Islamic Jihad, and was accused of making "nationalistic, incendiary" speeches. The third was Jamal Shati Hindi, a Fatah activist from Nablus, the only one of the three indicted on weapons charges, having confessed that he had trained to lay explosives. The military commander of the West Bank, Major General Amram Mitzna (who would go on to become chairman of the Labor Party), issued the deportation orders, arguing that each of the three men was a "senior" member of his organization, and therefore their removal from the area would help calm it down.

The panel selected to hear the case was made up of a new generation of Supreme Court justices, including former state attorney Gabriel Bach, who had represented the state in the trio case. Given that each of the deportees belonged to a different Palestinian organization, it was no wonder they were represented by three different lawyers: PFLP member al-Affo was represented by Leah Tsemel; Islamic Jihad member Rafia was represented by Palestinian-Israeli lawyer Darwish Nasser; Hindi, a member of Fatah, was represented by Jawad Boulos, who would later serve as legal counsel to the Palestinian Authority.

The difference in this case from previous hearings was that for the first time in the fight against Palestinian deportations, the petition was joined by a large human rights organization—and not just any organization, but Israel's largest and oldest, the Association for Civil Rights in Israel.[74] ACRI was represented by two lawyers: Avigdor Feldman, one of Israel's most important human rights lawyers and greatest legal orators; and David Kretzmer, a founder of ACRI and an esteemed jurist and professor at Hebrew University, an expert on constitutional law, and a future vice chair of the UN Human Rights Committee, the most senior international human rights position ever filled by an Israeli. The fact of ACRI joining the proceedings and Kretzmer appearing as counsel amplified the legal and public message that deportation is a serious human rights violation. Kretzmer wrote and presented, on behalf of all the petitioners, the argument regarding Article 49, and he asked the court to abandon its earlier rulings, given the "obvious interpretive error" that had been made.

But even before any arguments were advanced, the petitioners faced a vexing question. The panel appointed to hear the case included President Shamgar, who, as chief architect of legal policy in the West Bank for years, had given the legal seal of approval to the practice of deportation. And Shamgar had not stopped at giving counsel; he had also published his position on the inapplicability of the Geneva Convention in the Occupied Territories in a legal journal while serving as attorney general.[75] This was a key issue in the case. Were Shamgar's fully formed opinion on the subject, his prior history with deportation, and his operational ability to give orders that reflected his fully formed opinion cause to recuse him? In many respects, the petition, which required Shamgar to consider arguments he had previously rejected as military advocate general and as attorney general, effectively put him in the position of serving as an appellate instance, deciding appeals against his own decisions. While not true in a practical sense, since he had no involvement in the decision to deport the three petitioners in the case, this was the situation in the theoretical sense. In a legal world where a justice is meant to be neutral, counsel for the petitioners had problems with Shamgar's neutrality.

As the hearing began, Kretzmer and Feldman raised the issue and asked Shamgar, on ACRI's behalf, to consider the difficulty it caused. They focused on the fact that Shamgar clearly had a set position on the status of the Geneva Convention, as it was articulated in the article he had authored. They did not make a formal request to Shamgar to recuse himself, but he responded as if they had. It is not every day that doubts are raised about whether it is appropriate for the president of the Supreme Court to preside over a case, especially not in one so publicly and politically charged. But Feldman, arguing for ACRI, did not hold back and clarified the difficulty:

> While the Honorable President of this Court served as Attorney General, he expressed his clear opinion regarding doubts that the Convention applies in the Territories, for reasons that have to do with the sovereignty of the Hashemite Kingdom of Jordan over these territories, as well as other

reasons. The opinion of the Attorney General obviously has a guiding, or directing status with respect to the policy of the executive branch. The opinion of the Honorable President was expressed, *inter alia*, in a discussion published in the first volume of the Israel Yearbook of Human Rights. As such, this statement of opinion is more than an abstract academic view, but was rather applied in practice with regards to the topic of the matter herein. The rule is that: "In Israel, a norm has taken root, whereby a justice who held a position in the public service prior to his appointment does not hear a matter in which he was involved prior to the appointment, whether as the executing agent, or in a position of approving or directing policy." See, Meir Shamgar—On Judicial Disqualification following Yadid, Tarta Mashma, published in Shimon Agranat's Eightieth, 87, see p. 94.[76]

The reference to an article Shamgar himself wrote about recusal was a rather clever move that no doubt embarrassed Shamgar, but the argument, which turned into a motion, was doomed to fail. Justices often come to the court from public service and often hear matters concerning legal issues they dealt with as part of the executive branch. The motion for recusal was presumably submitted with the idea that even if rejected, Shamgar would have to be extra careful and his neutrality would be under close public scrutiny. Or that maybe he would even refrain from writing the main judgment.

According to the law, a motion to recuse a Supreme Court justice is heard by the justice himself, and, unlike judges in lower instances, there is no appeal.

Shamgar denied the motion and his outrage and repugnance at the maneuver were almost palpable. "There is no basis for the argument presented to us by the Petitioner," he wrote. "Expressing a legal view on a certain topic does not preclude subsequently taking part in a judicial proceeding in which the same legal issue is examined with respect to a different set of facts. In this regard, there is no difference whether the issue in question involves contract law, criminal law or public international law, as is the case herein." Shamgar also ruled that if the criteria cited in the recusal motion were always applied, any judge would be precluded from hearing "any matter that raises a theoretic issue to which he made reference in the past, whether as a lawyer appearing in court, in a lecture given in an academic context or in an opinion expressed as the Attorney General or the State Attorney."

Since the motion focused on the article he wrote, Shamgar ignored the fact that his active involvement in approving deportations, both as military advocate general and as attorney general, went beyond expressing an academic opinion.

At any rate, the petitioners were stuck with the panel headed by Shamgar. In the hearing, the petitioners once again presented the main argument regarding the applicability of Article 49 of the Fourth Geneva Convention, and the clear interpretation that deportations of residents of an occupied territory was always prohibited ("regardless of their motive"). The judgment was issued in April 1988 and covered seventy-eight pages, sixty-eight of them written by Shamgar.

His analysis of Article 49 found that, despite its clear language (which prohibits "mass or individual" deportations), the article does not refer to deportation of individuals for security reasons, which is what Israel was doing. "It is my opinion," he wrote, "that in accordance with the applicable rules of interpretation, one should not view the content of Article 49 as anything but a reference to such arbitrary deportations of groups of nationals as were carried out during World War II for purposes of subjugation, extermination and for similarly cruel reasons."[77]

Shamgar essentially adopted President Zussman's position in the Abu Awad case, but while Zussman devoted only a single paragraph to this topic, Shamgar thoroughly dissected it, suggesting an interpretive theory whereby the purpose of the article (preventing the type of atrocities perpetrated by the Nazis in territories occupied during World War II) takes precedence over the literal meaning, even when the latter is self-evident. Shamgar rightly referred to the important interpretive principle in international law, whereby international conventions should be interpreted in light of their *object* and *purpose*.[78] Therefore, he ruled that though the article clearly refers to "individual or mass" deportations, the prohibition applies only to "arbitrary deportations of groups of nationals," because, according to his analysis, the article's purpose is to prevent deportation for motives of "subjugation, extermination, and for similarly cruel reasons."

Shamgar also ruled that though the article prohibits deportations "regardless of their motive," it in fact only prohibits deportation for the commission of atrocities of the sort the Nazis committed against deportees. He even went so far as to accuse dissenters, petitioners included, of worshipping the literal interpretation, no less. Finally, Shamgar asserted that, in any event, the entire discussion was academic, since, in his opinion, being a treaty provision that has not attained customary status, Article 49 could not be invoked as a basis for remedy under Israeli domestic law—contrary to Haim Cohn's position in the mayors' case.

In the fight over the correct interpretation, Shamgar argued that his position was rooted in a "purposive" legal philosophy, one that first prioritizes the purpose of the norm and then requires an interpretation that conforms to that purpose; he characterized the petitioners' position, on the other hand, as literal, narrow, and formalistic. But by trying to limit the prohibition on deportation only to cases that are analogous to the Nazis' mass deportations, Shamgar in fact adopted a narrow conservative approach that identifies a law's purpose according to the historical context in which it was enacted (in this case, the background to the drafting of the Geneva Convention). Legal interpretation that puts great stock in the concrete-historical context of the legislative act is not, in fact, purposive. Rather, it is a conservative approach that looks for the legislator's original intent and assumes that this fiction exists (even when the "legislator" is in fact representatives of scores of countries, each possibly with its own "object" and "purpose" for supporting the language of the article).

True purposive interpretation involves identifying the norm's purpose in line with the values and principles that the specific legal field seeks to realize and that the law in general tries to promote. Had Shamgar used a purposive interpretation focusing on values, he would have had to conclude that the Geneva Convention is one of a body of conventions and legal principles meant to protect civilians during armed conflict and minimize their suffering to the extent possible. More specifically, the Fourth Geneva Convention, which includes the famed Article 49, is meant to protect residents of an occupied territory, govern their lives under occupation, and keep them from harm and abuse. The convention's purpose is, therefore, to implement the notion of protecting civilians' human rights during conflict and the rights of the occupied during a military occupation. As such, the articles of the convention are a type of charter of fundamental rights for people under occupation, and one of them is the right to live in their own country. Well established in human rights law, it does not change with the reason for the deportation. The right is to continue living in one's own country, among one's own people and community. On this issue, there is no conflict between the purpose and the text. The text fulfills the purpose and the purpose matches the text.

But what is odder still in Shamgar's judgment is the effort he put into his creative interpretation, when ultimately he ruled that Article 49 was customary and therefore not binding in Israeli domestic law. If that is the case, why go to all the trouble of interpreting Article 49 in a way that allows for deportation? The answer has nothing to do with the law, of course, but with politics and foreign relations. Israel was unhappy with its image as a state that violates the Geneva Convention, and Shamgar—military advocate general, attorney general, and now president of the Supreme Court—came to the rescue, enlisting his colleagues, the other justices.*

Except Shamgar got an unexpected surprise that meddled with his attempt to put an end once and for all to the debate on Article 49. One of the justices in the extended panel took a different view on the article's interpretation, and he wrote a powerful dissenting opinion. It was the same Justice Bach who, serving as state attorney, had defended deportation, and who now showed that the bench can sometimes offer great freedom. Bach agreed with Shamgar that Article 49 did not apply since it was treaty rather than customary law, and that therefore there was no cause to revoke the deportation orders. However, Bach felt compelled to disagree on the interpretation of Article 49. "I find no contradiction between this 'historical approach' and a broad interpretation of the Article in question," Bach wrote.

> The crimes committed by the German army in occupied territories empha
> sized the need for a convention that would protect the civilian popula
> tion and served as "trigger" for its framing. But this fact does not in any
> way refute the thesis that when framing that convention, the draftsmen
> decided to formulate it in broad forms, in a manner that would, inter alia,

---

* Another possible explanation is that in light of Justice Bach's opinion (detailed later), which sided with the petitioners on the correct interpretation of Article 49, while holding the view that the article is not customary and thus cannot be invoked in the domestic court, Shamgar felt obliged to respond and reason the contrary position. But even if that is the case, Shamgar's lengthy ruling was not written to allow the deportation but to defend Israel from charges of violating international law.

totally prevent the deportation of residents from those territories either
to the occupying state or to another country. The language of the Article, seen in its own context and in light of the treaty in its entirety, does
not admit, in my opinion, the construction that it is intended to prevent
only acts such as those committed by the Nazis for racial, ethnic or nationalistic reasons. We must not deviate, by way of interpretation, from the
clear and simple meaning of the words of an enactment when the language of the provision is unequivocal and when the literal meaning does
not contradict the legislative purpose or lead to an illogical and absurd
result.[79]

If Shamgar had intended his judgment to remove the legal and moral
question from Israel's and the world's agenda, he had failed. Bach's dissenting opinion along with Haim Cohn's dissent and legal criticism from
all over the world left deportations in place as a controversial practice considered by many to be a war crime.

BEFORE THE FINAL BATTLE

After the ruling in the al-Affo, Rafia, and Hindi cases, the court refused
to revisit the legality of military deportations of Palestinians. Lawyers kept
trying to bring it to court, but the justices rejected all attempts, referring
back to previous judgments, particularly to al-Affo's.

In late 1987, the First Intifada erupted. Protests, marches, and clashes
with security forces were an everyday occurrence in West Bank and Gaza
cities and in East Jerusalem as well. As always, the Israeli government
looked in its toolbox and once again brought out Regulation 112. The regulation was used time and time again against groups of local leaders, the
next generation of Palestinians in the territories. People like Bilal Shakshir, a member of the Democratic Front for the Liberation of Palestine,
Popular Front activist Muhammad al-Labadi, and Fatah member Muhammad Matour were deported by the military administration.

Given the restricted field of battle, lawyers again had to focus on the
procedural elements of deportation. Avigdor Feldman, who came on as
counsel in many of Langer's and Tsemel's cases, drafted a strong indictment against the use of confidential material to justify deportation. He
filed petitions for disclosure of such material, which the Supreme Court

justices then had to review to decide whether any of it could be disclosed to the petitioner.[80] During advisory committee hearings, he demanded to cross-examine the military commander who signed the deportation order.[81] He even argued that given the high number of deportations, each individual one was in fact part of a mass deportation of a group of nationals, and therefore (even under Shamgar's creative interpretation) prohibited by Article 49.[82] Finally, he argued that without the deportee's consent for the justices to review the confidential material ex parte, the justices could not sanction the deportation, since they had no idea on what basis it had been ordered.[83]

All of these ploys failed. The justices rejected the argument that the large number of deportations amounted to a mass deportation. When each deportation is examined and decided individually, it cannot be a mass deportation, Shamgar ruled. Bach, in a judgment that was a bitter disappointment for Feldman, ruled that if the deportee did not allow the justices to view confidential material ex parte, they would have to assume that the material proved the state's allegations against him, given the "presumption of propriety" carried by actions of state authorities. His demand to cross-examine the military commander was denied, and his requests to disclose confidential material yielded little. Feldman even tried at some point to get permission to present the minister of defense with a questionnaire to examine the efficacy of deportation,[84] in response to reservations the minister had expressed, which were reported in the media, but this also failed.

One by one, the Supreme Court upheld the deportation orders. In the whole history of the legal effort to prevent deportation, the Supreme Court had not struck down a single one.

And yet, beneath the surface, some cracks began to form. The final curtain was about to fall on Israel's use of Regulation 112.

HAMAS OVER AND OUT

In 1992, Israel experienced a great political upset. The right-wing government, in power since 1977, was replaced by one of the center-left, led by the Labor Party and headed by Yitzhak Rabin, the man who was chief of staff in the 1967 war. Rabin put together a majority government by forming a coalition with two profoundly different parties: Shas, a religious party that represented the Orthodox Sephardic community, and the liberal Meretz, which supported a two-state solution for Israel and Palestine and was led by the grande dame of human rights in Israeli politics, Shulamit Aloni. With a Knesset majority, the government was able to make the biggest change in Israeli policy since the occupation, the Oslo Accords, but the coalition was unstable, due to the stark differences between its member parties.

Israel had used deportation continually from the start of the occupation until the Rabin government was sworn in. Research by the human rights organization B'Tselem revealed that 1,107 deportation orders for Palestinians had been signed from 1967 to 1992, 990 of them in the first twelve years of the occupation, or up until 1979, the year Abu Awad was deported. In the subsequent eleven years, 117 orders had been signed.[85] The research shows that although deportation never stopped, use of the measure had significantly decreased.[86]

The first two weeks of December 1992 were harsh. The First Intifada continued to take its bloody toll. In Gaza, Palestinian militants shot and killed three IDF reserve soldiers, and one other was shot dead in Hebron. Hamas claimed responsibility for both attacks. The Hamas movement had been established in the early stages of the intifada as an Islamic Palestinian organization that served as an alternative to the PLO and had the support of the Muslim Brotherhood active throughout the Arab world. Ideologically, Hamas favored jihad against the State of Israel and operated through both a network of charities throughout the West Bank and Gaza Strip and an armed wing that executed armed attacks against Israeli soldiers and terrorist attacks against Israeli civilians. Thanks to its charity network, Hamas won increasing support from Palestinians and gradually became a significant political force. The movement's founder, Sheikh Ahmad Yassin, was arrested by Israel in 1989 and sentenced by the military court to life plus fifteen years in prison for religious rulings permitting the execution of Palestinians suspected as Israeli collaborators.

On December 13, 1992, a border police officer, Nissim Toledano, was kidnapped. The kidnappers, a Hamas cell, gave Israel an ultimatum: free Sheikh Yassin by 9:00 p.m. or Toledano would be executed. Toledano was murdered that same night and his body found two days later, bound and stabbed. Israelis were shocked by the cruelty of the murder and demanded decisive action against Hamas. The next morning, the government passed a resolution to deport a large number of activists from Hamas and its sister organization, Islamic Jihad. The resolution stated:

A. In light of a state of emergency and in order to maintain the security of the public [the Government has resolved] to empower the Prime Minister and Minister of Defense to instruct and authorize the military commanders of the areas of Judea, Samaria and Gaza to issue orders, according to the requisite and immediate security needs, concerning temporary deportation and without prior notice, to remove agitators, those inhabitants of the areas who in their activities endanger human life, or who agitate to such activities, and this for a period to be determined by the Military Commanders and not to exceed two years.

B. Whoever is deported as stipulated above will be permitted, within 60 days, to appeal his deportation before a special committee through his family or attorney, according to the regulations to be determined in the orders.[87]

The resolution breached the few principles the High Court of Justice had insisted on over the years: the deportation would take place without prior notice, the hearing would be convened retroactively, and the deportees would not be present. These were precisely the issues over which the Supreme Court went head-to-head with the government during the mayors' deportation, and the court had ruled that any hearing must take place before the deportation, not after the fact, and that the deportee must be able to attend.

The government resolution attempted to circumvent the difficulties by first stipulating that the deportation would be "temporary," for two years, and then by granting authority to enact legislative amendments to the emergency regulations that would allow immediate deportations. In this the government was aiming to take advantage of the opening introduced by Supreme Court president Landau in his judgment on the mayors' case: he had clarified that should the government wish to do so, it could change the Defense Regulations and stipulate that the hearing would take place retroactively rather than ahead of time. Prime Minister Begin had been interested in the change, although ultimately it was never made.

In line with the resolution, military commanders in the West Bank and the Gaza Strip signed orders permitting temporary deportations and retroactive hearings.[88] Based on these orders (which constitute primary legislation in the Occupied Territories), the commanders issued temporary deportation orders against 415 Hamas and Islamic Jihad activists. The criteria later cited by the attorney general for selecting the deportees were that some of them "took part in planning and supporting acts of violence, or in directing, inciting or preaching for such acts. Others aided the activities of the organizations in economic or organizational infrastructure, recruitment, procurement of funds, and writing and arranging for the circulation of flyers." Essentially, these were Hamas and Islamic Jihad activists at the neighborhood level and up.

The authorities quickly set out to collect the deportees. Those who were prisoners were taken from their cells; others were arrested by IDF troops in their homes. The military censor banned any reports of the deportations to prevent a public outcry, and perhaps also to block the flow of information that would allow a High Court petition. In the evening of December 16, buses with 415 deportees on board left central Israel heading toward expulsion at the Lebanese border.

But the plan to deport hundreds of people before anyone could file a petition failed.

That same evening, a journalist had called Leah Tsemel. "Did you hear scores of Hamas activists are about to be deported?" he asked. Tsemel was shocked. "No way! What are you talking about?" The reporter confirmed: "The buses are already at the prisons!" Tsemel knew this was a violation of the restrictions the High Court had placed on deportations back when she represented Abu Awad.[89]

From that point on, things moved quickly. Tsemel recruited Andre Rosenthal, who had interned at her office before becoming a lawyer and now had his own office. She alerted Avigdor Feldman as well. Without seeing the deportation orders and in absence of prior hearings, Tsemel and Rosenthal had to look up the names of Hamas prisoners they had represented in criminal and administrative detention proceedings so they could file a petition on their behalf, just in case they were included in the group. Throughout the night, they kept receiving names of more Hamas prisoners and activists who had been taken from their homes, and they added more petitions.

As the night went on, it became clear that individual petitions would not result in a general order against the entire deportation, so they deci-

ded to name public petitioners as well. Tsemel spoke to Yehoshua Schoffman, then ACRI's chief legal counsel, urging him to file a petition on
ACRI's behalf. At the same time, Tsemel, Feldman, and Rosenthal got
power of attorney from the human rights NGO HaMoked, which they had
represented on various matters involving human rights violations in the
territories, including it, too, as a petitioner. Together, the three lawyers
wrote three High Court petitions at lightning speed. In one, Rosenthal
represented HaMoked and two prisoners and their families; in the second, Tsemel represented a group of prisoners; in the third, Feldman represented another group of prisoners and Tsemel herself, who decided to
act as a public-interest petitioner.

ACRI also managed to file a public petition to cancel the deportation.
The organization's lawyers, Yehoshua Schoffman and Dana Briskman,[90]
argued that the deportation defied the procedure set in the Regulations
and denied the deportees their hearings. They also contended that the legislative amendment process had been flawed, that the revocation of the
right to an advance hearing made the orders illegal, and that a piece of
legislation aiming to deny access to the court and to legal counsel could
not stand. In the short time they had at their disposal, they managed to
cite the justices' criticism during Dr. Natsheh's case and that of the mayors of the attempts by the state to "outsmart" the court, as Landau and
Haim Cohn referred to it. The parallels to the current deportation were
obvious. All the petitions would later be combined.

The lawyers understood that an immediate court injunction was needed
to stop the buses on their way to the Lebanese border. To do this, they
had to contact the duty justice at the Supreme Court, and since it was very
late at night, they had to get to the justice's home. It just so happened
that Aharon Barak was duty justice that night. Barak, who had served as
the attorney general during the Natsheh affair, would have been touched
personally by the breaches in legal procedure involved in the group
deportation.

Barak is a wunderkind of Israel's legal system. He became a law professor at thirty-two. At thirty-nine, he was appointed attorney general, the
youngest lawyer to hold that position, and at forty-two he received his
Supreme Court appointment. Barak's keen intellect and rare charisma were
undisputed. His pleasant personality disarmed even his greatest opponents, and as a justice who served for more than twenty-eight years in the

Supreme Court—eleven as president—he left a bigger mark on Israeli law than any other president. His record as justice is a matter of colossal debate, but everyone agrees that Barak took a liberal, activist line that created a legal defense system for human rights in Israel. But his judicial record on security activities in the Occupied Territories is quite different, a sharp contrast to Barak inside the Green Line, to a certain degree clouding his legacy.

On the night of December 16, 1992, several lawyers made their way to Barak's home. Did they all go in? Or just some? And what exactly happened there? The events were already dramatic, with the clandestine deportation of hundreds exposed before it was accomplished; with hasty petitions, compiled even as the names of the deportees continued to stream in; with the urgent need to get an injunction to stop the deportation in the eleventh hour. What happened that night has become a bit of a war story for Israel's human rights lawyers, and, like any war story, it suffers from the Rashomon effect.

At least three lawyers claim they were at Barak's house, though none of them met there. Rosenthal says he returned to the house "four or five times."[91] The first time, Barak signed only a specific injunction, preventing the specific petitioners named in Rosenthal's petition from being deported. Rosenthal says Barak refused to issue a general injunction to stop the entire deportation, and so he kept coming back, each time with a new petition naming more deportees whose names had been provided by journalists or family. Barak signed each injunction he brought. Rosenthal remembers that during every one of the trips, Barak had him wait in the foyer and then returned with the injunction, which he had written in his study.

Dan Yakir, now chief legal counsel for ACRI, remembers how Schoffman "scribbled" a handwritten public petition, ran to Barak's building, and "waited in the stairwell" until Barak gave him a general injunction prohibiting the deportation of all the individuals on the buses.[92] Schoffman says he arrived at Barak's house together with Briskman at around 1:00 a.m. Somehow, television crews were already there. Barak was on the phone, listening as the secretary of the Supreme Court read him the government's decision allowing the deportations. According to Schoffman, he then brought the lawyers into his living room and issued the general injunction after reading their petition.[93]

Feldman also says he was at Barak's that night, and Feldman has a different, more detailed story. He remembers his shock when the door opened.[94] He was warmly greeted by Barak's wife, Elisheva, then a Labor Court judge. Over her shoulder, he could hear the sounds of a social gathering. It turned out Feldman had arrived in the middle of a reception for a Harvard professor, an acquaintance of Barak's visiting Israel. Feldman discovered he knew the American professor from time he had spent at Harvard as a visiting scholar. He looked around and saw the elite of Israel's legal world—State Attorney Dorit Beinisch, former attorney general Yitzhak Zamir. "Everyone was very relaxed, drinking wine and eating crackers and all sorts of dips," he recalls.

Barak invited him into his study. In that intimate setting, Feldman told Barak what was happening out there. He left Barak's home with an interim injunction prohibiting the deportation of the Hamas activists he was representing, pending a hearing.

It is hard to know, based on the limited research carried out, what exactly happened at Barak's home that night, but it seems that between two and seven visits by different lawyers, who disturbed either the justice's restful evening or a party for some Harvard professor, resulted in interim injunctions forbidding the deportations until the hearing scheduled for 10:00 a.m. the next morning. Schoffman remembers that a conference on Canadian constitutional law was taking place in Jerusalem at that time, which explains the event at Barak's residence. But he believes that Feldman's visit occurred a day or two later, when he came to submit an urgent motion related to the case.

Either way, once the State Attorney's Office got wind of the injunctions, the government urgently tried to push up the hearing, and the Supreme Court president announced it would be held at the unprecedented hour of 5:00 a.m. The buses, with hundreds of deportees on board, halted at the Lebanese border, waiting for the High Court's decision. It was now impossible to keep the deportations out of the media. The very thing the government had wanted to avoid was about to happen: a media circus producing headline after headline, even before the act had been executed.

On December 17, Israeli citizens woke up to drama. Busloads of deportees were parked near the border while the High Court of Justice debated in depth the legality of the government's maneuver. Prime Minister Rabin was furious that the deportation had been thwarted. He called ACRI "the

Association for Hamas Rights" and caustically remarked that Hamas victims don't get a hearing before they are murdered.[95]

At 5:00 a.m., the petitioners' lawyers reported to the new Supreme Court building opened with much ceremony a month earlier. For most of them, it was their first appearance in the monumental structure and their first time litigating before dawn. Representing the state was not State Attorney Dorit Beinisch but Attorney General Yosef Harish instead. His presence hinted at the drama that had gone on in the State Attorney's Office, where Beinisch thought the move, which contradicted the jurisprudence of the High Court, was unacceptable and refused to represent the state. This was a most bold step from someone who aspired to the bench and whose judicial appointment in no small measure depended on the politicians orchestrating the deportation. Her refusal also sent a strong message of dissent over the legitimacy of the deportations from within the state's own legal service. Beinisch's red line may not have denied the government legal representation or led to its defeat in court, but it did add to a long list of acts that eroded the legitimacy of deportation and put another crack in the ground on which it stood.

The deliberations were heated and long. Since none of the would-be deportees had had a hearing, there was no point or possibility of deliberating on the justifications for any of the deportations. Instead, the discussion focused on two arguments made by the petitioners: Could military legislation legitimately reduce the right to a hearing to one that is only retroactive, without the deportee present (but represented through a relative or a lawyer)? And is not the deportation of 415 people at once, in fact, a mass deportation, which, even according to Shamgar's position in al-Affo, is prohibited under Article 49 of the Geneva Convention?

Attorney General Harish, who unusually appeared in person, argued that the question of retroactive hearings had been answered in the mayors' case, where Justice Landau had ruled that they were prohibited in the absence of a legislative change to provide for them. Indeed, in the present case, the military commanders had signed orders (on the government's instructions) permitting the retroactive hearings. As for the mass deportation, Harish argued that it was ludicrous to classify the removal of 415 handpicked individuals as a "mass" action. Even if the deportation involved hundreds of people, it was a collection of many individual orders rather than one single order, he said, adding that each deportation had been individually examined. To this Feldman replied that according to the amount of time between the government's resolution and the issue of the deportation orders, which he had calculated with his colleagues Tsemel and Rosenthal, the West Bank's military commander must have dedicated one (!) minute to each of his decisions on each of the deportees, while the Gaza commander, who was "slower," devoted one minute and ten seconds to each deportee. This is not a collection of individual deportations. This is a classic mass deportation, Feldman pronounced.

THE HEARING LASTED fourteen hours, and the justices were clearly divided. While Shamgar appeared to support the state's position, Barak was extremely critical. At a certain point, the exchange between Barak and Harish sounded like a cross-examination.

JUSTICE BARAK: Next to each name, what is the terrorist act that justified the deportation and which may be disclosed, because this touches upon the question of the factual basis. Is it possible to deport everyone who is a member of an organization and more, meaning that it is possible to deport all ten thousand?* You yourselves agree that there must be individual guilt of some kind. My question is, at what level of gravity does one decide to deport? Every member of a hostile organization?

HARISH: Maybe so. It may be that if one wishes to uproot the organization, it is necessary to deport all of them.

BARAK: Is there an estimation of how many [Palestinian prisoners] are members of terrorist organizations in the Gaza Strip?

HARISH: Everyone, I think.[96]

The pressure on Harish caused tension in the Prime Minister's Office, where officials were waiting for the interim injunction to be lifted, and so they decided to do something unusual—send the chief of the general staff, Ehud Barak, to testify before the justices. This rare move would send a

---

* In its report on the mass deportation, B'Tselem noted that Barak was apparently referring to the total number of Palestinian detainees. B'Tselem also pointed out that the actual number was lower than the one quoted.

clear message about the importance the executive attached to completing the deportation successfully.

In the meantime, the three justices reviewing the case were engaged in a dispute. Barak was inclined to leave the interim injunction he had issued intact, while Shamgar and his deputy, Menachem Elon, wanted to lift it. Shamgar decided to expand the panel and added four justices. This was meant to strengthen the legitimacy of whatever decision was made.

Ehud Barak, the most decorated soldier in the IDF's history, arrived at the court in uniform, wearing all of his medals and badges, and gave an impassioned speech before the seven-justice panel about the deportation being crucial for Israel's security. Tsemel's motion to cross-examine him was denied.[97] The court was also presented with security briefs on Hamas and Islamic Jihad, containing a review of their actions and ideology. The deportation was hailed as a central tool in Israel's fight against these terrorist organizations, which had made it their purpose to establish an Islamic state in the entire territory of Palestine and to do so by waging armed struggle. The veiled threat was there between the lines: a High Court decision to return the deportees could lead to bloodshed.

After fourteen grueling hours, during which blunders came to light—people with the same or similar names to individuals marked for deportation had been mistakenly put on the bus—the court, by majority opinion, lifted the interim injunction and the deportation went ahead. No reasons were given for lifting the injunction; instead, a hearing in the petition itself was scheduled for mid-January. Before the High Court justices issued the decision, the *Yedioth Ahronoth* daily conducted an opinion poll among Israel's Jewish population, measuring the level of support for the deportation. The paper published the results on its front page on the next day, after the court had issued its decision. The results were unusually clear-cut: 91 percent supported the deportation and only 8 percent opposed it (in a typically Israeli manner, very few had no opinion—only 1 percent).[98] The justices were simply men of their people.

The "deportation of the four hundred," as it came to be called in the press, became an international incident, garnering even more media attention once it turned out that Lebanon had refused to allow the deportees into its territory. Newspapers published daily updates on the deportees, who had set up camp on the northern border of the "security belt," an area inside Lebanon controlled by Israel since 1982. Israel claimed the Lebanese government was responsible for the deportees, while the Lebanese government said that since it had not granted them entry into the country, the responsibility remained with Israel. The Lebanese army built a dirt barrier to prevent the deportees from entering Lebanese territory, while the IDF laid land mines on the road back through the security belt to prevent them from returning toward Israel. Journalists now had a juicy story about the hundreds of Palestinians who had been forcibly exiled and were now stuck in no-man's-land.[99]

On December 18, the UN Security Council convened to discuss the deportees and passed a resolution condemning Israel and demanding it revoke the deportation.[100] The High Court was inundated with more petitions, some filed by members of Knesset, some by deportees' relatives demanding their return, partly in response to the predicament in which the deportees now found themselves, which the petitioners said threatened their safety.[101] Relatives of Israeli terror victims also filed petitions, including the family of Nissim Toledano, whose murder had been the casus belli for the whole affair; they wanted the court to forbid the government from backtracking.

Another motion for an interim injunction was filed, stating that since the deportees were now stranded and Lebanon refused to assume responsibility for them, they must be returned to Israel pending a final ruling on the petitions or, at least, be given adequate living conditions, including a supply of basic commodities required for subsistence.

The court held a hearing four days after the deportation, in which the state submitted an affidavit from the head of the Military Intelligence Research Department, Yaakov Amidror, claiming that the location where the deportees were camped was under Lebanese control and Lebanese officials had supplied them with food and medicine. Feldman, Tsemel, and their colleagues were joined by Palestinian-Israeli lawyers Imad Dakwar, Anis Riad, and Jawad Boulos, each of whom represented a group of deportees. Three days later, the court sat again, recalling Chief of Staff Ehud Barak, except this time the justices agreed to let the petitioners' counsel examine him.

What took place in the courtroom was exceptional by any measure. Counsel for the petitioners, especially Feldman and Dakwar, got into a nail-biting duel with the chief of staff, during which Ehud Barak revealed, more than once, that he was not aware of the dangers awaiting the deportees in South Lebanon, and he gave evasive answers.[102] Dakwar kept up the assault on Barak, recalling the Sabra and Shatila massacre in 1982, and the ministerial responsibility ascribed to then defense minister Ariel Sharon.* The courtroom audience no doubt could not believe what they were seeing: a Palestinian-Israeli lawyer from Haifa cross-examining the Jewish state's chief of staff—a reversal of the balance of power, even if momentary, that defied comprehension.

The justices ultimately accepted the state's position that the Lebanese government was responsible for the deportees and they did not seem to be in danger.

Either in response to this decision or not, the Lebanese authorities decided, the same day, to stop allowing the Red Cross and the UN Relief and Works Agency for Palestine Refugees in the Near East (UNRWA) to supply food or medicine to the deportees via its territory. This made matters far worse since the deportees now seemed to have been abandoned in the middle of winter without any means of subsistence. Pressure on the Israeli government to take action mounted, but it held fast. In a majority vote, the government decided for the time being not to capitulate to the Lebanese move and refused to allow provisions to reach deportees via the security belt, which would have made the entire deportation questionable.[103] The many petitions that had been filed were heard on January 17 and 20, 1993, giving fodder to media reports and headlines.

A story that had begun with the abduction and gruesome murder of an Israeli police officer, and a move the government wanted to pass off as the necessary response to a ruthless terrorist organization by a functioning democratic state, had turned into a scandal about a belligerent act, devoid of due process, that made hundreds of Palestinians (who were never accused of involvement in the murder) destitute refugees, deported to a

---

* A massacre perpetrated by the Christian Phalange militias who entered the Palestinian refugee camps of Sabra and Shatila when the IDF took over West Beirut in 1982, during the Lebanon war. Four hundred and sixty people were murdered in the massacre. The Kahan Commission, which investigated Israel's responsibility for the massacre, determined that while IDF troops did not take part in it, the military and political leadership ignored the danger, and recommended Defense Minister Sharon be removed from office. It also severely criticized Chief of Staff Rafael Eitan and other senior officers.

no-man's-land they could not leave, perhaps without the means to survive. Israel's government had made every mistake they could have made and had lost the sympathy of the international community, even if at home a clear, strong majority supported the deportation.

The High Court issued its ruling on January 28. In a rare exception, the judgment was signed by the entire panel, without indication of who had authored it. In *His Honor*, journalist Naomi Levitsky's book about Justice Barak, she revealed that the panel had been divided between a majority that opted to dismiss the petitions, headed by President Shamgar, and a minority, led by Barak, that wanted to condemn the state's conduct. Levitsky disclosed that Shamgar had been perturbed by the prospect of the court being split over such an important case and therefore toned down the majority opinion: he agreed to avoid a ruling that the deportation did not contravene the prohibition stipulated in the Geneva Convention, leading Barak to agree to forgo the dissenting opinion.[104]

The justices accepted the state's position that this was not a mass deportation but a "set of personal orders."[105] They also reached the conclusion that the obligation to hold a hearing in advance cannot be canceled through legislation, since this right stems from the principles of administrative law, but that in certain special cases security considerations and the urgency of implementing the deportation do allow for retroactive hearings. In this the court adopted Justice Isaac Cohen's dissenting opinion in the mayors' case, and it was a clear departure from the principle the court itself had laid out for the executive—a principle that precluded dodging judicial review prior to deportation. Thus, the judgment states, there is no need for the explicit determination in the military orders that allows for deportation prior to a hearing: if circumstances justify departing from the rule that a hearing should precede deportation, the military may do so. A ruling that such a departure is always permissible would have been unlawful. In the case at hand, there was no point examining whether the particular circumstances had justified the exception, since the deportees had already been deported. And so, in line with the majority opinion in the mayors' case, a hearing (for those deportees who asked for one) could be held retroactively.

This was the final nail in the coffin of the notion that deportation without a hearing was a breach of law: if there is no review (even retrospectively) of whether the conditions that allow for a retroactive hearing had been met, what would be the remedy for a deportation carried out without a hearing and without justification? Still, the panel did reject the idea of holding a hearing without the deportee present and therefore ruled that those deportees who asked for a retroactive hearing must be allowed to meet with their lawyers. The court realized that the ruling could result in the deportees returning to appear at their hearings, which would be a humiliating blow to the government. Therefore, they ruled that "the committee may hold its hearings at any place where the IDF can guarantee that they can properly take place."[106]

The judgment in the case of the four hundred was the state's biggest victory in the long fight against deportation. In the moment of truth, the court bowed down and agreed to the violation of the few principles it had put in place over the years, which had procedurally constrained the act of deportation. A court that strove to appear as the guardian of human rights and the rule of law had failed to withstand public pressure at a time of bloodshed; it had succumbed to the executive branch's belligerent demand for almost unchecked power to violate the fundamental rights of hundreds of people. The judgment drew a great deal of criticism, severely wounding the court's prestige.[107]

Still, this was the last deportation. Caution compels adding—for now.

Despite the court victory, the deportation of the four hundred amounted to a great defeat for Israel's government. International pressure had its effect, and four days after the judgment was issued, the government heeded the American administration's demand and said that a hundred of the deportees would be allowed return.[108] The deportees, who had meanwhile gained international sympathy and the status of heroes among their people, refused any arrangement that did not let them all return. Live television broadcasts from their makeshift camp, the surge of international interest in the Palestinian struggle, and the political power they had accrued in the camp had blunted their zeal to return.

Israel was in over its head.*

---

* In the months that followed, international efforts to find a solution continued fervently. Israel increased the number of deportees it was willing to allow back, and the deportees turned the camp they had set up in Marj al-Zuhur into a training camp under Hezbollah sponsorship. The next generation of the Hamas leaders was born in this camp and ultimately returned to the Occupied Territories, stronger, and hailed as heroes.

CAN SUCCESS BE THE SUM OF DEFEATS?

Lawyers who represented deportees have different views on the contribution made by the legal battle against deportation. Tsemel believes the fight played a major role in combating the practice and that it was a huge success. "It turned deportation into a losing venture," she says.[109] "We created a situation where the establishment had to think eight times before deportation. That was my theory: make it hurt, make it annoying. If the whole thing takes months, with all the appeals, and meanwhile we pound them, talk about it, give lectures, mobilize public opinion abroad as well, it becomes difficult." Tsemel rejects the claim that the High Court's approval of deportation and the legitimacy this gives it, at least in the eyes of the Israeli public, tip the scales against legal action. This drawback, she argues, is nothing compared to the advantage of having created a written corpus of the authorities' position on the issue, and the possibilities that legal action creates for the struggle, even if the court does not revoke the deportations themselves.

Feldman is much more skeptical. He concedes that the legal battle had an erosive effect and led to disputes that might not have otherwise occurred, but ultimately, he thinks, "deportations stopped for reasons that aren't related to the High Court of Justice."[110] From his experienced vantage point, he sees little value in legal proceedings that end with a loss, and he estimates that other forces bring about policy change. "The decision to stop demolishing terrorists' homes," he says, referring to a temporary decision gained after years of concerted legal effort against what was seen as wrongful collective punishment, "was changed in a second. When they wanted to, they went back to demolishing them."

There are likely many reasons why use of deportations against Palestinians stopped. The Oslo Accords, signed a year after the deportation of the four hundred, brought an end to the First Intifada and established the Palestinian Authority. The peace accord with Jordan in 1994 and the IDF's withdrawal from the security belt in Lebanon in 2000 made it difficult diplomatically to deport people across those borders. International condemnation, resolutions in the UN General Council and Security Council, scathing reports by international human rights bodies, and domestic criticism raining down on the government all served to up the political ante of deportation.

If the legal fight against deportation did not yield a legal victory, it was nonetheless a crucial secondary tool for the public and international fight. It bought the opponents of deportation time, gave them information, and, most important, a set the terms of a moral and legal fight that seriously hurt the legitimacy of the deportation orders. The two strong dissenting opinions by Justices Cohn and Bach split Israel's legal community, and State Attorney Beinisch's refusal to defend the deportation of the four hundred also helped discredit the policy. Concern over a possible change in the High Court's position after Barak took over from Shamgar as president in 1996 may have also helped deter the executive branch.

But all this notwithstanding, it is important to remember that the security establishment's faith in deportation as an important means of achieving its goals has not gone away. In the years following the deportation of the four hundred, Israel's security establishment came up with alternatives, such as forcibly removing West Bank activists to the besieged Gaza Strip,[111] and deportation by consent and as part of international agreements to countries that agree to receive the Palestinian deportees.[112] However, forced deportation outside the Occupied Territories has not since taken place.

In an interview published the day after the dramatic High Court hearing, as the Hamas deportees were waiting at the Lebanese border, Reuven Hazak, then the Shin Bet's second in command, said, "In a law-abiding country, deportation is a long, complicated, and ineffective process."[113]

Hazak had succinctly summed up the success of the legal battle.

3

Settlements: Banging One's Head
Against the Wall of the Political

THE MASTERS ARE COMING

No other policy pursued by Israel in the Occupied Territories has had the devastating effect of the settlements. In the years since 1967, Israel has created a network of 125 settlements, which, since the end of 2015 have been home to 588,000 Israeli citizens (205,000 of them in East Jerusalem).[1,2] The municipal territory of the settlements, excluding East Jerusalem, covers about 9.73 percent of the total area of the West Bank.[3] Each settlement is the epicenter of a ripple effect of abuses affecting the rights of the surrounding Palestinian communities.

First and foremost, a settlement consumes Palestinian land. It violates the property rights of its neighbors on every level imaginable: land is confiscated from its owners and handed over to the settlement to use as its own; access to additional land is denied either legally and officially, or unofficially through settler violence that the authorities fail to address or sometimes assist; and the area's natural resources are plundered by Israeli companies, with some of the plunder serving the settlement economy. Palestinians unfortunate enough to live in villages near settlements see their freedom of movement constantly stifled and reduced: movement in vast areas allocated to the settlement is banned by law; travel near roads used by the settlers is limited through legal and de facto means; a requirement

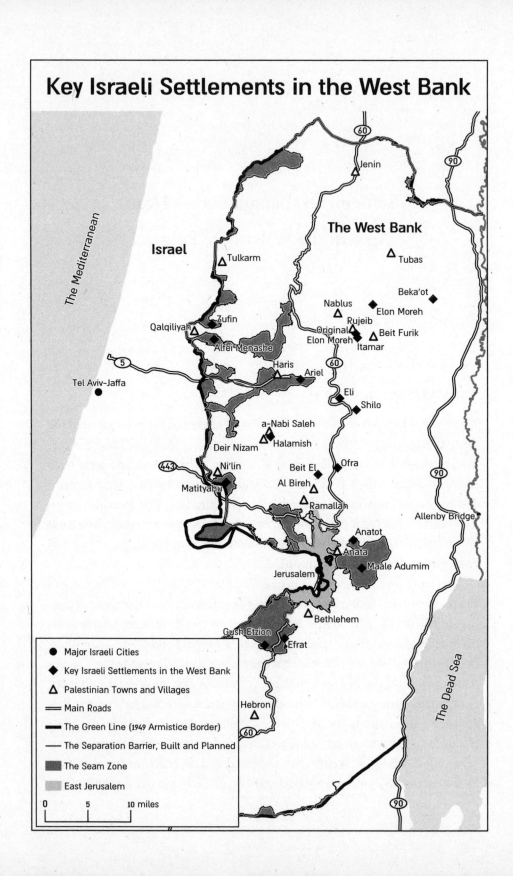

Key Israeli Settlements in the West Bank

The Mediterranean

Israel

The West Bank

Jenin

Tulkarm

Tubas

Beka'ot

Nablus

Elon Moreh

Zufin

Rujeib

Qalqiliyah

Original
Elon Moreh

Beit Furik

Alfei Menashe

Itamar

Haris

Tel Aviv-Jaffa

Ariel

Eli

Shilo

a-Nabi Saleh

Deir Nizam

Halamish

Ni'lin

Beit El

Ofra

Al Bireh

Matityahu

Ramallah

Allenby Bridge

Anatot

Anata

Maale Adumim

Jerusalem

Bethlehem

Gush Etzion

Efrat

The Dead Sea

Hebron

- ● Major Israeli Cities
- ◆ Key Israeli Settlements in the West Bank
- △ Palestinian Towns and Villages
- ═ Main Roads
- ━ The Green Line (1949 Armistice Border)
- ─ The Separation Barrier, Built and Planned
- ▓ The Seam Zone
- ░ East Jerusalem

0   5   10 miles

to "coordinate" arrival at certain areas reduces Palestinians' access to their farmland that borders on settlements.

These restrictions impede agrarian life, often completely preventing landowners from using their land. The personal safety of Palestinians living near settlements grows increasingly precarious. Settler violence has escalated over the years of occupation. Some of it is random, motivated by racism, hatred, and occasionally revenge, but some is part of a deliberate strategy to increase the areas controlled by settlements. This violence includes daily attacks on Palestinian property (setting fire to fields, damaging agricultural vehicles, and the widespread practice of uprooting olive trees—the symbol of Palestinian farming), physical assault, stone throwing and shooting, and recently, Ku Klux Klan–style attacks on families in the dead of night.[4] The authorities remain criminally passive in the face of this widespread violence,[5] with the depth of their negligence inviting conspiracy theories about Israel's interest in perpetuating the situation.

The footprint of the destruction wreaked by the settlements extends to every aspect of Palestinians' lives, and the assault on the fundamental rights of each Palestinian who lives near, or even passes by, a settlement only worsens over the years.

The Israeli settlement project is more than just settlements—that is, Israeli communities built within Palestinian territory. It also includes a network of roads and infrastructure, as well as five industrial zones housing factories and companies that are often financially unsuccessful yet enjoy generous government subsidies.

The magnitude of the settlement enterprise in the West Bank has created a reality of two distinct national communities living in a single geopolitical area, with one, accounting for 80 to 90 percent of the population,[6] composed of civilians living under occupation and governed by military law that they have no say in formulating (notwithstanding the very limited legal powers of the Palestinian Authority). The other is made up of citizens of the occupying power. One community has no civil rights by definition (or has had its civil rights suspended by the occupation), while the other enjoys full political power, with connections to, access to, and membership in the centers of power that determine the future for all. This civic reality, in which rightless subjects live in the same territory and under the same rule alongside masters who enjoy both power and rights, inevitably leads to systemic, institutionalized discrimination between the two groups through practice, policy, and legislation.

The legal means by which Israeli laws are applied to settlers living in the West Bank involve a "pipelining" technique: military orders, which constitute the primary source of governance in the occupied territory, stipulate that Israeli legislation, mostly administrative, shall apply in the settlements. This way, Israeli government ministries are able to exercise powers in the settlements without annexing them de jure. This also allows Israel's legal principles to apply to settlers only. In addition, extraterritorial legislation enacted by the Knesset directly applies to "Israeli residents of the Area" (the occupied West Bank), bringing Israelis living there (and formerly in Gaza) under Israeli law, though they do not live in Israel.

Creating these "enclaves"[7] of Israeli law applicable to settlers only contravenes a fundamental tenet of modern law, that is, legislation is applied on a territorial rather than a personal basis. Legal systems from ancient times had different norms for different groups of people (distinguished by gender, religion, nationality, ethnicity, or social status, among others). Since the French Revolution, however, the notion of personal law has been gradually replaced by the idea of territoriality, meaning that legal norms apply to all persons within the territory over which the legislator has jurisdiction. The Fourteenth Amendment to the United States Constitution, adopted in 1868, succinctly expresses this principle: "No state shall . . . deny to any person within its jurisdiction the equal protection of the laws." It seems so obvious today that no explanation is required.

Sticking to the principle of territoriality would have turned the Israeli settlers into civilians living under a military regime, putting them, at least legally, in a similar position to Palestinians. But the settlers did not migrate to the West Bank to live abroad. They did not aim to leave Israel but rather to expand it, a desire shared by their government. Thus, enclave law allowed the settlers to feel as if they had remained in Israel and also exercise their supremacy over Palestinians in legal terms. To achieve this goal, Israel sacrificed one of the fundamental principles of a just legal system and enshrined systemic institutional discrimination.

It is hard to look at the way Israel controls the West Bank, with separate legal and administrative systems governing Palestinians and Israelis, and with all local resources used to benefit one group at the expense of the other, without being reminded of a legal term from the not-so-distant past. A person would have to be unconscious not to pick up the whiff of apartheid everywhere there is a settlement. Israel has created not only an occupation that has persisted for generations but also a regime where one group oppresses and discriminates against the other for the sole purpose of preserving its control and supremacy. This is the very core of the legal definition of apartheid, which is an international crime.[8] The raging dispute in recent years over whether the apartheid analogy applies neatly to Israel's control of the West Bank is of great legal significance, but it has little bearing on the question of moral responsibility.[9] The character of the occupation regime is a direct attack on the very value the prohibition against apartheid protects: that of our inherent, shared humanity, and the particular cruelty attributed to a system of discrimination based on group affiliation. And there is another inextricable link to the crime of apartheid—separation.

UPPER JUDEA AND SAMARIA, LOWER WEST BANK[10]

Two roads lead to the settlement of Zufin, winding and twisting to the top of the hill overlooking the Palestinian town of Qalqiliyah from the north. One road comes from the west, from Israel, and another from the east, from deep inside the West Bank. Travelers on the road from Israel have no way of knowing that they are crossing a border. Not only is there no fence, gate, or roadblock between Zufin and the communities of Israel's Sharon region, but there's not even a sign to tell people that they have left Israel's sovereign territory. Not even the European Union has erased borders so completely.

The road from the east is another story altogether. The separation fence divides Zufin from Qalqiliyah, and if you want to get to the settlement from the east, you have to go through a gate installed in the fence, with a watchtower next to it, both staffed by Israeli soldiers. Israelis and tourists are free to pass. Palestinians need a special permit from the Civil Administration—the Israeli governing body in the West Bank. In June 2006, I was waiting by the gate to meet a client when a horse-drawn cart arrived from Qalqiliyah. It was driven by two Palestinian youths, about fifteen years old. "We're on our way to our uncle's field, which is trapped on the other side of the fence," they told the soldier at the gate, and proudly showed some scraps of paper they took out of a disintegrating envelope. The soldier took the permits, waved them about, and shouted to his invisible comrade in the tower. "This kid doesn't have a permit. It's his uncle's permit. The other kid has a permit, but not for entering with a vehicle!" "What about the horse?" the tower asked. The soldier rummaged through the papers again and shouted, "The horse has a permit."

The Israeli occupation spent three decades trying to merge the occupied land with the occupying country. Settlements were built, borders erased, Israel's road system was connected to the West Bank's, the two economies were intertwined to the point where a single customs zone was put in place. The object was clear: to incorporate the occupied land, connecting the capillaries there to the arteries here.

In the fourth decade, Israel gave up. The transplant showed serious signs of rejection, so Israel decided to try a new method of control and gave it a fitting name: separation. But "separation" is not just a magic word used by spin doctors and shrewd media advisers. It is an overarching political and security philosophy that has shaped Israel's rule over the West Bank since the outbreak of the Second Intifada in 2000, and dictated a physical and legal reality of separation and control based on nationality.

In 1999, Ehud Barak ran for prime minister on a slogan of separation—"We are here and they are there"—an instant formula for resolving the conflict. But the separation of populations began long before then; it was latent in the occupation from the very beginning, like a virus biding its time, and the time came.

The notion is as simple as it is malicious: the territory is split into two and governed by two realities—one Jewish, one Palestinian. The dissection is not two-dimensional but multidimensional, physical and legal. Jewish areas and Palestinian areas, Jewish roads and Palestinian roads, Jewish infrastructure and Palestinian infrastructure. In the fourth decade of the occupation, water pipes became Jewish and electrical lines became Muslim in quiet conversion ceremonies held by the Civil Administration, all in a bid to rearrange the area into two layers, Upper Judea and Samaria, and Lower West Bank.

The separation was modest at first: In 1992 Palestinians were prohibited from entering settlements. A system of orders was put in place, and settlement security officers were empowered to block Palestinians from passing through settlements. These orders were supported by a bureaucratic apparatus for issuing entry permits to the Palestinian laborers who cleaned and gardened for the settlers. It was there, in this system, that the principle was enshrined that would accompany the separation project for years to come: Palestinians need a reason. If they have a good reason, they can ask for a permit. If they don't, they can stay in Jenin or Hebron or Ramallah. But for Jews, the land is their patrimony. What business does a Palestinian have in a settlement?

In the mid-1990s, separation architects came up with the notion of a Special Security Area, the SSA. The SSA is a sterile radius surrounding the settlements, free of Palestinians. Areas covering hundreds of dunams, surrounding dozens of settlements, much of them cultivated Palestinian farmland, were fenced. Settlement security officers were given the keys to the gates installed in those fences and with them the power to allow or deny landowners access to their land.

Then, in the early 2000s came the long separation fence and the seam zone. Roughly 10 percent of the West Bank was torn away using fences and walls. On one side, fifty-five Jewish settlements remained connected to Israel, sweeping with them a few dozen Palestinian villages and hundreds of thousands of dunams of land, leaving most of the Palestinian population on the other side.

But barbed-wire fences and concrete are, alas, insentient objects. They cannot tell a Jew from a Palestinian and so treat them equally. To overcome the fence's lack of intelligence, the separation masterminds came up with a permit system for the seam zone (the area between the fence and the Green Line, which demarcates Israel's 1967 border), a clever legal weapon to do the selection that the fence and wall cannot do themselves. The West Bank military commander declared the entire seam zone a closed military area, off-limits to everyone but three "types of people" (this is the language in the order) to whom the declaration does not apply.[11] The first two "types" are tourists and Israelis. The military commander chose an interesting definition for "Israelis": in addition to citizens and permanent residents, an Israeli is also anyone who is entitled to citizenship under the Law of Return, in other words, anyone who is Jewish. For them, the fence is invisible, no more than a mirage. That the area between the fence and the Green Line is a closed military zone is as relevant to them as the labor laws in Bangladesh. The third type, the other people who enjoy a fence exemption, are Palestinians with permits to work in the settlements or in Israel, people considered essential to cleaning up the occupiers' mess.

Thus, the physical and legal reality of separation began to take shape. A Palestinian whose land was passed down to him from his father, and his father's father before him, and so on down the generations, must go to the District Coordination Office and ask for a permit to pass through a gate to get to his land, while any Brooklyn yeshiva boy is entitled to cross the fence with no trouble.

The settlements, the SSAs, and especially the permit regime have tainted the land. Entire areas were now painted with national colors—Jewish and Palestinian, white and black. An elaborate network of separate roads ("bypass" roads) was built so that all the hard work that was put into separation would not come to nothing at the road intersections.

Take Road 443 from Atarot to Ben Shemen, for example. Parts of the land on which the road was built were confiscated from a Palestinian teachers' association that planned to build a neighborhood for its members. The teachers petitioned Israel's High Court of Justice (an administrative bench of the Israeli Supreme Court) against the confiscation. The State Attorney's Office rejected their claims, explaining that the road was meant for them, for the Palestinian public. As occupiers, we, the State of Israel, have an obligation to improve roads in the occupied country. We can't just leave the roads the way they were in 1967, so what are you complaining about? Judge Aharon Barak liked this argument. His judgment in the case is the pinnacle of the rhetoric of "enlightened occupation." The land is confiscated for their benefit, he said. It is our duty toward the civilians we have come to occupy so they can travel on a two-lane road. The road was built and today it is de facto, if not de jure, limited to Israelis. Slabs of concrete and steel fencing were placed at every intersection that gave access to Palestinians. It has become a second major traffic artery between two major cities, Jerusalem and Tel Aviv, and it serves only Israelis.*

Road 443 is not alone. There are many like it. Contrary to the euphemism by which these roads are known, the "bypass" roads system does not seek only to bypass the Palestinian population but to erase it. Traveling on the Trans Shomron Road or the Ramallah Bypass Road, it is shock-

---

* The High Court struck down the legal ban on Palestinian cars using the road but did not rule out an "equal" ban on Israelis and Palestinians using the part of it that leads to Ramallah, ensuring Palestinians would have no reason to use the road. See HCJ 2150/07, *Abu-Saffya, Head of the Beit Sira Village Council and 24 Others v. the Minister of Defense et al.*, Takdin Elyon 2009 (4): 4474 (2009).

ing to see that the vision has been realized. The Palestinians are gone, vanished. The names on the green road signs posted by Israel's National Roadworks Company are exclusively in Hebrew—Eli, Shilo, Revava. Arabic names like Ramallah and Nablus have disappeared.

While contractors were making millions installing fences, building walls, and paving roads to dissect the two-dimensional space, Civil Administration officers and government officials made sure that Israeli and Palestinian water, electricity, and sewage do not mix. So, for example, the pipes that bring water to the settlement of Alfei Menashe and take away its waste run right under the small Palestinian village of Wadi a-Rasha, located about half a mile away. The settlement's electricity lines are overhead. Wadi a-Rasha itself got its electricity from a generator for years, and water came in tankers from Qalqiliyah twice a week.[12]

All of these physical splits joined the separate legal system put into place in the West Bank, which emerged through a consistent process that produced two parallel legal systems—one for Jews and another for Palestinians.

This is the essence of separation, a physical and legal wedge between occupier and occupied, ruler and subject, with the terms dictated by the stronger party. Israel's "separate and unequal" doctrine emerged more than five decades after the US Supreme Court eliminated the "separate but equal" paradigm used by the southern states to justify racial segregation.

The Israeli occupation was marked from the first day by an extraordinary ability: to invent a world of euphemisms that cleanse every injustice and crime we commit in the Occupied Territories and against its residents. This special talent turned assassinations into "targeted prevention," the obliteration of residential neighborhoods into "clearing," and the use of Palestinians as human shields into an "advance warning procedure." But when it came to separation, someone was asleep at the helm. Because what is separation? How can we translate it? The answer is "apartheid," the noun that describes a policy of creating "apartness," the eponym for a regime of segregation.

POPULATION TRANSFER

All of these terrible things happened because of the settlements in the West Bank (and before the 2005 disengagement, also in the Gaza Strip). They are precisely the reason international law specifically forbids transferring the population of the occupying power into occupied territory. The prohibition appears in the final paragraph of Article 49 of the Fourth Geneva Convention:

> The Occupying Power shall not deport or transfer parts of its own civilian population into the territory it occupies.

Israel has never deported Israelis to the West Bank. But it has and continues to transfer them there. It runs a governmental, legal, and bureaucratic system that enables its citizens to emigrate to the Occupied Territories, and even encourages them to do so to varying degrees. Israeli government officials have, through the years, made two arguments in international forums: One is that the Fourth Geneva Convention does not apply to Israel's control over the West Bank and the Gaza Strip because Jordan and Egypt, from which they were seized, were never their rightful sovereigns. Seeing as this is so, Israel claims, the test used to decide whether the Fourth Geneva Convention applies, namely, "partial or total occupation of the territory of a High Contracting Party"[13]—a signatory to the convention—is not met in this case. This argument, which seems to follow the same logic as a common Hebrew phrase that roughly means "it's okay to steal from a thief" (which is, in fact, a rather childish misinterpretation of a Jewish rule that exempts payment of restitution on the theft of stolen goods), was conceived by law professor Yehuda Blum, who served as Israel's UN ambassador in the late 1970s and early 1980s.[14] The second argument that Israel usually makes on the legality of the settlements has to do with how the ban in the Geneva Convention is defined. Israeli officials claim that "transfer" refers to a coercive act by the state, and since Israeli settlers move to the settlements voluntarily, the article does not apply.[15]

Neither of Israel's arguments has been accepted. In fact, they have both been scornfully rejected.

Consensus is rare, especially in an adversarial profession, entirely rooted in argument, such as the law. But on these two points—the fact that the land seized by Israel is occupied territory and that the settlements there are unlawful—there is broad legal international consensus. It is so broad, in fact, that it rivals the level of agreement on issues of hard science and is certainly unusual in a debate in the realm of social science. The position shared by all experts on international law is that the Fourth Geneva Convention unquestionably applies to the territories Israel occupied (which constitute "occupied territory" in the legal sense), that Israel is bound by it, and that the settlements violate the prohibition stipulated in Article 49. There is no country in the world today that espouses the position that the settlements are legal. There is no international body whose legal advisers dispute the position that the settlements are a violation of international law. The International Committee of the Red Cross, which is entrusted with interpreting the Geneva Conventions, wholly rejected the thesis offered by Blum,[16] which became the official position of Israel's government. Many international tribunals, most notably the International Court of Justice, have ruled that establishing settlements and allowing Israelis to live in them defies the prohibition on transferring population into occupied territory.[17] The academic community is as unequivocal on this as legal practitioners are. In hundreds of books, thousands of articles, and countless lectures, law professors reiterate that building settlements contravenes the fundamental principle of international law as expressed in the final paragraph of Article 49 of the Fourth Geneva Convention.[18]

This makes a lot of sense. The international laws of occupation seek to organize the regime of occupation in such a way that will allow the occupied population to resume their normal lives as much as possible, while at the same time enabling the occupying power to maintain its security and the security of its forces. Article 2 of the Fourth Geneva Convention relates to the application of the convention and has two paragraphs. The first stipulates that the convention applies in any case of armed conflict between countries that are party to the convention. The second clause, the one Israel relies on, applies the convention also to a situation of full or partial occupation of a territory belonging to another state party, "even if the said occupation meets with no armed resistance." The ICRC, followed by all experts on international law, clarified that the second clause elaborates on the first one, to cover cases in which occupation is not the result of armed clashes, like the Nazi occupation of Denmark in World War II, which did not meet armed resistance. Thus, Israel's interpretation of the second clause of Article 2 is misguided. The Fourth Geneva Convention applies to Israel's occupation whether the state from which the territory was seized was the rightful sovereign or not, seeing as it was a result of Israel's armed conflict with Jordan and Egypt, both of which are parties to the Geneva Convention.[19]

But what is more important than the textual interpretation is the purpose of the laws of occupation. These laws also seek to create a reality that will facilitate the end of occupation and a peaceful solution. They do so by limiting the changes an occupier can make to the necessary minimum. They are predicated on the modern notion that sovereignty is not obtained by force and that a territory's status can be changed only by virtue of agreement between the parties to an international conflict. Therefore, the prohibition in the Geneva Convention against population transfer must be seen as a fundamental principle of the way the laws of occupation seek to organize a regime of occupation. This prohibition has a purpose, one that runs through the entirety of Article 49, which also prohibits the deportation of residents of the occupied territory or their forcible transfer within it. The purpose is to prevent demographic changes that would end the occupied population's prominence in the area and its "ownership" of the land without its consent. The purpose is to prevent the occupying party from creating facts on the ground that would impede a peaceful solution to the conflict. The purpose is to minimize any infringements on the rights of the occupied population, which would undoubtedly be compromised if a community of the occupying nation were to be planted in its territory. The purpose is to prevent precisely all that has happened in the West Bank as a result of the Israeli settlements.

To complete the picture, it is worth noting that the prohibition on transferring the population of the occupying power into occupied territory is considered not just a breach of international law but a war crime. Not every violation of international law makes those who perpetrate it guilty of a war crime. Sometimes the ramifications extend only to the realm of international relations. The Geneva Convention concludes with a short list of prohibitions whose violation requires investigation and prosecution. The prohibition on transferring the occupying power's population is not included in this list.[20] But the 1998 Rome Statute of the International Criminal Court includes an article that explicitly defines the transfer of population from the occupying country into the occupied territory as a war crime. Initiated by Egypt (with vehement opposition from Israel), this definition of the crime went beyond the definition contained in Article

49 of the Fourth Geneva Convention, adding three words: the crime now involves transferring the population of occupying power into the occupied territory *directly or indirectly*.[21] Even the most submissive lawyers working for Israel's government would find it hard to claim that the state's countless actions and immense investment in settlements and encouraging migration to them do not constitute, at the very least, indirect transfer of Israeli civilians to the West Bank.

Clearly, the creation of settlements raises a legal question regarding violation of a fundamental tenet of the international laws of occupation. In addition to this question, the settlements have given rise to two other legal issues, which are no less important. The first is the legality of using residents' private property in the occupied territory to serve the needs of the occupying power's civilian population. The settlements began as communities built on privately owned Palestinian land. The laws of occupation address the confiscation of residents' property in both the 1949 Geneva Convention and the earlier Hague Convention of 1907.[22] Both conventions contain articles prohibiting damage to private property other than for imperative security needs, and completely prohibit confiscation without any exceptions.

The second issue relates to use of public property to serve the settlement project. A pivotal article in The Hague Regulations stipulates that the occupying power is to act as trustee of public property (public land and buildings, natural resources) and manage them according to the rules of trusteeship ("rules of usufruct") for the benefit of the occupied population.[23] How, then, can land and other resources in the occupied territory be allocated to individuals who are clearly not the beneficiaries of this trusteeship, citizens of Israel?

These three legal issues have been the focus of litigation in Israel's High Court of Justice since the 1970s in a bid to prevent or at least minimize the settlement project.

OUT OF THE ASHES OF RAFAH

Although the first settlements were built immediately after the 1967 war in various parts of the West Bank,[24] the earliest pertinent High Court petition addressed the evacuation of Bedouin from the Rafah Approach, an area on the Mediterranean coast in the northern Sinai Peninsula, south of Gaza City. The seeds of destruction that would eventually legally enable the monstrous settlement project in the West Bank were originally sown in this case: it embodied the main tenets of the court's approach to the settlement issue, as they would be expressed in its jurisprudence in years to come. The court bowed its head to the argument that settlement activity is guided by security considerations and, as the security argument grew weaker, that the settlements are a political question in which the court has no business meddling, despite its clear legal aspect.

The Rafah Approach was captured from Egypt along with the rest of the Sinai Peninsula and the Gaza Strip in 1967, and, as with all the territories Israel seized (with the exception of East Jerusalem, which was annexed immediately, and the Golan Heights area, which was annexed in the early 1980s), Israel imposed a military occupation. There is, however, a distinction between the Gaza Strip and the Sinai Peninsula. While the Egyptians never considered the Gaza Strip to be Egyptian territory and, like Israel after it, held Gaza under military rule from 1948 until 1967, the Sinai Peninsula was part of sovereign Egypt.

The Rafah Approach Affair, as the newspapers referred to it, was born as an initiative to create a barrier between the Gaza Strip and any future border with Egypt through settlement in the area. Documents recently uncovered as part of a fascinating research project by legal scholar David Kretzmer and journalist Gershom Gorenberg reveal that the notion of building settlements in the Rafah Approach had been on the agendas of Defense Minister Moshe Dayan, the Israeli government, and settlement authorities since the fall of 1968.[25] In a government session held in late January 1969, Dayan, mincing no words, said he believed the Bedouin should be evacuated and that the action should be presented as a security necessity: "First we must expel the Bedouin from this area, get up there with a tractor, and uproot all the almond orchards. . . . If we decide to do this for military purposes, we have to say: We're putting up a military post here."[26]

As far as Dayan was concerned, the government moved too slowly and too cautiously on the issue. Over the course of 1969 and 1970, detailed plans were drawn for settlements in the area, and one of them, Dikla, was started by soldiers with the object of becoming a civilian community in the future. Seizure orders were issued for sixteen thousand dunams of land but were not implemented as there was no final government resolution approving the settlements.

Nonetheless, the plan received support not only from the minister of defense but from other ministers and from the commander of the army's southern district in the 1970s, Ariel Sharon. Though still in uniform, Sharon had strong opinions on political issues and had no compunctions about making politically significant moves couched in security imperatives. At the time, the public thought of the newly occupied territories as something held in trust, to be returned as part of a peace agreement, and Sharon was concerned that the government would decide to return the Sinai Peninsula to Egypt.* Like Dayan, he believed that returning the area would bring the Egyptian army back to the Gaza Strip, where it would pose a strategic threat to Israel. Sharon therefore thought that there should be a buffer zone between Egypt and the Gaza Strip to prevent this scenario from materializing and that building settlements was the means to creating this zone.[27] To this day, it is still not clear just how much Moshe Dayan knew, when in late January 1972 Sharon began carrying out the plan by ordering the expulsion of the Bedouin tribes in response to a request made by the Jewish Agency to receive land for the purpose of settlement in the area.

On January 27, 1972, nine heads of Bedouin tribes in the Rafah Approach received notice from the IDF's Khan Younis district commander instructing them to remain home the next day because he was planning to visit.[28] The next day was a Friday. The tribe leaders gathered in the home of one of them and greeted the commander, Lieutenant Colonel Nissim Kazaz. During the meeting, Kazaz told them that the IDF Supreme Command had decided that the area where they lived was needed for security reasons and they would therefore be required to vacate their villages and land within three days. The tribe leaders said he threatened that anyone remaining after January 31 would have "his house demolished with him inside." Kazaz also pledged that those who owned immovables such as a house or a water well would be compensated.

The next day, IDF soldiers came on camels[29] and reminded the tribespeople that anyone who stayed would come to harm. In the days that followed, the tribes migrated from the site to the edges of the Rafah Approach, an area Sharon's headquarters allocated to them. After the

---

*   The irony was that the government did make this decision at the close of the decade, as part of the Camp David peace treaty between Israel and Egypt, and Sharon oversaw evacuation of the land as defense minister in 1982.

expulsion, which was carried out based on the seizure orders issued back in 1969, Sharon declared a huge expanse covering about forty-seven thousand dunams a closed military zone, and a fence was built around it to prevent the Bedouin from returning. The expulsion and dispossession of the Bedouin was kept secret by the military censor.

But the censor could not stop the information from flowing in through Israeli reserve soldiers who served in the Sinai Desert. Some of them, members of kibbutz communities in the Negev, came home shocked and told their friends and families about what was going on in the Approach. Members of the kibbutzim who belonged to the more dovish stream of the movement, Hakibbutz Haartzi, began investigating.[30] They went to tour the Sinai and were astounded by the scope of the destruction and the huge number of displaced people. Sharon's persona and image were undoubtedly a motivating factor in the kibbutz members' willingness to raise their voice against the cruel dispossession of the Bedouin. At the time, the party representing the Hakibbutz Haartzi movement was a member of the Labor-led coalition government and included several ministers. The kibbutz members asked them to bring the matter for discussion in the government. In early March, activists fighting the Bedouin expulsion held a conference in Kibbutz Nir Oz, attended by some 250 members of thirteen Negev kibbutzim. Party leaders could not ignore a conference attended by a core of their electorate in the south of the country. At that point, the IDF and the government were still denying the extent of the displacement, claiming that it was an evacuation of nomads who had invaded state land.[31]

After the Nir Oz conference, ministers demanded a government discussion and an explanation from the military as to what exactly had happened and why the government had not been informed. Minister of Health Victor Shem-Tov demanded that the Bedouin be returned to their land. Once the issue had reached the ministerial level, it could no longer be hidden from the public, and the press started reporting on it. What shocked people, no less than the cruelty of the displacement, was that it had been done without the knowledge or approval of government ministers. The Rafah displacement became a scandal.

After the government debate, which took place in mid-March, it emerged that the chief of staff had already appointed a military investigation several weeks earlier to look into what the media were calling "the aberration." The chief of staff had also asked for an opinion on what to do with the displaced Bedouin. The investigation concluded that there had been an act of insubordination and recommended reprimanding two senior officers and removing a civilian employee of the army. The military censor blocked publication of the names of the reprimanded personnel, but from that point on, the press began referring to Sharon as "the reprimanded officer." In their research, Kretzmer and Gorenberg confirm that Sharon was reprimanded for deciding to implement the 1969 orders without government approval. At any rate, the committee's decision, which has only recently come to light, indicates that both its members and everyone who testified were fully aware that the Bedouin were expelled for settlement or strategic-settlement reasons and that there were no security reasons that compelled their removal. Still, no recommendation was made to return the Bedouin to their land, only to help them start over in the location to which they had been transferred.

At this point, it is worth considering the difference between a security objective and a political objective. Legally, there is an immense difference between an act taken for security reasons and one to advance a political goal. While the laws of occupation allow the occupying power and military to carry out certain actions, including some that impinge on the fundamental rights of the occupied population, to maintain its security or that of the occupied territory, they do not offer similar exclusions for politically motivated initiatives. The laws of occupation run on two axes: the good of the occupied population and the security of the occupying power. Political motivations are not located on either of these axes and therefore cannot be considered a legitimate consideration for the military commander, unless they do not harm the occupied population.

The motivation for building Israeli communities in the Rafah Approach—shared by the government, Dayan, and Sharon—was clearly political: to influence the future border between Egypt and the Gaza Strip. Even if Dayan and Sharon thought a reworked border was strategically preferable, a move that is meant to shape future international treaties, rather than avert a specific security threat (such as arms smuggling or armed attacks by the enemy), is political.

Interestingly, the Israeli public did not buy the security argument, even when IDF spokespeople insisted that the area had been "fenced in" for security reasons "to improve military surveillance in the area."[32] The understanding that the displacement had been driven by settlement considerations led to a national debate and op-ed polemics on whether settling the area was wise. The military tried to convince the public that this was not dispossession for its own sake or for a political end, and the weapon it used was the doomsday device of Israeli army public relations: the claim of security needs. The Bedouin had been evacuated to prevent terrorism. Suddenly, the Israeli media were brimming with reports on terrorist activity among the Bedouin of the Rafah Approach and military explanations about the need for a security buffer to prevent such activity by separating it from Sinai.[33]

With the IDF insisting there was an immediate security need to uphold the displacement, and despite the ministers' call to allow the Bedouin to return to their land, the government accepted the military's recommendations. The dovish ministers preferred not to trigger a political crisis and so, using characteristic bullying tactics, Sharon got his way. The situation he had forced on the government in an act of subordination became a fait accompli.[34]

Still, the Negev activists did not give up. They staged a protest at the Ministry of Defense in Tel Aviv[35] and took politicians and journalists on tours to see firsthand the extent of the destruction and displacement.[36] The press continued reporting on both the aberration and the left wing's fight to get the Bedouin back to their land.

In the summer of 1972, as the political battle began to seem fruitless but leftist pressure to support the Bedouin continued, the party decided to help the displaced tribes in a petition to the Supreme Court.[37] Tel Aviv lawyer Haim Holtzman, who represented the activists, was retained by the nine tribe leaders and filed two High Court petitions on their behalf. Holtzman argued that some twenty thousand people had been displaced,[38] and that this was a violation of the prohibition on deporting occupied populations set out in Article 49 of the Geneva Convention. His main argument, however, was that the expulsion was not meant to serve security and that the presentation of it as such by the government and military was disingenuous. Holtzman had spilled the open secret of the plan to build Israeli communities in the evacuated area, showing that the motivation for the displacement was political rather than security-related. These were the legal arguments. But in his petition Holtzman made other serious allegations: "The Petitioners face a joint campaign of pressure intended to deter them from exercising their basic right to bring their case to the High Court of Justice." Holtzman accused the IDF district commander of lobbying the petitioners to abandon the case and warning them against contact with Holtzman himself, "because he is, allegedly, a communist."[39]

Holtzman noted that although the displacement had already occurred, the petition was urgent because earthwork had begun destroying orchards and field crops that belonged to the tribes. In response, Supreme Court justice Moshe Etzioni issued an order nisi compelling the state to respond to Holtzman's arguments within fourteen days.

Despite the great urgency, it would take nine more months for the court to rule on the case. During this time, the state submitted its response, which concealed the clear settlement motivation for the expulsion and cited only security considerations. The state provided figures on scores of terrorist activities, including shooting at Israeli forces, laying mines on roads, and even murders that took place in the area in 1970 and 1971. The state explained that since the Rafah Approach was a sensitive place and the site of increasingly hostile activity, there was a need to "isolate the Gaza Strip from weapons and ammunition supply sources in the Sinai area, and cut off access roads from Sinai to the Gaza Strip."[40] This explanation was in fact at odds with the military investigation's conclusion regarding the settlement motivation.[41] For its arguments, the state relied on an affidavit signed by Yisrael Tal, the head of operations in the General Staff. The court did not pause to wonder why Tal had provided an affidavit addressing the motives for an act carried out by Sharon, and it refused Holtzman's request to examine Tal.[42]

The state's lawyers went so far as to claim that the petitioning tribes were involved in the terrorism they had described. The proof for this alleged involvement, as presented in Tal's affidavit, was expert opinion that "the Bedouin's tribal structure and their way of life does not allow for any of the types of activities mentioned to take place in the area without many tribespeople, and mostly the tribe leaders, knowing about them."[43] But the accusation was baseless. It was concocted as a response to the petition and relied on a ludicrously orientalist analysis.[44] To show that the IDF was not entirely deaf to the Bedouin pleas, the state mentioned a plan to allow the tribes to continue cultivating some of their land inside the evacuated, fenced-off area for some part of the day.

However, the state, which was deep into planning the city of Yamit, to be built on the Bedouin land, as the proceedings were ongoing, was careful not to completely deny the possibility of establishing a civilian community in the evacuated area. Yisrael Tal cautiously addressed the issue in his affidavit. There are three ways to create a buffer zone, he explained: close the area and prevent locals from accessing it, establish a Jewish presence and settlement, or carry out a combination of both. Tal did not say which method had been chosen, only that "at this point," only the first method had been used.[45] Holtzman attacked the state's ambiguity on future plans for his clients' land, and in his written summation, he attempted to convince the justices that in the absence of a denial, intentions to build communities on the Bedouin territory must be considered the motive for the displacement.[46] If the goal was political, no legal argument could legitimize it.

The judgment was delivered in May 1973. Presiding Justice Moshe Landau chose to ignore the true purpose of the evacuation on the legality of which he had to rule, although this came up in the public debate over the questionable sense of settling in the Rafah Approach, and could be inferred from the absence of an affidavit from Sharon and the fact that the state's response never decisively denied the possibility of settlement.

"It appears from the affidavit that of the measures that could be taken, the IDF has, at least for the time being, taken only the first, that is, sealing the area and turning it into a buffer zone," Landau wrote in his judgment. "I shall therefore focus on reviewing matters in this light and shall not address the question of settlement for security purposes outside the jurisdiction of the state—a question that has its own legal aspects and was not addressed in the arguments before us."[47] To avoid the truth, Landau covered himself with a fiction that was aided by his refusal to allow questioning of Yisrael Tal. He gladly agreed to create a gap between public and legal discourse to avoid the need to review the legality of the settlements.

Unlike Landau, his bench mate Alfred Witkon was ready to take the bull by the horns and confront the undenied plan to build settlements in the area. However, he was willing to uphold the displacement, even if it had been done with the intention of housing Jewish settlers. His view about this possibility went on to set the legal foundation for the settlement project throughout the 1970s:

The Petitioners argued before us that their removal from their places of residence is not a security need and that the security arguments are no more than a pretext for preparing the land for Jewish settlement. The Respondents, on the other hand, argued that there certainly is a security need to evacuate the Petitioners and their tribe members from their places of residence and that the presence and settlement of Jewish settlers in the evacuated areas also serve security needs in this area. With regards to the removal of the Petitioners, there is no doubt that it is within the powers vested in the Respondents, so long as they were guided by security considerations. *It is clear that the fact that the land, in whole or in part, is designated for Jewish settlement does not completely negate the security nature of the action.*[48]

Witkon accepted a revolutionary thesis that establishing Israeli settlements in the Occupied Territories may be considered a security-related act rather than a political one.

The third justice on the panel, Yitzhak Kister, like Landau, ignored the question of settlement in the evacuated area. He too accepted that the existence of security justifications for the evacuation was enough reason for the court not to order the Bedouin's return. All three justices agreed that the court should practice a very conservative policy when it comes to intervening in security decisions. Witkon even thought that the doubts raised by the petitioners regarding the security need for a buffer zone were "nonjusticiable." "For a military-security act (unlike an administrative act within the military)," Witkon said, "if it is based in law and if we are satisfied that it is motivated by security considerations, the Court is not the appropriate venue to question said act and ask whether it really was necessary given the security situation, or whether the security issue could have been resolved in other manners as well."

Two other issues the court briefly addressed were the Geneva Convention's prohibition on deportation and the prohibition on damaging the property of an occupied population, which is enshrined in both the Geneva Convention and The Hague Regulations. Landau rightly explained that deportation means removal outside the occupied land, whereas the Bedouin had been removed to a different area inside it.[49] As for the damage to property, the court ruled, as it would in hundreds of cases over the coming decades, that the prohibition is not absolute and can be trumped by security needs. In other words, the property of the occupied population may be damaged, even destroyed, for security reasons.

The court rejected the petitions filed by the Rafah Approach Bedouin, and shortly after that, work on building the Yamit district settlements began.[50]

Although two of the justices on the panel refrained from addressing the legality of placing settlements on occupied land, the Rafah Approach judgment heralded the golden age of the "security settlement." This legal construct views the creation of civilian communities as a security act (rather than just a political or ideological one) and thus was permitted under the various exclusions set out in the international laws of occupation. Landau's willingness to make a ruling while ignoring the likely possibility that Jewish settlements would be built in the areas cleared of Bedouin, and Witkon's judgment that settlements could be construed as an act with "security attributes," showed the state's lawyers the way forward. In the years that followed, every settlement was said to serve a security purpose. A thesis emerged whereby the permanent presence of Israeli civilians in the Occupied Territories helps security because it creates pockets of communities sympathetic to the military and serves as an extra set of "eyes." During the 1970s this thesis enabled the creation of numerous settlements.

THE STORY OF the Rafah Approach Bedouin, who were the first to petition the High Court, had a happy ending. In 1982, Israel pulled out of the Sinai Peninsula as part of its peace agreement with Egypt. Before leaving, it destroyed the Jewish settlements, including those built in the Approach, and the Egyptian authorities gave the Bedouin their land back. One of the activists from the Negev who had helped with the campaign against displacement in the 1970s visited them in 2002 and discovered that their plots had been replanted and comfortable homes had been built with the help of the Egyptian government.[51]

ELIAS KHOURY

The exchange in the Supreme Court's large hall in Jerusalem's Russian Compound was acrimonious.

"We are not at war. There are no hostilities on the ground, and according to The Hague Regulations, land cannot be seized for military purposes if no hostilities are taking place in the area." Elias Khoury, a Palestinian

Christian lawyer and a citizen of Israel, charged at the armada that is Israeli security considerations. Legally speaking, this was a kamikaze mission.

Presiding justice Yoel Zussman sneered at him. "Perhaps they'll sign a peace accord by day's end?"

Khoury took a deep breath, trying to ignore the sarcastic derision.

He tried the human angle. "This is private property. It's the Petitioners' livelihood."

"If counsel would sign a guarantee against war breaking out, I'm willing to accept it," Zussman proposed.

"There are about a million dunams of land in the West Bank that belong to the state. Why deliberately take a plot that belongs to someone?"

The state attorney, Dorit Beinisch, had no need to do a thing. Zussman was doing the work for her.

"I can't determine what area is important for military purposes. I'm not a general," he said, and ended the discussion.[52]

It is hard to think of a greater asset to the cause of peace between Israelis and Palestinians than people like Elias Khoury. When asked about his four decades of litigation on behalf of his Palestinian clients, however, he spoke with great sorrow. "I believed. I didn't just think that I was right. I believed there would be legal success," he said.[53] "At the time, I believed in the justices of the Supreme Court. I believed in the fairness and liberalism of the late Haim Cohn, in Justice Zussman, Justice Witkon. I believed in those people with all my heart."

Khoury's entire demeanor is nothing but goodness. Even in his mid-sixties, it is easy to imagine him as a young lawyer, full of worthy intentions. But his early naïveté has all but gone. Growing extremism, Jewish racism toward Arabs, the settlers' grip on Israeli politics, and, of course, his bitter disappointment with the court system and its failure to protect his clients—West Bank Palestinians—have all played their part, but not alone. In 1975, in a Fatah terrorist attack in Zion Square in Jerusalem, a booby-trapped refrigerator blew up, killing fifteen people. One of them was Khoury's father. Thirty years later, at the height of the Second Intifada, a Palestinian cell murdered his son George as he was jogging in the French Hill, the Jerusalem neighborhood where he lived. The killers mistook him for a Jew. When the misidentification came to light, Yasser Arafat called Khoury to pay his respects and asked to declare his son a martyr. Khoury refused. In an interview given a few years later he explained:

"This [condemnation of the attack] cannot be lip service, just an obligatory gesture. The young generation must be taught, must understand that even in war, there are rules that cannot be broken. You cannot harm innocents."[54]

Khoury was born in 1951 in Acre but grew up in Nazareth. He finished law school at a young age and began practicing at twenty-two. For several years he worked for a Jerusalem lawyer who specialized in real estate and planning and construction laws, then opened his own practice in 1977, a time of political change in Israel. The new ruling party, the Likud, and its leader, Menachem Begin, called to expand the settlement project.[55] Khoury, who had ties to Israel's Communist Party, was in touch with key Palestinian leaders in the West Bank, the mayors who established the National Guidance Committee: Karim Khalaf of Ramallah, Fahd Qawasmeh of Hebron, and Bassam Shaka of Nablus.[56] In his new practice, Khoury handled land disputes for clients who came to him through his political contacts, and he made a name for himself in real estate law.

At the time, Palestinian leaders in the West Bank and Gaza Strip were debating how to respond to the plans the Israeli government adopted on an almost daily basis to increase settlements. Khoury was an avid supporter of challenging settlements through legal means. He read up on international law, an area in which he had no expertise. He borrowed books, read articles, and consulted with more experienced lawyers. He found that the laws of occupation contained important principles that could help the legal attack on the settlements, and especially that there were prohibitions on using privately owned Palestinian land for purposes other than security. Palestinian leaders in the West Bank were skeptical but eventually were won over.

Nineteen seventy-eight was a decisive year. The Begin government began executing its plans, and the military signed orders for the seizure of thousands of dunams of land in the West Bank—all for "security." Based on the rationale presented in the Rafah Approach case, and on the security exclusion to the prohibition against breaching the property rights of an occupied people, the government's legal advisers saw a way to circumvent the barrier to building settlements on Palestinian land—by arguing on the grounds of an imperative, urgent security need. Another issue government and military lawyers thought they were solving with the seizure orders was the prohibition against confiscating occupied land. The ban in this case is absolute. There are no exceptions.[57] The legal thesis intended to get around this hitch was that the land being taken was not confiscated, just "seized." In other words, ownership of the land has not been transferred to the state, as in the case of confiscation, only the right to use it for a period of time. While confiscation is deemed to be a permanent, forced transfer of ownership, seizure is a forced and, well, temporary, transfer of possession. How temporary? International law does not specify a time frame. A Palestinian whose land was "seized" by military order remains the owner of the land and is entitled to receive user fees from the military. He or she is also entitled to regain possession of the land as soon as the security need for it expires. How can such a temporary seizure be reconciled with the creation of settlements where civilians live within a community? This question would be answered in the cases Khoury brought to court.

The state's legal advisers offered ways to get around the difficulties settlements raise in terms of Palestinians' property rights, but they did not tackle the major, principled prohibition on transferring the population of the occupying power into the occupied land, the prohibition that appears in the final clause of Article 49 of the Geneva Convention.

In any event, this was the legal thesis that provided the basis for the establishment of settlements ever since the Rafah Approach case, during Labor Party rule, and it continued to provide the basis on which the Likud government built settlements in its early years.

FIRST TO ARRIVE at Khoury's office were residents from the West Bank villages of a-Nabi Saleh and Deir Nizam. In early 1978, a plan was made to build an Israeli settlement on land belonging to these neighboring villages. Two settler core groups, one religious and one secular, moved to the area, which they named Neve Tzuf. The religious settlement movement Gush Emunim had stood behind this initiative and lobbied with politicians to promote it. The government supported the establishment of the community and allocated it state land, not privately owned. The Taggart Building, an old British Mandate police station located in the area and used as a base by the border police, was evacuated, and the settlers moved in. The trouble was that state land in the region was scarce and scattered, and Gush Emunim demanded that the settlement be allocated more.

Ariel Sharon, by then out of uniform and serving as minister of agriculture, was one of the major political forces behind the acceleration of the settlement process. He asked Attorney General Aharon Barak to look into the status of land nearby, in a bid to find more to assign to Neve Tzuf. The Begin government, which viewed settlements as an ideological-Zionist enterprise, did not want to manufacture a security reason, which meant avoiding the use of private land if at all possible. The delays in building put the settlers in an uncomfortable situation. They huddled in the British police station without basic living conditions. In February 1978, the secular group decided to leave until the fate of the place was clarified. They found the conditions too difficult and had fallen out with the religious group, who they claimed received preferential treatment.[58]

One morning, in April 1978, residents of a-Nabi Saleh and Deir Nizam woke up to find that someone had fenced off some three hundred dunams around the police building, trapping a large part of their privately owned and cultivated land behind the fence. Heavy equipment brought into the fenced-off area began razing the land, harming seasonal crops planted by the owners. Investigation revealed that the local commander had signed a seizure order for security purposes for an area of about ninety dunams, designated for the settlement. The Palestinians were outraged but felt apprehensive about launching legal proceedings in Israel. "The landowners worried that the Palestinian leadership would object to them litigating in the Israeli court,"[59] Khoury recounts. "They were afraid that a High Court petition would be seen as legally legitimizing the actions of the occupation regime and that they would be accused of betraying the struggle."

Until that time, ten years after the occupation began, other than the Rafah Approach case brought by the Bedouin—which had challenged only the evacuation, not the settlement—no Palestinian had initiated this kind of legal battle. The only court with the jurisdiction to hear such a case was Israel's Supreme Court, sitting as a High Court of Justice, and concern about going to the occupier's court ran deep. Khoury used his contacts with the chair of the Communist Party in the West Bank, Bashir Barghouti, to call in a consultation with the National Guidance Committee, a forum of West Bank leaders. The Quakers, who provided humanitarian aid in the West Bank, also came to Khoury's aid. This was the only NGO in the early 1970s to fund legal services to West Bank and East Jerusalem Palestinians. They had gained the trust of farming communities and advised them to mount a legal challenge to the land takeover, which they agreed to fund. This funding was important, both because it provided an income for the few lawyers willing to represent the poor, disempowered communities and because even those who agreed to work pro bono on these cases were reported to the Israeli bar's ethics committee. At the time, lawyers were forbidden to provide services free of charge.

Khoury held a few meetings with the Palestinian leadership. He explained that aside from the possibility of winning, the court could be the central stage for resistance to the settlement project and would bring attention to the dispossession both in Israel and abroad. After hours of debate, the leadership was finally convinced and gave its blessing. Having received political backing, the villagers signed a retainer with Khoury. He petitioned on behalf of six landowners, asking to revoke the land seizure and dismantle the fence that had been put up.

The Supreme Court panel selected for the case was made up of Deputy President Justice Moshe Landau and Justices Moshe Etzioni and David Bechor. This was the first petition against a seizure of private land that was indisputably intended to serve the settlements. As the issue had become a hot political subject with the Begin government's rise to power a year earlier, the case attracted a lot of public attention.

Khoury did not raise the broad issue of the legality of establishing settlements on occupied land. Instead, he focused on the harm to private property and the illegality of seizing land for settlement purposes.

In a hearing held on May 26, 1978, Dorit Beinisch, counsel for the state, declared that the land seized by military order was not privately owned but rather public land (state lawyers use the phrase "state land," perhaps in a bid to create the impression that it belongs to Israel, though this, of course, is not the case). A review conducted by Attorney General Barak revealed that the ninety dunams seized in the military order had not been cultivated in recent years and therefore, under Ottoman law, must be regarded as public land.[60] Thus the state avoided relying on the security argument, since it denied that the area designated for the settlement had encroached on private property. But the land fenced off was three times larger than those ninety dunams, undoubtedly including land privately owned by the petitioners. On this issue, Beinisch told the astonished justices that she did not know who had put up the fence and confirmed that it was illegal.

"Did two kilometers of fence just fall out of the sky?" Justice Etzioni asked.

"I was unable to find out who put up the fence while preparing for the hearing," Beinisch replied.

Etzioni fired back: "It's safe to assume that it was not the Petitioners who built it."[61] These kinds of comments from a Supreme Court justice must have brought hope and satisfaction to Khoury and his clients. Beinisch pledged that the fence would come down.

Then the discussion focused on the ninety dunams seized by the military order. Beinisch said the government would not be building the settlement on private land. The only private land that had been confiscated, she said, would be used for an access road, and the law permits confiscation for public needs. Etzioni was still skeptical. How could a settlement be built on just ninety dunams? "Is this the first step, with more land seizures expected?" he asked.[62] He took the opposite approach to Landau's in the Rafah Approach case, seeing beyond the specific act and paying attention to the wider context. He also knew how the government and the military operated; he knew exactly who he was dealing with. Beinisch wanted to keep the wider context out of the discussion. "We are only talking about ninety dunams right now," she said, and refused to make any promises about the future.[63]

The court issued an order nisi that day, requiring the state to submit an affidavit of response explaining why the judges should not revoke the order for the seizure of the ninety dunams of village land, as well as an interim cease-and-desist order for all the work carried out on land belonging to a-Nabi Saleh and Deir Nizam. The heavy equipment came to a halt, and the razing stopped that day. Two days after the hearing, the settlers admitted that they were the ones who had built the fence, "to protect saplings we planted on Tu Bishvat," they wrote to the Israeli military governor in Ramallah and the minister of defense, pledging to take the fence down.[64]

Though the order nisi was not the final word, the a-Nabi Saleh hearing caused a stir in Israel and the Occupied Territories. For the first time, settlement building was halted by judicial decree. Palestinians all over the West Bank were introduced to a new way of fighting the creation of settlements on their land, a route that proved itself, in the case of a-Nabi Saleh, tangibly, on the ground, as the tools of destruction ground to a standstill.

Khoury's office was flooded with calls. Villagers from Tubas, in the northeastern West Bank, said a thousand dunams of privately cultivated land had been taken to build the settlement of Beka'ot. Residents of Haris, near Nablus, complained that two hundred dunams had been seized for a settlement in their area. Landowners from Tel Shilo produced documents showing that the new settlement there had been partly built on their territory. Communities from the Bethlehem region also came to Khoury's office with documents attesting to the seizure of thousands of dunams of their land for settlements in Gush Etzion, including the planned city of Efrat.[65] Everyone heard that the work in a-Nabi Saleh had stopped and everyone wanted in on the action. File a Supreme Court petition. Pull a Nabi Saleh for us, too, they asked.

But the order nisi in the a-Nabi Saleh case was the high point for the Palestinian petitioners. It all went downhill from there. The affidavit of response submitted by the state and signed by the Coordinator of Government Activities in the Territories, Avraham Orly, stated that on further legal examination, no seizure order was in fact required, because those dunams were state-administered public land. The order had been issued by mistake.

Khoury vehemently objected. His clients had been cultivating the land for generations, he said. It is private land. The focus of the debate shifted to whether or not the entire land allocated to the settlement of Neve Tzuf was public or private. The lack of clarity on the question of ownership was a result of the fact that the area had not been subject to land registration, a process in which the title to land is listed in the official land registry (known as the Tabu). In the absence of registration, disputes as to title may arise.

After the state submitted its response, Civil Administration and State Attorney officials contacted Khoury. They wanted to negotiate. Instead of years of litigation over the status of every morsel of land the military claims is public, they said, let's reach a settlement. Khoury was in favor. His contacts in Israel's top legal circles told him the state was prepared to reach a generous agreement and declare only sixty dunams as public land. "It's impossible to build a settlement on sixty dunams," they said with a wink, knowing that the battle was not just over land ownership.

But Khoury was up against a Palestinian leadership that refused to negotiate with the occupier over, as they saw it, the extent of the theft to which Palestinians would consent. The National Guidance Committee believed any compromise meant giving legitimacy to the Israeli settlement. "If they want to decide in their committees what is and isn't private, what is and isn't legal, they can do it themselves," Khoury was told. "We will never agree." Without the leaders' green light, the Palestinian landowners also refused to allow Khoury to negotiate on their behalf, even though they very much wanted a compromise to save their land. "They don't agree, so we can't agree either," they said.[66]

Khoury lamented the decision: "I saw there was no chance, no feasibility, no possibility of a settlement on sixty dunams, and I thought it was worth paying the price of the Taggart Building and its surroundings, because that was going to stay in the hands of the military anyway, and the settlers would remain there. I tried to convince the heads of the National Guidance Committee, but they said 'No. We will make no compromise.'"[67]

The state's position that the land in question was not private was followed by a motion to dismiss the petition. The land's status was not a matter for the High Court of Justice, Beinisch said. Since the only issue Khoury had presented to the court was interference with private property, and since the High Court is indeed not the venue for clarifying the status of land, the court agreed with Beinisch and the petition came to an end.

Neve Tzuf was established under a different name, Halamish, and today it is a midsize settlement with a population of 1,275 (as of 2015). The settlement that was planned on 90 dunams now spans 760, 250 of them privately owned by Palestinians from a-Nabi Saleh and Deir Nizam.[68] The village of a-Nabi Saleh was repeatedly hit by land theft over the years, based on the salami method. In 1980, the Halamish settlers cut down the rare arbutus forest that grew on village land to expand the settlement. The forest was destroyed even though it had been declared a protected nature reserve. The Council of Jewish Settlements in Judea and Samaria claimed that because the government insisted the community limit itself to state land, residents had no choice but to cut down the trees to build a neighborhood. "We prefer the land of Israel with Jews and without a forest than with a forest and without Jews," the council was quoted in the daily *Ma'ariv*.[69] A-Nabi Saleh continued to choke from the force of the occupation and the settlements, and gained fame, at the end of the Second Intifada, as a center of nonviolent, popular resistance. Village residents protested every Friday for years, persisting even under tremendous pressure and unprecedented violence unleashed by the military. Today the village is one of the only ones that refuses, as a matter of principle, to take any sort of action in Israeli courts. The unwavering position of the resistance leaders in a-Nabi Saleh is that there can be no dialogue with the occupier and its institutions.

It is tempting to ask "what if?" How would things have turned out had the landowners agreed to the compromise Khoury proposed? Khoury believes that just as the secular group had left because of the harsh conditions, the religious group would also have found it too hard to make do with the limited territory given to them in the compromise. But looking at the current map of Halamish, seeing just how much private land it covers and how many illegal structures have been built, including an entire neighborhood put up without permits, it is hard not to wonder whether the compromise would have really stopped the project or just put a small dent in its tracks.

THE SERIOUS RESPONSE Khoury and his clients received in court (which was soon to be replaced with cynicism) and the precedential achievement of the interim order to cease building spurred Khoury's ambition and strengthened his faith in the legal route. Before the a-Nabi Saleh case ended in disappointment, Khoury filed a number of petitions on behalf of clients who had come to him after the Palestinian leadership had given its blessing to litigation (though not to compromise). But in those cases, relating to three new settlements, Khoury did not have to grapple with property rights. On the contrary: the state did not deny that the seized land was privately owned by Palestinians. Now, Khoury had to face the security argument head-on.

In the first case, regarding the creation of Anatot, north of Jerusalem, the state denied plans to build a settlement on the seized land. Khoury had petitioned on behalf of forty landowners who together had seventeen hundred dunams of land seized by military order. Military government officials had reportedly told them that the area was meant for a settlement. The court issued an order nisi and an interim order prohibiting construction, but after Beinisch notified the court on behalf of the state that there was no plan to build a settlement in the area, just to use the land for the military's needs, the justices changed their tune. The fact that everyone knew a Jewish settlement was planned for the site made no difference to the legal case, established exclusively through Beinisch's declarations and an affidavit from a colonel who said the land was needed for "essential military installations." Khoury did everything in his power. He questioned the military purpose of the seizure and asked why it was needed in the absence of hostilities in the area. But he was facing a court that was not only unwilling to question security arguments but scorned those who did.

No exchange between judges and lawyers is a meeting of equals. But the Zussman-Khoury exchange that ensued and was recorded by journalists was a rare parade of judicial sarcasm and patronization. It was quoted several pages earlier but is worth repeating here:

KHOURY: We're not at war. There are no hostilities on the ground . . . land cannot be seized for military purposes if no hostilities are taking place in the area.

ZUSSMAN: Perhaps they'll sign a peace accord by day's end.

KHOURY: There are about a million dunams of land that belong to the state in the West Bank. Why deliberately take a plot that belongs to someone?

ZUSSMAN: I can't determine what area is important for military purposes. I'm not a general.

KHOURY: The military needs 1,700 dunams? It's unreasonable.

ZUSSMAN: It wasn't enough for the American army or the Russians.[70]

Khoury, undaunted, raised the suspicion that the security justification had been conjured up to keep the landowners from the land until the settlement was built. Zussman turned to Beinisch for help in assuaging the concern: "Do you have some sort of time frame in mind? It [the seizure] doesn't need to stay in place until kingdom come."

Beinisch was unable to give a time limit. "I don't know. If there's a policy, security consideration, it has to do with policy and security changes. This is about IDF deployment until the situation changes."

The panel dismissed the petition then and there and revoked the order nisi.[71]

Almost four decades have gone by since. The situation has apparently not changed, because the seizure order has never been canceled. On the other hand, no "essential military installations" were ever built on the land.

What did happen was that a settlement, Anatot, was built there, partly on the land discussed in that petition.

In the next case, Khoury no longer argued that the seized land was meant for settlement. Instead he brought to court the essential question of the legality of building settlements on private Palestinian land.

AYYUB'S TRIALS

Khoury knew Suleiman Taufiq Ayyub from his days working as an associate in a Jerusalem law office, before he opened his own practice. Ayyub was a certified surveyor who worked as a land registration official when the Jordanians ruled the West Bank. Once the IDF took over, Israel decided to halt the land registration process, partly based on the idea that an occupier should not engage in legal proceedings with long-term effects. This approach quickly changed, and Israel of course went on to make vastly long-term changes in the territories it occupied, but the land registration was never resumed. When Israel stopped the process, only about 30 percent of land in the West Bank had been registered, with the remaining 70 percent frozen at various stages.

Originally from Jerusalem, Ayyub and his family had some land in the Ramallah area, near an old Jordanian military base. Ramallah was one of the regions in which the land registration had been completed, so the territory belonging to Ayyub and his family was listed under their names in the central land registry, the Tabu.

In 1970, the military commander of the West Bank signed a seizure order for the Ayyub family land. This was done for security purposes, the order stated, to expand a Jordanian military base, now used by the IDF. Over the next few years another base was installed at the site, near the original Jordanian base and on the Ayyub family plot, and soldiers moved in. The military offered the landowners payment for using the land, but they refused to accept it.

Ayyub meanwhile continued working as a surveyor. He knew Khoury, a young lawyer specializing in real estate who occasionally needed a report from a certified surveyor familiar with the West Bank. Ayyub's reports were submitted to the courts in cases Khoury worked on, and sometimes Ayyub counseled him on the exact location of one plot or another.

Fast-forward to 1978. The Begin government was desperately seeking land for settlements. Gush Emunim was sending founding settler groups all over the West Bank, attaching a biblical story to every hill as justification for building a Jewish settlement. Israel's messianic surge that had begun with the great victory over the Arab armies in 1967 reached full height with the change in government. Begin spoke the same language as Gush Emunim. Though not a religious man himself, he was nonetheless captivated by the notion of the Jewish people returning to their homeland after two thousand years in exile and the reconstruction of landmarks mentioned in the Bible. Gush Emunim leaders took full advantage of Begin's Zionist romanticism. There, they told him, right there between the Palestinian villages of Turmusaya and Sinjil, between the olive trees, is where the Tabernacle once stood! This is where the Tabernacle stood before the Temple was built! We must rebuild Shilo! And over there, that's where the city of Shomron once stood, the capital of the kingdom of Israel. And here, right here, on the land of Ayyub the surveyor, was biblical Beit El! In the new army base, between the recruits' mess hall and the officers' club, that's where Jacob dreamed of a ladder with angels ascending and descending! And here, by the armory, God promised the land to Jacob and changed his name to Israel. We must rebuild Beit El!

Begin wiped away a tear and agreed to every demand. He initially allowed settler groups to live inside various military camps; then his government approved building the settlements. In the case of Beit El, the government decided to evacuate the military base to allow the settler group to establish their community. The purported biblical history set roots in the present, sowing the seeds of future disaster.

The decision to replace parts of the military base with a settlement was front-page news in the Israeli media. Jewish settlement in the Occupied Territories was a topic that stirred up emotions in the Israeli public and naturally enraged Palestinians, and every decision the government made at the time reached the headlines. Ayyub read and understood that his land was about to become a new settlement. He contacted Khoury. "This is my land and my family's land!" he said. "And now they're giving it to the settlers. Can anything be done?"

This was the case Khoury had been waiting for. "If they're handing it over to settlers, it means there's no security need to seize your land." Khoury explained some clear legal principles to his new client. Ayyub did not ask for the Palestinian leadership's blessing for the legal move. He knew the Israeli justice system through his own work and did not think he needed anybody's approval. He convinced his family to take the case to the High Court, and Khoury, who had gained a reputation thanks to the a-Nabi Saleh case, was the natural candidate to represent them.

In the petition Khoury submitted, he argued, first and foremost, that the decision to establish a civilian community on land that was seized in 1970 for the purpose of building a military base was proof that there was no longer a security justification and therefore the seizure order should be revoked. So long as the land was used for a military purpose, said Khoury, the seizure was sanctioned under international law. Once the use is no longer military in nature, the exclusion regarding a military imperative does not apply, and the land seizure becomes a violation of the prohibition on taking private property. In the case of Beit El, this was plain and simple, he said. Beit El was built as a result of settler pressure and as an ideological, political project.

But Khoury did not stop there. He argued what he had not argued in the a-Nabi Saleh case: that international law prohibits the transfer of population from the occupying country into the occupied territory, and that building a settlement is, in any event, not "temporary." Neighborhoods, schools, synagogues, and shopping areas were planned for the land, Khoury charged. How can that be said to be temporary? The seizure had to be seen as a veritable confiscation, and confiscation is peremptorily prohibited under The Hague Regulations pertaining to occupied land.

Khoury filed another petition at the time, on behalf of residents of the village of Tubas against the seizure of their land for the creation of a settlement, Beka'ot. In this petition, too, Khoury argued that the allocation of the land for settlement purposes indicates that there was no military need to support the seizure order and therefore it could not stand.

Justice Zussman understood that these cases were a political bombshell. They touched on the most controversial policy introduced by the new right-wing government, a policy over which the Israeli public was deeply split. He decided to hear the two cases, Beit El and Beka'ot, together, before an extended panel of five justices, a rare occurrence at that time. The decision expressed his view that the cases were of great significance, and the extended panel would lend greater legitimacy and validity to any decision. An order nisi compelled the military to file an affidavit explaining why seizing the land for the purpose of building settlements was lawful.

"The hearing before five justices next week is generating a lot of interest, as this is the first time the Supreme Court will issue a general decision on settlements in the Judea and Samaria area," a *Ma'ariv* reporter
wrote,[72] reflecting the feeling that this case would decide the fate of the
entire settlement project. The Palestinian National Guidance Committee,
consulted by the people of Tubas but not by Ayyub, had given its approval
to the proceeding. The committee leaders actually came to the November
1978 hearing and with them, in the crowded courtroom, were the leaders
of Gush Emunim and many Israeli and foreign journalists.

Ahead of the hearing, the military submitted its response in an affidavit signed by Avraham Orly, the Coordinator of Government Activities in the Territories. Though the military had not initiated the settlements
and, at least in the case of Beit El, did not decide where they would be
built, Orly agreed to give them a security veneer. It was not just Beka'ot
and Beit El that he described in security terms. Orly's affidavit was a manifesto for the thesis that civilian settlement in the West Bank as a whole
served security needs:

> [Settlement] is part of the government's security paradigm, which sees
> security as based, inter alia, on Jewish settlements. Under this concep-
> tion, all Israeli settlements in the territories held by the IDF form part of
> the IDF's regional defense deployment. Additionally, these settlements are
> given the highest classification in said regional defense deployment, which
> is expressed in the allocation of human resources and equipment. In times
> of calm, these settlements are used mostly for a show of presence and con-
> trol over essential areas, for observations and the like. The importance
> of these settlements grows during times of war, when the regular forces
> are usually deployed from their bases to operations, and the aforesaid set-
> tlements serve as the main element of presence and security control over
> the areas in which they are located. . . .
>
> The settlement itself is located on elevated terrain, overlooking an
> essential, important intersection where the Jerusalem-Nablus road,
> running the length of the territory, meets the west-east road running
> from the coastal plain to Jericho and the Jordan Valley. In addition, the
> area where the settlement was built allows control over infrastructure
> (water, electricity, communication) that are important for many areas. It

was for these reasons that the aforesaid location was selected for building the settlement of Beit El.[73]

This section of the affidavit is quite possibly the most striking example of conflating two statuses that the laws of war were intended to separate as much as possible: civilian and combatant. If the settlers' role is security, if they are expected to be part of the IDF's "regional defense" system, if they are expected to maintain a presence and help exercise control, if members of their communities are to serve as lookouts—if all this were true, then what are settlers? Civilians or combatants? This distinction is of the greatest importance, since civilians are protected from harm during hostilities, while combatants may be targeted. On behalf of the IDF and the government, Orly presented the court with the image of a community that might be home to civilians but its object, essence, and function are military.

Moreover, Orly's account of how Beit El was established was the opposite of what actually happened. The government created Beit El under pressure from the settlers, not at the military's behest or according to its needs. In fact, the military had to evacuate a base to make way for the settlement. The military accepted the dictate that a settlement should be established at the site, but if there was a security rationale, it was pulled out of the hat retroactively. Orly's description of the strategic point selected for the settlement was at best a manipulation and at worst a revision of history. Khoury protested Orly's affidavit. He argued that its arguments were false, intended to cover up the real motivation for Beit El, the desire to settle Jews in the West Bank for political, ideological reasons.

Orly also said that according to legal advice he received from State Attorney Gabriel Bach, the Geneva Convention was not customary law and therefore could not be enforced in Israel's courts. Orly was also apprised that the issue of settlements was being discussed by Israel and Egypt, who were negotiating a peace treaty at the time, and therefore the court should withdraw from the matter as it was "nonjusticiable." Indeed, Orly's affidavit reflected the legal strategy formulated by State Attorney Bach, who personally represented the military and the government in this case: the settlements are a security necessity, the Geneva Convention is treaty law, and the whole thing is nonjusticiable anyway. Thus the court faced three central questions, with two opposing views on each. Are the settlements a matter of security or not? Does the Geneva Convention ban on settlements apply or not? Is the matter justiciable or not?

A third position was also trying to make its way into the courtroom: the settlers' view. Members of Gush Emunim did not like the idea that their right to settle the land hinged on a security argument. The right, they believed, derived from patrimony. It was already Jewish land, to which they had returned after two thousand years in exile. Above all, the land had been promised to the people of Israel by God. This was the "*kushan*," the title deed, that gave them the right to settle it, and it trumped any private ownership by any Palestinian. The settlers wanted to present the court with their position that the settlements were justified as a historic, religious right rather than use some security trick. For all of Beit El's militarily strategic location, the site had been chosen for entirely different reasons. Two settler leaders asked to be named as respondents to Khoury's petition and contradict the thesis offered by the state attorney. The court, however, rejected their motion, and they were kept out of the hearing, fortunately for Bach.[74] No matter: the settlers did not give up on presenting their theological-legal position. They would return to court and play a pivotal role very soon.

Emotions at the hearing ran high, both because of the politically charged topic and because the courtroom was too small for the crowd wishing to attend. The Palestinian landowners, who were locked out of the courtroom, banged on the door and clashed with police officers who did not think they had a right to enter. In the commotion, the mayors of Ramallah and al-Birah were arrested and taken for interrogation.[75] Inside the courtroom, Bach explained the security advantage gained by having a civilian Jewish community "on the road" to the military base in Beit El that was used as the Judea and Samaria Division headquarters. On a map he also showed the importance of Beka'ot, located on the most convenient route from Jordan, an area where, he claimed, hundreds of terrorists infiltrated Israel. Khoury, for his part, argued that establishing settlements may be a political, ideological act, but certainly not a security one. Holding back his anger, he challenged the justices: They say this is a temporary seizure. How is it temporary if a community is built there? If civilians, entire families, move to live on my client's land? If they build neighborhoods there? Does this look temporary to you? This is a permanent settlement!

The panel of five issued its judgment four months later. One by one, they rejected Khoury's arguments and accepted Bach's, with the exception of the nonjusticiability argument, which was largely rejected. On the applicability of Article 49 of the Geneva Convention, which prohibits the transfer of population from the occupying country to the occupied country, Witkon ruled, based on an article written by Professor Yoram Dinstein, Israel's foremost authority on international law at the time, that the Geneva Convention was treaty law and therefore not enforceable in domestic courts.[76] According to Dinstein's position, Witkon had erred in the Rafah case by claiming that *both* the Geneva Convention and The Hague Convention were treaty law, and therefore unenforceable. In a critique of the High Court's judgment in that case, Dinstein clarified that Geneva is indeed treaty law but the older Hague Convention had attained the status of customary law and must therefore be enforced by Israeli courts. Unlike the Geneva Convention, The Hague Convention does not explicitly prohibit transferring civilian population into the occupied country, and therefore, wrote Witkon, the prohibition is not enforceable. Witkon refused to decide whether the Article 49 prohibition would have precluded the establishment of settlements, a question he said was "academic." "We cannot rule on this issue,"[77] he wrote. Witkon's position that it was not the court's role to rule on the settlements' legality under international law became a tenet that shaped the Supreme Court's approach for decades to come.[78]

However, Witkon ignored the fact that even if Article 49 was not customary law in the 1970s, it is not the only source of prohibition on building settlements. As one, the justices of the Supreme Court overlooked the fact that the laws of occupation are based on the fundamental principle that requires the occupier to maintain the status quo. In other words: preventing long-term changes in an occupied territory is one of the central guidelines of the laws of occupation. This general rule expresses these laws' underlying philosophy that the occupation is temporary and the occupier is a trustee rather than sovereign in the occupied land. Therefore, the occupier is not meant to take steps only a sovereign may take, such as building new communities and changing the demography of the area. The occupier merely administers the territory on a temporary basis. But, again, Witkon and his fellow justices avoided delving into the fundamental principles of the laws of occupation and rather focused on their more specific provisions, such as those pertaining to the property of protected persons and the security exclusions to the prohibition on destroying or seizing their property.

On the central issue of whether establishing the communities of Beit El and Beka'ot could be considered an act of security, Justice Witkon wrote:

> The main point is that in terms of the pure security consideration, there is no doubt that the presence of communities, even "civilian" communities, of citizens of the holding power in the held territory makes a significant contribution to the security situation in the area and helps the military carry out its mission. It does not take a security and military expert to understand that terrorist elements have less difficulty operating in an area that is exclusively inhabited by a population that is either apathetic or sympathetic to the enemy, than in an area where there are persons who may follow them, and inform the authorities of any suspected movement. Terrorists will not find shelter, assistance and equipment among them. The matter is simple and there is no need to elaborate.[79]

Quite aside from the legal difficulty of ascribing a military role to a civilian community, Witkon and his colleagues simply ignored reality. As every child in Israel knew, Beit El had not been established for security purposes but as a political-ideological step. Justice Witkon knew it, too. This might be why he began his judgment with the following dumbfounding statement, a sort of apologetic explanation for the fiction he was about to manufacture:

> The court—unlike other institutions and bodies—is sustained from the evidence contained in the affidavits submitted by the parties. On a sensitive issue such as the one before us, it is appropriate to emphasize that various statements, declarations and decisions, whatever their source may be, do not enter the scope of our judicial discussion, unless they are common knowledge, or evidence has been brought forward to support them.

Get it? Yes, the context of building Beit El was known and obvious. It was an ideological move. The government of Israel had not concealed its position that settlements as a whole and Beit El in particular should be built as a matter of ideology, not security. But State Attorney Bach provided the affidavit of an army general who said something else, and so we will ignore the hullabaloo outside. Government declarations, public discourse, media reports, Gush Emunim maneuvers designed to force the government to build settlements—all of these went in the trash. When it came to the context and motivation for creating Beit El, only Orly's affidavit counted.

The art of ignoring reality is one in which many justices excel. They rely on this dodge when convenient, or when they need an excuse to avoid stepping out of their comfort zone and making a courageous decision. I have often seen judges, especially those conducting a judicial review of an executive act, like the High Court of Justice, ask questions that rely on the general knowledge citizens have about events in their country. But when it is expedient to shut out general information available in countless media stories and politicians' public declarations, when a party to proceedings seeks to rely on statements made in the public sphere, the justices resort to legal procedure and the laws of evidence and use them as a barricade to keep the truth from entering the courtroom. This is the art of judicial disregard. Witkon was a master of it, and his colleagues were no amateurs either.

The pinnacle of the court's self-deception, or what we might call deviousness, was its ruling on the issue of the allegedly temporary nature of the military seizure. Khoury had posed a tough question about the temporary seizure of land that would be used for a permanent settlement. In response, the state attorney supplied a relative philosophical approach to the concept of temporality: something that is temporary has an expiration date, even if it is not marked on a calendar, and the settlements have an expiration date, which is the end of occupation. In other words, the settlements are, in fact, permanent in terms of the occupation, but the occupation itself is by definition temporary. Ergo the settlements are also temporary. According to this thesis of relativity, we cannot claim that a house stands in one place because the earth moves: if you look at it from the sun, the house is actually moving quite rapidly.

The thesis was groundless in every respect; most important, it completely ignored the purpose of the prohibition on confiscation that it sought to circumvent. What sort of meaning can the difference between "permanent" and "temporary" have for someone whose property has been "seized" if the seizure may last his entire life? What sort of restriction does the law impose on an occupying power if it prohibits the confiscation of private property yet also allows a "seizure" for generations? What is the value in this type of protection of private property? This was clearly not the intention behind the distinction international law draws between confiscation and seizure.

But the Supreme Court justices warmly embraced the semantic workaround Bach offered them. Witkon may have ignored the contortion, but Moshe Landau did address it briefly: "I accept Mr. Bach's response that the civilian community will only be able to remain at that location so long as the IDF holds the area pursuant to the seizure order," he wrote. "This seizure may itself end one of these days, as a result of international negotiations which may result in a new arrangement that will be validated under international law and decide the fate of this community, as all other communities in the held territories."[80] Their colleague, Justice Miriam Ben-Porat, wrote explicitly that for her "permanent" is a relative term. "[The settlers] are not passersby who are spending the night, or guests who are visiting for a few weeks or a few months. These are people who will view this place as their home," she wrote. "But one must remember that the state of emergency the country is in has lasted since its establishment, for more than thirty years." The idea was clear: if a state of emergency is temporary by definition and has been in effect for thirty years, then a community can exist for generations and still be considered temporary. And when will all this temporariness end? "The terms of an agreement will ultimately decide the fate of each specific community."[81] Given that scientists say the earth will not exist in a few billion years, is there anything that is permanent?

To put it baldly: the justices had done a Mickey Mouse job. Their interpretation of the overall laws of occupation, of the security exclusion to the prohibition on interference with property, and of the temporal aspect of the seizure was forced and unnatural and it ignored both the natural meaning of the terms and the purpose the norms sought to serve. The justices also went along with the fiction the respondents created with respect to the reasons and motivation for building the settlement, blatantly disregarding reality. All this to allow the government to have its way at the expense of Palestinian landowners. The interpretation was particularly egregious given the moment when the judgment was issued, just before the settlement project exploded, when there were still only a few thousand settlers. At this point in time, the only state institution tasked with enforcing international legal principles, the court, would have been able to stop this most far-reaching violation of the laws of occupation. And it chose not to.

Suleiman Taufiq Ayyub lost. His land and his family's land was given over for (temporary) use by a Gush Emunim settler group, and today, almost thirty years after the judgment, Beit El is home to a population of almost six thousand. It expanded to other areas seized (for security purposes, of course) shortly after the judgment was issued, and has also taken over many other privately owned plots that were never seized, at least not formally.*[82]

The judgment in the Beit El case, like all judgments, was named after the first petitioner, in this case, the surveyor and Jordanian land registry official Suleiman Taufiq Ayyub. Israel's official law report included a typo in Ayyub's name, rendering it as *oyev*, the Hebrew for "enemy." Perhaps it was not a typo. Omitting the Hebrew markers for vowels, the name can also be read as "Job" (which is, in fact, the origin for the Arabic Ayyub). It certainly serves Israel's case better to consider him an enemy.

SECURITY, SECURITY, AND MORE SECURITY

The Beit El judgment taught the lawyers who fought against the settlements that Supreme Court justices do not care about the context and motivation for seizing land as long as there is an opinion from an IDF officer saying that the settlement is required for security needs. A month after the court sanctioned the establishment of Beit El, attorney Ibrahim Nassar filed a petition on behalf of ten residents of Ni'lin, a village west of Ramallah, whose land had been taken for the new settlement of Matityahu. The court issued an interim order halting work until the petition was decided. State Attorney Bach, who had given the Israeli government an impressive victory in the Beit El case, was not about to change his winning horse, so he argued that Matityahu was necessary for security reasons. Extremely

---

* In 2008, Yesh Din, via my law office, helped Palestinian landowners file a High Court petition seeking the demolition of five structures with thirty housing units built on their land on a hill north of Beit El that had been overtaken by residents of the settlement. In 2014, the structures were demolished by court order. For this and another petition regarding a southern expansion, see chapter 6: Unauthorized Outposts.

necessary. It was located at a sensitive spot overlooking Israel's Ben Gurion International Airport, and therefore security needs dictated building a settlement there, Bach said, attaching an expert opinion from the Coordinator of Government Activities in the Territories.

Given the Beit El judgment, Nassar knew that he would never be able to pop the security bubble and that arguing that the settlement was politically motivated would get him nowhere. Instead, he decided to try to confront the security argument head-on—with a counter–expert opinion.

This was the first time the military's opinion was challenged in this way. Nassar managed to obtain an expert opinion from Matityahu Peled, a major general in the reserves. Peled had been a fighter with the one of the pre-state military organizations and later a senior IDF officer. After the 1967 war, he had undergone a process of political change that aligned him with Israel's left wing on the question of the Occupied Territories. Peled avidly supported ending the occupation and staunchly opposed Jewish settlement there. At the time of Israel's decision to build Matityahu on Ni'lin land, Peled was a leader in the Israel Peace Party, known as Sheli. In the expert opinion he wrote for Nassar's clients, Peled argued that the army's claim of the necessity for building a settlement at that spot—to prevent the enemy from using it to observe the airport—was a cover for ideological motives. Peled said that since the enemy—the Jordanians and their army—were on the other side of the Jordan River, the hill in Ni'lin, located far from the armistice line, had no strategic importance. Peled added that the military could provide any security needs in the location without dispossessing the Palestinian population and settling Israelis there. He disagreed with the "regional defense" concept and argued that the contribution civilians might make to security would be negligible.

In August 1979, the Supreme Court dismissed Nassar's petition. With regard to the security-military question, Justice Landau wrote that the court would always prefer the opinion of "those charged with maintaining security in practice" over security experts who were not in office.[83] Thus if serving security personnel, who receive orders from the political leadership, sign an opinion confirming that a certain area should be seized or a settlement established for security purposes, that's the end of the story.

So what was left for landowners fighting the creation of settlements on their land? The prohibition on transferring the occupying population into occupied territory was deemed unenforceable in a domestic court;

the political-ideological context for the settlements had been trumped by the claim of security needs. Statements by a serving officer outweighed counter-opinions from someone no longer serving. It seemed that the door, window, and chimney had been sealed off to victims whose land was used for building settlements, with the security argument an insurmountable hurdle.

Unless . . . unless one of those people "charged with maintaining security in practice" objected to a settlement. Then the whole construction would fall apart. And this is what happened a few weeks after Matityahu was approved.

WHEN TRUTH COMES TO COURT

While Khoury and his clients were in court fighting Beit El and Beka'ot, Gush Emunim was waging a battle on the ground to establish a new settlement on the outskirts of Nablus. Settler leaders had identified an area to the east of Nablus as the first stop in Canaan on Abraham's journey from Harran, the place where God promised the entire land to the patriarch and his descendants.[84] With the fervent belief that the creation of Israel and the occupation of the territories signaled the coming of the Messiah, the settlers put their finger on the map, on a hill overlooking what they claimed to be the biblical city of Nablus, now called Mount Huwarah, and said: Here, where our father rested, we will build the settlement of Elon Moreh.

On December 30, 1978, twenty families set out to settle on the hill.* They had no permits from the authorities and certainly no permission from the owners of the land they were planning to take over, but they had the Bible, and they thought that was more than enough. An IDF force stopped them on the Qalqiliyah-Nablus road. In protest, they decided to stay by the side of the road with their children and belongings.[85] This

---

* This core group was part of an effort made over a number of years to establish a settlement in the northern West Bank. Some of its members had attempted to settle in the ruins of a disused train station near the Palestinian village of Sebastia a few years earlier and had clashed with the Israeli government, until, in 1975, they received permission from Prime Minister Yitzhak Rabin to live in the military camp in Qadum, south of Nablus. Some of the group remained in Qadum when their comrades left to establish Elon Moreh. Those who remained went on to establish the settlement of Kedumim.

protest camp attracted attention and politicians who supported the settlement movement descended on it, making combative declarations about the nation's right to the entire land. Gush Emunim put tremendous pressure on Prime Minister Begin to approve a settlement at the site. This is where the divine promise was given to the People of Israel, they told Begin. How can you not approve a settlement? The government's attempts to appease the settlers and convince them to leave the protest camp failed. Without a pledge to establish Elon Moreh, we will not leave, the settlers said. The twenty families remained by the side of the road day and night and waited for Begin or the Messiah, whoever came first. Though this drawn-out demonstration was staged without the necessary permit for protesting in the West Bank (a requirement always fully enforced for Palestinians), the government preferred not to remove the Elon Moreh group by force.

Eight days after the families were stopped on the Qalqiliyah-Nablus road, Begin brought the issue for discussion at the Ministerial Committee on Security Affairs. At the end of the meeting, the committee decided to find a site for the families, with the exact location to be determined by the government "with consideration, as much as possible, for the group's wishes."[86] The opposition was furious, claiming that the government had caved in to Gush Emunim. But the settlers got what they wanted, and the protesters left the roadside camp.

Though the decision to establish Elon Moreh was made by the Ministerial Committee on Security Affairs, the prime minister tasked the chairman of the Ministerial Committee on Settlement Affairs, Minister of Agriculture Ariel Sharon, with locating a site for the settlement. A few weeks later, a site in the area of Mount Huwarah was identified and the military agreed. The matter was returned to the Ministerial Committee on Security Affairs, which received confirmation from Chief of Staff Rafael Eitan that the plan served security needs. In May, the ministerial committee gave the army permission to issue seizure orders for security purposes. So far, everything followed the Beit El script.

But that was where things took an unexpected turn. Minister of Defense Ezer Weizman, who had commanded both the air force and the IDF's operations division, was deeply invested in the Egyptian-Israeli peace process and thought the feverish settlement activity undermined these efforts. He challenged the ministerial committee's decision and demanded a government discussion. Weizman argued that there was no security need to build Elon Moreh. Thus the minister of defense, a former major general, disputed the position of the chief of staff. To make matters even more complicated, Weizman was supported by Deputy Prime Minister Yigael Yadin, a former chief of staff. So a minister of defense and a former chief of staff were ranged against the serving chief of staff.

Two days after the government discussion, the IDF commander in the West Bank signed seizure orders for seven hundred dunams of land belonging to residents of the small Palestinian village of Rujeib, near Nablus. Two days after that, on June 7, 1979, the twenty Elon Moreh families, escorted by IDF troops, stormed the area that had been seized, and, in a maneuver that looked every bit like a military operation, they established the settlement. It was only on the morning of the storming of their land that Rujeib's leaders were summoned to the governor's office to be told that their territory had been seized for "security reasons."

As this political affair was brewing, Khoury received a visit from Ibrahim Mattar, an old friend from his student days at the Hebrew University. Mattar was working with representatives of the American Mennonite Church, which gave humanitarian aid to Palestinians in rural parts of the West Bank. Through this work, he got to know the Rujeib landowners and remembered that Khoury was the champion of legal battles against land seizures for settlement purposes. Mattar wanted to connect the landowners to Khoury to fight the seizure.

As in the case of a-Nabi Saleh and Tubas, the Rujeib landowners wanted to oppose their dispossession, but only on condition that the Palestinian leadership supported their decision to go to Israel's court. Khoury once again had to persuade the National Guidance Committee. After the loss in the Beit El case, this was no easy task. This time it's different, he told them. The minister of defense opposes the seizure and denies the security need, which is highly significant. There is a chance this time. Besides, we may have lost the Beit El case, but restrictions were also imposed on the government, because the court ruled that no settlement could be established without a security need. Also, the Beit El case put the dispossession of Palestinian land on the international agenda.

Finding the upside in losses, explaining to clients why what looks like a loss is in fact a hidden success, is part and parcel of the work of a lawyer, especially one who represents disempowered communities, and Khoury was good at it. The National Guidance Committee was convinced. They mostly saw the public benefit of these proceedings, the international interest they would garner for the Palestinian cause.

A week after the Elon Moreh group settled, Khoury filed a petition on behalf of seventeen landowners. He made all the arguments he had made before, including the prohibitions in international law of transferring the population of the occupier into occupied territory and the confiscation of property. But Khoury stressed that the security need touted as the reason for the land seizure did not exist in this case, that it was driven by ideology, and proof of this lay in the fact that top security officials were divided on the issue, with some major figures denying the existence of a security rationale.

Khoury knew that the security question would make or break the case. He turned to Matti Peled, who had provided an expert opinion in the Ni'lin case, and asked him to provide an opinion in this case, too. Peled gladly obliged, helping Khoury with advice on security issues and refusing to take payment for his work, saying his involvement in these cases was part of his effort to promote peace. He offered to have Sheli's lawyer work on the case, too. The legal battle against Elon Moreh had drawn huge political attention in Israel and Peled wanted his party to be identified with it.[87] The lawyer Peled wanted to bring in was Amnon Zichroni.

Zichroni was a well-known lawyer in the 1950s and a left-wing figure. As an army conscript, he refused to carry a weapon, citing pacifism, and he was one of Israel's first conscientious objectors. He was later involved in the creation of several left-wing parties, including Sheli. Khoury suggested Zichroni be formally retained by the last named petitioner, number seventeen. That way, Zichroni could appear alongside him, but Khoury would remain the lead in the case, both publicly and in terms of the order of appearance in court. Zichroni enlisted a young bright associate from his law office to work with him. This was Avigdor Feldman.

The petitioners from Rujeib now had an impressive battery of lawyers, one Palestinian Israeli and two Jewish Israelis. The addition of Zichroni and Feldman, with Zichroni's political association, helped brand the case as a challenge to the entire settlement project, one that would determine the whole thing.

The legal team knew that Peled's opinion was not sufficient, based on the experience in the Matityahu case. Their hope that Defense Minister

Weizman's objection to the establishment of Elon Moreh would be reflected in the state's response was dashed. State Attorney Bach submitted a security expert opinion from none other than Chief of Staff Eitan. The security issue, which was debated in the pages of the Israeli press, required an opinion from the most senior ranking security official possible. Eitan's opinion relied on the hashed-out argument of strategically important "regional defense" achieved through Jewish civilian settlements on Elon Moreh's location next to a major traffic artery.

And then, as if by special request, while driving his car Khoury heard an interview with an ex–chief of staff, one of the leaders of the Labor Party, Haim Bar-Lev. An authority on security, Bar-Lev said there was absolutely no security need for the hill on which Elon Moreh was located, that the argument was nonsense, just a cover for the right wing's ideological agenda. Khoury wondered whether Bar-Lev would agree to sign an affidavit repeating what he said on the radio. Through a *Haaretz* journalist he knew, he was put in touch with Yossi Sarid, a Labor Knesset Member, who helped him make contact with the former chief of staff. Surprisingly, Bar-Lev agreed to sign an affidavit. In it, he said that Elon Moreh contributed nothing to Israel's security, not in fighting terrorism during a time of relative calm or in the event of a war on the eastern front. A civilian settlement on a hill about a mile from the Nablus-Jerusalem road would do nothing to help secure this traffic artery, especially since there was a large army base right next to the road, overlooking traffic arteries leading south and east. In fact, Bar-Lev wrote in his affidavit, in the event of a war, IDF forces might find themselves confined to protecting the civilian community instead of fighting the enemy.[88]

Another week went by, during which the settlers put up mobile homes and prepared to settle permanently at the site, and then the first hearing of the petition was held. Landau presided along with Justices Shlomo Asher and David Bechor. In the hearing, Khoury asked for an interim order to restore the status quo ante, that is, for the removal of the mobile homes along with the families. State Attorney Bach, representing the respondents, the minister of defense, and the military commanders of the West Bank and Nablus district, fervently objected. He claimed that Khoury's petition should be dismissed because Bar-Lev's affidavit had been submitted at the last minute, contrary to accepted practice. Bach also submitted an opinion from a Ministry of Agriculture expert stating that the land in question had barely been cultivated, going so far as to call its cultivation by the petitioners "political farming."

The justices dismissed Bach's claims and, after the hearing was over, signed an order nisi compelling the state to respond to the arguments made in the petition. They also issued an interim order to halt work at the site but did not compel the removal of the structures already in place. The order permitted settlers already at the site to remain but prohibited others from joining them. Khoury asked the justices to clarify that the interim order also precluded laying a pipe to bring water to the site. He knew this was an imminent plan. The justices confirmed that laying the pipe was prohibited. As in the Beit El case, here, too, the panel was extended to five justices. The court sessions were scheduled for September.

As soon as word of the interim order got out, Nablus military governor Yosef Lunz went to Elon Moreh, made sure the work stopped, and ordered a meticulous recording of the names of the settlers present, to ensure the court order was upheld. The court order stopping work in Elon Moreh was front-page news.[89]

Was there a security need or not? The Elon Moreh case would focus exclusively on this question. Some did not like the security discourse that had overtaken the question of the right to build settlements in the Occupied Territories. Menachem Felix and Avraham Shvut, two leading Gush Emunim activists and members of the Elon Moreh group, decided to repeat their failed attempt in the Beit El case to join the case and present their narrative. Their motion was heard by a single judge, Ytzhak Kahan, who found they had a personal stake in the hearing and therefore should be allowed to join as respondents.

The justices of the Supreme Court devoted five more sessions to Elon Moreh, an unusual occurrence, especially for an extended panel. On the first day, State Attorney Bach tried to argue that the Elon Moreh case was identical to the one in Beit El, but this time he faced justices who actually heard what was going on outside the courtroom. "This is the first time in our history that a petition has been filed against a respondent for an action he himself opposes, and someone else responds on his behalf and contrary to his opinion,"[90] Justice Witkon said, referring to the dispute between the minister of defense and the chief of staff. "I wonder," Witkon continued, "what would have happened if the minister of defense himself had submitted the affidavit and had been questioned." Though the defense minister's objection to Elon Moreh had not been formally presented to the court, it was known via the media. The papers had even run a story about the minister's visit to the site when one of the settlers made him coffee and, to protest his objection to the settlement, added salt instead of sugar.[91]

Witkon's comment made it clear that the defense minister's position seemed important to the justices and created some difficulty. Bach was prepared: "The minister of defense did object to the establishment of Elon Moreh," he said, "but after the government voted and decided, by a majority vote, to establish the settlement, the minister of defense supports the decision and the state's request to revoke the order nisi." But Bach's answer did not solve the problem, which was not whether the minister of defense supported the petition but whether he, as a security figure "charged with maintaining security in practice," believed that Elon Moreh was necessary for security purposes. Was his position not proof that the legal condition stipulated in the Beit El case—the security requirement—had not been met?

Khoury listened to this exchange and Justice Witkon's remark got him thinking. The debate focused on the reason for establishing Elon Moreh, whether it was driven by security or ideological reasons. He rose and said he had a motion. "We wish to examine the chief of staff about the pressure he was under and about the intervention of the minister of agriculture." This was an unusual request, and not just because of the affiant's position. The rules of procedure in the High Court of Justice do allow examining affiants, but they are not normally cross-examined. The High Court of Justice is meant to rule on questions of law, not fact, and therefore witness examinations in a bid to uncover facts are rarely held. The justices consulted and decided to rule on Khoury's motion at another time.

The hearing resumed a week later. According to the High Court rules of procedure, once an order nisi has been issued, the respondents plead first. Since Bach had already argued on behalf of the government and the military, it was the Elon Moreh settlers' turn. Their attorney Moshe Simon had a preliminary request: He explained that the twenty families were living at the site in poor sanitary conditions, he said. They asked that the interim order be amended so that they could dig a cesspool. A what?, the justices asked. A pit to drain the refuse.

Absolutely not. Zichroni and Feldman were outraged. No one had forced the settlers to live there. If life under the restrictions imposed by the interim order was too hard, they could go back to where they came from! Five justices of the Supreme Court, in a courtroom full of Israeli and foreign journalists, the ICRC, security officials, and members of Gush Emunim were debating the settlers' sewage. The discussion went on and on. Bach said the state supported the settlers' request as a humanitarian issue. Zichroni pulled out of his sleeve a procedural argument: the interim order could not be changed at the settlers' request because it was issued before they were party to the petition and therefore did not address them, he argued. The justices retreated for consultation and returned with a decision to allow the cesspool.

With the settlers' sewage problem solved, the parties moved on to the main course: arguments from Rahamim Cohen, also representing the Elon Moreh settlers. Menachem Felix's affidavit, submitted to the court, was directly at odds with the line of argument put together by Bach. The reason for building Elon Moreh, he said, was the divine edict to inherit the land. "The settlement of the People of Israel in the Land of Israel," Felix declared, "is the real, the most effective, the truest act of security." And for the finale: "But settlement itself does not arise out of security reasons or physical needs, but by the power of destiny of the return of Israelites to their land."[92]

Pop went the security bubble. The most important part of Felix's affidavit was two statements about the actions and claims of government ministers and the prime minister that contradicted the security arguments. These statements were made in response to the state's thesis that the land for Elon Moreh had been seized on a temporary basis: "The temporary status is incongruent with the government's decision regarding our settlement in this place," declared Felix. "In all the discussions and the many promises we received from government ministers and primarily the prime minister himself, and the seizure order was issued at the prime minister's personal request, everyone considered Elon Moreh a permanent Jewish settlement, no less than Degania or Netanya." Felix's claim touched on two immensely important legal points: the motive for issuing the seizure order—security or politics, and the planned status of the settlement—temporary or eternal.

Justice Landau was perturbed by what he had heard. The settlers' lawyer elaborated: There had been an argument in the government, he said, and the prime minister had intervened personally. Landau asked for State Attorney Bach's response, since the prime minister's intervention seemed to indicate that the decision to issue the order was, in fact, political. Bach promised to supply an answer.

The session ended with Khoury's assertion that the settlement had been established as a result of political pressure from Gush Emunim, and that the security argument was a pretext, a cover for dispossession carried out for ideological reasons. He called the court's attention to the fact that the Ministerial Committee on Security Affairs had discussed building Elon Moreh even before it had heard from the chief of staff, offering this as proof that the motive had nothing to do with security. He criticized the way in which the seizure had taken place, the fact that the landowners learned of it only after the land had been taken, and argued that this had been done in order to prevent the court's intervention.

On the next day, Bach submitted a notice on behalf of the prime minister:

> The prime minister stresses the right of the people of Israel to settle in Judea and Samaria on many occasions, both in Israel and abroad. This fact does not necessarily bear a connection to discussions held by the Ministerial Committee on Security Affairs with respect to national and state security, when it considers and decides on a specific question regarding the seizure of a specific site for security purposes. The prime minister believes that the two matters are not contradictory but that they are, nevertheless, distinct. With respect to statements made about the prime minister's intervention, such intervention was made in the form of bringing the matter for discussion by the Ministerial Committee on Security Affairs, while the prime minister is chair of the committee. . . . He took part in the discussion held by the committee, where he expressed his clear, unequivocal opinion favoring issuance of the seizure order, partly in consideration of the chief of staff's opinion.[93]

At the fourth hearing, the final date scheduled, the petitioners' lawyers repeated their request to question the chief of staff. In a dispute between a serving chief of staff and a defense minister and two former chiefs of staff, and given the concern that the settlement was established due to political pressure rather than military need, an affiant on behalf of the state should respond to questions. The justices were at a loss. Never before had a chief of staff been examined in the High Court of Justice.

Ultimately, they denied the request. However, the justices did order the chief of staff to answer several questions put to him in writing. These focused on the motivation for seizing the land and the process that resulted in the order. This was a dramatic development, and the newspapers reported it with huge headlines.[94] Very few doubted that the Elon Moreh case would decide the fate of the entire settlement project.

The responses, delivered a few days later, gave the lawyers a lot to argue about. In one answer, the chief of staff said, "To the best of my knowledge, the initiative for establishing a community in the Nablus area came from the Ministerial Committee on Security Affairs." In another he said, "I did not approach the government with a suggestion to establish the community of Elon Moreh." Thus Elon Moreh was initiated by a political body, not a professional security agency. Along with the prime minister's confirmation that he put the issue on the committee's agenda to promote the seizure order, the picture that emerged was quite a thorn in the state's side. Still, Eitan insisted that, regardless of the political machinations, creating a community in the designated location served security needs. The case was ready for a ruling.

On Monday, October 22, 1979, the court issued its judgment. The five justices accepted the petition and gave the government thirty days to remove the settlers and their mobile homes. The seizure order was revoked and the state was ordered to pay the petitioners ten thousand liras for their legal expenses. The justices dismissed the petitioners' argument based on the Geneva Convention prohibition on transferring the population of the occupier to the occupied land, repeating the position that the convention was treaty law and therefore not enforceable by domestic courts.[95] But they were persuaded that no security justification existed for the interference with property. Moshe Landau wrote the main opinion in which he preserved the chief of staff's dignity, ruling that there was no reason to doubt that he truly believed the settlement served military purposes. He did, however, conclude that the seizure order was not motivated by this belief:

I have reached the conclusion that the professional view of the chief of staff would not, in and of itself, have led to the decision to establish Elon Moreh, were it not for another reason, which was the driving force behind the decision made by the Ministerial Committee on Security Affairs and the government plenum, that is, the fervent desire of Gush Emunim to settle in the heart of the land, as close as possible to the city of Nablus.[96]

It took five justices, a declaration from the prime minister, five hearings, written questions for the chief of staff, and expert opinions from two former chiefs of staff to reach a conclusion anyone in Israel who listened to the radio already knew full well: Elon Moreh (like Beit El and the rest of the settlements) had been created for political-ideological reasons, not for security. Had the court accepted the state attorney's arguments, it would have, at best, broken the record for naïveté or, at worst, been immortalized as nothing but a rubber stamp.

And so, of all the justices, Moshe Landau, perhaps the most right-wing member of the Supreme Court at the time, a man who after retiring opposed the Oslo peace process, found himself leading the precedent-setting ruling in which the court struck down a decision to build a settlement on privately owned Palestinian land. For him this was no easy task. Feldman recalls how Landau's body trembled and his face paled as he read the judgment. In one of the best apologetic texts written by an Israeli judge, Landau explained that he was left with no choice but to strike down the seizure order:

We must not, when sitting to pronounce judgment, bring into the mix our personal views as citizens of the country. Yet there is still grave concern that the court would appear to be abandoning its proper place and descending into the arena of public debate and that its ruling will be applauded by some members of the public and utterly vehemently rejected by others. In this sense, I see myself here as one whose duty is to rule in accordance with the law on any matter lawfully brought before the court. It forces me, knowing full well in advance that the wider public will not heed the legal reasoning, only the final conclusion, and that the appropriate status of the court, as an institution, may be harmed, to rise above the disputes which divide the public. Alas, what are we to do when this is our role and duty as justices.[97]

Here Landau laments the price he believed was attached to ruling on this type of case: the danger that the court would be tainted as political and perceived as an institution that deals in politics. This is a characteristic concern of judges who imagine there is a clear line that separates politics from the law and who believe that as part of the court, they are on the clean, pure, apolitical side of the line. But Landau had not rued his fate when he gave approval to Beit El or wrote the judgment allowing the land seizure for the settlement of Matityahu. He did not fear being branded as political when he approved settlements; only revoking a seizure order made him feel the heat of politics.

After explaining that his role was to pass judgment on purely legal matters, and asking that he not be attributed with political motives, Landau went on to praise the settlers: "Even those who do not share the beliefs of the affiant and his comrades respect their deep religious convictions and the dedication that drives them."[98]

But the most important section of the judgment did not address Elon Moreh, rather the entire Zionist enterprise, in a text that is not so much legal as it is propagandist: "This petition provides a definitive answer to the argument that seeks to interpret the historic right promised to the People of Israel in the book of books as harming property rights under private property law."[99] Thus the petition filed by the Palestinians of Rujeib, whose land Israel's government sought to hand over to Jewish settlers, turned into a statement of defense for the morality of Zionism, which, Landau asserted, respects the property rights of non-Jews. Khoury, Zichroni, and Feldman's clients, who celebrated a historic, precedential victory that day, obviously focused on other parts of the judgment. They had no way of knowing how much this apparent side note would come to represent the role the Supreme Court saw itself fulfilling while overseeing the authorities of the occupation.

The victory in the Elon Moreh case was immense in every respect. It caused a serious crisis in the coalition that nearly resulted in the government disbanding.[100] The leaders of Gush Emunim, who held a meeting the day the judgment was issued, decided to refuse any offer to relocate the settlement.[101] The National Religious Party, from which Gush Emunim had emerged, demanded emergency laws to bypass the judgment. Agriculture minister Sharon demanded legal avenues be identified to "inoculate" the settlements against the court, prompting a confrontation with Attorney General Yitzhak Zamir.[102] The settlers were ultimately offered a new location for Elon Moreh, on public rather than private land, north-east of Nablus on the slopes of Mount Kabir, some five miles from the original site. With the exception of a handful of core settlers who insisted on remaining at the Rujeib plot and were forcibly removed, the group accepted the offer. The relocation did not stop Elon Moreh's settlers from asserting the claim that the new site was also the spot where Abraham had stopped upon entering Canaan.[103]

In the victors' camp, the feeling was not just that history had been made but that they had thrown a serious wrench into the settlement enterprise. Feldman was sure the Elon Moreh case meant the end of settlements in the Occupied Territories. "Anyone who was close to or involved in it knew how important and significant it was. The right wing also saw it as if the whole settlement project was up for debate." But Feldman also considers the Elon Moreh case a major stepping-stone in the process of wrapping the occupation in legalism.

> Suddenly there was a new player in the system. No one knew back then, no one foresaw how pivotal the High Court would become in the fight over the territories. A toxic player, as it turned out later, but we didn't know that at the time. The justices could have done a thousand other things. They could have said, 'This is a political case. It's a political issue and we're not going to intervene.' They said it to us in other cases. Or they could have found another excuse, but no, and it was . . . a very conservative court, very traditional, but with a moral compass. We won the case like you win a regular case. The state makes an argument: security reasons. The argument doesn't hold water, the argument is dismissed.[104]

Khoury, however, was skeptical about the significance of the judgment. "I didn't leave the courtroom with a feeling that the settlements were over. We were witnessing a barrage of declarations of land as state land,"[105] he said, referring to a shift toward building on territory not burdened by the restrictions of private land.

And sure enough, a little over two weeks after the judgment, under pressure from the settlers, the government held a discussion on settlement policy. An argument developed between Sharon, who supported building many more settlement clusters, according to a map he presented, and Weizman, who believed only in expanding existing settlements at that point, and nothing more. The government decided on a compromise.

Sharon's ambitious plan to settle the entire West Bank immediately was rejected, but his position on building new settlements did go through, albeit without specifications: "It is (unanimously) resolved to expand the settlements in Judea, Samaria, the Jordan Valley, the Gaza Strip and the Golan Heights, by increasing the population of existing communities and building new communities on state-owned land."[106] The decision conformed to the Supreme Court's jurisprudence, which had confined its view on settlements to question of interference with private property. If the land is not private, there is no issue, and the security exclusion never need be addressed.

But shifting the focus to non-private, "public" or "state" (as it was called) land created a new problem: the West Bank had limited reserves of such land. Israel would very quickly come up with a conniving legal solution: a new practice of declaring "state land," clearing the way for settlements, which worked as long as one ignored the prohibition on transferring population, as the Supreme Court had conveniently done in its judgments thus far.*

And what about Rujeib? Four years after the last of Gush Emunim were evacuated, a new settlement, Itamar, was built close to the village. It has expanded over the years and today includes some of Rujeib's land. It is still there today.

AVIGDOR FELDMAN

Israel has been blessed with a small community of lawyers who have dedicated their professional lives to cause lawyering. Their numbers might be modest (especially considering how much work they have), but their quality and the central role they play in public life far outweigh their quantity. Rights-oriented lawyers have become familiar figures in Israel since

---

* The drive to apply the classification of "state land" began with the Elon Moreh judgment and continued intensively through the 1980s and the first half of the 1990s. About a million dunams in the West Bank were declared state land, bringing a threefold increase to the reservoir of land considered public ("Under the Guise of Legality: Declarations of State Land in the West Bank," B'Tselem, February 2012, p. 13). As of March 2010, almost 40 percent of West Bank territory considered state land had been allocated by the Civil Administration to the settlement enterprise, and only 0.7 percent to Palestinian needs ("Scope of State Land in the OPT and Its Allocation to Different Entities," figures from a Freedom of Information Petition filed by Bimkom, March 2010, http://bimkom.org/2013/04/3480/ [accessed January 30, 2017] [Hebrew]).

the 1970s, with significant influence in various political circles, mostly left-wing, and there has hardly been a public issue in which they were not involved, usually in a leading position. Many are interesting people, with broad interests and activities, and talents that go beyond their chosen profession. Still, one outshines them all. It is hard to think of a more fascinating, challenging, original, and creative lawyer than Avigdor Feldman.*

The son of Holocaust survivors released from the Auschwitz and Buchenwald death camps at the end of the war, Feldman was called to the Israeli bar in 1974 after an internship with Amnon Zichroni. He had only five years' experience when he won the great Elon Moreh victory with Zichroni and Khoury. In 1984, he left Zichroni's office to pursue a master's degree in human rights law at American University's Washington College of Law with a scholarship from the New Israel Fund. Upon his return he fulfilled his scholarship requirement by working for a year at the Association for Civil Rights in Israel. Having been exposed to the tradition of human rights litigation by organizations in the United States, he worked to convince ACRI that the association should add litigation to its public and educational activities. Despite quite a bit of inside opposition, Feldman finally established the Center for Litigation, marking ACRI's first foray into the legal pursuit of human rights in Israel. Over the years, legal action became central to ACRI's work. Feldman was also one of the founders of B'Tselem—The Israeli Information Center for Human Rights in the Occupied Territories and the Public Committee Against Torture in Israel (PCATI).

When Feldman opened his own practice, he quickly became the most notable lawyer representing Palestinians in Supreme Court petitions and criminal trials, mostly in military courts. Throughout the 1980s, he focused on cases involving Palestinians and challenging occupation practices, from expulsion and torture to land confiscation, family unification, conscientious objection against serving in the Occupied Territories, and settlements. There was almost no issue related to the occupation in which Feldman was not involved. Add to these administrative constitutional cases the fact that he also developed a rich criminal defense practice in trials involving state security, and Feldman emerges as the most prolific of occupation lawyers.

---

* Feldman was my mentor during my legal internship and my employer for five more years, during which I was a lawyer at his office.

Feldman's reputation did not result only from his legal case involvement. He is also a prominent intellectual, an academic who teaches critical courses on law (one focused on Franz Kafka's *The Trial*, another on miscarriage of justice as an unavoidable by-product of the justice system). He writes scholarly essays, prose, and poetry, across genres and published in a wide range of venues: legal journals, activist literature, social media, and the daily press. His philosophy is so critical and subversive that it is aimed at all targets, even his own milieu of civil society organizations, lawyers, judges, and the elitist, pretentious left. But above all, Feldman is a rare orator. His gift for oral argument is so exceptional that it draws crowds to the courtroom who come just to hear him speak. A group of Tel Aviv retirees regularly followed him from case to case in the Tel Aviv District Court to watch him defend and cross-examine. The best show in town, they said, and for free. They would even place bets on the outcome of the cases, but there was no question of who was the best lawyer in Israel. I remember my elation whenever I heard his oratory skill in the courtroom, filling the air with so much tension that it felt as if lightning were about to strike—once because a police officer had breached protocol, once because a ministry official had been particularly cruel, and once because of the dubious morality of the chief of staff himself. When legal philosophers say the judicial process is also therapeutic, I think of the scores or maybe hundreds of Feldman's clients who have left the courtroom feeling that whatever the judges might say, they had already won. His extraordinary capacity to present their pain, his ability to crush the opposition's positions, dismantling them to the point of ridicule, and his construction of his own arguments and the rich intellectual experience observing all this gives his listeners satisfaction that even a court loss cannot erase.

Almost poetically, the Feldman of the podium is entirely different from the Feldman outside the courtroom. Everyone who knows him has experienced this contradiction. The confident man who shines before the bench and courtroom spectators, skillfully navigating between his visible emotion and the feeling he evokes in his listeners, becomes a painfully shy person who appears self-conscious and awkward in ordinary dealings. Those who are close to him always feel as if the courtroom is where he is most comfortable, like the observation about theater actors who can do things onstage that they could never do offstage. It seems to me that the unique warm human sensitivity that characterizes Feldman's court presence is what paralyzes him outside the court. He simply sees too much.

In any event, the Elon Moreh case was Feldman's first that related to the occupation. It is hard to avoid speculation that this great success significantly influenced Feldman's career path. It is no speculation, however, that the victory led young Feldman to believe that the law was the right tool for fighting for the occupied population's human rights, and maybe even against the occupation itself. "This case deluded us into thinking that the court, Landau's court no less, really could take down settlements," he said, years later.[107] "And not just any settlement. One that the settlers viewed as *the* settlement. You have to remember that Elon Moreh wasn't just another place. For the settlers, Elon Moreh was where God made his promise to give the land 'to you and your descendants' and then we won the case. And who won it? Elias Khoury, Zichroni, Feldman, people who have no means of making things happen in any other way. So you say to yourself, 'So . . . it works . . . then it's worth going to court.' "[108]

But as Feldman would learn the hard way, the Elon Moreh case did not finish off the settlement project. It became clear that the victory was nothing more than a mound of dirt in the path of the bulldozer. Memorandums from the attorney general commissioned by the prime minister confirmed that the judgment did not prevent building settlements.[109] Contrary to the public's understanding, Attorney General Yitzhak Zamir said, the High Court had not prohibited building settlements, not even on privately owned land. The court had simply ruled that land seizures must be based on true security need. Also, "As stated, the Elon Moreh judgment does not apply to settlements built on government land," Zamir wrote, "to which there is no impediment. This conclusion is quite significant, as government policy is to generally build new settlements on government land."[110]

Since the court had refused to discuss the application of the prohibition on transferring population into occupied territory—basing its refusal on the argument that Article 49 of the Geneva Convention was only legally binding at the level of international relations and not enforceable under domestic law and in local courts—no legal challenges to settlements built on state land were brought in the years after the Elon Moreh judgment. The right-wing governments of the 1980s were free to build, and the number of settlers in those years increased exponentially. In 1977, only 5,000 settlers lived in the West Bank.[111] By 1983, the number had jumped to 23,700, and by 1995 there were 133,000.[112]

These figures, and the reality behind them, whereby all resources in the occupied land underwent a process of subjugation to the new and growing community of masters at the expense of the locals, were a source of frustration for lawyers representing Palestinians, and drove Feldman simply crazy.

THE UGLY FACE OF NONJUSTICIABILITY

In the early 1990s, a nongovernmental body that had thus far avoided using the court to promote its agenda gained visibility in the fight against the settlements.

Peace Now, Israel's oldest and largest peace organization, was created in 1978 when a group of reserve soldiers and officers wrote a letter to Prime Minister Menachem Begin, calling on him to take advantage of the diplomatic window of opportunity and sign a peace treaty with Egypt, even if it meant giving up conquered territories. They also called on him to avoid building settlements that would stand in the way of peace. The Peace Now movement, which sprang up from this letter, became active against the settlements, which it saw as sowing the seeds of a future disaster. Members demonstrated in front of settlement sites and tried to convince the public that the settlements were an obstacle to peace, particularly between Israel and the Palestinians. The movement engaged in public political action only, including protests, petitions, articles, and media activity.

In 1990, the organization set up a special team to monitor building in the territories. The team was the brainchild of one of Peace Now's founders, Amiram Goldblum, a microbiology professor by day and the sole member of the settlement monitoring team he started in his spare time. This reflected a change of direction for Peace Now, which had until then reacted as issues came up: now it was seeking a more preemptive course of action.[113] The initiative also reflected the belief that if only everyone knew what was going on, political opposition would increase. Goldblum visited construction sites and counted the number of places where groundwork had begun. Peace Now published reports and updates that the Ministry of Housing did everything in its power to hide. Publicizing the numbers was politically significant in the absence of reliable official figures. Over the years, the settlement monitoring team envisioned and established by Goldblum became a major player in challenging the settlement policy and a source of reliable information for anyone interested in the subject.

The research success prompted Peace Now's leaders to consider legal action. After the Elon Moreh judgment and the shift toward building on non-private land (including lands declared "state" lands, as explained), the only argument that had not been decided by the Supreme Court was the prohibition on transferring population to the occupied territory set in Article 49 of the Geneva Convention. Tzali Reshef, a leader and founder of Peace Now and a lawyer, later explained that ACRI had been reluctant to fight the settlements because the issue was "controversial,"[114] thus encouraging Peace Now to take the legal reins.[115]

ACRI's legal counsel, Yehoshua Schoffman, sent Reshef a communication it had received about a plan to build a cemetery for Jerusalem residents in the settlement of Ma'ale Adumim. Reshef filed a petition on behalf of Janet Aviad, another Peace Now leader (represented as a Jerusalem resident who did not want to be buried in the Occupied Territories), and Ghassan al-Khatib, a Palestinian who lived in the area of the planned cemetery. Reshef argued that building a cemetery on occupied land for citizens of the occupying power defied international law as the land was not being used for security purposes. This was a cautious argument, skirting around the prohibition on population transfer. The petition required no hearing to succeed, as the State Attorney's Office, determined that burial was certainly not temporary and therefore could not be sustained, given the "temporary" nature of the occupation. The state attorney at the time, Dorit Beinisch, accepted this position and warned politicians that the case could result in the court reducing the latitude given to settlement activity on non-private land. So the state retracted the plan. This successful attempt boosted Peace Now's confidence and assuaged concerns about taking the legal route.

In the summer of 1991, Goldblum convinced the Peace Now leadership to initiate a public-interest petition to challenge the legality of the entire settlement project. After many conversations with key legal scholars such as David Kretzmer and Yoram Dinstein and journalist and law commentator Moshe Negbi, Goldblum realized that the High Court of

Justice had never actually ruled on the question of whether the settlements were a violation of the prohibition on the transfer of population. It was either naïve or crazy to think that at that point, twenty-four years after the territories had been conquered, with 150,000 Israelis living in the West Bank and Gaza Strip and with settlements being the most controversial political topic in Israeli society, the court would declare them illegal, compelling the evacuation of thousands. But Goldblum was not intimidated by the enormity of the task. He believed that making the argument in court, along with the attention it would garner, was important in and of itself. Besides, Goldblum was forever out to make the world a better place, and progressive activists are innately undeterred by low odds, otherwise they would not be activists in the first place.

So Goldblum went full speed ahead with his all-or-nothing case, enlisting a lawyer who was himself unafraid of legal suicide missions as long as they provided an outlet for rage: Avigdor Feldman. In Feldman, Goldblum found not just an excellent lawyer but a legal activist who was furious by how things had turned out after the Elon Moreh judgment. It was supposed to have been a game changer but was instead a one-off success, strategically insignificant. A decade after the case, Feldman had had his share of battles that ended in disappointment with the High Court's reluctance to intervene on behalf of his Palestinian clients and protect them from the occupation regime. Goldblum had found a lawyer who was not afraid to lose, as long as he got the opportunity to raise his voice in the courtroom and make everyone feel, deep inside, ashamed of their complicity in the crime.

The petition Feldman filed in October 1991, on behalf of Peace Now executive director Gavriel Bargil and the movement itself, said everything that could be said against the settlement enterprise. It raised the prohibition against population transfer as the main argument, taking the position that the norm had become so widely accepted and had sunk such deep roots in the laws of occupation that it had attained customary status and was now binding on domestic courts as well. The petition demanded recognition that Israel was violating the prohibition and de facto annexing occupied land, another violation under international law. Feldman repeated the arguments Khoury had made in the Beit El case that the settlements create irreversible facts and a permanent reality; as such, they contradict the main philosophy underlying the laws of occupation, namely that occupation is temporary and the occupier may not make permanent or long-term changes in the territory.

Feldman even constructed an argument that the generous government housing subsidies offered the settlers exploit the financial hardship experienced by many Israelis for whom emigration to the occupied territory has become the only option for a reasonable quality of life, amounting to their effective forcible transfer.[116] But perhaps Feldman's most innovative argument related to the reality created and sustained in the Occupied Territories as a result of planting members of the occupying community in the area alongside the occupied, who had no rights. "The creation of a large community of Israeli citizens," wrote Feldman, "who live in the held territories and enjoy physical assets, political rights, economic rights, legal rights, and fundamental rights that far outweigh those granted to the Arab residents of the held territories, leads to wrongful discrimination which humiliates the residents of the held territories and creates a social-political system that contradicts the values of the State of Israel as a free and democratic country."[117] The whole kit and caboodle.

The petition filed demanded that the court declare any settlement action not backed by a true security need as unlawful. Being well acquainted with the ideologically motivated settlers and their declarations in the Elon Moreh case, Feldman asked the court to rule that even in the case of "security" settlements, the state must only allow settlers who undertake to leave as soon as the "security reasons expire." He knew that ideological settlers would never agree to such a demand. The court was also asked to declare that using public funds to build settlements constitutes a violation of international law, and that the involvement of civilian housing and development agencies such as the World Zionist Organization and the Jewish Agency was unacceptable. Feldman and Peace Now were going for broke.

From the vantage of time, the petition could appear desperate or naïve. In what possible scenario would the Supreme Court—the same court that sanctioned the concept of settlement in the Beit El and Matityahu cases, that allowed the legal status of dunams and dunams of land to change to serve the settlements, that was, in effect, the state institution that laid the legal groundwork for a colonial occupation that maintains the permanent presence of its own civilians in the occupied land—be expected to put an end to this enterprise? Was it reasonable to imagine that the court would agree to arbitrate the core ideological dispute between Israel's Left and

Right? Did Feldman, Goldblum, and Reshef really believe the High Court of Justice would put a stop to the most significant government policy enacted in Israel's history?

Looking back, Feldman says there was no expectation of a seminal victory. "We went for broke thinking that the High Court of Justice would rule on something out of the whole package of issues we presented." Feldman's comment is noteworthy. The expectation was not to *win* "something" from the "package" of issues brought before the court, but to *get a ruling*. A rather modest hope for a party to a legal proceeding, is it not? The justices are not obligated to rule in favor of a certain party, but they are obligated to rule. In fact, ruling on the questions presented to them is their entire raison d'être as judges. They get paid to decide if A or B is right, if A's argument is legally sound, or perhaps B's. And yet there are cases in which the court would rather avoid a ruling, and the legal strategy then is to do what it takes to get a decision either way, as long as the judges rule.

"It was a win-win situation," says Feldman. "If we win, obviously it's a huge victory. If we lose, then at least there's a judgment that sanctions settlement, with everything that goes with that."[118] Let us linger on this point: Feldman considered a loss, a judicial ruling by an Israeli court that the settlements are legal, would be a step forward in the fight against them and the occupation. In an op-ed he wrote in 2013, Feldman called the High Court of Justice jurisprudence on occupation "the great library of the occupation."[119] This statement goes along with Feldman's theory that the documentation achieved through judgments is a significant contribution of the anti-occupation litigation. "A regime of evil writes itself to oblivion. It leaves behind, with historic generosity, not a paper trail but a highway of words that will feed PhD theses, master's theses, and scholarly conventions until kingdom come," he wrote.

Thus, a court loss would nevertheless contribute to the fight by extracting a detailed confession of injustice from those responsible, even if those details are supplied as a justification and defense (and perhaps especially then). "The history of the occupation is in fact written by the Supreme Court. It produces texts, the judgments, that tell the story of the people who were sitting on the bench. What? They approved the settlements? What, Meir Shamgar, allegedly *the* expert on international law, didn't know the settlements were illegal?"[120]

The State Attorney's Office submitted its response to the petition in December 1991. For the third time in a settlement case (after Beit El and Elon Moreh), the state claimed the court should not hear the petition. In fact, the state's aspiration was the opposite of Feldman's and his clients'. If the petitioners wanted a ruling, the state wanted to avoid one, or so it seemed from the state's arguments. The state asked to dismiss the petition *in limine*, as it "seeks a High Court ruling on issues of policy, which are the purview of other governmental arms."[121] The nonjusticiability argument had been rejected in Elon Moreh and in Beit El. In both cases, the court had ruled that when a case involves questions concerning fundamental rights, such as private property, the fact that it also involves political questions and public controversy does not make it nonjusticiable. "A military administration which seeks to infringe upon individual property rights must present a legal source for doing so and cannot exempt itself from judicial review of its actions on the claim of non-justiciability," Landau wrote in the Elon Moreh case.[122] However, the current petition filed by Peace Now was not based on interference with private property but on the prohibition on population transfer, and, therefore, state lawyers thought this time, they might win the nonjusticiability claim.

On August 25, 1993, several days after news of the agreement signed between Israel and the PLO in Oslo broke in Israeli and international media, the court issued its judgment.

Feldman's and his clients' hopes were dashed.

The court accepted the nonjusticiability tactic lock, stock, and barrel. "In my opinion," Supreme Court president Meir Shamgar wrote, "this petition should be denied, for it is defective in that it relates to questions of policy within the jurisdiction of other branches of a democratic Government, and it raises an issue whose political elements are dominant and clearly overshadow all its legal fragments. The overriding nature of the issue raised in the petition is blatantly political."[123]

The Supreme Court of the 1980s and early 1990s, led by Shamgar and his deputy, Aharon Barak, was at the time the most activist in Israel's history. Its justices did not shy away from repeatedly inserting themselves into delicate matters of church and state, or even into the internal workings of the legislature. They dared to rule that political agreements are subject to judicial review and went so far as to introduce a new cause for administrative intervention, "unreasonableness," which allowed for unprecedented judicial involvement in the actions of the executive branch. Aharon Barak, who took over the Supreme Court presidency from Shamgar in 1996, was renowned for the slogan attributed to him by his detractors: "everything is justiciable." The Supreme Court's judicial activism dragged it into a colossal battle with the executive branch, with politicians harshly criticizing what they perceived as the liberties the court took to intervene in matters under the purview of other state authorities, defying the prevailing constitutional order. Conservative jurists also disapproved of the court's "lack of restraint," as they saw it. The court's character and the degree to which it intervened in policy matters was a controversial topic and the subject of bitter dispute. And now, all of a sudden, at the height of this activist trend, the Supreme Court justices managed to find one topic where they were able to exercise great restraint, control, and judicial passivity: the settlements.

It is not that they thought they had no answer anchored in law to the question of the legality of the settlement project. Justice Eliezer Goldberg, who presided over the Peace Now case along with Shamgar, wrote that the matter must be ruled nonjusticiable "not because we lack the legal tools to give judgment, but because a judicial determination, which does not concern individual rights, should defer to a political process of great importance and great significance."[124]

The same court, with the same president, just two weeks after rejecting the Peace Now petition for nonjusticiability, infuriated Prime Minister Yitzhak Rabin by ruling that he had to fire Minister of Interior Aryeh Deri because he had been indicted on charges of bribery, though no law requires firing an accused minister.[125] Two years later, the same court declared that it had the power to repeal legislation it thought contradicted the protection afforded to fundamental rights in two recently enacted basic laws. The judgment that declared this new power expressed Barak's view that the two basic laws in question had brought a "constitutional revolution."[126] Yet the same court that was accused of judicial imperialism had dodged a ruling on the legality of the settlements. The Peace Now case showed that the court's glorious conquests ended at the Green Line.

In its evasive maneuvers to avoid ruling on the legality of the settlements, the court not only departed from its own judicial activism, but it created an enclave of nonjusticiability within the universe of justiciability. To escape giving a ruling, the justices relied on two lines of reasoning, ones that hardly conform to the court's professed loyalty to liberal values and the protection of human rights. The first involved Justice Goldberg's argument that the issue before the court did not "concern individual rights." The Peace Now petition was entirely based on the apartheid-like reality the settlements created in the Occupied Territories (even if the phrase did not appear in the petition). It spoke of the harm to the equality and dignity of the occupied population, which is forced to live in conditions of systemic, structural discrimination, without rights, alongside a community of people who do enjoy rights, connections, power, and all the resources of the occupied land. How can it seriously be said that the petition did "not concern individual rights"? True, it was not based on the property rights of specific individuals but on the argument that the general policy creates a systemic structure of institutional discrimination of one national group by and for the benefit of the other. It is difficult to think of an argument more pertinent to human rights. Goldberg's position that building settlements on public land, with all the attendant ramifications for every aspect of Palestinian life, is not a human rights issue because the land has not been confiscated is akin to saying that the "separate but equal" approach to education was not a human rights issue because nothing had been taken from the segregated group. This is a kind of argument the justices would have said "should not have been made in the first place."

Second, the justices suggested that even if there were a legal aspect to the settlement issue, the petition's "dominant" elements were political and therefore must be left for a diplomatic or political process. But this ignores the fact that the West Bank and Gaza Strip are under occupation, and only Israeli citizens have the civil and political rights that allow them to influence decision making, while the millions of Palestinians are denied any influence over settlement policy. In this context, placing emphasis on the diplomatic-political process as the appropriate venue for deciding the fate of the settlements means giving a seal of approval to an undemocratic, discriminatory political system. Thus, Shamgar's reference to "democratic government" in his reasoning is particularly aggravating. What democracy was he talking about?

The truth is that the court probably knew that a genuine, exhaustive judicial deliberation of the issues raised in the petition would inevitably lead to one of two outcomes, and the justices were not prepared to pay the price of either. One would have been the significant restriction of Israel's settlement activity. This would have made the court the object of unprecedented attacks from Israel's right wing, the intensity of which would have probably severely undermined the court's status and power. The second would have been to dismiss the petition on its merits, to decide that the prohibition on transferring population did not apply to Israel's control over the West Bank and Gaza Strip, that the prohibition was not customary, or that settlements and emigration of Israelis did not constitute "transfer." Taking this path would have compromised the court's standing in the international legal community. It had been more than a decade since the court had ruled on these issues, and since then the legal and political consensus that the prohibition on population transfer does apply to the Israeli occupation and that settlements are a serious breach had gained significant momentum. An Israeli judicial finding to the contrary would have undoubtedly raised some eyebrows and quickly turned into a bit of a joke. A jurist of Shamgar's stature would not have jeopardized his reputation in this way.

This was exactly the corner into which Avidgor Feldman wanted to push the court: either do the right thing or make another contribution to the great book of the occupation, the library of evil, and sign your name to it. Justice Goldberg seemed to refer to that trap in the conclusion to his judgment: "The petitioners have the right to place a 'legal mine' at the court's threshold, but the court should not step on a mine that will shake its foundations, which are the public's confidence in it."[127] Nonjusticiability was the escape route from the petition's legal guerrilla attack—an inelegant, immoral escape route, but an effective one.

TO LITIGATE OR NOT TO LITIGATE

The judgment in the Peace Now case put an end to efforts to challenge the legality of the settlement project head-on in the court. The settlements had been granted asylum in the shape of nonjusticiability. They officially became the only entity in Israel that is neither above nor beneath the law but beside it. The justices held on to nonjusticiability as if it were a lifeboat in a stormy sea, and the few attempts made to revisit the issue in some creative way were abruptly dismissed. In 1998, Feldman and I represented five villages in an area known as E1, east of Jerusalem, in a challenge to a master plan approved for a vast new neighborhood in Ma'ale Adumim, on public land designated for the future development of the five villages.

According to the master plan, the neighborhood was meant to alleviate a severe housing shortage in Jerusalem and serve its economic needs. We attempted to attack the plan without resorting to the prohibition on population transfer, using the argument that the laws of occupation prohibit exploitation of occupied territories for the economic needs of the occupying power. This is a fundamental principle in the international laws of war, and the High Court of Justice has acknowledged it in its jurisprudence.[128] Accepting this argument in the context of building and expanding settlements would have restricted civilian development in them only to cases in which it could be demonstrated that there was no economic benefit to Israel.

The court dismissed the petition, citing the Peace Now case. Justices Eliyahu Mazza, Mishael Cheshin, and Tova Strasberg-Cohen took refuge in the comforting embrace of nonjusticiability, latching onto the peace process between Israel and the PLO to once again avoid making a decision: "The issue of Israeli settlement is one of the topics being discussed by Israel and the PLO in negotiations for a permanent arrangement. The fate of Israeli settlements in the area will be decided in the arrangements reached. The court need not address this issue whilst diplomatic negotiations are taking place, and indirectly intrude upon the map-drawing process. This is clearly the role of the government and its various arms."[129] This was not the only case in which the court recruited the peace process in order to avoid granting relief to Palestinian petitioners.

Is it right (it is certainly tempting) to accuse the justices, who for four decades failed to stop the settlement enterprise, of cowardice? Or must we accept that the legal battle against the main axis of the Israeli occupation brought the petitioners to the edge of the judicial world, a place where the justices, like Samson, could well lose their hair? In other words, is it true, as Shamgar maintained, that ruling on an issue with conspicuously political dimensions, on a topic that divides the nation and defines its political camps, would force the court dramatically to exceed the mandate society has given it? Or, as Goldberg claimed, would such a ruling amount to a suicide mission that no judicial authority concerned with its survival should take? It is hard to counter the notion that when Feldman petitioned the court to reverse the tide of twenty-five years of settlement and more than a hundred thousand settlers, he was asking the justices to be superheroes.

Still, a number of points do put a dent in the justices' desperate justifications. First, in the days when the settlement project was still young, stopping it with legal tools would not have exacted the heavy social, political, and perhaps even constitutional price the court came to fear so much in the 1990s and after. At the time of Elon Moreh and Beit El, and certainly during the early challenge of Rafah Approach, the court could have put an end to the clear violation of international law, when the operative repercussions would have been quite limited.

Second, even if we accept the apocalyptic scenario of the court's fate had it ruled the settlements unlawful, the notion that the justices had only two options is not persuasive. In fact, the panel presiding over the Peace Now case could have, even without declaring every last settlement unlawful, set limits on the settlement project, restricted the government's investment and encouragement, clearly articulated the settlements' temporary nature, or produced a framework for the temporary status of the Israelis living in them. Shamgar's court could have done all this without ordering the evacuation of all existing settlements. It chose not to, in a choice made of free will.

Third, and perhaps most important: the court of the 1980s and 1990s was an activist institution that elected to spend its political capital by intervening in the fight between the branches of government over matters that were important to Israel's upper middle class, such as religious coercion and government corruption, especially after the political shift of 1977. The justices made a choice to use their limited power in this way. Even if we accept that the court could not fight the government on several fronts simultaneously, the justices had the option of setting their priorities differently. They could have decided that the most urgent moral, ethical, and legal claim on their constitutional power was Israel's undemocratic control over millions of rightless Palestinians rather than the liberties of Israel's upper class.

The political, historical evidence shows that choosing the second option allowed the court to form an alliance with Israel's elite, which in return protected it from harm by those on the losing side of its judgments. The first option would have benefited people who have practically no political power. This might explain the choices the court made as an institution. But still, is this not the ultimate judicial mission, to protect the disempowered, the rightless? And if both fights cannot be fought at once, shouldn't the preference be to protect those who have no ability to protect themselves? In the end, the court, as an institution, chose to absorb the anger unleashed in religious circles when it defended the right of secular people to watch movies on the Sabbath and eat nonkosher food rather than face the wrath of the right wing had it been more active in limiting the settlements.

Reviewing the legal conflict over the settlements, it is hard to imagine a more colossal failure. In the most important battle of the occupation fought in Israeli courts, directed against the one policy with the harshest, most long-term effects—the settlements—the only achievement was to restrict the use of private land. And even this, which should not be taken lightly, was massively diluted by the system of declaring state land (also upheld by the High Court of Justice), which transformed more than a million dunams of private land into public land during the 1980s. If Gush Emunim and Israel's government fathered the settlement project, the High Court of Justice was its godfather.

Then again, some other important outcomes cannot be ignored. Thanks to the legal proceedings, the process of building and expanding settlements became more transparent, and the public received more information about how and why it was pursued, making it perhaps the most well documented and thoroughly reported crime of Israel's occupation. The proceedings also provided a platform for drafting a manifesto against the crime of settlements (peaking with Feldman's petition on behalf of Peace Now). This manifesto was used for other proceedings and later by the political movement fighting Israel's colonization of the Occupied Territories. The High Court cases also helped brand the settlements as one of the worst violations of the fundamental rights of the Palestinians living under occupation.

In many ways, the courtroom became one of the most important centers of protest against the settlement project. The hearings drew both local and international media attention, fostered a debate over the various dimensions of harm the settlements wreak on Palestinians, and forced the government to lift the veil of security from the endeavor. Finally, the challenge in court also exacted a political price by forcing the government to articulate its settlement policy according to the court's schedule, when the timing was not always politically convenient, thus compelling it to find some midpoint between the settlers' eagerness and the more moderate approach of the political center.

What about the Israeli public? Justice Landau was correct when he wrote in the Elon Moreh judgment that "the wider public will not heed the legal reasoning, only the final conclusion." By declining to intervene in building settlements on public land, the court sent a message that there were legal ways to establish settlements. Limiting their creation to public land allowed the illusion that Israel respects Palestinians' rights. Israel tried to sell this illusion in international circles and failed miserably, but its own public's belief in it was, at certain points, a major price paid for litigating against settlements. Over time, however, with growing international discussion about the settlements and findings by international bodies that they are a legal violation and a daily assault on Palestinians' fundamental rights, it appears that the price has dwindled. Israelis now know that their government stands alone against the entire world on this issue.

This list of failures and achievements begs us to ask, "What if?" What if Khoury, Feldman, Zichroni, and others had not taken the legality of the settlements to the Supreme Court? What if the court had declared it nonjusticiable early on without waiting twenty years? Are the results of what might be over-litigation worse than its absence? Israel's human rights community and its activity every day in the High Court is the answer. Even if the decision to take the fight to court was made without exhaustive strategic consideration, the fact is the organizations prefer to use litigation rather than leave the courtroom empty. Their challenges to the settlements' legality have never stopped, not even after the nonjusticiability blow dealt in the Peace Now case. The front door may have been shut, but human rights organizations have continued to bang on every window, chimney, and air vent not sealed off by the court. Five years after the Peace Now petition, the legal battle continued, now against unauthorized outposts—settlements built without official approval but with the authorities' generous help, a subject to which I shall return at length. Here, too, the court was prepared to grant relief only in cases pertaining to private property, blatantly ignoring other hardships inflicted by the outposts and claiming they were a political issue. Again, the main achievements of the litigation were information, protest, public discourse, and (sometimes heavy) political damage.

We cannot assess the wisdom of the legal fight against the settlements without acknowledging the support it gave to the political forces opposing the settlements as well as the support it received in return. Would the litigation have yielded a different result had those forces been stronger or more determined? Litigation on such obviously public issues is always an aid to a movement, bringing its values to court. Litigation can help a public movement, providing tools and information. It can also compel the authorities to make a decision or take a position. But it is not the main tool for change: it cannot replace a public movement and is rarely able to effect clear social change without one.

Given that all Israeli governments have built settlements and invested in them, on both the right and the ostensible left, the view that all settlement is wrong and illegal exists only on the political margins. Thus, the court has had trouble mustering the necessary courage to adopt such a position, just as it would have been unrealistic to expect a judicial ruling in favor of same-sex marriage in the United States if neither political camp supported it. So court proceedings cannot be considered a first-order tool for social change, that is, one that could tip the scale in favor of change. Instead, and especially when the remedy sought goes against the political grain, legal action is a second-order tool, one that can help change the political trend. The outcomes of such legal battles create new ways to fortify the camp that is seeking change.

This is why it is dangerous to assess "what if" in legal terms only. The role the legal battle played in bolstering opposition to the settlements (even without decisive wins) is difficult to gauge. It is impossible to know how much weaker the opposition might have been without the information that came to light thanks to the litigation, the manifesto it produced, and the spotlight it put on the settlements.

And besides, the fight isn't over.

4

Against Torture

THE PICTURE OF THE BAD COP

Since the start of the occupation of the West Bank and the Gaza Strip, thousands of Palestinians have been tortured in the interrogation rooms of the Shabak, Israel's secret service.* "Thousands" is a careful estimate. It may well be tens of thousands. Use of physical measures against detainees, such as forcing them to sit in painful positions for long periods of time, sleep deprivation, exposure to extreme cold and incessant noise, hooding for hours and days, painful binding, violent shaking to the point where detainees lose consciousness, and "ordinary" beatings and choke holds were daily staples for Palestinian interrogees. Along with these measures and others like them, Palestinian detainees were also subjected to psychological torture such as threats to hurt them or their family members and various types of humiliating and degrading treatment.

If the settlements are the most significant and most lasting crime of the Israeli occupation, torture is the most heinous. Torture is a grave crime that has no exigent circumstances. The many individuals who have perpetrated it over the years remain free, none having been held accountable for their actions. Shamefully, torture still goes on in twenty-first-century Israel, even if to a much lesser degree both in terms of frequency and the types of torture used than in the past. The great decrease in the use of

---

* "Shabak" is the Hebrew acronym for Sherut Habitachon Haklali, or General Security Service, Israel's internal security service. It is also referred to as the Shin Bet.

torture is almost exclusively the result of the steadfast legal campaign waged against it.

The legal challenge against torture in Israel is as old as the country's use of it. Initially, given the Shabak's sweeping denial that torture was used, legal efforts focused on proving that it was. Later, after exposure of the fact that it had been used and lied about for years, the practice itself was directly challenged by Israel's human rights community in a series of intense legal proceedings aimed at declaring torture illegal and prohibited.

Just as torture forms a dark and shameful chapter in Israel's history, the legal fight to end it is a serious contender as the country's most successful campaign of human rights litigation.

The story of this fight could begin at a number of different points. We might, for instance, start with the many criminal trials heard by the military courts in which defendants tried to convince the judges that the main proof of their guilt—a confession signed during their interrogation—had been extracted from them using torture. Or we could focus on the Shabak interrogators who, in the sixteen years between 1971 and 1986, testified in countless trials that no one had touched the defendants during interrogation and that the confessions were a result of their incredible investigative prowess or of the suspects' overwhelming guilt, which compelled them to confess. Instead, we could open with the immense frustration felt by lawyers who, over the years, represented scores, hundreds, of Palestinian defendants who all gave disturbingly similar descriptions of the many measures used on them during their interrogations, yet faced a brick wall of Shabak interrogators who accused their clients of hallucinations and judges who never, not once, favored their clients' accounts over that of the Shabak. Indeed, we could turn the spotlight onto the military judges, the officers who sent Palestinian defendants to years in prison after rejecting their allegations of torture. The judges went on dismissing their claims even though they sat trial over many people from different parts of the Occupied Territories, members of different political and organizational groups, who all spoke of the small chair with the sawed-off front legs in which they were forced to sit, tied, in a painful position, for hours; who all talked about the stinking sack pulled over their heads, which, together with sleep deprivation, caused disorientation and mental distress; who all had accounts of being slapped and punched; forced to sit in a "frog" crouch, on the tips of their toes, for varying periods of time or in the "banana" position, where their wrists and ankles were tied behind their backs, and more. The judges heard and chose not to believe, although undoubtedly in some cases, believed but chose to say they didn't.[1]

Or we could begin with the day that something happened that would set in motion a chain of events ultimately tearing down the false façade. This downfall would finally, after many years, allow a change in the discussion on torture in Israel: no longer whether detainees were being tortured but whether this was legal and moral. By coincidence or, more likely, not, the crack in the wall of lies surrounding what went on in the Shabak's interrogation rooms began with an unusual case in which an IDF officer was the victim of torture. By coincidence or, more likely, not, the officer was not Jewish but Circassian. His name was Izzat Nafsu.

In the early 1980s, Izzat Nafsu served in Lebanon as a liaison between the IDF and various Lebanese militias. He was arrested on suspicion of having contact with Palestinian elements in Lebanon that he did not report. Nafsu was interrogated by the Shabak and convicted by a court-martial in 1982 of a number of serious crimes, including treason, espionage, and aiding the enemy in its fight against Israel. The conviction was entirely based on Nafsu's confession during the interrogation that he had met with a senior Fatah leader in Lebanon and supplied his organization with weapons. Nafsu was sentenced to eighteen years in prison.

During his court-martial, Nafsu said his confession had been extracted using torture. His interrogators used violence, including shaking him, pulling his hair, pushing him to the ground, kicking, and slapping. He testified he had been deprived of sleep by being forced to stand for hours in the holding facility yard, and that he had been forced to take ice-water showers. Nafsu said the Shabak interrogators insulted him, threatened to arrest his mother and wife, and even blackmailed him using personal information they had on him. At Nafsu's trial, the Shabak interrogators denied everything he said. After his conviction, in late June 1986, his appeal filed in the Military Court of Appeals was also rejected. All the military judges, in both instances, ruled he had concocted the allegations against the Shabak interrogators.

By sheer coincidence, around the time his appeal was rejected, the Knesset had passed an amendment to the Military Justice Law that was meant to allow, in exceptional cases, a second appeal against decisions made by the military court system, this time to Israel's Supreme Court—in other words, a civilian instance. The amendment introduced a right to file a motion for leave to appeal against a military court judgment, and it gave the Supreme Court president the power to decide when such leave would be granted. After the rejection by the Military Court of Appeals, Nafsu was among the first to file a motion for leave to appeal to the Supreme Court, pursuant to the new amendment. President Meir Shamgar granted his motion, and the hearing was scheduled for May 1987.

At the same time, prior to the hearing of Nafsu's second appeal by the Supreme Court, the country was up in arms over an explosive national controversy dubbed "the Shabak affair." What seemed entirely unrelated to Nafsu's case was about to save the Circassian officer from his long incarceration and open up a Pandora's box. The importance of this event merits attention.

The details of the Shabak affair read as if they were lifted straight from a conspiracy theory. In fact, the affair deserves (and got) its own book.[2] It began on the night between April 12 and 13, 1984, when an IDF unit, under the command of Brigadier General Yitzhak Mordechai, the chief paratroops officer, stormed a number 300 bus that had been hijacked by four young Palestinians armed with knives. The press initially reported that all four hijackers had been killed in the rescue mission, but three days later, in defiance of the military censor, the daily *Hadashot* reported that two of the hijackers had been brought out of the bus alive.[3] Two days after that, *Hadashot* published a photograph of the two hijackers, standing outside the bus, handcuffed and in the custody of two Shabak agents.[4] The image, shot by photojournalist Alex Levac, proved that the two hijackers had not been killed during the rescue but had been captured and no longer represented a danger. It caused an uproar. The bloodcurdling truth was that the head of the Shabak, Avraham Shalom, had ordered the service's senior agent on the scene, Ehud Yatom, to liquidate the two hijackers who had been captured alive, and a Shabak team commanded by Yatom executed the chief's orders. They took the hijackers to a secluded field and beat them to death with rocks and an iron bar.

This sordid truth was about to be exposed, given the media reports that two of the hijackers had been taken out of the bus alive. Under pressure from the public and the attorney general, Defense Minister Moshe

Arens was compelled to appoint a commission of inquiry to look into the deaths of the two men. But Avraham Shalom was determined to prevent exposure of the truth, which would undoubtedly have led to his dismissal and perhaps even his prosecution, since the killing of the hijackers while in custody was nothing short of murder. He demanded to have his own man appointed to the commission of inquiry, which was headed by a retired IDF general, Meir Zorea. Shalom's demand was met. The man he chose for the mission was Yossi Ginosar, a veteran Shabak interrogator.

To keep the commission from learning the truth, Ginosar acted as a Trojan horse.[5] He reported the commission's internal discussions back to his friends in the agency every night and helped coordinate the agency's officers' testimonies about their role in the affair. The Shabak added insult to injury by pointing a finger at Brigadier General Mordechai as the man responsible for the hijackers' death, testifying that they saw him beat them. Though the Zorea Commission completed its work without conclusive findings and without determining where the responsibility lay, Mordechai remained the prime suspect in the killings, both legally and to the public.

In any event, the web of lies, witness tampering, and interference with the investigation proved disastrous for the Shabak. The agency was consumed by the task of keeping up its deception, and its officers soon learned the truth my mother taught me as a child: every lie inevitably leads to another lie until you have to create the whole world all over again. The Zorea Commission was succeeded by a commission of jurists headed by Jerusalem district attorney Yona Blatman. The lies and deceit continued there, too. The Shabak continued to hide its actions and give testimony that cast suspicion on Mordechai. Avraham Shalom had to constantly make sure that the men who had been directly involved in the affair maintained their lies, that people who had not been involved but knew what had happened continued to keep the secret, and that the weaker links would not break. Feeding and protecting the lie became a consuming mission for the Shabak's leadership, which had become entangled in its own fantastic web. At the same time, many in the agency were horribly afraid that a senior military officer might take the fall for something he had not done, leading some to have moral compunctions. The officer, Mordechai, was eventually brought before a major general for disciplinary action but was acquitted.

About a year and a half after the incident, three senior Shabak officials who had been aware of the conspiracy, the deputy head and two division heads, decided to demand Shalom's resignation. Shalom staunchly refused. The deputy head, Reuven Hazak, then went to the prime minister, Shimon Peres, with the whole truth of what had happened. To Hazak's amazement, Peres gave him the cold shoulder, and Hazak was ultimately forced to leave the agency.[6] The second in command, Peleg Radai, was shunned by Shalom, to the point where he, too, decided to leave, and the third official, Rafi Malka, was dismissed by Shalom after another division head said that Malka was speaking ill of him.[7]

In early 1986, Hazak met with Dorit Beinisch, the deputy state attorney, who wondered why the shoo-in for the top position in the Shabak had decided to retire just as he had been about to receive the appointment. Hazak shared the truth with her, and Beinisch was flabbergasted. This led to a meeting among Hazak, Radai, Malka, and Attorney General Yitzhak Zamir in which he, too, was made privy to the entire story. In May 1986, the affair returned to the headlines with reports, limited by censorship, that the attorney general had ordered an investigation into a "senior official."[8] Days later, after the senior official's identity was published abroad, circumventing Israeli censorship, the Israeli public learned that he was none other than the head of the Shabak.

For a month, more and more details were leaked about the suspicions that had led the attorney general to make the unusual (and courageous) decision, in any regime, to pursue a criminal investigation against the head of the secret service. The public learned how the hijackers had been killed, that the work of the investigative commissions had been sabotaged, and that a senior military officer had almost been framed for murder. Zamir's term as attorney general was not extended. He had announced his intention to step down even before the affair blew up, and the government used his announcement to appoint a successor, Justice Yosef Harish, midway through handling the affair.

It all ended with Shalom's resignation and a pardon by the president, at Peres's request, of Shalom, Ginosar, Yatom, and several other Shabak officers, including the agency's legal counsel, who had either been involved in the murder or in the cover-up. A High Court petition against the pardon, which was granted even before an indictment had been served, was dismissed.[9] The police continued investigating the affair after the pardon was given, mainly because of Avraham Shalom's contention that he had received the order to kill the hijackers from Yitzhak Shamir, prime minister at the time of the incident. A legal team that included Yehudit Karp, a senior attorney in the Attorney General's Office; Edna Arbel, who later became the state prosecutor; and Itzhak Elyasuf, a deputy attorney general, published a final report on the affair in December 1987, accepting Shamir's denial that he gave the order to kill the hijackers. The report included a statement attributed to one of the implicated Shabak officers, Ginosar, that hiding the facts from the Zorea Commission was not unusual conduct for the Shabak. This was a most troubling statement, and yet it did not fully open the Shabak's can of worms.

As THESE EVENTS were unfolding, Izzat Nafsu was waiting for his appeal to be heard before the Supreme Court. At that point, Nafsu was represented by two skilled and experienced defense lawyers. Zvi Hadar, who had served as military advocate general, represented him in military court, and, as defense counsel, examined the Shabak agents who vehemently denied having harmed his client. For Nafsu's appeal at the Supreme Court, Aryeh Kamar, a well-known veteran lawyer with a lot of experience in security cases, both as a senior state prosecutor and as a defense attorney, joined the legal team. Just at this time, Ginosar's identity was exposed in connection with the Bus 300 scandal. The press initially referred to him as "G," but somewhere along the line his full name and even his picture were published. This was about to change Nafsu's fate dramatically.

When Hadar saw Ginosar's picture in the media, an alarm bell went off. He identified Ginosar as the person who had headed the team that interrogated his client Nafsu.[10] The fact that Ginosar had deceived the Zorea Commission, tampered with testimonies in the Bus 300 scandal, and thought that dishonesty was no aberration in the Shabak significantly boosted Nafsu's claim that his interrogators were lying, not he; that he had confessed under torture; that he, not his interrogators, should be believed.

Hadar and Kamar sent an urgent letter to State Attorney Harish. How could any credence be given to the Shabak's claims that Nafsu had not been tortured?

This chain of events was reported to the military advocate general, seeing as it was the military that had prosecuted Nafsu. The MAG, Amnon Shtrasnov, ordered a comprehensive review of the Nafsu file. The military might have handled the case against Nafsu, its officers having served the indictment and held the trial, but the military had not carried out the interrogation; the Shabak had. With the Supreme Court hearing less than a month away, information started leaking to the press about the serious findings uncovered in Shtrasnov's review. "There are many doubts surrounding the credibility of the testimonies given in the case," the press reported.[11] The public was outraged. It was the second incident within a year that cast grave doubts on the Shabak's integrity.

On June 24, 1987, Nafsu, his defense counsel, and the military attorneys arrived at the Supreme Court. In a dramatic move that would destroy the Shabak's ability to avoid scrutiny of its methods of operation, the MAG notified the bench, presided over by Supreme Court president Meir Shamgar, that:

> Following an examination conducted by the Shabak at its own initiative, after objections and doubts were raised with regard to the entire affair within the agency . . . and following questioning I personally conducted during the past month since I was apprised of the findings of the Shabak examination, new evidence and facts have been revealed and the following doubts arose in the matter at hand. . . . Most of the claims made by the defendant at the voir-dire about the pressure exerted on him to confess, and which, he argues, affected his free will, with the exception of direct means of violence, such as kicks and slaps, were examined and found to be fundamentally correct.[12]

And so Shtrasnov told the court that Nafsu's allegations about his interrogation were true, meaning that the Shabak agents who denied it were lying. Indeed, Shtrasnov declared before the court that the agents had perjured themselves in Nafsu's trial: "The testimony of the Shabak interrogators in the court of the first instance, denying use of undue pressure, were not truthful. Except for their contention that there was no hitting or slapping, most of the appellant's claims regarding the conduct of the investigation have been validated."[13]

The parties notified the court that they had reached a settlement that would reverse the military court's judgment while Nafsu would plead guilty to the offense of exceeding authority to the point of posing a threat to the state (he had stumbled upon a Fatah member in Lebanon, who later tried—and failed—to blackmail him, and he failed to report this to his superiors). In keeping with the plea bargain, the Supreme Court reversed Nafsu's most serious conviction, convicted him of the lighter offense, and cut his prison sentence from eighteen to two years. Since he had already served seven and a half years, Nafsu was immediately released.

In its judgment, the Supreme Court addressed the seriousness of the information that had come to light, but a reading of the judgment reveals that the bench was mostly concerned by the lies, not by the torture:

> Nothing can detract from the gravity of this conclusion, which points to these witnesses' dereliction of their duty to speak truthfully when testifying before a judicial instance. These actions constitute a severe blow to the credibility of the agents of the aforesaid arm of the state. The court was thereby deprived of the ability to decide the case of the appellant on the basis of true information, and the status and force of the court that was misled by the statements of the interrogators have been compromised. The reprehensible acts revealed in this case, which led the court to make findings and conclusions based on confessions obtained in a manner on which the court was misinformed, require decisive measures to uproot such practices. We direct the attention of the attorney general to this matter. . . . We are also given to understand, from the words of learned counsel for the state, that an examination by a special team is now underway regarding the methods of interrogation employed by the Shabak. The present case illustrates the urgency and importance of this matter.[14]

This was such a momentous blow to the Shabak that even Israeli society, which usually worships its security agencies, could not just carry on as if nothing had happened. The media reflected the general sentiment that a full inquiry must probe the extent of the agency's lies. How many times had interrogators lied to the court? How many government authorities had they deceived? Besides, the finding of perjury in the Nafsu case demanded a criminal investigation. There was no way out.

But was there?

A week later, in an effort to appease the public, and instead of a criminal investigation, the government decided to appoint a state commission of inquiry. Israeli law provides several tools for investigating issues of national importance: parliamentary commissions of inquiry, government commissions of inquiry, police investigations, and state comptroller reviews. But the most powerful investigative body is a state commission of inquiry. Although the government plenum is empowered to establish such commissions, the commission members are appointed by the president of the Supreme Court. According to the law, the commission of inquiry is to be chaired by a serving or retired Supreme Court or District Court judge. A state commission of inquiry has broad powers that include summoning witnesses, compelling answers to questions, issuing search and disclosure warrants, and punishing those who fail to comply. The commission also has the liberty to deviate from the evidence and procedural laws that apply to courts. These commissions have gained a reputation in Israel as strong, independent bodies, and governments do whatever they can to avoid appointing them when it comes to probing their own work. The letter of appointment of the commission established by the government after the Nafsu affair defined its area of inquiry as follows:

[T]he matter of the Shabak methods of interrogation regarding Hostile Terrorist Activity [HTA] is—in the wake of Criminal Appeal 124/78 [Nafsu]—a subject of vital public importance at this time which requires elucidation. Therefore, the government decided: To establish a commission of inquiry . . . regarding the investigation methods and procedures of the GSS on HTA, and the giving of testimony in court in connection with these investigations. The commission will make recommendations and proposals as it sees fit, also regarding the appropriate methods and procedures concerning these investigations in the future, while taking into account the unique needs of the struggle against Hostile Terrorist Activity.[15]

The president of the Supreme Court selected the members of the commission. It is hard to imagine a more prestigious group: Moshe Landau, a former president of the Supreme Court; state comptroller Justice Yaakov Maltz; and reserve major general Yitzhak Hofi, the former head of the Mossad, Israel's foreign espionage agency, and a member of the Palmach, the elite fighting unit of the pre-state underground army.[16] Given the scope of the investigation, the inquiry presented a rare opportunity to erase the shame of torture from Israel's investigative apparatus.

NO SUCH THING AS LEGAL TORTURE

Let's spend a moment on torture in Israel and torture in general.

Human rights philosophy, and international human rights law in its footsteps, recognize very few absolute rights. Most rights have exceptions. As US Supreme Court justice Oliver Wendell Holmes famously said, even the broadest protection of free speech would not allow a person to falsely cry "Fire!" in a theater full of people.[17] Even the mother of all rights, the right to life, has exceptions. A clear example is self-defense. Every legal system accepts the taking of a life in circumstances of self-defense. Another example is the fact that combatants may kill enemy combatants under international law, including in circumstances that do not involve self-defense. These are just two consensually accepted exceptions (there are also the disputed exceptions, such as euthanasia, the death penalty, and abortion).

Since humans are social beings, and their lives involve constant interaction, one person's right is necessarily a restriction of another person's liberty: a person's right to property is a restriction on another's liberty to use this property without permission. A person's right to privacy is a restriction on others from invading this privacy. In fact, any recognition of a right is necessarily a restriction of a freedom, and recognition of an absolute right is the imposition of an absolute restriction, which is one of the reasons why absolute rights are so rare. Also, the recognition of absolute rights creates a hierarchy between absolute and non-absolute rights, with the former preferred over the latter in case of a clash. The more absolute rights that are recognized, the greater the risk of irreconcilable clashes between them. For example, it is impossible to recognize both the right to health and the right to property as absolute rights; if the former is absolute, those who have means must be taxed to fund health care for those who have not, in which case the right to property is no longer absolute. Or, to respect the right to property of those who have it, no taxes should be extracted, which amounts to sacrificing the right to health of those who do not have the means to buy health services, making this right non-absolute. There is no way to uphold both these rights fully.

In this sense, the notion of absolute rights is almost an oxymoron: the more absolute rights are recognized, the more absolute restrictions would have to be imposed, chipping away at liberties, which then become non-absolute.

One right that has attained absolute status is the right to be free of slavery and servitude. Slavery—the ownership of one person by another—is as old as humanity. Servitude is complete subjugation to another person, even without ownership. A dedicated campaign by one of the first international human rights movements during the Age of Enlightenment made slavery, servitude, and forced labor illegal in most countries in the world. The legal restrictions imposed on individuals (and states) to protect the right to remain free of slavery, servitude, and forced labor involve prohibitions on recognizing human beings as property, on human trafficking, and on holding people in servitude by force (and even by consent, as a way of paying back a financial debt, for example). When these rights were included in the UN International Covenant on Civil and Political Rights in 1966, the first two—freedom from slavery and servitude—were phrased in absolute terms, with no exceptions. But on the prohibition on forced labor, drafters had to introduce an exception: compulsory military service. However compulsory military (and even civic) service might be framed, it is nonetheless a type of forced labor, if not actual servitude. And so the international community found an exception even to this right.[18]

The right not to be subjected to torture is, like slavery, one of the very few rights that are absolute. Torturing people to extract confessions out of them or others, along with cruelty, inhuman treatment, and degradation as a means of punishment or revenge are, also like slavery, horrifying practices that are as old as humanity itself. Torture is meant to achieve a purpose that puts it at the top of the heap of inhumane acts: obliterating the autonomy of the victim, turning him or her into a vessel stripped of independence and ready to meet the torturer's every demand. This state is achieved by inflicting physical or mental pain at a level that creates complete subjugation, along with humiliation and degradation. Given this effect, it seems that aside from slavery, torture is the worst possible assault on the essence of humanness that lies in every person. Once torture peels away a person's ability to choose and decide how to act, through physical or mental pain, that person becomes a puppet, controlled by others; one of the features that makes this person human is fatally wounded. A

Kantian way of putting it would be to say that torture is the ultimate treatment of someone as a means rather than an end. This is why it is important to stress that physical and mental violence against a person need not be sadistic in order to be considered torture. "Conventional" violence, perpetrated by an agent of the state, or on behalf of same, with the object of extracting information or a confession, or punishing the victim, is torture. The degree of violence certainly aggravates the crime, but does nothing to change its lineage.

The fight to eradicate torture, like abolitionism, began during the Enlightenment and made some achievements during the eighteenth and nineteenth centuries. Yet, unlike abolitionism, the fight saw colossal defeats during the first half of the twentieth century, when totalitarian and colonial regimes widely used various forms of torture. After World War II, the prohibition on torture was written into the Universal Declaration of Human Rights, which states, in no uncertain terms: "No one shall be subjected to torture or to cruel, inhuman, or degrading treatment."[19] This phrasing, which contains no exceptions, was subsequently adopted in every convention, every international normative document, international and regional human rights conventions, constitutions, and domestic legislation.

It is important to grasp the enormity of the prohibition as absolute: it means that the prohibition on torture trumps every other right, including the right to life. The contention that torture can be used as a means to save human lives is unacceptable under international law (if such a clash where the life of one person depends on torturing another even exists; it is entirely unclear that such a "clean" juxtaposition between the right to life and the prohibition on torture ever occurs in reality). There is another crucial distinction to be made here: "torture" does not refer to any use of physical or mental violence to extract information. The prohibition focuses on institutional violence, rather than violence perpetrated by individuals. Torture is distinct from "ordinary" violence.

In 1984, the International Convention Against Torture and Other Cruel, Inhuman, or Degrading Treatment or Punishment was opened for signature.[20] Article 1 of the convention defined what torture is. Torture, according to the definition, is an act that meets the following, cumulative, criteria:[21]

1. Intentional infliction of pain or suffering (both physical and mental) at a high degree of severity;
2. By or at the instigation of a public official, or with the public official's consent or acquiescence;
3. In order to achieve one of the following purposes: extracting information from the victim or from a third party, extracting a confession from the victim or a third party, punishing the victim for acts they or a third party committed, intimidating the victim or coercing them or a third party into carrying out a certain act.

According to this definition, torture is a special strain of severe, deliberate violence used against a person by state officials, or with their involvement, to achieve a specific purpose. Violence instigated as a "private initiative" with no connection to the authorities does not count as torture in the legal sense, regardless of how cruel it is. The meaning of the phrase in public discourse is much broader and includes any particularly cruel or sadistic instance of violence.

It is worth mentioning, in this context, that the Rome Statute, which established the International Criminal Court, contains a much broader definition of torture, and that is the infliction of severe pain or suffering (physical and mental) on a person in custody (detention, prison) by a torturer or under his or her control.[22] This definition does not require that the violence be perpetrated to achieve one of the objectives listed above, and it includes torture that is not inflicted by a public official. However, the UN convention definition is more broadly accepted (at least for the time being) and it is the definition that has been adopted by most countries.

In any event, the egregious nature of instrumental violence carried out against a person by a public official, someone who has government powers and is superior to the victim by virtue of their position,* is what makes torture something distinct from violence in general. Violence against individuals by public officials, inflicted for the purpose of extracting information or a confession, is considered so grave that torture has been recognized both as a crime against humanity and as a war crime.[23]

---

* Or, under the ICC definition, also by a perpetrator who is not a state representative but is in a position of control over the victim.

This brings us to torture in Israel.

Allegations of torture in Shabak interrogation facilities began surfacing a few years after the occupation of the Palestinian territories in 1967. Charged with thwarting subversive activity and terrorism, the Shabak had focused mainly on the Arab population inside Israel; with the occupation, it faced a new reality, one of hundreds of thousands of Palestinians who were not Israeli citizens living under Israel's control and who were not happy about it. Many organizations were active in the newly occupied Palestinian society. All of them were anti-Israel and many opted for violent resistance to achieve their end.

The task the Shabak had to shoulder was heavy and complicated, and the people at the helm chose the easiest route to execute it: importing oppressive techniques from the undemocratic world; outlawing any political organization; arresting and detaining anyone involved in political activism (including nonviolent); and terrorizing and intimidating the civilian population. To do all this, the Shabak needed information. A lot of information. Who are the members of the scores of political and military organizations? What is the resistance strategy of each organization? How are they funded? Who are their contacts in the Arab world? Who supports which organization? What personal secrets are local leaders hiding? What is this or that person's weak spot? The Shabak had to be fed a constant stream of this information, because material received yesterday would be irrelevant tomorrow. The main way to get this information was to extract it from people under interrogation, who, naturally, were rather reluctant to provide it. It did not take long for the Shabak to adopt methods of interrogation to overcome their reluctance.

However, from the 1970s on, extracting information from interrogees was not done necessarily just to get intel, but also to prosecute and convict individuals suspected of hostile activities. Shabak interrogators, whose chief mission remained to frustrate "subversion," suddenly found themselves in the service of the occupation's criminal investigation system. Confessions detainees made to their Shabak interrogators became a pivotal tool in establishing the evidence for their prosecution and long prison sentences.

The reports of beatings and use of humiliation and degradation as techniques to break detainees' spirits began trickling out in the early 1970s. Felicia Langer published several testimonies by clients who had been severely beaten by Shabak agents, held in small isolation cells for weeks, and threatened by police that they would be sent back to the Shabak if they did not confess. She complained to the judges who presided over her clients' trials and to the authorities about the interrogation techniques reported by her clients: the *falaka*, or foot whipping, in which the soles of the feet were beaten with a cane or a pipe; beatings of the genitals; and days of hooding or isolation. Langer's complaints to the minister of police and the attorney general were all dismissed as unfounded, and she was fiercely ridiculed for believing her clients' "wild oriental imaginations."[24]

Since the only proofs of her serious allegations were the testimonies of the accused, Langer's attempts to obtain remedy from the High Court of Justice ended in failure and won her ridicule there, too. In one High Court hearing, Deputy Attorney General Mishael Cheshin (who went on to become a justice and then vice president of the Supreme Court) berated her after she complained about not having been allowed to examine complaints made by one of her clients by visually inspecting his bruises: "Ms. Langer has a duplicating machine and she files petitions on any trivial matter, all accompanied by a great hullabaloo about how detainees are allegedly tortured. She wanted [her client] to do a striptease in the Ramallah prison. Of course she was denied!"[25] Cheshin likely dropped his incredulity when, several years later, as a private-sector lawyer, he represented the three senior Shabak officials who exposed the agency's lies in the Bus 300 affair.

At any rate, the derision came to an end in 1977 when the *Sunday Times* of London published an investigative report spanning four pages, which included grave findings based on more than forty testimonies from people who had been interrogated by the Shabak, half of them identified by name. The report was the fruit of five months of digging by the paper's Insight Team, headed by reporters Paul Eddy and Peter Gillman. The article determined that Israeli interrogators used torture methods such as beatings, electric shocks, sexual degradation, and isolation for days and weeks in special cells called "the closet," which were so small a person could not stand up. The article claimed the torture was "systemic" and appeared "to be sanctioned at some level as deliberate policy."[26]

The story generated instant shock waves. Media outlets around the world quoted it. The Associated Press reported on it the day the article appeared and kept on reporting, and its coverage was picked up by many other newspapers. Israel's government responded with an aggressive denial, accusing the *Sunday Times* of disseminating Arab propaganda against the only democracy in the Middle East, which only fanned the flames. In a rather unusual move, two weeks after the *Sunday Times* article's publication, the *New York Times* reported on the paper's findings and the subsequent debate.[27]

Despite Israel's flat denial and its posture of injury, Menachem Begin, the incoming prime minister, was deeply affected by the *Sunday Times* story. Whatever happened behind closed doors, it seems that Begin, who had only just been sworn in, asked for more information about the interrogation rooms and issued instructions to tone down the interrogation methods. Lawyers say that after the story was published and the uproar it caused, and during Begin's six years as prime minister, the reports of Shabak torture decreased significantly.[28]

But in 1984, incidents of violence during interrogation seemed to be on the rise again. A report published by Amnesty International that year included information gathered by its researchers that indicated systemic, frequent ill-treatment of people interrogated by the Shabak, including beatings, deprivation of sleep, food, and access to toilets, repeated exposure to cold showers and cold air ventilators, hooding, forcing detainees to stand for extended periods of time, and degradation and humiliation directed at women in the detainees' families.[29]

Reports of this type continued to reach the press and the public through the 1980s. On top of these allegations, the news repeatedly featured incidents of people dying during interrogations in circumstances that suggested the deaths resulted from violence. But the Shabak's denials and the habit of disbelieving Palestinian detainees' accounts prevented a critical mass from forming that would have made the issue a national subject of debate. This would all change in 1987 with the appointment of the Landau Commission, when the Shabak's methods of interrogation could no longer be swept aside.

GO AHEAD, TORTURE, BUT JUST DON'T LIE

On November 8, 1987, four months after its appointment, the Landau Commission submitted its final two-part report to the prime minister. The first part addressed the commission's findings regarding Shabak agents' court testimonies and presented recommendations on the principles of using "physical pressure" during interrogations. The second part, which still remains classified, included an analysis of the Shabak's interrogation methods and detailed guidelines for its agents on what may and may not be done during an interrogation. Although it seemed that nothing about the Shabak could shock the country after the past year—with its revelations about the Bus 300 scandal and the Nafsu affair—the Landau report managed to deliver yet another shock.

The commission's findings confirmed what the Shabak's detainees had been saying for years: the interrogators were authorized to use torture—or, to use the commission's euphemism, "physical pressure"—in interrogations, and use it they did. The commission even admitted that this "pressure" was of such force that it "could be expected to appear to the court as violating the principle of the person's free will, and thus causing the rejection of the confession."[30] Meaning, had the courts known that the accused had been subjected to physical violence, and had they been aware of the force of this violence, they would have probably acquitted the accused. In fact, the commission said this explicitly: "In trials of the type discussed here such a rejection is tantamount to an acquittal of the accused."[31] But that had not happened. Confessions had not been ruled inadmissible and defendants had not been acquitted—and not by accident. The commission found that the Shabak had routinely given false testimony in court, denying that "physical pressure" had been used against interrogees, which is why hundreds, perhaps thousands, of defendants were not acquitted. The judges had always believed the Shabak agents' false accounts that they never touched the interrogees. The commission made the following astounding comments about the practice of false testimony:

> The method in question seemed to have been spontaneously generated, and the interrogators were dragged along and slid into it as a matter of course. One top Investigation Unit member defined it as "lore handed down from father to son." . . . False testimony in court soon became an unchallenged norm which was to be the rule for sixteen years.[32]

Senior Shabak officials, including the most senior, knew about the practice of perjury, the commission found, as did the Shabak's legal advisers.[33] The commission gave full vent to its fury at this culture of falsehood and deception, but it stopped short of recommending that the attorney general prosecute the perjurers. They had obstructed justice, lied in court, and caused miscarriage of justice, but the Shabak agents would be given immunity for the same reason that state offenders are always granted immunity: bringing them to justice would harm the state. In this case, prosecuting Shabak interrogators and senior officials would, it was said, be extremely damaging to the secret agency, and therefore to the public and the nation. Although the commission had the courage to expose the Shabak's criminal conduct, its recommendations undercut the principle of accountability. And the worse the practices the commission exposed, the more dangerous was its recommendation to give the offenders a pass.

In any case, what concerns us more is the second part of the commission's report, the one addressing the Shabak's interrogation methods and the question of whether these may involve the use of violence. While the commission condemned the Shabak's "culture of lies" in the bluntest terms, it saw the violence used on detainees in an entirely different light. The Shabak managed to convince the commission that "recourse to some measure of physical pressure in the interrogation of HTA [hostile terrorist activity] suspects is unavoidable." In its recommendation, the commission committed to paper words that would be etched on the bodies and souls of thousands of detainees, almost all of them Palestinian, over the coming years:

> The effective interrogation of terrorist suspects is impossible without the use of means of pressure. . . . The means of pressure should principally take the form of non-violent psychological pressure through a vigorous and extensive interrogation, with use of stratagems, including acts of deception. *However, when these do not attain their purpose, the exertion of a moderate measure of physical pressure cannot be avoided* [emphasis added].[34]

This was the first time in Israeli law that the use of violence during interrogation was officially legally sanctioned. The courage the Landau Commission had shown in exposing and denouncing the Shabak's lies was eclipsed by the crime of legitimizing torture.

The commission addressed the legal sources for its recommendations. In fact, even before exploring the legal authority that empowered Shabak agents to use "moderate physical pressure" in interrogations, the commission had to confront a basic question: What legal authority empowered Shabak agents to carry out any state act, including interrogations, even without physical pressure? The need for the Landau Commission to look into the source of the agency's power was due to the astonishing fact that at the time of the report and for many years later, the Shabak was not a statutory body. That is, there was no law that defined it and granted its powers.

The Shabak lived in the shadows, not just in terms of intelligence but also in terms of its legal existence. In later torture trials after the Landau Commission, Avigdor Feldman, a leader in the legal fight against the practice, referred to the Shabak as a "governmental leech." With no governmental power of its own, the Shabak latched onto other statutory bodies or officials and fed off their power. In one example, the director general of the Ministry of Education has the power to appoint and dismiss school principals. The Shabak does not. So the Shabak would latch onto the director general, "advising" him on the appointment of principals in the Arab sector. Understandably, the director general and other civil servants tend to listen to the Shabak's advice. As advisers go, the Shabak is hard to refuse. This is how it feeds off others who have statutory powers. So whom does the Shabak latch onto for interrogations and use of violence? That's just it: no one. The power to interrogate lies with the police, and the Shabak did not want to advise them on who and how to carry out interrogations; it wanted to do this itself. Besides, police officers are not allowed to use force, so leeching off them would not help.

The Landau Commission was hard pressed to find a legal basis for Shabak interrogations. It pinned this core activity of one of the most powerful governmental agencies in Israel on an article in the law that regulates the government's general powers. The article stipulates that the government has all powers that have not been granted by law to other state authorities.[35] This residual section, the commission determined, allows the government to set up an intelligence agency and give it tasks that have not been assigned to another statutory body. However, this far-reaching interpretation contradicts the basic tenets of the rule of law, which hold that the authorities have no powers other than those explicitly granted to them by law (unlike citizens, who are permitted to do anything that is not explicitly prohibited by law). The commission's understanding would mean that the government can do almost anything without any need for legislation empowering it to do so. It could, for instance, set up new armed forces, or build a system of secret detention facilities, or perhaps even detain people without trial—all without authorization from the legislature—because these are acts that no other body has the power to do. A general power to do anything contradicts the essence of the idea of the rule of law.

Still, the committee determined that the Shabak is a product of the government's general power to act. But what gives it the power to use "moderate physical pressure" during interrogations? On the face of it, using violence is a criminal offense, and this is even before we get into torture as a crime under international law.

Well, in the absence of a legal license to torture people, the Landau Commission pulled out a defense plea available under criminal law—the defense of "necessity"—and determined that even if the use of "physical pressure" is a criminal offense, Shabak interrogators may invoke "necessity" as a defense against conviction. In other words, the Landau Commission was unable to find a legal provision that allows Shabak interrogators to use force against interrogees. Instead, it determined that the power derives from the non-criminality of the use of force. The difficulty this maneuver raises is immense, even before we get to the question of whether, in fact, a criminal defense exists for use of force against an interrogee. Criminal defenses are invoked to prevent criminal convictions. They do not give advance permission to carry out criminal acts, certainly not to state agents. Law enforcement powers—the power to search, arrest, or use force against people—are among the most hazardous powers granted by law. As such, in law-abiding countries, these powers are normally explicitly regulated in laws that also articulate the conditions for using them.

According to the "necessity defense," which the Landau Commission cited as the foundation for Shabak interrogators to use "moderate physical pressure," a person will not be held criminally liable if they are forced to commit an offense to save their own or another person's life, person, or property, as long as the offense was proportionate and immediately necessary to avert danger. The Landau Commission found that since Shabak interrogations were done to prevent terrorist attacks, they come under the necessity defense. So even if the interrogators use "moderate physical pressure," their acts are lawful.

Oceans of ink were spilled over the question of whether the legal

thesis adopted by the Landau Commission was correct. Lawyers for interrogees and human rights organizations claimed that the necessity defense
is intended to prevent a conviction *retroactively*, in cases that meet the stipulated conditions, and that the commission's proposition to use it as *pro-
spective* authorization for criminal conduct was entirely baseless; they
argued that giving license under the necessity defense repudiated its logic
as a defense for people who find themselves forced to commit an offense
in *unforeseeable* circumstances; that the necessity defense was never
meant to serve state agents acting within their state powers, for which
purpose there is another defense—one of "justification"[36]—but that does
not protect against torture; that a significant proportion of Shabak interrogations are carried out to gather general intelligence and therefore fail
to meet the requirement of immediate necessity; and more.

The question of whether there is a legal source of authority for using
"moderate physical pressure" during interrogations will come up again.
For the meantime, let's assume that there is. What does "moderate physical pressure" include exactly? What distinguishes "physical pressure" that
is not moderate—and which, even according to Landau Commission standards, is not permitted—from "physical pressure" that is moderate and
hence, as per the commission, allowed? The commission refused to enu-
merate the techniques it permitted publicly, arguing that detainees should
not be given advance knowledge of interrogation practices. This position
is also highly problematic, suggesting that people under interrogation may
be kept in the dark about their rights. The commission stopped short of
committing this to paper, but the logic behind veiling the exact defini-
tions of physical pressure implies that the committee members were willing to leave a threat hanging over interrogees, who would be ignorant of
the limits placed on the use of force. This approach favors the use of torture, since torture does not involve just physical pain and suffering, but
also the psychological kind. Detainees who fear they are about to undergo
torture are already experiencing a form of torture. Thus the Landau Commission put the "code of guidelines" for Shabak interrogators, which defines
"the boundaries of what is permitted to the interrogator and mainly what
is prohibited," in the second, classified, part of the report.

In the coming years, thousands of Palestinian detainees would learn,
up close, what the Landau Commission considered to be "moderate physical pressure," and their testimony would help opponents of torture map

out the Shabak's methods. The patterns that emerged from the descriptions of people who had been interrogated provided the fight against torture with the facts it needed; eventually the methods adopted in the wake of the Landau Commission made their way into the petitions filed against torture at the High Court. Throughout these years, in countless lectures and press interviews, Avigdor Feldman condemned the seal of approval the commission had given to torture. "There is no doubt in my mind," he would say, "that the second part of the Landau report was written in Yiddish, because only Yiddish has enough words for pain to describe every kind of it."

ATTORNEY ROSENTHAL WOULD LIKE TO SEE HIS CLIENTS

In December 1987, six weeks after the Landau Commission report was published, the First Intifada erupted. A volcano of subterranean rage that had brewed during twenty years of occupation and dispossession exploded in a popular uprising against the Israeli regime. Thousands of Palestinian civilians took to the streets in clashes with the military. A new reality surfaced in the Occupied Territories overnight: demonstrations, commercial strikes, violent altercations between Palestinians throwing stones and burning tires and the symbols of Israel's authority. The uprising went on for months.

New self-governing Palestinian organizations defying Israeli rule at the local and national levels, coupled with intensified activity by more veteran organizations, gave Israel a great deal of trouble. The security forces tried to quell the protests and break the uprising by using force on a massive scale, sometimes cruelly, exacting a heavy toll on the civilian population. One of the methods was the "broken bones" policy, attributed to a directive given by then minister of defense Yitzhak Rabin to "break" the protesters, and rioters' "arms and legs." But to confront the new challenge head-on, Israel needed information, and a lot of it. Extracting information about "subversive" organizations was, of course, the job of the Shabak, which now had the official green light to use "moderate physical pressure" during interrogations.

No wonder that the years after the Landau Commission's report were tough for the fight against torture. The reports streaming in to human rights organizations indicated a significant increase in scope compared to previous years,[37] and the odds of whipping up public dissent against a practice that had been sanctioned by a state commission of inquiry, headed by a former Supreme Court president, justified as necessary for national security, and during a time of uprising were rather slim. The testimonies received by the different organizations, whether Palestinian, Israeli, or international, included frequent descriptions of the *shabach* method: detainees were forced to stand for entire days with their hands cuffed behind their backs, a sack over their heads, and their cuffed wrists tied to a post, requiring them to arch their backs, or to sit on a low chair tilted forward while their hands were tied to a post behind the chair, exerting painful pressure on the detainees' hands if they slid down the seat[38]; they were also deprived of food and sleep, or locked in the "closet," where they could not stand straight, or received the *falaka*, or suffered partial suffocation by pressure exerted on the thorax. In both 1988 and 1989, nine Palestinian detainees died while in custody (compared to one or two cases on average in previous years).[39] B'Tselem concluded that in at least five cases, the deaths could be attributed to the methods of interrogation used against the detainees. The Landau report, commissioned in response to the torture that had led to a miscarriage of justice in Nafsu's case, and which, many believed, was meant to restrain the Shabak, in the end strengthened the security service's violent interrogation techniques by sanctioning it.

The intifada prompted the creation of a new human rights organization in Jerusalem, with the object of helping Palestinians who had been subjected to beatings by Israeli security forces. Initially called the Hotline for Victims of Violence, the name was later changed to HaMoked (Hebrew for hotline): Center for the Defense of the Individual. At first, HaMoked handled only complaints from Palestinians who were the victims of violence, but it quickly became a place to turn to with many other issues and complaints.

One type of call for help was particularly common: requests from families whose child or spouse or sibling had been detained, trying to find out where their relatives were. The IDF and the police were not in the habit of letting families know when someone was taken into custody, let alone where they were being held. Detainees were pulled off the streets and transferred to detention facilities where they might be held for weeks without anyone knowing where they were or even whether they had in fact been detained. HaMoked decided to help systematically with this issue and began contacting the security authorities to locate the detainees. But Ha-Moked quickly understood that locating them was only half the work. The families also needed to know how the detainees were faring. For that, a lawyer had to see them. HaMoked decided to provide this service as well. A visit from a lawyer would also give the detainees a chance to get some preliminary legal advice.

One of the lawyers was Andre Rosenthal. He had finished his internship with Leah Tsemel several years earlier and opened a small practice in Jerusalem, not far from HaMoked's office. As Rosenthal and HaMoked soon found out, a lawyer's visit to the Palestinian detainees was not a given. Martial law in the West Bank and the Gaza Strip, as well as Israeli law, which applies in East Jerusalem, gives the Shabak the power to deny a detainee a meeting with counsel for several weeks. Such severe, sometimes catastrophic, harm to due process rights was the fate of many Palestinian detainees. In fact, orders denying meetings with counsel became a fixture during interrogations that were defined as "security" cases. Thus HaMoked decided to file High Court petitions against these orders, and Rosenthal embarked on a project of submitting petitions to lift them.

Every time HaMoked traced a detainee and Rosenthal was denied a visit, he filed a High Court petition with a motion for an urgent hearing. One petition, and another, and another—a steady flow of petitions. Because Rosenthal knew nothing about the allegations against his clients at the time of filing, each petition was identical, other than the detainee's name and general background. Rosenthal became a serial petitioner. He soon realized that the Shabak took advantage of the interval during which he was not allowed to see his clients to inflict some "special interrogation measures" (or "moderate physical pressure"). When he was finally allowed to see them, his clients had usually confessed, the case was done, and there was little he could do as a lawyer to help.

Sometimes frustration is the mother of invention, and Rosenthal was extremely frustrated. He and his colleagues at HaMoked were helpless against the systemic violation of Palestinian rights—the right to receive legal counsel; the rights of families to know where their relatives are and what is happening to them; and above all, the right to freedom from constant egregious torture during interrogation. Rosenthal decided to take action. He began adding to his petitions a motion for an interim order, or temporary order, until the petition is resolved, forbidding the interrogators from using "physical pressure." And so, indirectly, torture during interrogation made it to the High Court's agenda for the first time. As months went by, and Rosenthal heard from clients, once the order denying meeting with counsel was lifted, exactly what had been done to them during the interrogation, his requests became more specific: do not deprive my client of sleep, do not put my client in "the *shabach* position," and more.

The petitions filed by Rosenthal and HaMoked were a strange hybrid. They did not challenge torture and the legal source for it directly. They focused on the demand to let the interrogee see their lawyer and get legal advice, but they demanded that until that was made possible, the interrogee would not be subjected to torture. Since the Landau Commission report was the official legal document that established the Shabak's power to use force against interrogees, for the first time, the allegations were not denied, at least not flatly.

The hundreds of petitions filed by Rosenthal and other lawyers at that time, the late 1980s and early 1990s,[40] did not produce a single judgment. These cases all followed a trajectory that precluded exploration and a reasoned resolution of the torture question: after the petition was filed, the court would normally call an urgent hearing, sometimes within a day or two of the filing. If the Shabak had concluded its interrogation using "special measures," its counsel would let the court know, and the specific order against the use of "physical pressure" would be removed. If the interrogation was still under way, the Shabak would insist that the court dismiss the motion for the interim order. The lawyers representing the state would repeat that the use of "moderate physical pressure" during interrogations was "a necessity." The hearing might be postponed and the proceedings drag on until the Shabak was finally able to tell the court the motion for the interim order against the use of physical modes of interrogation had become "moot."

HaMoked has stacks of letters from the State Attorney's Office asking it to withdraw petitions in cases in which the Shabak no longer needed to use "necessity interrogations," as state attorneys had come to call interrogations under torture. The justices never once used a petition to hold a meaningful, exhaustive discussion on the legality of torture. At the end of the day, the issue of meeting with counsel, which was the main demand in these petitions, turned into an arbitration process in which the court decided how long it could deny a meeting with counsel; once the Shabak was done using torture, it invariably no longer had an objection to allow the detainee to meet with counsel. So these petitions almost always ended in a court order to remove the case from its docket, thus in practice dismissing it, or with a very short judgment describing the proceedings and concluding with the option of a meeting with counsel at some date.

However, Rosenthal believes that his petitions put pressure on the Shabak to cut down the time of his clients' maltreatment, and that they brought the issue to public attention. HaMoked made efforts to interest journalists in the topic, and over the years the Israeli and foreign press did report extensively about Israeli torture practices, thanks to Rosenthal's petitions and the work of HaMoked and other organizations.

But this wave of petitions led to two other important by-products. First, they opened the Supreme Court justices' eyes to the Shabak's use of torture, to the way it was used and its systematic application. The petitions appear to have laid the groundwork for Supreme Court president Aharon Barak's willingness, a few years later, to take the bull by the horns and review the legality of torture. In this sense, the petitions provided an introductory course on the subject.

Second, in a handful of cases the justices granted the motion for an interim order and forbade continued use of physical pressure on a particular petitioner. Rosenthal estimates that there were five or six such cases. They were rare but dramatic, although they made no mark, since the decisions were brief and gave no reasoning, and therefore were not entered into the law reports. The drama sometimes intensified when the Shabak, through the State Attorney's Office, made a motion to revoke the order and allow the interrogations under torture to resume.[41]

In one of those cases, the Shabak's motion was filed urgently, and the hearing took place at night. The client was an Islamic Jihad activist named Muhammad Hamdan. He had been taken into administrative detention in 1992, was removed to Lebanon in the deportation of the four hundred, and then returned to the Occupied Territories. He was placed in administrative detention again, and after some time, taken into interrogation on suspicion of planning terrorist attacks. When Rosenthal filed a petition on Hamdan's behalf in 1996, demanding an order against the use of physical pressure, the Shabak notified the court that it did not intend to do so and the court issued the interim order prohibiting the use of force.

However, the next day the Shabak asked the court, in light of new information, to revoke the interim order, essentially requesting permission to torture Hamdan.

At the High Court convened that night the Shabak was represented by the State Attorney Office's brightest star, one of the civil service's best litigators and a future state attorney, Shai Nitzan. He had a reputation for having bought into the Shabak's arguments with more conviction than the Shabak itself, and he would resort to any dramatic ploy to make the case for intensive interrogations using physical pressure. In Hamdan's case, Nitzan claimed that the interrogation would literally save lives.[42] He denied that physical pressure was torture, yet angrily also said that even if it were, it would be justified when human life is at stake. The interim order, Nitzan argued, was preventing the extraction of important life-or-death information.

On the panel with Aharon Barak, now president of the Supreme Court, was Justice Mishael Cheshin, possibly the most tempestuous judge ever to sit on the bench. With the impressive lineage of a father who sat on the Supreme Court when it was established in 1948; an education among the giants of Israeli law at Jerusalem's Hebrew University; years in civil service, where he reached the position of deputy attorney general; and a short three-year private practice followed by his appointment to the Supreme Court, Cheshin was a beloved son of Israel's legal aristocracy. He had a fiery temperament, immense intellect, and vast knowledge, and he expressed them boisterously thanks to his gift for language. Lawyers feared him because on the bench he was the polar opposite of the sphinx-like model of the British judiciary. He had the soul of a Sophist and the personality of a lawyer rather than a judge: he quibbled with lawyers, chastised them for errors, and reprimanded them for what he saw as inconsistencies or immoral stances, often roaring in the courtroom at anyone whose arguments annoyed him or who was not properly prepared.

That night, Cheshin and his colleagues had to make a decision no modern court should have to make: whether to allow the torture of an interrogee. A court hearing usually proceeds in a fixed way: the parties make their case, and the judges give their decision. Judges all over the world occasionally pose questions to the parties. But when Cheshin was in the courtroom, hearings never followed the formula. If Cheshin was on the bench, everyone knew the justice would talk as much as the opposing attorneys. He has his opinions and he will give them, argue for them, and work at persuasion. Sometimes this was a recipe for a real treat. Sometimes Cheshin's performance pulled the parties into a high-level intellectual dispute, an ideological fencing match. At other times it made for an unpleasant exchange, which, given the inherent imbalance of power, had the effect of gagging the lawyers.

At the hearing over Hamdan's interrogation, Cheshin dragged Rosenthal into a theoretical-ethical debate. He demanded that Rosenthal state a clear position on the "ticking-time-bomb" dilemma. Suppose there is a ticking bomb in the Shalom Tower in Tel Aviv, Cheshin thundered, and the bomb will go off if it is not located and defused in time. There is a detainee who knows where the bomb is. Should we not use "physical pressure" on him? Rosenthal, despite an appearance of fragility, stood his ground. No, he answered. The prohibition on torture is absolute. Torture is not permitted no matter the circumstances. Cheshin could not contain his anger. "That's the most immoral position I have ever heard!" he bellowed. "A thousand people are about to die and you expect us to do nothing?"

Rosenthal gave all the standard answers to the ticking-time-bomb conundrum: there are no such clear-cut cases in real life, the Shabak never knows with absolute certainty that a particular detainee has specific information about a bomb; he added that in Hamdan's case, the Shabak was only estimating that his client had information that could save lives, that the necessity defense could only be applied with hindsight, and torture cannot be approved in advance. Cheshin could not bear to listen. "Do not beat around the bush! Are you prepared for people to die? Answer me!!" he bellowed. At that climactic moment, with Cheshin's voice reverberating through the room, the lights went out. The court had an automated system that turned the lights out at 8:00 p.m. Still, maybe they were cowering at Cheshin's rage.

The justices accepted the state's motion and revoked the interim order.[43] Rosenthal went home knowing that at that very moment, his client was being tortured.

THE PUBLIC COMMITTEE AGAINST TORTURE

In late 1989, the Public Committee Against Torture in Israel (PCATI), a new human rights organization, was founded. Hannah Friedman, its founder, a surgical nurse by profession, had been an ACRI volunteer for a number of years, and had formed a group that handled public complaints against police conduct. Members of the group wrote letters, lodged complaints, and referred particularly serious cases to ACRI's lawyers. Among the many files on the team's desk was one folder containing a number of complaints made by a lawyer who represented Palestinian suspects and defendants. The folder had sat on the desk for a long time. Friedman's team had brought up the complaints, alleging serious torture during interrogation, with different forums within ACRI. But Friedman felt that ACRI, which then kept closer to the public consensus than in later years, shied away from the subject.[44] Friedman had not been told to ignore the file, but the fact remained that these serious complaints were never addressed.[45] As time went by, Friedman surmised that ACRI preferred to keep a distance from this hot potato. Yehoshua Schoffman, then ACRI's legal adviser, does not recall any discussion about the complaints and says there was no policy to avoid responding to claims of violence during Shabak interrogations.[46] Either way, the dusty folder would not leave Friedman in peace. She decided to establish a public body dedicated to fighting torture.

One Friday in 1989, Friedman got a group of friends together. She had been born in the Netherlands before the war. When the country was occupied by the Nazis, her parents fled with her and her sister to Brussels, where they stayed in a hotel, but the Nazis soon came to Brussels as well. German soldiers raided the hotel just as Friedman and her sister were playing in the garden. A neighbor who saw the soldiers arresting Jews, sneaked the sisters into her home and saved their lives. She gave them a home and took devoted care of them until the end of the war. Friedman's parents had been sent to Auschwitz, but were apparently murdered on the train to there, since German records do not list them as having arrived at the extermination camp. After the war, a Jewish couple who had lost their two sons to the Nazi murder machine adopted Hannah and her sister. This background might explain Friedman's incomparable tenacity: a good-hearted woman, a loving aunt at first glance, who stubbornly mobilized psychiatrists, lawyers, journalists, and politicians to take action against torture. On that Friday afternoon, each friend at the meeting contributed NIS 100 to set up the new organization. Among the founders were professionals from a variety of fields: Yehoyakim Stein, a psychiatrist;[47]

sociologist and criminologist Stanley Cohen;[48] psychiatrist Ruchama Marton;[49] journalist Haim Baram; and lawyers Avigdor Feldman and Leah Tsemel.

The task that PCATI took upon itself was ambitious and extremely challenging: to end torture in Shabak interrogations even as the intifada was raging, when Palestinians were seen as enemies and dangerous terrorists. The public's first instinct has always been to give the security forces as much power as possible, and discussion at the time did not even recognize "torture" as related to the "physical pressure" exerted during interrogations. It was a terrible starting point for a public campaign.

PCATI first chose public advocacy as its core activity. Its members began collecting information about torture and bringing it to public attention through media articles and conferences in an attempt to raise awareness and kick-start a critical debate. PCATI also filed complaints with the state attorney when they learned of cases in which the detainees said they had been tortured during interrogations. These complaints were sent with a demand to order an investigation. The letters, sent in the early 1990s, are still awaiting a reply.

In the first eighteen months or so of its operation, PCATI made inroads into triggering a public discussion on torture. A number of serious cases exposed were covered by the local and foreign media. One especially grievous episode involved two brothers, Isma'il and 'Ali Ghul, from Silwan in Jerusalem. They were interrogated by the Department of Minorities of the police, on suspicion of murdering a Palestinian who had collaborated with the Israeli authorities. After two weeks of interrogation, Isma'il broke down and confessed to the murder, incriminating his brother and a cousin in the process. When Tsemel was permitted to see him, he said he had confessed because of the severe violence inflicted on him, which included beatings, the *falaka*, and standing with his hands raised in the air for extended periods of time. Despite her protests, the judges kept extending his arrest. His brother 'Ali did not confess even though he described even worse abuse, which culminated in him losing consciousness and being taken to a hospital.

About a month and a half after their arrest, the brothers were indicted for murder, based on Isma'il's confession. But then the police caught someone else who confessed to the murder, and the Ghul brothers were released.[50] When PCATI learned about the interrogation techniques the

Jerusalem police had used, it decided to hold its first press conference, thus introducing Israeli society to the organization. The story sent shock waves across the country; a commission was appointed to investigate the allegations of torture, and several police officers were prosecuted.[51] PCATI had scored a great success, but, not coincidentally, the case related to police officers, not Shabak agents. They remained shielded by their agency's secrecy and the protection of the Landau report.

In March 1991, B'Tselem published a comprehensive report about the interrogation methods used against Palestinians.[52] It was based on the testimonies of forty-one individuals who had been interrogated and many other sources. A large proportion of the testimonies and other materials had been gathered by PCATI. The B'Tselem report was the first Israeli document to describe torture methods in the minutest detail and to link them legally to the term torture (though not definitively, as the report's title— "The Interrogation of Palestinians During the Intifada: Ill Treatment, 'Moderate Physical Pressure,' or Torture?"—is posed as a question). Like other B'Tselem reports, this one marked a turning point in a campaign that it helped frame and conceptualize.

Later that year, PCATI decided to petition the High Court of Justice against the Landau report's authorization to use "non-violent psychological pressure" and "moderate physical pressure." Its assumption was that the lack of legal authority (other than the commission's report) to use physical pressure, in conjunction with the absolute prohibition on torture in international law, would pose a powerful and potentially successful legal challenge. Convincing the public seemed like an extremely long-term mission, and the severity of the practices PCATI was fighting understandably created impatience. Often, impatience in a struggle is the impetus to take it to court. Activists feel that legal action offers a shortcut. In any event, in the petition, which Avigdor Feldman filed on behalf of PCATI and a Palestinian who said he had been tortured during a Shabak interrogation, the court was asked to issue an order compelling the prime minister and the head of the Shabak to instruct the agency's interrogators to refrain from following the recommendations made by the Landau Commission. Feldman also asked for the declassification of the second part of the Landau report.

Feldman included all possible arguments in the petition in a bid to show that the Landau recommendations were unlawful. Chiefly, he claimed that the necessity defense was not a recipe for advance authorization for violence, and that it certainly did not apply to all the interrogations conducted by the Shabak, most of which were designed to collect general information and only very few to avert planned terrorist attacks. In practice, he argued, implementation of the Landau recommendations had resulted in more Palestinian deaths in custody during the interrogation phase. Finally, the recommendations in fact permit torture, which is a violation of the strict prohibition in international law.

The case was so important that the state was represented by the state attorney herself, Dorit Beinisch. The panel appointed to preside over the case, Deputy President Menachem Elon and Justices Shlomo Levin and Dov Levin, was in no rush to rule on the explosive issue it had been handed. The first hearing took place in April 1992, and concluded with the justices deciding to wait for the annual review by the small ministerial committee tasked by the Landau Commission to periodically appraise the directives given to Shabak interrogators. The justices also ordered that the code of guidelines and the classified portion of the Landau report be referred to the panel for review.

More than a year later, in June 1993, after considering the classified material, the panel concluded that the secret part of the Landau report should remain secret. No reasons were given other than that the interest in not disclosing the report outweighed the need to make it public. Over the next few months, the court held hearings on the petition's main issue, the legality of the Landau Commission recommendations regarding use of psychological and physical pressure. Feldman offered an important new argument related to two basic laws that set limits on Israeli legislation in order to protect fundamental rights (Basic Law: Human Liberty and Dignity and Basic Law: Freedom of Occupation). The two laws had been recently passed, in March 1992, after the petition had been filed. Feldman argued that the enactment of these laws made it impossible to institute normative arrangements that violate human rights other than through Knesset-enacted primary law that must meet the requirements of the basic laws. Human rights cannot be violated outside the law, and a report by a state commission of inquiry is—no matter how you spin it—a document, not a law.

The panel issued its decision in August 1993 to dismiss the petition *in limine*.[53] The court determined that the petition raised a general question—

that is, an issue that is not a dispute between two parties who seek the court's intervention. Therefore, the court should not address it. The court believed that the legal question (whether "moderate physical pressure" was lawful) being raised was hypothetical, unrelated to a concrete case to be decided. The interrogation of the Palestinian petitioner in the case, Adnan Salahat, had ended months before, so a decision would have no impact on his interrogation. "The matter may arise incidentally during deliberations concerning a specific set of facts, whether in a motion to have confessions collected by Shabak agents excluded," wrote Justice Shlomo Levin, "or during criminal trials of interrogators the state alleges had acted unlawfully."[54]

Levin referred to a judgment issued in another one of Feldman's cases, a petition filed on behalf of a veteran human rights activist, Yoav Hass, who had asked for a pronouncement that the open-fire regulations given to soldiers during the intifada were illegal. In that case, the panel decided by majority opinion to dismiss the petition on the argument that the court is meant to rule on questions of principle only as part of deliberations on a concrete case; in terms of the open-fire regulations, that would be a case concerning a specific incident in which firearms were used.[55] In the Hass case, Feldman had filed a motion for a further hearing by an extended panel of the Supreme Court, but that hearing had not yet occurred when the PCATI petition was decided. And so, a decision in one Feldman case helped dismiss another Feldman case. Later, a dramatic turn of events in the first one would result in a change in the second one as well. We will get to it.

At any rate, PCATI's first attempt to use the law to effect changes in a policy that had full government backing and public support ended in bitter defeat. Not only had the legal action failed, but also the court had refused to rule on its merits.

MODERATE LEGAL PRESSURE

The judges' decision in the PCATI petition was based on a fallacy: the notion that an exhaustive debate on the legality of torture could be carried out only in deliberations over a concrete case was profoundly wrong. The only concrete contexts in which the subject came up were petitions filed on behalf of interrogees who were asking the court to stop the "moderate physical pressure" being used on them in interrogations. One reason why such a "concrete context" would not serve as an occasion for a broad investigation of torture is that the pace and intensity of interrogations, certainly security interrogations, are worlds apart from the rhythm of legal proceedings, especially if they pertain to serious questions of principle. Interrogations continue all day and all night over a period of several days to several weeks. Trials, on the other hand, proceed slowly, over months and years, to allow a thorough discussion of the disputed issue, sometimes at a scholarly level.

Petitions filed on behalf of people in interrogations were always heard under tremendous time constraints, with the Shabak pushing to end the deliberations quickly, given that the bomb was ticking or the arrest period was drawing to an end. And even when the Shabak admitted there was no ticking time bomb, such cases still could not serve as an opportunity to explore the principle of the issue: the Shabak would notify the court that it no longer intended to use moderate physical pressure against the detainee named in the petition, and so, to use the court's language, the case would have become "hypothetical." Scores of petitions of this kind were erased from the court's docket. The second track Justice Shlomo Levin had mentioned as a possible avenue for probing the legality of the Landau recommendations—trying Shabak interrogators for the methods they used—was a nonstarter. Interrogators following the Landau recommendations and the guidelines contained in the second, classified part of the report were not brought to trial. Why would they be? Levin and his colleagues had dismissed PCATI's petition with recommendations for alternative ways to explore the issue, but these suggestions were bogus.

MOUNTING LEGAL PRESSURE AND THE TORTURE PETITION RELAUNCHED

Throughout the early 1990s, Rosenthal, working through HaMoked, and another lawyer, Allegra Pacheco,* working with PCATI, continued to file

---

* Pacheco, a New York City lawyer and Israeli citizen, was the first Jewish litigator to open an office in a Palestinian city, in Bethlehem. She fought various Israeli policies in the Occupied Territories, including house demolitions, land seizures, and administrative detention.

petitions on behalf of Palestinian detainees. Pacheco's petitions, unlike Rosenthal's, directly addressed torture. Both demanded the right of detainees to meet with counsel and to be spared the use of "physical pressure." PCATI filed seventy such petitions during these years.[56] Still, the lawyers found no way to confront torture in the courts by going through the front door. So Feldman went through the back door.

Feldman's earlier case, calling for a review of the army's open-fire regulations in the Occupied Territories,[57] had acquired new relevance. The High Court had cited this case in its dismissal of PCATI's petition, on the grounds that it could not adjudicate an issue of principle or a general policy or practice unless it is based on a specific case requiring judicial remedy.

Feldman had requested a further review of the open-fire regulations, and, as it happened, the case was heard by an extended panel of five justices a month after the court dismissed PCATI's petition.

Feldman had asked the court to adopt Justice Eliezer Goldberg's minority opinion: the judge was of the view that regarding a petition challenging the legality of a norm (a law, a regulation, or an order), there was no reason to require a concrete case in need of remedy. In the extended panel hearing, two justices, President Shamgar and Justice Eliyahu Mazza, concurred with Goldberg's minority opinion, overturning the ruling on the open-fire discussion by a majority of three against two. The panel decided that when a petition addressed "issues related to respect for the law and the principles of the rule of law," no specific dispute was required to justify a hearing; as long as the case was not "a political question artificially disguised as a legal question," a hearing should be granted.[58]

This pulled the rug out from under the dismissal of the PCATI petition against the Landau Commission's recommendations. Feldman raced back to court. In September 1994, he re-filed the PCATI petition, this time with no actual, live petitioner, no sample Shabak interrogee, with only PCATI as petitioner. A purely public petition. Feldman copied the one he had filed three years earlier almost word for word, adding only the argument pertaining to the basic laws that had passed in 1992 (after the original petition had been filed), and an argument for the validity—after the open-fire regulations ruling—of a public petition challenging the Landau Commission's recommendations.[59]

What happened to this new PCATI petition happened often in the

1990s when an explosive petition came before the justices, demanding a ruling that could have gotten the court into hot water. It simply got stuck in stasis. The system has different ways of dealing with tough, complicated, sensitive cases. Only one of them involves deliberating and ruling—an option that often scares judicial institutions. And the torture petition was a perfect example of a case that would land the Supreme Court in trouble if it ruled on its merits. A ruling that pronounced torture unlawful would bring down the wrath of the security establishment and most of Israeli society; the justices might even be accused of compromising security and enabling the death of civilians. On the other hand, legitimizing torture would do irreversible harm to the court's international prestige. The court was in a classic lose-lose situation, and the path of least resistance was to avoid a ruling. Throwing out the petition on a technicality would have been one way of going about it, as the court had done in the first PCATI petition. Except that now that the legal basis for dismissing the first petition had been eliminated, the court had no more cards to play to avoid deliberating on this searing subject.

In this state of affairs, with its back against the wall, the Supreme Court pulled out its doomsday device: a work-to-rule. The new PCATI petition simply lay on the shelf. An order nisi was issued, but no hearing was scheduled. Months went by—years, in fact—and Feldman's office received no call from the court secretariat to summon him for a hearing.

There is no doubt that the failure to schedule a hearing was in response to a directive from the justices. The backlog of cases waiting for High Court hearings is always quite sizable, much larger than is reasonable for a judicial system, but it is still no more than several months. Even during the busiest times, the first hearing is held eight or nine months after the state submits its response, but not two years later and certainly not three. Feldman was stuck with a petition that was fated to remain "pending."

There is another perspective. The case was being handled by the man who would go on to replace Justice Shamgar as president of the Supreme Court in 1996, Justice Aharon Barak. Famed for his mastery of the art of timing, Barak planned his judgments to coincide with favorable political and national security conditions. It may well have been that Barak was waiting, first for his appointment as Supreme Court president and the ability to control the case as he wished, and second, for calmer days, when it would be easier to give a ruling that was inevitably going to ruffle the feathers of the security establishment. This interpretation assumes that Barak felt there was no way to reject PCATI's new petition, and so he was waiting for the right timing, when the court would sustain the least damage from pushback by the state.

In any case, there is no way to know what sort of exchanges went on between the justices' chambers and the court secretariat; the fact is that the new PCATI case was shelved for more than three years, until January 1998. There is very little that the lawyer who filed the petition can do in a situation like this. The justices are the undisputed overlords of scheduling and pushing cases forward. Meanwhile, as the new PCATI petition hibernated in the Supreme Court secretariat, the torture continued and with it the unending stream of petitions the lawyers called the "small petition," the ones filed in real time to stop the torture of a specific interrogee (the "big petitions" being the first and second PCATI efforts). The pressure on the court was relentless.

Then, on April 26, 1995, before dawn, 'Abd al-Samed Harizat, a computer programmer from Hebron, died at Hadassah Hospital in Jerusalem. Five days earlier, he had been arrested in his home in Hebron on suspicion of being a "senior commander" of the Hamas armed wing. Prime Minister Yitzhak Rabin had declared an all-out war on suicide bombings, which had intensified that year, and on Hamas, which was responsible for most of them and became a major target for security forces. Harizat was taken to the Shabak interrogation wing at the Russian Compound detention facility in Jerusalem. The next day, Saturday afternoon, he was rushed to the hospital with irreversible brain damage. His family contacted Andre Rosenthal, who immediately set out to determine what had happened to his client. Harizat died four days later. The news was quickly picked up by the media, and the public was exposed to the death of an interrogee in Shabak detention in real time. Usually slow to report allegations of fatal violence by Shabak officers, the press now demanded some answers. The Ministry of Justice opened an inquiry and the Jerusalem Magistrates' Court was asked to order an autopsy.[60] The inquiry turned into an inquest, which lasted several weeks.

The Department of Police Investigations, tasked with investigating Harizat's death, concluded that on the day after his arrest, his interrogators had used a technique known as "shaking." This is a method of torture in which the victim is "shaken violently by the upper body, forward and backward, in a manner that causes the neck and the head to oscillate rapidly, such that the brain is thrust against the cranium and is shaken severely."[61] Having been subjected to twelve "shaking sessions" over an eleven-hour period, Harizat's condition suddenly deteriorated and fluid began bubbling from his mouth and nose.[62] He lost consciousness and did not regain it. The report of the Institute of Forensic Medicine, a government institution that then had a monopoly on postmortem examinations, confirmed Harizat's death was caused by hemorrhaging and edema, which were results of "rotational acceleration" of the head—that is, shaking.[63]

The Shabak would later argue that Harizat had a "thin skull," that he was a frail man, that the technique did not inherently cause this kind of damage. However, their claim did not quite fit with the findings of the Institute of Forensic Medicine. The interrogators also argued that they had intelligence pointing to Harizat being in charge of a Hamas cell that was about to carry out attacks; therefore extreme interrogation methods such as shaking were legitimate to extract information about the cell's location and plans. The goal was to save Israeli lives.

When the inquest concluded, State Attorney Dorit Beinisch and Attorney General Michael Ben Yair had to decide whether to prosecute any of the Shabak agents and, if so, which ones. Ben Yair had tried to constrain the use of torture, leading to a very public dispute with the head of the Shabak, Carmi Gillon, who wanted to expand it.[64] Ultimately Ben Yair and Beinisch decided on disciplinary action at an internal Shabak and Mossad tribunal against one interrogator. Beinisch and Ben Yair concluded that the interrogators could not have anticipated the fatal outcome and therefore should not be subject to criminal prosecution. However, since one of the interrogators had exceeded the approved guidelines with respect to "shaking," he would be disciplined. The interrogator in question was acquitted on most of the counts, convicted only of what the disciplinary tribunal called a "technical failure." The tribunal also held that Harizat had been a "ticking time bomb," which justified the use of shaking. Years later the High Court dismissed a petition to criminally prosecute the interrogators submitted on behalf of Harizat's family by Andre Rosenthal, who was working with HaMoked.[65]

Still, Harizat's death was a watershed. Torture kills. Although death in custody had happened before, and news of it had been made public (in B'Tselem's important 1991 report, for example), this was the first time the country was made aware of the details without question marks or denials. People in ACRI felt that an opportunity had opened up to challenge the practice of torture, focusing on a specific technique. They thought a legal challenge to a technique that had proven to put interrogees' lives at risk and even kill them would have a fair chance of success. The court would not be able to avoid the case by dismissing it as "general" or "theoretical."

In June 1995, two months after Harizat's death, with the results of the DPI investigation in their hands, ACRI petitioned the High Court of Justice to prohibit the use of shaking. ACRI also asked for an interim order to prevent its use while the petition was pending. ACRI joining the ranks of the fight against torture with a "big" petition was a most significant development. Israel's oldest and largest human rights organization, ACRI was founded and led by the pillars of the country's legal community. The leaders of ACRI were consistently the most prominent members of the Hebrew University Law Faculty, the crucible of Israeli law. Among them were David Kretzmer, a future vice chairperson of the UN Human Rights Committee; Ruth Gavison, who was not just a renowned jurist and scholar, but also a foremost champion of individual rights in Israel; and Mordechai Kremnitzer, an expert on criminal law and one of the country's standard-bearers of liberalism. Over the years, retired Supreme Court justice Haim Cohn and former Supreme Court president Shimon Agranat served as presidents of the organization. ACRI was part of Israel's legal elite, with special reverberations in legal circles.

The petition was initially handled by several ACRI lawyers, including Dana Briskman, Eliyahu Avram, and Dan Yakir. Eventually, Yakir, the lawyer most closely associated with ACRI over the past two decades, took the reins. Unlike ACRI's founders, who were academics and members of the establishment, Yakir is the quintessential activist lawyer. With unwavering allegiance to human rights, Yakir, both as a regular lawyer with ACRI and later as its legal counsel, has covered almost every area of Israel's human rights violations: discrimination against Palestinian citizens; discrimination against members of the LGBTQ community; violation of freedom of expression; and of freedom of art, and of due process rights, prisoners' rights, and social rights, which were not even on ACRI's radar when he joined it as a volunteer in 1982. Over the years, Yakir became not just the face of ACRI's legal work but also synonymous with the fight for human rights in Israel. After Harizat's death, Yakir was convinced that ACRI should take legal action against shaking, and he pushed strongly for it within the organization.

But despite the enormous push ACRI's petition gave to the anti-torture campaign, it was still not enough to jolt the Supreme Court out of its paralysis. ACRI's petition joined PCATI's petition on the shelf and languished there for months.

The "big" cases were in stasis, but that did not mean the pressure had no effect. Every new case pressed a little more against the dam that was holding back a court deliberation on the legality of torture. The PCATI and ACRI petitions could not stay on the shelf forever. The justices were well aware that something had to be done with these legal time bombs. Media coverage of torture had increased, with more and more reports of allegations of torture and coverage of the ministerial committee that approved "special investigation measures." After Harizat's death, Avigdor Feldman published a scathing op-ed in *Haaretz* that asserted a broad indictment: "For one torturer to go about his business uninterrupted there have to be several dozen people, about the number of people who live in an apartment building. They surround the torturer like a loving, caring family: office staff, prison guards, police officers, doctors, judges, and about a hundred other people who look the other way."[66] The harsh condemnation was not lost on the justices.

At the same time, the stream of individual petitions filed on behalf of detainees continued to arrive, and the issues the petitions addressed became clearer with time. If the early wave of petitions had sought to lift the ban on meeting with counsel and only added deliberations over interrogation methods as a side issue, the methods themselves were now becoming the main focus. Harizat's death accelerated this trend. One such case that played out with drama and public attention was a petition filed by Islamic Jihad activist Abd al-Halim Balbisi, who was arrested in December 1995. Andre Rosenthal, working on behalf of HaMoked, filed a petition on Balbisi's behalf demanding that he not be subjected to shaking or the *shabach* technique.

Supreme Court justices Eliyahu Mazza, Mishael Cheshin, and Dalia Dorner issued an interim order restricting the use of physical measures in Balbisi's interrogation, but more than two weeks later Shai Nitzan, the state attorney most involved in torture cases, filed a motion on behalf of the Shabak to revoke the interim order. Nitzan told the court that during his interrogation, Balbisi had confessed to his part in one of the deadliest terrorist attacks in Israel, a double suicide bombing at the Beit Lid intersection, which killed more than twenty people. Balbisi had revealed that a third terrorist had never made it to the site and also disclosed the location of a bomb he had planned to use. Security forces located the bomb and defused it. All this information had been obtained without using physical pressure, but now, Nitzan argued, the Shabak had intelligence that Balbisi knew about other groups preparing attacks in Israel. Balbisi was not giving any further details, though, and so Nitzan claimed there was an immediate need to use "physical interrogation methods."

The court heard the state's motion the day after Nitzan filed it. The panel that was hastily composed to meet included Justices Gabriel Bach, Cheshin, and Yitzhak Zamir. Rosenthal went for an unusual line. He did not deny the Shabak's information or ask the court to inspect its credibility. There was little point, since Rosenthal would not be privy to the material or able to question its reliability. (Lawyers often think it preferable that justices do not see material rather than seeing it ex parte; the risk of their minds being "poisoned" by information the lawyers are not able to critique is too great.) However, Rosenthal's consent could allow the justices to presume that the Shabak had good reason to believe in this important information that Balbisi was supposedly keeping to himself. So Rosenthal decided to focus on the shaking. He asked the court to deny the state's motion to revoke the interim order prohibiting physical pressure, but, failing that, he requested that the prohibition on shaking, which had already killed Harizat, remain in place.

The justices decided to accept the state's motion, also rejecting Rosenthal's request to bar shaking.[67] Aware that their decision could be seen as granting the legality of various measures of physical pressure, including shaking, the justices added a reservation: "Our decision relates solely to the interim order issued in this case. It does not constitute a final position on the issue of principle raised by the Petitioner in the petition for order nisi, which we did not discuss today, at the petitioner's request." It is hard to imagine a stranger judicial decision. Three Supreme Court justices permit an intelligence agency to use a measure impugned as torture—an act that is unambiguously prohibited, defined as a crime under international law—but also proclaim that their permission should not be taken to mean that the measure is legal. Their decision speaks to the bind in which the justices found themselves. On one hand, the deed was prohibited. On the other, they feared that prohibiting it would prevent the Shabak from saving Israeli lives. The justices' dilemma resulted in a decision that basically says, do whatever you want, but don't claim we said it was legal. The justices' distress cries out from the page, but it does not absolve them of responsibility.

The headlines soon followed, and they used the *t* word: "The High Court Allows Torture of Suspected Planner of the Beit Lid Attack," *Haaretz* said.[68] "Shin Bet Gets Go-Ahead to 'Violently Shake' Suspects," decried Britain's *Independent*.[69] The pressure on the Supreme Court and its justices was mounting.

In the months that followed Harizat's death, the number of cases in which the court granted a motion for an interim order against the use of torture increased. The petitions mainly focused on shaking, the *shabach* method, and sleep deprivation.[70] Rosenthal and Leah Tsemel, who filed similar petitions, managed to get such orders from different panels of the court; and by the time the petitions had been filed, the Shabak had usually either finished its torture or had no need to use it in the specific case and so seldom asked to have the orders revoked. It did ask for revocation in two cases—Balbisi's and Hamdan's—and the court granted the requests both times. The court was inundated with these sorts of cases throughout 1996 and 1997, while the two big petitions filed by PCATI and ACRI stayed on the shelf, with no hearings scheduled and no interim orders issued. Meanwhile, the descriptions from different interrogees that were included in the various petitions uncovered more and more torture techniques. Each technique had its own name, apparently the invention of Shabak agents, which hinted at how it worked: "the frog crouch," "the banana position," "the closet," "the fridge," "the bathtub," "the shower."[71] Exposed to the steady stream of harsh allegations, the justices eventually took action.

In late 1997, PCATI filed two petitions on behalf of two Palestinians under interrogation, Abd al-Rahman Ghneimat[72] and Fouad Qur'an,[73] who were represented by Tsemel and Allegra Pacheco. The petitions focused on the *shabach* method. Having litigated in the military courts on behalf of clients who had been subjected to this form of torture, Feldman's intellectual curiosity led him to investigate the origins of the term "shabach." Palestinian interrogees told him it was an ancient Arabic word denoting a special type of ghost. Shabak interrogators, on the other hand, said the term applied to a hitching post or some other station where horses are tied.[74] Both explanations are bloodcurdling. In its publications and petitions, PCATI notes that detainees were often held in the *shabach* position for days, even weeks, with five-minute bathroom breaks two or three times a day, during which they would also receive their meals, on the bathroom floor.[75] In the affidavit enclosed with his petition, Ghneimat said:

> I am Abd al-Rahman Ghneimat and I have been under interrogation since November 13, '97.* The interrogation has ended, but I am still being held in *shabach*, with a sack over my head. This has been the situation the entire time, five days a week, without sleep or rest. The handcuffs are hurting my hands, and have caused them to swell. In addition, the loud music has affected me and is making me constantly dizzy. I am now going into day forty of the interrogation in the same state. I also have pain in the wrists, the back, the entire body. Everything I have written is true. This is my signature.[76]

In various petitions, including those filed by Ghneimat and Qur'an, the Shabak claimed that what the detainees call "shabach" was, in fact, the "waiting period" between interrogations. They explained that there were time slots for interrogation, rest, and waiting, and provided different and not very persuasive justifications for each element of the waiting period. The music prevented the detainees from speaking to each other. The cuffs stopped them from assaulting their interrogators. The cloth sack blocked detainees from seeing who was being held with them and other things they were not supposed to see. Sleep deprivation was an unintended byproduct of intensive interrogation (begging the question why interrogees were not able to sleep during the waiting periods), and so on. However, in his petition Ghneimat noted that he had been held in the *shabach* position for forty days, with breaks only on weekends—hardly a waiting period between interrogations. Both petitions naturally asked for an urgent interim order to prohibit more torture.

Qur'an's petition was heard on December 26, 1997. Justice Barak, now president of the Supreme Court, presided, with Justices Tova Strasberg-

---

* His petition was filed on December 24, six weeks later.

Cohen and Dalia Dorner at his side. The state pledged that Qur'an would be able to sleep and eat and declared no shaking had been used. These types of declarations had been sufficient in previous years to end the deliberations on such petitions. But this time the justices took a different approach. They asked for Qur'an's interrogation logs to examine his claims about the time he had spent in *shabach* (or "waiting"). The hearing was put off for several days so the Shabak could produce the log, which was expected to contain exact information about Qur'an's interrogation. When the hearing resumed, however, the justices had difficulty getting Yehuda Shaffer, who represented the Shabak, to give them any clear account of how much time the petitioner had spent in the *shabach* position. The hearing produced an unprecedented decision: a demand for precise data about a torture method:

> We ask the Respondents to provide us with details (within forty-eight hours)—in a notice to the Court—on the following:
>
> a. During the time the Petitioner was not resting, how long did he spend under interrogation, and how long did he spend waiting?
>
> b. What measures—such as music, hooding, sitting on a low chair, use of hand cuffs—are the Respondents using during the Petitioner's interrogation and what is the rationale for these methods?
>
> The notice shall be provided to counsel for the Petitioner, unless a request is made to withhold some or all of this information. Upon receipt of such request, we shall review it and make a decision.[77]

On January 5, 1998, the panel of judges decided to join the two petitions and issued an order nisi (a conditional order to stop the physical measures in interrogations, compelling the state to provide a response affidavit). President Barak further ordered that an unprecedented panel of nine justices hear the petitions. A hearing by the extended panel was scheduled for January 8. Suddenly everything moved very quickly. In the briefs that were submitted with lightning speed, Tsemel and Pacheco had to reckon with the state's disavowal that the so-called waiting period was an interrogation method. They showed that the state's explanations for a position in which interrogees were held for hours and days was preposterous, and argued that this was in fact torture, which is absolutely prohibited. Tsemel's and Pacheco's briefs included quotes from scores of interrogees' affidavits collected by HaMoked that showed exactly the nature of the *shabach* position. According to one affidavit:

> They put a tight sack over my head, which made breathing very difficult. They put cuffs on my hands and feet. They bound them tightly, which made my hands and feet swell and bleed. They sat me on a small, low chair, and tied my hands behind the backrest. . . . This went on with no breaks until Thursday night. It paralyzed me. I felt I could not take it any longer. My nerves were shot and paralyzed.[78]

This was the signal to bring the two big petitions out of stasis. At the January 8 hearing, the nine justices decided to join the PCATI and ACRI petitions to Tsemel's and Pacheco's and hear all four together. Torture had finally been taken out of deep freeze and was on a course toward a decision. However, on the same day, the court was also scheduled to consider the motion for an interim order to end Ghneimat's torture, who by then had allegedly been held in the *shabach* position for fifty-four days. All nine justices, almost the full complement of justices of the Supreme Court, were present to rule on the motion. They had differing views, and the ruling was decided on a single vote: five justices were against issuing the interim order, and four were in favor, so the Shabak was not compelled to end Ghneimat's torture.

What looked like a defeat in fact contained some encouraging news: both the Supreme Court president, Aharon Barak, and his vice president, Shlomo Levin, were among the minority. The two justices could not have been more different: Barak viewed the law as a means of achieving moral values, and hence was a proponent of the purposive interpretation of constitutional issues; Levin, an expert on civil rules of procedure, was known for his formalistic approach to the law. Presumably, one objected to torture for moral reasons, while the other was persuaded that the Shabak simply did not have the legal authority to use physical pressure. In any case, the lawyers campaigning against torture saw reason for hope in the majority-minority split, and their expectations began to rise. They understood that when a majority opinion wins by a single vote, and the minority has on its side so charismatic and influential a president as Barak, along with his vice president, then the majority is not all that stable.

In the weeks that followed, two more individual petitions filed by Rosenthal were added to the big PCATI and ACRI petitions and to those filed by Ghneimat and Qur'an, and suddenly a massive torture case was under way. It is hard to imagine a more impressive battery of lawyers working on behalf of the petitioners: Feldman, Yakir, Tsemel, Pacheco, Eliyahu Avram (representing HaMoked), and Rosenthal. On the opposite side were state attorney lawyers Shai Nitzan and Yehuda Sheffer.

"DECIDING THESE PETITIONS WEIGHED HEAVILY ON THIS COURT"

The joined petitions addressed several, but not all, physical measures. The ACRI petition focused on shaking. The individual petitions filed by Ha-Moked and PCATI addressed the *shabach* position, sleep deprivation, and the frog crouch. Other measures that had been reported over the years—exposure to extreme cold, the closet, and the *falaka*—were not discussed, though PCATI's "big" petition sought an order against any and all use of "moderate measure of physical pressure." Some of the methods had possibly fallen into disuse by the time the joined petitions were heard. According to HaMoked's and PCATI's records, the methods change over the years. Challenging the legality of "non-violent psychological pressure" had also been dropped somewhere along the line, though it had been included in PCATI's original petition.

The hearings in the joined petitions were held in May 1998 and January 1999. Because the court had issued orders nisi, proper procedure required the State Attorney's Office to plead its case first; the petitioners would follow with their rebuttal. Shai Nitzan mounted a passionate defense of the formula for special interrogation methods handed to the Shabak by the Landau Commission ("moderate physical measures"). He had a lot to say. First, some of the individual petitioners were none too endearing—to put it mildly. Ghneimat had been convicted of involvement in a lethal attack on the Apropos Café in Tel Aviv in which three women were killed and thirty people injured. Nitzan argued that the information extracted during his interrogation revealed the existence of another bomb, hidden in his village, ready to be used in a similar attack. One of Rosenthal's clients, Hatem Abu Zeideh, was convicted of recruiting Hamas operatives and helping to plan to kidnap soldiers and attack security forces. According to Nitzan, the information extracted from him, during an interrogation that included physical pressure, helped foil planned attacks against soldiers.

Nitzan refused to disclose in open court which interrogation methods used by the Shabak met the criteria of "moderate physical pressure." Counsel for the petitioners refused to allow him to present the methods ex parte. However, Nitzan did not deny the use of some of the measures alleged by the petitioners: sleep deprivation, the *shabach* position, the frog crouch, and shaking. He repeated explanations from previous cases: these were not interrogation methods in and of themselves but incidental outcomes of legitimate interrogations; interrogations are often urgent and intense (hence the sleep deprivation); detainees must be prevented from communicating with each other (hence the loud music and hooding); the imperative to ensure the interrogators' safety (hence the handcuffs and binding during "waiting" periods).

Nitzan admitted that shaking had been used as a means of interrogation, but it was a rare exception, he said, applied only when lives were at stake. Harizat's case was also an exception, a result of a rare complication. "Shaking is indispensable to fighting and winning the war on terrorism," he argued. "It is not possible to prohibit its use without seriously harming the ability of the Shabak to effectively thwart deadly terrorist attacks." The state took the position that the need to save lives is pitted against the clear difficulties raised by shaking: "Using it has in the past helped prevent murderous attacks," Nitzan said, juxtaposing the pain inflicted on murderous terrorists against the lives of innocent Israelis. Nitzan filed an affidavit from Shabak head Ami Ayalon, who made similarly unequivocal statements:

These measures . . . are—to the best of my knowledge and judgment—highly essential to the fight to thwart terrorism and cannot, at present, be relinquished without seriously compromising the agency's ability to prevent terrorist attacks.[79]

Ayalon, who later joined the Israeli peace camp, justified the use of shaking and the *shabach* position to the Supreme Court by deploying the ticking-time-bomb dilemma. Neither Ayalon nor Nitzan articulated precisely the range of cases that presented a ticking time bomb, or defined interrogations that were meant to "prevent terrorist attacks." The purpose of the vast majority of Shabak interrogations was to collect information, and any such information could be relevant to "preventing terrorist attacks." Nitzan argued that the protocol, which was approved by the ministerial committee and limits use of shaking and other measures to cases that are considered exceptional, together with the tight oversight and monitoring of the Shabak, strikes a proper balance between the need to protect individuals under interrogation and the need to protect national security.

On the legal issues, Nitzan closely followed the Landau Commission conclusions. Shabak agents may conduct interrogations pursuant to the government's general, residual powers; Shabak interrogators are authorized—by name—by the minister of justice, pursuant to his legal powers, to conduct interrogations, just as police officers are; the Shabak's agents' power to use physical interrogation methods derives from the "necessity" defense, which prevents an act from being considered a criminal offense if it is carried out to avert immediate, serious danger to human life. Nitzan was furious with the petitioners' contention that the physical measures at the center of the discussion should be classified as "torture," and he went so far as to say that they did not even reach the level of the lesser categories, more softly prohibited under international law, of cruel, inhuman, or degrading treatment. These acts did not cause the severe pain and suffering that would justify classifying them as such, Nitzan concluded.

In the months that elapsed between the two hearings, in May 1998 and January 1999, the government tried to pass a law to authorize the use of "moderate physical pressure" during Shabak interrogations. The attempt was prompted by comments the justices made during the first hearing, to the effect that the court would be hard pressed to sanction use of such drastic measures without having a legal source on which to rely. The justices also expressed discomfort at being asked to do the dirty work of upholding the controversial practice when the legislature had shunned the task. The fact that the two hearings were scheduled so far apart might not have been a coincidence; perhaps the court wanted to give the government time to pass a law. But despite having seven months to do so, the government failed in its attempt.

The petitioners were scheduled to make their arguments in a third hearing, in May 1999. As counsel on the earliest of the cases, PCATI's big petition, Feldman was the lead. In the run-up to the hearing, the lawyers filed many supplementary briefs. Yakir, for ACRI, and Avram for HaMoked, showed in their briefs that there is a full consensus under international law that torture and cruel or inhuman treatment are absolutely prohibited with no exceptions. They referred the court to decisions made by international tribunals, to opinions penned by experts, and to the decisions of the UN Committee Against Torture, which oversees the implementation of the International Convention Against Torture, ratified by Israel in 1991 (in three different reports, issued in 1994, 1997, and 1998, the committee rebuked Israel for the methods used by the Shabak).

One judgment the petitioners brought up again and again, because of the similarities between the interrogation methods it describes and those under scrutiny in the High Court hearing and because it dealt with the legality of the use of physical means in interrogations in general, was the European Court of Human Rights' seminal decision from 1978 in Ireland's case against the United Kingdom for the interrogation methods used against members of the IRA. Those methods, which included forcing detainees to stand against a wall in a position that stretches the body; hooding; subjecting them to noise, sleep deprivation, and withholding food and drink, had been inflicted intermittently over a period of four to five days.[80] The European court ruled that the combined use of the five techniques undoubtedly amounted to inhuman, degrading treatment. The degradation, the European court stated, stemmed from the potential these techniques had to induce feelings of fear, anguish, and inferiority among the victims, which together could break them mentally or physically. Still, the majority opinion was that the suffering endured by the detainees did not reach the particular level of severity and cruelty that characterizes torture.

However, the crucial differences between the five interrogation methods used by the British forces and the Shabak's, Avram argued in his brief for HaMoked, were duration and continuity. "The durations practiced in Israel are far longer than the four or five days of interrogation in total, during which the methods were used, intermittently,"[81] he wrote. Another difference, he added, was that the Irish detainees appeared to have suffered no long-term injuries from their interrogations, while Israel's High Court was presented with several expert opinions about real injuries sustained by Shabak interrogees. One expert report revealed that one of the petitioners had suffered a permanent psychiatric disability while another had neurological damage resulting from shaking—this apart from Harizat's death by shaking.

Yakir concluded his supplementary brief for ACRI by clarifying that the torture case was also about Israel's moral character. "The spirit and moral fortitude of any enlightened regime is measured precisely by its ability to overcome primal urges, its ability to remain true to basic moral standards, even during difficult times, and even while confronting the most difficult enemy," he wrote.[82] Feldman was the most damning. He sharply criticized the state's defense of the interrogation methods and made sure not to let a single one of the many accomplices to the practice off the hook:

> The picture that emerges from the responses given by the Respondents in the various petitions is one of a bureaucratization of torture, physical pain, and mental suffering, based on an internal moral code concocted by the Shabak, replete with self-persuasion regarding the righteousness of these measures while waving the primitive, lest we say barbaric, banner of the necessity defense. This is an alarming picture which indicates a dangerous direction toward the state shedding fundamental rights in favor of the pseudo-ethical, pseudo-philosophical self-justification of the necessity defense.[83]

The nine justices delivered their judgment in September 1999. On his way from Tel Aviv to the court in Jerusalem, Dan Yakir got stuck in traffic caused by a garbage-truck drivers' strike. He had to take a detour and had a hard time convincing other drivers, whom he asked for use of a cell phone to let the court know he was delayed, that a man without a phone was in fact a lawyer. When he finally made it, half an hour late, the petitioners were just coming out of the great hall. His colleagues' smiles gave away the news. The court had accepted the petitions, unanimously ruling that the Shabak had no power to use the frog crouch, shaking, sleep deprivation, and the *shabach*—including playing loud music and using hooding and painful binding. Eight justices favored issuing a final order prohibiting these methods, while one justice, Yaakov Kedmi, advocated holding the decree absolute off for a year to allow the legislature to write these or other techniques into law.

The judgment, written by Supreme Court president Aharon Barak, would define his career, and he clearly knew it. He had managed to achieve consensus on a major issue among all the justices of the court he headed, and this was no small feat. Aware that many in Israel would be angered by the judgment, that it might be perceived as detrimental to security and fighting Palestinian terrorism, Barak opened with an impassioned acknowledgment of the security challenges facing the country: "Ever since it was established, the State of Israel has been engaged in an unceasing struggle for its security—indeed, its very existence," Barak wrote. "Terrorist organizations have set Israel's annihilation as their goal. Terrorist acts and the general disruption of order are their means of choice." Before getting to the question of the legality of the interrogation methods, Barak gave a detailed account of the methods used by terrorists, the number of people murdered, and of the Shabak as the government agency charged with protecting Israel's citizens. With this preamble, Barak set out to sugar-coat the ruling at the core of the judgment: the interrogation methods used by the Shabak and discussed in the case were unlawful.

After giving a description of the interrogation methods in question, Barak moved on to examine their legality. He ruled that the power granted by the minister of justice does authorize Shabak agents to conduct interrogations, similarly to police officers, but that the necessity defense cannot serve as a source for authorizing use of physical measures during interrogation. With one simple statement, Barak ended years of heated debate and invalidated the power to allow interrogators to use physical pressure: "The lifting of criminal responsibility does not imply authorization to infringe a human right."[84] Shabak interrogators, Barak ruled, have the same powers as police interrogators, no more and no less. With no statute giving them additional powers, they do not have any.

However, Barak did not deny the relevance of the necessity defense, stating that it may be invoked by an interrogator being prosecuted for resorting to physical measures during an interrogation. "The defense deals with cases involving an individual reacting to a given set of facts," Barak wrote. "It is an improvised reaction to an unpredictable event."[85] Thus Barak distinguished between using "necessity" as a source for authorizing use of physical measures during interrogation and "necessity" as a defense against criminal conviction. An interrogator cannot receive prior authorization to commit an act that constitutes an offense, certainly not in the form of general guidelines, because the necessity defense applies only when a person is forced to take an action in unexpected circumstances where it is the only thing that could save life. Even then, the fact that the act is shielded from criminal liability does not make it legal. The defense simply prevents a conviction. Barak concluded the discussion of the necessity defense with a statement that would later be interpreted in a way that he probably did not intend: "The attorney general can establish guidelines regarding circumstances in which investigators shall not stand trial, if they claim to have acted from 'necessity.'"[86] Subsequent attorneys general took Barak's statement to allow an exclusion that permitted the use of physical interrogation methods after all.

Barak stopped short of classifying the interrogation methods as torture, or even "just" degrading and inhuman treatment, though he did allude to the decision of the European Court of Human Rights, which had considered similar methods to be inhuman and degrading treatment. He also dismissed the state's argument that the government's residual powers—the provision that the government has any power not already held by another state authority—could serve as a legal source for use of physical interrogation methods. The government's "residual or prerogative powers" cannot serve as a source for powers that infringe on individual liberties. They authorize the government to act "whenever there is an 'administrative vacuum,'" but "there is no so-called 'administrative vacuum' in this case, as the field is entirely occupied by the principle of individual freedom. Infringing this principle requires specific directives."[87]

In conclusion, Barak returned to the threats facing Israel and acknowledged the fact that the judgment made fighting terrorism more difficult. However, he argued that in the broader sense it would actually make the country stronger:

We are aware that this decision does not make it easier to deal with that reality. This is the destiny of a democracy—it does not see all means as acceptable, and the ways of its enemies are not always open before it. A democracy must sometimes fight with one hand tied behind its back. Even so, a democracy has the upper hand. The rule of law and the liberty of an individual constitute important components in its understanding of security. At the end of the day, they strengthen its spirit and this strength allows it to overcome its difficulties.[88]

Concerns over the public's reaction took Barak one step further. Beyond recognizing, even glorifying, Israel's fight against its enemies, he revealed his own struggle with the case: "Deciding these petitions weighed heavily on this Court," Barak wrote candidly. "We are, however, judges. We must decide according to the law. This is the standard that we set for ourselves. When we sit to judge, we ourselves are judged."[89]

WITHDRAWAL PAINS

"At 10:00 a.m., torture stopped," wrote Amir Oren, *Haaretz*'s military correspondent, the day after the judgment was issued. "Shortly after 10:00 a.m., fax machines in the interrogation facilities began churning out the High Court's decision, with particular emphasis on Paragraph 38, which denied the legality of the permits. At that moment, the head of the investigations division in the Shabak ordered that any sort of torture allowed by the cleansing term 'permit' must stop."[90]

The judgment sent shock waves throughout the security establishment and caused political-legal strife. The papers reported a dispute between Attorney General (and future justice and vice president of the Supreme Court) Elyakim Rubinstein, who favored legislation that would reinstate some or all the interrogation methods the court had struck down, and Minister of Justice Yossi Beilin, who opposed such a move.[91] Over the next few years, various attempts were made to initiate legislation that would either permit the use of torture or absolutely prohibit it and stipulate penalties for doing so. All of these attempts failed. Torture was never permitted by law, but also never prohibited to any extent greater than the High Court's judgment.

Although the justices had determined that advance permission could not be given to use the interrogation methods listed in the judgment, they had not ruled out situations where such use would not be considered criminal if the interrogator had acted out of necessity. A succession of attorneys general, beginning with Rubinstein, interpreted this intricate position very differently from the public understanding of the judgment. Barak's comment that the attorney general could "establish guidelines regarding circumstances in which investigators shall not stand trial, if they claim to have acted from 'necessity,'" was taken by the attorney's general to mean that they, as head of the general prosecution, could produce a protocol that will determine when the prosecution of interrogators who had used "special" interrogation methods should be carried out and when it shouldn't.

About a month after the judgment was delivered, Rubinstein published a document titled "Shabak Interrogations and the Necessity Defense—A Framework for Discretion."[92] Rubinstein explained that as he understood it, "the ongoing, routine work of collecting information about terrorist organizations and their general activities" could not be considered to meet the necessity defense requirement for "present danger." On the other hand, if the information pertained to a specific and certain threat to human life, the interrogator's sense of "necessity" would more plausibly meet the requirement. Rubinstein determined that the necessity defense would, naturally, apply in "extremely" rare cases, and could not be a routine feature of interrogations.[93] So far, a rather reasonable interpretation of the judgment. Except Rubinstein added a controversial directive that would dull the judgment's great success, instructing the Shabak to institute "internal directives with respect to the required internal process of consultation and authorization."[94]

Crucially, the High Court judgment did not subscribe to the radical position (the position of international law) that torture and cruel and inhuman or degrading treatment are always prohibited, no matter the circumstances. Without reaching a direct judgment on this question, the justices under Barak's leadership accepted, as a working premise, that use of physical pressure may be unavoidable in ticking-time-bomb situations.[95] The court rejected Feldman's legal view that the "necessity" defense cannot serve agents acting pursuant to statutory powers. It accepted the possibility that a Shabak interrogator using physical pressure might subsequently be deemed to have acted out of necessity and therefore should not be prosecuted. However, the judgment frames the necessity defense as applicable just to individual interrogators who find themselves in a situation where they believe that only physical pressure, used on the specific person in front of them, could save lives. The judgment envisions an interrogator who *takes a risk* and carries out an illegal act to save lives, knowing that the lawfulness of the act would later come under scrutiny. Placing the risk on the individual interrogator creates a chilling effect. The fact that the scenario involves an individual agent taking a huge personal legal risk, without authorization from his or her superiors, greatly reduces the odds of it actually occurring. Rubinstein's directive to institutionalize a process of consultation and authorization within the Shabak seriously reduced the chilling effect, regressing to a situation very much like that in which prior authorization was given for certain methods, a system that the High Court had fully rejected.

Nonetheless, the code of interrogation guidelines, which had established when detainees could be forced to sit on a low, tilted chair; deprived of sleep; or exposed to loud music—all ruled unlawful by the court—was replaced with internal guidelines and a system of consultations within the Shabak that determined when using these measures would not constitute a basis for prosecution. Information leaked from the Shabak indicated that following Rubinstein's directive, the agency came up with a "necessity interrogation protocol" and that the consultation process for using physical force involved approval granted by the interrogation team leader or sometimes by the head of the Shabak.[96] These internal guidelines meant that physical interrogation methods remained in use.

In the fifteen years following the judgment, Israeli human rights organizations documented a significant number of interrogations in which the prohibited methods were used, as well as new methods such as beatings, sudden body pulling, sudden head twisting, back bending (the banana position), and psychological pressure involving threats to arrest family members, verbal abuse, and humiliation.[97] There are no exact figures on the prevalence of torture since the judgment, but the information gained by human rights workers and lawyers who represent Palestinian interrogees suggests that there are between a handful and several dozen cases each year, with spikes in times of heightened security tension.[98] Figures obtained by PCATI under the Freedom of Information Act show that between 2001 and 2008, the inspector of complaints by Shabak interrogees received six hundred complaints regarding degrading, abusive treatment and physical violence during interrogations.[99] Not one of these complaints resulted in a criminal investigation.*

---

* In 2015, for the first time since the interrogation of the Shining Path activists in the 1970s, the Shabak used its "special" methods on Jewish interrogees. This occurred during the detention of members of a far-right group after the home of the Dawabsheh family in the Palestinian village of Duma was set on fire, and three family members were murdered. According to press reports, this time the Shabak did not settle for approval from the head of the agency, as in the case of Palestinian interrogees, but asked for and received permis-

In 2011, Avigdor Feldman filed a motion for an order under the Contempt of Court Ordinance against Israel's prime minister and the head of the Shabak. Feldman argued that by instating a system of guidelines and permissions to use physical force they had violated the judgment. The motion was denied a year later, on the grounds that the judgment the petitioner alleged was violated was of the "declarative" kind. In other words, it was a judgment that stated a legal situation, rather than an operative order that must be executed, and therefore could not be violated.[100] The panel, headed by Supreme Court president Dorit Beinisch, implied that the correct path would be a petition challenging the internal directives rather than a contempt-of-court procedure. No such petition was ever filed.

DEFEATING THE SECURITY ARGUMENT

The litigation campaign against torture in Israel is rightfully seen as a tremendous achievement for the human rights community. When the campaign began in the 1970s and 1980s, almost every Palestinian interrogated on security issues was subjected to violent procedures. These methods were not just concealed from the public, both in Israel and internationally, but also actively denied while the perpetrators lied to the courts. Some tens of thousands of Palestinians most likely suffered some kind of abuse during interrogation and use of violent methods was routine. While torture was not eradicated after the 1999 High Court judgment, there is no doubt that the use of violent interrogation methods dramatically declined. Once a regular, ordinary practice, torture became an exception, even if it was used in more than a handful of cases. No one, not even people who believe the prohibition on torture and inhuman and degrading treatment to be absolute and therefore do not consider the judgment a complete success, can deny that it brought about an immense change.

Throughout the years of the legal battle, both parties were keenly aware of the weapons in the other's arsenal. The Shabak and its legal representatives had on their side the most effective version of the security argument: the interrogation methods are necessary for the fight against

---

sion directly from the attorney general. Chaim Levinson, "Sources: Attorney General Approved Torture of Jewish Suspects in Duma Murder Case," *Haaretz* English website (last accessed July 17, 2016).

terrorism. They are the most direct, clear-cut instance of measures required to save human lives, in the most concrete sense. Ordinarily, less of a rationale would have sufficed. In Israel's legal and political spheres, almost any interest or argument is vanquished as soon as the state convincingly raises the cause of security, especially when that cause touches the very heart of the security mandate: protecting civilians against terror that strikes in coffee shops, on buses, on streets, and in shopping malls.

But for their part, the human rights organizations and their lawyers had rare support: an international legal consensus that did not just deny the legality of the torture policy but also considered it one of the gravest conceivable violations of a basic norm of international law. The European Court of Human Rights, various UN bodies, friendly democratic states (the George W. Bush administration and its post-9/11 interrogation methods came later), international conventions, and jurists the world over shared this position. The Israeli court would have had no leg to stand on had it chosen to uphold the use of "physical pressure," which is why torture opponents fought so hard throughout the 1980s and 1990s to bring the issue to the court. Their instinct, which proved true, was that a court considering itself part of the democratic-liberal tradition would not be able to issue a judgment approving torture, or even methods "merely" defined as inhuman. After the Landau Commission published its report and brought "moderate physical pressure" out of the shadows, all that was left was to push the court to confront the issue.

Given the potent weapons in each party's arsenal, it is no wonder that the court was reluctant to make a ruling and for years evaded a thorough review of the subject. But NGOs such as HaMoked and PCATI gave durability to the pressure applied to the court. Indeed, the anti-torture litigation campaign was the finest hour of Israel's civil society organizations, which, with the exception of ACRI (established back in 1972), became active in the late 1980s. It is hard to imagine isolated private lawyers filing the scores, even hundreds, of petitions that were filed on behalf of interrogees over the years. The different organizations changed the world of human rights advocacy in Israel into one where repeat players, with consistent funding and personnel, made sustained campaigns possible. While the individual petitions failed to get the court to confront the issue head-on for many years, they did produce a certain "disquiet," as Feldman calls it, within the legal system.[101]

President Barak's personality was also a critical factor in this success story. He, more than any other Supreme Court justice, thought it paramount that the jurisprudence of the court he headed conform to major international norms. In this sense, the court's (and the president's) self-image as a member of the international democratic-liberal community is in itself a powerful tool, which, in extreme cases, can even trump the security wild card.

Some might say that this analysis overlooks the moral aspect of opposing torture, which quite likely played a role in the justices' decision; that the court should be given more credit that its judgment was mainly driven by a moral objection to the Shabak's interrogation methods. Perhaps. It is plausible that the horror of torture played an important role in forming the position of Justice Barak, who displayed a great deal of sensitivity to human rights violations. Still, the fact that the court and its many justices, who knew of the interrogation methods, avoided doing anything about them for many years lends support to the theory that the international legal consensus featured prominently in the ultimate result. The judgment was, to use Feldman's words, "morally thin" and had no "historic outlook, no perspective," as if the entire question were "examined through a keyhole";[102] it also left the door open for different legislation and an exception in the shape of the necessity defense. We therefore may doubt how strongly the justices were influenced by moral considerations.

5

The Separation Barrier

TERRORISM

The Second Intifada broke out in late September 2000, two months after the collapse of the Camp David talks. After more than thirty years of occupation, the end had appeared on the horizon with the 1993–1995 signing of the Oslo Accords, only to slip away after the breakdown of the talks. This was the background to the Palestinian uprising. The spark that started the fire was Ariel Sharon's media-hyped visit to the Noble Sanctuary/Temple Mount in Jerusalem,* a provocation intended as a show of force, asserting Israel's dominion over the holy place.

While the First Intifada, which lasted from 1987 to 1993 and was known as the "intifada of the stones," had been a popular uprising that mostly took the shape of protests, strikes, and clashes between Palestinian civilians and the Israeli regime and military, the Second Intifada quickly took a different turn. The popular committees that had organized the First Intifada were replaced by paramilitary groups that engaged in an armed struggle against Israeli security forces, and planned and executed large-scale terrorist attacks aimed at civilians inside Israel and the Occupied Territories. Suicide attacks, which had been used in the early 1990s, became the main mode of operation for some of the armed groups. Terrorists wearing explosive belts blew themselves up on buses and in cafés, restaurants,

---

* Haram el-Sharif in Arabic, Har Habayit in Hebrew, the site is home to the Dome of the Rock and Al-Aqsa Mosque, and is also where the First and Second Temples once stood.

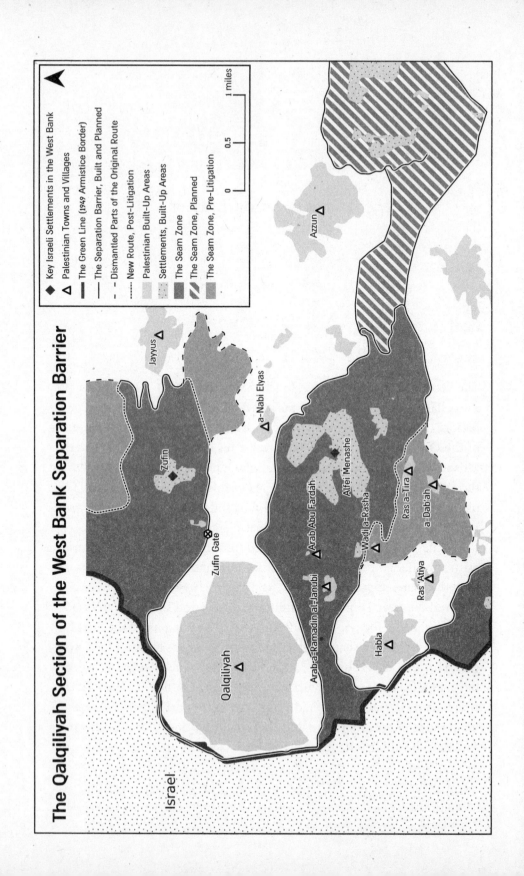

The Qalqiliyah Section of the West Bank Separation Barrier

Legend:

◆ Key Israeli Settlements in the West Bank
△ Palestinian Towns and Villages

The Green Line (1949 Armistice Border)
The Separation Barrier, Built and Planned
Dismantled Parts of the Original Route
New Route, Post-Litigation
Palestinian Built-Up Areas
Settlements, Built-Up Areas
The Seam Zone
The Seam Zone, Planned
The Seam Zone, Pre-Litigation

0   0.5   1 miles

Israel

Qalqiliyah

Zufin

Zufin Gate

Jayyus

a-Nabi Elyas

Azun

'Arab Abu Fardah

Araba-Ramadin al-Janubi

Wadi a-Rasha

Alfei Menashe

Ras a-Tira

a-Dab'ah

Ras 'Atiya

Habla

shopping centers, and main streets in Israel. At the height of the intifada, these unfathomably cruel attacks were a daily horror. According to B'Tselem's figures, 675 Israeli civilians were murdered, mostly in suicide attacks, from September 2000 to the summer of 2005, when Israel evacuated the Jewish settlements in the Gaza Strip. During this time, 313 members of the Israeli security forces were also killed.[1] Seventeen suicide attacks were committed in March 2002 alone, in which 94 Israeli civilians lost their lives. In the armed struggle in Gaza and the West Bank that same month, 30 security personnel were killed. No wonder that month was called Black March.

Israel responded with massive force during the first days of the uprising, when it still consisted mostly of popular protests. In the first week after Sharon's fateful visit in Jerusalem, more than 50 Palestinians were killed. At the one-month mark, there were more than 100 Palestinian fatalities. The terrorist attacks in Israeli cities, which in time replaced the popular protests, brought further clampdowns from Israel. According to B'Tselem figures, by the summer of 2005, 3,270 Palestinians had been killed.[2] Over the course of the intifada, Israel invaded Palestinian cities, assassinated the leaders of armed Palestinian groups, and took measures to pressure the civilian population. People on both sides lived with fear and violence, with the conflict taking a deadly, painful toll.

But let's go back to the suicide attacks for a moment. If the word "terrorism" means anything—its exact meaning has and will forever be a matter of controversy—then suicide attacks take center stage. Aimed entirely at harming civilians—the more the better—and carried out in supremely civilian locations, they are meant to put fear in the hearts of the population, Israel's civilian population, in this case. They are meant to terrorize. At the height of this period, people were faced with daily images of charred buses, bodies and body parts strewn around them. Streets were awash with blood. Children lost their parents, parents lost their children, and every foray to a shopping center, a café, or a stroll down the street was undertaken with great fear. A struggle that deliberately kills civilians as a means to achieve political goals is terrorism, and using suicide attackers who sacrifice their lives, who blow themselves up in civilian population centers, is one of its most bloodcurdling incarnations. There will come a day, maybe when the conflict is over, when Palestinians will be unable to escape the duty to reckon with some of their organizations' tactics.

Suicide terrorism, like any other type of terrorism (with the possible exception of using unconventional weapons), painful and difficult as it may be, does not, however, pose an existential threat to the nation it targets. It disrupts life. It causes indescribable suffering. It muffles the voices that call for peace and moderation. But it cannot bring a country to its knees, overthrow its government, or replace the regime in the way that a conventional war can. But terrorism can produce significant changes in the character of the society it targets. As Israel learned firsthand, a reality of terror is perfect breeding grounds for ideas and acts that threaten that society's principles and values. Terrorism can elicit exceptional cruelty and extinguish any compassion that society might have had. In fact, in many cases, herein lies terrorism's triumph.

MANIPULATION

The separation barrier* Israel's government decided to build, along a route that mostly runs well inside the West Bank, may hold the title for the most cynical manipulation of pain caused by suicide terrorism. And it's not as if the title has no other contenders. Israeli politicians have often used the suffering resulting from terrorism to promote themselves, inflame hatred, and justify immoral acts. In that they may not differ much from politicians the world over, who feed the fear of terrorism and exploit it. Except in Israel terrorism has hit long and hard, and the potential for its use has been considerable. Still, given its chosen route, the separation fence wins the title, because under the guise of a measure taken solely for security and to protect Israeli citizens from terror, the government advanced a grandiose political plan of settlement.

Worse still: even if we accept the claim that physical separation between Palestinians and Israel enhances security, then the government's plan for the fence, with a route designed with settlement goals in mind, in fact sacrificed its civilians' safety, as well as the safety of the security forces

---

* As with many controversial issues, the disagreements over the barrier were translated into wars of terminology: the IDF calls it a "security barrier" or "security fence"; those who oppose it prefer "separation wall" or even "apartheid wall." Most Israelis refer to it as the "separation fence." I have chosen to use "separation barrier" because it constitutes a physical system of separation that includes several components, among them fences and walls. Nevertheless, barrier, fence, and wall are used interchangeably.

stationed along the fence, in pursuit of a political goal. After Israel's territorial demands were rejected during negotiations, the staunchest annexationist opposition to the notion of any boundary between Israel and the West Bank got together and plotted how to exploit the public demand for a physical barrier that would stop free entry by Palestinians; their goal was to dispossess thousands of Palestinians of their land—de facto annexation of as much of the West Bank as possible—and establish unilateral facts on the ground. While we must revile terrorism, we must also repudiate the exploitation and manipulation of the fear it creates.

The idea of a fence that would separate Israel from the West Bank had been brought up in the 1990s in response to terrorist attacks at the time. Israel had begun imposing closures to legally prohibit Palestinians from entering Israel in the early 1990s. This was a reversal of the policy put in place shortly after Israel seized the West Bank in 1967, which sought to erase the Green Line and allowed freedom of movement across both territories. Palestinians from the West Bank who wished to enter Israel, whether to find work (and there were a great many) or harm Israelis, had little trouble doing so. During the Rabin government, which signed the 1993–1995 Oslo Accords, the leadership shied away from building a physical barrier for fear that it would mark the final borders at a time when Israel and the PLO were negotiating them.[3] During Ehud Barak's tenure as prime minister in the late 1990s and early 2000s, the concept was in fact (physical) separation between the West Bank and Israel, but with the exact borders to be determined through negotiations. After the failure of the Camp David talks, Barak's government resolved to build a double fence, one along the Green Line to prevent Palestinians from entering Israel and one around the West Bank settlement blocs to protect the people living in them. The Barak government was voted out of power shortly thereafter, and the decision was never implemented.

Supporters of creating a physical barrier, mostly from the center and center-left political camps, realized that it would significantly shape the future border between Israel and Palestine, which was precisely why the right wing vehemently opposed the idea. The right-wing opposition feared that creating a fence along the Green Line would greatly increase the risk that Israel would eventually withdraw to that boundary, which is internationally recognized as its sovereign border. The settlers and their supporters understood that the pool of Israelis willing to move to the settlements would dwindle significantly once such a fence was up, as the specter of withdrawal would be hanging over the territory that lies beyond it. This opposition, spearheaded by Ariel Sharon, first as leader of the opposition and then as prime minister, was fearful that physical separation could undermine the settlement project and put an end to the notion of Greater Israel.[4]

As the price exacted by suicide terrorism increased, however, the public demand for a fence grew stronger. In a poll taken in June 2002, 69 percent of Israelis expressed support for the fence and only 29 percent opposed it.[5] In 2004, support rose to 80 percent.[6] Security experts told Israelis that a system of fences, walls, and ditches would make it significantly harder for suicide bombers to reach Israel. The public thought this made sense. Every time a Palestinian wearing an explosive belt managed to detonate himself in one city or another—and at the height of the Second Intifada this happened every few days—it turned out that they had easily crossed the virtual border on their way from the West Bank to the site of the attack. Sharon and his government could not explain to the public why they wanted to avoid building a physical barrier. Ultimately, he and much of the opposition succumbed to public pressure and the government passed a series of resolutions on a system of fences and walls, beginning in June 2002.

The same Ariel Sharon who had opposed the fence and any separation of Israel from the West Bank, one of the greatest supporters of the settlement project and Israel's expansion into vast areas of the Occupied Territories, now became the fence's chief planner. Except it turned out that Sharon had never really retreated from his position; he merely redeployed. Sharon took the fence that Ehud Barak's government had intended to build along the Green Line and pushed it eastward, into the occupied West Bank. Under pressure from settler leaders and true to his own ideological beliefs, he devised an invasive route that penetrated deep into occupied territory to include the main settlement blocs. The fence ballooned around them to keep much of the land on the west side, attached to Israel. It is clear that the route Sharon's people planned follows the Zionist principle of claiming "as much land as possible with as few Arabs as possible."

A series of resolutions passed by Sharon's government in June and December 2002 and October 2003 green-lit the theft of more than 16 percent of the West Bank (355 square miles) to be trapped between the fence and the Green Line. The route would split the West Bank, keeping almost a sixth of it contiguous with Israel. Sharon also started working on plans for an eastern fence that would separate the rest of the West Bank from the Jordan Valley, a vast and sparsely populated area. Whatever was left would be locked in, between fences on the east and the west. This eastern route, which had not yet been discussed by the government, would have taken another bite out of the West Bank, bringing the sum of land either partly or completely inaccessible to Palestinians to well beyond 25 percent.

Thus, Israel's largest national project was launched: a winding, invasive, thieving route that, according to the original plan, would have sliced open hills and mountains, cut across valleys and canyons, following a 447-mile course, well over twice the 200-mile length of the Green Line. The separation barrier is in fact a system of fences, walls, ditches, and patrol roads several hundred yards wide, with a ten-foot-high electronic detection fence running down the center. In some spots, where the route runs alongside populated areas, the barrier is an ominous concrete wall. Whatever its construction, the separation fence repartitioned the country.

PERMITS[7]

What prevents an athletic Palestinian from climbing the fence or the wall and crossing to the other side? What gives a soldier stationed at a gate installed in the fence the power to deny a Palestinian access to the other side, which is also part of the West Bank? What gives the soldier the power to let an Israeli settler cross?

The physical barrier was not sufficient to accomplish full separation, the fence's underlying purpose. A system was needed for also differentiating between people. For this reason, the separation fence has two dimensions. One is physical, made of concrete, barbed wire, and steel. The other is legal, made up of military declarations, orders, and a permit system. This legal fence is applied to the physical fence to do what the physical fence is not smart enough to do: selection. This legal fence prevents the Palestinian from crossing to the other side. It gives the soldier the power to impose the prohibition against doing so by using force. And it allows free passage to anyone who is not Palestinian. To enforce the separation but also use the fence as a filter, the military had to cast a complicated legal net around it, impenetrable to Palestinians but open to Israelis, tourists, and almost everyone else. This legal fence is known as the "permit regime," a system that prohibits Palestinian presence in the area between the fence and the Green Line—the seam zone—absent a special military-issued permit. This is a system of separation and discrimination based on nationality.

IN THE EARLY 2000s, Majed 'Adwan was about fifty years old. 'Adwan lives in Azzun, a town east of Qalqiliyah in the West Bank. His father had left him a fifty-dunam plot of land with about two hundred olive trees and sixty almond trees. 'Adwan says that fifteen of the olive trees date back to the Roman period, meaning they are two thousand years old or more. The rest, with the exception of seventy that he planted himself, were planted by his father fifty years earlier.

'Adwan worked as a teacher in Azzun and nearby villages. The farming on his plot was done mostly by hired hands. He would visit the plot every day, usually in the early morning, to help out with the cultivation, removing stones, plowing, weeding, but also to just walk among the trees, drink tea, and take in the view. The plot yielded about sixty barrels of olive oil in an average year and provided income for the extended family. In 2003, the IDF finished building the separation fence near Azzun, and 'Adwan's land was on the other side.

According to the permit regime, 'Adwan and his family had to obtain permission from the military to cross the fence to reach their land. To get their permits, they had to submit an application form to the Civil Administration with various documents indicating their places of birth, ownership of the land, where they lived, and more. The family collected the required documents, filled out the forms, and submitted the application. Still, for about a year, 'Adwan did not have a permit and could not access his land.

In 2004, after he missed the 2003 olive harvest, 'Adwan received a six-month permit to cross the fence, but without a car. He filed two applications for a permit to enter with a car but these were denied. As a teacher, he was given a permit to cross a different gate in the fence to reach the villages where he taught, with permission to take his car, but the security establishment deemed that as a farmer he could not bring his car through the gate that led to his land.

At some point, 'Adwan was granted a permit to take his car through Gate 34. He tried to find out where Gate 34 was but to no avail. Even the soldiers he asked about this mysterious gate did not know its location, but they knew it would not lead to his land and so did not let him pass. 'Adwan had to take a taxi to get to his land. It drove him and his family to the closest gate, and from there, after the obligatory wait in line, they continued on foot, a distance of about one and a half miles. The short drive from the house to the plot, which ordinarily takes just a few minutes, became an arduous journey involving a taxi, a wait in line, and walking. 'Adwan scaled down his visits to once a month. Before the 2004 harvest 'Adwan was granted a permit to cross the fence with a car and this time it was not restricted to a certain gate. But then the Civil Administration told 'Adwan that his laborers had been denied permits. He missed the 2004 olive harvest, too.

'Adwan related this story to researchers working for HaMoked in preparation for a petition I filed in 2005 on behalf of the villages of Azzun and a-Nabi Elyas against the segment of the fence in their area.[8]

As soon as the first phase of the separation fence was completed, the IDF commander of the West Bank issued a series of declarations, orders, and directives to put the legal fence in place. One declaration designated the seam zone, the area between the Green Line and the fence, a closed military area,[9] off-limits to Palestinians except by permit issued by the military. However, the orders exempted certain groups of people who needed no permit to access the seam zone, neither in principle nor in practice. According to Section 3 of the declaration, "No person shall enter the seam zone or remain in it. Any person present in the seam zone must exit it immediately." But the declaration went on to state that the prohibition does not apply to Israelis or to people who are included in general permits to be issued by the military commander. One such "general permit" issued on the same day granted automatic permits to foreign nationals who hold a valid entry visa to Israel, in other words, tourists. As for "Israelis" to whom the closed military zone does not apply, they are defined as each of the following three categories: "a citizen of the State of Israel, a resident of the State of Israel . . . and any person entitled to immigrate to Israel under the Law of Return." *People who come "under the Law of Return"*—that is, Jews.

The meaning is clear. While Palestinians who live in villages where they may have been born, where perhaps their parents and grandparents were born as well, which unfortunately wound up on the west side of the fence, need a permit to continue to work their land or reside in their own homes, any yeshiva student from Brooklyn visiting Israel may cross the gate and stay in the seam zone without a care. The closed military zone order does not apply to him. So, for example, while the military prevented residents of the Palestinian village of Bil'in, who demonstrated every Friday together with activists from Israel and abroad, from crossing the fence to access their farmland on the other side, dozens of youth from Europe and the United States, some tourists, some permitted under the Law of Return as Jews, could cross the fence freely.

Thus, the military regime—the commander of the West Bank, with his legal advisers and the highest personnel in the Ministry of Justice—created a legal system that unabashedly and explicitly grants and withholds rights based on nationality. This system governs a broad swath of territory, spanning hundreds and thousands of dunams. Though this is not the first piece of the occupation's military legislation to distinguish between Palestinians and Israelis—or Jews—it is the most blatant and extensive legalization of discrimination, and it comes with a huge bureaucracy created specifically to serve, apply, and enforce this discrimination. It is legislation that has the unmistakable markings of what we have no choice but to call apartheid.

The most conspicuous feature of the wording of the permit regime's various orders is its shamelessness. In an era when discrimination based on group affiliation has acquired a particularly bad reputation, when human rights activists the world over dig deep into ostensibly equitable regulation to uncover hidden bias, the Israeli occupation committed to law a series of clauses that overtly refer to "types of people" who may or may not receive permits, that distinguishes between "Israelis" and "foreigners with a valid Israeli visa," who enjoy a special status exempting them from the permit regime, and Palestinians, who are subjected to it.

The military commander empowered the head of the Civil Administration to institute arrangements governing Palestinian access to the seam zone. What resulted is a labyrinthine bureaucracy with myriad forms with which Palestinians who wish to enter the closed zone must wrestle. There are application forms for Palestinians who need a special permit to continue living in their own homes; forms for farmers seeking a permit to access their land; forms for workers in various trades and for aid agency staff who need to reach the other side of the fence; forms for business owners, hired help, and ordinary Palestinians who need to visit friends and family for "humanitarian reasons" (weddings, funerals, visiting the sick). There are fifteen different kinds of forms for Palestinians who for some reason need to enter the seam zone.

The permits issued by the Civil Administration are ordinarily limited to certain hours or certain seasons. The permits issued to olive grove owners are only good for the harvesting season, as if the groves do not need tending between harvests. Permit holders are limited to crossing only the gates that are specified. Another mechanism governs permits to cross with vehicles, and it, too, involves a variety of forms: the "permanent resident passage with vehicle"; the "permanent resident entry of new vehicle to seam zone"; and the "personal permit holder application for passage with vehicle." The military commander also created a fourth caste, in addition to the first three (Israeli citizens and Jews eligible for citizenship; tourists; and Palestinians who must apply for permits): Palestinians who work in Israel or in the settlements have a general permit to access the seam zone, but only for work, and only during work hours.

The permit system, which radically altered the demographic and sociological space to which it applies, is a classic example of how a regime can use bureaucracy to control its subjects. The ingenuity of the system is in its lack of a blanket rule denying all access to the area. But there is vast denial of access, which is achieved through a bureaucratic division of the Palestinian population into subgroups from which permits are denied for different reasons.

One subgroup includes people who are denied access because they cannot prove they have "business" being in the seam zone. They previously traveled freely in the area (or at least had the right to travel freely) and now cannot show any ties to it (such as land or property ownership or having clients there). No appropriate form exists for this group. The other group is made up of Palestinians who do have an "interest" in accessing the seam zone but are unable to navigate the bureaucratic web the army has woven around them and simply give up. The mess of permits, forms, inconsistent gate opening hours, and the difficulty of obtaining information about eligibility pushes many Palestinians who do have "business" in the seam zone and used to have freedom to come and go just to abandon the possibility of reaching it.

THE BARRIER OF DISPUTE

The legal frame in which the lawfulness of the barrier was discussed had been set, to some extent, by the High Court's jurisprudence regarding the settlements. Those judgments had determined that private Palestinian land may not be confiscated (ownership cannot be forcibly denied and transferred to the regime); that private land may, however, be seized (possession or use of it may be temporarily transferred to the regime), but only for security purposes; and that Israeli settlement on public land is nonjusticiable.

The building of the barrier was launched using land seizure orders issued by the military in the first half of 2002, before the earliest government resolution on the barrier in June of that year. The orders pertained to strips of land roughly sixty to one hundred yards wide along the route planned for the north-south Tulkarm-Qalqiliyah stretch. At that stage, before the entire route had been determined, no one anticipated the full extent of the barrier's impact on the lives of hundreds of thousands of Palestinians—not the Palestinians themselves or the international or human rights communities. At that point, the seizure orders framed the barrier as a property rights issue only, an injury to the landowners who lost possession and use of the lands on which the fence was to be erected and to people whose land was slated to remain on the other side. It would take more than a year for the human rights organizations—and through them, the public and media in Israel and abroad—to fully grasp the profound repercussions of a fence that redrew the boundaries of the West Bank.

One of the reasons it took so long was that the route was not clearly discernible at first, a fact that shaped the early litigation. The seizure orders revealed only discrete parts of the plan, since they were issued just for privately owned land, leaving gaps in information where the route cut through public land. Also, these initial orders related to fairly short segments of the fence, between several hundred yards and a few miles in length. Perspective is everything, and at this scale what was visible was just the fence's local impact—the harm to farmers losing access to their land, to children unable to reach their schools, to patients cut off from their clinics and doctors, to businesses severed from their customers. Widening the perspective to take in the whole village or district revealed the harm to the community, to its fabric of life and its residents' human rights. Naturally, lawyers who worked on the early cases focused on these localized effects. They represented individuals, families, or communities and addressed the damage the fence inflicted on their particular area.

But this localized view obscured crucial information about the nature and the impact of the fence as a whole, information that only became clear from a panoramic perspective that showed the entire route. This revealed two factors that could not be gleaned from the local view: The first was that the seam zone between the fence and the Green Line was undergoing a process of de facto annexation to Israel. Overall, the diminishing connections (among others links of commerce, transportation, and services) between this area and the rest of the West Bank were putting the zone on a path to separation, while new connections with Israel were gradually filling the void, since there was no physical barrier between the two spaces. The second factor related to the pattern of the fence's incursion into the West Bank. As noted, only a small part of the barrier followed the Green Line, while most penetrated into the occupied territory, swallowing vast tracts of land. The many enclaves created by the route consistently occurred in two places: near settlements or settlement blocs and in areas that were relatively close to the Green Line but devoid of Palestinian communities. The bird's-eye view confirmed that the route sought to sever from the West Bank as many settlements and as much Palestinian-free land as possible.

Legally, these two factors are extremely important. First, international law absolutely prohibits unilateral annexation of land that was captured by force (which is why the international community does not recognize Israel's annexation of East Jerusalem and the Golan Heights). Second, if the route was determined with settlement interests in mind (which constitute a political rather than a security consideration), then, according to the jurisprudence on settlements, the land seizures were illegal.

The overview of the fence's route is also invaluable for measuring its impact on the human rights of the people living next to it, as certain effects are not visible from the local perspective. A wide-angle view shows, for example, that the fence cuts villages off from the urban centers that provide them with vital services, harming the educational, cultural, religious, commercial, and social connections formed over centuries. The entire Jerusalem area, which served as a metropolitan center for a great many Palestinian communities, would be closed off behind fences and walls, forcing the smaller localities nearby to look to Ramallah instead. With bottomless arrogance and the stroke of a pen, the planners of the fence presumed to reorganize the sociology of Palestinian space. It was hard to see all of this when our view was limited to two or three miles of barrier, and so petitions against individual segments of it were missing the crucial arguments of the larger injuries inflicted by the entire route.

The first person to take a panoramic look at the fence was the head of B'Tselem's research department, Yehezkel Lein, and constructing this overview was no simple feat. Although the government had already passed its resolution on the fence's route in the northern West Bank, the Ministry of Defense refused to release a map, so the staff of B'Tselem had to piece it together like a puzzle, using the land seizure orders that had begun streaming to Palestinian farmers and observing work being carried out on the ground.[10]

I vividly recall the day in early 2003 when I was invited to HaMoked's office by Dalia Kirstein, the organization's legendary executive director, to hear Lein explain the findings of a report B'Tselem would soon release about the implications of the fence that would soon be built. HaMoked was considering asking me and Avigdor Feldman, in whose office I was working at the time, to suggest a strategy for challenging the fence in court. But before planning a legal move, we needed to understand this creature we were taking on, and Lein and B'Tselem were the first to have studied it in depth.

In that meeting, Lein laid out the effect the fence would likely have on all areas of life. A quarter of a million Palestinians stood to be harmed, he said. Dozens of villages would lose much of their land, thousands of Palestinians would be trapped on the "wrong side" of the fence. They would have trouble reaching hospitals in Qalqiliyah, Tulkarm, and East Jerusalem. The twists and turns in the route and the placement of the gates the military planned to install would result in restricted access to services in urban centers to Palestinians on both the west and east sides of the fence. Education, welfare, trade—it would all be compromised.[11] At the time, Lein's forecast seemed wildly overblown, but it has paled in comparison to what really happened over the years. His perspective also revealed the truth about the fence's route: one of the chief criteria guiding it was the location of the settlements.[12] His presentation convinced HaMoked to file a petition against the fence—all of it.

As WE KNOW well by now, the international laws of occupation seek to protect the rights of the occupied population, but they contain exclusions that allow the occupying regime to infringe on those rights if security requires it. The security in the name of which these rights may be curtailed is that of the occupying power (Israel), the occupying army (the IDF), and the occupied population itself. Still, even when security is at play, not every infringement is permissible and not every right may be curtailed. For the most part, the kind of infringement that may be permissible is a *proportionate* one, meaning one that is unavoidable to avert a security threat where the harm of the threat, should it be realized, would be greater than the harm caused by the infringement.

Thus, the laws of occupation contain at least two cumulative legal conditions to render infringing on the rights of the occupied population lawful: the violation of rights must be necessary for pure security reasons and for no other purpose, and it must be proportionate. These two principles apply to the barrier.

So, it was clear to us that the first and principal legal battleground would be the condition of security: Had the fence's route been determined by security reasons, or, as in case of the Elon Moreh settlement, by ideological reasons or to advance a political agenda, in which case it had to be struck down? This dispute could either be fought out over each segment of the fence separately or over the entire fence. To us, it was obvious: the smoking gun that proved the political purpose of the fence was the pattern of its route, and showing this required a panoramic view.

Over the next decade, litigation against the barrier would keep the High Court of Justice busy through thousands of sessions and hundreds of petitions that fought this battle on three legal fronts: Did the barrier amount to prohibited annexation? Was the fence designed to serve lawful security needs or prohibited political goals? Did it properly balance Palestinian rights with the security threat it was meant to prevent? To these we added a fourth and particularly fierce front: the legality of the permit regime. Did it distinguish between Palestinians, on the one hand, and

Israelis (along with Jews, who are eligible for citizenship) and tourists, on the other, on permissible grounds, or was this wrongful discrimination—perhaps so wrongful it could be considered apartheid?

To be clear, the Israeli human rights organizations that spearheaded a significant number of these cases (along with many private lawyers) did not espouse a legal position against building a barrier. The state can fence itself to kingdom come if it wants. It can surround itself with fences and walls. It can dig ditches and fill them with water and even grow alligators in them if it so wishes. Any country may close itself off with barriers, isolate itself from the world, and forbid foreigners from entering. There would have been no legal case of any kind had the separation barrier been built on the Green Line, the recognized border between Israel and the West Bank. The legal dispute stemmed entirely from the decision to put most of the fence deep inside the West Bank, pilfering great parts of it in the process. Legally speaking, the alternative to the barrier designed by Israel's government was not necessarily no fence but a fence that was lawfully placed. There is also the issue of whether fences and walls create the kind of space in which we want to live, whether separation is our vision for the next generation. But that, of course, is not a question for the law.

EARLY CASES

Residents of four villages to the south of Tulkarm were the first to file High Court petitions against the fence being built on their land: Far'on, Jubara, Kafr Sur, and a-Ras. The seizure orders were signed by the military commander even before the government resolution was passed, based on an April 2002 decision by the security cabinet to build a "temporary barrier" (until the ministerial team headed by the prime minister decided on long-term measures to prevent entry of Palestinians into Israel).[13] The temporary barrier was planned for three sectors, including Tulkarm.[14] The orders were issued within days of the cabinet decision, and the military took over the land and began leveling earth and uprooting trees. The horrified village residents contacted a young Jerusalem lawyer, Ghiath Nasser, who worked around the clock to submit two High Court petitions, one on behalf of several families from Far'on and the other on behalf of the a-Ras village council and 132 local residents. Since every passing moment brought further destruction by the army's heavy equipment, the petitions were filed urgently and sought an interim order to halt the work pending a decision. Nasser also asked for and received the leave of the court to file within a few days an expert opinion on the harm that the fence's route would do to the villages.

These two cases launched a routine that would be repeated countless times and feature on the High Court's agenda for many years: the IDF issues seizure orders for a segment of the fence; landowners run to a lawyer to file an urgent petition with a motion for an interim order to prevent irreversible damage; the interim order is issued to allow for an effective hearing; the trial takes up the proportionality of the harm to the Palestinians versus the security benefits.

The two expert opinions Nasser submitted were meant to shed light on this question of the harm being done to his clients. They were prepared by Bimkom—Planners for Planning Rights, an exceptional human rights organization that would play a pivotal role in petitions against the fence. Bimkom had been established three years earlier by a group of planners and architects to promote justice and equality through spatial planning and development. Though the full route and the real nature of the fence had not yet been determined, Bimkom's experts were still able to translate the seizure orders issued in the four villages into the damage they would cause to property, freedom of movement, and livelihoods. Being planning professionals, they were also able to offer alternative routes that made geographic and engineering sense.

The opinion prepared by architects Efrat Cohen-Bar and Shmuel Groag explained that the route would leave 75 percent of a-Ras's land and about half of Sur's inaccessible. The fence would cut off some four thousand dunams, which provide income to two thousand residents. The enclave created between the fence and the Green Line would be roughly one to two miles wide, and the fence would run very close to people's homes.[15] The opinion did not say what the map made clear: the reason for the fence's route was the nearby location of the settlement of Sal'it. The fence planners had decided to do whatever it took for the fence to encompass the settlement, creating an enclave east of the Green Line to do so, even at the cost of grave harm to thousands of residents in Palestinian villages.

Because the settlement was built at some distance from the Green Line, the fence took a sharp turn to the east, penetrating into the West Bank and creating a sizable bubble around it, trapping much land in the process. In the opinion prepared by architects Eli Ilan and Cesar Yeudkin regarding Far'on, the two explained that the fence would impede the access of twenty-six families (80 percent of the families in Far'on) to land containing 80 percent of the village's olive orchards.[16] Both opinions submitted by Bimkom planners offered alternative, less greedy routes for the fence that ran much closer to the Green Line and utilized existing roads, thereby reducing the destruction the fence would inflict.

The two cases were scheduled for a joint hearing in early May 2002. Black March had ended just a month before the hearing, with seventeen suicide attacks and close to 130 Israeli fatalities. April had been a hard month, too: three suicide attacks took the lives of ten Israeli civilians. In the eighteen months since the start of the Second Intifada, about 300 Israeli civilians and some 140 security personnel had been killed. In late March, Israel had launched a military campaign, Operation Defensive Shield, during which its forces invaded Palestinian cities and fought against armed Palestinians. The operation lasted throughout April and was still under way in early May. It was in this atmosphere that the court heard the petitions filed by the Tulkarm area villagers.

The state thoroughly exploited the security situation. Though the hearing was scheduled for two weeks after the petition had been filed—lightning speed for the High Court of Justice—the state signaled greater urgency, asking the court to lift the interim order prohibiting work at the sites. In his affidavit, the head of the IDF's Central Command argued passionately that operational needs required that the fence be built immediately. It was so pressing that the work could not wait for even ten days. The panel selected to hear the case, headed by Supreme Court president Aharon Barak, granted the motion and lifted the interim order.[17] Leveling work and tree removal resumed although the petition had not yet been heard.

It is hard to imagine worse circumstances for a lawyer to argue a case. The bullets are flying and people are being killed, while the legal suit seeks to prevent an act the military claims is essential for it to win the war. How many justices anywhere have the backbone to focus on the merits of the case and ignore the background noise?

The judgment in both petitions was given at the conclusion of the hearing, with the justices dictating it in the parties' presence. Ordinarily, the court gives its decision at the hearing itself only when the case is straightforward, free of complex legal questions requiring deep reasoning. The lawfulness of building the separation barrier was hardly a simple issue that needed no weighty legal consideration. It was far from cut-and-dried. Still, the justices casually denied the petitions:

> We have reviewed the petitions and the responses thereto. We have been presented with the Respondents' plans and the Petitioners' proposal. We have studied the various maps. We are satisfied that the Respondents' decision contains no flaws that require our intervention. We have taken note of the notice given by Respondents' counsel that the Petitioners (and their workers) would be issued permits that would give them access to land they own and cultivate that is located beyond the checkpoint. The petition is dismissed.[18]

The security situation, the justices' trepidation about intervening in something considered vital for fighting terrorism, and the state's promise to allow farmers access to their land persuaded the court. Within several months, a system of barbed-wire fences and patrol roads separated the villages from their land. And then it turned out that the state's promises were not worth much. The residents of Far'on discovered that the gate placed in the fence near their village was locked. It never opened. They had to reach their land via another gate, closer to Tulkarm. A three-block walk turned into a two-mile trek. Eighteen months after the judgment was delivered, villages in the area petitioned the High Court, through ACRI, to order the state to fulfill its promise and open the gates to allow the farmers to cross.[19]

IN JUNE 2002, the government passed the resolution to build a contiguous barrier, approving, as a first phase, a route running from the northern tip of the West Bank to the settlement of Elkana, south of Qalqiliyah—a seventy-two-mile stretch of fences and walls.[20] Seizure orders began raining down on communities all over the northern West Bank. In September, a group of young Palestinian-Israeli lawyers from the Jerusalem Legal Aid Center* filed two more High Court petitions, this time on behalf of

---

* The center has operated out of East Jerusalem since the 1970s, offering free legal aid to marginalized populations. It is now called the Jerusalem Legal Aid and Human Rights Center.

landowners from the Qalqiliyah area. After the Supreme Court's smooth approval of the earlier land seizures, the military had pressed southward, claiming land belonging to the villages of Jayus and a-Nabi Elyas.

Representing fifty-five of the landowners who were affected by the orders, the center's lawyers—Azzam Bishara, Sliman Shahin, and Hassan Khatib—argued that the expected harm to the petitioners and their communities was immense and therefore disproportionate. They also raised more principled arguments, among them the claim that an occupying regime had no authority to seize privately owned land and use it to prevent movement by the occupied population in parts of their territory. Lawyers from the Jerusalem Legal Aid Center made similar arguments in a third case, in which they represented residents of villages north of Tulkarm, who had also been served with seizure orders for their land.[21] An interim order prevented work on the fence, and the Qalqiliyah petition was scheduled for an urgent hearing before a panel headed by Justice Dorit Beinisch in mid-October 2002.

The timing of the Qalqiliyah hearing was not quite as bad as in the Tulkarm case, but it was still 2002, the worst year of the Second Intifada. A suicide bombing on a bus in central Tel Aviv in mid-September had killed five people and wounded dozens more. Soldiers were injured in ongoing operations in the West Bank and the Gaza Strip. The Israeli preoccupation with the need for a barrier became obsessive. The fence was the cure-all that would put an end to terrorism. The Ministry of Defense was pushing to build it in a rush, and the lawyers representing the state piled on the pressure. They asked for urgent hearings, within days; they objected to the interim orders when they were issued, asking for them to be lifted. They argued that work on the fence was progressing at such great speed to seal the gaps that allowed terrorists to infiltrate and prevent unnecessary risks to the laborers, insinuating that any delay caused by legal proceedings could mean loss of life. The justices got the message loud and clear.

But the legal team handling the fence cases for the state wanted more than just a dismissal of the petitions; they wanted the court's seal of approval. As they saw it, the Supreme Court was not just an institution that could get in the way but one that could be of great assistance. There were early signs that the fence might trouble the international community. The resounding condemnation and legal and diplomatic opposition from the rest of the world was still some time in the future, mostly because the fence had not yet been built and its disastrous effects on the lives of Palestinians had not yet been felt, but everyone involved knew that the project would be highly controversial. A judgment from the Supreme Court hailing the fence as lawful could be very helpful in the fight for Israel's image and legitimacy. The court had already dismissed one petition against the fence, but that did not give the authorities quite what they needed, since the judgment was brief and gave no reasoning. It was difficult to yoke the fence's 450 miles of dispossession to its narrow shoulders.

And so in response to the petitions filed by the Jerusalem Legal Aid Center, which argued that the land seizures for the fence were unlawful and ultra vires, the state filed long, detailed briefs that included a full legal thesis about the military forces' power in the West Bank to implement the project under international law. In the unspoken code between state attorneys and Supreme Court justices, the length and detail of the state's response, with the background to the barrier and the legal basis for it, in a case scheduled for an urgent hearing (which would have allowed for a short, perfunctory response), was a clear signal that the state was after a reasoned judgment. Indeed, that it needed one. Beinisch, who had worked in the State Attorney's Office for some thirty years, seven of them as the state attorney, was well versed in the unspoken code.

On the state's legal team were two senior lawyers, Orit Koren, who was in charge of High Court petitions at the State Attorney's Office, and Avi Licht, then a deputy state attorney. The legal construct they offered was this: the separation fence was meant to prevent terrorists from infiltrating Israel. The seam zone it would create was intended to serve as "a geographical security zone that would allow troops to engage in pursuit" if a Palestinian managed to penetrate the fence.[22] This purpose made the project a matter of security, thereby meeting the conditions stipulated in international law for infringing on the property rights of an occupied civilian population. The attorneys referred the court to an article of The Hague Regulations concerning the Laws and Customs of War on Land, which prohibits the military from destroying or seizing enemy property unless imperatively required for security reasons.[23] The state's lawyers argued that the fence fell under the exception to the prohibition.

To substantiate the claim that the fence's route in the Qalqiliyah area had been chosen according to security considerations only, the state submitted an affidavit from Lieutenant Colonel Dani Tirza, the man at the helm of the authority created to oversee the fence's construction. Tirza explained the security factors that dictated locating the fence on such an invasive route and seizing so much land. Here it passes through a key strategic point for control of the topography. There it creates a pursuit zone, and here it secures a road used by Israelis. We will return to Tirza and his affidavit, which, we hope, he has since come to regret.

What about the fact that the fence encircles Israeli settlements? What is the security concern here? The State Attorney's Office approached the topic with great caution and such brevity that the reader could almost miss it: "The placement of the barrier at some distance from the territory of the State of Israel might have also stemmed from additional reasons, including topographical considerations or consideration for conditions on the ground, *such as the presence of communities near the seam line, on either side thereof* . . . another security consideration that was taken into account was the protection of *Israeli communities near the barrier.*"[24] Did you catch that?: "communities near the seam line" and "the protection of Israeli communities." These two half sentences, hidden in a twenty-five-page document, account for the ruin the fence would bring to thousands of people. Just ten words to explain why the fence spliced the West Bank in two.

Take, for example, the route around the Qalqiliyah villages (see map, p. 258). The reason why Jayus, Azzun, and a-Nabi Elyas were cut off from their densely cultivated farmlands, the reason their communities were slated to lose virtually the entire income they made from the olive groves owned by families who have lived in the area for generations: it was clearly not the need to create a "security zone" to protect Israel, or even because of "topographical considerations." The only reason was to locate the Israeli settlement of Zufin within the seam zone, and—as it would later turn out in one of the most dramatic fence cases—to include land designated for the settlement's future expansion.

On October 14, 2002, the Beinisch panel dismissed the petition filed by the residents of Qalqiliyah-area villages. Again, the justices responded to the state attorney's request to rule without delay, and again the petition was dismissed as soon as arguments had been heard, with the decision dictated in the courtroom. However, this time the judgment included reasons—short, but rationalized. The justices quoted the state's explanation that the fence was required for security purposes and therefore met the exception to The Hague Regulations prohibition on destroying or seizing private property in occupied territory. They went on to state:

> We have found no flaw in the seizure orders that were issued, or in the actions taken by the Respondents that would justify our intervention. Although the seizure would cause damage, difficulties and discomfort to the residents, we accept that these are measures that were meant to serve as an important element in the IDF's combat strategy, designed by the officials in charge of security, and as is known, this court does not tend to intervene in operational, security considerations.[25]

THE FENCE'S JOURNEY: GENEVA, NEW YORK, THE HAGUE, TEL AVIV

The early petitions' dismissal helped boost the fence project. Over the next few months, work progressed rapidly, while desperate Palestinians looked on as their space was constricted and sealed off and their property and source of livelihood was trapped behind barbed wire and concrete. Stories began to appear about how the fence was harming farmers, mostly in the foreign press but also, increasingly, in Israel as well. B'Tselem's report, published in April 2003, laid the initial groundwork for estimating the damage caused by the fence. The building work produced terrible haunting images that made for great daily features in the media: ancient olive trees being uprooted by bulldozers made in the United States or Europe; Palestinian farmers, trying to stay on their land, being dragged away by soldiers equipped with state-of-the-art American weapons; green orchards and ancient terraces reduced to rubble, then replaced by concrete and barbed wire. For Israel the fence was a photojournalistic disaster.

Over the course of 2003, the government passed two more resolutions that extended the fence's route. The full route, as planned and now approved, included countless enclaves. The seam zone adjacent to the Green Line encompassed fully 16 percent of the West Bank; an additional zone planned for the east, along the Jordan Valley, would have taken another significant bite out of the territory. To place the settlement of Ariel inside the seam zone, for example, the fence penetrated deep into the heart of the West Bank, about thirteen miles from the Green Line. The Americans and the

Europeans cried foul. The government resolutions attempted to assuage the international community by calling the fence "a security measure intended to prevent terrorist attacks" and claiming that "it does not reflect a political border," but anyone could see that it was creating facts on the ground.

In the summer of 2003, the George W. Bush administration expressed staunch opposition to the route's penetration into the northern West Bank.[26] The Americans and the Europeans realized that the fence would hurt the contiguity of Palestinian territory and the viability of a future state. The fence made Israel's commitment to the Road Map, a path toward peaceful resolution of the conflict backed by the Quartet (the United States, Europe, Russia, and the UN), meaningless. And so it drew strong political condemnation. At the same time, NGOs and journalists warned of the catastrophic humanitarian harm the fence would cause. The chosen route ended up uniting different groups opposed for different reasons. With every mile, the controversy over the fence's legitimacy increased—mostly abroad, but to some degree in Israel as well.

The opening shot for the international community's legal fight against the separation fence came in September 2003. The UN Human Rights Commission's Special Rapporteur on the Palestinian Occupied Territories[27] filed his periodic report. The special rapporteur is an important institution in the UN's professional human rights protection system. Special rapporteurs are experts in their fields appointed by the Human Rights Commission (now called the Human Rights Council) based in Geneva.[28] Their task is to report to the commission on the state of human rights in a certain country or conflict area, or on a specific human rights issue (extrajudicial executions, for example). While the commission is a political body of state representatives, often including envoys from countries with the worst human rights records, the special rapporteurs bring the authority of their expertise. In 1993, the commission appointed a special rapporteur for the Occupied Territories; in 2003, the position was held by John Dugard, a South African professor.

It is difficult to imagine anyone better suited for this complicated and sensitive job. A renowned scholar of international law and an expert on human rights and international criminal law, Dugard ran a human rights litigation center at Johannesburg's University of the Witwatersrand during the 1970s and 1980s. The center was prominent in the legal fight against

apartheid. Dugard's academic career had also been spent at the most prestigious universities in Europe, the United States, and South Africa, and,
with his parallel work at the UN, he was highly regarded in both legal and
diplomatic circles.

The main chapter of the report Dugard submitted to the commission
in September 2003[29] was devoted to the separation barrier, which he
referred to as the separation "wall," the term the international community came to adopt. In the chapter, Dugard determined for the first time
that the fence was a project of annexation rather than security. While there
had been no official act of annexation, he wrote, meaning Israeli law had
not been applied to the seam zone, the nature of the barrier, the resources
invested in it, and the considerations dictating its route all pointed to
the fact that the area ripped away from the West Bank and attached to
the State of Israel had effectively been annexed—a unilateral act prohibited under international law.

Dugard noted the disastrous implications of the fence, even quoting
the B'Tselem report, which had undoubtedly influenced his own research.
He described how thousands of Palestinians and hundreds of businesses
had begun relocating for fear of being trapped behind the fence, which,
he said, was creating a new generation of refugees and internally displaced
people. Dugard added what was obvious to anyone looking at the fence's
route: the main consideration behind it was to include the greatest
number of settlements—themselves a violation of international law—on
the "Israeli" side. Thus, the barrier was unlawful for three separate reasons: the de facto act of annexation; the grave harm to Palestinian human
rights; and the absence of a legitimate military need to deviate from the
Green Line, given the illegality of the settlements. Overall, Dugard saw
the barrier much as the settlements themselves: a force of dispossession;
a unilateral fact on the ground; a severe violation of Palestinian human
rights; a breach of international law. Dugard's sharp recommendation to
the UN was, therefore, to condemn the creation of the barrier as an act
of forcible, unlawful, prohibited annexation with all the legal ramifications of such a condemnation.

About a month after Dugard filed his report, the UN's major bodies
convened to discuss the legality of the separation fence. The Security Council was presented with a motion for a resolution that the fence's deviation
from the Green Line was unlawful and that Israel must dismantle it.

When the Security Council debated the resolution, on October 14, 2003, ten member states voted in favor, four abstained, and one objected. The single objection came from the United States, which used its veto power as one of the five permanent members of the Security Council. The resolution was dropped despite the clear majority in favor because of the American veto.

However, the Palestinians had made sure that the UN General Assembly would consider a draft resolution calling on Israel to dismantle the parts of the fence not located on the Green Line. There are a number of advantages in going to the General Assembly: as a body in which all the world's countries are represented, a favorable vote there would represent an important moral and public victory. And there is no veto power in the General Assembly. A majority is a majority. On the other hand, its decisions do not have the binding legal significance of Security Council resolutions. In any event, a group of twenty-five countries submitted a draft resolution demanding that Israel dismantle the parts of the fence that deviated from the Green Line and calling on the Palestinian Authority to do everything in its power to prevent attacks on Israeli civilians and arrest those responsible for them. The draft resolution also requested that the UN secretary-general report on Israel's compliance with the resolution within a month.[30]

The resolution passed with a huge majority: 144 in favor and 4 against—Israel, Micronesia, the Marshall Islands, and the United States, which opposed the resolution, despite agreeing with its contents in principle, only to protect its ally. Israel announced it had no intention of obeying the resolution; on the contrary, it intended to step up work on the fence. Two days after the General Assembly vote, Israel's Ministry of Defense defiantly posted a map of the fence on its website.

A month went by, and the UN secretary-general filed the report he had been asked to write. In a rare departure from cautious diplomatic speech, his statement was direct and unequivocal: "I have concluded that Israel is not in compliance with the Assembly's demand that it 'stop and reverse the construction of the wall in the Occupied Palestinian Territory.'"[31]

Ten days later, a group of Arab states rallied by the Palestinians submitted a new draft resolution to refer the issue of the fence to the UN's top judicial body, the International Court of Justice in The Hague. The idea was to use articles in the UN and ICJ constitutions that allow UN bodies to request an advisory opinion from the court on a legal issue. In this way, the Palestinians would be able to circumvent the barrier to bringing a case before the ICJ, which cannot hear claims made by one country against another unless both parties have accepted its jurisdiction, either permanently or ad hoc. This is not the case with an advisory opinion, which the court may give if it is asked to do so by a competent body, such as the General Assembly. An advisory opinion, however, is a weaker judicial tool than a decision in a contentious case. While international law requires compliance with the ICJ, an advisory opinion does not have the enforcement power of an operative order. Still, the legal analysis and conclusions of an advisory opinion are internationally binding and remove any legal question marks. All countries and UN bodies would be obliged to adhere to the legal finding and demonstrate compliance with it in their dealings with Israel over the fence. In this sense, the process initiated by the Palestinians could cause Israel significant diplomatic difficulties.

The draft resolution requesting an advisory opinion from the ICJ had been distributed on December 3, 2003, and was debated five days later. On December 8, 2003, the General Assembly passed the resolution with ninety votes in favor, eight against, and seventy abstentions.[32]

The question of whether or not the fence was lawful moved from the court in Jerusalem to the court in The Hague.

WHILE THE UN Human Rights Council and Security Council were debating whether or not the separation fence was legal, three thousand miles from The Hague and fifty-seven hundred miles from New York, I sat in a room in a dilapidated building in Tel Aviv, somewhere between the Matmid porn cinema and the falafel and shwarma stands of Allenby Street, in Avigdor Feldman's office, drafting a public-interest petition on behalf of HaMoked and waging a full frontal assault on the fence with my keyboard.

With no coordination, without having read Dugard's report, our draft petition included the same three arguments he presented to the UN Human Rights Commission: the fence's construction was an act of de facto annexation and therefore a violation of international law; its infringement on Palestinian human rights was disproportionate; and, most important, the only reason for the fence to penetrate deep into the West Bank was to protect settlements, but since they themselves are unlawful, they cannot justify the claim for a legitimate security need that allows the harm inflicted upon Palestinians.

The legal strategy we suggested to HaMoked was a departure from previous petitions. We wanted to take on the fence's entire route rather than just parts of it, to challenge the basis for its existence by claiming that any departure from the Green Line was unlawful. We suggested attacking the notion that the military had the authority to build any system of fences and walls that separates parts of the West Bank, contrary to its power to build a physical barrier on the Green Line, which we did not dispute. We thought the right thing to do was attack only the invasive parts of the fence rather than the very notion of a fence. The idea was to highlight the fence's political and settlement purpose, to show that pattern, which could only be done if the entire route came up for debate rather than just one segment of it. This approach allowed us also to challenge the permit system designed for the seam zone. Both Feldman and I saw this system as the height of shamelessness on the part of the military and state lawyers. We could not help but think of a term that at the time was not as widely applied by progressives to the occupation as it is today: apartheid.

But the legal arena in which Feldman and I were about to launch our assault was profoundly different from the one in which Dugard and The Hague lawyers operated. Things that are a given in international law, the starting point in debate in an international forum, are not self-evident in Israel's Supreme Court. The two key differences in terms of the fence were the status of Jerusalem and the status of the settlements. We faced legal challenges that would not come up in an international forum.

We'll begin with Jerusalem. Some of the invasive parts of the wall were planned to run through East Jerusalem, territory that Israel had annexed and to which it applied Israeli law. Since the world does not recognize Israel's annexation, Dugard could address East Jerusalem in the same way he addressed the West Bank. We could not: the annexation was an act of Israel's parliament and therefore considered binding on its Supreme Court, which applied Israeli law to East Jerusalem rather than the international laws of occupation. If our petition, as it pertained to East Jerusalem, would be decided according to local law, much of our argument, which was based on the restrictions to Israel's authority under international law, became irrelevant. Our petition was certainly bold, and asking the High Court to recognize that East Jerusalem must be treated according to the laws of occupation seemed hopeless. So we thought it better to leave out the East Jerusalem part of the fence.

The other difficulty concerned the status of the settlements. In international legal arenas there is not even the faintest doubt that the settlements are unlawful, their creation is a violation of international law, and Israel must evacuate them. However, that is not the situation in Israel, where the Supreme Court has declined to make a ruling on the settlements' legality, effectively allowing them to flourish. It was clear to us that what Feldman had been unable to do in the early 1990s—force the court to rule on the settlements' legality*—would be no more successful a decade later, especially as a side issue in a case about the fence. Ironically, the settlement project had been dramatically accelerated in the 1990s, particularly after the Oslo Accords were signed, and the number of settlers had grown dramatically. A court that feared the consequences of ruling on the settlements in 1993 would not dare to open its mouth in 2003.

This presented a huge stumbling block for our petition: the settlements' legality was central to the question of the legitimacy of the route for the fence. It seemed a requisite stop on the road to a ruling that the fence's invasive route does not serve a legitimate security purpose. How could we square the circle? After pondering the issue, we decided to circumvent the question of the settlements' legality. In our draft petition we explicitly wrote that we were not asking the court to rule on the legality of the settlements, but that: "The Petitioner shall claim that the 'military necessity' (or 'military imperatives') interest, recognized in humanitarian law and in the laws of occupation as permitting a proportionate injury to the rights of civilians, extends to the security interests of the occupying power and of the occupying forces, *but not to those of citizens of the occupying power who have chosen to immigrate to and settle in the occupied territory.* Their interests are expressed in the powers to administrate and restore order and safety alone, which cannot, in themselves, serve as a source of authority for violating so many of the residents' rights."

We filed the petition in November 2003, a few weeks before the UN General Assembly asked the ICJ to provide an advisory opinion on the fence's legality. We opened with our bottom line:

The Petitioner's claim, which is an argument of principle, is this: That a colossal construction project such as that of the separation wall, the effects

---

* For the Peace Now case, see chapter 3.

of which on the occupied civilian population, on the economy of the Occupied Territories and on all aspects of civilian life there, are far-reaching and long-term, to the extent that one might say that they are permanent—violates the principles of international law and is categorically prohibited by the laws of belligerent occupation, insofar as its route runs inside the occupied territory and materially alters the fabric of civilian life in the occupied territory, effectively isolating considerable portions of the occupied population, creating hermetic enclaves and constituting de facto annexation of parts of the occupied land.

And then, still on the first page of the petition, we raised the argument that the fence was not a security measure but rather a political maneuver, and that in any event the settlements could not serve as a cause for the intrusion of the fence into the West Bank:

We would be exposing no secret if we were to state that every deviation of the route of the wall from the Green Line . . . is designed to include Jewish settlements located deep inside the Occupied Territories in the area fenced in by the separation wall, thus turning them into an inseparable part of the State of Israel. Such inclusion of the settlements sweeps with it also occupied lands and communities, but in order to prevent dangers they allegedly pose, the wall twists and turns like a coiled snake around the living spaces of these residents of the Territories, isolating them from the State of Israel on the one hand and from the Territories—the rest of the West Bank—on the other and, as aforesaid, all in order to wrap the wall around settlements, the mere establishment of which was, from the outset, at the very least, problematic and dubitable according to international law.

We saved our introduction's harshest statements for the end. We demanded that the permit system be revoked. In January 2004, three weeks after we filed HaMoked's petition, ACRI filed its own petition, focusing on the permit system and demanding its cancellation due to its infringement on a slew of fundamental rights.[33] While ACRI remained relatively reserved, Feldman and I, with HaMoked's consent, used extremely harsh language. To the best of my knowledge, this was the first time an act of the Israeli authorities was referred to, in the Supreme Court, by the word we used:

And, finally, the physical injury to the residents of the enclaves goes hand in hand with the legal travesty that was designed in order to administer the seam zone, which creates, in practice, two types of residents in this zone: "Israelis," who are defined in the declaration on the closing of the area as citizens of Israel, residents of Israel and those entitled to citizenship by the Law of Return (!), to whom the declaration does not apply, and who are free to travel into, out of and within the zone; and others (in practice: Palestinians) who are subject to the declaration and who require all sorts of permits to enter the zone, work in it, remain in it overnight, and exit it. Let us correctly define the legal structure described above by its full name: The web that the declaration and the orders have spun in the seam zone is an intolerable, illegal and immoral *apartheid*. In other words, the discriminatory and oppressive topographical structure rests upon a shameful normative infrastructure, unprecedented in Israeli law.

MUHAMMAD DAHLEH SAVES BEIT SURIK

Supreme Court president Aharon Barak was fully cognizant of the fact that such a precedent, in which a single issue was simultaneously under review by both the international court in The Hague and his own court in Jerusalem, could have far-reaching ramifications for the institution he headed. Those parts of international law that have been assimilated into domestic law are considered part of the country's law of the land. Thus, local justices are expected to be familiar with international norms, even if they have not been enacted by the local sovereign, and to treat them as they treat the laws of their own country's legislature. As always, the truth is more complicated.

Domestic courts often treat international law as a stepchild. They discriminate against it and are hostile to it. They do not understand it the way they understand, embrace, and sympathize with the offspring of their local legislature. Israeli justices, certainly those who obtained their legal education decades ago, before international law had thawed from its Cold War deep-freeze, are no exception. When news broke of the ICJ's discussion of the barrier, Barak realized two things: first, the barrier cases piling up in his court would receive greater international attention than usual; second, whereas the Supreme Court usually has a monopoly on determining the law in the issues it adjudicates, it had a competitor of sorts in this case. This exceptional situation resulted from two conditions that allow for such judicial overlap: first, the international tribunal has jurisdiction over an issue under review at the same time by a local (in this case, Israeli) court; second, the two courts are expected to base their decisions on the same normative framework, in this instance, the international laws of belligerent occupation and perhaps international human rights law as well. Thus, the two courts' rulings, based on the same legal principles, are comparable.

Barak, I believe, was very concerned. He had devoted his life to making a name for the Israeli justice system, glorifying it both at home and abroad. He had succeeded, like Shamgar before him, in establishing the Supreme Court as a highly professional and in some respects innovative, groundbreaking institution. The court's liberal judgments on various individual liberties, its constitutional revolution, and the power it demonstrated to strike down Knesset law—that is, the court's activism—were highly regarded, almost idolized in some circles. And now all this esteem was threatened by his justices reviewing segments of the fence and issuing thinly argued rulings with little juridical depth on the core question of its legality. I am convinced Barak was worried about future judgments in which the analysis of international law would fall short of the standard that had established the court's reputation in international academic and legal circles, thus diminishing its status. It was obvious that the Supreme Court would not fare well in any decision issued by the court in The Hague if the international tribunal were to review just its brief decisions made in the early cases of the villages south of Tulkarm or north of Qalqiliyah.

Besides these concerns, Barak had to face another challenge concerning the barrier. In the year and a half that passed between the first government resolution on building the fence in mid-2002 and the referral of the issue to The Hague, a large number of petitions against different segments of the fence had piled up in the court secretariat. Regardless of The Hague, the situation required the attention of the president of the Supreme Court. He is responsible for managing the flood of cases to prevent different panels from reaching different decisions or using different legal standards to rule. Barak decided to do something common when a single issue produces multiple legal cases: choose one barrier petition and issue a guiding judgment, with comprehensive, detailed reasoning, that would serve, once and for all, as a decisive ruling on its general legality and on its basis in law. Such a judgment would promote coherence in different future rulings on the fence and provide legal certainty on what is allowed and what is not. This sort of guiding judgment might also render some of the pending cases moot. And with thorough and comprehensive analysis of the legal intricacies, such a judgment could represent Israel in The Hague.

MANY YEARS have gone by since Barak picked the case for the guiding judgment, and I still wonder how the story of the barrier might have turned out had Barak taken what Feldman and I considered to be the natural step, which was to choose our principled public-interest petition representing HaMoked. We had after all raised arguments of principle challenging the legality of the barrier—the same arguments under consideration by the international court.

But Barak preferred to focus on a case that addressed one specific segment of the fence rather than deliberating on a range of questions about the legality of the project. His decision reflected a material position, in which the degree of the barrier's legality (or illegality) is not necessarily identical in all of the four hundred miles planned for it. From this perspective, the fence's legality is a function of its impact on the life around it; therefore, one mile might be legal while another might not. Barak's decision to review distinct segments of the fence meant ignoring the unmistakable patterns of its route as a whole. The focus on segments might have served to expose facts that were not visible through a wide lens, but it left other facts, only clearly seen from a broad perspective, out of the picture. Barak later wrote that the great discrepancy between the conclusions of Israel's High Court of Justice and the ICJ was due to the different judicial techniques used by the tribunals,[34] with one looking at the entire route and the other looking at each segment separately. There is another possibility: the discrepancy between the conclusions was not the result of different judicial techniques but rather the opposite; the methods were selected in advance to provide judgments with different outcomes.

THE SPECIFIC CASE Barak chose concerned a twenty-five-mile stretch of the fence planned for an area northwest of Jerusalem. The route was planned to wind its way between Israeli towns and Palestinian villages. Mevaseret Zion, a Jewish suburb of Jerusalem within the Green Line, and three Israeli settlements (Giv'at Ze'ev, Givon, and Har Adar) across the

Green Line were on one side of the fence, and eight Palestinian villages, including Beit Surik, Biddu, Qatanna, and Beit Iksa, were on the other. This route would have been disastrous for the eight villages. According to figures the petitioners provided to the court, 42,000 dunams of their land would be affected: 4,800 were to be used for the fence itself, and 37,000 would remain on the other side of it. They calculated that 26,500 dunams of the land to be cut off from its owners was cultivated, serving as the main source of income for the thirty-five thousand residents in this group of villages. The situation in Beit Surik was the worst: with settlements on two sides—Givon to the east and Har Adar to the west—the fence would fully encircle the village, penning it into a sort of cage, with only one small opening to the north.

The villages enlisted one of the most prominent Palestinian lawyers in Israel, Muhammad Dahleh. He had opened his own practice in East Jerusalem two years earlier, together with his wife, Suhad Hammoud, after working as a partner at a different law office for a decade. Dahleh quickly became one of the most sought-after lawyers dealing with real estate and commercial law as affected by the Palestinian Authority, Israel, and international involvement. Through his practice, Dahleh stood out in cases relating to the conflict, especially in litigation against settler groups aggressively seeking to Judaize Palestinian neighborhoods in East Jerusalem.

As a Palestinian with Israeli citizenship, Dahleh is a minority wherever he goes and has had to use his talent to the greatest extent to succeed. In Jewish Israel, he is an Arab; for Palestinians in the West Bank, he is in many respects an Israeli and therefore cannot be a member of the Palestinian bar. Despite all this, he was the first Palestinian to intern with a justice at Israel's Supreme Court and the first to be appointed to the board of one of the largest and most powerful Israeli companies, Israel Chemicals. At the same time, he was the first and only Palestinian Israeli to join the committee recommending a draft for the Palestinian constitution. Quick thinking, eloquent, with a Hebrew that few Israelis have mastered, Dahleh broke multiple glass ceilings and became a successful lawyer much in demand.

In the February 2004 petition that he filed on behalf of the eight Palestinian villages, Dahleh did not just describe the loss of his clients' land. He asked the court to take a wider look at the implications of the barrier for the villages. He analyzed how the fence would create a fragmented space, how it would not only impede access to land and harm livelihoods but would also sever economic and social ties between the villages and

nearby urban centers. He argued that the fence would block any possibility of development, strangling the villages within their built-up
areas; it would impede access to and from the villages, making it hard
for students to reach school, suppliers to reach their customers, and rescue
teams and ambulances to reach patients in need.

All this on top of what Dahleh described as the erasure of the villages'
main source of income: farming. Legally, he argued—as Dugard had
claimed in his report and we in the HaMoked petition—that building the
fence meant annexing occupied land, which is prohibited under international law. He asserted that the security grounds cited by the state were a
smoke screen for the fence's real purpose, which was to annex the settlement areas to Israel. Knowing that the principled argument against the
fence had been dismissed in the Tulkarm and Qalqiliyah cases, Dahleh
added another expansive argument: that the measure of harm caused to
his clients makes the fence disproportionate; that is, that the harm to the
rights of the Palestinian residents exceeds the security benefit achieved
by the fence, if such exists. This position regarding the proportionality of
the fence and the need to consider alternative, less injurious routes was
an important innovation in the litigation.

The Beit Surik case, as it came to be known, was expeditiously heard
by the Supreme Court over an unprecedented seven days of sessions
between March and May 2004. President Barak decided that the most
senior panel—the justices serving the longest on the Supreme Court—
would hear it, and so the panel included Barak himself, together with Deputy President Eliyahu Mazza and Justice Mishael Cheshin. During the
hearings, the justices pushed the State Attorney's Office and the military
to consider less harmful alternatives to the current route. They also inquired
whether the farmers could be compensated for their loss of land with alternative plots. They did not accept the state's arguments that the damage
would be much lighter than the petition claimed because the fence would
include access gates. The justices understood that the permit system would
make access complicated and exhausting.

To allow time for the negotiations the justices requested, the hearings
were postponed repeatedly for several days. Dahleh very much wanted to
convince the court that any fence that incurs into occupied territory is
illegal under international law, but he reached the conclusion that his
chance of winning for his clients was better if he suggested an alternative

route. He believed that offering an alternative would expose the weakness of the security argument, delay the fence's construction, and maybe even see the decision reversed.[35] It would also serve the argument of proportionality by showing a less injurious route.

The problem, however, was that any alternative route that did not adhere to the Green Line meant essentially accepting the right of the occupying forces to erect a fence in occupied territory. Thus, Dahleh made it clear to the court that he did not think the alternative route was lawful, just that he was presenting it to illustrate that the military had chosen their route for reasons unrelated to security. Dahleh obviously knew his proposal carried a measure of risk. The court just might accept it, resulting in an invasive route, ostensibly at his suggestion. But he wanted to win. He also believed the catastrophic damage his clients would suffer precluded the privilege of plunging into these ethical-political dilemmas. In the negotiations that took place in response to pressure by the Supreme Court justices, at meetings in the basement of the Ministry of Justice, Dahleh sat alone, across the table from lawyers, military officers, and planners, and felt as if he were "negotiating Palestine's borders."[36] But he was convinced that suggesting a route along the Green Line that left the settlements outside the fence would never have been taken seriously, and he would have lost the support of the justices. The route he eventually proposed followed the Green Line as closely as possible, but it also penetrated into the West Bank to create tight, minimal enclaves around the settlements in the area.

At this point the case took an unexpected turn. After the petition had been filed, a group of residents from Mevaseret Zion, which bordered on Beit Surik, asked to join and support the case. They argued that the fence would destroy their neighborly relations with Beit Surik, and that the loss of land and the permit system were a violation of the Palestinians' dignity. The group also initiated a move that would have a significant impact on the results of the case, and consequently on the fence's entire route. They contacted Shaul Arieli, a former brigade commander in Gaza, and more recently the head of the Interim Agreement Administration, an Israeli military body that had advised the government on Israel's security demands during talks with the Palestinians.

After retiring from the military, Arieli joined dovish research groups and became active in the Council for Peace and Security, an organization of former Israeli security officials engaged in promoting a resolution of the conflict between Israel and its neighbors. The council was enthusiastic in its support for building a barrier as a security measure but opposed the route the government had chosen. Members of the council thought vast parts of the route lacked any security logic and believed that its invasiveness was a serious liability for any chance of a future agreement with the Palestinians. Arieli was the council's top expert on the West Bank and Israel's interests there.

The Mevaseret group asked Shaul Givoli, the council's managing director (and also a retired police major general and military brigadier general, the chief education officer in both the police and the military), to consider preparing an alternative route and submitting it to the High Court. Several council members, including Givoli and Arieli, came to a meeting the Mevaseret group had organized with delegates from Beit Surik to tour the area. The scene was most unusual: retired Israeli generals on a tour with Palestinian villagers to consider a move against government policy. After the tour, the council proposed a different route, "thinner" than the one considered by the court. Life really is full of surprises.

The interests the Israeli generals were promoting were in line with the interests of the Palestinian farmers. While the council did not agree with the route suggested by Dahleh, its own offering was closer to his than to the government's plan and did not extend too far from the settlements it surrounded. The council then filed a motion to join the proceedings as amicus curiae and submit its proposal. True to his belief that an alternative route, certainly one supported by Israeli security figures, increased the chances of a favorable outcome, Dahleh asked the court to accept the council's affidavit. The affidavit itself was signed by several members, including Givoli and Avraham Adan, a major general of mythic status, the man who held the handmade ink flag Israel raised in Eilat in the event that ended the 1948 War of Independence.

On June 25, the secretariat of the ICJ in The Hague issued a communiqué: the court would issue its advisory opinion on the separation wall on July 9. Two days later, Israel's Supreme Court secretariat issued a summons to the parties in the Beit Surik case: the court would deliver its judgment on June 30, nine days ahead of The Hague.

THE HIGH COURT panel struck down eighteen of the twenty-five miles of the route from Beit Surik to Beit Anan. Barak authored the fifty-two-page judgment; Cheshin and Mazza signed their names to it. The judgment was a judicial masterpiece that gave a win to the position that Israel could build a fence *and* to the petitioners and the protection of their rights. "We accept that the military commander cannot order the construction of the separation fence if his reasons are political," Barak wrote. "The separation fence cannot be motivated by a desire to annex territories to the state of Israel. The purpose of the separation fence cannot be to draw a political border."[37] Barak meticulously followed the distinction established in the settlement cases: land may be seized for security purposes but not for ideological-political purposes. And Barak had been satisfied by the affidavits filed by the commander of the military's Central Command, which claimed that the separation fence was motivated by and intended for security; he rejected Dahleh's principled argument on the illegality of the entire fence.

Of course, the information the court had received was limited to the specific section of the fence in question, focusing on topography, on whether a particular mountain should or should not fall on one side of the fence or the other, on whether the fence had to be protected from "flat-trajectory fire," and the acceptable distance from settlement homes. These were security considerations only—not a word had been uttered about any political program. And the fact that Dahleh's proposed route agreed with attaching the settlements to Israel obviated the need to discuss whether or not protecting settlements is a legally valid reason for having the fence penetrate into occupied territory. The principle that the military commander may seize land to build the fence was approved once and for all. The court ruled that his power to do so draws from the international laws of war and occupation, from the provisions of various articles in The Hague Regulations and the Fourth Geneva Convention, all of which prohibit damage to property but also include an exclusion for imperative, urgent security needs.[38] This principle, together with the acceptance that the rationale for the route was purely security-driven, allowed the court to reject the allegations of annexation.

Barak then proceeded to examine the proportionality of the harm caused by the route. He ruled that even though a fence may be built in occupied territory, that does not necessarily mean any route would be legal. It must properly balance the security benefit with the injury it would cause to Palestinians. On this point, Barak accepted Dahleh's argument:

More than thirteen thousand farmers (falahin) are cut off from thousands of dunams of their land and from tens of thousands of trees which are their livelihood, and which are located on the other side of the separation fence. No attempt was made to seek out and provide them with substitute land, despite our oft repeated proposals on that matter. The separation is not hermetic: the military commander announced that two gates will be constructed, from each of the two villages, to its lands, with a system of licensing. This state of affairs injures the farmers severely, as access to their lands (early in the morning, in the afternoon, and in the evening) will be subject to restrictions inherent to a system of licensing. Such a system will result in long lines for the passage of the farmers themselves; it will make the passage of vehicles (which themselves require licensing and examination) difficult, and will distance the farmer from his lands (since only two daytime gates are planned for the entire length of this segment of the route). As a result, the life of the farmer will change completely in comparison to his previous life. The route of the separation fence severely violates their right of property and their freedom of movement. Their livelihood is severely impaired. The difficult reality of life from which they have suffered (due, for example, to high unemployment in that area) will only become more severe.[39]

Barak saved his most scathing statements for the route that threatened to imprison Beit Surik: "The original route as determined . . . leaves the village of Beit Sourik [sic] bordered tightly by the obstacle on its west, south, and east sides," Barak wrote, adding, "This is a veritable chokehold, which will severely stifle daily life." Faithful to a principle established in one of the first settlement cases, when the High Court rejected the opinion of a major general in the reserves, preferring the professional opinion of standing security officials, Barak ruled in favor of the military's stance when it came to determining which route promised the greatest security. However, Barak affirmed that the test of proportionality means that a perfect route for security purposes cannot always also be lawful. He noted the duty to forgo some of the security advantage to avert a human rights catastrophe for the victims of the fence, but only if an alternative was available. "Such an alternate route exists," Barak wrote in the most important section of the judgment, referring to the Council for Peace and Security's proposal. "It is not a figment of the imagination. It was presented before us."[40] The military had not disputed the security expertise of the council members, thus allowing Barak to rely on their proposal to adequately—if not maximally—meet security needs:

> In the opinion of the military commander—which we assume to be correct, as the basis of our review—[the route suggested by the council] will provide less security in that area. However, the security advantage reaped from the route as determined by the military commander, in comparison to the proposed route, does not stand in any reasonable proportion to the injury to the local inhabitants caused by this route.[41]

The High Court of Justice did not compel the state to build the fence on the route suggested by the council. It sufficed to strike down 75 percent of the military's original route as disproportionate in light of a plausible alternative and sent the military back to the drawing board.

Barak knew that his judgment, the first in which the High Court had struck down a segment of the fence, would send shock waves through the political system. Just as in the case of interrogation methods—that is, torture—the panel he headed had intervened in something considered pivotal to Israel's security doctrine, which could prompt rage. And again, as in the torture case, Barak added an apologetic final paragraph to articulate his misgivings and attempt to convince the public that its safety also hinges on respect for the law:

> Our task is difficult. We are members of Israeli society. Although we are sometimes in an ivory tower, that tower is in the heart of Jerusalem, which is not infrequently hit by ruthless terror. We are aware of the killing and destruction wrought by the terror against the state and its citizens. As any other Israelis, we too recognize the need to defend the country and its citizens against the wounds inflicted by terror. We are aware that in the short term, this judgment will not make the state's struggle against those rising up against it easier. But we are judges. When we sit in judgment, we are subject to judgment. We act according to our best conscience and understanding. Regarding the state's struggle against the terror that rises up against it, we are convinced that at the end of the day, a struggle according to the law will strengthen her power and her spirit. There is no secu-

rity without law. Satisfying the provisions of the law is an aspect of national security.[42]

The judgment came as a shock to the commander in charge of planning and building the barrier, Dani Tirza—the same lieutenant colonel who had signed the affidavit regarding the early case of the villages near Qal-qiliyah, which claimed that the route had been determined according to security considerations. Tirza, a settler from Kfar Adumim, had replaced Shaul Arieli as the head of the military's negotiation administration and had also been appointed during Prime Minister Ariel Sharon's tenure to head the barrier authority. In a 2008 book about the barrier, which I wrote with Shaul Arieli, Arieli explained that most military officers pre-ferred to stay out of the fence-planning process, fearing that involvement in the project, which was largely motivated by settlement consider-ations, would implicate them politically.[43] But Tirza was unafraid. He served Sharon faithfully, becoming his confidant and trusted adviser on this issue.

As soon as the Beit Surik judgment was delivered, everyone understood that this particular segment of the fence was not the only one that would have to change; the entire route would need revising. The High Court of Justice had introduced a standard that necessitated changes in many segments, some of which had already been built, that up to that moment had almost entirely disregarded Palestinians' rights. The court had also sanctioned the project as legal—just ten days before the ICJ was set to pronounce its own judgment—but Dani Tirza only saw his glass as half-empty. The realization that a lot of the land he had managed, in consulta-tion with Sharon, to envelop inside the fence would now be left outside of it made him livid.

Tirza is a quiet man who does not easily lose his composure (I clocked many hours with him on different fence cases, and he gave the impres-sion of being polite and courteous), but he could not contain himself as he exited the courtroom, and he gave the press, who asked for his response, a statement that a civil servant should not have made: "Today the Palestin-ian Authority was handed a resounding victory by an Israeli court. . . . To my great sorrow, today, in my view, is a black day for the State of Israel. This judgment is terrible. It makes a mockery of all victims of terrorism . . .

we will pay for it with human lives." Two days later, Tirza was publicly scolded for his statements by both Attorney General Meni Mazuz and the minister of defense.[44] None of this prevented him from continuing to serve in the same capacity for several more years—until another one of his failures was exposed, as we shall see.

The Ministry of Justice and the Prime Minister's Office reacted with more restraint. They recognized what Tirza had failed to see: the judgment gave Israel an important asset with which to respond to the world and possibly even The Hague. Quotes attributed to sources close to Sharon noted: "The High Court's ruling will help the Israeli argument that there is no room for UN intervention in the implementation of the recommendations the court in The Hague is set to deliver next week."[45] The Ministry of Justice praised the judgment as "an extremely important contribution to Israel's international struggle, particularly in the court at The Hague."[46]

The fence was ultimately built more or less along the route suggested by the Council for Peace and Security. It encircled the settlements and attached them to Israel, but tens of thousands of dunams with many orchards and groves remained contiguous with their owners' land, and the fence authority had to plan many parts of the route anew, bringing them closer to the Green Line.

But the Beit Surik case posed no small number of dilemmas for lawyers who represented Palestinian landowners in fence cases in subsequent years. One question was whether to continue to suggest alternative routes. Dahleh's petition, which was filed in an early phase of the fence litigation, had attempted to propose an alternative route while still maintaining the argument that the entire project was unlawful. But once the High Court had issued a definitive reasoned ruling dismissing this argument of principle, suggesting other routes would amount to engagement in the fence's planning and legitimizing its intrusion into the Occupied Territories. After the Beit Surik ruling, most lawyers who worked on fence cases, myself included, refused to propose alternatives that did not sit directly on the Green Line or inside Israel. We believed we had to stay true to the principle that a fence that penetrates into occupied territory cannot be legal and that presenting a different route may be construed as legitimacy for violating this principle. We were also not prepared to accept the notion that Israeli settlements, which we considered a serious breach of international law, justified the fence's incursion into the West Bank. We insisted on this position, even at the cost of giving up the advantage we knew could be gained, as in the Beit Surik case, by proposing an alternative and less invasive route.

FROM BEIT SURIK TO THE HAGUE TO ALFEI MENASHE

If Barak thought that delivering a precedent-setting, principled Israeli judgment on the question of legality of erecting a barrier in the occupied territory, ahead of the ICJ's advisory opinion, would influence that institution, he was wrong. Although the advisory opinion came nine days after the Beit Surik judgment, no mention was made of it. The judges of the ICJ accepted all the arguments Israel's court had rejected, the same arguments we had made in the HaMoked petition.

The ICJ had taken a bird's-eye view of the barrier. It cited the UN secretary-general's report, which addressed the entire seam zone, and effortlessly identified the pattern of its twists and turns around settlement blocs. The court included the fact—true for the planned route at the time—that 80 percent of all settlers would reside within the fence area and that the route had clearly been planned to incorporate the greatest possible number.[47] Focusing on altitudes and topography and their military significance, as Central Command had done in its affidavit to Israel's High Court, was not possible given the ICJ judges' approach to the route. The ICJ predicted that the fence would help effect a change in the demographic makeup of the seam zone, thereby impinging on the Palestinians' right to self-determination in that area.

The court went on to rule that despite Israel's official position that the fence was not a case of border marking and therefore not annexation, the network of fences and walls and the legal regime associated with it (the permit system) would create a fait accompli—an act of de facto annexation of the area west of the barrier.[48] The advisory opinion stated unequivocally and unapologetically that every last one of the settlements was illegal and therefore could not stand as a legal cause for the fence to deviate beyond the Green Line.

The ICJ reviewed the multifaceted violation of Palestinian human rights, which emerged from the information the court had received (particularly the secretary-general's report, which had been updated for the court, and Dugard's report), and found no justification for it. Israel's claim that the fence was an act of self-defense could not stand, in the ICJ's view, since the threat it faced originated in an area under its control, while self-defense relates only to external threats[49] (a very weak argument that was rightly widely criticized). The court recognized that Israel is vulnerable to serious attacks on its population and that it is the country's right, even duty, to protect itself. However, this right must be pursued with respect for international law, whereas building a fence inside occupied territory is a violation of it.

Of the fifteen justices of the court, fourteen concluded that the fence was unlawful. Only one, Thomas Buergenthal, an American, had reservations. He believed the court did not have enough information to reach its findings regarding the fence's security purpose. He expressed views similar to Barak's that the fence should not be considered in its entirety because some parts might be legal while others were not. Still, he also ruled that the settlements were a violation of international law and, inasmuch as parts of the fence were planned to protect them, these sections were also a violation.[50]

The ICJ's approach to determining the fence's legality differed from that of Israel's High Court of Justice in a number of respects, not only in terms of a whole-versus-segments perspective. The ICJ's sensitivity to Israel's security needs was unlike that of the Israeli court, which naturally gave considerable weight to the fight against terrorism and viewed the imperative to counter it as a security issue that justifies even drastic measures. The ICJ, on the other hand, never bothered to detail the type of terrorism that occurred in Israel's streets. It dismissed the challenge with the laconic statement that Israel must fight its legitimate battle within the confines of the law.

But perhaps the most important difference concerned the settlements. While Israel's High Court judgment did not address the question of whether protecting the settlements can justify the fence's incursion into occupied territory, the ICJ made this a central issue. The settlements are not lawful and therefore cannot be used to validate the evils caused by the fence. This was a unanimous finding by all fifteen judges of the court.

The ICJ's opinion breathed new life into the principled fight against the fence in Israel, which had taken a beating in the High Court's ruling on the Beit Surik case. Immediately after publication of the opinion from

The Hague, Israeli lawyers working on fence cases pending before the High Court filed briefs, basing their arguments on the ICJ's findings. I was one of them, and my case involved the enclave around the settlement of Alfei Menashe.

IN THE EARLY months of 2004, the legal fight against the barrier received significant reinforcements: ACRI decided to procure funding dedicated to representing Palestinian communities that would be harmed by the fence. Since the Supreme Court president's ruling required a separate examination of each fence segment, there was a large number of cases, and ACRI's own legal staff could not handle them all. In an unusual move, ACRI decided to outsource some of the work. It also hired a Palestinian citizen of Israel, Khuloud Badawi, to serve as a field researcher, help maintain contact with the affected communities, and collect necessary information for the cases. ACRI's staff and field researchers visited the villages with the lawyers, explaining the meaning of the seizure orders to the residents, collecting facts and figures on the impact they would have on every aspect of life, filing objections to the seizure orders, and offering to represent the communities in the High Court of Justice pro bono.

I had just started my own practice. After six years with my mentor, Avigdor Feldman, I decided I wanted to run my own cases. I had also had my fill of the criminal litigation that formed a large part of Feldman's work. We parted as friends and agreed to continue collaborating on several cases I had begun in his office, including the HaMoked petition against the barrier. I took a monthlong vacation in India and then rented a tiny office in Tel Aviv. It was a magical time, if not too efficient. When I finished typing a letter, I would print it, sign it, put it in an envelope, lock the office, and walk to the nearest post office. It took a few weeks for me to realize this was not going to work, and I hired a secretary to come to the office twice a week. When she was there, I would have to leave—there wasn't enough room for the two of us. The office was so small and the air conditioner, which could not be turned away from the guest chair, was so old that anyone visiting the office would have to run to the bathroom a few minutes into the meeting. On the days I was exiled from the office to make room for my secretary, I worked out of cafés, a work environment I still love.

Despite being a fledgling lawyer and thanks to my involvement in the

HaMoked case, I was a natural port of call for the director of ACRI's legal department, Dana Alexander, herself a lawyer, who enlisted independent attorneys for ACRI's fence cases. We met in my new office, and she suggested I represent the residents of one of the enclaves created by the fence.

The enclave in question had been formed around Alfei Menashe, a settlement built in the 1980s and located south of Qalqiliyah and north of Hablah, a large Palestinian village (see map on p. 258). At the time, about five thousand Israelis lived in Alfei Menashe, and it sprawled over several hilltops, two and a half miles from the Green Line. To include the settlement within the fence but leave out Qalqiliyah and Hablah, which border on the Green Line, the route had to create a bubble around it by penetrating deep into the West Bank, surrounding Alfei Menashe, and then tracing a course back to the Green Line.

As always, the fence architects did not stop at the built-up portion of the settlement; they expanded the bubble to include a lot of land beyond it, mostly farmland and pastures. This left five very small Palestinian villages, which well predate Alfei Menashe, imprisoned on the wrong side of the fence. The villages were home to more than one thousand people. Three of them in the southern part of the enclave were quite old—according to some residents, stretching back to Roman times. The two northern villages were communities of tin shacks set up by Bedouin from the Negev who became refugees in 1948 and purchased land there. The second-generation refugees were now facing another exile. The fence had gates and a checkpoint, which supervised access between the enclave and the rest of the West Bank, while the settlement enjoyed territorial contiguity with the State of Israel.

The fence around Alfei Menashe was completed in August 2003, before ACRI set out to help communities in the area, and the enclave was placed under the permit system that forced the Palestinian residents to get permission to continue living in their own homes. Unlike other cases, which challenged future segments of the fence and their potential violation of the petitioners' rights, this case would show the court the actual harm the fence had inflicted on the lives of Palestinians—and this particular segment had had an especially disastrous impact on the five villages. They had been cut off from their surroundings and the villagers' lives had changed beyond recognition. Places that had been within walking distance (the school, the clinic, the market) now required a car journey and a set of permits to cross through checkpoints. The cost of gas and water soared, now that they were hauled through the checkpoints. Many children, mostly girls, dropped out of school because parents objected to their crossing checkpoints staffed by armed soldiers. A large number of patients no longer went to the clinic and farmers had lost the ability to sell produce to their customers on the other side of the fence. In one fell swoop, the enclave's Palestinian residents were cut off from their source of income, from the urban centers that supplied them with services, from family and friends who now needed permits to visit, and, of course, from the rest of their people. For these villages, the fence spelled doom, as they could not live under these conditions indefinitely.

When we researched how the route had been decided, we discovered that the Israeli communities seeking to influence the plans had lobbied for it. The head of Alfei Menashe's town council, the late Eliezer Hisdai, was an influential member of the Likud Party who understood the fence's political implications early on. He met with the defense minister and senior army officials dozens of times to demand that the fence include the settlement, connecting Alfei Menashe to Israel. The route proposed by the security establishment was changed several times due to pressure from Hisdai, who insisted the fence surround not only the built-up part of the settlement but also areas where he planned to build more neighborhoods in the near and distant future. Residents of Matan, a community on the Israeli side of the Green Line, also lobbied to prevent a situation where the main access road from Alfei Menashe would go through their town. This pressure, not pure security considerations, is what ultimately determined the route.

On my first visit to the enclave with Badawi and Alexander, I encountered the terrible sight of communities that were neglected, frightened, and very poor. In one village, all the men were sitting in a central square. I thought perhaps they had gathered there for our visit; I was wrong. Unemployment had reached such monstrous numbers that everyone was home. "This fence," said one of the elders of Wadi a-Rasha, sitting stooped over with a cigarette dangling from his mouth, "even Allah can't move it." I told him this was a clear instance of a route that had been determined for political rather than security reasons and was causing disproportionate harm. I thought we had a strong case. "If you manage to move the fence even one yard I'll slaughter a sheep for you," he said as his comrades laughed. "Don't slaughter the sheep," I said. "I'm a vegetarian." The man did not know the term, but some of the younger men in the village said something in Arabic and his eyes opened wide in amazement. "Okay. If you move the fence, I'll give you the sheep," he said finally. "Do whatever you want with it."

ACRI offered the villagers legal aid. The heads of the villages hesitated. They wanted the help but were very fearful of retaliation from Israel's Civil Administration, the military, and the settlers. The council head of Wadi a-Rasha said he was worried about the people from Alfei Menashe, who had a lot of influence over the Civil Administration and the army. They could lobby for demolition of houses in his village as an act of vengeance, he said. I thought he was exaggerating and told him he had nothing to worry about. In the end, the village found its nerve and joined the petition. Shortly after, the Civil Administration issued three demolition orders for the homes of two of the village petitioners and the council head. So ACRI filed a petition against the demolition orders, too.

In the end, only two of the villages decided to join the petition. The other three supplied information about the harm caused to them but remained fearful about formally joining the petition. Later, however, the Attorney General's Office and the Alfei Menashe council claimed that the three villages had not joined the petition because they had no problem with the fence's route. The villages were so angry that they changed their position and gave me power of attorney to act on their behalf in the case.

The petition I filed on behalf of the villages trapped behind the fence gave a detailed account of the injustice they had suffered and included some of the residents' anecdotes. I wrote about the father who tried to take his sick four-year-old to the doctor in Qalqiliyah, but the car he was driving was not his own and so was not listed in his permit. At the checkpoint he was told to find the owner or walk to the clinic with his feverish son. I wrote about the wedding of the council head's son, which no one attended because the family's guests were all denied permits to enter the village. I wrote about how one village lost half its cattle when a disease went untreated because the veterinarian, who lives in Qalqiliyah, could not get a permit to enter the enclave. I wrote about the grave disruptions in the water supply because the tankers that arrive once a week were having trouble getting permits.

I concluded with this: "The reader might ask: Is a normal human life truly possible under these conditions? How long will residents of the enclave last before they become destitute refugees (some for the first time, some for the second)? How long will it take before the village names of Arab a-Ramadin, Arab Abu Fardah, Wadi a-Rasha, Ma'rat Ad-Dab'a, and Ras al-Tira are erased from the map of Samaria?"[51]

Legally, I made the same arguments I had made in the HaMoked case and that had been accepted in the ICJ's advisory opinion: the fence was unlawful because it meant de facto annexation of the enclave to Israel, which is prohibited under international law; the fence was clearly meant to protect the settlement rather than Israel, and therefore the seizure orders fail to comply with the central condition for their validity: a legitimate military need. I also argued that the fence disproportionally violated the fundamental rights of the people living in the villages. The first two arguments challenged the authority to build the fence in the enclave. The third related to the proportionality of the route selected. Arguing on the authority to build a fence to protect the settlements forced me to assert that the settlements were unlawful, an issue the High Court of Justice had ruled was nonjusticiable. I had hoped to get around this impasse with the workaround suggested in the HaMoked case: I asked the court to rule that the settlements cannot be considered a military need that justifies violating the rights of the occupied population, regardless of the question of their legality. "Military need" serves the occupying power or its forces, not its citizens who choose to relocate to the occupied territory. Their protection should not involve impingements on the rights of the occupied population.[52]

Finally, I highlighted the dependency the enclave created between its Palestinian residents and the settlement of Alfei Menashe, which had become almost their sole source of income. These circumstances produced a particularly ugly situation:

> The sad truth is that the fence and the permit system have cast the Palestinian residents of the enclave in the role of servants to the settlers of Alfei Menashe. This completes the terrible process of creating a world of masters and servants, lords and serfs, settlers and Palestinians, a reality of division along ethnic lines into superior and inferior castes. A criminal reality of systemic, institutionalized legal discrimination.[53]

ISRAEL'S HIGH COURT could not indefinitely avoid addressing the ICJ's findings of de facto annexation and the absence of a legitimate security need for a route designed to maintain territorial contiguity between the settlements and Israel. The ICJ's prestige cast a shadow over Barak's ruling in the Beit Surik case—that the route had been chosen for security reasons—and he knew the High Court would have to issue another principled judgment that would decisively address the questions of the power to build an invasive fence and the political annexationist motivation for its route.

The first fence cases to be heard after the ICJ opinion had been filed by two Palestinian villages located near the Green Line; Budrus, which was represented by Ronit Robinson on behalf of ACRI, and Shuqba, which was represented by Muhammad Dahleh, who had been inundated with calls from victims of the fence after his Beit Surik success.

In the first hearing, Barak instructed the parties to submit briefs on the impact they believed the ICJ ruling had on the rules set forth in the Beit Surik case. Was it necessary—he appeared to be asking—in light of the ICJ ruling, to change the High Court's ruling on the authority to build a fence inside occupied territory? Because the discussion was so important, Barak extended the panel from three to nine justices, a rare number reserved for particularly far-reaching cases.

For the human rights organizations involved in the petitions, the Budrus and Shuqba cases were the worst possible choice for such a momentous deliberation. They were ill suited for the heavy burden placed on them. In Budrus and Shuqba the fence did not veer too far from the Green Line, and the quantity of land snatched from Palestinians was relatively small (several dozen dunams), which meant the fence had caused fairly limited harm to their residents. Also, the route near them had not been shaped by a settlement. The two cases had been selected at random, but the selection hurt the fight against the fence.

ACRI decided to try adding a stronger case to the hearing before the extended panel, a case in which the harm was severe and clearly motivated by political, settlement-oriented considerations. The Alfei Menashe case was the best candidate. On the date scheduled for the Alfei Menashe hearing, I asked the court to add it to the petitions set to be heard before the extended panel that would consider arguments on the impact of the ICJ ruling. The State Attorney's Office grasped what was going on and vehemently objected. The last thing it wanted was a discussion of the ICJ findings in a case where the fence was disastrous for Palestinians' lives and its route had been driven purely by the desire to keep a strong, politically influential settlement contiguously connected to Israel. Yet the state's lawyers were unable to explain their objection to adding the case to the extended panel. They could not openly admit that the injustice in this case was greater, or that the route had been influenced by political considerations. Barak repeatedly tried to get to the bottom of their resistance, but they provided no satisfactory explanation. He then ruled that since the petition raised issues that did not come up in the other petitions, the Alfei Menashe enclave case would be heard by the extended panel as well.

The Supreme Court heard the case in June 2005, in a hearing that lasted close to five hours. I focused my argument on the issue of authority, saying that the fence meant annexation and that there was no legitimate need for building it, given that international law does not recognize protecting the settlements as justification for violating the rights of the occupied population.

With the help of an expert opinion prepared by Bimkom and signed by renowned architects such as Moshe Safdie and Ernst Alexander, I showed the justices the declining spatial reality in all its aspects, the result of the centuries-long connection between the villages in the enclave and the Palestinian communities to the east having been severed. On behalf of Bimkom, anthropologist Shuli Hartman had conducted research showing that the deep social connections between villages had begun to disintegrate.

With the passion of a rookie lawyer who felt as if he held the lives of hundreds of people in his hands, I argued that the same force that had cut the strings tying the villages to the rest of the West Bank was now forging new connections, chains that were shackling the enclave to the west, to Israel. All the commercial, political, social, and legal channels linked the enclave in one direction only, to the west. A map drawn by Bimkom experts showed the roads that had been cut off by the fence and the ones that had been built to replace them, providing a visual depiction of annexation. The justices observed a large aerial photograph of the enclave, showing the fence; I indicated the land grabbed and reserved for Alfei Menashe's future development to the south, north, and east. "This fence is motivated solely by considerations that are meant to serve the settlement," I said with restrained anger. "The security explanation crumbles under the real, political reason that determined its route."

Addressing the justices directly, I said that everyone knew the fence was political. The Palestinian villagers, who had seen to their amazement that the IDF symbol on their permits had been replaced with Israel's state emblem—they knew it; the residents and developers of Alfei Menashe, whose real estate had soared in value now that the settlement had become de facto part of Israel (the price of a four-bedroom apartment there rose by 15 to 30 percent in the six months after the fence route was fixed)—they knew it, too; and of course the military commanders knew it, particularly those working for the fence authority. The person who knew it best, perhaps, was Dani Tirza, who was working with Ariel Sharon on deciding Israel's future borders.

In the recesses during the hearing, I had a chance to speak with Eliezer Hisdai of Alfei Menashe. Hisdai was a man of about fifty, average height, full of confidence and energy. He knew, just like me, that arguments in court are one thing and reality another. "It's not about the fence, it's about the new neighborhood," I told him, hinting at his plans to build throughout the enclave, which would never be realized if the route were to change. Hisdai looked at me in silence for a moment and then nodded his head. "So . . . tell it to the court," I suggested. He smiled and kept silent.

At the end of the hearing, I warned the justices against the dissonance between the discourse outside and inside the courtroom. "Everyone is talking about the fence as a border: the left, the right, the settlers, the Palestinians," I said. "It is only here, inside the courtroom, that everyone is playing the security charade, only here are people cautiously stepping around the political argument."

What I failed to realize at the time was that the security charade did not only serve Israel in its quest for a belligerent, unilateral solution to its conflict with the Palestinians; it served the court, too, in its quest to preserve its legitimacy both in Israel and abroad. The justices needed the security argument, which is inherently an issue of fact and professional expertise, rather than a matter of law, to issue rulings that would remain legally sound. The security excuse allowed the court to approve the fence, thereby avoiding a clash with Israeli public opinion, which overwhelmingly favored building it, while also taming Israel's voracious appetite by

striking down parts of it, thus avoiding a severe blow to the court's stand-
ing and legitimacy in world opinion. This was why Barak chose the Alfei
Menashe case for his response to the ICJ ruling. Not Budrus, not Shuqba.
Alfei Menashe.

Barak had sought a case with which he could give the government a
broad victory and Palestinians a local one; a case in which the fence would
remain permissible in general terms but rejected in concrete specifics, just
as in Beit Surik. This way, both sides could leave the courtroom with their
hands raised in victory. No one would be able to blame the court. No case
was better suited for this purpose than Alfei Menashe. The harm the
enclave had caused to the Palestinians was immense, and so the route could
be easily struck down based on proportionality.

THE COURT HANDED down its judgment on the Alfei Menashe enclave
on September 15, 2005. It was longer than eighty-five pages, which President Barak had written with all eight colleagues concurring. When I
entered the courtroom before the reading of the judgment, I was shocked
to see two sets of copies prepared by the court's spokesperson's office—
one in Hebrew and one in English. I asked a court administrator angrily
whether the judgment had also been translated into Arabic—unlike
English, it is one of Israel's official languages and the one spoken and read
by the petitioners. I was told that it wasn't in the budget.

The judgment's opening section was titled "Terrorism and the Response
to It." It related the history of the Al-Aqsa Intifada and proceeded to give
a detailed account of the process of building the fence and the Alfei
Menashe enclave as part of it. This structure implied a cause and effect
between terrorism and the fence and indicated that the court adopted the
security thesis in its analysis of the fence's legality.

A central part of the judgment was dedicated to Barak's grappling with
the ICJ's advisory opinion. The legal framework the court had used to
examine the fence's legality was the same one used by the ICJ, he wrote.
Both instances rested their legal analysis on the law of belligerent occupation, on the provisions of The Hague Regulations and the Geneva
Convention. So why the difference between our conclusions in Beit Surik
and the ICJ's? Barak had the answer: The facts before us are different
from the facts presented to the ICJ, especially with regard to the security
need. Israel did not cooperate with the ICJ and did not present its judges

with the security thesis underlying the fence. But we, the Israeli justices, have been privy to this thesis. In addition, Barak wrote, the ICJ reviewed the fence in its entirety. We look at each segment separately.

Treading carefully to give the ICJ its due respect, while rejecting its advisory opinion for being based on incomplete security information, Barak laconically dismissed both aspects of the argument regarding the lack of authority to build a fence in occupied territory (the absence of a military need and de facto annexation). On the first element (military necessity), Barak ruled (again) that the military had the power to build a fence for security reasons. This time he addressed the question of whether the settlements constituted a security need and explicitly ruled that protecting the settlers was a "military necessity." He skipped over the hurdle of the legality of the settlements by using an artificial distinction between the settlements and the settlers, or in Barak's own words:

> Our conclusion is, therefore, that the military commander is authorized to construct a separation fence in the area for the purpose of defending the lives and safety of the Israeli settlers in the area. It is not relevant whatsoever to this conclusion to examine whether this settlement activity conforms to international law or defies it, as determined in the Advisory Opinion of the International Court of Justice at The Hague. For this reason, we shall express no position regarding that question. The authority to construct a security fence for the purpose of defending the lives and safety of Israeli settlers is derived from the need to preserve "public order and safety" (regulation 43 of The Hague Regulations). It is called for, in light of the human dignity of every human individual. It is intended to preserve the life of every person created in God's image. The life of a person who is in the area illegally is not up for the taking. Even if a person is located in the area illegally, he is not outlawed.[54]

There was a bit of sleight of hand in this, because protecting the Israeli settlers could be achieved by returning them to Israel. Protecting them where they live is protecting the settlements.

The same court that in the 1970s had accepted the settlements as a military necessity, required for protecting Israel's national security, now accepted the thesis that there is a military necessity to protect the settlements using a fence. The settlements, justified as a security need in the 1970s, begat a new security need in 2000. Much like the woman who swallowed the fly, each move Israel made, ostensibly for the sake of security, seemed to yield another, and it did not stop with the fence. After the fence was built, seizure orders were issued for more Palestinian land. Military necessity required observation towers, and then additional land was seized to protect the towers. Israel built the settlements to protect itself, then the fence to protect the settlements that protect Israel, then the towers to protect the fence that protects the settlements that protect Israel, and then the special security areas to protect the towers, that protect the fence, and so on: a long cumulative tale of occupation.

To be clear: we had not argued that the military was not required to protect the settlers. We granted the premise that the military has a duty to protect everyone in the occupied territory, including citizens of the occupying power. Our argument was different: the military cannot violate the fundamental rights of the Palestinians to protect its own citizens in the occupied territory. As long as Alfei Menashe is not evacuated, I argued at the hearing, the settlement should be surrounded on all sides by the fence, not the Palestinian villages. Let the military dig a tunnel for the settlers to reach Israel instead of annexing the entire space just to give them convenient access. The justices laughed. For them, it was a moment of comic relief.

The lengthy judgment contained no analysis of the many facts presented to the court about the settlement-related considerations behind the fence—the plans to build more neighborhoods, the change to the route to avoid having a road running through Matan. There was no reference to the myriad evidence that the fence was unilaterally creating a new geopolitical entity in occupied territory. They chose not to look at the role of political interference in deciding the fence's route, or at the long-term effects of the fence and the permit system. In fact, other than a section detailing the parties' arguments, the judgment made no mention of the claim of annexation.

Indeed, Barak had deflected the argument about annexation in violation of international law by accepting the contention that the fence was built to protect the safety of all Israelis—those living in the settlements, those living in Israel, and those traveling between them.

The High Court of Justice chose to hide behind the security blanket. It was the only way the court could sanction the fence and the consequent landgrab without reaching legally ludicrous findings. It was the only way the court could reject certain parts of the fence without alienating the Israeli public. The High Court needed the security narrative just as much as the security narrative needed the High Court.

However, the judgment concluded by finding that the route of the fence around the Alfei Menashe enclave was so harmful to the villages that an alternative had to be considered, surrounding only the settlements and leaving out as much of the village land as possible. The route could not otherwise be deemed proportionate. The court gave some indication of an alternative route, bringing the fence right up to the settlement on the north and south. The sting of the loss on the principled argument gave way to joy at the result for my clients, who received me with victory cries when I came to the enclave after the judgment was read. One of the residents, thrilled at the prospect of his nightmare being eased or even ending, gave an emotional interview to a television network that had come to the enclave. He had faith in the Israeli courts, he said.

The Alfei Menashe enclave was not eliminated, but it did change. For the first time a part of the fence that had been built was taken down in response to a court order. The fence that had been so oppressive for the three southern villages was dismantled, replaced by a new one farther to the north. The villages renewed their connection to the West Bank. The Palestinian Authority began directing resources to the villages and their situation quickly improved. It would not be an overstatement to say that the villages were saved from extinction. The two northern villages, however, the small, disempowered Bedouin tin shacks, remained in the enclave. Another petition we filed on their behalf, through ACRI, was dismissed. Alfei Menashe also filed a petition, after the plan to expand southward was derailed by the fence's relocation. It too was dismissed.[55]

In all the petitions brought against the fence thus far, the High Court had accepted the security argument, believing the state's assertion that political considerations had played no role in deciding its route. In the following two years, two cases—Azzun (Zufin) and Bil'in—would expose that lie.

THE ZUFIN INDUSTRIAL ZONE (A FUTURE PLAN)

"Please explain to me why it extends so far in that direction," I said, pointing at the fence surrounding a large area dense with olive trees.

"The distance between the houses in the settlement and the fence is several miles, and you tell the court you only need an area in the range of a light weapon, just a few hundred yards." My interlocutors smiled at each other and said nothing. The council heads of Azzun and a-Nabi Elyas could not follow the Hebrew.

This was the scene: February 2005, two Palestinians, a Jewish Israeli lawyer, a Bimkom architect, and four Israeli military officers standing on a patrol road on the western side of the fence. It had taken the military almost six months to arrange a tour for my clients and me along the segment of the fence that surrounded Zufin, the settlement north of Qalqiliyah (see map on p. 258). Its route had stolen thousands of dunams of land from the villages near Zufin and no security explanation had been provided. Many months earlier, in the summer of 2004, during my first meeting with the council heads, I was shocked at the brazen invasiveness of the route. At this point I was deeply involved in fence cases—the Ha-Moked principled petition with Avigdor Feldman and the Alfei Menashe enclave. I knew the security argument and I didn't buy it. But I also knew that a fence located at a distance of two to three miles from settlement homes failed to meet even the fence administration's own criteria.

As readers might remember from chapter 1, at that meeting I advised the potential clients to petition to dismantle the fence, which had undermined their income, made mostly from farming, primarily in orchards that were now beyond their reach. The council heads, suspicious of this enthusiastic thirtysomething lawyer's grasp on reality, asked me to help them get a gate installed in the fence, nearer to their villages. The closest gate was a long way away, and it did not give them access to their land, certainly not with agricultural vehicles. So they asked for another gate. For me, this created a dilemma. I wanted a fight against the fence, and now I was being asked to help manage it.

The council heads reminded me that the petition filed two years earlier by these same villages against land seizures in the Qalqiliyah area had been dismissed on security grounds. I insisted that no security explanation could possibly account for the Zufin fence, which poked a long bulging finger westward, inexplicably engulfing twelve hundred dunams. The fence's location could and should be revisited. At the end of the meeting, we agreed that I would do both: ask for a gate and start work on a petition to dismantle the fence.

Now, walking along the patrol road, I tried to trip up the legal advisers from the Civil Administration and get them to explain the bulge in the fence. But I already had the answer. The fence administration had lied to the court in 2002 when it claimed that this big swath of land was needed to protect the road that ran through it, connecting Israel with the settlements. How did I know? Thanks to Alon Cohen-Lifschitz, a Bimkom planner and architect and childhood friend from Jerusalem.

From the beginning of the battle against the fence, the planners and experts of Bimkom had joined the teams set up by HaMoked and ACRI to study the various parts of the route. One of their goals was to obtain the master plans for the settlements and explore their relation to the fence's route. The importance of this was that claims about security considerations would be undermined if it turned out that the route followed plans for future settlement expansion. The professed purpose of the fence was to protect living people, not future expansions.

Cohen-Lifschitz worked in the Bimkom department that dealt with planning in the Occupied Palestinian Territories and did whatever he could to uncover the master plans. Together with ACRI, he filed an application under the Freedom of Information Act to get the Civil Administration to divulge its information. At some point, he went to the offices of the Samaria Regional Council, posing as an architect looking into projects for investors in the northern West Bank. He ended up getting his hands on a range of master plans for settlement expansion that were not publicly available. Then he came with me to Zufin. I stayed in the car, fearing I might be recognized, while he—or rather his architect persona working on behalf of investors—collected information on future expansion. More plans were uncovered by B'Tselem. In short, Alon had a pretty good understanding of settlement expansion plans, including in Zufin. When Alon saw the bulge in the fence, he knew that it correlated to the exact location of an industrial zone that had been planned for Zufin even before the fence's route had been determined. The fence, touted as a security need, meticulously followed the contours of a future industrial zone. Case proved.

"So what is this bulge for? Can you explain it to me?" I pressed the two twentysomething military legal advisers. The two were intelligent, pleasant, and had a sense of humor. In another time and place, we might have been friends. They were two of Israel's finest. Just like them, dozens of young Israeli men and women, educated in middle- or upper-class neighborhood schools, had imbibed a worldview of Jewish nationalism blended with basic liberal values, studied law in the best schools in the country, and then enlisted to serve in the army's legal service. This is part of Israel's tragedy: the best of the best, driven by a genuine desire to serve their society and do good, end up serving the machinery of occupation and dispossession.

The two officers exchanged glances and sheepish smiles but said nothing. I believe they had probably voiced criticism of the settlement considerations that dictated the route of the fence in internal deliberations, but revealing the secret to me would mean a break with convention that neither of them was prepared to make. So they were careful not to lie, but neither did they tell me the truth. They simply promised to add a gate in a convenient location for my clients.

In the petition I filed in March 2005 on behalf of the Azzun and a-Nabi Elyas council heads, I charged that the fence's route had been planned to accommodate the settlement's future expansion and any security explanations were false. We showed that the bulge in the fence followed a master plan for an industrial zone that had not yet been approved or even begun the lengthy application process to be submitted to the authorities.

The attorney representing the state was Avi Licht, another good, talented, decent man. Now a senior attorney in the State Attorney's Office, he would, I believed, speak truthfully about the motives for building the fence on my clients' land. Unlike the officers, who were under no obligation to answer my questions, Licht had to respond to the accusations in the petition and explain the reasons for the route to the judges. I was right about him being truthful. In his response to the petition, he asked for it to be rejected for every reason imaginable, but one sentence gave away the fact that the bulge was not the result of security considerations: "In the planning of the route prior to its construction," Licht wrote, "weight was given to a plan that was in the design process but has not yet entered into effect."[56] Licht even cited the number assigned to the plan.

This flew in the face of the testimony the state had given in the 2002 case of the Qalqiliyah area villages: that the route was meant to provide a buffer zone, to allow troops to chase terrorists who infiltrate the fence before they reach houses in the settlements, and also to create a protected observation point over a road that ran along the bulge, outside the fence, and was used by the settlements. Suddenly there was no buffer zone and no protected observation point. The plan had been to build an industrial zone for the settlement. Three years earlier, Dani Tirza, the head of the fence administration, had signed an affidavit, submitted to the High Court, that stated the security considerations. The state's response in this case was also supported by an affidavit from Tirza. Which Tirza were we supposed to believe, the earlier Tirza or this one? The significance of the state having misled the court in this way was beginning to dawn on me.

But the state took the position that the route should still remain as it was, even though an illegitimate consideration had gotten into the mix. "Had this segment of the barrier been planned today, it would have been done in a slightly different manner and would not have included the entire area of the plan," Licht wrote, but added: "Most of the land beyond this segment is public land rather than agricultural land. . . . The cost of dismantling and rebuilding the barrier in this section is prohibitive."[57] The first argument was factually wrong. The second was shameless. First they put up a fence in a way they themselves consider illegal, and now they're too cheap to put it right?

The justices immediately grasped the egregiousness of the state's actions and the absurdity of its position. As usual in fence cases, the panel presiding was composed of senior justices: President Barak, Deputy President Cheshin, and Justice Beinisch, who had been on the panel in the Qalqiliyah villages case and realized that she had been misled. She shook her head in astonishment. "I remember that hearing," she said angrily. "It was in the middle of the terrorist attacks and the intifada, and you wanted a quick judgment, you said security, security, security." Once again the security establishment had not told Beinisch the truth. Once again it had misled the court. Just like in the Shabak affair.

The justices issued an order nisi compelling the state to reconsider its position. Several months later, the state announced its stance had changed. "It has been decided to construct a new route. . . . The new route will not include the southeast corner of the old route."[58] The state had decided to remove the bulge and reconnect some twelve hundred dunams of cultivated farmland to the rest of the West Bank. My clients were going to be reunited with their land. The thinking behind this move must have been that deciding to relocate the route might have allowed the state to avoid a harsh judgment of its conduct. If that was the plan, it failed miserably:

The petition at hand uncovered a grievous practice. In the original petition, the Supreme Court was not presented with the full picture. The court
dismissed the original petition based on information which was only partially substantiated. The State Attorney's Office acted properly in having
notified the court of the fact that plan 149/5 had been taken into consideration upon learning that this was so. The Respondents acted properly
in having changed the route of the fence at their own initiative, given this
information and given our judgment in the Alfei Menashe case. However,
the petition at hand reveals an incident that cannot be condoned, in which
the information provided to the court did not reflect the full scope of considerations taken into account by the decision makers. This led to the dismissal of a petition that even the Respondent now agrees should have been
accepted.[59]

The court ruled the fence unlawful and ordered it dismantled within
six months of completion of the construction of the new segment. The
court also ordered the state to pay the petitioners 50,000 shekels in costs.
There is no rule that mandates ordering costs against the losing side in a
High Court petition, but justices often use the orders to express dissatisfaction with a party's conduct. The amount the state was ordered to pay
was extremely high for the High Court and reflected the justices' anger.

The scathing criticism by Israel's highest judicial instance was extensively covered by the media. It was proof that considerations that favor
the settlements had influenced the fence's route. Still, the security establishment and the Ministry of Justice treated this case as a mishap, an aberration. Didi Remez, a founder of Yesh Din and a friend, filed a police
complaint against Tirza for perjury. The attorney general probed Tirza's
conduct. In response to a parliamentary question, Deputy Defense Minister Efraim Sneh said that since Tirza's contract with the Ministry of
Defense was soon to expire, and given his "extensive track record with
the security fence project and other projects," the attorney general had
decided against disciplinary measures. However, Sneh said, the attorney
general did recommend against Tirza's future employment "in any position that requires presenting the state's position on the separation fence,
and likely on anything else as well."[60]

Nonetheless and in spite of the defense minister's order barring Tirza
from appearing in the High Court on behalf of the security establishment,

Tirza did represent the state in several hearings before his contract ended.[61] Tirza was later appointed by Prime Minister Ehud Olmert to serve as adviser and liaison with settlers on unauthorized outposts. In February 2007, the State Attorney's Office announced that it would not order an investigation into Tirza's actions and that the complaint filed by Didi Remez would be archived. An appeal filed against this decision was dismissed.

"WHY ARE THEY DEMONSTRATING IN BIL'IN?"

The intrusion of settlement considerations into the barrier planning process was no mishap. Everyone working on barrier-related issues knew it. It was an open secret. Politicians spoke about the barrier as Israel's future border, and the settler leadership worked tirelessly to have land designated for future settlement development included in the seam zone. The public debate around the subject was entirely uncensored. Still, it was hard to bring this awareness into the courtroom. There were security explanations attached to every possible route of the barrier: If it extended to the highest elevation, then that was to allow observation. If it was built at two-thirds of the height, that was to avoid exposing the troops. If it was built at the bottom of the valley, the purpose was to protect the hill. No matter how it was built, there was a security justification.

This doublespeak around the fence was so entrenched that it led to an embarrassing incident between Justice Minister Tzipi Livni and Supreme Court deputy president Cheshin in late 2005, when the two participated in the same law conference in Caesarea. Livni stated that the fence marked Israel's future border and that in practice, "the High Court of Justice, in its rulings over the fence, is drawing the country's borders."[62] Cheshin had to respond, publicly chastising the justice minister: "That is not what you have contended in court." Though visible in plain sight, however, the fence's political goal was blocked from entering the court. Most of the petitions filed against the fence were dismissed, with the justices accepting the security arguments, and much of the fence was erected deep inside the Occupied Territories. But there were rare cases in which the court simply could not avoid the clear evidence before it that the route was selected to serve the interests of the settlements.

The battle waged by the small Palestinian village of Bil'in against the construction of the fence on its land has been recounted by many. I wrote about it in *The Wall of Folly*, a book coauthored with Shaul Arieli.[63] At least three books were published by photojournalists who covered the struggle,[64] and two films were made, *Bil'in Habibti*, by Israeli filmmaker Shai Carmeli-Pollak, and *Five Broken Cameras*, by village resident Emad Burnat and Israeli director Guy Davidi. The film was nominated for an Academy Award for Best Documentary in 2013.

Before the resistance to the fence, Bil'in was unknown, not only to Israelis but to many Palestinians as well. Located west of Ramallah, amid larger, richer villages, Bil'in is home to farmers and civil servants and had never made a name for itself during the intifadas. But as the fence began to take shape and the residents realized that more than half of the four thousand dunams they still owned would be cut off on the other side (most of their land had been lost in the war of 1948), the village underwent a metamorphosis. From a sleepy farming community with scant political activism, Bil'in turned into a vibrant hub of resistance to the occupation, and the methods it used were novel.

Village youths set up a popular committee to organize the struggle, and it was they who steered the course toward nonviolent resistance. Together with activists from Israel and around the world, they staged weekly demonstrations on Fridays that attracted progressives from all over the region. With unprecedented creativity, the protest marches included spectacular installations—cages built to represent the fence's effect on Palestinians, farmers handcuffed to olive trees slated for uprooting, even protesters dressed up as characters from American film and television starred in the protests. The popular committee leaders studied the writings of Martin Luther King and Mahatma Gandhi and did everything they could to prevent the youth who joined the protests from nearby villages from throwing stones at the Israeli troops (with great though incomplete success). After two violent intifadas, this was a very different Palestinian fight. The popular resistance enjoyed tremendous success in the public opinion. The international press had a field day. The unarmed Palestinian practicing nonviolence quickly took over the screen.

This success was certainly helped by Israel's violent overreaction. The military, the border police, and the Shabak set out to do what they had done before in villages that protested the fence—crush the marches with might. The security forces confronted the crowds with tear gas, rubber bullets, and arrests. These strong-arm tactics did not stop with the marches. Bil'in was officially termed a "hostile village." The Shabak was brought into the picture, and military forces carried out nightly raids, breaking into houses and making arrests. Some of the popular committee members were arrested as if they were the heads of terrorist organizations and accused of . . . organizing illegal protests.

Among those detained were Abdallah Abu Rahmah, a teacher and one of the central leaders of the protests; my friend, Deputy Council Head Muhammad Abu Rahmah (Abu Nizar) who, despite being beaten after he was pulled out of his bed, was glad to be arrested, as he was ceremoniously led to the cell where his fourteen-year-old son (!) had been held for five days; my good friend Muhammad Khatib, who, with his youthful, optimistic personality, was the life of the marches, and whose ingenuity produced a ceaseless stream of creative ideas for nonviolent protest—all arrested in the dead of night.

Their homes were raided by armed men, faces covered by black masks, who loudly woke up horrified family members. Khatib's house was invaded by a border police platoon accompanied by men from the Shabak. They broke down the front door and charged into the bedrooms with guns pointing. The horror of the nightly arrest is deeply etched in the souls of Khatib's young children. In his interrogation at the Ofer detention facility, it turned out this arch-terrorist was suspected of inciting illegal demonstrations and throwing stones.

When I heard about the arrest, I was enraged. Khatib and I are the same age, and in the years I represented the village we became friends. What began as a political alliance developed into a close personal relationship. My eldest son, who often came with me to Bil'in, befriended his sons. The arrest was a reminder that even though we were involved in the same struggle, we were not equals. I am Israeli and Jewish. I will not be arrested in this way. He is Palestinian and none of his connections with Israelis and foreign journalists will help. If the Shabak wants to prevent him from demonstrating and terrorize his family, so it shall be. They knew that had Khatib been summoned for questioning, he would have come. But no. The raids, the terror, the humiliation—they were all part of the goal. In the end, and it took about a year, Khatib made history, becoming one of very few Palestinians to be acquitted in a military court, but the damage was done.

Unlike other villages, Bil'in did not give in. The presence of Israeli and international activists brought attention from the media, and Israeli lawyers like Gaby Lasky and Tamar Peleg-Sryck, who had long experience representing activists, now represented Bil'in's detainees. The security forces' violence was documented and televised, and the fight began to resemble a Palestinian David fighting an Israeli Goliath. All of this gave the fight staying power. Nothing like it had happened before with any segment of the fence.

But the popular committee knew that nonviolent resistance alone would not move the fence. Previous attempts to challenge the fence in the High Court, made through a lawyer appointed by the governor of the Qalqiliyah district, had failed. However, conversations with Tamar Peleg-Sryck and research by Nir Shalev, one of the Israeli activists, suggested that there had been a missed legal opportunity, that maybe something could still come out of going to Israel's court. I was invited to a meeting in the village and accepted the mission of trying to revisit the Bil'in case.

Again I turned to Bimkom for help. It appeared that the placement of the fence—at a great distance from the homes in the nearby Orthodox Jewish settlement of Modi'in Illit—had been determined by reasons that had nothing to do with security. The route conspicuously ran at the bottom of a valley overlooked by the built-up part of Bil'in. It did not need a general to see that something was off militarily. Any forces would have to patrol a route commanded by Bil'in. The objective instead was to take over two hills located about a mile away from the settlement.

Alon Cohen-Lifschitz and Nir Shalev looked into the record and their findings were unequivocal: a plan for a huge neighborhood that would cover the entire area between Modi'in Illit and Bil'in, and the separation fence traced its precise outline. This new neighborhood of East Matityahu would have thirty-three hundred residential units. Two Canadian development companies and one from Israel were about to make a lot of money from Bil'in land.[65] The security establishment always makes an argument for preserving space between the fence and the built-up part of the settlement it protects, but in this case the huge expanse was about to be filled with houses reaching all the way to the fence. Construction of part of the neighborhood, several large five- and six-story apartment buildings, had already begun, some of them on private plots belonging to residents of Bil'in. Most of these structures were slated for land that had been declared in the 1990s as state land through a very dubious procedure.[66] The buildings that had been started were located in the western part of the area, close to the part of Modi'in Illit that had already been built, but construction was moving eastward.

In the petition I filed on behalf of the village, I again made the argument that the fence's location had been chosen to serve settlement interests, not security needs. We had all the proof we needed, but still I was very concerned. I knew that the slow progress of High Court cases could result in a judgment being handed down after the neighborhood was completed. The first hearing in the case was scheduled for February 2006, about six months after the petition was submitted. Twenty-two large apartment buildings, with dozens of units in each one, were already at various stages of construction. Some of the units were already occupied, to establish facts on the ground. If the houses were built and people were living in them, the state would be able to say that the fence perhaps should not have been built the way that it had, but now its route was justified because the people living there needed the protection of the fence. Besides, I felt the court would be hard pressed to order a change to the route if that meant appearing to abandon people already living at the site. Once the petition had been filed, the race was on: What would come first, a court ruling or the completion and occupancy of the homes?

The solution was hidden in a detail in the state's response to the petition. The state attorney lawyer who handled the case, Aner Helman, had openly included many details of which we had not been aware. The plan approved for the neighborhood involved fifteen hundred housing units only. The developers had asked to amend it to accommodate denser housing and double the number of units, and had begun construction according to this amended plan before it entered into effect. All of the construction was illegal.

Illegal construction in West Bank settlements is no surprise. In fact, it is quite common. What was different in this case was the massive scale of the illegal construction—thousands of housing units in a large, established settlement—which is why it had caught the attention of Peace Now. Dror Etkes, coordinator of Peace Now's Settlement Watch, which monitors construction in settlements, had gladly mobilized to help Bil'in. Etkes is a veteran peace activist who turned Peace Now's Settlement Watch into a well of reliable information—information Israel's government would prefer to hide. He combed the West Bank on a daily basis and had gained a reputation as someone with unrivaled knowledge of the territory who could spot any rock that had been moved. He knew the people of Bil'in well and had been wondering how to help them for quite some time. Finally, he had the opportunity.

We decided that Peace Now would file its own petition, while Bil'in's petition was pending, to stop the construction. The new petition would seek the demolition of the illegally built structures and an interim order prohibiting any continued construction, on the grounds that the plan under which the buildings were advancing had not been approved. A halt to construction would buy some critical time. Aside from Peace Now and Etkes, the head of the Bil'in village council was also named as petitioner, to show agreement between the Israeli peace organization and the Palestinian village council. Adding Peace Now, a well-known and well-established Israeli organization, to Bil'in's struggle was without a doubt valuable in terms of public perception.[67]

We made sure that the massive illegal construction project received extensive media coverage. In December 2005, *Haaretz* ran with a story by senior journalist and commentator Akiva Eldar about the illegal construction in Modi'in Illit of a neighborhood of thousands of housing units. Interestingly, the headline referred to the building being "near Bil'in."[68] The village had become such a household name that the editors chose to run the story mentioning the Palestinian location rather than the large settlement housing tens of thousands of Israelis.

Our legal strategy began to bear fruit. In early January 2006, Supreme Court justice Ayala Procaccia issued a temporary order prohibiting the construction, new occupancies, and use of the buildings.[69] Having been caught red-handed engaging in illegal construction, the developers could only get the order lifted and resume work if they pushed their amended plan through the various Civil Administration bodies. We followed these proceedings closely, submitted objections, and even filed a High Court petition against the plan's approval.[70] The temporary order ultimately remained in effect for a year and nine months, until the amended plan was approved and the petition we filed against it was dismissed. At that point, the petition filed by Peace Now to stop the expansion became moot, but the long delay meant that the situation on the ground had changed very little when the High Court justices were ready to deliver their judgment on the fence in Bil'in. This was a great achievement because a large stretch of Bil'in's land, slated for the settlement's expansion and included inside the fenced-off area, was still vacant. Thus, it was still possible to redraft the route of the fence and restore the land to the village.

The High Court sessions made it clear that the impact of Bil'in's popular struggle had reached the courtroom. The senior panel was busy considering scores of petitions against different segments of the fence. They saw monstrous parts of the route that caused grave harm to Palestinian communities as well as places where the damage was relatively mild. Bil'in was somewhere in the middle. Aside from the demonstrations, the public attention, and the illegality of the construction on village land, there was nothing special about that portion of the fence. During the first court hearing, just a few minutes into my oral argument, Aharon Barak stopped me and asked, "Mr. Sfard, what's so special about Bil'in that they're always demonstrating there?" The harm inflicted by the fence was not exceptional, but the extraordinary public campaign was.

The High Court delivered its judgment on September 22, 2007. It was authored by newly appointed Supreme Court president Dorit Beinisch, who had to choose between our position and the state's. We had argued that the route had been chosen to serve the interests of settlement expansion, and therefore it failed to comply with the criteria set out by the High Court in the Beit Surik and Alfei Menashe cases, that the route must be determined by security considerations, not a political agenda. The state maintained that it was permissible when planning the route to take into consideration areas in which new construction had begun. The president and her colleagues on the panel, Justices Eliezer Rivlin and Ayala Procaccia, chose our position. First, they ruled, planning that had not been approved at the time the route was determined should not have been taken into account:

> Nonetheless, in the case before us it is clearly apparent that the determination of the fence route was significantly affected by the plans to erect new neighborhoods east of Modi'in Ilit. To the extent that the planning schemes considered in determining the route were in advanced stages of implementation and inhabitation, their consideration does not present difficulty, for various reasons. . . . Due to the planning situation of the "East

Mattityahu" neighborhood, and the decisive weight which the military commander granted the defense of this future neighborhood, difficulty arises regarding the legality of the route that takes that consideration into account.[71]

Second, the justices accepted that the route itself quite clearly had nothing to do with security. The phrasing was restrained, but the findings were unprecedented:

> Given the factual basis as it was presented to us, the current route of the fence also leads one to wonder about the security advantage it provides. It is uncontroversial that the route passes mostly through territory which is topographically inferior both to Modi'in Ilit and Bil'in. It leaves a number of hills on the Palestinian side and two hills on the Israeli side. *It endangers the forces patrolling the route* [emphasis added]. Against the background of the security outlook presented to us in many other cases, according to which it is important from a security standpoint to construct the fence on topographically controlling territory, the current route leads one to wonder. In general, the military commander presents the possession of controlling hills as a significant security advantage in many cases regarding fence route planning, but in this case a route has been determined that is at least partially on territory which is inferior vis-à-vis the hills.
>
> *This route cannot be explained by anything save the desire to include the eastern part of "East Mattityahu" west of the fence, otherwise it is doubtful whether there is a security-military reason for determining the route of the fence where it is now* [emphasis added].[72]

This was everything the people of Bil'in, the Palestinians, and opponents of the barrier had argued over the years: the fence's route had been chosen to serve the interests of the settlements, not security considerations; in fact, security was sacrificed for the settlements. The decision was a colossal defeat for the state, a humiliation. Having consistently resisted questioning the sense of the decisions made by the security establishment, the High Court now gave voice to unheard-of criticism of purportedly professional security claims. The media covered the victory extensively, with *Ma'ariv* going so far as to run the headline "Bil'in Beats IDF."[73]

Still, as we had expected, the High Court did not order the removal of the entire fence. It instructed the fence planners to draft a new route to include the expanded part of Matityahu East where the structures had already been built and some even occupied, but to leave the rest outside the fence. This meant canceling the plans for some one thousand housing units in the settlement, but also that only half the land taken from Bil'in would be restored to the village.

On the day of the High Court's order to move the route, Bil'in's residents left work and marched toward the fence with drums and flags. When I reached the village in the early afternoon, Bil'in seemed to be at the center of the universe. TV vans with satellite dishes were parked on every corner. Reporters from Israeli, Western, and Arab media were standing on rooftops overlooking the fence, broadcasting live. One of the braver Bil'in villagers hoisted me on his shoulders, despite my protestations and warnings that it would end with an injury to his back. Three army jeeps were stationed on the other side of the fence; the soldiers inside them watched the crowd but this time did nothing to disperse it. They knew it, too: this was Bil'in's day.

The leaders of the popular committee were ecstatic. Palestinian politicians sought them out, with their official state cars winding their way up the rough road leading to the village. Everyone celebrated the judgment as a win. Few paused to consider the final outcome: of the village's four thousand dunams, the fence had taken two thousand and the judgment returned about one thousand. The village had lost one thousand dunams. Still, there was much joy. There's a Jewish folktale about a man who complained to his rabbi that his house was too crowded. "Bring in a goat," the rabbi told him. After a week, the man was at his wit's end. "Now take out the goat," the rabbi said. "Doesn't that feel better?" Bil'in was like that man. After losing two thousand dunams, the village was overjoyed in the end to have lost only one thousand. The goat was gone from the house.

Bil'in had become an icon and so any achievement by the village was bound to be overblown. Nonetheless, its adoption of an alternative strategy of struggle, of nonviolent, popular resistance, had proved to be more than an empty slogan: it had led to a concrete, positive result, and in this sense, too, the judgment was perceived as a great victory.

I gave interviews to the Israeli and foreign media all that day, explaining the meaning of the judgment. I answered many questions, most of them predictable. But one question troubled me deeply, even the very need to ask it. I had heard it before, but usually from journalists with the Arab networks, and occasionally from Western journalists, too. That day, though, for the first time, it came from Israeli reporters: "Do you think the IDF will uphold the High Court's judgment?" "Of course," I answered each time. "I cannot imagine it wouldn't."

In practice, though, the state did everything in its power, even brazenly, to avoid upholding the judgment. It took four years and two scathing High Court decisions holding the state in violation of the ruling for failing to comply until the new fence was built and the old one dismantled, as the original judgment had ordered.[74] This effort to avoid complying with the court's judgment was new at the time, but it became a common challenge for lawyers representing Palestinians in the High Court in subsequent years.

The weekly protests in Bil'in continued during the four years after the High Court's ruling on the fence. On April 17, 2009, in a small, quiet protest in which no stones were thrown, Bil'in resident Bassem Abu Rahmah was hit in the chest with a gas canister that was fired directly at him, in violation of IDF regulations. He died instantly. A year and a half later, at a protest on December 31, 2010, the military dispersed a massive quantity of tear gas, and Bassem's sister, Jawaher Abu Rahmah, who did not participate in the demonstration, suffered tear gas inhalation near her home. She died several hours later. Bassem and Jawaher were killed in demonstrations against a fence that remained in place after the High Court had ruled it unlawful.[75]

TO LITIGATE OR NOT TO LITIGATE

The judgments issued in Beit Surik, Alfei Menashe, Zufin, and Bil'in were exceptions.[76] There were many more petitions against other segments of the fence, and in the majority the justices upheld the route. In some, a compromise was reached, usually with only minor success for the Palestinians. The invasive separation fence was eventually built, with a seal of approval from the High Court justices, who suppressed its appetite but satisfied it nonetheless. Eighty-five percent of the fence (completed or under construction) is inside the West Bank. It is twice as long as the Green Line and when it is fully built, more than sixty settlements and 85 percent of settlers will be on the western side, attached to Israel.[77]

According to figures from July 2013, more than 11,000 West Bank Palestinians are now trapped on that side of the fence and need permits to
continue living in their homes.[78] Approximately 250,000 residents of East
Jerusalem are also cut off from the West Bank because of the fence.[79] More
than 150,000 Palestinians on the other side, still in the West Bank, live
in enclaves, surrounded by the fence. For some 150 Palestinian communities, the fence has severed them from their land, which they can only
reach with a permit from the Civil Administration.[80] Over the years, the
number of permits and their duration have declined.[81]

The process that human rights organizations warned would happen
is now under way: the area on the wrong side of the fence is gradually losing its connection to the rest of the West Bank, and Israel treats this land
as its own. Annexation has arrived; through belligerence, Israel has managed to place facts on the ground that will be extremely difficult to undo.
Litigation against the fence failed to prevent this massive landgrab. The
High Court of Justice dismissed the arguments of principle against the
fence's construction and thereby effectively allowed Israel to expand into
the West Bank.

Still, even with these failures—the High Court's denial that building
a fence in the West Bank is an act of dispossession and a breach of international law; the vast tracts of land that are now restricted or out of bounds
for Palestinian communities—we cannot overlook the achievements of the
litigation. The Beit Surik and Alfei Menashe rulings forced the Israeli government to make substantial changes to the fence's route to meet the proportionality requirements stipulated by the High Court. Other cases in
which the court ordered changes to the route, such as Bil'in and Azzun,
resulted in the fence being moved closer to the Green Line. International
pressure, mostly from the United States, stopped the fence from connecting to Israel two large settlements deep inside the West Bank—Ma'ale
Adumim and Ariel.

The fence, which would in its original bloated version have grabbed
more than 16 percent of the West Bank, was slimmed down to 8 percent;
it is mostly thanks to the High Court cases that 8 percent of the land was
rescued, tens of thousands of dunams, mostly farmland. Bimkom's Alon
Cohen-Lifschitz estimates that some four hundred thousand dunams
slated to fall beyond the reach of Palestinians were ultimately left intact
in the West Bank thanks to the legal campaign. This 8 percent is the live-

lihood of tens of thousands of people. It is a reservoir for development for hundreds of Palestinian communities, many of which are among the poorest and most disempowered in the West Bank. The litigation against the fence kept many from plunging into deep poverty and losing their connection to basic services. For the Palestinians, the fence cases were quite literally a lifeline.

The fence litigation posed a hard dilemma for human rights lawyers. While it failed to prevent the harm caused by the fence, its reduction of that harm by a substantial degree should not be underestimated. On the other hand, the lawyers behind the litigation became part of the creation of the barrier. Like a hill or an engineering impasse, we too were a factor that shaped the route. I did not like this insight. It took me a while, but at some point it dawned on me that I was one of the architects of the barrier, that there were sections where my signature might as well appear next to the Ministry of Defense Barrier Administration and the High Court of Justice, even though I objected to these sections, even in their mitigated format.

But that was the price we, the lawyers who represented the communities harmed by the fence, had to pay to gain entry to the world of remedy, and our litigation did indeed achieve remedy for a significant number of people and even had a mitigating effect on the entire route. At the same time, our cases helped give a seal of approval to the government's policy of building a barrier inside the West Bank and to the wholesale violation of human rights that came with it. We constantly asked ourselves whether public opposition to the fence would have been stronger had there been no legal challenge. For many Israelis, the Supreme Court's judgments legitimized the barrier. Israelis who might have strongly objected were appeased when it seemed that justices of the High Court had made sure that the harm caused by the fence was "proportionate." This reassurance was surely amplified by the extensive media coverage of the few judgments that went in favor of the petitioners and the scant coverage of those that did not, which were the majority of cases.

From the perspective of human rights legal activism, two planes of the purpose of litigation were on a collision course: securing remedy for the clients ostensibly meant being part of the mechanism that designed the barrier and sacrificing the fight against its legitimization. As for results, if the goal was to obtain remedy for individual clients and prevent violation of their rights, the results were, at the least, mixed; if the goal was a change in policy, the legal fight was an utter failure. This kind of failure in a court that is highly regarded by many could, theoretically, make it harder to garner public protest against a controversial policy. I took some solace in the thought that so few Israelis objected to the fence; it would be hard to claim that the price on that front was terribly heavy.

But the fence litigation taught us another thing. It clearly showed how, in the twenty-first century, a domestic court has the power to make rulings that translate into actions on the ground, a power that international tribunals have yet to possess. Neither the UN General Assembly nor the ICJ managed to move one inch of the separation fence. Only Israel's High Court of Justice was able to do so. This understanding made our dilemma even more acute. Given Israel's international political strength, it could seem that abandoning the domestic legal sphere to focus on the international legal fight would yield few results and the fence's route would remain as it was in the government's June 2002 resolution, that is, the fat fence. But that does not mean that the international arena was unimportant. The impact of the battles outside the country, the ICJ opinion, the demonstrations in Bil'in, the stories in the international media were all strongly felt in the halls of Israel's High Court. This is obviously speculation, but it is hard to believe that the High Court would have reduced the seam zone by as much as it did without the external pressure.

THE LEGAL FENCE: APARTHEID?

After Israel's High Court had ruled on the legality of the fence, there was still one small matter: the permit system.

Throughout the years in which the Beit Surik, Alfei Menashe, Bil'in, and Azzun cases were litigated, the principled petition that Feldman and I had filed on behalf of HaMoked, which challenged the fence in its entirety along with the permit system, remained pending. Aharon Barak had decided to avoid the question of the fence's legality and instead to look at each segment separately. Immediately after the court ruled in the Alfei Menashe case, we were instructed to clarify what still remained to be ruled in the HaMoked petition. The High Court had combed through the issue of the fence's legality, ruled as it had ruled, and the HaMoked case had seemingly become moot. This was mostly true. Of the many arguments

we had raised against the barrier, only one question had not been decided by the High Court: the legality of the permit system. We asked for
and received leave of the court to amend the petition and expand on that
question.

In April 2006, we filed an amended petition that was perhaps the
boldest I had ever written. An entire section was dedicated to a description of the Pass Laws that restricted travel by black people in apartheid
South Africa. We argued that there was a lot of similarity between the
Israeli seam zone permit system and the disgraceful Pass Laws of that
dark era. In that case, as in this one, the freedom of movement of a certain group of people was restricted and made subject to permits. In that
case, as in this one, the restriction was not individual but based on group
affiliation—there it was race, here it was nationality, but the principle
was the same.

For the sake of accuracy, it had to be said that the division between
Jews and Palestinians was not absolute, as Palestinian citizens of Israel
did not require permits. But anyone familiar with discriminatory regimes
knows that sometimes the division is not just between black and white.
Palestinians with Israeli citizenship shared some of the privileges Jews
enjoyed, but this did not change the fact that, as a rule, the permit system,
like other systems employed in the Occupied Territories, discriminated
on the basis of nationality with some exceptions.

For this reason we used the word "apartheid" explicitly, saying: "the
web of the declaration and the orders applicable to the seam zone constitutes an intolerable, illegal, immoral legal apartheid."[82] We charged that
Israel was creating a feudal system of masters and servants and described
how the legal structure we objected to met the terms of the definition of
apartheid as it appears in the apartheid convention[83] and the definition
of the crime against humanity of persecution written into the Rome Statute of the International Criminal Court.[84] "Is it for this that we have established a country?" I wrote with pathos in the amended petition. "Is it for
this that we have gathered from every corner of the world, the survivors
of regimes that persecuted us, discriminated against us and denied us every
possible right simply because of our origin, in order to establish a state
whose army will implement a discriminatory regime over millions who
are not us?"[85]

The HaMoked case, which we had called "the fence case," had turned into "the permit case." It was joined with the petition ACRI had filed against the permit system,[86] with the hearing scheduled for November 2007. The state's response was more or less security, security, security. The permit system was an inseparable part of the fence, which, as everyone knew, is a paramount security project. Without the permit system, the fence would mean nothing,[87] because anyone crossing it can easily enter Israel. There is no barrier between the fence and Israel, after all, so canceling the permit system would be tantamount to taking down the fence. Since the danger to Israel and to Israelis comes from Palestinians rather than Israelis or tourists, imposing restrictions on Palestinians follows from a rational distinction, not racial discrimination. This is not wrongful discrimination, and certainly not apartheid, the lawyers representing the military commander seethed. It is a "legitimate distinction."[88] This is a rational distinction, not a racist one.

For us, this line of argument amounted to twisting the knife. The knife had been struck when the fence was built not on the Green Line but inside the West Bank itself. The Israeli government was now twisting it, using the security circumstances it had itself manufactured by attaching part of the West Bank to Israel in order to justify controlling who could and could not enter and distinguishing between them on the basis of nationality.

The hearing took place before President Dorit Beinisch, her deputy, Eliezer Rivlin, and Justice Ayala Procaccia. It was tense and sometimes heated. Two different organizations requested to be added to the petition as respondents, Shurat HaDin—Israel Law Center, a right-wing organization of Jewish jurists, and Fence for Life, an organization advocating for the fence. The Fence for Life lawyer opened his oral arguments with incitement against the petitioners. He accused us, HaMoked and ACRI, of serving terrorists. This type of accusation has become run-of-the-mill for human rights activists in Israel, but back then it was novel; the justices were not impressed, going so far as reproaching the lawyer.

On the merits, though, it was the petitioners' message that drew the justices' disapproval. ACRI's lawyer, Avner Pinchuk, did not use the word "apartheid," but I vividly recall him saying "Your Honors. It walks like a duck. It quacks like a duck. I'm afraid it is a duck." I was far less subtle. With a very specific legal argument before us about the similarities between the permit system and apartheid Pass Laws, I could not help but express in court what grieved me. I could not avoid using the actual word. President Beinisch was clearly uncomfortable. "Must we use this word?" she asked. "And if I don't use it," I answered, "will it disappear?"

THE JUDGMENT WAS not delivered until April 2011, a year and a half after the hearing.[89] Beinisch drowned our grave allegations of institutionalized discrimination, collective punishment, and apartheid in a gluey puddle of "proportionality." In a process that began with her predecessor, President Barak, and continued during Beinisch's tenure, proportionality took over the Supreme Court. The judgment given in the permit system petition was the pinnacle of the proportionality rhetoric, which seems to suggest that no policy or practice is prohibited per se. Everything is a function of circumstances and of the benefit produced. According to the logic of proportionality, the legality of an act is always examined mathematically against its benefits and never independently in terms of binary principles of right and wrong. The notion that there are some things regarding which the question of benefit should never be asked, that there are some things to which proportionality is irrelevant, has vanished. The court's judgment revealed that even discrimination is a question of proportionality—yes, even discrimination.

It is true that only Palestinians need a permit to cross the barrier, Beinisch conceded, with her colleagues Rivlin and Procaccia concurring. True, only they have to show a "reason," a "legitimate interest," to be eligible for that permit, while Israelis and tourists get a free pass. They need no reason. But the rationale for treating Palestinians differently isn't their religion or nationality, it's . . . *security*, and the harm this discriminatory system causes to Palestinians must be weighed against the interests that are served by restricting passage. According to the judgment, these interests are weighty—stopping terrorism, preventing fatal harm to civilians. Beinisch rejected our suggestion that anyone who wants to enter the seam zone should have to go through a security check, accepting the military's position that "a physical search does not, in and of itself, guarantee prevention of entry by terrorists or persons barred entry for security reasons who will receive weapons or explosives in various ways once in the seam zone or inside Israel."[90]

So a policy of annexation and settlement begat a seam zone that separated Palestinians from their land, Palestinians from themselves; a seam zone that in turn was used to justify institutionalized systemic legal discrimination between those entering based on nationality, all in the name of security. If the fence had been built on the Green Line, Israel's sovereign border, denying entry to Palestinians who had no permit, or visa, would not have been an issue. Denying Palestinians access to and within their own land was justified by the fact that the intrusion of the fence into the Occupied Territories meant there was no barrier between the seam zone and Israel. Deliberately or not, the justices failed to see in the state's argument that annexation, which had turned the seam zone into a place where Palestinians were guests and Israelis were owners, was staring them in the face. And what about apartheid? Well, Beinisch did not like the sound of this harsh word:

> The comparison drawn by the petitioners between the policy which was applied in the seam zone, and is founded on security reasons, and the apartheid regime which was applied in South Africa, is inappropriate, extreme, and far reaching. This comparison disregards material aspects which concern the unique situation in the seam zone and it seems that it would have been better had it not been raised.[91]

In any legal system, the judges get to have the final say. It is written in the judgment. Authors, however, get to say one more thing, and that is what I am going to do now. In the final submission I filed in the permit system case I wrote:

> This is not a slippery slope but a well-lubricated water slide on which it is impossible to remain in one spot—for indeed, if it is legitimate to create a zone in which we distinguish among people based on their national origin, then why not build separate roads or perhaps even special beaches in the Dead Sea for Palestinians and separate toilets and drinking fountains? This has to be said loud and clear: There is no difference between the regime which is the subject of this petition, which the respondents created, and the regime of racial segregation in the southern United States in the first half of the twentieth century. And should the respondents claim that the two have entirely different motives and purposes, we shall reply that this difference may be an argument for leniency in sentencing, but has no bearing on the question of the commission of the serious crime.[92]

6

Unauthorized Outposts

AMONA

I left the hearing at the Eshel prison near Beersheba at about noon. I walked out of the ugly prison complex scarring the desert vista, and, as lawyers tend to do, I conducted a postmortem of my argument—mostly what I hadn't said and perhaps should have. I got into the taxi and asked the driver to turn on the news. An Israeli habit. It had been two hours since I'd last heard it, maybe the apocalypse had arrived. My cell phone started pinging, indicating the many messages I'd received. It took me a few seconds to realize what had happened while I'd been sequestered with no cell phone in the makeshift prison courtroom. At 10:00 a.m. that February morning in 2006, military and police forces had begun evacuating and demolishing nine homes built in the unauthorized settlement outpost of Amona, near Ofra and east of Ramallah. This was the result of a petition I had filed on behalf of Peace Now and the coordinator of its Settlement Watch, Dror Etkes.

There was much excitement on the radio. The state was now fulfilling its pledge to the High Court to tear down the nine stone buildings, but this was not going over quietly. Journalists reported that hundreds of mostly young right-wing activists had barricaded themselves inside the homes slated for demolition, clashing with the police officers who had besieged the site in an effort to execute the judicial ruling. Both sides used violence, but after a few hours of clashes, the nine homes, which had been built on private land owned by residents of the nearby Palestinian villages

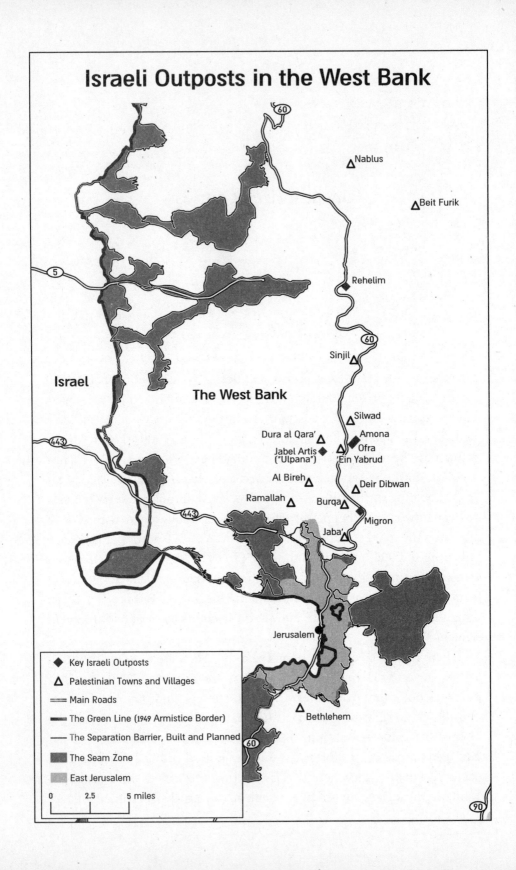

Israeli Outposts in the West Bank

Nablus

Beit Furik

Israel

The West Bank

Rehelim

Sinjil

Silwad

Dura al Qara'

Amona

Jabel Artis ("Ulpana")

Ofra

Ein Yabrud

Al Bireh

Deir Dibwan

Ramallah

Burqa

Migron

Jaba'

Jerusalem

Bethlehem

◆ Key Israeli Outposts
△ Palestinian Towns and Villages
≡ Main Roads
▬ The Green Line (1949 Armistice Border)
— The Separation Barrier, Built and Planned
■ The Seam Zone
■ East Jerusalem

0   2.5   5 miles

of Silwad and Ein Yabrud, were demolished. Scores of protesters and police were injured in the clashes. This was quite possibly the most violent skirmish to have ever occurred between settlers and Israeli security forces. The live broadcasts showed a mass brawl with club-wielding mounted police ramming into the hundreds of people who had holed up at the site, mostly teenage boys and girls with passionate religious-nationalist beliefs. I had wanted those homes removed. I had worked for it. I was pleased with the court win, but the visions of violence were hard to watch and put a damper on the victory.

The demolitions in Amona became a symbol. They brought home to Israelis the high cost of evacuating settlements (which was the protesters' intention). Less than a year after Israel's disengagement from the Gaza Strip, when Israel succeeded in removing civilians from Gaza settlements with no serious violence, the settlement movement felt the need to restore its deterrent power, which is what the protesters did in Amona. This unauthorized outpost, where some forty families lived in prefabricated homes, was not in fact evacuated that morning—only nine permanent homes that had been constructed and were not yet occupied. Still, the settlers fought the demolition order as if the entire settlement enterprise hung in the balance.

That was my first evacuation. It was also the first petition I had filed for the removal of homes built on privately owned Palestinian land.

Twelve years after the traumatic demolition of those nine homes, Amona faced another evacuation; this time it was the entire outpost, with all its structures and hundreds of residents. In the interim between then and now, dozens of petitions to remove Israeli construction in the West Bank, ones that I had helped file and litigate, had resulted in changes in settlement building practices. They had also prompted dramatic political shifts, both internally and in Israel's relations internationally.

HAVING ONE'S CAKE AND EATING IT, TOO

Israel is obligated to build no new settlements, not just in terms of international law but also by virtue of international agreements to which it is a party—namely, the Oslo Accords, signed from 1993 to 1995. Even before the first agreement was signed, Yitzhak Rabin's government decided to halt settlement construction.[1] All of the various accords adopted between

Israel's government and the PLO since 1993 include an implicit Israeli commitment not to start new settlements,[2] although Rabin insisted that no settlement would be evacuated prior to final status negotiations. However, one of the key points of contention between Rabin and PLO chairman Yasser Arafat during the Oslo negotiations involved the growth of existing settlements. Israel later interpreted the article stipulating that neither party would take unilateral measures to change the territory's status to mean that it could expand existing settlements to meet the needs of "natural growth." This exception was manipulatively read by successive governments to the point where settlement expansion became the rule.

Still, the settlement movement took several years to recuperate from the shock of Oslo and the freeze on new settlements. But beginning in 1996, with redoubled efforts after the start of the Second Intifada in late 2000, its leadership initiated large-scale construction of new communities and expansion of existing ones—all without the necessary government approvals. There was no planning by the Civil Administration authorities, no building permits, no formal agreement from the government, something required for every stage of West Bank construction because of its political significance. Dozens of new settlements sprang up all over the West Bank—"outposts," mostly small and isolated, usually satellites of established ones that supplied them with electricity and water through unofficial hook-ups. In addition, developers stepped up building new neighborhoods in old settlements, a process that bypassed the required legal procedures. Most important, the majority were built completely or partially on privately owned Palestinian land.[3]

As we have seen, the early attempts in court during the 1970s and 1980s to challenge settlement building (based on the prohibition in international law against transferring population into occupied territory) had failed because the court cited nonjusticiability as a reason to refuse to discuss the issue. But the argument produced one achievement: the 1979 Elon Moreh judgment, in which the court ruled that settlements could only build on privately owned Palestinian land if a real security need was proven. The achievement was significantly eroded through a policy, implemented during the 1980s and 1990s, of declaring land Palestinians considered privately owned as state land. But in the 2000s, the settlement enterprise reverted to building on privately owned land, without the Civil Administration even bothering to declare it as state land, and even on registered private land, which cannot be declared public under any circumstances.

More than one hundred new settlements were built this way. Calling them "outposts" is a way of distinguishing them from settlements built with government approval and according to military administration rules. Of course, the legal consensus worldwide, based on international law, is that all the settlements are illegal, whether or not they have been approved by Israel's government and built on public land, according to master plans and with permits. Israel denies this view, however, and its High Court of Justice has avoided ruling on the question. Still, even the government accepts that building without approval and permits or a master plan, on land that belongs to someone else, is illegal. To differentiate between the overall illegality of the settlements and the specific illegality of failing to comply with building and planning laws or obtaining government approval I use the term *unauthorized* settlements (or outposts or construction) to refer to the second group. Nonetheless, all are illegal.

Back to the outposts. To the outsider, this all probably looks quite astounding. Massive construction of communities, some of which are home to dozens of families, taking place right under the authorities' nose and without any form of enforcement to put an end to this criminal enterprise. Dozens of communities, hundreds of housing units, thousands of residents—much of it rising right in their neighbor's backyard, none of it approved, and no one lifting a finger to stop or investigate it. Maybe I'm going too far. Someone did lift a finger: the relevant agency, the Civil Administration Enforcement Unit, which is tasked with oversight of planning and building laws in most of the West Bank, sent its officers out into the area to take decisive action. They identified and documented all this unlawful construction. Whenever they saw work under way on a new construction site, done without permits (often on privately owned Palestinian land), they did what they were supposed to do: issue stop-work orders and demolition orders for the structures already built. For years, Civil Administration enforcers pasted orders on walls in illegal construction sites and served copies to the site supervisors. Wherever Israelis monitoring settlement expansion went they found that Civil Administration enforcers had already been there, issuing orders in their thousands. But not a single one was carried out. They went no further than the paper they were written on, trapped in a dimension of bureaucratic forms but never realized.

How is it possible that orders from the authorities are ignored on such a wholesale scale? Under the rules of the military administration, carrying out a demolition order in the Jewish sector of the West Bank requires approval from the minister of defense. When politicians have to give the green light and the orders are directed at people with political power, well, it's no surprise that the orders are nothing but worthless pieces of paper. So the enforcers gave out orders and the builders kept on building. The orders piled up and the construction continued at full steam. The enforcers were like chickens, desperately flapping their wings but unable to lift off. It might be a bird but it nonetheless cannot fly.

But the reason for the failure of law enforcement is not only the politicians' refusal to allow execution of the Civil Administration's demolition orders. The truth is far worse. While a significant number of the outposts may have been built without government consent, they had plenty of help from government ministries and the military administration. One hand might have been signing demolition orders, but the other was channeling funds and helping with planning and infrastructure for illegal construction, sometimes taking private land.

How is this possible? Sometimes when I give talks about the outposts to people who aren't familiar with Israel, I liken the situation to a gigantic aircraft carrier moving in a certain direction for a long time. The vessel's course is etched into the DNA of its navigation systems, its engines, its tiniest screw. The metaphorical direction of the sea vessel is the Zionist principle of creating settlements as a means of taking control of land. For more than a century, this principle has been the driving force of Zionism in which all state and social institutions are invested and which all strive to realize. Suddenly a new captain comes aboard in Oslo, and orders an immediate change of course—no more settlement construction, no new settlements.

Many government and public institutions had difficulty internalizing this new course and continued pushing in the direction they had been following for generations. The Ministries of Housing and Agriculture still provided funding, the police and the military left the builders in peace, and the leaders who came after Rabin's assassination took an approach somewhere between turning a blind eye and providing quiet support. They never gave official approval but let the settlers know to head for the hills. They promised the American administration that they would evacuate the outposts but instead funneled money and obstructed enforcement. For years, Israeli governments told the world they were not building new settlements, all the while enabling a massive increase in the number of Israeli communities in the West Bank. The government managed to avoid getting in trouble with both the international community and the settler community, the strongest political lobby in Israel. To have its cake and eat it, too.

For a critical number of years, this sleight of hand worked without a hitch. But reports compiled by organizations such as Peace Now, which were monitoring West Bank building activity, together with the glaring facts on the ground made the international community and primarily the US administration aware of the diplomatic scam. The staunchly pro-Israel George W. Bush administration, one of the least critical American governments in terms of Israel's settlement enterprise, began to show signs of impatience. The roadmap for peace presented in April 2003 by President Bush on behalf of the Quartet (the United States, Russia, the European Union, and the United Nations) with Israel's consent, included an Israeli undertaking to dismantle all outposts built after Ariel Sharon took office as prime minister in March 2001.

However, a pledge and its implementation are two very different things. Israel failed to dismantle a single outpost. The problem of the outposts gradually became a focus of diplomacy between Israel and the United States, and Israel did not always supply accurate information. Washington got wind of this and stopped relying on Israel's reports. At one point, a senior American official embarrassed an Israeli emissary in a meeting when he disputed Jerusalem's information about the status of the outposts and it turned out the American was right.[4]

In July 2004, as part of an attempt to ease American pressure, Sharon commissioned Talia Sasson, an attorney formerly with the State Attorney's Office, to write a comprehensive report on the unauthorized outposts so that the Israeli government would, for the first time, have full and accurate figures. This allowed Sharon to tell the Americans that the outposts were being addressed, with a government study as the first step. Sasson worked under impossible conditions, with many government agencies failing to give her data and figures or supplying erroneous or partial information, but she completed her task in March 2005 and her voluminous report became the outpost bible.[5]

Ever since the report was compiled more than a decade ago, not one of its thousands of facts has been disputed. The report exposed a system of cooperation between the settlement movement and very senior officials inside the government who helped fund and build outposts, all without any official decisions having been taken. The government adopted the report's many recommendations involving legislative amendments, policy and personnel changes, punitive action for some responsible parties— and set up a ministerial committee to implement them,[6] but in practice the report was buried.

The rapid development of new unauthorized settlements established concrete facts on the ground. Considerable pastureland and cultivated farmland belonging to Palestinians were seized for building outpost homes or as farmland for the intruders. The Israelis settling in the outposts were often from the more militant, nationalist, annexationist wing of the settler movement, and many of the outposts became hotbeds for violence against Palestinians living nearby.

For organizations such as Peace Now, which had fought to end settlement activity, the outposts posed an immense challenge. For years, Peace Now had focused its attention on fighting the government on settlements, staging protests, publishing reports, and lobbying politicians. Any expansion or development of settlements had always required a political decision, which created the possibility of a political struggle of opposition. But how to organize against unofficial criminal activity? What does one do when the police refuse to catch the thieves? In 1998 and 2002, Peace Now and Yesh Gvul, another leftist group, made two attempts to challenge the lack of enforcement on outpost activity. In both cases, the petitioners asked for orders addressing the entire practice. The court deflected both attempts as too general.[7]

Then in 2005, Dror Etkes of Peace Now's Settlement Watch concluded that giving up on a legal fight was not an option: given the new circumstances, the court had to be called to task. He showed up at my office with photos he had taken of Amona, an outpost built entirely on privately owned Palestinian land with no government decision, planning approval, or building permit (which could not have been issued as the land belonged to someone else). Etkes had been following construction in the outpost for years, and had learned several months earlier that construction had begun on nine permanent homes. His inquiries revealed that the Civil Administration had issued stop-work and demolition orders for all nine structures, but of course the orders were never executed and construction went on. In his correspondence with the Civil Administration, Etkes asked about plans to stop construction and implement the demolition orders. The response he received was the Civil Administration's stock answer to questions about illegal construction in the West Bank: Yes, they intended to carry out the demolition order. Certainly. Just not right now.

Little did we know that the case of the nine Amona homes[8] would be a trial balloon for a much larger project to come.

A DELUGE OF AMONAS

The demolition of those structures in Amona in 2006 did not result in the Palestinian landowners returning to their land. The outpost stayed at the top of the hill, preventing farmers from Ein Yabrud and Silwad from reaching their plots, where the buildings' ruins remained. But the demolitions caused a political stir, putting the outposts in the spotlight and creating, for the first time, a balance of threat.

Until then, the settlers had been able to build without permits with no interference. The Amona demolitions showed that they would not be able to get away with this forever. A lot of money had been put into these homes, and like the hopes of the families who had been planning to move into them, the money was lost. Most important was that the legal proceedings forced the government to pick a side. Before this case, Israeli leaders could have it both ways. They could tell the world they never approved construction in the outposts—after all, there were no government decisions or Civil Administration building permits. They could continue to give vague promises about removing the outposts, all the while avoiding blocking their construction and expansion, and certainly not forcing their evacuation.

The High Court petition had backed the government into a corner: it could not avoid stating a clear position. Asked for the state's response, the government had to say whether it stood with the victims or the criminals. There was no middle ground. What's more, it is harder to skirt fulfilling a pledge made to the court than one made to the public or even a diplomatic commitment. In the case of the nine Amona homes, the legal pressure coincided with a significant change in the political climate. Ariel Sharon had fallen into a coma in early January 2006, and Ehud Olmert, appointed acting prime minister and designated to lead his party in national elections in late March of that year, pledged to the court to execute the demolition orders issued by February 1. Olmert presumably thought a tough stance toward the settlers and demonstrable loyalty to the rule of law would be electoral assets.

Before the Amona demolition orders were carried out, Peace Now decided to file another High Court petition against two more outposts in which Etkes had noticed intense construction activity: Haresha, west of Ramallah; and Hayovel, near the village of Qaryut, between Ramallah and Nablus. The Civil Administration's enforcement unit had issued demolition orders in these two outposts, too, and, like in Amona, they had not been carried out and there was no intention of that happening. Using the Amona model, I filed another public petition on behalf of Peace Now and Etkes rather than the direct victims of the illegal construction, asking for an interim order compelling the military and the police to prevent further construction, and a judicial order compelling the demolition of structures that had already been built.[9] As with Amona, the court issued the interim order to stop construction, creating the deterrent we sought. I filed a third petition on behalf of Peace Now, after the 2006 election. It targeted six outposts flagged in the Sasson report: the government had taken all the steps toward evacuation (under American pressure), including issuing orders to evacuate (known as delimitation orders), but implemented none of them.[10] In this petition, we no longer targeted individual structures but demanded the evacuation of entire outposts.

As a political movement working for peace and toward a two-state solution to the Israeli-Palestinian conflict, Peace Now's venture into settlement litigation was not an obvious step. And unlike other NGOs, its legal engagement was not primarily prompted by concern for Palestinian human rights (although violation of those rights is a concern for Peace Now members, whose decisions are often influenced by the desire to reduce injustice). The legal route was forced on the movement. As long as settlements were being built according to the law and the orders of the military administration, Peace Now's fight was in the political realm and for public opinion. But the emergence of large-scale construction and new settlements built in defiance of the legal restraints Israel had placed on such construction—a situation with serious political implications—made the political battle meaningless.

The government approval required for all settlement building (in addition to the necessary planning and building permits) comes with a price, a foreign one if approval is given and a domestic one if it is denied, which turns the relevant decision makers into lightning rods for political pressure. Building without permits was a way around all the planning and political hurdles, but through criminal behavior. Peace Now was forced to divert its resources and energy to the legal sphere because its political foe had stopped playing by the rules. The settlers managed not only to circumvent the Palestinian population, which had no role in Jerusalem's decision-making process anyway, but also Israel's, which is supposed to have a say in politically significant decisions. Turning to the court, whose role is to protect the rules of the political process, was therefore necessary.

But beyond their political importance, the outposts also involved a clear breach of human rights. They were often built on privately owned land and blocked access to even more land, some of it also privately owned or used for pasture. As a political movement with a political goal, Peace Now naturally focused on the larger outposts, but many Palestinians lost land in smaller or less significant locations, which could get overlooked in the legal fight. This vacuum was filled by the NGO Yesh Din, an Israeli human rights organization set up in 2005.

Yesh Din Volunteers for Human Rights (the literal Hebrew phrase means "there is law") grew out of a group of women who had started another organization, Machsom Watch, which monitored activity at the IDF checkpoints throughout the West Bank. They had become disenchanted with the passivity of their action and looked for more effective ways to fight abuse of Palestinian rights. In the living room of Tel Aviv art collector Mooky Dagan, the women set up an organization with a mission to strengthen human rights in the Occupied Territories by empowering law enforcement against the settlers and security forces. Along with my good friends Didi Remez, a strategic adviser of rare talent, and Lior Yavne, who became one of Israel's leading human rights researchers, and myself as legal adviser, the group established Yesh Din, a women-led, volunteer-based NGO, and enlisted a professional team to transform their findings into public and legal advocacy.

Within weeks of Yesh Din's creation, its volunteers spread through West Bank villages, initially on their own, and then with the help of paid Palestinian field workers who became a central part of the organization. The volunteers and the field researchers collected evidence and testimony of harm to Palestinians and their property. Yesh Din developed a unique methodology that included the investigation of alleged incidents; accompanying the victims to the police or the military; making sure their complaints were processed; and then monitoring the investigation and prosecution. Over the years, Yesh Din helped thousands of Palestinians, representing them in Israel's system of law enforcement. I carry the title of Yesh Din's cofounder with great pride. In just a short time, it became one of the most important human rights NGOs in Israel. Its findings, published in reports, position papers, and information sheets, provide a deep understanding of some of the most egregious and complex aspects of the occupation, and, as we shall see, its legal activity has had a profound impact on Israel's settlement policy.

In any event, after Peace Now fired the starting gun for litigation against the outposts, Etkes suggested that Yesh Din join the effort. Our success in Amona, which had been extensively covered in the media, prompted many Palestinians in West Bank communities to ask whether something could be done about the unauthorized outposts or new settlement neighborhoods built on their own land. Yesh Din's approach, which was less concerned with the political significance of the site and sought to aid anyone who had lost property, was well suited for a more expansive legal campaign against illegal construction.

Yesh Din's first petition related to illegal building was filed in mid-2008 jointly with B'Tselem. In parallel, B'Tselem published a report on Ofra,[11] which revealed that the settlement, home to many leaders of Gush Emunim, was built mostly on privately owned Palestinian land that had been properly registered in the land registry. The settlement had started life, toward the end of the 1970s, as a "work camp" established on a military base on land that had been designated for use by the Jordanian army.[12] The work camp's site had purportedly been expropriated during Jordanian rule, although there is some doubt about the facts.[13] The work camp quickly metamorphosed into a settlement and construction spilled out to cover vast areas around it. The Yesh Din–B'Tselem petition—also joined by five landowners from nearby villages—was directed at nine red-roofed homes that were under construction in the center of the settlement.[14]

Etkes, who was now coordinating Yesh Din's involvement, had identified the construction and monitored it. I joined him on one of his trips to Ofra to take pictures of the structures. It was one of the last.times I was able to go into a major settlement without being recognized and risking violence. Etkes, more experienced and better known, had to wear a wide-brimmed hat and sunglasses to avoid being spotted.

In the petition we asked for an interim order to halt construction, but the duty justice, Edmund Levy, hesitated and asked for the state's response. In petitions of this sort, the question of occupancy plays an important role. Occupancy complicates matters because demolition will mean evacuating people from their homes, sometimes entire families. Legally, occupancy should have no bearing on the court's decision: if structures are illegal, they should come down. Practically, however, and especially politically, occupancy turns an already sensitive case into an especially charged one. When people in Ofra heard that a petition had been filed to halt construction (but with no subsequent order to compel them to stop building), the settlement's rabbi reportedly ruled that the non-Jewish workers on the site could continue working through the Sabbath. The aim was to speed up the work and move occupants into the homes before the High Court could step in.[15]

Early petitions like this one against the buildings in Ofra heralded a change in the rules of the game. Since the mid-1990s, the feverish illegal construction of outposts and settlement expansion (carried out with the authorities' willful ignorance at best, and their support in funding and planning at worst) had allowed the settlers to expand their hold on the land with no interference. The military and the police turned a blind eye and the Palestinians had no means of defense against the landgrab and the contraction of their living space. But the intervention of two NGOs with the means to support research and fund litigation opened the door to a new strategic campaign. No longer limited to isolated legal challenges, the fight to stop illegal construction could take the long view and work for change through cumulative efforts: we were freed from the limitations of just one Amona case to rain down a deluge of Amonas.

A REPEAT PLAYER

A cumulative litigation campaign works somewhat like water on limestone: each procedure extends the impact of the one that comes after it. If done wisely, the effect is synergetic, the sum being larger than its parts. A cluster of procedures involving the same agent makes that agent a repeat player. Party to different court cases, all relating to the same subject, the repeat player is a very different creature from the one-time player, who comes to court, makes his argument, receives a judgment, and disappears. Repeat players benefit from knowledge and understanding that one-timers do not have. They might lose the first time around, but they will then apply what they have learned to the next case. They can litigate one case with full awareness of the court or state's position in other related cases because they are involved in those as well. They have a broad view of the topic of litigation. They know about the shifts that take place over time, in geography, politics, or any other axis. In some cases, they can choose the order of litigation that comes to court, which allows them to plan which issues will be decided first and which later. While the one-time player has a role in one case, one judicial ruling, repeat players are partners in creating the evolving body of jurisprudence on their topic of engagement.

Between 2005 and 2016, Peace Now and Yesh Din litigated High Court cases involving more than thirty outposts and settlements where illegal construction had caused direct harm to some fifty Palestinian communities and indirect harm to many more. All told, Yesh Din filed upward of eighty procedures and Peace Now another seventeen. Additional petitions were filed by lawyers in private practice and in other organizations, such as Rabbis for Human Rights and the Society of St. Yves. Most of the cases were filed on behalf of Palestinian landowners who had been harmed by the settlement activity and received legal aid from the organizations. In the majority, settlers had built on the petitioners' land. In others, the settlers had cultivated their land or denied the owners access to it with fences and other physical barriers. The litigation amounted to a cumulative campaign pursued by classic repeat players: social change organizations. Most of the activity was comprised of High Court petitions, but there were also freedom of information cases, administrative procedures in Civil Administration tribunals, and several civil suits.

This is a huge number of procedures, which in sum had the potential for change that no one case could possibly effect. The cluster resulted in the same fifteen justices of the High Court repeatedly ruling on cases involving illegal construction in the West Bank. The press followed the litigation as it had weighty political ramifications, both domestically and internationally, and its reporting would appear periodically. Most important, the accumulation of legal activity gradually forced the realization, among the justices, the press, and the public, that the cases were not isolated instances of unauthorized building, but systemic; they grasped that wherever you might turn in the West Bank, you would see unchecked Israeli landgrabs.

The legal campaign dragged the court into the political arena, into the rivalry between the settlement enterprise's supporters and opponents, and turned it into a central player. The High Court abhors intervening in matters of bitter political debate, but these cases left the justices with little choice. They were required to rule on an issue that was politically complicated but legally straightforward: construction was under way on land belonging to others, in defiance of planning laws and without the necessary permits; the state was unable to deny the facts given the information collected by its own agents (in the Sasson report and the security establishment's settlements and outposts database)[16] and the demolition orders they themselves had issued.

Whatever one's ideological position on the settlements might be, there was no legal way to avoid executing the demolition orders. Or was there? As long as the construction was on privately owned Palestinian land, the orders to destroy it were incontrovertible; but if the structures were going up on public land, perhaps they could be retroactively approved under certain conditions. But such a move would still come with a political and diplomatic price tag, still being a breach of general and specific promises Israel's government had given to the international community, the Palestinians, the American administration, and yes, its own population. So the government preferred to do nothing.

The settlement movement found itself in a bind, too: it could fight law enforcement and call for retroactive approval of the structures, but that would confirm its reputation as a group of land thieves with no scruples about grabbing private Palestinian land or disdaining international and Israeli law. Or it could disavow illegal construction, thus paving the way for the distressing images of evacuation and demolition. In the end, there was no debate, or if there was one it took place behind closed doors. The settler leadership near-unanimously stood behind the outposts (some were deeply implicated in building them in the first place). They not only gave their support to the more established outposts, home to the sons and daughters of the settler aristocracy, but also to those on the fringe, set up by radical extremists who did not recognize their leadership. They threw their full and substantial political weight behind preventing evacuations and demolitions, even in cases where there was no legal avenue to approve the construction retroactively.

Given the array of forces involved, illegal construction became a volatile political issue that plunged the governing coalition into crisis every few months. The litigation forced the government to do precisely what it sought to avoid: make a decision on the outposts, and—even worse—act on it. The government had to close the gap between its official stance that the outposts are illegal and must be removed, as it had pledged to the world, and its capitulation to settler lobby pressure.

The litigation served the interests of two parties: the petitioners, who wanted their stolen land returned, and the opposition to the settler enterprise, with its vastly expanded landgrab. It resulted in two important strategic by-products: the legal action pushed the government out of the comfortable position that had allowed it to benefit from criminal activity ostensibly perpetrated by others without paying the price; it also, to some extent, drove a wedge between the settlement movement and the government and the military, which until then had fully cooperated with the settlers.

These outcomes were all made possible through the total effect of the campaign's unusual features: repeat players engaged in a large accumulation of proceedings, with research and legal support, as well as access to information, which allowed them to go up against the ultimate repeat player, the state, with its unlimited access to information. The importance of information cannot be overstated. Peace Now and Yesh Din amassed a body of knowledge about the settlement project that had never before been available to the opposition. With this, the opposition was able to face the settlers and the state on a near-equal footing.

People such as Dror Etkes and Hagit Ofran, who took over from him at Peace Now, or Muhammad Shakir, a lawyer from Yesh Din, as well as my good friend Shlomi Zachary, a lawyer who worked with me in my practice on all the outpost cases—they all had minute knowledge of both the terrain and its history. They learned how to analyze aerial photographs and extract information from the Civil Administration's databases. Etkes and Ofran, who traveled the length and breadth of the West Bank daily, knew the territory so well they could often tell just by looking at a hill or a slope through binoculars whether the settlers had put up a new prefabricated home or even just a shed. Ofran, a charismatic, kind-hearted activist with a deep sense of mission, is a prominent leader of the Israeli peace camp. She independently schooled herself on the mechanisms for funneling government funding to the settlements and has fought to expose information about the Israeli council budgets in the Occupied Territories.

Over the years, the organizations involved—mainly Yesh Din, Peace Now, and Bimkom—managed to assemble databases listing the legal status of every parcel in the West Bank and learn their way around the practices used to take over land and build on it. Additionally, as often happens with repeat players, we developed extensive knowledge of the state's involvement in unauthorized construction and of the evolving changes in its official position and practical policies. The wave of legal proceedings on outposts let us leverage this mass of information to refute misleading arguments and inaccuracies put forward by the state or the settlers. Furthermore, the organizations' fund-raising meant that we could represent victims pro bono. This allowed us to file petitions even in cases with a limited chance of success, or where the remedy, if granted, would be minor in relation to the investment of effort and resources.

For all these reasons, a campaign of this magnitude could not have taken place without the support of the NGOs. The earlier fight against the settlements was similar in many ways to this struggle against the outposts, but it was waged exclusively by private lawyers retained by the victims. Though some one hundred and twenty settlements were officially built in the West Bank prior to the Oslo Agreements, only a few legal proceedings were launched against them. In private cases, funded by individuals, the probability of success plays an important, even decisive, role in the decision to go to court. Saving a small parcel of land might not be financially viable given the resources that the fight might demand, even if the outcome is successful. The resources available in the cases that were launched in the 1970s and 1980s were inevitably limited. Given the state's monopoly on information and on framing and defining its policies, the state of course had a significant advantage.[17] That advantage was erased in the outpost cases of the early 2000s. In fact, we sometimes had more accurate and reliable information. The justices noticed and, as repeat players, we could see how much they trusted the information we supplied.

Of the legal battles fought over the fifty years of occupation, I find it hard to think of a better example of a broad, concentrated, strategic legal campaign driven by a clear methodological approach. The challenge to the separation fence also involved multiple cases, but they were neither centrally managed nor guided by a clear strategic plan that coordinated everyone involved in the different petitions. The dozens of proceedings against outposts and illegal settlement construction in the last decade were almost exclusively launched by NGOs that funded the work and maintained a system of research and information to support it. These circumstances made this legal campaign exceptional and ground-breaking.

SO WHAT'S THE POINT OF ALL THIS?

The early outpost cases were filed as public-interest petitions, with the NGOs named as the petitioners, not the victims, the Palestinian landowners.

We quickly realized that only so much could be done with public-interest petitions. The argument of principle regarding unlawful actions is strong, but it pales in comparison to the proprietary claims of a landowner whose plot had been invaded and used for construction or farming. Countering our legal challenges by claiming the land had been purchased by the settlers or that it is owned by the state is much less viable if the landowner is the petitioner. These legal considerations were in sync with a wave of calls from Palestinian communities, who, after the demolition of the Amona homes, wanted to look into the possibility of fighting to get their land back. I remember a meeting in 2006 in the village of Deir Dobwan. The outpost of Migron had been built on village land, and the remains of the nine Amona homes were visible from the window of the local council building. The landowners were skeptical about our ability to have the outpost removed, but wanted the legal fight. From that point on, petitions were filed on behalf of actual victims. Sometimes organizations that represented the victims, and served as public petitioners, were also named parties to a petition.

Any litigation for social change on behalf of victims of the policy being challenged has several purposes. The outpost cases were no different. The specific purpose was to win every case and retrieve the land for its owners. Any lawyer who has lost the zeal to win a remedy for his or her client and is blinded by a grander purpose should get out of the profession. On the Yesh Din cases, Zachary, Shakir, and I represented actual people whose meager holdings had been stolen through criminal action, driven by a racist ideology of Jewish supremacy, and effectively backed by the authorities. Some of our clients had lost their livelihoods. Others were humiliated by their impotence against the invasion of their ancestral land. Most were farmers, and their land was not only the source of their livelihood but part of their culture and their being. They remembered when the land was thick with vineyards and olive trees, and now, before their eyes, it was all uprooted, bulldozed, covered in gravel and structures that were aesthetically and architecturally foreign. There was nothing we wanted more than to see our clients return to their land.

The second purpose of our litigation was to change policy. We wanted to inflict a decisive blow on this settlement construction, which ignored even the few restrictions Israel imposed on its colonization. We wanted to stop the building on Palestinian land. To do so, we sought to raise awareness of the settlement project as a crime, a landgrab. Should we fail in the primary purpose of returning the land to its owners (which also served the goal of ending the whole practice), we wanted the government to pay a political price for aiding and abetting the crime. We believed that in the long run, a hefty price would curb or even stop the practice.

So for us activist lawyers and the NGOs leading the petitions, every case served both the client's specific interest of recovering their land and the general interest of changing government policy.

Could these different purposes collide? Could there be a conflict of interest? At first glance, it appears not. After all, our clients, Palestinian landowners, presumably want to regain their land and impede illegal construction. Still, conflicts may come up. One example is if the settlers offer to purchase the land from the petitioners. A client might be interested in the offer to receive financial compensation for his land, especially if they realize that the odds of the land being evacuated and returned are slim. But if accepting the offer serves the interest of the specific client, the sale of the land would severely undermine the general interest of fighting settlement and illegal construction.

Another potential conflict of interest is the danger that a legal case on behalf of a specific client could backfire, accelerating the chance of the land being confiscated and the construction retroactively approved. Although retroactive approval of construction was one of Israel's tactics, it could not be deployed while we were in the process of litigation if the land was formally registered in the name of the Palestinian owners. This was the case in Amona. Retroactive approval could only be granted if the land had been confiscated, and the Ministry of Justice confirmed that confiscating privately owned land is prohibited for any purpose under international laws of occupation, let alone for transferring it from the occupied population to settlers.

Throughout the years of litigation on these cases, the settler movement pushed the Knesset to pass a law to sanction the confiscation of private land, which would open the door to retroactive authorization of outposts and prevent evacuations. The name of the bill—the Law for the Regularization of Settlement in the Judea and Samaria Area (popularly known as the Regularization Law)—suggests that retroactive approval is a technical, procedural act, concealing the fact that it is actually an act of dispossession. The settler movement lobbied for the bill ahead of every evacuation as a solution for the political crisis it had itself created; the bill was blocked repeatedly by the staunch opposition of every senior figure in the government's legal agencies; the politicians feared the international community's response to such a brazen violation of a fundamental legal prohibition and of Israel's own undertakings not to build new settlements. Still, the settlers never gave up on the idea, and like the gun that appears in the first act, the bill would eventually come back and change everything.

In any event, during most of the years of the Yesh Din and Peace Now litigation, the effort to win retroactive authorization was applied when the land in question was not registered in the name of a private owner. In these cases, the Civil Administration would first declare that all the rights to land use resided with its authorities—this was a way of effectively confiscating land without it legally being considered confiscation.[18] Then, the Civil Administration would draw up master plans that could be used to legalize construction retroactively. This move also drew its share of scathing international criticism and some domestic denunciation, leading Israel's government to prefer to maintain the outposts' unauthorized status, as long there was no judicial pressure to evacuate them.

At the beginning of this process, after Israel had made international commitments to curb settlement, the government's official position was that illegal construction should be demolished and removed. Given the settlement agenda of the governments of Benjamin Netanyahu, however, this position changed and since 2011, the preferred course of action was to declare any territory that is not privately owned or otherwise out of bounds as state land, and then to approve the construction retroactively. This approach is extremely troubling, as it rewards criminal behavior and doubly harms Palestinians who have already been injured. But for Netanyahu, this is preferable to clashing with his political allies.

In this situation, the activist lawyer faces a potential conflict of interest: Once a specific case is threatened by the danger of retroactive authorization for the construction that's been built on the land in dispute, should the lawyer abandon the case (which would almost certainly halt the authorization process)? By doing so, the client's legal claim to his land would remain intact. Or would it be better to continue to push for a decision, even at the risk of the land being declared "state land" and the construction on it authorized, thereby triggering a hefty political price for Israel? And what if there is a danger of confiscation, through, for instance, the Regularization Law?

As lawyers and human rights activists, we had no doubt as to what came first. Professional ethics compel us to work on behalf of our clients and to their advantage. And our ethics as human rights activists also preclude us from sacrificing the interests of the individual for the good of the many. If a humanistic worldview that places human beings at the center of consideration means anything, it means not sacrificing the individual's interests to advance the general good, especially when the individual belongs to a disempowered, oppressed community.

So what did we do in these cases?

In the course of the litigation, we received several offers to purchase land that had been taken over by settlers and which we had asked the court to order evacuated. We made a decision that seemed self-evident to us as lawyers: we would not prevent any offer from reaching our clients. Only the client could decide how to respond. Selling land to Israelis is condemned by Palestinian society and those who do it are marked as traitors. Lawyers who cooperate with land deals are seen by Palestinians as impeding the fight against the occupation and as collaborators of the settlement movement. I would never be part of such a transaction between master and serf, between the privileged and the occupied. To me, these conditions are exploitative by definition, the opposite of a legitimate deal, which involves a transaction between parties with equal rights who are free to choose to enter them or not. Still, I did not want to take the paternalistic approach and resolved to leave the decision to the client. Should the client accept the offer, I would propose finding another lawyer for the negotiations, but I would not get in the way and I'd certainly maintain the client's confidentiality.

Luckily, the clients who received an offer to purchase their land for settlers rejected it with disgust. They would rather lose their land with no compensation, they said, but go down fighting than sell it to settlers, even for an astronomical price.

Most of our clients also shared our strategic view of the danger of retroactive authorization. They saw value in the fight itself, even if it might end with a loss. Many felt that silence and resignation in the face of the theft of their land were worse than a fight that could end with defeat. In any case, they knew the battle would be waged in the institutions of the occupier, and they pinned little hope on those institutions. Additionally, they had already lost possession of their land in any concrete sense, so losing it formally would leave them no worse off. It would just make the landgrab official. I felt that they chose to fight because it allowed them to hold their heads high. It negated their position as helpless prey and drew attention from other Palestinians and the international press, which made their plight visible. They ceased being the ultimate victims, silenced as well as hurt.

THE LEGAL CAMPAIGN'S FIRST DECADE, AN INTERIM SUMMARY

The wave of petitions began to produce results—a trickle at first and then a downpour. There were many successes, but taking stock also reveals the limitations of the litigation, as well as the danger of triggering a backlash by fighting a policy that powerful political actors hold dear. Any measure of our specific successes—that is, winning material remedy for the client—

is distinct from the campaign's overall accomplishments, in terms of bringing about broader change, easing the contested policy, or even stopping the practice altogether.

Let's begin with the concrete level.

In about twenty cases, the remedy sought was obtained in full (some one hundred were filed, but not all sought concrete remedy).[19] In some of them, the court gave a final judgment ordering the demolition and evacuation of unlawful construction, or the removal of construction that obstructed the Palestinian farmers' access.[20] In other cases, the demolition or evacuation was carried out under pressure from the court but without need for a judgment. Two particular judgments related to entire outposts.

In the first, the court ordered the state to remove and demolish the largest outpost in the West Bank, Migron.[21] Established in the late 1990s on a hill southeast of Burqa, Migron was, by 2009, home to some fifty families, or 250 people. The outpost was built on land owned by Palestinians from nearby villages, mostly Burqa and Deir Dobwan. The legal challenge to Migron lasted from 2006 to 2012 and included a great many proceedings undertaken in tandem with a High Court petition filed by Peace Now and the landowners. In one proceeding, the settlers demanded recognition of their right to keep the land based on various promises allegedly given by the authorities over the years. In another, we sued the state on behalf of some of the landowners for damages due to the harm they had suffered as a result of the state's failure to evict the settlers. That case was designed to put a different form of pressure on the government, and we withdrew it once the High Court ruled on the original case. Settlers brought other petitions in response to our victory in the High Court in a failed attempt to have it revoked, based on claims—eventually refuted—that they had purchased and owned some of the land in the outpost.

The Amona case was the second judgment in which the court ordered the full evacuation of an outpost (the same one named in Peace Now's first petition, which ended with the order to demolish nine permanent dwellings).[22] After Migron had been evacuated, Amona was the largest outpost in the West Bank. In 2008, Yesh Din and landowners from the villages of Silwad and Ein Yabrud, on whose land the outpost stood, filed a petition to have it removed. In 2014, after six years of litigation, which, as in the Migron case, was carried out in tandem with many other proceedings, the High Court ruled that the entire outpost had to be evacuated by the end of 2016. For two years, the government grappled with this political bombshell and how to handle it. Amona's residents had direct connections to the country's leadership and strong political backing from the ruling Likud Party and Habayit Hayehudi (the Jewish Home), the party most identified with the settlement movement and a key member of the governing coalition. The violent evacuation of the nine dwellings a decade earlier had turned Amona into a national symbol, and symbols are very powerful, especially to fundamentalists.

One option the government considered was to convince Amona's settlers to move to a different site (essentially establishing a new settlement), but they vehemently opposed this. Another was to pass legislation that would allow confiscation of the land on which the outpost was built and explicitly vacate the High Court's ruling, hoping that the court would not strike the legislation down as unconstitutional. Aside from undermining the High Court, this option would mean violating the absolute prohibition in international law on confiscating the property of residents of an occupied territory, as well as making an official declaration that Palestinian property rights mean nothing to the Israeli government. We will return to Amona and the momentous impact of this case.

Two more judgments ordered large-scale demolitions and evacuations in neighborhoods north and south of the settlement of Beit El, near Ramallah. The first neighborhood was on Jabal Artis (Ulpana Hill to the settlers).[23] All construction there was done on land owned by residents of the nearby village of Dura al-Qara' and registered in the land registry. There were fourteen permanent structures with six housing units in each and several more prefabricated homes. Yesh Din petitioned on behalf of two of the Palestinian landowners. Five of the structures had been built on their land, a total of thirty housing units, which were all occupied by the time the judgment was handed down. In this instance, the judgment incorporated a pledge given to the court by the state to demolish and remove the structures, a pledge that was later broken. The second case related to construction begun on land owned by a resident of Dura al-Qara' and seized by the IDF in the 1970s for security purposes, though it was never used. The developer took advantage of the fact that the landowner was not permitted to access his land, building two multi-unit buildings and clearing land for more. Here, too, a pledge made by the state was broken.

Each of the judgments for evacuation caused a political uproar and led to outrageous attempts by the government to avoid upholding the rulings of Israel's highest judicial instance, even when the rulings were based on the state's own commitment to evacuate. Both in Migron and in the southwestern neighborhood of Beit El, the state asked for many years of delays implementing the judgments. In Migron, the state requested the delay on the pretext that it would take time to build a new neighborhood for the evacuees. In the second case, the delay was intended to allow time to consider retroactively authorizing the outpost, thereby avoiding the demolition. These deferral motions were submitted in the eleventh hour before the evacuation deadline, which meant that the High Court was facing a fait accompli.

In other words, Israel's government defied the court's judgment in the first case and ignored a pledge it had undertaken in the second. Regarding Migron, the High Court was not fooled and rejected the attempt to subvert its judgment, voicing harsh criticism of the government's conduct.[24] In the other case, the court gave the state many extensions to allow it to pursue retroactive authorization, thereby effectively accepting its breach of promise. Yet once the court realized these efforts were going nowhere, it ordered the structures demolished.[25]

As for Jabal Artis, the state conceded that it was obliged to tear down the illegal five structures built there, and the court issued its judgment based on this concession. But when the time came for the demolition to begin, the state, in its most brazen attempt to override the court and under great pressure from right-wing Knesset members affiliated with the settler movement, applied to withdraw its own consent and have the judgment reversed. Accepting the state's request would have involved a grave violation of one of the fundamental tenets of the judicial process (primarily, the finality of judgments); moreover, the state's approach to the court at the eleventh hour, as the evacuation was about to take place, effectively meant that the judgment was not upheld. If a private individual were to do such a thing, they would likely be charged with contempt. In any case, the High Court wholly rejected the state's maneuverings and in this case, too, severely criticized its conduct and ordered it to pay the petitioners' costs.[26]

Jabal Artis and Migron were ultimately evacuated in June and September of 2012. The construction that began in southwestern Beit El was also demolished, in late July 2015. But all the signs indicated Amona's evacuation, scheduled for completion by the end of 2016, would be politically far more complicated and difficult.

The pattern of last-minute attempts to derail the evacuations was not limited to state motions asking for more time. Settlers, who had denied in court that the land they had taken had ever been owned by Palestinians, suddenly showed up with documents allegedly proving they had bought the land from its Palestinian owners, demanding the evacuation be halted. In the cases in which I was involved, these allegations proved to be based on forged documents, but these efforts worked to buy the settlers some time.

Aside from these cases, each of which related to an entire outpost or neighborhood, in seven more petitions there were rulings or agreements that the state must demolish and remove smaller-scale construction consisting of a few structures.[27] Nine more struggles led to the removal of settler invasions into Palestinian farmland, and of fences put up by the settlers to deny Palestinian farmers access.[28]

Another judgment was issued in the case of the nine permanent homes built in the center of the settlement of Ofra. As in Amona, the court gave the government of Israel two years, until February 2017, to execute the demolition orders.[29] The order on the nine Ofra homes joined the evacuation order for nearby Amona to compound the political hell storm that was brewing for Israel's right-wing government toward the end of 2016.

In many other cases, the result was not as clear-cut. In 2011, in a petition filed by Peace Now for the evacuation of six outposts against which the military had issued evacuation orders back in 2004, though they were never executed, the state announced its new intention to evacuate construction located on privately owned Palestinian land but pursue retroactive authorization on public land.[30]

In many cases the distinction between private and public land in the West Bank is complicated, at best. Since two-thirds of the land is not registered in the Tabu land registry, the status of many plots is in dispute. The High Court therefore often granted the state's requests for delays, and waited, sometimes for a very long time, for the government to pursue proceedings to retroactively approve some of the illegal construction, while at the same time pushing for the demolition of other construction, which the state admitted was on privately owned land.

Beyond the demolished construction, many petitioners managed to
return to their land after the settlers had been evacuated. Residents of Sinjil returned to their plot after a long and exhausting legal battle and resumed
cultivating it. Residents of Jaba' returned after many years to plots that
had been fenced off by settlers from Geva Binyamin. Residents of Beit Furik
returned to cultivate some of their land adjacent to the outpost bloc around
the settlement of Itamar. Residents of Silwad and Ein Yabrud, who had
been denied access to their farmland because of a fence built by settlers
from Ofra, returned after the fence was removed. Every phone call we
received from Yesh Din's field workers with the news that farmers had
managed to reach their land after years of dispossession filled the office
with joy and gave us the fuel for a few more miles of Sisyphean battle.

Now LET'S MOVE to the impact of the legal campaign on the level of
policy change.

There's no question that the legal proceedings made it difficult for the
settlement movement to continue its building boom. Peace Now and Yesh
Din monitored every instance of construction, however small, and Zachary and I, representing the petitioners in all the proceedings, notified the
court of these developments on the ground even as the petitions were pending. The immediate ancillary outcome of the litigation was a freeze,
sometimes complete, on construction in the outposts. In many of them
construction had already begun, and the structure's skeletons remained
standing, often for years, waiting for a decision. On every trip I took in
the West Bank, I saw these white elephants, born out of the cases we brought
to court, such as the sewage treatment facility built by the Binyamin local
council, without permits, on land that belonged to our clients. The facility was never hooked up to the grid and never went into operation, thanks
to a court order.[31] There were also the ten skeletal buildings in the Rehelim outpost in the northern West Bank near the settlement of Tapuah,
where construction was halted thanks to another High Court order (which
was initially disobeyed but ultimately put into effect).[32]

The overall success documented by Peace Now and Yesh Din has
resulted in other far-reaching effects. There have been clear quantitative
and qualitative changes in the practice of illegal construction. Creating
new outposts ground almost to a complete halt. In less than a decade, since
the latter half of the 1990s and until the first Amona petition was filed in

2005, more than a hundred outposts were built; in the subsequent decade, only a handful have been established, all on land considered public rather than private.[33] Our litigation campaign was so vigorous that, at certain points, we petitioned to have the construction of single structures stopped.[34] We sought to send a message that no construction would go unchallenged, and the message was received. The price paid for building in this way, with interim orders to stop construction and final demolition orders, was too high. The outpost movement and the Israeli local councils in the West Bank (the greatest outpost builders and supporters) had to devote too much of their resources and energy to defending themselves in court, and they began practicing caution.

Beyond this, *construction on privately owned Palestinian land stopped completely.* The settlers finally grasped the legal quandary involved in building on land that belongs to someone else. It is regrettable that the practice stopped only because the price became too high, not because it is immoral. The smaller-scale unauthorized construction, which continued even after the legal battle against it began, was no longer undertaken on privately owned land. It is true that the Sasson report and the directives issued in its wake, which prompted criticism over taxpayer funds being funneled into outposts, also contributed to this shift, but the legal proceedings were the main factor. Managing to eradicate widespread criminal activity that had political backing, in a fairly short space of time, is a phenomenal success.

THE SUCCESSES WERE numerous and significant and clearly the litigation against the outposts and illegal construction produced real change. But there were heavy costs, too, and far-reaching implications for the fight against the settlement project as a whole.

On the concrete plane, despite the legal victories, many of our clients were still denied free access to their land, and some were unable to regain any use of it. The landowners in Burqa, where Migron had been built, could not fully return to their land. Though some shepherds have been able to graze their flocks on the hill intermittently, there has been no permanent cultivation, mostly due to fear of the settlers who still maintain some presence in the area.

Harbi Ibrahim Mustafa, one of the petitioners in the Jabal Artis case, returned to his land, but only for short visits. Shamefully, the military

demanded that any such visits be prearranged and carried out with a sizable military escort, including jeeps, on the pretext that Mustafa needs
protection from the settlers. This is not something the military is ready
to do on a daily or even weekly basis. He had dreamed of planting vines
on the land, telling me during a court recess about his father's vineyard
and his childhood memories of spending time there. The dreams of this
charming, gentle man, who astonishingly maintained a moderate tone in
all his dealings with us and in his interviews with the press, remained
beyond reach. But the fight for him to exercise his rights on the land continues.

In other similar cases, settler violence and security pretexts meant the
most we could win for our clients was watered-down access to their land,
subjected to prearrangements and military escorts. In some places, where
the demolished structures were in the midst of intact buildings, the landowners were denied any access, despite the judicial recognition of their
ownership.

At the same time, the political cost of evacuating outposts stoked the
government's desire to appease the settlers and "compensate" the settlement movement for the demolition of its illegal construction. The
compensation—something of a political pact between the government and
the settler leadership—took the form of new construction: expanding the
number of housing units in existing settlements and finding alternate sites
for the outposts. Compensation—and revenge—for merely enforcing the
law. Thus the state built a new settlement for the Migron evacuees, just a
mile away from the outposts' original location, on state land. The government also made ambitious promises to the Beit El settlers to compensate
them for demolishing the five structures on Jabal Artis. Details have not
been divulged, but the press has uncovered that these promises involve
approvals for a four-hundred-unit expansion in the settlement and funding for four public buildings.[35]

Perhaps the most significant cost of the outpost petitions at that point
was the surge of retroactive approvals and permits that they prompted.
Since Israel had undertaken not to build new settlements, the government
artificially "attached" outposts to settlement jurisdictions and passed
them off as developing neighborhoods (probably presented as "natural
growth") in existing settlements, denying that they were, in fact, new
settlements. And so, in the few cases we litigated regarding unauthorized

construction on public land, retroactive authorization led to the dismissal of the petition.[36]

In the course of the campaign against the outposts, the prime minister appointed a commission, headed by retired Supreme Court Justice Edmund Levy, to investigate "the status of construction in Judea and Samaria." The Levy Commission was set up in 2012 as a means to circumvent the attorney general in exploring possible legal avenues to remove the obstacles in the way of illegal construction in the West Bank. The commission's recommendations were radical even by the standards of the Netanyahu government. It proposed the adoption of an official position that international law "intends" the West Bank to become sovereign Israel territory and to retroactively approve all the outposts built on public land as well as some on private land. The government did not dare adopt the Levy Report openly for fear of the international reaction, but in practice it has implemented many of its recommendations.[37]

This acceleration of retroactive authorization resulted in the fact that by 2016, nineteen outposts had been approved retroactively and thirteen were undergoing the same process.[38] Thus there were more than thirty new settlements that were a direct outcome of the legal fight against outposts. Israel's government did not recognize a single new settlement between the signing of the Oslo Accords in 1993 and 2008; in the course of a few subsequent years, first in a trickle and then in a deluge, new settlements cropped up all over the map of the West Bank.

Finally, one argument made the claim that the outpost petitions led to intensified legal proceedings against unlawful construction in the Palestinian sector. The settlers invested a great deal of effort and money into creating organizations with the purpose of mimicking our petitions, asking the courts to order the demolition of building undertaken by Palestinians without the necessary permits, and targeting illegal construction in our clients' villages.

While these petitions have been a nuisance and a cause for anxiety for Palestinians, attributing significance to the settlers' involvement is misguided. House demolitions have always been more prevalent in the Palestinian sector, and they are politically motivated. Unlike the outpost petitions, which were the only way to produce pressure for demolitions within the settlements, legal proceedings against Palestinian construction have played a very small role in the balance of power that determines the extent of demolition orders imposed in the Occupied Territories. More-over, building without permits in the Palestinian sector is an entirely dif-ferent creature from unauthorized settlement construction. It is done mostly by people who build on their own land for lack of choice: Israeli policy is aimed at curbing Palestinian development, a goal realized by denying the vast majority of Palestinian permit applications. The impact of the settlers' "mirror petitions" is therefore significantly smaller than that of the outpost petitions, and they also yielded no legal achievements.

BEYOND THE ACHIEVEMENTS and the setbacks on the ground, the legal battle also bore significant political fruit. It put illegal construction and the landgrab at the forefront of the debate about the settlement project. Out-posts made the headlines time and time again thanks to court cases, and the government was compelled to sacrifice a great deal of political, legal, and diplomatic capital to avoid their evacuation, and then more political capital to implement the instructions of the court. Had the government been able to preserve this capital, it would likely have spent it on other ways to support and expand the settlements.

Additionally, the court judgments confronted the Netanyahu govern-ment with a dilemma: whether to stay true to the rule of law and fulfill its duty to uphold the directives of the court, or to cling to its radically pro-settlement worldview. For the right-wing regime, upholding the Migron or Jabal Artis judgments was the political equivalent of a thumb-screw. Every evacuation left it scarred and ensured that the next one would be even harder. The hardest of all, everyone agreed, would be the evacu-ation of Amona, which had only become a more potent symbol of the entire settlement enterprise since those first demolitions in 2006. Evacuation would be so hard, in fact, that one cabinet minister said the government could not survive it.[39]

But the government did survive, and the events in Amona provide a fascinating lesson in what happens in the physics of the collision of law with politics.

AMONA STRIKES BACK

The judgment was handed down on Christmas Day 2014, stating that Amona had to be evacuated within two years, by December 25, 2016.

Amona's settlers immediately began preparing for a political and public onslaught. Throughout the two-year period before the evacuation, they took full advantage of the settler movement's immense political sway within the parties in the governing coalition.

Though the forty-plus families who called Amona home had taken land that did not belong to them—which was why they were facing eviction— it seemed self-evident to everyone involved that the government owed them alternate housing. The political challenge to the government was huge: it had to implement the judgment while avoiding a coalition crisis that could bring it down. The prime minister thought this circle could be squared with a tempting compensation package, which, if large enough, would buy consensual evacuation. The formula had worked with the evacuation of the five buildings in the Ulpana neighborhood (Jabal Artis) and in Migron. First the package would have to include a generous solution for the evac- uees, but also some notches on the settlement movement's belt in the shape of settlement expansion, master plan approvals, and money—an offer the settlers could not refuse.

So the same state that destroys unauthorized Palestinian construction without the slightest misgivings, leaving whole families homeless, includ- ing children and the elderly, set out to coddle the Jewish intruders. And as the clock ticked, the price it was willing to pay to secure the settlers' cooperation and avoid a confrontation with the security forces that would need to enforce the High Court's order kept rising.

Ministry of Defense officials searched for a site to relocate the com- munity of Amona (in the West Bank, of course—the settlers would never agree to move to Israel proper), all at Israeli taxpayers' expense. The site that was finally selected was east of the settlement of Shilo, an area that had been declared state land, and they began planning the new settlement.*

The people of Amona, however, would have none of it. They demanded to stay right where they were, on the hilltop they had seized two decades earlier. All the promises of red-roofed cottages, the speeches praising them as pioneers and victims of leftist agitators who put ideas in the heads of

---

* The plan was presented at that stage as authorization for a neighborhood in Shilo, to avoid the international costs of officially building a new settlement. The site itself was not contiguous to the settlement; it was in fact located quite far from its eastern boundary, in Shvut Rachel, which was itself an outpost that was authorized as a neighborhood of Shilo in the same way.

the Palestinians (who otherwise cared nothing for the land they owned), the visions of grand investments and settlement master plans—all this only fueled the settlers' conviction that they had the political power to beat the court's orders. The settlers of Amona refused all offers. Every last envoy sent to beseech them to agree to relocation, to a compromise, came back empty-handed. Amona would not give up the mountain.

Instead, its leaders demanded that their political representatives renew the efforts to pass the Regularization Law, which would pave the way for confiscating the land and retroactively revoke the evacuation order. That, the settlers said, was the only solution.

Netanyahu opposed the law. He feared the international ramifications of a law that would essentially be an act of annexation (the occupying power's parliament would be instituting norms in the occupied territory) and a violation of the laws of occupation, specifically the absolute prohibition against confiscating the property of the occupied population. Netanyahu even expressed concern that the Regularization Law would land Israel in the International Criminal Court in The Hague.[40] But most of all, Netanyahu feared the reaction of the American administration.

During its eight-year term, the Obama administration followed Israel's settlement policy and exerted varying levels of pressure to stop it, or at least tone it down. Despite this pressure, Netanyahu had built thousands of housing units and led the policy of retroactive approval for the outposts. For this and other reasons,[41] he had had his share of clashes with the American president, sometimes openly, through the media. For its part, the US administration issued frequent condemnations of Israel's settlement policy. Considering Israel's absolute dependency on its largest ally, the American president had a very powerful stick, but his use of it had been constrained. However, with his administration in its last year, free of electoral pressure, Jerusalem feared that Obama would bring the stick out in full force.

One scenario that kept Netanyahu up at night was the specter of the US administration withholding its support for Israel in the UN Security Council. The Security Council's resolutions have far-reaching implications and the legal consensus considers them binding.[42] A resolution against Israel could accelerate its growing political isolation, hurt its trade relations, and spark a legal domino effect on a conflict that had already made an appearance in foreign courts and international tribunals. The Obama administration had devoutly defended Israel up until that point—in 2011, it had even vetoed a resolution against the settlements that echoed its own policy. But Netanyahu feared that this protection was weakening. Certainly, the US administration strongly opposed the Regularization Law. And the Israeli-Palestinian conflict was already on the Security Council's agenda in the winter of 2016. This was an explosive combination that should not be triggered with a provocation like the Regularization Law.

These considerations show that there were and are constraints to Israel's policy choices. The outposts and the fight against them were shaped by a great number of factors and uncertainty surrounding the government's actions and reactions, but the major international pressure points imposed limits and everyone, lawyers included, calculated their steps accordingly. My assumption was that Netanyahu would not risk political defeat at the Security Council and that the Regularization Law did not stand a chance of being adopted.

But on November 8, 2016, all our assumptions about international pressure and the leverage of Israel's greatest ally were upended when Donald Trump, a real estate tycoon, was elected forty-fifth president of the United States. The Trump campaign's statements on Israel sounded as if they had been lifted straight from the settler playbook. He had promised to overhaul the American approach to the conflict. He did not see the settlements as an impediment to peace (unlike every administration since the 1970s), accused the Obama administration of treating Israel unfairly, and pledged to move the US embassy from Tel Aviv to Jerusalem (thereby recognizing Israeli sovereignty over the entire city, something no previous president had dared to do). But Trump had said a lot of things during his campaign. On the morning of November 9, the whole world was waiting to see whether those things should be taken seriously.

The settlers were sure they should. The day after Trump's win, Minister Naftali Bennett, head of the settler-allied Habayit Hayehudi party, said this was the moment to renege on the two-state solution.[43] Jerusalem's deputy mayor and head of the city's Planning and Building Committee said of plans to build and expand settlements in East Jerusalem, "We intend to take the plans out of deep freeze."[44] And when Trump picked his Jewish lawyer David Friedman, a New York right-wing settlement supporter and donor, to fill the post of US ambassador to Israel, the settlers thought the messiah had come. This surge of confidence was expected to have an immediate impact on the balance of power in the Amona crisis.

Still, as we know, timing is everything, and unfortunately for the settler movement, Barack Obama was still president. Trump would not be inaugurated until January 20, 2017, while the court's judgment required evacuation of the outpost by December 25. Meanwhile, draft proposals for a resolution on the Israeli-Palestinian conflict were making the rounds at the UN headquarters in New York and Netanyahu knew that Trump's election had not removed the danger. At least, not yet. So he continued to oppose the Regularization Law. As the days went by and the evacuation deadline drew nearer, tensions grew inside the coalition and with them the threat to its existence. What to do?

In yet another attempt to appease the Amona settlers' insistence on staying on the mountain while avoiding passage of the Regularization Law, a new idea was suggested: move the outpost a few dozen yards north, to other plots on the same hill. This would both uphold the court judgment and give Amona's setters a public victory, since they would essentially remain at the same site. This solution would also block the Palestinian landowners from using their land because their plots would still be very close to the new site, and security considerations would prevent them from gaining free access.

However, the "Amona North" alternative, as it came to be known, suffered from the same flaw as the original Amona: the land was privately owned, registered in the name of Palestinians. The military had concluded that many of the owners were not physically present in the West Bank, but still, the land was privately owned.

THE GOVERNMENT NEEDED some other savior to deliver it from this legal conundrum. And in November, deliverance came, hailing from the Ministry of Justice on Salah a-Din Street in East Jerusalem.

Avichai Mandelblit, who served as military advocate general from 2004 to 2011, became Netanyahu's cabinet secretary after his military service ended. In January 2016, Mandelblit went on to become attorney general. As the person who held the top military legal position through some of the turbulent years of the Second Intifada and during Operation Cast Lead in Gaza, Mandelblit was no stranger to legal disputes involving moral dilemmas. His decisions as MAG were frequently and highly criticized by the human rights community in Israel and abroad, many believing that the military's already questionable approach to the fundamental rules of the laws of war and occupation deteriorated further during his tenure. Though the criticism failed to change Mandelblit's approach, he did seem to care about it and even accept some of it as legitimate. A native of largely secular Tel Aviv who became religiously observant in his twenties, Mandelblit was rooted in neither the Zionist religious movement nor the legal elite.

The central issue awaiting him, as he assumed the role of attorney general, was the explosive case of Amona. Within just a few months, he became the first attorney general, since the 1980 Elon Moreh judgment (in which the High Court prohibited seizure of land for the use of a settlement), to lend his hand to the use of privately owned Palestinian land for settlement purposes. In fact, Mandelblit did much more. In a string of memos and directives, he approved practices his predecessors had not dreamed of and severely undercut what was left of the restrictions the legal system imposed on the West Bank landgrab.[45]

To enable the idea of moving Amona to the north, to land also privately owned by Palestinians, Mandelblit determined that "abandoned" land—that is, registered to people not currently living in the West Bank—could be used temporarily to settle the people of Amona. This determination was predicated on a military order that allows the transfer of possession of property belonging to an absent person to the military, with an instruction that the property must be protected and held in trust until the absentees return.[46] But the legal position maintained over the years was that such land could not be allocated for settlement, since it was to be managed in trust, temporarily, for the absentee's benefit.[47]

Mandelblit undid the prohibition. It is possible, he determined, in the case of a *pressing public need*, to allocate abandoned land to settlers, and even prefer them over the absentee's relatives or village brethren, although it would be safe to assume that the owner would want the latter to have the property.[48] Mandelblit decreed that solving the Amona problem was just such a pressing public need and therefore permitted allocating the abandoned land for the settlers' temporary use. The same people who were ready to invade land belonging to others and refused to leave it, even under court order, would be entrusted with guarding the land until the owners returned. Thanks to Mandelblit, the government and the settlers were able to reach agreement: they would resettle in Amona North.

For us lawyers and our clients, this was a nightmare. After eight years of fighting and winning a favorable judgment, the Amona settlers would stay on the mountain, moving their caravans a few symbolic yards and keeping the rightful owners from returning to their land.

As the evacuation deadline was drawing near and the proceedings for either solution—Amona North or Shilo East—required more time, Mandelblit filed a court motion to delay implementing the judgment for seven months. The settlers still would not hear of the Shilo East idea and also refused to move to an interim site until the Amona North location was ready. The grounds Mandelblit cited for the motion was that a nonconsensual evacuation would end in violence. His lawyers even asked to show the court, ex parte, a Shabak report on the risk of conflict and unrest in case of a nonconsensual evacuation.

Zachary and I strongly objected to the motion. We reminded the court that the state had had two years to prepare for this moment and argued that the real reason for the requested stay was political, meaning the fear of a coalition crisis. We accused the government and Mandelblit of making shameful false use of security grounds and giving in to settler pressure. We withheld consent to let the justices view the Shabak report without making it available to us and the public, stating that using privileged material to delay implementing a court judgment was a very dangerous precedent for the rule of law.

In mid-November, the court dismissed the state's motion. In a long, detailed decision, the panel, headed by President Miriam Naor, reproached the state for seeking yet another delay "at the eleventh hour" and ruled that no grounds justifying the delay had been presented.[49]

This loss did not stop the government's race toward Amona North. Just a little over a month was left before the evacuation, an undeniably short time, but this option had become the only consensual one. Under government orders, the army declared dozens of plots in the northern part of the hill abandoned, and with a military order to expedite planning procedures within days rather than months, a master plan was drawn up for a caravan compound.

But the government, the attorney general, and the military had to contend with Yesh Din's indefatigable team. Zachary and Shakir, together with the head of the Silwad village council, Abd a-Rahman Saleh, worked around the clock to let the plots' owners know that their land had been declared abandoned and file objections on their behalf. It turned out that for almost every plot whose owners the military had claimed were abroad, there were at least a few owners or their heirs in the West Bank, meaning the plots were not abandoned. In most cases, the present owners lived right next door to Amona, in Silwad. The military's review appeared to have been extremely cursory and the number of abandoned plots kept shrinking. At first, the Civil Administration tried to adjust the master plan to match the changing map of abandoned plots. They tried to reduce the number of caravans, bring them closer together, cancel public spaces, erase parking spots. We joked that this would be the first outpost where the caravans were piled one on top of the other. Finally, only two plots remained, non-adjacent. Amona North seemed to be off the table.

It was the final act. The gun from the first act of the legal campaign against the outposts, before Amona threatened the government, was now the only weapon the settlers had left: the Regularization Law. Most coalition party MKs supported the law, with the exception of Kulanu, headed by Finance Minister Moshe Kahlon. Without his backing, the bill did not have a majority. Kahlon's objection had to do with the issue of revoking court judgments: he could live with the harm to Palestinian property, but the affront to the court's dignity was too much.

The bill's sponsors wanted it passed and agreed, just before the first reading, to drop the article addressing prior court judgments. They thought they could bring it back prior to the bill's second and third reading.* Besides, even without that article, passing the law would be a great achievement. It would not save Amona or the nine homes in Ofra, but it would open the door to the confiscation of tens of thousands of dunams of private land and authorization of dozens of outposts and thousands of homes. The sacrifice of Amona would not be in vain.

On December 7, the bill was brought to the Knesset plenum for its first reading, omitting the retroactive cancellation of High Court judgments. The pressure on Netanyahu was enormous. On one side was the interna-

---

*   Bills must pass three readings in the Knesset before becoming law.

tional community, Obama, and the Security Council; on the other, key partners in his coalition government with the power to bring it down.

Those opposed to the law were joined by the executive branch's entire body of legal counsel: the legal adviser to the Defense Ministry, the military advocate general, and even Attorney General Mandelblit, who in a rare move announced that he would not defend the law against any petition contesting it in the High Court of Justice. This law, Mandelblit held, was unconstitutional and a breach of international law.

Whenever Netanyahu has had to choose whether to bow to pressure from within or from without, he has buckled to pressure from within. The Regularization Law was no different. It passed the first reading with a majority of 58 to 51 of 120 MKs. Netanyahu had opposed the law and often spoken against it, but he voted in favor, although he demanded that coalition members now hold off advancing it until the change of US presidents. He hoped that the stalled legislative process would persuade the Obama administration to refrain from taking action against the government. He was wrong.

Two days before Christmas, the Security Council debated a resolution that deemed all West Bank and East Jerusalem settlement illegal, demanded that Israel cease its settlement activity immediately, and called on all states to "to distinguish, in their relevant dealings, between the territory of the State of Israel and the territories occupied since 1967." It is hard to imagine a text more detrimental to Netanyahu's policy.

Fourteen of the Security Council's fifteen members voted in favor. The fifteenth member, the United States, abstained.[50] The American veto that had protected Israel through the eight years of Obama's presidency was withheld. US Ambassador to the UN Samantha Power explained in her speech that the Americans had decided to withhold their veto power because settlement expansion and outpost approval threatened the two-state solution, and because Israel was advancing a law to authorize the outposts rather than evacuating them. This may have been Israel's greatest UN defeat since the start of the occupation in 1967.

AFTER THE REGULARIZATION Law passed its first reading, there was one more attempt to implement the Amona North option. The idea was to issue a military order to empower the military commander to dissolve the partnership between the present and absent landowners by force and re-parcel their property. The plots belonging to the absentees would then be declared abandoned property. A dissolution of partnership at the request of one co-owner, without the consent of the other, is a complicated procedure done only by a court of law. In this case, the military commander was given the power to do as he saw fit for the ultimate goal of giving the so-called abandoned plots to the residents of Amona.

Mandelblit put his stamp of approval on this brazen defiance of the basic tenets of property law and the order was signed.[51] Because of the complexity of this legal maneuver and the fact that few people understood it, Mandelblit maintained his public reputation as having opposed the Regularization Law rather than as someone who approved unprecedented harm to Palestinian property.

The clock was running out. The government now offered the Amona settlers an agreement based on its undertaking to re-parcel and reallocate the abandoned sections in Amona North. It also offered generous monetary compensation to each family, in return for a quiet consensual evacuation. We'll build you a new settlement, Netanyahu promised. And on the same mountain.

Ahead of the date of evacuation, hundreds of supporters, mostly youth, poured into the outpost. They were set on confronting the evacuation forces and fighting to prevent it. Reporters camped out at the site so as not to miss the evacuation, whether it took place at night or early in the morning, and news channels were planning continuous live coverage. Israel had Amona fever.

A week before the final court deadline, Amona's settlers decided to take the government deal. State counsel hurried to the court with the signed agreement and filed another motion to stay the evacuation—for "just" six weeks. Given the government's agreement with the settlers, a deal that would avoid confrontation and civil unrest, counsel asked for time to implement the improved Amona North plan.

We objected once more: whatever agreement had been reached, there was no reason to delay returning the land to its owners. But we knew the court would find it hard to resist. After all, the parties had indeed reached an agreement to quietly evacuate an outpost that had been standing for two decades, whose dismantling was shredding Israel's political system and roiling its people. Could the court really refuse six more weeks?

Still, the court required more than a government-settler deal to approve a delay, especially in light of the public turmoil and the power struggle that had ensued between the executive and the judiciary. Should the agreement on Amona North collapse for one reason or another, the evacuation could still escalate to violence and the stay of judgment would have been granted for nothing. In an unusual decision, the High Court demanded that the Amona settlers sign an undertaking to "evacuate peacefully and without confrontation or resistance," without linking this undertaking to implementation of the Amona North plan, which was marred by legal issues. The settlers hesitated but eventually signed, and the court granted a six-week stay, until February 8, 2017.

In the following weeks, the Amona North plan did indeed fall apart. The patchwork effort to conceal its illegality did not hold. Every move toward carrying out the plan took time and prompted objections, even from legal personnel within the military and the State Attorney's Office. Finally, when three plots were about to be re-parceled, Yesh Din and the landowners filed a High Court petition, with Zachary arguing that the order allowing the forced re-parceling was a violation of international law. High Court Justice Salim Joubran signed an interim order prohibiting the re-parceling pending a hearing. The time was up.

ON FEBRUARY 1, 2017, eleven years to the day after the evacuation of those nine Amona homes, the outpost's dismantling began. Hundreds of police officers were brought to evacuate some one thousand people, most of them youth from outside the outpost who had barricaded themselves in the homes. The evacuation took two days and more than sixty officers and some twenty civilians sustained minor injuries.[52]

Also on February 1, the High Court delivered its judgment on re-parceling: Zachary had convinced the court that the military order was illegal and it was quashed.[53] Amona North was over.

THE ENRAGED RIGHT wing received its payoff four days after the evacuation. With Obama on vacation and Trump in the White House, and with stiff competition from Habayit Hayehudi on his right, Netanyahu accepted the Regularization Law. Shortly before 11:00 p.m., with a majority of sixty to fifty-two, the bill approving confiscation of private Palestinian land and its allocation to settlers passed. The Knesset ordered Israel's authorities in the West Bank to commit a war crime.

WAS IT WORTH THE FIGHT?

The battle against the outposts and illegal construction in the settlements is still under way, but there is enough history now for readers to take an informed position on its effectiveness and wisdom.

Success in a campaign of litigation aimed at changing policy—especially one waged over many years involving many proceedings—does not boil down to a count of the judgments that granted remedy against those that did not. Any measure that looks only at the direct results of judgments and ignores the campaign's contributions (or damage) on multiple planes is misleading. For this reason I remained unfazed by settler activists who tried to demoralize us by pitting the number of houses demolished against the number of houses retroactively approved or added as compensation.

The test of the campaign's success is not whether there are more or fewer buildings in the West Bank, or even more or fewer settlements. That is a factor, but not a central one. My colleagues and I embarked on a journey that had several goals, and we designed a legal strategy to achieve them. To measure its accomplishments, we have to look back at the goals we set.

Clearly, a central purpose was to win relief for our clients. On this front, our success was far from complete, but many clients did see the settlers removed from their land. In other cases, barriers constructed by the settlers that prevented our clients' access were taken down. The wins were certainly greater than the alternative of taking no legal action.

Our broader goal was to end construction that bypassed the stages of planning and state approval, and particularly to stop all construction on private land. On this front, the success was quite impressive, not necessarily as a result of a change in the state's motivation to enforce the law, but because construction, especially on private land, was made too costly. New outposts were greatly reduced and construction on private land was all but eradicated.

Another important goal was to jolt the government out of the comfortable spot it had occupied for years, one that allowed it to sit on the fence regarding the outposts. As Dror Etkes used to say, "They have to decide who they're with—the cops or the robbers." We sought to end the government's ability to expand the settlements without paying the attending political and diplomatic price. Although we of course strove to win every case and achieve evacuation or demolition of all illegal construction, this goal meant that we would still prefer to see the building authorized than remain as is, with the government managing to evade its responsibility.

This goal was achieved, to a great extent. When the government declared it was with the cops, conceding its duty to remove illegal construction, it found itself in confrontation with the settlers. When the state declared it was with the robbers, authorizing outposts and adopting the Regularization Law, it found itself politically isolated, essentially prompting the Security Council to pass its resolution. Time will tell how far the resolution's impact will extend.

Some might look at the backlash against the litigation and the passage of the Regularization Law and wonder whether the campaign was worth it. This doubt is rooted in the terrible implications of the Regularization Law, which, if implemented verbatim, will result in massive confiscation of tens of thousands of dunams of privately owned land[54] and inflict harm on untold thousands of Palestinians. But the doubters should remember that the land that might be confiscated (if the High Court upholds the law—a very big if*) has already been invaded by settlers, and is therefore off-limits to its owners irrespective of the law.

Was the state of affairs before the legal battle really preferable? Was it better for land to be stolen while the government neither sanctioned nor stopped the theft? Whoever prefers the status quo ante would undo more than just the Regularization Law. They would cancel all the successes described here: the evacuation of Migron and the Ulpana homes, the southwestern compound of Beit El, and Amona. They would deny the many farmers who have been able to recover their land, the dramatic drop in incursions into private land, the end of creating new outposts, even the Security Council resolution.

The Regularization Law and the Security Council resolution are two far ends of the spectrum of events that would not have happened without

---

* Two petitions were filed to repeal the law, and Attorney General Mandelblit stayed true to his word, announcing he would not defend the government in court. These petitions are still pending, while implementation of the law has been postponed. In one of the petitions, my colleague and friend Shlomi Zachary and I, together with Dan Yakir and Roni Pelli, lawyers from ACRI, are representing ten human rights organizations and twenty-five local Palestinian councils.

the outpost petitions. They are testament to the fact that the ground beneath the settlement project is not stable.

For these reasons, I am convinced it was worth it.

DURING ONE OUTPOST case, I ran into a lawyer in the Supreme Court cafeteria who was working in one of the government's many legal counsel offices. "You're doing a tremendous amount of damage to your own goals," he said angrily, as someone who shared our opposition to the outposts. "Because of your petitions, we're forced to plan approval of whole outposts!"

I looked at this talented, qualified Israeli, who surely was a star student in his law school and presumably knew that all the settlements are illegal. "Who's forcing you?" I wanted to ask. "Why don't you refuse to pledge your talent to defy the law?" But I said nothing, because the fight was necessary, whether successful or not, and that is hard to explain in a brief encounter in the cafeteria.

7

Security and the Piccolo

THE THREE PILLARS OF THE OCCUPATION

The occupation rests on three legs: the gun, the settlements, and the law. Take out one and the regime topples over like a two-legged chair. The *gun* is the foundation, the trunk that grows the occupation's branches, feeds and supports them. It repels resistance from the occupied people. It imposes the will of the occupier on the occupied land and its inhabitants. It gives the occupiers the power, the freedom to make policy decisions. The *settlements* clinch the hold on the occupied territory. Colonization is a process of planting roots deep into the soil, and these roots have a double effect: they anchor the tree of occupation firmly in the ground so that it holds steady even in a storm, and they suck the water from the soil at the expense of local vegetation. Last, the *law*. It formalizes the systems of control and colonization, anchors them in an organized framework, and gives them legitimacy. Put to work in the service of the occupation, the law provides its DNA, the code that determines the growth of its roots, trunk, and branches, ensures their development, protects them against disease or mutations that might weaken them.

In the three previous chapters I described the legal battle against the settlement branch of the occupation: challenging the lawfulness of the settlements, fighting to remove the outposts, and opposing the separation fence (itself a tool in the service of both colonization and control). Two other chapters addressed the gun, or the use of force in the form of deportations and torture during interrogations.

There are three more practices in the arsenal of force that the occupation uses to entrench its hold: administrative detention, house demolitions, and extrajudicial executions. The first policy has led to imprisonment without trial for thousands of Palestinians for months, even years. The second has meant the destruction of thousands of homes belonging to the families of people suspected of engaging in violence, although the families themselves had done nothing wrong. The third policy involves the assassination of hundreds of Palestinians suspected of hostile activity (the precise cause for suspicion is unknown but could range from involvement in violence against Israeli security forces or civilians to holding a leadership role in political groups fighting Israeli control). The evidence of their involvement is always classified and the determination that they deserve to die is made secretly according to confidential criteria and without external oversight.

Administrative detention and house demolitions have been at the center of a decades-long legal fight that is still ongoing. The challenge to extrajudicial killings has consisted mainly of a single petition that directly contested the legality of the practice. The thread common to all three is the violation of the basic principle of legal fairness—the notion that individuals cannot be deprived of their fundamental rights without due process. At the very minimum, the person has a right to know the accusation against them and to mount a defense against it. House demolitions defy another principle as well: that no one shall be harmed for the actions of another.

ADMINISTRATIVE DETENTION

Administrative detention has been used by the occupation since day one. Of all the powers vested in Israel's security forces to maintain control over the occupied territory, to prevent revolt, political resistance, attacks on the military, and terrorism against civilians,* administrative detention seems to be the most widely used.

---

* Israel uses the term "terrorism" to denote any violence by Palestinians against Israelis, civilians as well as combatants. However, according to the international definition, terrorism is the use of violence against *civilians* for political gain. In this chapter, I attempt to adhere to the international definition without getting into the complicated question of when it is legal for civilians to fight occupation forces.

Administrative detention is detention without trial. Many legal systems provide for various types of such incarceration, but here we focus on administrative detention for security reasons. The legal thesis is that it is a preventive measure. Unlike post-conviction imprisonment, which is retribution for the prisoner's past actions, or punishment, administrative detention is forward-looking. It is intended to forestall the danger that the detainee poses to future security, to protect, not punish. This leads to another important distinction between criminal and administrative incarceration: criminal law, as a matter of principle, does not impose punishment for thoughts or plans that have not come to fruition or were never put into action. It usually is not applied to preparations for committing an offense (with an important exception—conspiracy to commit a crime or misdemeanor, which, in effect, does punish for preparations rather than the offense itself). In contrast, administrative detention allows the authorities to deny a person's liberty based on plans or preparations, which serves as an indication that the person will likely commit an offense in the future.

These distinctions mean that administrative detention must not be used as an alternative to criminal prosecution.* Where the authorities believe they have evidence of a crime, they are required to serve an indictment and allow defendants to challenge the evidence against them in court. If there is no evidence, the presumption of innocence applies.

It does not take a jurist to see just how dangerous administrative detention is to the fundamental right to liberty. It is one thing to deny liberty following *proof* of a crime. It is an entirely different proposition to deny liberty because of an *assessment* that a person will commit a future crime.

But the forward-looking nature of administrative detention is only one of its problematic aspects. What makes it fatal to a detainee's human rights is the fact that it is almost always based on classified intelligence material. All over the world intelligence agencies and secret police assess security threats and they are extremely zealous about the secrecy of the materials they collect and produce. The result is that people are not only

---

* It is important to note that the criminal track in the Occupied Territories is the military courts. Though defendants in these courts have many more rights than administrative detainees, Israel's military courts in the Occupied Territories have a grave record of violating due process rights. See Lior Yavne, *Backyard Proceedings*, Yesh Din (2007).

arrested for things they have not yet done, but the justification for their arrest is based on materials that they never see.

That's not all. By definition, administrative detention has no end date. Unlike post-conviction imprisonment, which has a set duration, administrative detention goes on for as long as the assessment of the threat posed by the suspect remains in place. The threat is re-evaluated periodically based on . . . classified material.

The bottom line is that a person may be detained without knowing the security threat they allegedly pose, the basis for being deemed a threat, or the duration of the detention. If anything deserves the clichéd term "Kafkaesque," it is administrative detention for security reasons.

Still, despite the clear difficulties presented by administrative detention, international law recognizes that sometimes there is no choice but to use it. The classic scenario put forward in its support is this: The authorities have reliable information that a person or a group is planning to carry out a terrorist attack and kill civilians. If the information can be used to arrest and prosecute the conspirators in a court of law, great. But what if the information does not translate into evidence that can be used in a criminal trial? A possible reason why the information may not be used as evidence is that it might expose intelligence sources or the operations of intelligence agencies. Say, for example, that one of the conspirators is an informant. Exposing him would not just place him in jeopardy, but would also hamper the ability to uncover future conspiracies—either because the agent was exposed or because others fearing exposure would refuse to serve as informants.

Another possible impediment to prosecuting is that the evidence might be inadmissible, for instance, hearsay. Perhaps the informant recounted something he was told about the suspect by another coconspirator. Evidence law considers hearsay inadmissible as the defendant is denied effective cross-examination. A third reason could be that there is no evidence criminal activity has taken place, only indications of plans to carry out future crimes. One scenario is that one person tells another about their plan to carry out an attack and the plan is reported to the authorities. No crime has been committed, there is only the possibility of a future crime. Thus, administrative detention is intended to allow authorities to detain someone who poses a danger to the public when criminal arrest is not possible and when there is a degree of likelihood that the person will commit a serious crime if left at liberty.

But the practice violates a great many democratic values and fundamental legal principles; most important, it creates an extremely slippery slope by giving authorities an easy tool that is free of any real scrutiny, certainly public scrutiny. The latent danger in a draconian power to detain people without trial, based on confidential evidence, is immense: the term "security" is so fluid that there is a risk of it being used to cover an ever-expanding range of *contributions* to security, some of them indirect, which extend well beyond the clear and present danger of innocents being hurt. Because the process is closed and devoid of public scrutiny, there is the threat of it being put to use for extraneous purposes—political, for example. And because of the departure from the laws of evidence and principles of due process, which means the accused does not know the substance of the suspicions against them and cannot mount a defense, there is a great danger of harm to innocents who might be detained on the basis of erroneous intelligence, unsubstantiated rumors, or even deliberate settling of personal scores. Critics of administrative detention argue that all these dangers amount to a risk that far outweighs any benefit the measure provides.

International law does not offer a clear way out of the collision between the right to liberty and due process, on the one hand, and the important interest of public safety, life, and bodily integrity, on the other. It does, however, provide guidelines for navigating the clash, which are: Administrative detention is bad. It may be a necessary evil, but it is still bad. International human rights law, which stipulates that where liberty is denied, the detainee's right to know the charges and mount a defense against them must be respected,[1] still allows for suspending this right in cases of a "public emergency which threatens the life of the nation."[2] International humanitarian law (that is, the laws of war, which include the laws of occupation) permits administrative detention, but limits its use to "imperative reasons of security."[3] Commentary from the International Committee of the Red Cross states that administrative detention is lawful only when "real and imperative reasons of security" mandate it, and as long as its "exceptional character" is preserved.[4] Thus administrative detention is allowed only in extreme, rare cases when the security threat is particularly grave.

In the West Bank (and previously in the Gaza Strip), administrative detention is carried out pursuant to a military order.[5] The order empowers the military commander to sign an order of detention for up to six months, when there are "reasonable grounds to believe the security of the area or public safety require the detention." This provision is meant to be subject to another provision, which stipulates use of administrative detention only "for imperative security reasons,"[6] but even so, the bar set for the degree of certainty that the feared harm will materialize—"reasonable grounds to believe"—is quite low, a rather elastic probability test. No clear danger. No near certainty. The text also allows for a broad interpretation of the threat's severity: "the security of the area or public safety" is not, say, a danger to life and limb. This broad wording undermines what is supposed to be the exceptional character of administrative detention, according to the language of international humanitarian law and the commentary.

The order also empowers the military commander to extend the detention for six months at a time, with no cap on the number of extensions, and stipulates judicial review by a military judge who may view the material on which the order is based. The material itself remains confidential and is not divulged to the detainee or their counsel. The military judge has the power to revoke, reduce, or approve the detention order. In East Jerusalem (which has been annexed by Israel) and Gaza (following Israel's ground retreat in 2005), administrative detention is based on Israeli legislation that is very similar to the military order.[7] However, the power to sign the detention order rests with the minister of defense and the judicial review is conducted by the district court. And, as if it weren't enough that the very core of the procedure—the allegations and the classified material supporting them—is kept from the detainee, the entire process is hidden from the public, taking place in camera.[8] There is no pertinent reason to hold a closed hearing when the classified information involved will be discussed anyway, with only one party present. Someone must have realized that the whole thing looks bad, and had therefore better be hidden from the public and its representatives.

Israel is not the only country in the Western world that holds people in administrative detention for security reasons. Both the United States and the United Kingdom, for example, have laws that allow preventive detention, and in both places judicial review is crippled. But Israel is singular among democratic countries in its widespread use of the measure, to the point where we cannot say that its "exceptional" character was preserved.

Since the beginning of the occupation, thousands of Palestinians have been held in administrative detention for periods ranging from several months to several years. The number of detainees at any given moment is directly related to the level of tension in the Occupied Territories at that time, which is clearly illustrated by its fluctuations. According to figures provided to B'Tselem by the Israel Prison Service and the IDF spokesperson, the number of Palestinians held in administrative detention peaked in November 1989 during the First Intifada at 1,794 detainees. Overall, 3,300 people were held in administrative detention that year. After the first Oslo Agreement was signed in 1993, that number dropped to reach a low of no more than a handful, although the average fluctuated between 100 and 350 administrative detainees. At the outbreak of the Second Intifada, the number shot up again, reaching 1,000 in late 2002. Between 2005 and 2007 the figures stabilized at a 700-to-750 average. The end of the Second Intifada brought another decline, and by January 2011, 219 Palestinians were held in administrative detention. Since Operation Protective Edge in Gaza in 2014 and the wave of violence in 2015, the number has risen to 600 administrative detainees at the end of 2015 and 696 in April 2016.[9]

IF ANYONE KNOWS about administrative detention, it is Tamar Peleg-Sryck. In the 1980s as she approached sixty, after serving as vice principal and dean of students at an art school, she decided to head to law school. She was attracted to the field because she believed it would allow her to act on her values and for the mundane reason that there is no mandatory retirement age for lawyers. The energetic Peleg-Sryck was hardly the sort of woman to stay at home and watch television.

As a former Communist, she originally intended to devote her time to representing workers. But she did her internship with Avigdor Feldman, and, just like me over a decade later, realized that her legal skills were most needed in the netherworld beyond the Green Line. After she was called to the bar, she started working in the litigation center Feldman had set up in ACRI. This was in the early days of the First Intifada. Hundreds of detainees flooded the military courts, and the one in Gaza instituted an expedited detention procedure.

Defense Minister Yitzhak Rabin had allegedly recently told the army to "break arms and legs" and the press was filled with reports of violence by the security forces. ACRI decided to investigate whether the expedited procedure in Gaza violated detainee rights, and Peleg-Sryck wanted to go. She thought she would also collect testimonies about the violence used against the detainees. But Gaza was undergoing an explosion. General strikes and mass demonstrations with stone throwing and tire burning were taking place daily. But Peleg-Sryck, like Felicia Langer and Leah Tsemel before her, gave no thought to the danger posed by the Palestinian uprising, especially to Jewish Israelis. She got into a Palestinian taxi and went to Gaza.

Since that trip, Peleg-Sryck has devoted her more than twenty-year career, first at ACRI and then with HaMoked, to representing Palestinians on many issues, though mainly in the fight against torture and administrative detention. The mission she undertook to collect testimony of violence against Palestinians forced her to visit complainants in detention facilities. She became a regular sight in Ketziot, the main military detention facility for Gazans, and through her work wove professional and personal relationships with Gaza lawyers. They welcomed the prospect of an Israeli lawyer filing complaints against the abuse of their clients, especially Raji Sourani, the lawyer who would go on to establish the Palestinian Center for Human Rights.

These contacts gradually led to Peleg-Sryck representing Palestinians in judicial reviews over administrative detention orders. As these grew, the proceedings troubled ACRI, whose approach was to focus on principled cases only. But Peleg-Sryck's commitment to the detainees, her loathing of administrative detention, and her anger at its gratuitous and escalating use only sharpened her interest.

And so, this Jewish lawyer, a native of Pinsk, who arrived in Palestine as a young girl during World War II and served as an IDF officer, became, in the seventh decade of her life, a familiar figure first in Gaza and then in the West Bank to Palestinian administrative detainees, military judges, and prosecutors who were young enough to be her children, even her grandchildren. Representing administrative detainees grew into a project, which found a home in HaMoked, where Peleg-Sryck worked until she retired in 2012 at age eighty-six. She estimates the number of detainees she represented throughout her career to be in the thousands.[10]

With such extensive experience, no one is better positioned to evaluate the only mechanism intended to serve as a safeguard against abuse of administrative detention: the judicial review. After the order of administrative detention has been signed, a military judge in the Occupied Territories (or a district court judge if the resident is in East Jerusalem or present-day Gaza) reviews the justification for the order. Detainees may have legal representation in this proceeding, but the lawyers, or more accurately, their effectiveness, are limited: the material reviewed by the judge is classified and the defense receives only a gist of it, usually a short sentence containing a very general description of the allegations. With secret evidence and undisclosed allegations, the detainee's lawyer has an incredibly difficult task. How can she find an alibi for her client if she doesn't know when and where he was alleged to have done whatever it is he allegedly did? How can she argue that the source who incriminated her client is a business competitor if she doesn't know who the source is? Did we say Kafkaesque?

In these circumstances, the role of the court as critic is crucial.[11] Ordinarily, the court is meant to play a mostly passive role, listening to parties' arguments and observing the evidence; in a judicial review based on classified material submitted ex parte, the judge should play a more active role. In the jurisprudence of the High Court of Justice, its role when reviewing classified material is defined as "acting as the detainee's 'mouth,'"[12] even as the detainee's "temporarily appointed defense counsel."[13] The court is supposed to raise questions about the material, review the source material itself, and question the security officials about its reliability.

Peleg-Sryck says that in the late 1980s and early 1990s there were still judges who saw their work in this light and took it seriously. They would call the Shabak agents involved with the classified material for cross-examination by the defense and to answer questions in an ex parte hearing. Also, Peleg-Sryck claims, military prosecutors used to be more willing to question and entertain doubt. Ultimately, most of the administrative detention orders were upheld, but still, the judges occasionally reduced the duration of the orders or even revoked them altogether.

This approach eroded over the years. Administrative detentions by the thousands flowed through the pipeline of the military courts during the Second Intifada, especially in 2002 at the time of Operation Defensive Shield, when IDF forces invaded West Bank cities. Judges were asked to approve them daily, and fewer and fewer judges had the nerve to stand up to the military commander. The Shabak claimed that its officers were too busy to come to the hearings and would send an edited summary of the classified information. The military prosecutor, usually a young twenty-something just out of law school, was ill equipped to answer the judges' questions or respond to the defense. Even when she knew the answers, she wasn't sure she was allowed to divulge them. The military judges, for their part, did not protest the Shabak agents' absence from the courtroom and the practice of summoning them faded.

Gradually, the judges came to apply a much broader interpretation of what constitutes a security threat, and people were routinely held in administrative detention not for suspected violence or aiding violence but for involvement in Palestinian organizations outlawed by Israel. Administrative detention became a primary tool for decimating political and not just military organizations. Peleg-Sryck did the math and found that no more than 20 percent of the administrative detainees she represented in 2002 were alleged to have participated in military rather than political or civilian activity in outlawed organizations. By 2008, they counted for just 9 percent of her clients.[14]

There have been grave accusations that the security agencies have exploited the tool of administrative detention, that the threat of it has been used as a way to recruit collaborators,[15] as an alternative to a failed arrest on criminal charges, and as a way to pressure community and political activists. A study conducted by HaMoked and B'Tselem revealed that between August 2008 and July 2009, 95 percent of the administrative orders brought for judicial review before the military court of first instance were approved as issued. In the military court of appeals the rate of approval was 85 percent. An examination of individual cases concluded that military judges were failing to take the activist approach required when reviewing a procedure based on material that is concealed from the defense.[16] When judicial intervention did occur, it resulted in the reduction of the detention time rather than it being revoked. Lawyers who represent security detainees have developed a cynical approach to a procedure they have come to see as no more than a formality.

It must be said that the system of judicial review of administrative detention involves two elements that inherently bias the judges in favor of giving their approval. First, the judge is disproportionately influenced by the classified information, which is presented by the prosecution ex parte, thus precluding any response from the defense. Second, judges are unnerved by the prospect of denying administrative detention only to learn that their decision was a mistake. It can be hard to blame a judge who fears releasing a man who might then go on a killing spree. There is no serious risk involved in the opposite decision—that approving administrative detention might later turn out to have been based on flawed evidence. The basis for the arrest is secret so there is no way to prove that a detainee was falsely imprisoned.

And in the very few cases of administrative detention where the military judge reduced the length of the order, the remedy often proved meaningless: just as the detention came to an end, the military commander would order an extension.

THE BODY THAT oversees and guides the work of the military courts is the High Court of Justice. Over the years, hundreds or even thousands of petitions were filed with the High Court against approval of administrative detention orders. The court's jurisprudence on administrative detention is perhaps the most extreme example of the gap between judicial rhetoric and action.

The rhetoric is striking. In dozens of judgments, High Court justices have emphasized—sometimes passionately—the gravity and dangers of administrative detention and its profound violation of the right to liberty. In fact, Israeli jurisprudence produced some of its best thinking on the importance of judicial review as a rearguard against arbitrary denial of liberty in response to administrative detention cases.[17] The High Court justices have always insisted that administrative detention can only be used as an exception, and that the military commander and judge must carefully examine the intelligence to be sure that detention is unavoidable, that there is no other way to defuse the threat. They have endlessly repeated the dictum that administrative detention is a preventive measure and so may not be used to detain people for alleged past actions. They have ruled that a criminal procedure is preferable, and where that is available, the court must avoid administrative detention.[18]

In a seminal judgment given in a case litigated by Peleg-Sryck and Dan Yakir on behalf of an administrative detainee, HaMoked, and ACRI, the court ruled that the military commander may not extend an order of administrative detention that was reduced by a military judge unless new material indicated a threat emanating from the detainee, or if the reduction was ordered for the express purpose of considering a further extension.[19] The judgment initially seemed like a tremendous achievement, as it appeared to give meaning to reductions. But a workaround quickly emerged to allow post-reduction extensions: in their few decisions to reduce the length of detention, military justices began to add that the reduction was "insubstantial," meaning that it did not derive from any weakness in the intelligence material, but was intended to speed up the military commander's decision on whether to extend the detention. "A very grand judgment with no effect in reality," Dan Yakir said, looking back.[20]

The High Court worked hard at presenting administrative detention as a necessary evil and an exception, and the judicial review over it as sharp and powerful. The results, though, tell a different story and the dissonance is intolerable.

Pioneering research by legal scholar Shiri Krebs of Stanford University revealed that not one of the 322 petitions against administrative detention decisions heard by the High Court between 2000 and 2010 resulted in the detainee's release and rejection of the classified evidence.[21] In fact, of the hundreds (perhaps thousands) of such petitions filed with the court during the occupation, there is only one reported case in which the judges ordered the detainee's release, and this in a brief decision containing no reasoning.[22]

The study, which included probing interviews with justices, state attorneys, and defense lawyers, also showed that, as in other occupation-related issues, informal practices evolved in administrative detention cases, too: these produced more than a few compromises in which detention was reduced. Krebs calls this "bargaining in the shadow of the court," and notes that although the justices avoided intervening in the detention orders, they did take on a quasi-mediation role.

Although the law provides that the courts have the last say on administrative detention, it is nevertheless the child of another agency, the Shabak. Its agents decide who will be detained and why, and they collect the material that ostensibly justifies detention. They also determine what counts as related to "the security of the area"—acts of terrorism or also organizational and political activity. The military commander might sign the order and the military judge approve it, but in practice, as lawyers representing security detainees have noted, everyone bows to the Shabak—military judges in the first instance and appellate instances as well as High Court justices. These judges all have far-reaching powers, yet they abstain from using them to carry out a genuine incisive review. "They sanctify the Shabak's position and don't get to the bottom of the classified material," says Peleg-Sryck.[23]

ISRAEL'S USE OF administrative detention in the Occupied Territories has never been challenged in court in a general proceeding seeking its wholesale eradication. No petition has argued that it is never permissible to detain people without trial, based on secret evidence, when there is no admissible evidence that they committed an offense. The reason for this is clear: administrative detention is legal, and not just under Israeli law but also under international law. The difficulty presented by Israel's practice is not its legality but its prevalence, and the very low bar set for using it. International law stipulates that administrative detention is an exception. Israel has made it the rule. International law requires that its "exceptional character must be preserved." Israeli law preserves the rhetoric of exceptionality but has turned it into the norm.

In such circumstances, when the illegality stems not from the measure itself—as in the case of torture or the settlements—but from how it is used, human rights lawyering is hard pressed to come up with a battle plan. The sense that administrative detention is often misused for purposes that are not clearly or at all security-related is hard to shape into a legal argument, given the authorities' denial. And the low threshold that Israel uses to determine the probability of a threat and its relevance as justification for detention is also more likely to come up on a case-by-case basis rather than as a principled claim.

But perhaps the greatest difficulty is the question of what constitutes a security threat that might justify administrative detention. Despite the veil of classified, confidential material, it is still evident that the military courts and the High Court of Justice apply a broad interpretation of the "security reasons" that warrant administrative detention. While legal human rights activists believe that the option of administrative detention must be reserved for the very rare cases in which classified information indicates that the detainee poses a clear and present danger to life and limb, Israeli jurisprudence seems to recognize more marginal and far less direct contributions to security as a basis for justifying its use.

Thus the measure has been justified if the detainee has served in a senior position in an organization defined as a terrorist organization,[24] or on the basis of the detainee's "status" in such a terrorist organization,[25] or on the detainee's "connections" to terrorists.[26] In many cases, the judges provide a general outline of the detainee's actions as they emerge from classified material. They have sometimes revealed that this activity is not necessarily "military" by nature.[27] Perhaps the judges revealed less than they knew in their decisions to avoid specifying detailed allegations given the secrecy of the material, but the sheer number of administrative detainees over the years, along with the fact that Israel considers the civil and political activities of organizations it defines as terrorist to be part of its security mission, tend to support the conjecture that undermining organizations, not just thwarting terrorist attacks, has been approved as grounds for administrative detention.

IN THE PAST few years, Palestinian administrative detainees have increasingly turned to a means of protest practiced by political prisoners around the world: hunger strikes. One reason why detainees have embraced so extreme a measure could be the futility of the legal fight. As I learned early in my career, when I was mostly involved in criminal cases, the law is built on hope. Defendants hope to be acquitted. Appellants hope their conviction will be overturned. Convicts hope to get clemency or early parole. If none of these happen, maybe exculpatory evidence will turn up, maybe there'll be a retrial. Each and every individual has good reason not to break the rules. What do administrative detainees have? All they can do is punch at the wind. Their despair is great; their hopelessness (and that of their lawyers) is absolute.

On December 18, 2011, the day after he was taken into custody, administrative detainee Khader Adnan, in his early thirties and a resident of Araba, went on a hunger strike. It lasted for sixty-six days, a record at the time. His hunger strike drew much media coverage in Israel and abroad and interest in administrative detention altogether. Deep into the strike, Adnan collapsed. He was taken to a hospital, with his life hanging by a thread. The Israeli government blinked. Adnan's lawyers reached an agreement with the military, which undertook not to extend his detention. He ended his strike and was released on April 17, 2012. Adnan's actions inspired other Palestinian administrative detainees to follow suit over the course of 2012.[28] In April of that year, 1,600 Palestinian prisoners declared a general hunger strike. A month later, a prisoner delegation reached agreement with the authorities, and a gradual decline began in the number of administrative detainees, from 310 in the beginning of the year to 156 in November.[29]*

Since Adnan's detention, hunger strikes have become a common form of protest and resistance. According to Physicians for Human Rights—Israel, between 2012 and 2015 dozens of Palestinians went on a hunger strike. Every few months, the fear grows in both Palestine and Israel that a hunger striker will suffer irreparable damage or die. As soon as a hunger striker has to be hospitalized, his or her lawyer petitions the High Court for the prisoner's release. After all, who can be considered dangerous in such a physical condition? As for the High Court, it found a formula to avoid being implicated in a detainee's death, on the one hand, and avoid the appearance of succumbing to pressure, on the other: "suspending" the detention order, not canceling it. As long as the detainee is frail and hospitalized, he is not legally considered a detainee. Once he recovers, the administrative detention resumes.[30] And if they do not recover? What then?

"We naturally work on the assumption that should the situation become irreversible, heaven forbid, the order shall be revoked immediately, and we shall not say more."[31]

PUNITIVE HOUSE DEMOLITIONS

The judgment in Mahmoud al-Fasfous's case is brief and provides very little information about him. All we know is that in May 1989, when he filed the petition, he was already quite old. We know he lived at home with his son, Taha. We know that Taha had been arrested and confessed to

---

*   Incidentally, Khader Adnan was rearrested after his release and again placed under administrative detention. He went on a second hunger strike, which lasted 55 days and ended with his release. See: Avi Ashkenazi and Avi Issacharof, "After Almost a Year: Khader Adnan, the Hunger-Striking Administrative Detainee Is Released Again," *Walla!*, July 12, 2015.

throwing rocks and Molotov cocktails at cars to stop the passengers from going to work in Israel and to target people he and his friends suspected of collaborating with Israel. We don't know whether anyone was hurt by the son's actions, but had they been it would most likely be mentioned in the judgment. We know that Taha was tried in a military court and that in addition the military commander decided to demolish their home.[32]

Al-Fasfous's lawyer, Muhammad Aweisat, who filed a High Court petition against the demolition, did everything he could. He asked the panel, headed by Supreme Court president Meir Shamgar, to consider his client's age, the fact that he would be left homeless if the demolition order were carried out. He argued that international law prohibits such harm to an elderly man who had done nothing wrong and was not even aware of his son's wrongful actions. Finally, he noted that it was the month of Ramadan, and that this, at the very least, should be taken into account, and that no man (especially an elderly person) should be made homeless during the holidays. Shamgar and his two colleagues, Dov Levin and Yaakov Maltz, rejected al-Fasfous's pleas in two short paragraphs. "Given the proliferation of firebomb throwing, which, by nature, is nothing short of an attempt to kill or injure people by burning them, we have seen no room to intervene in the discretion of the third respondent"— the West Bank military commander—declining also to stay the demolition order until after the holiday.[33]

ISRAEL'S POLICY OF demolishing the family homes of people suspected or accused of attacking IDF soldiers or Israeli citizens has been in place since the occupation began in 1967. A document uncovered by the Akevot research institute indicates that as early as June 13, 1967, just two days after the fighting ended and a week before the military administration was put in place, IDF forces demolished eight homes in the Gaza Strip because people who had laid mines left tracks leading back to those houses.[34] The frequency of the policy's use has fluctuated over the years, and it has twice been abandoned for several years, both times after harsh criticism and doubts about its effectiveness escalated. The policy was renewed, first in a trickle and then in a downpour, in 2015.

Over the years, more than a hundred High Court petitions were filed against demolition orders, all of which were issued pursuant to Regulation 119 of the Mandatory Defense Regulations.[35] This regulation permits not only the forfeiture and demolition of homes belonging to the families of terrorists, but also the forfeiture and destruction of all the houses on the street where the suspect lives, and even, if the military commander so wishes, the entire neighborhood.* The High Court delivered more than a hundred judgments on the issue over the years, but with the exception of five recent cases, in which the court revoked the demolition orders for reasons unrelated to the lawfulness of the measure,[36] all the petitions were rejected.† Thousands of homes have been demolished since 1967. According to figures from Israeli human rights organizations, from the start of the occupation until the beginning of the First Intifada in 1987, the military demolished or sealed more than 1,300 homes pursuant to Regulation 119. Most of the orders were carried out in the dead of night with no real judicial process.[37] During the first four years of the First Intifada, in 1987–1991, Israel demolished some 430 homes and in the first four years of the Second Intifada, 2001–2005, another 660.[38]

Demolishing a home is always a tragedy. Imagine a bulldozer tearing your house apart. Whatever you managed to save from its iron claws is scattered on the ground where your refuge once stood. Imagine your life after the place where your very core was housed—where you realized yourself and your family, personally, and privately—is nothing but rubble. Each home demolition leaves utterly innocent children, the elderly, men, and women on the streets, ruined and shamed. The house demolition policy has inflicted dreadful pain on thousands of Palestinians, many of them

---

*   The regulation reads (emphasis added): "A Military Commander may by order direct the forfeiture to the Government of Palestine of any house, structure, or land from which he has reason to suspect that any firearm has been illegally discharged, or any bomb, grenade, or explosive, or incendiary article illegally thrown, or of any house, structure, or land situated in any area, town, village, quarter, or street *the inhabitants or some of the inhabitants of which* he is satisfied have committed, or attempted to commit, or abetted the commission of, or been accessories after the fact to the commission of, any offence against these Regulations involving violence or intimidation or any Military Court offence; and when any house, structure or land is forfeited as aforesaid, the Military Commander may destroy the house or the structure or anything on growing on the land."

†   There was, in fact, one exception in 1993, when a panel headed by Aharon Barak revoked a demolition order and replaced it with a partial sealing of the house given that a mother and seven sisters lived in the assailant's home. The court ruled in that case, that though the military commander did have the power to order the house demolished, discretion requires a less drastic, more proportionate measure. HCJ 5510/92, *Turqman v. Minister of Defense*, IsrSC 48 (1): 217.

young, who watched as the home their parents built was destroyed within minutes. That pain turned of course to anger and hatred. Israel has come under scathing criticism for using this policy. The position that house demolitions are unlawful and constitute a violation of international law enjoys broad consensus among Israeli and international jurists. Israel's abandonment of Regulation 119 twice is partly the result of the severity of the criticism leveled at the policy and the damage its use caused to the country's reputation,* but the state always returned to it when the security situation became more volatile.

Israel says the policy is predicated on the need to deter people from committing acts of violence. It is not punishment of family members, state counsel has told the High Court time and time again. It is a tool for fighting potential terrorists. Anyone thinking of harming Israelis needs to know that their family will be thrown out on the street and their home demolished. We have information, counsel added in several cases, showing that even people who are willing to die to hurt Israelis fear what will happen to their families after their death. It is a deterrent and it is effective.

Demolishing the family homes of suspected or convicted offenders (demolition is carried out even prior to a conviction, based on alleged evidence)—even if the offense is horrific—is a crime. It is a clear case of collective punishment of men, women, and children for another's actions, usually a family member, and is therefore an immoral and unlawful act every legal system must reject as part of its fundamental principles. When

---

* The policy was halted between 1998 and 2001 and again between 2005 and 2008. In late 2004 and early 2005 a committee headed by Maj. Gen. Ehud Shani examined the efficacy of house demolitions as a counterterrorism tool. When it completed its mission, the committee recommended a moratorium. Then Chief of the General Staff Moshe Ya'alon adopted the committee's recommendation, with a caveat that the military may depart from this new policy in "extreme cases." A presentation of the committee's recommendations that was provided to HaMoked states that while "the house demolition tool is part of the (small) toolbox the IDF has for fighting terrorism," its negative effects, such as reinforcing the collective Palestinian national identity, the fact that house demolition is considered collective punishment which does not conform to the principle of human dignity and private property, and contradicts liberal value, in fact reinforces the Palestinian refugee trauma, enhances the "occupation corrupts" argument, and creates an unbridgeable gap. The presentation ends with an unequivocal statement: "The IDF, in a Jewish, democratic state, cannot walk the line of legality, let alone the line of legitimacy!!! [sic]."

house demolitions occur in occupied territory, they also violate the prohibition against harming the property of protected persons stipulated in international law.[39] The only exception to this prohibition is destruction that occurs in the course of combat as a military necessity, which has no relevance to Israel's policy.[40] Any demolition in occupied territory that is not covered by this exclusion[41] is unlawful as a violation of the full protection of private property. Thus the policy is illegal first and foremost due to its violation of this principle.

But the chief moral and legal difficulty with the policy is of course the punishment of innocents. Punishing people who are not guilty is an absolute evil under any theory of justice (and any legal system) built on humanistic values that sanctifies the individual and seeks to protect individual rights and freedoms. Incidental harm to innocents is not an absolute evil. Both morality and law tolerate it in certain situations, and this is essentially Israel's line of defense. Family members are incidental victims, the state says. Our fight is not with them. We wish to effect deterrence. But the question of what constitutes incidental harm or punishment of innocents rests on the issue of purpose. If the purpose is to harm the guilty party, the person responsible for the prohibited act, and the harm to others is collateral, an undesirable side effect, then the injury is indeed incidental. If the harm to innocent parties is a desired purpose, the goal of the act, then it is a punishment.

We have to distinguish between purpose and motivation. Whatever the motive is for punishing innocents, the purpose of causing them harm is wrong. For the sake of argument, let's accept Israel's claim that its motive for demolishing the homes of suspected assailants is to deter future assailants. The method it has chosen for such deterrence is to harm innocents. Therefore, these innocents are not incidental victims. They weren't hurt by shrapnel from a missile aimed at some other target. They *are* the targets. Their suffering is a means for achieving the goal of deterrence, and they were selected from a variety of potential victims because of their relation to someone suspected of engaging in terrorism. It follows that they are being punished for that person's actions. This is a classic case of punishing the innocent. Incidentally, as any student of criminal law knows, one explicit purpose of punishment is deterrence; so even if we accept the motivation of deterrence for demolishing the homes of families of suspected terrorists, that does not rule out characterizing the practice as punishment. And since it is punishment for another's actions, it is also collective punishment.

IN THE EARLY years of the occupation, the use of Regulation 119 to demolish or seal houses of suspected or convicted security offenders was carried out with no judicial oversight. Once again, it took the illustrious Felicia Langer and Leah Tsemel to come up with the idea of challenging the orders to demolish homes in the High Court of Justice, in much the same way they had challenged deportation for security reasons (Regulation 112). Since in the 1970s the duty to give people affected by the order advance notice and the right to a hearing had not been institutionalized, house demolitions, like deportations, were carried out without warning and with no time to challenge the order. So the two lawyers began filing pre-emptive petitions on behalf of clients who had reason to fear that the military planned to demolish their homes. The petitions were speculative, but they did at least help clarify the situation: as part of the state's response, the families would finally receive official notification regarding the military's plan to demolish the home.

The first judgment on the legality of the practice was given in 1979 (my description is generous, since just a single paragraph was devoted to the question of its lawfulness).[42] Tsemel represented two clients from the Ramallah area. In one of the cases, the military said it had no plans to damage the client's home. In the other, the military confirmed that an order had been issued to seal off one room in the house in response to actions by the petitioner's son. The son had been convicted by a military court of membership in an unlawful association (Fatah) and of sheltering a fugitive who had placed a bomb in Jerusalem. He was sentenced to five years in prison. Tsemel argued that damaging the home is prohibited given the Fourth Geneva Convention prohibition on collective punishment[43] and interference with the private property of residents of occupied territory.[44] In the single paragraph that addressed these arguments—which then formed the core of Israel's legal justification for its punitive house demolition policy—court president Shamgar dismissed the attempt to ban the use of Regulation 119. Whether the Geneva Convention applies or not, Shamgar explained, the Defense Regulations that constitute West Bank law predate the occupation and therefore continue to apply regardless of any possible violation of Convention prohibitions. In fact, Shamgar ruled, the laws of occupation require the occupier to respect the laws in force prior to the occupation.[45] Essentially, Shamgar had avoided answering whether house demolitions constituted collective punishment or prohibited destruction of private property by ruling that the law predating the occupation is impervious to international law. Shamgar repeated this position in another judgment, in 1987.[46]

The judgments issued in subsequent years in petitions that sought to revoke house demolition orders all avoided legal questions of merit, often referencing those earlier rulings. Research shows that despite scores of judgments upholding the practice (one study counted more than one hundred High Court rulings),[47] only the first two addressed the charge of violating international law, and here too in just a few paragraphs. In the past three decades, the court refused to deliberate on the main legal argument that Regulation 119 violates the provisions of a higher normative order, rooted as they are in international law. The High Court's rulings focused on other issues, such as the proportionality of the demolitions (for example, whether it is right to demolish the entire home, or should the destruction be limited to one floor only or sealing a room); the family's right to a hearing prior to the demolition and what that entails; and the application of the policy to the homes of suicide bombers (the court approved[48]).

When it comes to the basic questions of legality—that demolitions constitute collective punishment and violate the prohibition against destroying the property of protected persons—the rulings have been recursive, referring to earlier judgments, which themselves refer back to the argument[49] that Regulation 119 predates the occupation and is therefore not affected by the laws of occupation. From a legal standpoint, this argument is extremely weak: first, international law trumps local law, certainly in a regime of occupation that draws its power from international law; second, the laws of occupation confirm that local laws need not be obeyed if they contradict international law.[50] Yet at the same time, the court reinforced the interpretation of home demolitions as deviating from the principle of personal responsibility, thus strengthening its character as a collective punishment. The justices repeatedly, explicitly (and bluntly) asserted that the family's lack of involvement in or even knowledge of their relative's actions was immaterial. "Considerations of deterrence sometimes require, according to case law, the deterrence of potential perpetrators, who must understand that their actions might harm the property of their loved ones, even when there is no evidence family members were aware of the terrorist's actions," wrote Justice Hanan Melcer.[51]

The only one to break ranks was Mishael Cheshin, the tempestuous independent thinker, who, in a long line of incisive, conscientious judgments, dissented in rulings that sanctioned house demolitions because he deemed them collective punishment.[52] But he, too, ultimately toed the line. When another independent-minded justice, Dalia Dorner, suddenly joined his dissent, for the first time paving the way for a majority to revoke a demolition order, Cheshin got cold feet. "Even as the trumpets of war sound, the rule of the law shall make its voice heard," he wrote in one of the most famous passages in Israeli jurisprudence—and, in my view, one of the saddest. "But let us admit a truth: in such places its sound is like that of the piccolo, clear and pure, but drowned out in the din."[53]

HUMAN RIGHTS ORGANIZATIONS and lawyers representing the families affected by the policy did not give up. Most worked for HaMoked, which devoted a lot of effort into ensuring that no demolition order was executed without a hearing and a High Court petition. Felicia Langer, Leah Tsemel, Andre Rosenthal, Dan Yakir—joined in recent years by attorneys Gaby Lasky, Smadar Ben Natan, Yossi Wolfson, and Labib Habib—kept taking swipes at the seemingly immovable Regulation 119. This massive litigation activity managed to push the High Court to set some limits on the policy over the years.

Justices who addressed the issue found themselves on the horns of a very serious dilemma. They seemed to fully understand that they were sanctioning an act their judicial instinct told them was an outrage, but they feared being perceived as an impediment to counterterrorism. In their judgments, some gave voice to this dilemma and to the emotional disquiet that came with it.[54] They explained that if the policy saved lives, as the security establishment believed, how could they prohibit it? Elyakim Rubinstein, for instance, wrote: "Before us is a *hope* for deterrence that would save human lives, versus injury, although painful, to property."[55] When the possibility of saving life (even just the belief or hope of it) was pitted against the violation of rights entailed in house demolitions, life always won, despite the moral offense of using people as a means to an end and despite the slippery slope of harming innocents.

So the justices tried to limit the policy rather than abolish it. They ruled, for example, that the policy could only be used in response to the worst of acts, meaning killing. This was important because before this ruling, the military demolished the homes of people implicated in far lighter offenses.[56] They also ruled that any demolition must be proportionate to the number of individuals harmed, and that the military must consider partial demolition or sealing a section of the house as alternatives.[57] These important restrictions helped reduce the range of cases to which demolitions applied.

In 2004, a tribunal headed by President Aharon Barak hinted that the judges were, for the first time, considering intervening in the policy and could even rule that it was illegal. This came in response to a petition filed by Andre Rosenthal from HaMoked on behalf of the family of a Palestinian who had carried out a suicide attack in a Jerusalem cafe, killing seven and injuring many others. Hundreds of homes had been demolished in the preceding years and pressure on the judges to intervene had accumulated. According to Rosenthal, the justices (including Mishael Cheshin and Esther Hayut) were extremely critical of the state's position, with Barak adding that the court was seriously considering not upholding the demolition order.[58] After the hearing, the IDF formed a committee to rethink the use of house demolitions, and eventually recommended freezing the policy. As a result of the freeze, the judges declined to rule on the general legality of demolitions and stated that the petitioners in Rosenthal's case had received the remedy they sought.[59] The freeze lasted for three years, until 2008, when the policy was renewed. Of the tribunal's stark criticism there is no record, except in the memories of those who were in the courtroom.

Time after time, the court evaded arguments addressing the policy's overall legality, claiming that "all arguments raised . . . have already been discussed and decided by this court in previous judgments."[60] Tracing these claims back to the relevant judgments that had purportedly "discussed and decided" the issue leads us to the meager rulings of 1979 and 1987. The sole contribution that later judgments made to the question of legality was to accept—mostly rhetorically—the argument that demolitions were not punitive as their goal was deterrence. Judgments increasingly tossed this assertion into the air as a sort of knee-jerk defense against the claim that the justices were giving their approval to collective punishment, but they provided no elaboration. Not a single judge took the trouble to consider the distinction between punishment and deterrence. The rote assertion reads like heckling from the stands: "It's not punishment, it's deterrence!" And without deliberation or reasoning, the cumulative effect of inserting these claims into judgments had its own power. It is what allowed Supreme Court president Miriam Naor to pronounce categorically in the mid-2010s, "It has been held in case law that the purpose of house demolitions is not to punish but rather to deter."[61] In what case law? Where was the question discussed? The fact is that in his original judgment, Shamgar was ambivalent, characterizing the power to demolish homes as "a punitive act whose purpose is deterrence."[62]

IN NOVEMBER 2014, I took part in the most ambitious attempt to force the High Court of Justice to reckon with the two fundamental questions regarding the policy's legality. I filed a public petition[63] on behalf of eight human rights organizations led by HaMoked, which has represented most of the families facing demolition orders in the past twenty years. We argued extensively that the time had come to address whether the policy constitutes prohibited collective punishment.[64] The petition was filed as another wave of violence washed over the area. The abduction and murder of three Israeli teenagers had led to intensive military operations in the West Bank. Another war, worse than its predecessors, was being fought in the Gaza Strip, which was savaged from the air. Young Palestinians were stabbing Jews on the streets of Israel. House demolitions, which had been on the wane, were once again pulled out of the toolbox in a Pavlovian reaction by Israel's security establishment. One home was demolished after another. Entire families were left homeless. Given the huge body of jurisprudence approving the practice over the years, we concluded that it was time to challenge the court's staunch refusal to consider the legal arguments.

We decided to file a petition of principle rather than one that addressed a specific demolition, because we believed that one of the reasons the court had trouble diving into the issue was the fact that demolition cases have to be decided very quickly. Once it issues a demolition order, the security establishment pushes to end deliberations on questions of legality to carry out the order. As in the fight against torture, the pace of individual cases impedes a thorough review of the legal issues. So we decided to grant the court the time it needed by filing a petition in which the remedy sought was declarative rather than concrete.

Our petition was filed together with an unusual expert opinion provided by four Israeli law professors,[65] all of them specialists in international law, who expressed a clear position that the policy is not only illegal, but in some circumstances it could amount to a war crime; under certain conditions, it could even invoke the jurisdiction of the International Criminal Court.

In a hearing in early December 2014, I argued before a panel whose members—every one of them—had approved house demolitions in the past: Deputy President Elyakim Rubinstein, Esther Hayut, and Noam Sohlberg. In a judgment issued several months earlier, Sohlberg, a resident of the settlement of Alon Shvut who was appointed to the Supreme Court under pressure from the country's right wing and became the first settler to serve in Israel's highest judicial instance, wrote a sentence that stuck with me: "Indeed, injuring a family member—who committed no sin—in a manner that causes him to remain without a roof over his head, contrary to fundamental principles, is troublesome. But this should be well remembered, in criminal proceedings the purpose of which is punitive—as distinct from the purpose of deterrence herein—innocent family members are injured as well. The imprisonment of a person for a criminal offense he committed inevitably harms his spouse, children and other relatives, both physically and mentally."[66]

As the hearing began, I decided to respond to the analogy Sohlberg had drawn between the two kinds of harm—that suffered by a family who loses their home because of the actions or suspected actions of a family members and that of a family whose relative is imprisoned. I opened, however, by stating that three decades of jurisprudence in hundreds of High Court petitions had failed to grapple with the fundamental arguments against house demolitions. The time had come to take that bull by the horns. I raised the concern that the gap between the position of the Supreme Court and that of the academic legal community was intolerable, especially since it was unexplored. I referred to the professors' position that the policy might constitute a war crime, and even challenged state counsel, Yochi Genessin and Aner Helman, to cite one judgment, of the scores handed down in the almost four decades of jurisprudence on the subject, that truly addressed the question of collective punishment and whether house demolitions also violates the prohibition on destroying the property of the occupied.

On the merits, I explained that punishment and deterrence are not mutually exclusive: a punitive act can be motivated by deterrence and a policy whose purpose is deterrence can depend on a means that harms innocents. Then I reminded Justice Sohlberg of his analogy to the harm caused to children whose father is incarcerated. "With due respect," I said, "the analogy is wrong. The children are indirect victims of the incarceration. When their house is demolished, they are direct victims. The correct analogy would be sending the children to prison for the actions of their father. Would that not cause deterrence?" Sohlberg did not reply. His response came in the judgment.

THE RULING WAS delivered on the last day of 2014. The justices refused to discuss the questions we posed. The panel decided there was no reason to revisit the legal questions, citing as grounds that two judgments delivered several months earlier had addressed them.[67] Except that those two judgments, like the scores of judgments before them, did not in any way address the arguments regarding violating the prohibition on collective punishment and the destruction of property of the occupied. In fact in those specific cases, the State Attorney's Office had pleaded with the justices not to address these questions because they had already been decided. When? Back we go through the spiral of self-referencing judgments, all the way to the 1970s.

Justice Hayut added another reason for her refusal to break with jurisprudence, one that has oft been repeated in subsequent judgments. Though she admitted that the "issues raised in the petition are difficult and troubling," and though "toeing the line of case law on this issue is not easy," she could not "agree" to revisit the legality of the subject "without turning this court of justice into a court of justices."[68] Justice Hayut was alluding to the danger that despite the existence of clear case law, each justice would reach their own decision, undermining the unified voice of the institution to which they belonged. This position is an expression of a thesis of "narrow personal discretion,"[69] as I called it. The thesis is that the personal position of a justice is subordinate to previous rulings by the court, but it has two weaknesses. First, the Supreme Court is not bound by its own precedent and a justice sitting on the panel has no collegial duty toward the other justices presiding on the same panel or to previous panels. Instead the justice may—indeed must, if her conscience so demands—dissent. Second, bowing down to previous judgments is a self-fulfilling prophecy that creates the mirage of a broad, unified body of jurisprudence.

This result is most poignantly seen in the case of house demolitions: the argument that the court has an "authoritative voice" on the issue is deceptive because it is based on an accumulation of judgments that, as noted, never addressed the arguments against the policy on their merits. Still, following Hayut's statements, judgments related to Regulation 119 were marked by an odd rule of loyalty to the supposed collective voice of the court. Many justices reviewing challenges to the legality of the power to demolish homes echoed Hayut's statement.[70] What has happened here? Has the Supreme Court adopted a new legal precept that requires its justices to be bound by the rulings of their predecessors? No: the justices who choose only to defer to those who came before them are seeking to avoid the burden of moral responsibility for approving collective punishment. They are looking for a principle that will compel them to dismiss the petitions.

Self-diminution and pinning responsibility on a higher norm is a known phenomenon in studies of cognitive dissonance among judges who are asked to cooperate with actions they oppose and choose to do so.[71] Judges who are caught in such dilemmas are in effect saying, "Everyone has ruled this way, and I am bound by that." They are giving their approval of collective punishment and taking cover in collective responsibility. They reach back to their predecessors—Shamgar, Levin, and Barak—seeking to diminish their own responsibility. "Come, collective responsibility," the justice whispers, "shelter me under your wing." Do none of them remember that moral responsibility is not divided because others share in the injustice? Moral responsibility only ever multiplies by the number of accomplices.

And Sohlberg? Sohlberg was the only judge on the panel who dared confront the outrage, even if just for a fleeting moment. He continued to deny that house demolitions were punitive but admitted that deterrence "necessarily involves harm to innocent people. Otherwise, how shall deterrence of suicide bombings and the like be achieved? . . . even at the cost of injuring family members of the terrorists." In response to our argument that Jewish religious law also prohibits collective punishment, Justice Sohlberg added the following: "The rule that 'every man shall be put to death for his own sin' is neither the most important nor an isolated rule, contrary to the petitioners' position that it is the last word. A distinction must be made between collective physical punishment and impingement on property."[72] I took this as an indication that deep down, Sohlberg agreed that house demolitions were collective punishment. But he thought they were necessary.

THE PANEL DISMISSED the petition and the president of the Supreme Court dismissed a motion we filed for a further hearing before an extended panel,[73] so it seemed as though we were back where we started. It looked as if we were facing a future of petitions unanimously dismissed because the court had to toe the line of case law.

We were wrong.

It began with Justice Uzi Vogelman, a judge on the liberal end of the court's spectrum, who in October 2015 heard a case involving the impending demolition of family homes of people who had murdered Dalia Lamkus, a twenty-six-year-old Jewish woman from the settlement of Tekoa. In his judgment, Vogelman strongly opposed using the power to demolish homes in cases where there was no evidence of family involvement in the act that prompted the demolition order. His position was predicated on the disproportionality of the measure, but Vogelman clarified that as long as case law had not changed, he remained bound by it.[74] In a dissenting opinion, he thought that the order should be revoked in this specific case because it was issued a long time after the murder and only after other violent incidents occurred, which indicated that the family would be paying for more than just the crimes of one of its own.

A month after this, for the first time since Justice Cheshin's judgments in the 1990s, a dissenting voice in the High Court denied the very legality of Regulation 119's power to order house demolitions. Menachem Mazuz, who served as attorney general from 2004 to 2010, was appointed to the Supreme Court in 2014, just as we filed the NGO's principled public-interest petition. The youngest justice on the bench had dared challenge the line of case law—and in the first house demolition case he participated. Mazuz referred to the arguments regarding violations of international law as "weighty." He bemoaned the fact that discussion of these arguments in prior case law had not been "exhaustive," "thorough," or "sufficiently comprehensive" and claimed they were worthy of "thorough examination."[75] In a dissenting opinion, he proposed revoking the demolition order.

In his next house demolition case, Mazuz's criticism was harsher:

> The conscious and deliberate infliction of harm on innocent people, and even more so, the severe violation of their constitutional rights, only for other potential perpetrators "to see and beware," would be inconceivable conduct in any other context. The consideration of deterring others is indeed recognized as one of the punitive principles in criminal law, but it is applied only against a convicted offender rather than against an innocent third party. . . . In my opinion, a sanction that is intended to harm innocent people cannot stand, whether we define the flaw as a violation of a right, a case of exceeding authority, unreasonableness or disproportionality.[76]

Mazuz's position that the use of Regulation 119 should be revisited, perhaps even by an extended panel, was supported within a few weeks by Justice Vogelman, with Justices Salim Joubran, Dafna Barak-Erez, and Anat Baron following suit. The justices carried out the conversation through their judgments, and since a large number of demolition orders were issued within a short period of time, the conversation was lively. Two more justices, Esther Hayut and Zvi Zylbertal, also expressed ambivalence about the merits of the regulation. Both clarified that they must approve use of the regulation as long as case law remained unchanged, but expressed misgivings about the existing case law. Within a few months, seven justices—almost half of those on the Supreme Court—indicated their sense that the case law warranted reexamination. Given their professed commitment to case law, this could only be done under the auspices of an extended panel.

Yet Supreme Court president Miriam Naor, the judge with the authority to convene an extended panel hearing, was staunchly opposed. It was Naor who had blocked our attempts in HaMoked cases to have them heard by extended panels or to have decisions brought for review by larger panels.[77] "I have not been convinced," she wrote in one decision, "that case law is currently so unstable as to justify an extended panel." One reason Naor gave for her refusal was that extending the panel would require putting other cases on hold pending the panel's decision, which in her view presented a great difficulty. Yet she also appears to have been concerned by the possible outcome of an extended panel hearing. Given the positions expressed by the justices, an extended panel would be likely to at least narrow the interpretation of the power to demolish homes. The political pressure on the court was already intense, and each interim order temporarily staying a demolition brought vicious attacks from right-wing politicians.[78] Things got so bad that Justice Vogelman was given security guards.[79]

But the winds of change were blowing. For the first time since Israel began demolishing homes in retaliation for terrorism in 1967, for the first time in the great many petitions to have come to the High Court, there were panel formations that yielded a majority in favor of revoking the orders.[80] In November 2015, the High Court accepted a petition to revoke a demolition order because it turned out that the home in question was owned by someone other than the family of a man implicated in a terrorist attack in which a civilian was killed.[81] The family lived in the house under an annual lease.[82] President Naor ruled that harming non-family members fails to produce the required deterrence and ordered the revocation of the demolition order, on condition, however, that the landlord evict the suspected terrorist's family.

Then in December of that year, Justices Mazuz and Zylbertal formed a majority that revoked an order issued eleven months after the incident that prompted it, due to the delay.[83] In March 2016, Mazuz and Baron outnumbered President Naor to revoke a demolition order issued for the home of a young man who stabbed and killed two Israelis in Jerusalem. The two justices ruled that the fact that the young man did not live in his parents' home and only visited it precluded use of Regulation 119.[84] In April 2016, a panel comprised of Hayut, Vogelman, and Zylbertal struck down three out of four orders to seal the homes of young men who had thrown rocks at passing cars, resulting in the death of a driver. The justices ruled that since the three had not thrown the rock that caused the death and their responsibility for the outcome came down to being present at the scene and aiding their friend, sealing their apartments, with the resulting forced eviction of their families, would be disproportionate.[85] Finally, in September 2016, a panel comprised of Yoram Danziger, Zylbertal, and Baron revoked a demolition order in a case where the evidence against the suspect in a shooting murder was not sufficiently definitive.[86]

While the military orders were revoked in all these cases, none was struck down in response to the argument that demolishing family homes is unacceptable collective punishment. The justices accepted ancillary arguments that limited the policy but they did not outlaw it. In eight more cases heard between mid-2015 and mid-2016, the demolitions were upheld, but the judgment included a dissenting opinion calling for its revocation.[87] In the space of two years, the military demolished or sealed a total of thirty-nine homes belonging to families of Palestinians suspected of terrorism.[88]

FOR A LONG time, the legal fight against punitive house demolitions seemed to be going nowhere; the human rights community appeared to be defeated. Lawyers asked themselves whether they were in the end only augmenting the terrible body of case law by filing petitions when they knew these would be rejected; whether we weren't sinking deeper into the mud. The lawyers who were part of this fight were sorely disappointed. "House demolitions are collective punishment, period," says Dan Yakir.[89] "Which is why the frustration over the High Court's rules was especially intense and the motivation to try and reverse them particularly high." House demolitions violate the fundamental principle of personal responsibility, which the legal system holds sacred—at least in every other context. The court's refusal to address this violation severely undermined the faith of legal activists in the highest judicial institute. "House demolitions are our collective open wound," Yakir concludes. Still, within one year, High Court panels revoked seven demolition or sealing orders, something that had not happened in the preceding thirty-six years of house demolition hearings.

Those judgments were due, at least in part, to HaMoked's determination and that of the lawyers who took cases on its behalf and fanned the embers of the cause, even when they seemed to have gone cold; to the existence of an international legal consensus on which they could rely; to the Israeli professors' willingness to speak out; and especially to their strong, compelling appeal to morality. All these factors cumulatively fostered internal opposition inside the court. Thus far, this is only dissent, and it has focused on limiting the policy. Its existence will likely reinforce a trend to reduce the use of house demolitions rather than eliminate them. Still, this is no small development. Judicial opposition is extremely important because it has the potential to become a majority. Until then, it provides a crucial alternative viewpoint. The fight to remove collective punishment from Israel's toolbox is in critical condition, but there is life in it yet. We have not yet heard the final word.

ASSASSINATIONS

On November 9, 2000, shortly after the start of the Second Intifada, a helicopter flew over the Palestinian town of Beit Sahur, near Bethlehem. Just before noon, the helicopter decreased altitude and fired a missile toward a jeep driving on one of the town's busy streets. The missile killed Hussein Abayat, an activist in Tanzeem, a military wing of Fatah, which Israel alleged was responsible for shootings in Gilo, a nearby settlement. Two women standing nearby, Aziza Danoun Joubran, age fifty-eight, and Rama Rashin Hindi, age fifty-four, were also killed in the missile attack. Abayat's assistant, who was with him in the jeep, and two other passersby were injured.[90] The next day, Prime Minister Ehud Barak said, referring to the attack on Abayat: "This . . . sets a new standard for action. Anyone who hurts us gets hurt."[91]

Abayat's assassination was the starting gun (a rare opportunity to use the expression literally) for Israel's official policy of extrajudicial executions. In English, the commonly used euphemism is "targeted killings." The Hebrew term used by the military and government is even more insidious. It translates literally as "targeted thwarting" or "targeted pre-emptions."

According to B'Tselem, from the beginning of the Second Intifada to Operation Cast Lead in Gaza in 2008—over the course of seven years— 384 Palestinians were killed in "targeted killings"; 232 were the people targeted while 152 were incidental bystanders.[92] Hundreds more were hurt, sustaining injuries that cause lifelong disability and suffering. Israel might not be the first country to assassinate its opponents, but it is the first to openly and officially undertake a policy of assassinations.

What is wrong with the policy should be self-evident, but after years of dealing with the subject, I've learned that even people who consider themselves humanists need to be convinced that "killing terrorists" is problematic.

The first problem is that killing a person deliberately is murder. Modern law recognizes a very small number of instances in which intentional killing is not considered murder. Self-defense and necessity provide a defense in cases where lethal force is immediately required to deflect an attack or another life-threatening situation.[93] The laws of war allow combatants to kill enemy combatants during armed conflict. These exceptions to the prohibition against taking human life are shared across legal systems. Other permitted killings are more debatable, and some are sources of bitter controversy: capital punishment (international human rights law takes quite an antagonistic approach, severely limiting capital punishment and pushing for its abolition); assisted dying; and abortion (which centers on the dispute over the start of life).

Killing suspected terrorists does not fall under any of these categories. Self-defense and necessity do not apply, since the killings do not necessarily take place in circumstances of an attack or immediate danger (in fact, the entire point of these assassinations is to strike the individuals outside of combat) and the targets are not combatants (more on that to follow). It appears that this is, in effect, a policy of extrajudicial execution, or, in other words, murder.

The second issue relates to the decision-making process. The list of targets is compiled in secret by the Shabak. The Shabak determines the level of suspicion that justifies death and the kind of evidence required to confirm the suspicion. Were the targets arrested and prosecuted, proving their guilt would require admissible evidence and judges to be convinced by it. Executions are carried out without any external oversight, not even the military judges' weak, perfunctory oversight of administrative detention orders. So in terms of evidence and procedure, it is easier for the military to decide to kill suspects than to prosecute them or even place them in administrative detention.

There is no better illustration of the gravity of this situation than the case of Hamas activist Abd al-Rahman Hamed. Throughout the 1990s, Hamed was held in administrative detention in various prisons. During his incarceration at Megiddo Prison, he was accused, along with two others, of murdering a fourth prisoner they suspected of collaborating with the authorities. Avigdor Feldman represented one of the accomplices, who was convicted by the district court and sentenced to life in prison. During the appeal, it turned out that the prosecution had failed to disclose valuable investigative material. This seemed to indicate that the main witness for the prosecution, who testified in exchange for his release, had likely perjured himself.[94] Hamed was acquitted of the murder charge by the Supreme Court, which also ordered his release after six years of incarceration as an administrative detainee and a convicted prisoner.

Less than a year after his release, on October 14, 2001, Hamed was reading the Quran on the roof of his home in Qalqiliyah when he was shot at close range by IDF soldiers. He was killed instantly. The Prime Minister's Office announced that it had evidence of Hamed's involvement in planning a deadly terrorist attack at the Dolphinarium nightclub in Tel Aviv several months earlier, in which twenty-one young Israelis were murdered. This alleged evidence was never made public.

Israel considered Hamed a dangerous Hamas activist, which is why he was apprehended in the first place. There was not enough admissible evidence to put him on trial for any specific offense, so he was placed under administrative detention, which was extended every few months, subject to some measure of judicial review. Israel then accused him of murdering a collaborator, a charge that turned out to be based on incomplete evidence, and convicted him by failing to disclose relevant documents to the defense. When he was acquitted by the Supreme Court and released, the IDF simply took him out. No shred of evidence was put before any sort of judicial body or the public, and none was required.

The third problem with the policy of "targeted killing" is that it is clearly anything but targeted. As the B'Tselem figures show, dozens of innocent bystanders are killed in these operations ("uninvolved individuals," according to the military), and hundreds more are injured. In fact, 40 percent of those who died as a result of this policy until 2008 were bystanders. To avoid exposing soldiers to the risk of approaching the targets closely, the IDF usually carries out the assassinations by firing missiles from aircraft. It seldom uses other more accurate methods, such as sniper rifles.

The arguments against the policy are, therefore, its fundamental illegality; the harm to innocent people; and the lack of safeguards, such as proof and oversight, to avoid harming those who are not involved in terrorism. If these arguments have merit, the policy is not just a breach of the laws of war, which prohibit deliberate harm to civilians; it is also a war crime.

In late 2001, when the executions intensified, I published an op-ed arguing that the policy was a violation of the laws of war, and that one day an Israeli officer might find himself facing the international criminal court in The Hague. After the article was published, Hannah Friedman, founder and director of the Public Committee Against Torture in Israel, asked me to author a report about the assassination policy. The report, written in collaboration with the Palestinian organization al-Qanun (LAW) and Renta Capella, a researcher working for al-Qanun, was published in June 2002.[95] At the same time, Friedman suggested that Avigdor Feldman and I should file a High Court petition against the policy on behalf of PCATI and al-Qanun. Feldman agreed and joined the fight.

ISRAEL'S RATIONALE FOR the assassination policy morphed as soon as the legal advisers came into the picture. Where the previous rhetoric was vindictive ("anyone who hurts us gets hurt"), it became preventive and forward-looking. Now the killings (called "pre-emptions") were not intended as punishment for past actions but as a preventive measure against the targets' future plans. The IDF spokesperson's statements in the past had referred to grievous actions already committed by the target; now they included assertions that the intelligence agencies had information about the target's deep involvement in the planning and execution of future terrorism.

The legal advisers also had to find a way out of the legal quandary posed by the executions. There are two main fields of law that address the state's power to use lethal force against individuals: the laws governing law enforcement and the laws of war.

The laws governing law enforcement address criminality and public disturbances. They allow law enforcement agents to use the force immediately necessary to defuse a public menace posed by a specific individual. However, if a suspect is not caught during the commission of the criminal activity, the extent of the force that may be used against them is only that required for arrest. Clearly these laws cannot supply the legal basis for assassinations by the state. The only killings they permit are those necessary for saving the lives of individuals who are in clear and imminent danger.

Under certain conditions, the laws of war allow the use of force even when the object of an attack poses no immediate danger. Combatants may target enemy combatants when the latter are not engaged in an attack.

However, the laws of war do not allow the use of force against just any-one. They recognize two statuses: civilians and combatants. Combatants are soldiers and officers in a regular army or they might belong to another armed group that meets the following conditions: it has an effective chain of command; its members carry their arms openly and bear insignia iden-tifying them as combatants that is visible from a distance (usually a uni-form); finally, the actions carried out by this armed group comply with the international laws of war. People who belong to such a group and meet these conditions are combatants. All the rest are civilians.[96]

Each status comes with rights and obligations. Civilians may not take part in hostilities; if they do, they may be tried. Civilians are protected from attack. They are not legitimate targets during fighting and enemy combatants may not direct their weapons against them. Combatants, on the other hand, may take part in hostilities; if caught, they are treated as prisoners of war and may not be tried for participating in action as part of the hostilities (unless they have committed war crimes). This right gives combatants license to kill enemy combatants, and not only when they pose immediate danger. Combatants may, for instance, bomb an enemy base even when soldiers there are resting or have no combat role. The combat-ants themselves are also legitimate targets for an enemy attack. This is the principle of distinction—the heart of an arrangement put in place by the modern laws of war. The principle requires a distinction at all times between combatants and civilians and demands that all operations be directed at military objectives, and it is the raison d'être for the laws of war. It is meant to minimize the suffering of civilian populations during armed conflict. The idea, in simple terms, is to leave war to the soldiers.

So are the targets of Israel's assassination policy civilians or combat-ants? If they are civilians, they cannot be targeted. If there is evidence that they took part in fighting Israeli combatants, and surely if they commit-ted acts of terrorism against Israeli civilians, they may be arrested and put on trial. If they are combatants, however, then they cannot be tried for participating in hostilities against the IDF, as that is their right (again, unless they have committed war crimes, such as deliberately attacking civilians). Israel was in no way willing to recognize members of Palestin-ian armed groups as combatants, as this would compel acknowledgment of their right to take part in fighting, and even lend legitimacy to the organ-izations in which they were active. On the other hand, recognizing them as civilians would make the assassination policy unlawful, perhaps even a war crime, as it entailed large-scale deliberate harm to civilians.

The question of how to classify members of armed groups similar to Palestinian militant organizations is obviously not unique to this conflict. It is relevant to many groups all over the world that use violence to advance political goals. Members of these groups see themselves as freedom fighters. To their opponents, they are terrorists. They often claim combatant status, while their opponents reject such claims and treat them as criminals. Prior to Israel's creation, Zionist resistance fighters considered themselves combatants,[97] while the British Mandate authorities viewed them as terrorists, or civilian criminals.

The IDF department of international law came up with a typical solution for an occupying army that also serves as the legislature, which has over many decades grown used to the idea that if the law is inconvenient, the law must be changed. The two statuses recognized in international law—civilian and combatant—were not applicable, so they created a third: "unlawful combatants." Let's take the worst of both options, the IDF's lawyers said to themselves, and come up with a new category of people: they cannot take part in hostilities, not being combatants, and are also a legitimate target for attack, not being civilians. This is a special status for people the IDF defines as terrorists. While the workaround is rather creative, it has nothing to do with international law, which recognizes only two statuses. It is a proposition that undermines the core principle of the laws of war and blurs the lines of a distinction that is meant to be razor sharp. It puts precisely those the laws of war intend to protect, civilians, in danger.

There is another point that merits a closer look: international law does recognize exceptional situations in which civilians are a legitimate target for attack—when they take part in hostilities. However, the window of opportunity for targeting them in such situations is extremely narrow, remaining open only "for such time as they take a direct part in hostilities."[98] Thus a civilian who takes part in the fighting—by, say, shooting at soldiers—may be targeted while he is actively doing so. This exception could reasonably be interpreted as applying also when the civilian takes up arms and engages in a military deployment preceding the launch of an attack in which he will participate.[99] The exception of *direct participation in hostilities* that allows targeting civilians follows the same logic as the concepts reflected in the self-defense and necessity defenses and the laws governing law enforcement. It only applies when these civilians pose a danger. Once they're done with fighting and return home, they may be arrested and tried, but they are no longer legitimate targets for attack. In that sense, they are like criminals who can be subjected to lethal force if they pose a danger to human life, but must be tried for their actions once the danger subsides. This, at least, is how we saw it when we set out to the courts to kill the targeted killings.

IN JANUARY 2002, Feldman and I filed the petition on behalf of PCATI and al-Qanun against Israel's government, the prime minister, the IDF, and the head of the Shabak.[100] In the petition we asked for an order to compel the revocation of the policy and prohibit the respondents from using it. "We are in no way arguing that security forces may not prevent terrorist attacks using painful measures, or even that they must refrain from fatally harming those who set out, armed with a pistol, gun, or explosive belt, to a busy center intending to kill anyone they might encounter," we wrote in the introduction. "What we are addressing is the equally unambiguous issue of what is lawful and permitted when fighting people who are *suspected* of terrorist activity, based on information of one nature or another, but who do not pose a danger *at the moment they are targeted*."

We argued that the targeted killings were in fact a policy of extrajudicial executions and that they were unparalleled in the democratic world. Israel was the first country to adopt an acknowledged policy of assassinations, but the American administration quickly followed suit as part of its war on terror after 9/11. The United States later expanded its policy into a program of assassinations using drones, which is still carried out primarily in Pakistan and Afghanistan. Our legal argument was divided into an analysis of Israeli law, international humanitarian law (the laws of war), and international human rights law. We showed that none of these legal fields offered an exception to the prohibition on murder that could serve as a defense for the policy.

Six months earlier, in July 2001, Naila Attiya, a Palestinian-Israeli lawyer, had filed her own High Court petition to have the assassination policy declared illegal. She represented the chair of the Hadash Party, Knesset Member Muhammad Barakeh. The case was scheduled for a hearing on January 29, 2002, five days after we filed our petition. As the two cases

were very similar, it was obvious the Barakeh hearing was extremely significant for the future of Feldman's and my case, so I went to Jerusalem
to attend it.

What happened there was unusual by any measure. Times were tense.
A bloody year in the Second Intifada had drawn to an end. The Israeli
government touted its assassination policy as one of its main tools to protect civilians from suicide terrorism. This was not a simple starting point
for arguing that assassinations are illegal. And as soon as Attiya began
her oral argument, hostility rained down. The justices interrupted her,
spoke over her, and used unusually sharp language. They put up little resistance against the legal arguments she raised, but they employed a most
caustic, even derisive tone: "There's such a thing called terrorism," presiding Justice Eliyahu Mazza said, in the condescending manner of a first-
grade teacher. "It is the enemy of all humankind, not just Israel." Attiya
tried to argue that targeted killings were extrajudicial executions. The
judges did not like that. Maybe the terrorists should be told of the prohibition on killing innocents, Mishael Cheshin suggested sarcastically. Mazza
added that a moratorium on the policy, as Attiya asked, might cost the
lives of many Israelis.

As much as Attiya tried to steer the justices toward a legal discourse,
they insisted on talking security. Things reached a boiling point when they
asked Attiya to suggest an alternative to the assassinations. The question
was no doubt rhetorical; the judges were probably not expecting an Arab
woman lawyer to venture a suggestion on the Jewish state's security methods. But Attiya answered: instead of executing suspected terrorists, she
said, Israel must arrest and try them. At that, Cheshin's anger erupted.
He turned red, his voice booming. "And who will go into the territories
to make the arrest?" he roared. "Your son, Ms. Attiya? No! My son will
have to put himself in danger!"

All the unwritten rules on the relationship between judge and lawyer
had suddenly been thrown out. Cheshin had expressed his private
concern as the father of a combat soldier as something relevant to his
decision in court. More important, he had made an unprecedented statement, one that could be interpreted as denying Arab citizens of Israel
legitimate participation in the conversation about the limitations of security action because they do not serve in the army. Sitting on a wooden
bench reserved for spectators, I was stunned. My heart sank. I had never

seen such vitriol in court, and I had been to many heated hearings. The convergence of what was going on outside—the armed intifada, the IDF fighting in Palestinian towns and cities, the suicide attacks on the streets—and the accusation of war crimes by an Arab lawyer in Israel's Supreme Court made for an extremely volatile situation, and it ended with an unconventional blast.

The panel, which also included Justice Edmund Levy, promptly dismissed the petition, dictating a single paragraph to the court secretary:

> We have read and heard, extensively, the arguments of counsel for the petitioners. It appears to us that the response filed on behalf of the respondents provides an exhaustive answer to the petitioner's arguments. The selection of combat tools used by the respondents to prevent murderous terrorist attacks is not an issue in which this court sees fit to intervene, all the more so in a petition that lacks any concrete basis and seeks a sweeping remedy.
>
> The petition is denied.[101]

The first hearing in our case was scheduled for April. We had three months to figure out how not to end up like Attiya. We didn't have to think too hard. Feldman and Sfard, both Jews, are not Attiya. Besides, we got a completely different panel, headed by Supreme Court president Aharon Barak, a man with a radically different temperament and worldview from the justices in the Barakeh case.

Barak arrived at the April hearing with a decision he had prepared in advance. He asked the state—which had until then mainly argued that the issue was nonjusticiable and our petition should be dismissed without a hearing on the merits—to provide its position on the normative framework governing the policy, both in terms of international and Israeli law. The decision even referred the state to a list of articles Barak (or his aides) had found and thought relevant. This was a signal that Barak was unfazed by the previous ruling that the issue was nonjusticiable, and he was going to treat our petition with utmost seriousness, as he had in the torture petition.

THE ASSASSINATIONS CASE lasted almost six years. Shai Nitzan, the State Attorney's Office lawyer who represented the state in the torture case and a future state attorney himself, was counsel this time as well. In his initial response, which centered on nonjusticiability and relied partly on the judgment in the Barakeh case, he argued that the court must refrain from telling the military how to fight. But when Aharon Barak demanded a response to our claim that the policy was unlawful, Nitzan's line of defense was the proposition concocted by the IDF international law department, that the targets for assassination were neither civilians nor combatants, but "unlawful combatants," who may be killed but may not take part in hostilities. Should the court decline to recognize this new status, Nitzan had another angle, based on the exception that removes protections from civilians who take part in the hostilities and allows the killing of civilians who engage in terrorism. The state argued that the restrictions set out in international law, namely that civilians may be targeted *only for such time* as they take direct part in hostilities, is not customary and therefore not binding on Israel. "There is no limitation as to the period of time such an attack is permitted," according to the state's summation.[102]

The state delayed filing its written briefs, but we continued to apprise the court of the growing number of people, both targets and bystanders, who were victims of the policy. Assassinations had become daily occurrences and these operations often left a body trail of civilians suspected of nothing. The most serious case occurred three months after our first hearing, in July 2002. An Israeli F-16 fighter jet dropped a one-ton bomb on a residential building in Gaza City in the middle of the night. The target was Salah Shehadeh, the commander of the armed wing of Hamas. Seven apartment buildings were destroyed in this attack and fourteen civilians were killed (in addition to Shehadeh himself and his aide). More than one hundred were wounded.[103] The not-at-all targeted killing of Shehadeh prompted much litigation. Feldman and I represented Yesh Gvul, an organization of conscientious objectors, and a slew of academics and artists who demanded an investigation into the incident and that Major General Dan Halutz, commander of the air force, be denied promotion.[104] The massive death toll in this assassination surely warranted a High Court interim order preventing any further assassinations until adjudication of the policy's legality. But the court dismissed our motion.[105]

The case meandered along. Altogether, the court held four sessions, and there were several rounds of written submissions that increasingly focused on an analysis of the relevant provisions in the international laws of war. We tried to push for a decision and filed numerous motions to schedule hearings, but the state delayed for months, and Barak put the case on the back burner—the place reserved for particularly sensitive rulings that could affect the court's standing in Israel and abroad.

The case generated a lot of interest in the media, among human rights NGOs, and among international law experts the world over. The more other countries appeared to resort to targeted killings, the more interest our case received. After all, it was the first and only case at the time in which a court had been asked to address the legality of killing operatives in organizations that the West had declared as terrorist entities.

In June 2003, a year and a half after filing our petition, we submitted an expert opinion commissioned from Professor Antonio Cassese. The first president of the International Criminal Tribunal for the former Yugoslavia, Cassese had served as a judge on the tribunal for seven years. He was one of the world's foremost authorities on international law, and the combination of his academic and judicial careers, both of which revolved around human rights law and the laws of war, made him an exceptional expert witness. He was also a charming Italian who accepted me warmly in his office at the University of Florence on my first-ever business trip abroad.

In his opinion, Cassese wholly rejected the notion of a third status of "unlawful combatants" and insisted on the importance of the distinction between combatants and civilians. Cassese also addressed an issue that had concerned us, the definition of "direct participation" in hostilities during which civilians may be targeted. Cassese clarified that the term should be interpreted narrowly, referring only to actual combat actions and military deployment preceding the launch of an attack. He indicated that these are actions in which the civilian openly bears arms and can be seen doing so. Therefore, civilians who at one point had been engaged in fighting but had since ceased, as well as people uninvolved in the actual fighting who had played a supporting role (training, teaching, fund-raising, or providing logistical assistance to those about to participate in fighting), are not legitimate targets for attack. They may be arrested and tried but not assassinated.

Then two international organizations of progressive lawyers filed an application to join the petition as amici curiae and present their position on the policy: the American National Lawyers' Guild and the International Association of Democratic Lawyers.[106] In February 2004, another organization, Shurat Hadin—the Israel Law Center, a right-wing group of Jewish lawyers (mostly Israeli and American), asked to be named respondent in the proceeding and argue against the petition. The case had become a microcosm of the international debate between those who viewed assassinations as crimes and those who believed them vital for the war on terror.

The final hearing was held in December 2005. The senior panel, headed by President Barak, alongside Deputy President Mishael Cheshin and future president Dorit Beinisch, heard the arguments and asked relevant questions. The passion and fury of the Barakeh case had vanished.

President Barak was set to retire in September 2006, and his deputy, Cheshin, even earlier. Eliezer Rivlin, the new deputy president, took Barak's place in the assassinations case. The law allows a justice to sign judgments up to three months after retiring. In the months after Barak left the court, his final judgments appeared every few days. December 14, 2006, was the last day of this three-month grace period and of his thirty-year judicial career. On that day Barak issued his judgment on legality of assassination.

THE HIGH COURT of Justice dismissed the petition.[107] This is the bottom line, but it is a bit deceptive, because the panel also threw out the state's argument of a third status that is neither civilian nor combatant.[108] And the court imposed several restrictions on the assassination policy, which it preferred to call "a policy of preventive strikes that cause the death of terrorists." The court also rejected the nonjusticiability argument and ruled that the issue raised in the petition *is* primarily a legal one and that "it is when the cannons roar that we especially need the laws."[109]

The court ruled that the assassination targets were civilians. This determination follows from the fact that the laws of war define civilians negatively, that is, those who are not combatants are necessarily civilians. The targets of the assassinations, people suspected of attacks on Israeli civilians, did not fulfill the conditions for being combatants. They did not have fixed insignia detectable from a distance (such as uniforms); they did not carry weapons openly; and their method of fighting was to target civilians, so it clearly could not be said that they ran their operations in accordance with the laws of war.[110] In light of all this, the people Israel targeted for assassination were not combatants and were not eligible for the privileges combatants have under international law. In fact, they were not permitted to fight at all. They were, however, eligible for the protections afforded to civilians and, therefore they were not legitimate targets for attack, unless and while they threatened other people's lives.

Barak wrote the main opinion in the judgment and his analysis centered on an interpretation of the exception of "taking a direct part in hostilities." The literal text rules that civilians may be targeted "only for such time" as they take part in hostilities and only when participation is "direct." In the range of actions that Barak ruled as "direct," he strayed far from the text's literal meaning, encompassing not only physical attack but also participation in the decision to perpetrate such attacks and planning and providing services for those who carry them out, "be the distance from the battlefield as it may."[111] Barak rejected the logic we and Cassese had offered, whereby the interpretation must be a derivative of the rationale of avoiding harm to innocent civilians, which, therefore, allows targeting only people who take part in the attack itself, rather than people who remain behind the scenes and whose involvement is necessarily a suspicion that requires proof.

Barak gave the phrase "only for such time" a rather broad interpretation as well. Though he rejected the state's position that the time exclusion is not customary law and therefore not binding, he nevertheless referred to attacks as a "chain of hostilities," and suggested viewing them as a continuum throughout which participating civilians are legitimate targets.[112] Civilians involved in a single act of hostility resume their immunity once the act is over. However, if the civilians are activists who repeatedly participate in hostilities, the exemption continues to apply during the intervals between the individual acts, when there is allegedly no participation in hostilities. In his judgment, Barak concluded that we must avoid allowing those participants in hostilities from going in and out of immunity from attack as if in a "revolving door."[113]

This broad view of "direct" participation and "only for such time" creates a category of people who remain civilians but may be targeted. Barak's interpretation departed from the relatively narrow confines of harm permitted due to necessity or self-defense because it allowed harm to members of organizations even when they posed no threat to others. Barak may have rejected the introduction of a third category, but in practice the breadth of his interpretation of "direct" participation did just that. His colleague, Deputy President Rivlin, noticed. He pointed out that Barak's proposed interpretation took the sting out of the obstacle to recognizing a third category, as it "in fact creates a new group, and rightly so."[114]

Still, Barak tried to resolve the difficulties presented by his interpretation, and his solution was a series of restrictions on the assassinations policy. First, information that the target has taken direct part in hostilities must be substantiated and verified. Second, assassinations should not be carried out if the target may be arrested and tried (though significant risk to soldiers' lives may be sufficient reason to choose assassination). Third, strikes that may cause disproportionate harm to bystanders should be avoided. Finally, an assassination must be followed by a thorough and independent examination to make sure the target was not misidentified and that the circumstances of the attack met the necessary evidentiary threshold and the proportionality requirement (otherwise, compensation for harm caused to innocent civilians should be considered).[115]

The panel led by Barak delivered an outcome that rendered the policy neither definitively legal nor illegal: "It has, therefore, been decided, that no determination should be made in advance that every targeted killing is prohibited according to customary international law, much as no determination should be made that every targeted killing is permitted according to customary international law. The laws governing targeted killings are stipulated in customary international law and the legality of any individual strike must be determined in their light."[116]

WHEN THE JUDGMENT was issued, the petitioners' camp felt a sense of loss. We had asked the court to prohibit the use of a policy we believed illegal through and through, a policy that was dangerous and caused massive loss of life, and we did not get what we asked for. In addition, the rejection of the argument regarding a third status was watered down by the broad interpretation of direct participation. The IDF and the Shabak were free to continue executing people who did not pose an immediate threat to life. The decision regarding whom to assassinate would still be made in secret, and the slippery slope inherent in the policy would only put more civilians at risk. A bitter defeat.

It took quite some time before our feeling of colossal defeat began to change. An analysis of the assassination numbers in the years after the judgment suggests that the court's restrictions on the policy did have a mitigating effect. According to B'Tselem, fatalities during assassinations dropped dramatically in the two years following the ruling, from forty-six in 2006 (twenty-two of them targets) to twenty-three in 2007 (fourteen of them targets) and fourteen in 2008 (eight of them targets).[117] The drop in the number of targets could be primarily due to the waning and demise of the Second Intifada and the improved security situation, but another factor indicates that the judgment did play a role. Prior to the ruling, a third of the assassinations were carried out in the West Bank. After it, all of them took place in Gaza, where Israel has no permanent presence on the ground. It is likely the military's legal advisers consider that assassinations in Gaza more readily fulfill the conditions laid out in the judgment, given the greater difficulty of apprehending suspected terrorists there.

NONE OF THE campaigns covered here ended with success, if success is defined as the abolition of the policy being challenged. But using a more nuanced definition of the term, one not synonymous with "victory," allows a more generous view of the proceedings' achievements.

First, important restrictions were imposed on the practice of punitive home demolitions and targeted killings, and the extent of their use diminished. Second, the legal battles preserved the legal and moral opposition to all three policies and defined their immorality. Third, the court cases focused the media on the question of these measures' legality and ignited a public debate on their justification.

The emergence of a camp of justices opposed to home demolitions proves that thirty years of uniform case law does not have to mean that the struggle is hopeless. A state of unease might be growing, out of view, that erupts when it reaches an intolerable level. This is something to hold on to in the darkest of days. Even if the wall we face seems impenetrable, our scraping at it might be making a dent. Tipping the scales in the legal struggle for human rights is sometimes accomplished by adding small weights over time—we see no change until the final weight shifts the balance.

I would like to believe that this is also true of the struggle against the wide use of administrative detention, and that the scarcity of achievements only means that the scales are still being loaded.

Conclusion: Sand on the Slope

REACHING FOR THE STARS

It happened in one of the dozens of court sessions litigating the outposts. Supreme Court president Dorit Beinisch headed the panel. Our petitions to remove illegal construction in the West Bank were filling up the court docket, and Beinisch began to grasp that this wave was not going to recede, that the justices of the institution she led would have to decide time and again over the coming years whether to remove settlers from their homes. She knew the trouble they would face from the politicians if the court was to grant remedy to all who deserved it. She did not like the predicament in which she found herself, in which we had placed her.

"Mr. Sfard," she said as she turned to me resentfully at the beginning of the session. "The Israeli-Palestinian conflict will not be resolved through legal action in this court." I was taken aback. Was that what I wanted? Was that what my friends and I were trying to do? To end the occupation through litigation?

If I were a director filming this scene, I would at this point have the camera come in slowly for a close-up of Mr. Sfard, standing in a black robe before the bench. Then I'd dissolve to the lawn at Jerusalem's Hebrew University campus. A young man, thin and with a full head of hair, sits on the grass with the registration forms and circles "law" as his first choice. The young Mr. Sfard is busy filling out forms until he notices the camera. Then he looks directly at the camera and says with youthful earnestness, "Yes! I want to file petitions to change the world! So, to answer your question, madam president, of course I want to end the occupation through litigation." But I'm not a film director. I'm a lawyer in mid-career, and I gave the president the only response appropriate under the circumstances: "Madam president, all we want is for our clients to get back the land that's been stolen from them."

LAWYERS WORKING FOR social change are destined to a life of disappointment. Their careers are full of bitter, often painful, defeat. They fight to change a reality created and supported by those in power. In nondemocratic regimes, this power is the regime itself. In democracies, it is an intricate combination of the governing institutions, the various elites, and the majority of the population. But in both situations, were the hegemon not invested in maintaining the status quo, there would be no need to involve the courts in the fight for change. Litigation is usually a tool used by the weak to force change indirectly; the powerful do not need this workaround. If they want change, they can use direct means to make it happen. Since these are the basic terms for any litigation for social change, the odds of success are inherently low. And since failure is part of the job, the graph charting the optimism of cause lawyers plummets over time. The process is inevitable.

This is why a social change lawyer's state of mind at the beginning of their career is so important. People who graduate from law school with the goal of devoting their new expertise to social change need to shoot for the stars. They'll have plenty of time to come to terms with the limitations of the profession, to learn the many shades of gray that lie between white and black, to compromise on subtleties. But when they're young and just starting out, they had better be the revolutionary type, sure that their cause is not only just but also achievable. They had better start high so that they don't end up too low. That way, there's always a chance that the initial spark will not burn out. That way, the spark is renewed with every victory, every success, and generates the energy for the battles to come.

Every veteran lawyer interviewed for this book has that spark. In some it shines bright, almost blindingly so, undimmed by the disappointments along the way or by the fact that the occupation has only become more deeply entrenched over the years. Others might have acquired a veil of cynicism, but I see it disappear the moment a good case comes along.

None of these lawyers describes their work in terms of only assisting clients. They see their cases representing victims as part of a larger vocation, not as individual unrelated events. They see themselves as part of a political movement. They see their legal battles as part of the struggle to end the occupation.

It wasn't always like this—there were times when some Israeli human rights activists tried to distinguish among the different fights, but that effort has faded away. Anyone trying to combat human rights violations carried out as part of the occupation *is* fighting to end the occupation. The occupation itself is one vast human rights violation. For this reason, the community of human rights lawyers representing cases involving the occupation would, I believe, respond to Beinisch with a resounding "Yes!" "Yes! We do want to end the occupation through litigation! But because we are experienced and know better than our interns, we realize the odds are high that the legal fight will be only an auxiliary means of ending the occupation, not the primary engine." The veteran lawyers recognize the limitations of what they *do* without giving up on and constantly aiming at what *ought to be done.*

THE CALCULUS OF LITIGATION FOR SOCIAL CHANGE: VICTORY AND SUCCESS

Professor Jules Lobel is a seasoned American human rights lawyer. He has worked at the Center for Constitutional Rights, one of the leading US human rights organizations, since the mid-1980s, now serving as its president. He is also a chaired professor of international and US constitutional law at the University of Pittsburgh, where he invited me to speak on occupation litigation in Israel. In the course of our long conversations about the legal battles we had fought, each in a different country and in a different political context, we found yet again that some of the dilemmas of human rights lawyering are universal, cutting across causes and continents. We also found that we shared a common background, both coming from progressive Jewish families with roots in Eastern Europe and both raised on values of social justice. I found in him the unusual mix, rare among lawyers, of a revolutionary dreamer, determined to mend the world, and a clear-eyed realist, a grounded individual who knows exactly where he is and how the world works. Lobel's compassion and human sensitivity—worthy qualities in any profession—made him a legend of human rights lawyering.

Through the Center for Constitutional Rights, Lobel had been involved in countless legal battles, some of which, he admits, were hopeless from the get-go. In the 1980s, he litigated challenges to US military involvement in Latin America. In 1990, he joined a legal team that asked the court to deny President George H. W. Bush the authority to enter the first Gulf War without the approval of Congress. After 9/11, under the presidency of his friend and colleague, famed human rights lawyer Michael Ratner, the center stood at the forefront of legal representation for detainees held in Guantánamo Bay and also tried to prosecute those responsible for torture there and at Abu Ghraib in Iraq. Lobel gave an expert opinion in support of a criminal complaint filed against Secretary of Defense Donald Rumsfeld in Germany for his alleged responsibility for torture.

The courts did not prevent US involvement in El Salvador and Nicaragua, close the Guantánamo detention facility, or release the detainees by judicial decree,* nor was Rumsfeld arrested. Like any human rights lawyer, Lobel has had his share of courtroom defeats. "By 1991, I was an experienced, accomplished, and well-polished loser," he wrote. The progressive agenda he and his friends brought to court did not win over the justices. Not only a bitter disappointment, these losses led Lobel to question whether litigation was an effective tool for social change. He took some time off and wrote his book *Success Without Victory: Lost Legal Battles and the Long Road to Justice in America*.[1] In the course of his research, Lobel discovered that he was part of a long line of distinguished losers: nineteenth-century lawyers who tried to abolish slavery, lawyers who turned to the courts for women's suffrage, and lawyers who tried through litigation to stop the Vietnam War. They all lost in court.

Still, slavery was abolished, women got the vote, and, after decades of legal disputes, President Barack Obama accepted the position that war requires congressional approval (when he failed to receive it, he

---

* However, most of the detainees were eventually released, and it is undisputed that the Guantánamo litigation, which managed to curb some of the government's powers regarding the detainees, played a major role in their release.

canceled the planned military intervention in Syria). Lobel's conclusion is astounding:

> I now began to see how "failure" could not really be measured adequately by the winner-takes-all model of American law. Certainly, on the face of it, the legal tradition I studied was unsuccessful. . . . But if success can be viewed like the pentimenti of a painting, as the unseen underside necessary to the final perceptible painting, then these cases take a different hue. Success inheres in the creation of a tradition, of a commitment to struggle, of a narrative of resistance that can inspire others similarly to resist.[2]

Lobel recast the way we should measure the outcome of a legal battle. His analysis places litigation in a historical context and measures its success partially in terms of its ability to contribute to changing the discourse, educating, inspiring a movement for change, and creating solidarity with disempowered communities. As he writes, this type of success is not always evident and calculable in the present.

The debate over what constitutes "success" in litigation for social change stems from the fact that there is an attractive and simple alternative to Lobel's refined analysis: *winning*. Ever since the National Association for the Advancement of Colored People gained its huge legal victory in the fight for the integration of African Americans in the US education system, in the famed *Brown v. Board of Education of Topeka*,[3] both human rights lawyers and the public have had a generic model for legal success. The case was born out of a meticulously crafted legal strategy, designed by the NAACP, with careful timing, choice of clients, and lines of argument.[4] The NAACP legal team, led by Thurgood Marshall (who later became the first African American on the US Supreme Court), made history: the court struck down the "separate but equal" doctrine, which was instituted in the late nineteenth century and allowed for separate schools for blacks and whites as long as the investment in them was equal.

The decision seemed poised to revolutionize race relations in the United States on a magnitude second only to the abolition of slavery, and all this thanks to written and oral submissions in a courtroom in Washington, D.C., before nine justices. The case ignited the imagination of legal activists the world over and continues to inspire them today, more than sixty years later. What human rights lawyer does not dream of being Thurgood

Marshall? What human rights organization does not hope for its own *Brown v. Board of Education*? The case gave the legal battle for human rights a simple, immediate model for success: *victory*. One case that changes the world in an instant, the sudden catharsis of the judge's gavel hitting the sound block. How different is *victory* à la *Brown* from the slow, gradual, quasi-philosophical *success* offered by Lobel, a process that advances at the snail's pace of political sociology.

Brown did alter how movements for social change work. The precedent resulted in resources and energy channeled into litigation campaigns in every field in which people were fighting for change. Other reality-altering legal victories since *Brown* have bolstered the perception of litigation as a major tool in such fights, an engine that can produce instant change. A US judgment from 2015 that compelled recognition of same-sex marriage,[5] for example, was received as an affirmation of the power of litigation.

But, contrary to the popular perception, these cases far from prove that meaningful social change for the disempowered, for people whose rights are violated, can come from courtroom victories. Research has shown that *Brown* did not really bring integration in the years that followed. The ruling caused a backlash in southern states opposed to desegregation and they found ways around it.[6] Some have even claimed that the ruling in fact delayed the delicate integration process already under way because of the strong pushback it caused.[7] They argue that desegregation was only truly implemented after Congress passed the 1964 Civil Rights Act a decade later, which mandated racial integration in educational institutions. This research suggests that sweeping social change can only come about when society is ready for it, rather than as a coercive decree of the legal elite. On the other hand, even if the change was the result of the Civil Rights Act rather than the court ruling, there is the argument that it would not have happened without *Brown*. That legal victory may be said to have changed public discourse. The Supreme Court ruling also gave the pro-integration camp political power, moral energy, and strong legitimacy, the importance of which cannot be overrated.[8] This analysis of *Brown* uses Lobel's language of success.

And if not *Brown*, then what about *Obergefell v. Hodges*, the 2015 Supreme Court decision that allowed same-sex marriage throughout the United States? Maybe that ruling offers proof that social change can come from the courtroom? Unlike black students, who for the most part were prevented from attending white schools after *Brown* by the opposition to racial integration, same-sex couples were granted the right of marriage across the country the day after the judgment was delivered. The judgment appears to have delivered immediate change. But a closer look at the social processes that formed the background for the ruling reveals that in fact society changed first and the court followed.

In the years prior to *Obergefell v. Hodges*, most states had already recognized same-sex marriage. Equality in marriage enjoyed tremendous public support across parties and candidates. The Supreme Court justices who ruled in favor of same-sex marriage were presumably influenced by the rapid change that had occurred in public perception, something commentators describe as a "sea change." Thus, the court did not *create* the change in public perception, it *declared* it. In this case, as in many others in which judgments appear to have effected a dramatic shift in the protection of human rights, the court was riding a wind of change that had already blown through society and was simply giving it the seal of approval.

I have focused on *Brown* and similar cases because they are responsible for the idea that litigation that does not end in victory—meaning the full and immediate acceptance of a position of social change—is a failure. All the evidence suggesting that *Brown* was not an overnight success—or, conversely, that the failed litigation to abolish slavery or win the vote for women was not a colossal defeat—does not help. Legal activists want a *Brown*, even if they could know for sure that seventy years down the road, despite the losses in court, their ridiculed arguments will be seen as self-evident wisdom.

These examples underscore the difference between *victory* and *success* in social change litigation: the first is an immediate event, obtaining the remedy sought through litigation, that is, a legal victory; the second is long-term, measured by the extent to which litigation advances social change by shaping the public discourse, educating, building a moral manifesto, and galvanizing a movement. Success may also be visible in the offshoots of legal action, which include heightening awareness and attention for the particular cause, extracting official information, compelling the state to take a clear position, exhausting domestic remedies (this enables action in foreign and international tribunals), empowering the affected community, and raising the political, public, and diplomatic costs of maintaining the status quo.

This distinction between success and victory is critical for evaluating the effectiveness of a legal campaign. It offers a broader perspective that extends beyond the immediate outcome of legal action. It also invites a distinction between their negative counterparts, *defeat* and *failure*. A defeat occurs when the remedy sought is denied by the court, whereas legal failure is, like legal success, a long-term effect. It occurs when the legal battle fails to change public discourse and perception or to educate. A central insight here is that victory and defeat do not necessarily correlate to success or failure. A victory in court might be a step on the road to success, but it could also be a fleeting moment in a process that ends in failure. Similarly, defeat might lead to failure, but it could also serve as a catalyst for a process that ends in success. The tendency to associate victory with success and defeat with failure is understandable, but the two are not inextricably linked.

Now that we have established the distinction between legal victory/ success and defeat/failure, can we assess the outcome of the legal battle against the occupation? Not yet. But knowing that there might be a price to pay for the victories, and that the defeats might, in fact, yield benefits, allows us to cost out the overall effect of the various legal campaigns. This will help us understand the dynamic that can turn victory and defeat into either success or failure.

THE CALCULUS OF LITIGATION FOR SOCIAL CHANGE: TWO COSTS OF DEFEAT (AND ONE OF VICTORY)

Human rights lawyering has three potential layers of purpose. The first is *remedy for the client*. Unless litigation is undertaken on behalf of a public-interest petitioner, there are always clients who are victims of the challenged practice or policy. That the remedy sought in a specific case might also serve as a tool for wider social change cannot cloud the fact that the litigation is a goal in its own right. If that goal is achieved, the harm to the client has been prevented or compensated. If it is not, the harm remains.

The second layer of purpose is the *policy* that is being challenged. On this plane, the purpose is to have the policy changed or canceled. If this is achieved, it results in an across-the-board change that applies to every case affected by that policy. This is the classic objective of battles for social change: ending racial segregation in schools; stopping the demolition of homes belonging to terrorists' families; removing barriers to abortion; prohibiting the use of torture during interrogations. The first two layers—individual remedy and a challenge to policy—are present in almost every legal fight for social change. Usually, test cases involve incidents and clients who have been chosen because they are most likely to convince the court of the illegality or unconstitutionality of the particular issue. But even when individuals volunteer their case for the cause, they are still living, breathing people, and they are clients, whose interests—the first layer of purpose—lawyers are morally and ethically compelled to serve.

The third layer is broader than the second and the most ambitious of all three. Not a factor in every fight for social change, it is, in fact, probably absent from most: this is *regime change*.

In my first chapter, I described the dilemma faced by a group of Israeli human rights lawyers about a decade ago: whether to keep filing petitions with the High Court of Justice. We were concerned that our achievements in court had been marginal, yet they were used to gloss over the most important human rights issue in the West Bank and Gaza Strip: the occupation. We considered ourselves part of a movement that sought to end a regime that suspended the civil rights and liberties of millions. So we asked ourselves whether our sporadic success in obtaining remedy for an individual victim, or even in changing policy, helped advance the goals of the third layer of purpose: changing the regime itself. To put it another way, we thought that one of the parameters for evaluating our work should be its impact on the occupation's shelf life, on its durability and stability. We suspected that this level clashed with the needs of the other two. Thus, we tried to find a way to have our cake and eat it—to win remedy for the victims but avoid sustaining the occupation by granting it legitimacy and positive publicity.

As stated, regime change is not a necessary or even common goal of legal battles for social change. But when it is present, it makes the calculus of success or failure even more complicated, involving three variables instead of two. Doing the math means being able to quantify the cost of legal defeat, that is, of judicial rulings that deny the remedy sought. But first we have to distinguish among the various arenas in which human rights struggles are fought, because different arenas involve different costs.

The arenas I analyze below are all *internal*, that is, they are institutions of the country in which the violation has occurred, unlike litigation in an *external* forum, meaning foreign or international.

Internal fights are fought in one of three possible arenas: The first is *democratic*. In this model, the legal battle is over human rights violations committed by a democratic country, one that is committed to basic liberal values and whose record in this context is at least reasonable. As we would expect in a democratic regime, the judicial system where the fight occurs is professional and independent. The second forum is *undemocratic*. Here, the battle is fought against an undemocratic regime that barely even (if at all) pays lip service to the notion of human rights and whose record of upholding them is usually somewhere between dismal and appalling. In this context, there is often real concern that the courts are not independent and their professionalism may be in doubt.

The third possibility is the most complex, the *mixed* forum. It has democratic foundations, both in the values underlying the legal and government systems and in the principle of representation they inherently entail. But it also has undemocratic elements. In one example, a democratic state might have independent, professional courts that are committed legally to the concept of human rights but are tasked with overseeing an undemocratic regime maintained by their country. Occupation by democracies is the obvious example of such a mixed theater. Another variety is a domestic court that is asked to rule on a conflict between its country and a foreign entity. In this situation, one party to the proceedings is the state, the country's executive branch, a sister to the court and part of the same regime, while the other is not only foreign and therefore bereft of influence over the forum (the law, the selection of judges, the procedures, and the moral and judicial culture) but is also in conflict with it. A domestic court ruling on an external dispute has lost the neutrality (or appearance of neutrality) it maintains (or is meant to maintain) in an internal dispute.[9]

Finally, one more example of a mixed arena is a technical democracy—a regime in which the checks and balances designed to preserve the power of the majority are deficient. This is a mixed theater because it is based on fundamental democratic principles, such as representation and majority rule, but operates under the influence of undemocratic rules, such as severe limitations on a minority's right to freedom of expression and political protest.

Now, having defined the different layers of purpose and arenas of human rights litigation, we can move on to assess the impact of losing in court. The immediate and obvious cost is to the client, who was denied relief, and to the social movement, whose morale has taken a beating. All this, as well as the waste of energy and resources that could have been put to more effective use. These are the ordinary costs that come with any defeat—costs in the narrow sense.

Added to these costs is the legitimacy gained by the impugned policy or practice. If the cost of defeat in the narrow sense is *passive*—that is, no remedy and no change—its effect in the wider sense is *active*, in that it helps to support the policy we were trying to change. Success recedes while the chance of failure increases. To understand this dynamic, let's return to basic concepts in political science and legal philosophy.

Modern societies follow the principle of the rule of law, that is, the idea that the rights and obligations of individuals and state authorities— what they are and are not permitted to do—are determined by general norms. To the extent possible (and it is not really possible), these norms are established through a veil of ignorance—that is, under the assumption that we do not know on which side of the norm we, who share in its creation, will find ourselves in the future. It is the generality of the norms that apply to all that is supposed to prevent arbitrariness and preserve equality. Modern society tasks the judiciary with resolving disputes over the exact substance of the norms and filling in gaps left by the legislature; to do so, the judiciary creates new norms that follow from principles of a higher order or from general unwritten principles.

A legal norm (a law, regulation, order, or judgment) does not have the power just to *dictate* but also to *justify*. There is a fervent debate among positivist and other schools of philosophy of law over the nature and characteristics of a legal norm, which I will sidestep. Suffice it to say that, for the most part, we obey statute and case law not just because they come with mechanisms for enforcement but because we accept that following them is the right thing to do. We accept, for the most part, that a norm established through the prevailing constitutional order is justified. A legal norm describes proper conduct and this conduct is proper because it has been established through a legal norm. And so a legal norm is at one and the same time an "is" and an "ought." It both binds and educates.

Therefore, a court ruling that affirms and validates the norm being challenged (that is, when we human rights lawyers lose) grants momentum not only to the dictating force of the practice (allows its ongoing implementation), it also reinforces its educative power (the legitimacy it enjoys through its simple existence). A defeat may therefore convince many that the policy being challenged is legitimate and justified or necessary, and weaken the call to change or abolish it. This is the active cost of defeat and the intuitive connection between a court loss—an immediate, localized event—and failure, which is a long-term process.

For the third layer of purpose—regime change—the active cost of our court losses would appear to be the danger of enhancing the regime's standing. The judicial process can give the regime an extremely important asset, shielding it from accusations of arbitrariness and lack of oversight. Paradoxically, it is not just our losses in court that help strengthen the regime but also—perhaps especially—our victories. When the court grants relief, it sends a message that the system contains a mechanism to remedy injustice. To those critical of the regime, this message could weaken the demand for change or at least suppress the sense of urgency. The logical conclusion, therefore, is that when (a) regime change is one of the goals of the legal campaign, and (b) success for the client will enhance the regime's standing, then (c) the win promotes failure in the long term. In such a case, there may be a clash between the interests of the three different layers of purpose.

Because the active effect of defeat extends to social perceptions and legitimacy of governmental policies, it has a different impact in different arenas. In general, the damage is usually highest in a democratic context and lowest in a nondemocratic one. Take, for example, a case challenging the prison conditions in a particular country, where they are so deplorable that they constitute a violation of prisoners' rights. That country's court reviews the case and rules that the conditions are acceptable, meet the required standards, and do not violate the prisoners' rights. For the prisoners, the defeat is passive; they see no change in their conditions. But the damage to society is active. In a democratic context, where many citizens would be troubled by the idea of living in a country whose prisoners are held in deplorable conditions, the court's ruling will allow them to rest easy. In a democratic country, the court is considered prestigious and reliable, and its judgments have significant educative force. The public usually trusts the court and will not delve into the fine details of the case. In a nondemocratic context, the chance is much higher that the citizenry and certainly the international community will view the ruling with skepticism. In an extreme situation, the population might be brainwashed, but in that case the legitimizing effect is not derived from the courts and their rulings.

The active impact in a mixed context is much harder to calculate and more subject to fluctuation. How the court rules will shape the public's perception of the legal force of the country's norms. But conversely, the degree of the court's influence depends on the nature of its rulings and the criticism they provoke. This two-way process also affects the active cost of defeat in other theaters, but the mixed theater is particularly susceptible to it.

In terms of the occupation, Israel is a classic mixed arena (both as an occupying democracy and as a domestic regime adjudicating an external conflict). Israel's Supreme Court enjoys the prestige of the democratic arena, although that prestige has eroded over the years as a result of the role it has played in legitimizing practices of the occupation. The active cost of defeat (and victory) in the High Court changes from case to case and from one period to another. The public is used to the court's liberal rulings on human rights in Israel, and this shapes the trusting reception of its judgments on the occupation, strengthening their active force. But as the occupation continues and criticism of the court's involvement has intensified, its legitimizing power has diminished, especially for international observers.

THERE IS ANOTHER potential cost involved in litigating for social change. Legal campaigns, especially in the democratic or mixed arena, have the potential to dominate the cause. They could take it over, weaken other sources of action, and possibly suppress them for their own needs. Think about campaigns for change: there is usually a pool of supporters. Some are victims; some simply believe the policy is wrong or unjust. There is a certain amount of energy for the fight, which might be applied to protest, writing, lobbying, civil disobedience, or even violence. Once the cause goes to court, much of the energy that might have led people to engage in other action is directed at the slow, organized channels of legal procedures. The movement switches gears, waiting for a judicial ruling and hoping it will effect immediate change. The drive to move mountains diminishes. Legal proceedings almost inherently jeopardize grassroots action because they set the course for change, while engaging the street or the media or the political process seems (but only seems!) to be the wrong locus of change.

Movements that began with grassroots activism risk losing that engagement when they take their cause to court. The legal system functions as a release, dispelling anger by subjecting it to the court's rules. This is not just a by-product of the legal system, it is one of the law's purposes. Still, we should avoid overstating this process of suppression, certainly in nondemocratic circumstances like occupation. The demonstrations in Bil'in neither stopped nor subsided because the cause went to court—they might have even been fueled by the parallel fight. The intifadas did not wait on the High Court. The Palestinian people are fighting for their freedom, so any rage diverted into litigation has been marginal.

But has the legal campaign weakened public engagement in Israel? In the absence of High Court litigation, would more Israelis have taken to the streets and more of the elite pushed to end the occupation? Possibly, but there is no reason to believe the difference would have been significant.

Now, with all these insights, we can begin to assess the costs and benefits of taking the occupation to court.

THE CALCULUS OF LITIGATING THE OCCUPATION

This book describes multiple legal campaigns against widespread human rights violations in the Occupied Territories. Analyzing the success or failure of these campaigns, each one separately and all of them together, is difficult, if only because there is no control group. There is no parallel occupation where no litigation took place or where the same violations were litigated in a different way. Since evaluating the worth of a legal battle partly depends on comparing it to an alternative, our results will inevitably be somewhat speculative.

With this caveat in mind, what can we take away from the vast, cumulative experience of this legal battle for human rights? From the perspective of the three layers of purpose in litigation, what can we learn from the victories, the losses, the successes, and the failures?

The first layer, winning remedy for the client, is the easiest to assess. Thousands, perhaps even tens of thousands, of Palestinians were granted relief thanks to High Court proceedings filed on their behalf. Some, like the landowners from Burqa, Silwad, and Deir Dobwan (where Migron and Amona were built) or Bil'in, actually won in court. For most, however, remedy did not come in the shape of a favorable judgment but as a compromise, or settlement, "in the court's shadow," as David Kretzmer named this process.[10] The expression refers to the pressure applied by the justices to the state in the course of a hearing, which often resulted in petitioners obtaining full or partial relief. Sometimes the relief came simply because petitioners had filed a petition, which prompted the State Attorney's Office to revisit their case.

Every lawyer who has represented Palestinians in the High Court has seen this happen. The clients start out as nobodies, weightless entities in space. The authorities ignore them, sometimes not even responding to their communications, batting them away like bothersome flies. Until they file a petition. As soon as the clients hire legal representation and enter the legal process, they gain heft and volume and visibility. The authorities might reconsider the case and even decide to reverse their actions. The justices might pressure state counsel to grant a petitioner remedy ex gratia, or even make a veiled threat to intervene in the process, which usually leads the authorities to change their decision. The petitioner ends up with a settlement to prevent or mitigate the damage, while the court has avoided issuing a binding precedent. This has happened in countless petitions every year. In some issues, such as the right of Palestinians to travel abroad, the number of petitions granted remedy without a ruling is huge, 75 percent or more.[11]

Settlement in the court's shadow is the oxygen that keeps Palestinians petitioning the High Court. After all, when it comes to rulings in favor of Palestinian petitioners, the statistics are rather grim as opposed to the overall outcomes.[12] News of the many compromises and out-of-court settlements travels fast, encouraging Palestinians to give the High Court a try.

Kretzmer also credits the effect of the court's shadow with influencing the second layer of purpose, policy. He suggests that this process has a mitigating effect, even if no concrete petitions have been filed. I concur: the authorities did sometimes avoid policy decisions for fear of the High Court's intervention. However, this fear, which was much in evidence fifteen years ago when Kretzmer made his argument, has since subsided.[13] Now military and state attorneys feel that on many issues of security, they determine the violation or preservation of fundamental rights, since the High Court will sign off on whatever they approve. In other areas, such as the retroactive authorization of illegal settlement construction, the High Court still has something of a restraining effect.

Either way, our assessment in terms of winning remedy for the client is simple, since every achievement is a net gain; the alternative, forgoing litigation, would provide no remedy. The legal track is unambiguously positive from the limited perspective of the first layer of purpose. It granted many Palestinians tangible relief over the years and spared thousands of families from all manner of harm in every area of life.

OUR EVALUATION OF the legal battle in terms of the second purpose plane, policy change, is less positive. There have been very few victories, certainly if we try to count full or nearly full wins.[14] The great majority of the policies challenged in the High Court of Justice were not struck down by the court. The legal campaign to end torture came the closest to victory, when the court declared the use of "moderate physical pressure" during interrogation unlawful. However, even that success did not secure full protection for interrogees.

Some of the legal campaigns achieved partial victory: the court intervened in the policy that shaped the route of the separation barrier; it imposed some degree of law enforcement over unauthorized outposts; and it framed the assassination policy, codifying the conditions for its use. While the legal fight yielded no victories challenging the deportation of Palestinian activists, it played a major role in eventually ending the practice. In other areas, the defeat was total or nearly total. While the court was willing to intervene in the implementation of settlement policy (raising the barrier to building on privately owned land), it flatly refused to deliberate on the policy's legality per se. The legal challenge to the permit system, which was tacked on to the fight against the separation barrier, also suffered a complete defeat, and with it the challenge to the lawfulness of building the barrier in the Occupied Territories.

Other legal battles not covered in this book also ended largely in disappointment: the fight against land seizure and confiscation, which left the military regime with broad powers to seize private land for security purposes; the challenge to Israel's wide interpretation of its power to amend legislation in the Occupied Territories, which failed to assimilate the restrictions on this power that exist in international law; the struggle for accountability and penalty for Israeli civilians and combatants who victimize Palestinians, which (with few exceptions) failed to prevent de facto immunity for Israeli assailants; the struggle against revocation of residency rights and for family unification, which won remedy for individual petitioners but did not change policy; the fight against restrictions on movement; the challenge to certain methods of warfare used during armed conflict, which resulted in no judicial intervention in policy, although it did have a (limited) mitigating effect; the fight against Israeli policies in East Jerusalem; and the campaign for due process in the military courts, the results of which cannot be summed up in a sentence, but suffice it to say that many injurious practices remained intact.

All of these struggles have involved a great deal of legal action, some of which continued for decades, while some are still ongoing.

CAN WE DRAW any conclusions about the chance of victory (distinct from success) and defeat (distinct from failure) in these legal struggles for policy change in the occupation?

First, it seems fair to say that *the likelihood of effecting policy change through court victory is inversely proportional to the perceived importance of that policy to Israel's overall Palestinian strategy.* The clearest example is the legal battle against the settlements. The settlement policy represents the government's core position on the future of the Occupied Territories and the Israeli-Palestinian conflict. It is the strongest manifestation of Israel's plans for these territories, and it expresses, for better or worse, the country's perception of its own future. Accordingly, any attempt to change this policy through judicial rulings, to get the court to declare settlement illegal, has ended in unmitigated defeat. Another example is the fight to restrain Israel's power to make legislative changes in the

Occupied Territories. There, too, lawyers have sustained total defeat. The High Court has stretched the exception to the international prohibition on legislative amendments in occupied territory to the point where the military government has become more powerful than the sovereign it is meant to temporarily replace. Just as in the settlement enterprise, the power to change legislation in the territories and make long-term plans is at the core of Israel's policy toward the West Bank (and previously, the Gaza Strip).

It seems that the barrier and the various permit systems that comprise Israel's separation policy are also part of the country's political strategy for the land it has occupied, serving the goal of long-term control. Similarly, Israel's policy of denying family unification and curtailing Palestinian residency—essentially interference in the demographics of the West Bank—is key to ambitions of control and colonization. Court intervention in any of these areas would have had a dramatic impact on the government's ability to pursue its political goals in the Occupied Territories and in the conflict whose outcome will define Israel's identity, no less.

The reason why the High Court avoids intervening in these core disputes, I believe, is rooted in the judiciary's view of its constitutional role. Due to the democratic component of the mixed arena, the court accepts that its role involves judicial review of government policy from the perspective of human rights. But the justices also believe that regime change is not part of their mandate, and so they shy away from decisions that could shake the regime's foundations or change its character. Injurious policy is certainly a matter for judicial review, but an injurious regime is not, even when it is clear that the regime's nature is the main source of the violation of rights. This is all the more true when a conflict between the state and an external body is thrown into the mix. Supreme Court president Beinisch's comment that "the Israeli-Palestinian conflict will not be solved through legal action" clearly expresses this approach. It comes from the justices' intuitive feeling that the separation of powers draws a line between judicial review over "ordinary" policy, which does come under the court's purview and is justiciable, and criticism of the very foundations of the regime, which should be left for "politics."

If we liken the regime to a building, then the experience of our occupation litigation in Israel's High Court shows that the court is willing to intervene in the interior design. It might even take down an internal wall from time to time or move it elsewhere. But the court explicitly refuses to deal with the building's exterior walls and supports. These foundational elements are seen as political, and the court avoids them. According to this division, "moderate physical pressure" during interrogation is ordinary policy, interior design, but establishing settlements is a supporting beam, a "legal mine" that involves "questions of policy within the jurisdiction of other branches of a democratic Government."[15]

My criticism of this approach is laid out in chapter 3, "Settlements: Banging One's Head Against the Wall of the Political." It ignores the mixed character of the Israeli arena: it is not really a democracy when only one segment of the people affected by the decisions the court cedes to politics participates in the political process—the occupiers. The occupied are excluded from the decision-making process, which makes the democratic argument false, even dangerous. The court's refusal to address these crucial questions leaves the least powerful, those who have no civil rights or representation in any governmental authority, defenseless. Yet this is the approach taken by justices who consider themselves part of the democratic side of the mixed arena and adjudicate as if there were no other darker side.

Studies of the legal battle for human rights in apartheid South Africa reached a similar conclusion. Among the South African judiciary, liberal judges tried to prevent or mitigate human rights violations perpetrated against blacks. However, they never dared, nor did they think it their role, to rule on the foundations of the apartheid regime. Thus, they never conceived of abolishing the laws of racial segregation or refraining from applying them. During the truth and reconciliation process that followed the end of the apartheid regime, established to investigate the violations of human rights, one complaint addressed the legal system's responsibility for the regime's crimes. A group of old-order justices, who served in the court before and after the end of apartheid, filed their response. They explained that they believed the supremacy of parliament precluded judicial intervention in such fundamental issues. "The courts had no choice but to apply the law as they found it, however unjust it might appear to be," they wrote.[16] There are great differences between apartheid South

Africa and Israel's occupation. Ignoring the illegitimacy of decisions made by only one population in a regime that controls two is not among them.

ANOTHER CONCLUSION TO emerge from this review of victories and defeats is almost self-evident and quite intuitive: *the High Court is extremely reluctant to intervene in practices that are presented and perceived as the regime's principle tools for maintaining security.* To put it less euphemistically: The court often served as a rubber stamp for the security establishment's demands. They did so even when those demands involved terrible violations of fundamental rights, as in the case of assassinations; even when a broad legal consensus accepted that the measure was illegal, as with the separation barrier; even when the justices sought to evade exhaustive judicial discussions to uphold the policy, as was the case with house demolitions; even when they lapsed into inconsistency, as in approving the deportation of four hundred Hamas activists to Lebanon, although the legal obligation to hold a prior hearing had not been fulfilled. The court approved assassinations, house demolitions, widespread use of administrative detention, denial of family unification, deportations, uprooting olive groves, school and university closures, mass curfews, withholding the supply of electricity to Gaza, and building of the separation barrier—the list goes on—all in the name of security.

Still, in times of relative calm, the High Court's wall of resistance when it came to security did crack.[17] In 1999, after the First Intifada had ended and before the Second began, the court struck down the use of torture. And at the end of the Second Intifada, the High Court indicated that it might intervene in house demolitions. This threat resulted in a temporary moratorium on the use of Regulation 119. But when the security situation deteriorated and the policy was resumed, the High Court went back to upholding house demolitions. Though the High Court justices like to say that "security is not a magic word," their rulings suggest otherwise.

The court's jurisprudence on cases related to the occupation suggests another conclusion: *the High Court tends to recognize the procedural rights of victims of injurious policies.* This includes the rights of deportees, of homeowners whose houses are designated for punitive demolition, and of administrative detainees to a hearing and a judicial review. The court also recognized attendant rights, such as the right to legal representation, public hearings, and judicial review of administrative decisions. In some cases, the High Court extended the victim's right to access the material used as a basis for the decision, although it did subject that right to security considerations, which undermined its efficacy.

So FAR, THIS review has focused on the victories and defeats of the legal campaign. But what about its successes?

The insights gleaned from our assessment of litigating the occupation support the findings of scholars who have studied other battles in other places and conflicts:[18] even if not victorious, litigation can generate success in the form of offshoots that advance the fight for policy change, protect human rights, and even promote regime change. But unlike victory, success has many parents. Legal action is only one of them. The outcome of the legal process can support and push political, diplomatic, and public pressure. It can spark a political dynamic, provide information or morale to a movement, increase the cost of human rights violations, buy time for an activist campaign, undermine the public's faith in the integrity of the regime, and dent its moral image. As just one parent, legal action cannot take sole credit for any success, but it has a claim as a partner.[19] *Achievements in a struggle for social change can fuel a movement. Without such a movement, the achievements would simply evaporate.*

The fight against deporting Palestinian leaders did not yield a single legal victory, but after it assured the deportees transparency and procedural rights, the other forms of struggle were able to raise the political cost of deportation, and ultimately the campaign ended in success. The fight against home demolitions has also supplied few victories, but it subjects the establishment to tremendous pressure, which has led it to moderate the use of the measure and even abandon it altogether. This campaign also produced transparency and procedural rights, which were important tools for those who opposed the policy.

The legal challenge to the settlements yielded no victories (aside from the limited win in the Elon Moreh judgment), but it ensured a flow of information that made the settlements the most documented crime of the Israeli occupation. This information was channeled into the political and public spheres, and if it failed to stop the settlements, that is due to the weakness of the political camp that truly wants them stopped. Both the fight against the settlements and the outposts forced the government to state a position. This particular by-product, unique to legal campaigns, is useful for the opposition movement. The state's articulation of a position, as it was compelled to do in the challenge to torture and assassinations, undermines its moral standing—an important step on the road to success.

All these struggles made a significant contribution to public awareness of the policies and their victims in Israel and abroad. The legal proceedings have particular traits that make them an efficient tool for focusing the media's spotlight. Perhaps it is the element of contest—at the end of a trial, one side loses and the other wins, which makes it engrossing and suspenseful. Perhaps it is the prestige associated with the decisions of judges in a democratic society. Either way, few tools are better or more effective in exposing an issue to the wider public than legal cases. Nearly all the struggles described here earned their place in the public discourse largely, if not entirely, thanks to the related legal proceedings.

Those proceedings also served as a platform for drafting the indictment against the specific policy being challenged, as well as the occupation overall. The opposition's manifesto is greatly influenced by the legal discourse because of its particular traits: the language of human rights lawyers is mostly constitutional and therefore has a powerful moral dimension; the methodology, based on argument and retort, a back-and-forth between two parties' positions, ensures that the facts presented meet a threshold of reliability; perhaps most important is the authority of the justice system as an arbiter of society's disputes, and of the law to set the boundaries of what is allowed and what is not.

In a society founded on the rule of law, clarity on the law's position is a significant step toward ending a dispute. No wonder, therefore, that each party to a dispute tries to argue that the law is on its side. For this reason, a party that does not have the law on its side will argue that a norm of a higher order (like international law) contradicts and trumps the local legislation that supports the opposing party, rather than simply ignore the legal dimension. This is what conscientious objectors to the Vietnam War did when they were told American law mandated their conscription. This is what the opposition to the Iraq War argued when they insisted the war was illegal, even if the competent authorities ordered it. And this is what the opposition to the occupation does in Israel. Israel, for its part, trying to avoid the price of a clear violation of international law, has never admitted to defying it and ignoring its instructions, presenting, instead, a different interpretation, one that enables its policies.

THIS IS ALSO why modern opposition movements need human rights lawyers, active as they are in societies where the law is a principal arbiter of questions of legitimacy. These legal experts draft the charges of illegality against a policy or the regime, and they do it in courtrooms. The indictment is drafted in cases of settlements, the separation barrier, house demolition, and instances of torture. The process of drafting and redrafting the charges continues through many cases, big and small, individual and public interest. This work, composing the manifesto of the opposition to the occupation, goes on daily and without pause. Lawyers constantly update, elucidate, refine, and develop that manifesto in response to changes in the reality of the occupation.

These are at least some of the by-products of litigation—securing transparency and disclosure of information, safeguarding procedural rights, raising awareness, forcing the state to articulate its position, and stating the ideological-moral foundation of the opposition movement. All these elements help shape the discourse, educate the public, and galvanize the movement for change. They are the fuel for the journey toward success. They are so important that despite my calling them by-products, a legal strategy might sometimes view them as the main goal.

WHAT ABOUT THE ACTIVE COST OF LITIGATION?

On March 23, 1983, South African law professor Raymond Wacks gave a talk in honor of his appointment as head of the Department of Public Law at the University of Natal in Durban. His talk caused an immediate stir in legal circles in South Africa, sparking a heated debate. A South African judge who believes apartheid is morally indefensible and wishes to reconcile his conscience with his vocation, said Wacks at the climactic point of his talk, must resign. Wacks's sensational call for the country's judges to resign was reported four days later in a widely circulating daily newspaper,[20] generating a string of commentary in the days that followed. The full text of the talk, together with a response and a counterresponse, was reprinted in the *South African Law Journal* several months later.[21]

In his talk, Wacks analyzed the predicament of liberal judges who opposed the obvious injustice of the apartheid regime, predicated as it was on racial discrimination and oppression of the opposition. Wacks argued that adhering to the principles of adjudication meant that liberal judges could not infuse their rulings with the principles of freedom and equality, unless they chose to lie about the applicable legal norms or base their decisions on morality rather than law. Given that a court loss would simply prompt the regime to change the law, and since the regime used the law and the independence of the judiciary to manufacture legitimacy, a morally conflicted judge who continued to serve within the system inevitably enhanced the regime's legitimacy without any real ability to make changes for the better. That judge must, therefore, resign.

Wacks's talk was mostly aimed at two particular liberal law professors who were critical of the regime but argued in their writings that South African judges could and should interpret laws and fill in the gaps left by the legislature using liberal values. One of the professors, John Dugard (who served as the UN special rapporteur on the Occupied Territories in the early 2000s), published a detailed response.[22]

Dugard denied Wacks's premise that South African law consisted solely of repressive, racist principles. South African law, Dugard said, also had many liberal elements that derived from the Roman-Dutch law on which it was founded, as well as from British common law. These elements had remained, even after the apartheid laws were enacted, beginning in the 1950s. The laws of apartheid severely undermined the legal presumptions regarding equality and freedom but did not entirely revoke them, nor did they abolish the regime's subordination to the principles of reasonableness, natural justice, and legality. These may have been violated by the state and the new laws, but it could not be said that they no longer formed part of South African law to the extent that would make a liar out of a judge who invoked these principles. To put it differently, Dugard argued that South African law was something of a mixed theater.

Dugard's view was that judges who had difficulty reconciling their position with their conscience needn't choose between falsehood and resignation. They had a third option: pushing their conscientious view within the law. The judges' discretion and latitude in upholding human rights was, Dugard admitted, severely curtailed, but they were not completely denied. Judges still had some freedom to promote human rights. The relevant point for our discussion is that Dugard never denied that the judges' service on the bench lent legitimacy to the regime, but he argued that this challenge was not unique to judges. Lawyers defending dissidents in political trials and lawyers who petitioned against human rights violations in the courts of the apartheid state also helped support the image of a serious legal system based on the rule of law. Their participation in the legal process might be perceived as indicative of its fairness, Dugard wrote. And this participation did not end in the courts. Getting in a dig at Wacks, he wrote that law professors who freely criticize what needs criticizing and educate students in a liberal worldview also cloak the system in progressiveness, tolerance, and freedom. Must they all resign, too?

On the question of whether engagement in the court helped legitimate the system, said Dugard, there is no clear line of moral responsibility distinguishing between a judge and a lawyer, a practitioner and an academic, but the price of legitimacy is worth paying, he believed, so as not to desert the fight for justice. Resignation would be abandonment, and a particularly grave act, considering that the victims of injustice sought representation, petitioned for protection, and hoped the courts would rule in their favor. The dispute between Wacks and Dugard earned a place of honor in scholarly discussions about fighting evil regimes.

Israel is not South Africa, and the occupation, though it has developed clear elements of apartheid over the years, is different from apartheid South Africa. Still, the debate between Wacks and Dugard has relevance for the internal legal fight against the occupation. In both situations, the question is whether the damage, in terms of lending legitimacy to the regime, outweighs the legal battle's benefits. To answer this question, Wacks and Dugard had to assess the extent to which the legal system could produce success; the degree of legitimacy offered by the court through the participation of liberal lawyers, organizations, and judges; and the potential effect of a mass resignation of judges or a boycott by lawyers.

Dugard mentioned the boycott of the military court system by Palestinian lawyers after the occupation of the West Bank and Gaza Strip, which, he believed, undermined the system's legitimacy. But he also cited a study conducted by Palestinian human rights lawyer Raja Shehadeh, which concluded that the damage caused by the lawyers' strike outweighed the benefits.[23] Wacks mentioned the resignation of Rhodesian judges after the enactment of draconian laws in the 1960s but admitted it had nearly no effect.[24]

It seems clear that the litigation against human rights violations of the occupation did produce some important positive outcomes over the years: a few victories, more successes, and many clients who received remedy. The few existing studies have all highlighted litigation as the most effective tool in the fight for human rights in the context of the occupation.[25] But the question remains: How much damage has been done by the legitimacy lent to policies upheld by the court and to the occupation regime itself? It is impossible to answer this fully, given the subjective nature of "legitimacy" and the lack of clear criteria to measure it. The way legitimacy is won in the legal community is different from the way it is gained in the media or among the general public. There is also a difference between local and foreign populations. Still, there are some yardsticks to help the evaluation.

First, the legal system's prestige is heavily influenced by the judiciary's readiness to intervene in the executive branch's decisions. Tension between the executive and the judiciary is inherent and required in a regime that maintains separation of powers and takes human rights seriously. Thus, there is a big difference in the legitimacy enjoyed by a court that is perceived as a rubber stamp for the authorities and one seen as bold and activist. And this is a source of paradox in legal defeat in human rights cases: the more progressive the court, the more it is willing to confront the authorities and protect victims of human rights violations, the higher the active cost of legal defeat. The contrary is also true: the more passive the court, the more routinely it rules in line with the authorities' approach, the lower the active cost of defeat and the cost of liberal lawyers' cooperation. This is an important conclusion: the danger of granting legitimacy to a particular policy (or, in a mixed arena, to the regime) is particularly high in a legal system in which the odds of winning an achievement are high.

Second, at least some of the cost of legitimacy that comes from participating in litigation can be offset if the repeat actors (the lawyers and human rights organizations) publicly criticize the absence of fairness of the system in which they work. According to the spillover theory of legitimacy, the system benefits from the prestige of the human rights lawyers: if they're willing to take part in the court's proceedings, the thinking goes, then they must believe the system is fair. But those same actors can use their prestige to mitigate this impression by letting people know how they see this system. This does not completely negate the effect created by their participation, and many people will never hear their critique, but it does offer one way to diminish any supposed harm.

Third, nonparticipation is not always a viable option. Sometimes only a full, collective boycott would be effective, which is usually difficult, if not impossible, to achieve. Human rights lawyers cannot choose that route when victims bring them their cases. A human rights worldview does not condone sacrificing the individual for the greater good (especially when this good is speculative and indirect).

THERE WERE CERTAINLY times when the cost of participating in High Court proceedings and losing was extremely high. The courts of Meir Shamgar and Aharon Barak in the 1980s and 1990s helped convince Israelis of the legitimacy of any occupation-related policy or practice that the justices approved. At the time, the High Court enjoyed a strong reputation as a standard-bearer of human rights and a bastion of protection of fundamental liberties. Thus, its judgments that sanctioned violations of Palestinians' rights were seen as unavoidable, the lesser of various evils. Widespread professional criticism from academics and human rights organizations of rulings on issues such as deportation, settlements, or house demolitions did reduce this effect, but only in narrow circles.

With the arrival of a new generation of judges in the 2000s, the High Court underwent a dramatic transformation. Many of its current justices share a conservative ethos that emphasizes national over universal values. Some important rulings from the court in recent years contradict the fundamental principles of equality, political freedom, and freedom of expression hallowed in liberal legal systems.[26] The court is losing its reputation as a fortress of protection for individual rights.

The sizable body of research focusing on the High Court's jurisprudence on occupation-related cases near uniformly confirms that, for all its reputation, even during the more liberal years, the institution tended to uphold the regime's practices. And the High Court's prestige has also been corroded by the proliferation of international tribunals and the globalization of law. International judicial bodies now adjudicate over matters that were previously the sole purview of Israel's High Court: the International Court of Justice, which issued an advisory opinion on the legality of the separation barrier; UN committees, which discuss a variety of occupation-related issues; and domestic courts in other countries, where disputes related to the occupation are sometimes heard. These have broken the Israel court's monopoly and mitigate the active cost of defeat.

All this leads to the conclusion that the active cost of High Court losses and participation in its proceedings has diminished over the years. The cost of losing ten years ago, when we wondered whether to stop bringing petitions connected to the occupation, was higher than it is today. The cost during the 1980s was even higher. The court had not yet been tarnished by its own decisions.

ONE DAY

This book was written as the clouds over Israel's skies darkened.

The occupation marked its fiftieth anniversary, and the processes that had strengthened its hold continue with full force. Israel's thrust toward annexation shows no signs of fatigue and the occupation adds to its inventory of ruthless methods of control every day. Its rightless subjects see no liberty on the horizon, and the peace process that brought hope to many has faded to irrelevance.

But the clouds of repression do not stop at the Green Line. Israeli society itself is undergoing dangerous shifts. The nationalist, antiliberal right has doubled in strength and declared all-out war on the many individual liberties, mostly political, of Israelis who oppose the government's policy. Human rights organizations and peace activists have become a lightning rod for the government's inflammatory rhetoric. The parliamentary majority is using its power to limit their activities and undermine their legitimacy. Right-wing organizations engage in political witch hunts in academia, the arts, and the judiciary, often with the support and encouragement of members of parliament, even ministers.

The price Israeli society exacts from anyone daring to criticize government policy is rising and now includes being labeled a foreign agent, even a traitor. Israel appears to have learned none of the lessons offered by history to the forces seeking to stifle freedom of expression and slander political opponents. Try being a lecturer in, say, sociology, political science, or law, who criticizes the treatment of Palestinians to your students—an experiment best conducted after tenure is secured. Try being an actor who refuses to perform in a settlement for reasons of conscience— you had better not be part of a publicly funded institution. Try the heresy of referring to May 15 as Nakba Day, the name given to the Palestinian catastrophe of 1948. Try calling for a boycott of settlement products or being a military prosecutor charging a soldier who killed a wounded terrorist. In today's Israel, it takes more than simply a decent person to do any of this. It takes a hero, and Israeli reality confirms what we already know about human nature: not all decent people are heroes.

Racism toward Israel's Arab minority is at an all-time high. A remarkable effort is invested in discrediting its political leadership, whose influence is in any case negligible, certainly in proportion to its constituency's numbers; and even greater work goes into trying to oust those Knesset members from parliament. Cynical politicians who pass themselves off as centrists exploit nationalist populism, spreading hatred and racism to curry favor with the voters, and they succeed. Israeli society is moving toward the isolationist, chauvinist, fascist end of the spectrum.

There is a different perspective. One result of these developments is that Israeli society's major disorder—"dissociative identity disorder syndrome," to use the professional term, or a split personality, in lay language—has shown signs of diminishing. Israel's soul is home to two personalities: at times their conflict was held in check by a balance of power, despite their mutual animosity. Now, one personality has gained dominance over the other, to the point that we can envisage somewhere down the line the Cain inside us rising up to kill our Abel.

Contrary to the arguments of certain radical circles, Israeli society and the state have deep, authentic liberal foundations. Its system of government includes an elected legislature, a separation of powers, and the principle of rule of law. Its High Court chose, from the beginning, to elevate freedom of expression and its many facets to the level of a fundamental right and has zealously protected it. None of this is an accident or for purposes of propaganda. At the same time, the state's definition of itself as Jewish, the exaltation of nationalism, the dispossession of the people who were here when the state was established, the violent conflicts with neighboring countries, and especially the de facto creation of an underclass subjected to systemic, institutionalized discrimination because they are Palestinian—these, too, are part of Israel's deep, authentic foundations, defining attributes of its society.

For many years these two personalities have danced around each other in the country's public space. Even as we enacted legislation that expressed respect for fundamental rights, the primacy of human dignity, and political, artistic, and academic pluralism, we also set up a bureaucracy and enacted policies to entrench hegemony, dispossession, and discrimination. More than any of these, we created the occupation, a half century of occupation, which gave weight to Israel's antiliberal identity. In time, the occupation gained heft, strengthening the country's undemocratic, nationalist, conservative forces.

This process was probably inevitable. It seems that an open, liberal democracy cannot be sustained over time alongside the undemocratic, belligerent rule over millions of people. A mixed theater, like a radioactive agent, is inherently unstable. The culture of domination intrinsic to a regime of occupation acts like ionizing radiation that produces mutations under prolonged exposure.

THE STORY I have told does not have a happy ending. It does not have an unhappy one, either. We do not know the end, because the fight against the occupation has yet to be concluded. It is important, though, as we near the close of this book, to acknowledge that the battles recounted here are not just about ending the occupation. In a profound sense, they are a struggle for the character of Israel's society. In their petitions, lawyers try to stop the mutation; in their arguments, they try to spread sand on the slope.

From that perspective, the significance of this legal fight for Israel's society is greater than the sum of its victories and successes. Based as it is on moral and ethical values, the fight preserves an alternative to the policies of settlement, belligerence, and dispossession, even when no one seems to be interested in that alternative. It is not only lawyers who do the work of preservation, but also public figures, artists and academics, journalists and politicians, all of those who fight for democratic values and against the occupation. However, the critical, cautionary, educating voice of legal activists has a special role and importance, constantly defining and articulating the evil to be uprooted and the good that should come in its stead.

The sound of the legal proceedings, playing through the occupation almost from its first day, disturbs the bugles, war drums, and battle cries that would have otherwise monopolized Israel's soundtrack. The voice of legal resistance, to paraphrase Justice Mishael Cheshin, is like the piccolo, light and pure, yet never drowned out in the din. On the contrary, it is clearly heard, rising above the roar of nationalism—sometimes even provoking the roar. It plays an important role in documenting the past, changing the present, and designing the future.

Because one day the occupation will end. Today it might look strong and stable, but it will end. It might be hard to believe that now, because rationally we expect to see signs of such a monumental change and they are nowhere in evidence. But historical processes are not necessarily linear. The ground beneath the occupation might look solid, but it may very well be that under that, just below the surface, cracks have formed and are growing wider. They are not visible to those aboveground to whom it seems as sturdy as ever. But at some point, without warning, the cracks may open and the ground will fall in like a sinkhole.

One day the occupation will end, like apartheid in South Africa, like the fall of the Berlin Wall—no one predicted those events, even shortly before they happened. And when the occupation ends, we'll find that we are not entirely bereft of a culture of good government, that we do have moral foundations to draw on. We'll discover that those foundations have been preserved by their guardians for the day after, among them the human rights organizations and activists.

This is why, until the occupation ends, human rights lawyers must hold their heads high and know that they have a role in the appearance of cracks in the occupation. They are forcing a gate in its wall by upholding the greatest idea in human history: that all humans are equal and all are deserving of rights because they are human. It is their role to sound the alarm, to remind everyone that, as Salmon P. Chase, one of the greatest American abolitionist lawyers, said, "There is no reliable security for the rights of any unless the rights of all are also secure."[27]

I am not saying the occupation will end tomorrow. I don't know. A lot more blood might be spilled along the way. I only know that the fight is not over—neither the fight to end the occupation nor the fight for the nature of Israeli society.

NOTES

INTRODUCTION: THE ZUFIN GATE

1. Zygmunt Bauman, *Modernity and the Holocaust* (London: Polity Press, 1989). For full disclosure, Zygmunt Bauman was my grandfather.
2. Abraham Joshua Heschel in an interview with Carl Stern in 1972: https://www.youtube.com/watch?v=WjDNPwVEHdE (starting at min 33:22) (last viewed on August 14, 2015).
3. Felicia Langer, *With My Own Eyes: Israel and the Occupied Territories, 1967–1973* (Ithaca, NY: Ithaca Press, 1975).
4. Jackson Diehl, "Israeli Defender of Arab Rights Quits in 'Despair and Disgust'; Lawyer for Palestinians Rarely Won a Case in 23 Years," *Washington Post*, May 13, 1990.
5. Mark Weisman, "ACRI Work in the Occupied Territories: Assessment Study (Litigation)," 2008 (Hebrew).

1: THE BATTLEGROUND

1. East Jerusalem was annexed by a government order: Law and Administration Ordinance (No. 1), 5767-1967; the Golan Heights area was annexed through Knesset legislation fourteen years later: Golan Heights Law 5742-1981.
2. HCJ 337/71, *Christian Society for the Holy Places v. Minister of Defense*, IsrSC 21 (1): 574 (1972). Majority justices were Yoel Zussman and Isaac Cohen; dissenting was Justice Haim Cohn.
3. Meir Shamgar, "Legal Concepts and Problems of the Israeli Military Government—The Initial Stage," in Meir Shamgar, ed., *Military Government in the Territories Administered by Israel 1967–1980: The Legal Aspects* (Jerusalem: Harry Sacher Institute for Legislative Research and Comparative Law, 1982), 13, 43n56.
4. Ibid.
5. See David Kretzmer, *The Occupation of Justice: The Supreme Court of Israel and the Occupied Territories* (Albany: State University of New York Press, 2002), p. 20.
6. *Johnson v. Eisentrager*, 339 U.S. 763 (1950).
7. See, e.g., *Hamdan v. Rumsfeld*, 548 U.S. 557 (2006).

8. As well as special tribunals, such as religious tribunals, land tribunals, courts for serious crimes, and tribal courts where disputes between Bedouin tribes, particularly in the Negev, were heard.

9. Yitzhak Zamir, "The Jurisdiction of the High Court of Justice," *Legal Studies in Memory of Avraham Rosenthal*, 255, p. 229 (Hebrew); Eliad Shraga and Roy Shahar, *Administrative Law* (vol. E), p. 13 (Hebrew).

10. One of its five wings, the Queen/King Bench, is an administrative instance.

11. For a discussion of this issue, see Shraga and Shahar, *Administrative Law*, pp. 13–15; and Yair Shraga, "For the Administration of Justice: On the Establishment of the High Court of Justice of Israel," *Iyunei Mishpat* (vol. 28), p. 225 (2005) (Hebrew).

12. Court Ordinance, 1924, Art. 5.

13. Basic Law: The Judiciary 5748-1984, Art. 15 (d) (2), English translation available on Knesset website (accessed November 14, 2016).

14. Ibid., Art. 15 (c).

15. "The Supreme Court sitting as a High Court of Justice, shall have jurisdiction to hear and determine such matters as are not causes or trials, but petitions or applications not within the jurisdiction of any other Court and necessary to be decided for the administration of justice." (The Palestine Order in Council, 1922, Art. 43, para. 2.)

16. See, e.g., HCJ 3511/02, *Negev Coexistence Forum for Civil Equality v. Ministry of Infrastructure*, IsrSC 57 (2): 102, where the High Court ordered the state to immediately build a bridge for the children of a Bedouin tribe who have to cross a river where sewage runs on their way to school. The court ruled it has jurisdiction to make this order even if planning and building laws do not allow for immediate construction thanks to its power to grant relief "for the sake of justice."

17. The Christian Society case was preceded by several petitions regarding actions taken by the military administration in the Occupied Territories, but the judgments given in them were not reported: HCJ 95/67, *Attallah Antoun v. Minister of Defense* (1967); HCJ 93/68, *Bouri Bishara v. MAG*; HCJ 126/68, *Darwish al-Zein v. Chief Warder at Ramla Central Prison*; and HCJ 283/69, *Muhammad Abdallah v. the Military Court*. For more information about these petitions, see Limor Yehuda, "The High Court and the OPT: Judicial Oversight or Stamp of Approval for the Occupation—Introduction," on the website of the film *The Law in These Parts*, https://www.thelawfilm.com/inside/ (accessed November 7, 2016) (Hebrew).

18. HCJ 302/72, *Sheikh Suleiman Hussein 'Odeh Abu Hilu v. Government of Israel*, IsrSC 27 (2): 169 (1973), p. 177.

19. In addition to this, laws enacted by the Palestinian Authority, established under the Oslo Accords, apply in the West Bank as well. These laws do not apply to Israelis and Israeli settlements. They are also subject to military legislation on issues that are not the purview of the Palestinian Authority under the Interim Agreement between Israel and the PLO. See Israeli-Palestinian Interim Agreement on the West Bank and the Gaza Strip (signed in Washington, D.C., September 28, 1995), Arts. XVII and XVIII.

20. "One Rule, Two Legal Systems: Israel's Regime of Laws in the West Bank," Association for Civil Rights in Israel (November 2014), http://www.acri.org.il/en/2014/11/24/twosysreport/ (accessed January 30, 2017).

21. Orna Ben-Naftali and Yuval Shani, *International Law Between War and Peace* (Ramot, Israel: Tel Aviv University, 2006) (Hebrew), pp. 117–22.

22. International custom is one of the primary sources of international law. A customary norm is created when states follow a certain practice in the belief that the practice is obligatory. Such a norm turns into a rule of customary international law that applies globally and is binding regardless of it being codified (with some restrictions). In Israel, like in many other countries, for an international convention signed by the state as per the decision of the executive branch to be binding under domestic law, its provisions must be "channeled" through a local legislative act. In other words, the provisions of the convention must be made part of Israeli law through statute. Otherwise, the international convention is binding only on the international relations plane. In contrast, international norms that have attained customary status are automatically part of the law applicable in Israel, unless there is a domestic law that explicitly contradicts them. For more, see Robbie Sabel and Yaël Ronen, eds., *International Law* (Tel Aviv: Nevo, 2016) (Hebrew); chapter 2, "Origins of International Law" (by Robbie Sabel), and chapter 3, "The Status of International Law in Domestic Law" (by Tomer Brodie).

23. See Eyal Benvenisty, *The International Law of Occupation* (Princeton, NJ: Princeton University Press, 1993), pp. 3–6; Orna Ben-Naftali, Aeyal Gross, and Keren Michaeli, "Illegal Occupation: The Framing of the Occupied Palestinian Territory," *Berkeley International Law Journal* 23, no. 3 (2005): 551–614.

24. "The Hague Regulations revolve around two central axes: one—is ensuring the legitimate security interests of the occupier in a territory which is under belligerent occupation; the other is—safeguarding the needs of the civilian population in a territory under belligerent occupation." HCJ 393/82, *Jam'iat Iscan Al-Ma'almoun et al. v. Minister of Defense*, IsrSC 37 (4): 785, at p. 794. Unofficial translation available on the HaMoked website, http://www.hamoked.org/items/160_eng.pdf (accessed November 15, 2016); see also Yoram Dinstein, "Legislative Powers in the Administered Territories," *Iyunei Mishpat* B (5732-3), 505, 509 (Hebrew).

25. Regulation 46 of the Regulations annexed to the Fourth Hague Convention.

26. Art. 49 of the Fourth Geneva Convention, first paragraph.

27. Art. 49 of the Fourth Geneva Convention, sixth paragraph.

28. The Jordanians and the Egyptians left intact some of the laws enacted by previous rulers, British Mandate orders and Ottoman Empire laws, such that local law is a legal-geological formation made up of legal strata put in place by previous rulers.

29. Meir Shamgar, "The Observance of International Law in the Administered Territories," *Israel Yearbook on Human Rights* (1971): 262, 263.

30. HCJ 337/71, p. 580.

31. See, e.g., HCJ 393/82, p. 792.

2: DEPORTATION: RAISING THE STAKES

1. Memorandum on the Palestine (Defense) Order in Council, 1937, *Palestine Gazette*, Extraordinary No. 675 of March 24, 1937, Supplement No. 2, p. 267. This 1937 Order in Council was preceded by the 1931 Order in Council, which empowered the high commissioner to issue emergency regulations, Palestine (Defense) Order in Council, 1931, *Palestine Gazette*, p. 2798.

2. Defense (Emergency) Regulations 1945 (hereinafter: Defense Regulations).

3. Regulations 108 and 112 of the Defense Regulations.

4. Regulation 112(8), referring to the advisory committee established under Regulation 111(4), to advise on administrative detention.

5. For instance, Menachem Dunkleblum, who served as president of the Jewish Bar Association of Eretz Israel (the precursor of the Israel Bar Association), sharply criticized the Defense Regulations at a conference held in Tel Aviv in February 1946: "Indeed, these regulations are a danger to the entire Yishuv"—the name for the Jewish communities in Mandatory Palestine—"but we, as lawyers, have a special interest in them: this is a violation of the elementary concepts of law and justice. The regulations sanction complete arbitrariness on the part of administrative and military authorities. This arbitrariness, even if authorized by a legislative institution is anarchy. . . . The Defense Regulations cancel individual rights and give the administration unchecked power." In the same conference, attorney Yaakov Shimshon Shapira compared the Defense Regulations to Nazi law and asked his colleagues to "publicly and internationally declare: The Defense Regulations of the Government of Eretz Yisrael destroy the pillars of justice in the country." See *Ha-Praklit* 3, no. 2 (1946): 58–62 (Hebrew). When the State of Israel was established, Dunkleblum was appointed one of the first five justices of the country's Supreme Court, and Shapira served as the first attorney general and later minister of justice.

6. Genesis 4:14 (KJV).

7. The transcripts were uncovered by the Akevot Institute for Israeli-Palestinian Conflict Research (hereinafter: Akevot Institute). The author is a member of the institute's board of directors.

8. Minutes of a meeting on the situation in Judea and Samaria headed by the prime minister (June 3, 1980), The Conflict Records' Digital Repository (Akevot Institute), Document no. 12954, p. 26.

9. Ibid., p. 34.

10. B'Tselem, "Deportation of Palestinians from the Occupied Territories and the Mass Deportation of December 1992" (June 1993), p. 17. The figure is based on the response of Defense Minister Ariel Sharon to a parliamentary question submitted by MK Mordechai Virshuvsky, *Knesset Record*, vol. 95, p. 1145 (1983). Another quote refers to 1,180 deportations. Quoted in Kretzmer, *The Occupation of Justice*, p. 165, from E. R. Cohen, *Human Rights in the Israeli-Occupied Territories 1967–1982* (Manchester: Manchester University Press, 1985), p. 106.

11. Letter from Yehoshua Almog, Foreign Ministry delegate in the Occupied Territories, to Moshe Sasson, Foreign Ministry deputy executive director, "Patient Operations," August 28, 1970, The Conflict Records' Digital Repository (Akevot Institute), Document no. 1004132. The document is stored in the National Archive, HZ 4470/05.

12. Letter from Yehoshua Almog to Moshe Sasson, "Planning measures to avoid further escalation in the Gaza Strip," January 4, 1971, The Conflict Records' Digital Repository (Akevot Institute), Document no. 1003521. The document is stored in the National Archive, HZ 4470/17.

13. One exception was a proceeding challenging a deportation order issued under the Defense Regulations against a Palestinian resident of East Jerusalem. Since East Jerusalem had been annexed and put under Israeli law, in terms of Israeli law, jurisdiction in the OPT (Occupied Palestinian Territories) was not an issue in this case. See HCJ 17/71, *Azmi Ibrahim Mrar et al. v. Minister of Defense et al.*, IsrSC 28 (1): 141.

14. In a letter to the prime minister, dated July 4, 1975, Yigal Alon describes the deportation of "several dozen" Palestinians and cautions that "there is little doubt that the deportation of residents of the Territories contravenes international law by which the country is bound." Letter from Yigal Alon to the prime minister, July 4,

1975, "Deportation of residents of the Territories to neighboring Arab countries," The Conflict Records' Digital Repository (Akevot Institute), Document no. 1008503. The document is stored in the National Archive, HZ 5833/3.

15. Felicia Langer, *My Way* (Tel Aviv: Dvir, 1991), p. 226 (Hebrew).

16. Ibid., p. 228.

17. Ibid., p. 64.

18. Ibid., p. 229.

19. Major General Shlomo Gazit, the first Coordinator of Government Activities in the Territories (then titled Head of the Policy-Security Coordination Committee), and later Head of Military Intelligence, claimed in his book that Mayor Ali Ja'abari asked that "Israel arrest some of his opponents or deport them to Jordan." S. Gazit, *Trapped Fools* (Tel Aviv: Zmora-Bitan, 1999), p. 170 (Hebrew).

20. HCJ 159/76, *al-Natsheh v. Military Commander* (unreported), quoted from J. Algazi, "In Memory of a Dear Friend and Human Being," http://www.defeatist-diary.com /index.asp?p=memories_new10044&period=20/7/2009-30/3/2010 (last accessed August 11, 2017) (Hebrew). See also Langer, *My Way*, p. 232.

21. In 2002, Colonel Shaul Gordon, president of the West Bank Courts Martial, led a change that ended adjudication by judges without legal training, and lawyers on reserve military duty were added to the bench.

22. HCJ 139/77, *A. et al. v. Minister of Defense et al.*, IsrSC 32 (1): 29 (July 13, 1977).

23. Art. 1 (9), Constitution of the Hashemite Kingdom of Jordan.

24. Convention (IV) Relative to the Protection of Civilian Persons in Time of War. Geneva, August 12, 1949 (hereinafter: Geneva Convention). Art. 49 stipulates: "Individual or mass forcible transfers, as well as deportations of protected persons from occupied territory to the territory of the Occupying Power or to that of any other country, occupied or not, are prohibited, regardless of their motive."

25. Arts. 146–147, Geneva Convention.

26. HCJ 97/79, *Riad Abu Rashid Abu Awad v. Commander of the Judea and Samaria Area*, IsrSC 33 (3): 309.

27. Order Regarding Interpretation (Additional Provisions) (No. 5) (Judea and Samaria Area), 1968, Section 2. Section 3 of this order stipulates that the version of emergency legislation that is considered valid is the version in effect on the eve of Israel's establishment on May 14, 1948, unless explicitly revoked. So, using a military order on interpreting legislation, the military commander made sure any effect of Jordanian constitutional law on emergency legislation would be erased.

28. Convention (IV) Respecting the Laws and Customs of War on Land and its annex: Regulations Concerning the Laws and Customs of War on Land. The Hague, 1907 (Hague Regulations), Regulation 43.

29. HCJ 97/79, p. 314.

30. Ibid., p. 317.

31. HCJ 785/87, *Affo v. Commander of IDF Forces*, IsrSC 42 (4), English translation available on Supreme Court website, p. 84 (English version).

32. HCJ 103/92, *Boulos et al. v. Advisory Committee Under Regulations 108 and 112 of the Defense Regulations et al.*, IsrSC 41 (1): 466.

33. *Haaretz*, November 7, 1979, p. 2 (Hebrew).

34. Quoted in Gazit, *Trapped Fools*, p. 95.

35. In his book, Gazit wonders why the Israeli authorities, which consistently forbade any political activity in the Occupied Territories, allowed the GNC to be active. Gazit, *Trapped Fools*, p. 95.

36. For more detail, see chapter 3: "Settlement: Banging One's Head Against the Wall of the Political."

37. "Weizman: We Will Take Measures Against Shaka," *Al HaMishmar*, November 8, 1979.

38. K. Amnon (Amnon Kapeliouk), "I Expressed Understanding for the Motives, Not Sympathy with the Coastal Road Murderers," *Al HaMishmar*, November 8, 1979.

39. Until 1999, courts-martial operated inside Israel under the British Defense (Emergency) Regulations, mostly trying Israeli Arabs on security charges.

40. This decision to ban airing interviews with people "associated with the PLO" made by Lapid, who later became minister of justice, was a bone of contention and ultimately the focus of a High Court petition, in which the directive, in its sweeping version, was struck down. HCJ 243/82, *Amnon Zichroni v. Broadcasting Authority Board of Directors*, IsrSC 37 (1): 757.

41. A description of the chain of events appears in Langer's book *My Way*, p. 237.

42. Ibid., p. 238.

43. Dani Rubinstein, "West Bank Mayors to Resign Tomorrow if Shaka Is Not Released," *Davar*, November 11, 1979, p. 1.

44. "Israeli Military Authorities Arrest Nablus Mayor Bassam Shaka Pending Deportation," *New York Times*, November 12, 1979.

45. "Israel's Arrest of Arab Mayor Sparks Protest," *Washington Post*, November 12, 1979.

46. "The United States reproved Israel Thursday for trying to deport a West Bank mayor and said the action could impede a Palestinian settlement," Associated Press, November 15, 1979; see also Mordechai Barkai, "The Administration Condemns Decision to Deport Shaka," *Davar*, November 15, 1979, p. 1.

47. "HCJ Sends Shaka to Military Advisory Committee," *Davar*, November 22, 1979, p. 3.

48. UN General Assembly Resolution 34/29 (16 November 1979), A/RES/34/29.

49. "Israeli High Court Blocks Deportation of Nablus Mayor Pending Final Appeal," *Washington Post*, November 23, 1979.

50. "Military Appeals Committee Recommendation on Shaka—Early Next Week," *Davar*, November 29, 1979, p. 2.

51. "Student Strikes and Protests in West Bank Ahead of Shaka Recommendations," *Davar*, December 30, 1979, p. 1.

52. Quoted in Gazit, *Trapped Fools*, p. 95.

53. Langer, *My Way*, p. 264.

54. Quoted in a report by Itim News Agency correspondent Shmuel Mitleman, "HCJ Orders Defense Minister to Explain Why He Should Not Revoke the Deportation Orders Against the Trio," *Ma'ariv*, May 22, 1980, p. 3.

55. Ibid.

56. "Major General Matt: The Change in the West Bank Began at the Meeting Held by Shaka a Year Ago," *Davar*, May 3, 1980.

57. Minutes of a meeting on the situation in Judea and Samaria headed by the prime minister (June 3, 1980), The Conflict Records' Digital Repository (Akevot Institute), Document no. 12954.

58. Langer, *My Way*, p. 272.

59. Ibid., pp. 272–73.

60. HCJ 320/80, *Yusra Qasem Qawasmeh on behalf of herself and her husband, Fahed Qawasmeh, et al. v. Minister of Defense*, IsrSC 35 (3): 113 (August 19, 1980), p. 117.

61. Ibid., p. 133.

62. Ibid., p. 124.
63. Order Regarding Interpretation. The order was mentioned in the Abu Awad case as well but was not needed in that case.
64. HCJ 698/80, *Fahed Daud Qawasmeh et al. v. Minister of Defense*, IsrSC 35 (1): 617 (December 4, 1980).
65. Art. 49, Geneva Convention.
66. Criminal Appeal 174/54 *Enosh Shtampeper v. the Attorney General*, 10 IsrSC, p. 5.
67. HCJ 698/80, p. 627.
68. Ibid., p. 637.
69. Ibid., p. 641.
70. Ibid., p. 647.
71. HCJ 629/82, *Mustafa v. Military Commander of the Judea and Samaria Area*, IsrSC 37 (1): 158.
72. HCJ 513/85, *Nazal et al. v. IDF Commander in the Judea and Samaria Area*, IsrSC 39 (3): 645. A motion for a further hearing by an extended panel was rejected. HCJ 513/85, *Nazal et al. v. IDF Commander in the Judea and Samaria Area*, TakSC 85 (3): 41.
73. Langer, *My Way*, pp. 225–26.
74. With the exception of the Human Rights Protection League, which was established in 1930 and was still in operation in 1987. This organization was considered anti-Zionist and therefore marginal in Israel.
75. *Israel Yearbook of Human Rights* (vol. 1) (1971).
76. HCJ 785/87, *Affo v. Commander of IDF Forces*, IsrSC 42 (4) (April 10, 1988). English translation available on Supreme Court website.
77. Ibid., pp. 31–32 (English version).
78. Vienna Convention on the Law of Treaties 1969, Art. 31: "A treaty shall be interpreted in good faith in accordance with the ordinary meaning to be given to the terms of the treaty in their context and in the light of its object and purpose."
79. HCJ 785/87, pp. 92–93 (English version).
80. The practice is based on the provisions of the Evidence Ordinance [New Version], 1971, Section 46, which allows filing a petition for disclosure of evidence regarding which the minister of defense or the prime minister had signed a confidentiality certificate. According to the section, a petition for disclosure of evidence deemed confidential for national security reasons shall be heard by a justice of the Supreme Court. See a sample petition filed by Feldman for disclosure of confidential evidence that formed the basis for a deportation decision: MApp. HCJ 497/88 (HCJ 768/88), *Bilal Shakshir v. IDF Commander in the West Bank*, IsrSC 43 (1): 529.
81. Ibid., 43 (2): 242.
82. Ibid.
83. HCJ 792/88, *Muhammad Matour v. IDF Commander*, IsrSC 43 (3): 542 (August 24, 1989).
84. HCJ 814/88, *Tayseer Nasrallah v. IDF Commander in the West Bank*, IsrSC 43 (2): 265 (June 21, 1989), para. 11.
85. B'Tselem, "Deportation of Palestinians from the Occupied Territories and the Mass Deportation of December 1992," (June 1993).
86. It is worth noting that according to B'Tselem research, most of the deportation orders issued in the first decade, 881, were signed between the years 1970 and 1974.
87. The 25th Government of Israel, Resolution No. 456 (translation from B'Tselem report).

88. Order Regarding Temporary Deportation (Temporary Order) (Judea and Samaria Area) (No. 1381), 1992; Order Regarding Temporary Deportation (Temporary Order) (Gaza Strip) (No. 1986), 1992.

89. This description is based on interviews the author conducted with Leah Tsemel (May 19, 2015), Avigdor Feldman (April 12, 2015), and Andre Rosenthal (November 9, 2015).

90. It is interesting to note that both of them later went to work for the High Court Department at the Justice Ministry, representing the state in petitions filed against it. Schoffman was later promoted to the position of director of the Counseling and Legislation Department and Briskman was promoted to a senior attorney position in the High Court Department.

91. Interview with the author, November 2015.

92. Aviva Luri, "Running to the HCJ," *Haaretz*, January 5, 2005 (interview with Dan Yakir).

93. Interview with the author, June 21, 2015.

94. This description is based on Feldman's interview with the author on April 12, 2015.

95. Quoted in M. Negbi, "The Legal Crisis," and in B'Tselem, "Deportation of Palestinians from the Occupied Territories and the Mass Deportation of December 1992," p. 67.

96. Quoted in a *Haaretz* report, January 18, 1993, and in B'Tselem, "Deportation of Palestinians from the Occupied Territories and the Mass Deportation of December 1992," p. 48.

97. Naomi Levitsky, *His Honor* (Jerusalem: Keter, 2001), p. 180 (Hebrew).

98. "For Deportation: 91%, Against: 8%," *Yedioth Ahronoth*, December 18, 1992. The same poll revealed another interesting figure. While 55 percent of the participants believed that the deportation would decrease terrorism, 26 percent thought it would increase it. In other words, at least 15 percent were in favor of the deportation, despite believing that it would exacerbate terrorism.

99. B'Tselem, "Deportation of Palestinians from the Occupied Territories and the Mass Deportation of December 1992."

100. S/RES/799 (1992).

101. Attorney Imad Dakwar filed two petitions, one on behalf of MK Abdulwahab Darawshe and one on behalf of one of the deportees. See an interview Dakwar gave about this case, "The Deportee Case," *BiDlatayim Ptuhot* (April–May 2008), p. 36 (Hebrew). Attorneys Anis Riad, Jawad Boulos, and Darwish Nasser each filed more petitions on behalf of groups of deportees. A total of twelve petitions were heard together.

102. Arieh Bender, "Fascinating Duel," *Ma'ariv*, December 23, 1992.

103. B'Tselem, "Deportation of Palestinians from the Occupied Territories and the Mass Deportation of December 1992," p. 43.

104. Levitsky, *His Honor*, p. 187 (Hebrew).

105. HCJ 5973/92, *Association for Civil Rights in Israel et al. v. Minister of Defense et al.*, IsrSC 47 (1): 267. English translation available on Supreme Court website, p. 21 (English version).

106. Ibid., p. 291 (English version).

107. See, for example: Eyal Benvenisti, "First Deport then Hear", *Mishpat uMimshal* 1 (1993) 442 (Hebrew); Behnam Dayanim, *The Israeli Supreme Court and the Deportations of Palestinians: The Interaction of Law and Legitimacy,* 30 Stan. J. Int'l L. 115, 186 (1994); Kretzmer, *The Occupation of Justice,* pp. 184–186.

108. Israel's consent was given in return for a pledge from the Clinton administration to block an attempt to impose sanctions on Israel for breaking the UN Security

Council calling for the return of the deportees. See "Israel to Return 100 Palestinians It Had Deported," *New York Times*, February 2, 1993, p. A8.

109. Interview with the author, May 19, 2015.

110. Interview with the author, April 12, 2015.

111. The State Attorney's Office euphemistically referred to this as "assigned residence." See main judgment on this issue, HCJ 7015/02, *Ajuri v. IDF Commander*, TakSC 2002 (3): 1021 (September 3, 2002).

112. For instance, in May 2002 an agreement was reached for the deportation of thirteen wanted men who barricaded themselves in the Church of the Nativity in Bethlehem; seven European countries agreed to take them in. The deportees consented, which means this was not a forcible transfer in the ordinary sense of the term.

113. "For Every Deportee, Three New Ones Emerge," *Yedioth Ahronoth*, December 18, 1992, p. 48.

3: SETTLEMENTS: BANGING ONE'S HEAD AGAINST THE WALL OF THE POLITICAL

1. Figures taken from B'Tselem website, http://www.btselem.org/hebrew/settlements/statistics (last viewed August 11, 2017).

2. According to the Palestinian Bureau of Statistics, the total number of Palestinians living in the West Bank in 2015 was 2.86 million and in East Jerusalem 420,000: http://www.pcbs.gov.ps/Portals/_Rainbow/Documents/gover_e.htm (last viewed August 11, 2017).

3. Peace Now's website: http://peacenow.org.il/settlements-watch/matzav/population (last viewed August 11, 2017).

4. An example of attacks of this kind is the torching of the Dawabsheh family home in the village of Duma, south of Nablus, in which a baby and his father and mother were killed and another child was severely wounded. See "Palestinian Infant Burned to Death in West Bank Arson Attack; IDF Blames 'Jewish Terror,'" *Haaretz*, July 31, 2015, http://www.haaretz.com/israel-news/1.668871 (last viewed February 1, 2016).

5. For an analysis of the ineptitude shown by the authorities and statistics on investigation outcomes, see reports and figures published by Yesh Din on the organization's website, http://www.yesh-din.org/. See also the reports published by B'Tselem, which has been investigating these issues since the late 1980s, at http://www.btselem.org/.

6. According to the Israeli Central Bureau of Statistics, the number of Israelis residing in the West Bank in 2015 was 385,000 and in East Jerusalem 208,000 (http://www.cbs.gov.il/shnaton67/st02_15x.pdf). According to the Palestinian Central Bureau of Statistics, the number of Palestinians residing in the West Bank in 2015 was 2.86 million and in East Jerusalem 420,000 (http://www.pcbs.gov.ps/Portals/_Rainbow/Documents/gover_e.htm). According to these figures, the ratio in the West Bank is 88 percent Palestinians and 12 percent settlers, and if adding East Jerusalem, then the ratio is 85 percent–15 percent.

7. "Enclave law" is a term coined by Amnon Rubinstein in his article "The Shifting of the 'Territories'—From Pawn Held in Trust to Legal Hybrid," *Iyunei Mishpat* 11 (1987): 439, 450 (Hebrew).

8. See International Convention on the Suppression and Punishment of the Crime of Apartheid, 1973, Art. II, and the Rome Statute of the International Criminal Court, 1998, Art. 7 (1) (j) and 7 (2) (h).

9. See John Dugard and John Reynolds, "Apartheid, International Law, and the Occupied Palestinian Territory," *European Journal of International Law* 24, no. 3 (2013):

867–913, doi: 10.1093/ejil/cht045; Yaffa Zilbershats, "Apartheid, International Law, and the Occupied Palestinian Territory: A Reply to John Dugard and John Reynolds," *European Journal of International Law* 24, no. 3 (2013): 915–28, doi:10.1093/ejil/cht043.

10. This subsection is based on a section of *The Wall of Folly*, which I coauthored in Hebrew with Shaul Arieli, *Homa uMehdal* (Tel Aviv: Aliyat Hagag, 2008).

11. Order Regarding Defense Regulations (Judea and Samaria) (No. 378), 1970, Declaration Regarding Closure of Area No. s/2/03 (Seam Area).

12. The route of the separation barrier has since been changed; the village was "reattached" to the West Bank and the Palestinian Authority connected it to the grid.

13. Convention (IV) Relative to the Protection of Civilian Persons in Time of War, 1949, Art. 2, para. 2.

14. Yehuda Blum, "Zion Redeemed Through Law," *HaPraklit* 27 (1971): 315 (Hebrew). This was Blum's response to the position presented by Yoram Dinstein in his article "Zion Shall Be Redeemed Through International Law," *HaPraklit* 27 (1971): 5. Dinstein responded in a third article: "She Has Not Been Redeemed, or Actions Not Protests," *HaPraklit* 27 (1972): 519.

15. See the explanation posted on the Ministry of Foreign Affairs website in November 2015: http://mfa.gov.il/MFA/ForeignPolicy/Peace/Guide/Pages/Israeli%20Settlements%20and%20International%20Law.aspx (last viewed February 8, 2016).

16. The position of the ICRC is presented in Meir Shamgar's essay, "Legal Concepts and Problems of the Israeli Military Government—The Initial Stage," in *Military Government in the Territories Administered by Israel 1967–1980, The Legal Aspects*, ed. Meir Shamgar (Jerusalem: Harry Sacher Institute for Legislative Research and Comparative Law, 1982), p. 32.

17. For a review of the resolutions and commentary made by international bodies, see *Unprecedented* (Yesh Din and the Emile Zola Chair for Human Rights at the Haim Striks School of Law, College of Management Academic Studies, January 2014). For the International Court of Justice Advisory Opinion, see Consequences of the Construction of a Wall in the Occupied Palestinian Territory, Advisory Opinion, ICJ (2004), 136. In December 2016, the UN Security Council reiterated its position that all settlements are illegal and a violation of international law: Security Council Resolution 2334 (December 23, 2016), S/RES/2334(2016).

18. For a review of some of the academic literature on the subject, see *Unprecedented*, pp. 24–25.

19. For more detail on this argument, see Kretzmer, *The Occupation of Justice*, p. 35.

20. Fourth Geneva Convention, Arts. 146 and 147.

21. Rome Statute of the International Criminal Court, Art. 8 (2) (b) (viii).

22. Convention (IV) Respecting the Laws and Customs of War on Land and Its Annex: Regulation Concerning the Laws and Customs of War on Land.

23. The Hague Regulations, Regulation 55.

24. Kfar Etzion was built a few weeks after the war on the ruins of the Jewish settlement that was located in Gush Etzion until 1948. It was followed by several more settlements in the Gush Etzion area and the Jordan Valley, in accordance with the Allon Plan, which sought to annex the Jordan Valley, Gush Etzion, and the southern part of the Gaza Strip to Israel. See Idith Zertal and Akiva Eldar, *Lords of the*

Land: The War over Israel's Settlements in the Occupied Territories 1967–2007 (New York: Nation Books, 2007).

25. David Kretzmer and Gershom Gorenberg, "Politics, Law, and the Judicial Process: The Case of the High Court of Justice and the Territories," *Mishpat uMimshal* 17, no. 1 (5775): 24–34 (Hebrew).

26. Ibid., p. 26, quote from the transcripts of a government session dated January 26, 1969.

27. S. Gazit, *Ptaim BeMalkodet* (Tel Aviv: Zmora-Bitan, 1999), p. 240 (Hebrew).

28. The description of the events appears in the petition filed by the tribe leaders to the High Court of Justice at a later stage, as well as in "Approach Tribe Leaders Go to the High Court of Justice," *Davar*, July 31, 1972. See also Kretzmer and Gorenberg, "Politics, Law, and the Judicial Process," p. 19 (Hebrew).

29. The IDF had established a camel cavalry that made quite a reputation for itself as violent.

30. Oded Lifshitz, "Return to Rafah," *HaDaf HaYarok*, February 7, 2002.

31. Ibid.

32. "The IDF Spokesperson Explains," *Al Hamishmar*, March 9, 1972, quoted in Kretzmer and Gorenberg, "Politics, Law, and the Judicial Process," 31n26.

33. For an article expressing skepticism about the veracity of the allegations against the Rafah Approach Bedouin, see Nahum Barnea, "The Jewish Side of the Rafah Approach," *Davar*, April 21, 1972.

34. Yosef Kharif, "Bedouins Evacuated in Rafah Will Not Return—Offered Choice Between Monetary Compensation or Reconstruction," *Ma'ariv*, April 17, 1972, p. 3.

35. "Demonstrate to Return Bedouins to Rafah," *Davar*, May 28, 1972.

36. Lifshitz, "Return to Rafah."

37. Ibid.

38. In its response to the petition, the state alleged that the number of displaced persons was much lower, around five thousand.

39. "Order Nisi Issued in Rafah Approach Case," *Davar*, August 8, 1982. The newspaper reported that the IDF spokesperson had said the allegations were under investigation and that "no flaw has been found in the conduct of IDF officers in these matters."

40. HCJ 302/72, *Sheikh Sulaiman Hussein 'Odeh Abu Hilu v. Government of Israel*, IsrSC 27 (2): 169 (May 23, 1973), p. 174.

41. In their research, Kretzmer and Gorenberg show that the state's arguments and affidavits included explanations that, though maybe not outright lies, were phrased in a very misleading manner, both with respect to the motives for the expulsion and the description of the conclusions of the various inquiry committees. Kretzmer and Gorenberg, "Politics, Law, and the Judicial Process," p. 50.

42. Ibid., pp. 41–42.

43. HCJ 302/72, p. 175.

44. Major General Shlomo Gazit, then head of the Policy-Security Coordination Committee in the Territories (now called the Coordinator of Government Activities in the Territories), says in his book that these were "peaceful Bedouin who cooperated with the Israeli authorities." Gazit, *Ptaim BeMalkodet*, p. 240.

45. Ibid., p. 176.

46. Holtzman passed away before the hearing took place and was replaced by Gavriel Glazer.

47. Ibid.

48. Ibid., p. 182, emphasis added.
49. However, the justices ignored the fact that the Geneva Convention also prohibits evacuations inside the Occupied Territories (see Art. 49, 2–5, and Art. 78).
50. "Dayan: The Approach Will Be Home to Hundreds of Thousands of Jews," *Davar*, September 26, 1973.
51. Lifshitz, "Return to Rafah."
52. Based on a report by Amos Levav, "High Court Rejects Petition Against Anatot Land Seizure," *Ma'ariv*, December 18, 1978.
53. Interview with the author, April 20, 2015.
54. "Palestinian for Better or Worse: Attorney Elias Khoury's Private Grief," *Zman Yerushalayim*, April 13, 2011. Also published on NRG website, http://www.nrg.co.il/online/54/ART2/232/003.html (last viewed February 1, 2016).
55. Up to this point, the settlement project had been governed by the Allon Plan.
56. For more details on the National Guidance Committee and its leaders, see chapter 2, "Deportation: Raising the Stakes."
57. Art. 46 of The Hague Regulations explicitly notes, "Private property cannot be confiscated."
58. "Neve Saleh Group Leaves, Neve Saleh Group Accepts New Members," *Ma'ariv*, February 17, 1978.
59. In an interview with the author, April 20, 2015.
60. For more details on Ottoman law and the status of public (or state) land, see below.
61. Amos Levav, "Did Two Km of Fence Drop out of the Sky?" *Ma'ariv*, May 26, 1978.
62. "High Court Forbids Work in Nabi Saleh," *Davar*, May 26, 1978, p. 3.
63. Ibid.
64. "Settlers: We Put Up the Fence," *Davar*, May 28, 1978, p. 1.
65. Dani Rubinstein, "More High Court Petitions on Land Confiscation Expected," *Davar*, June 4, 1978, p. 3.
66. Khoury's account was conveyed in an interview with the author.
67. Ibid.
68. According to Peace Now figures as provided to author.
69. February 13, 1980.
70. Levav, "High Court Rejects Petition Against Anatot Land Seizure."
71. HCJ 834/78, *Musa 'Abd a-Salam Salameh v. Minister of Defense et al.*, IsrSC 33 (1): 471 (December 17, 1978).
72. Amos Levav, "Hearing in Settlement Petition to Be Held in Front of Five Justices," *Ma'ariv*, November 14, 1978.
73. HCJ 606/78, 610/78, *Suleiman Taufiq Ayyub et 11 e. v. Minister of Defense et 2 al.*, IsrSC 33 (2): 113 (March 18, 1979), p. 125.
74. The attempt made by Gush Emunim to join the petition is not mentioned in the judgment. See Gazit, *Ptaim BeMalkodet*, p. 243, and Khoury interview with the author.
75. Amos Levav, "Someone Out to Embarrass the Government of Israel at Critical Negotiation Stage," *Ma'ariv*, November 24, 1978.
76. The article is Y. Dinstein, "The Rafah Approach Judgment," *Iyunei Mishpat* 3 (1973), 934.
77. HCJ 106/78, 110/78, p. 123.
78. His bench mate, Supreme Court deputy president Moshe Landau, wrote: "I have more willingly reached the conclusion that this court must refrain from discussing the issue of civilian settlement in an area considered held under international

law, knowing that this issue is a point of contention between Israel and other governments and may be discussed as part of the critical negotiations the Government of Israel is currently engaged in. Any opinion expressed by this Court on such a sensitive matter, which can only be made as a side comment, will neither add nor detract, and it is best for matters belonging in the sphere of foreign policy to be discussed in that sphere alone" (ibid., p. 128).

79. HCJ 606/78, 610/78, p. 119.

80. Ibid., p. 132.

81. Ibid., p. 135.

82. See HCJ 9060/08, *Abdalla v. the Minister of Defense* (judgment of September 21, 2011). Another petition filed by Yesh Din with respect to a southern expansion resulted in the plan being frozen. See HCJ 5165/15, *Qassem v. the Supervisor of Permits in Lands Seized for Military Purposes* (2017).

83. HCJ 258/09, *Falah Hussein Ibrahim 'Amira v. Minister of Defense*, IsrSC 34 (1): 90 (August 24, 1979), p. 92.

84. "Abram passed through the land to the place of Shechem, as far as the terebinth tree of Moreh. And the Canaanites were then in the land. Then the Lord appeared to Abram and said, 'To your descendants I will give this land.' And there he built an altar to the Lord, who had appeared to him."

85. Dani Rubinstein, "Settlement Attempt Thwarted Near Nablus," *Davar*, December 31, 1978.

86. Yosef Waxman, "This Is the Government Resolution on the Elon Moreh Core Group," *Davar*, January 11, 1979.

87. Khoury interview with the author.

88. Parts of Bar-Lev's affidavit are quoted in the judgment in HCJ 390/79, *'Izzat Muhammad Mustafa Duweikat et al. v. Government of Israel et al.*, IsrSC 34 (1): 1 (October 22, 1979), p. 8.

89. See, e.g., "High Court Forbids Work and Additional People in Elon Moreh," *Davar*, May 20, 1979.

90. Quotes taken from *Davar* daily newspaper: "Petitioners' Counsel Asks to Examine Chief of Staff," *Davar*, September 7, 1979.

91. Aaron Dolev, "A Settlement Post at Nablus Approach", *Maariv*, 19.6.1979 (Hebrew).

92. HCJ 390/79, pp. 10–11.

93. HCJ 390/79, p. 17.

94. "High Court Compels Chief of Staff to Say if Elon Moreh Motivation Was Security," *Davar*, September 24, 1979, p. 1.

95. However, the court also rejected state counsel's argument that the court must refrain from discussing settlement due to the topic's political nature, in other words, declare it nonjusticiable. See remarks of Supreme Court deputy president, Moshe Landau, p. 14 of the judgment, supra note 88. Justice Landau recalled that the argument had been rejected in the Beit El case and reproached the state attorney, saying, "Repeating it does not make it any more valid."

96. HCJ 390/79, p. 17.

97. Ibid., p. 5.

98. Ibid., p. 11.

99. Ibid., p. 130.

100. Dan Margalit, "Coalition Confused: How to Save Elon Moreh," *Haaretz*, October 23, 1979; Daniel Bloch, "Top Government Official Estimates Elon Moreh Affair to Lead to Government Resignation," *Davar*, October 28, 1979, lead story.

101. Zertal and Eldar, *Lords of the Land*, p. 469 (Hebrew version).
102. Transcripts of Government Meeting 7/5740, October 28, 1979, pp. 22–23, and Transcripts of Government Meeting 8/5740, November 1, 1979, p. 63; Zertal and Eldar, *Lords of the Land*, p. 469 (Hebrew version).
103. Video on settlement website, http://www.elonmoreh.co.il/ (last viewed November 13, 2015).
104. Interview with the author, April 12, 2015.
105. Interview with the author, April 20, 2015.
106. Resolution No. 145, dated November 11, 1979.
107. Avigdor Feldman interview with the author, April 12, 2015.
108. Ibid.
109. Memorandum Regarding Legal Status of Communities in the Judea and Samaria Area, February 25, 1980, published by Akevot: Institute for Israeli-Palestinian Conflict Research: https://akevot.org.il/en/news-item/zamir-opinion-on-settlements/ (last viewed August 11, 2017).
110. Ibid., para. 9.
111. Gazit, *Ptaim BeMalkodet*, p. 239.
112. Last two figures are from Israel Central Bureau of Statistics, "Statistical Abstract of Israel 2013," Table 2.15, "Population by District, Sub-District and Religion."
113. Tzali Reshef, *Peace Now: From the Officers' Letter to Peace Now* (Tel Aviv: Keter, 1996), p. 200.
114. ACRI's cautious approach, also reflected in abstaining from clearly saying that the occupation itself is wrong, changed in the mid-1990s.
115. Reshef, *Peace Now*, p. 203.
116. HCJ 4481/91, *Bargil v. Government of Israel* [1992–94], IsrLR 158 (official English translation).
117. Ibid.
118. Feldman interview with the author.
119. A. Feldman, "Which Side Are You On, Grandpa Weinstein?," *Haaretz*, July 25, 2013.
120. Interview with the author.
121. Quoted in Reshef, *Peace Now*, p. 204.
122. HCJ 390/79, p. 16.
123. HCJ 4481/91, p. 5.
124. HCJ 4481/91, *Bargil v. Government of Israel* [1992–94], IsrLR 158 (official English translation), p. 11.
125. HCJ 3094/93, *Movement for Quality Government et al. v. Prime Minister et al.*, IsrSC 47 (5): 404, judgment dated September 8, 1993.
126. CivA 6821/93, *United Mizrahi Bank Ltd. et al. v. Government of Israel et al.*, IsrSC 49 (4): 221, judgment dated November 9, 1995. Barak often wrote about the "constitutional revolution" after Basic Law: Human Dignity and Liberty and Basic Law: Freedom of Occupation were enacted in 1992. See, e.g., Aharon Barak, "The Constitutional Revolution: Protected Fundamental Rights," *Mishpat uMimshal*, A, 1 (1992), p. 9.
127. HCJ 4481/91, *Bargil v. Government of Israel* [1992–94], IsrLR 158 (official English translation), p. 11.
128. HCJ 393/82, *Jam'iat Iscan Al-Ma'almoun et al. v. Minister of Defense*, IsrSC 37 (4): 785.

129. HCJ 3125/98, *'Abd al-'Aziz Muhammad 'Iyad v. IDF Commander in the Judea and Samaria Area*, 55 (1): 913 (November 7, 1999), p. 918.

4: AGAINST TORTURE

1. Military Judge Yonatan Livni admitted in an interview for the film *The Law in These Parts* that he knew about what went on in the ISA's interrogation rooms.
2. See, for instance, Ilan Rahum, *The Shabak Affair* (Tel Aviv: Carmel, 1990) (Hebrew); Yehiel Gutman, "Shock in the Shabak," *Yedioth Ahronoth*, 1995 (Hebrew).
3. The news that two of the hijackers had not been killed in the rescue operation itself first appeared in the *New York Times*, circumventing the Israeli censorship, and was quoted in *Hadashot*.
4. The newspaper was "sanctioned" for breaching censorship orders: the paper was shut down for several days and its editors were criminally prosecuted. The trial and appeal process took nearly a decade, and they were finally vindicated by the Supreme Court, LCrimA 1127/93, *State of Israel v. Yossi Klein et al.*, IsrSC 48 (3): 485.
5. The facts regarding how he sabotaged the work of the commission were established in the jurists' report published in December 1986 (*The Karp Report*). See "The Command of the Head of the Shabak to Kill Two Terrorists Was Improper and Led to the Cover-up Process," *Ma'ariv*, December 30, 1986.
6. For Hazak's version, see Gidi Weitz, "Newly Released Papers Reveal How Shin Bet Tried to Hide 'Bus 300' Killings," *Haaretz* English website, September 27, 2011, http://www.haaretz.com/newly-released-papers-reveal-how-shin-bet-tried-to-hide-bus-300-killings-1.386889 (accessed July 17, 2016).
7. Ibid.
8. E.g., "Zamir Order to Investigate Senior Official Surprised the Government," *Ma'ariv*, May 24, 1986 (headline, Hebrew).
9. HCJ 428/86, *Yitzhak Barzilai v. Government of Israel et al.*, IsrSC 40 (3): 505 (August 6, 1986). Justice Barak, in a minority opinion, believed the president had acted ultra vires (beyond the scope of his legal authority) in pardoning individuals who had not been prosecuted, let alone convicted.
10. Amnon Abramovich, "The Nafsu Case: Not Every New Legal Case Is a New Affair," *Ma'ariv*, April 16, 1987 (Hebrew).
11. Yosef Valter and Ilan Bachar, "Senior MAG Officials Have Question in Nafsu Case," *Ma'ariv*, April 29, 1987 (Hebrew).
12. CA 124/87, *Lieutenant Izat Nafsu v. Chief Military Prosecutor*, IsrSC 41 (2): 631 (May 24, 1987), pp. 633–34. English translation available on the website of the Supreme Court of Israel, http://elyon1.court.gov.il/files_eng/87/240/001/Z01/87001240.z01.pdf, p. 3 (accessed June 23, 2016).
13. Ibid., p. 634.
14. Ibid., p. 637.
15. Government of Israel Decision on May 31, 1987.
16. Interestingly, the person appointed as commission coordinator was Justice Alon Gillon, whose brother, Carmi Gillon, was a top-ranking member of the Shabak at the time and was later appointed to head the agency.
17. *Schenck v. United States*, 249 U.S. 47 (1919), 52.
18. In fact, there were three exceptions: military service, work required of persons who are incarcerated by court order, and forced service in cases of emergencies that

threaten society. See Art. 8 (3) (b) and 8 (3) (c) of the International Covenant on Civil and Political Rights, 1966.

19. Universal Declaration of Human Rights (1948), Art. 5.

20. The convention was adopted and opened for signature on International Human Rights Day, December 10 (the day the Universal Declaration of Human Rights was signed in 1948), 1984. It entered into effect upon ratification by 20 countries, in June 1987. To date, the convention has been ratified by 158 countries.

21. The article reads, "For the purposes of this Convention, the term 'torture' means any act by which severe pain or suffering, whether physical or mental, is intentionally inflicted on a person for such purposes as obtaining from him or a third person information or a confession, punishing him for an act he or a third person has committed or is suspected of having committed, or intimidating or coercing him or a third person, or for any reason based on discrimination of any kind, when such pain or suffering is inflicted by or at the instigation of or with the consent or acquiescence of a public official or other person acting in an official capacity. It does not include pain or suffering arising only from, inherent in or incidental to lawful sanctions."

22. Rome Statute of the International Criminal Court, A/CONF.183/9 of July 17, 1998, Art. 7 (2) (e).

23. Torture is a crime against humanity when it is widespread or systematic; see Rome Statute above, Art. 7 (1) (f). Torture is a war crime when perpetrated as part of hostilities; see Convention (IV) Relative to the Protection of Civilian Persons in Time of War, Geneva, August 12, 1949, Art. 147; Rome Statute, Art. 8 (2) (a) (ii).

24. Langer, *My Way*, p. 226 (Hebrew).

25. Ibid., p. 327.

26. "Israel Tortures Arab Prisoners: Special Investigation by INSIGHT," *Sunday Times*, June 19, 1977; the article was reprinted in "Israel and Torture," *Journal of Palestine Studies* 6, no. 4 (Summer 1997): 191–219.

27. Report by Roy Reed, July 3, 1977.

28. Langer refers to this in her book *My* Way, p. 318. See also B'Tselem, *The Interrogation of Palestinians During the Intifada: Ill-Treatment, "Moderate Physical Pressure" or Torture?*, p. 26. English translation available on B'Tselem website, https://view .officeapps.live.com/op/view.aspx?src=http://www.btselem.org/download/199103 _torture_eng.doc (last accessed July 17, 2016).

29. Amnesty International, *Torture in the Eighties* (London: Amnesty International, 1984), p. 234.

30. Commission of Inquiry into the Methods of Investigation of the General Security Service Regarding Hostile Terrorist Activity, Report, Part One (Jerusalem, October 1987). English translation by the Government Press Office, available on Ha-Moked website, http://www.hamoked.org/files/2012/115020_eng.pdf, p. 23 (last accessed July 17, 2016) (hereinafter: *Landau Report*).

31. *Landau Report*, p. 23.

32. Ibid., p. 25.

33. Though the commission received testimony that judges were also "part of the game," Justice Landau—a former president of the Supreme Court—was outraged by the denigration of the judges serving in military courts, saying, "Even though no judges were called to appear before us and we heard no explicit denial, we find this allegation to be baseless, and wholly unacceptable. We can only regret that the allegation was made in the first place by a few GSS personnel." *Landau Report*, p. 34.

34. Ibid., pp. 79–80. Emphases added.

35. Basic Law: The Government (2001), Sec. 32 (Sec. 29 when the Landau Commission report was published) holds, "The Government is authorized to perform in the name of the State, subject to all laws, any act, which is not assigned by law to another authority." Unofficial translation available on Knesset website, http://knesset.gov.il/laws/special/eng/BasicLawTheGovernment.pdf (last accessed July 17, 2016).

36. The justification defense protects anyone who acts in accordance with their lawful duty, or under orders of a competent authority. However, the defense is not applicable for patently illegal orders, and therefore, it is not at all clear that it could help an interrogator who tortures an interrogee. The justification defense currently appears in Section 34M of the Penal Code 5737-1977.

37. Amnesty International spoke of "thousands" of Palestinians who suffered ill treatment or torture in Israeli facilities. Amnesty International, 1990 Report, pp. 129–32.

38. The description is taken from a PCATI publication: Allegra Pacheco, ed., *The Case Against Torture in Israel: A Compilation of Petitions, Briefs, and Other Documents Submitted to the Israeli High Court of Justice* (Jerusalem: Public Committee Against Torture in Israel, May 1999), p. 3 (hereinafter: *The Case Against Torture in Israel*). According to the description, the *shabach* is a combination of several interrogation methods and it included, at times, exposure to loud music and sleep deprivation.

39. B'Tselem Report of March 1991, p. 32.

40. In an interview with the author on November 10, 2015, Rosenthal estimated that there were hundreds of petitions.

41. Rosenthal recalled two such cases.

42. The description is based on the author's interview with Rosenthal on November 11, 2015, and the *New York Times* report "Israel Allows the Use of Physical Force in Arab's Interrogation," *New York Times*, November 16, 1996, p. 8.

43. HCJ 8049/96, *Hamdan v. Israel Security Agency* (published in Nevo) (decision dated November 14, 1996).

44. Hannah Friedman interview with the author, December 22, 2015.

45. In January 1990, Tamar Peleg-Sryck lodged a complaint, on ACRI letterhead, following allegations that the clients of Palestinian human rights lawyer Raji Sourani had been tortured. This was an important personal initiative on Adv. Peleg-Sryck's part, who was handling prisoner cases for ACRI. A copy of the letter is reprinted in B'Tselem, *Interrogation of Palestinians*, p. 113.

46. Correspondence with the author, June 22, 2016.

47. Shortly before PCATI was established, Dr. Stein testified at the trial of members of the leftist group Shining Path, who had had contacts with the Democratic Front for the Liberation of Palestine, an organization led by Naef Hawatmeh and considered by Israel to be a terrorist group. The four Shining Path members were arrested in 1988 and prosecuted for breaches of national security. The defendants claimed they had been tortured during the interrogation. Stein was a defense witness and spoke about the impact the interrogation methods had on the interrogees. The trial ended in plea bargains that included short prison sentences.

48. Professor Cohen was born in South Africa, where he had fought against apartheid. In Israel, he fought against the occupation. Cohen was also a member of the board of directors of B'Tselem.

49. Dr. Marton is the founder and president of Physicians for Human Rights–Israel.

50. See a brief account of the affair in B'Tselem, *Interrogation of Palestinians*, pp. 30–31.

51. Five of the ten accused were convicted: "Five Jerusalem Police Convicted of a Range of Crimes, Including Attacks, Against Palestinians," *Haaretz*, July 14, 1995 (Hebrew).

52. B'Tselem, *Interrogation of Palestinians*.

53. HCJ 2581/91, *Murad Adnan Salahat et al. v. Government of Israel*, IsrSC 47 (4): 837 (August 12, 1987).

54. Ibid., p. 419.

55. HCJ 873/89, *Yoav Hass v. Minister of Defense et al.*, TakSC 94 (3): 2163 (November 6, 1994).

56. *The Case Against Torture in Israel*, 3n38.

57. HCJ 873/89.

58. HCJFH 4110/92, *Yoav Hass v. Minister of Defense et al.*, IsrSC 48(2), 811 (April 11, 1994), p. 813.

59. When the PCATI petition was dismissed in August 1993, Feldman filed a motion for further hearing by an extended panel—HCJFH 4487/93. President Shamgar ruled that the motion would remain pending until the decision in the open-fire regulations case, because both petitions challenged the same case law. After a ruling was made in the open-fire regulations case, Shamgar ruled that there was no longer any need to hear the PCATI petition, which in fact means that the finding that led to the dismissal of the petition—i.e., that no public petition could be filed on an issue of principle without a specific case in need of judicial remedy—was void.

60. Uri Nir and Eitan Rabin, "Court Likely to Order Autopsy of Palestinian Who Died Following Shabak Interrogation," *Haaretz*, April 26, 1995 (Hebrew).

61. The definition is taken from the petition filed by ACRI, HCJ 4054/95, *Association for Civil Rights in Israel v. Prime Minister et al.* (joined with second PCATI petition).

62. "The Right Not to Be Subjected to Torture," from The State of Human Rights in Israel, ACRI website, https://www.acri.org.il/he/5494#fn40 (last accessed July 17, 2016) (Hebrew) (hereinafter: "The Right Not to Be Subjected to Torture").

63. This term was used by Amnesty International in its report on the case, https://www.amnesty.org/en/documents/mde15/023/1995/en/.

64. In an interview he gave to the bar association magazine, Ben Yair made very clear, and very novel, statements for a person who stood at the helm of Israel's public prosecution: "You can't give other tools, that are illegal, to replace intelligence. There's no such thing. We won't open torture chambers here in place of intelligence. . . . They [Shabak interrogators] get interrogation training not to go and use physical force, but to use their brains. The brain must be used based on intel. Torture cannot replace intel." *HaLishka*, October 1995 (Hebrew).

65. Moshe Reinfeld, "HCJ: No Prosecution in ISA Shaking," *Haaretz*, March 26, 2003 (Hebrew); HCJ 2150/96, *Abdallah Harizat v. Attorney General* (unreported).

66. Avigdor Feldman, "The ISA Lexicon," *Haaretz*, May 14, 1995 (Hebrew).

67. HCJ 7964/95 (HCJMiscApp 336/96), *Balbisi v. Israel Security Agency* (decision dated January 11, 1996).

68. "HCJ Allows Torture of Suspected Beit Lid Attack Planner," *Haaretz*, January 12, 1996 (Hebrew).

69. "Shin-Bet Gets Go-Ahead to 'Violently Shake' Suspects," *Independent*, January 12, 1996.

70. Details regarding interim orders issued in 1996 are available in "The Right Not to Be Subjected to Torture."

71. Feldman, "The ISA Lexicon."

72. HCJ 7563/97, *Abd al-Rahman Ghneimat et al. v. Minister of Defense et al.*

73. HCJ 7628/97, *Fouad Qur'an et al. v. Minister of Defense et al.*

74. Feldman, "The ISA Lexicon."

75. *The Case Against Torture in Israel*, p. 8.

76. Ghneimat affidavit, translated from Arabic, in *The Case Against Torture in Israel*, p. 53.

77. HCJ 7628/97 (decision dated December 28, 1997).

78. Affidavit of Nasser Daud al-Azraq, who was interrogated in Shikma Prison, near Ashkelon. The quote appears in "Supplementary Brief of the Petitioners" in HCJ 7653/97 and HCJ 7628/97, included in *The Case Against Torture in Israel.*

79. Ami Ayalon affidavit, published in *The Case Against Torture in Israel*, p. 103. The PCATI report places special emphasis on this quote.

80. *Republic of Ireland v. United Kingdom*, ECHR (5310/71), Series A, no. 25 (judgment dated January 18, 1978).

81. Para. 28, Sources in International and Comparative Law, Supplementary Brief and Annexes of Petitioner 3 in HCJ 5188/96, *Al Kaka v. General Security Service et al.* Published in *The Case Against Torture in Israel*, p. 132.

82. Supplementary brief on behalf of the Association for Civil Rights, para. 28, ACRI website, https://www.acri.org.il/he/524 (last accessed July 17, 2016) (Hebrew).

83. Para. 11 in Supplementary Brief of Petitioners in HCJ 5100/94, *Public Committee Against Torture in Israel v. Government of Israel*, published in *The Case Against Torture in Israel*, p. 89.

84. HCJ 5100/94, *Public Committee Against Torture in Israel v. Government of Israel*, IsrSC 53 (4): 817 (September 6, 1999). English translation available on Supreme Court website, http://elyon1.court.gov.il/files_eng/94/000/051/a09/94051000.a09 .pdf, p. 34 (last accessed July 17, 2016).

85. Ibid., pp. 34–35.

86. Ibid., p. 36.

87. Ibid., p. 17.

88. Ibid, pp. 36–37.

89. Ibid, p. 37.

90. Amir Oren, "At 10:00 a.m., Torture Stopped," *Haaretz*, September 7, 1999 (Hebrew).

91. "Rubinstein Supports Legislation to Bypass ISA Ruling," *Yedioth Ahronoth*, September 7, 1999; "Rubinstein-Beilin Quarrel over Response to Torture Case," *Haaretz*, September 7, 1999 (all in Hebrew).

92. "ISA Interrogations and the Necessity Defense—a Framework for Discretion," in *Accountability Denied: The Absence of Investigation and Punishment of Torture in Israel* (Jerusalem: PCATI, December 2009). The document itself was reprinted only in the Hebrew version of the report, p. 64.

93. Ibid., paras. G (2) (b) (2) and G (2) (b) (3).

94. Ibid., para. G (2) (b) (4).

95. HCJ 5100/94, para. 34.

96. See, e.g., Nir Hasson, "Complaints ISA Interrogators Tear Off Beards and Sodomize Detainees," *Haaretz*, November 8, 2011 (Hebrew). On November 10, 2006, a clarification was published that only the head of the Shabak may authorize use of physical interrogation methods.

97. B'Tselem and HaMoked, *Absolute Prohibition: The Torture and Ill-Treatment of Palestinian Detainees*, May 2007. See also *Family Matters: Using Family Members to Pressure Detainees Under GSS Interrogation* (Jerusalem: PCATI, March 2008); *Ticking Bombs: Testimonies of Torture Victims in Israel* (Jerusalem: PCATI, May 2007).

98. An investigative report by *Haaretz* revealed that the number of "necessity inter-rogations" significantly increased during the last six months of 2014. The report was based on a review of allegations of torture made during military court trials and on statistics regarding complaints filed by interrogees via PCATI. While only five complaints were filed during the first half of the year, nineteen were filed in the second. Chaim Levinson, "Torture of Palestinian Detainees by Shin Bet Investigators Rises Sharply," *Haaretz* English website, March 6, 2015, http://www.haaretz .com/israel-news/.premium-1.645587 (last accessed July 17, 2016).

99. *Accountability Denied*, pp. 86–87.

100. HCJ 5100/94, 4054/95, 5188/96, *Public Committee Against Torture in Israel v. Government of Israel* (decision dated July 6, 2009) (published in Nevo) (Hebrew).

101. Interview with the author, April 12, 2015.

102. Ibid.

5: THE SEPARATION BARRIER

1. These figures and the figures that follow originate in the B'Tselem database.

2. According to B'Tselem figures, 1,540 of them were men and women who had not taken part in hostilities, 1,117 had taken part, and, with respect to 553, whether or not they had taken part in hostilities is unknown.

3. Shaul Arieli and Michael Sfard, *Homa uMehdal: Geder Ha-Frada—Bitahon o Hamdanut (The Wall of Folly)* (Tel Aviv: Sifrey Aliyat Ha-Gag, 2008), p. 40 (Hebrew).

4. Ibid., p. 42.

5. Reported in *Ma'ariv*, June 21, 2002, and quoted in Arieli and Sfard, *The Wall of Folly*, p. 42.

6. Jaffee Center for Strategic Studies poll, March 2004; quoted in Yehuda Ben Meir and Dafna Shaked, "The People Speak: Israeli Public Opinion on National Security 2005–2007: Memorandum No. 90, May 2007" (Institute for National Security Studies, 2007), p. 62.

7. This section is based on Arieli and Sfard, *The Wall of Folly*, chapter 6.

8. Affidavit on file with author, submitted as part of HCJ 2732/05, *Head of 'Azzun Village Council v. Government of Israel et al.*

9. Proclamation Regarding Closure of Area No. 03/2/S (Seam Zone), October 2, 2003. The declaration closed only the parts of the seam zone where the barrier's construction was completed; the permit regime does not apply in other parts of it.

10. B'Tselem, *Behind the Barrier: Human Rights Violations as a Result of Israel's Separation Barrier*, March 2003, pp. 9–11.

11. Ibid., pp. 12–19.

12. Ibid., pp. 35–36.

13. Resolution B/64 of the Ministerial Committee for National Security Affairs, April 14, 2002.

14. B'Tselem, *Behind the Barrier*, p. 6.

15. Efrat Cohen-Bar and Shmuel Groag, *The Seam Zone Barrier from Shufa Intersection to Sal'it—Expert Opinion*, filed in HCJ 3325/02, *Abd al-Rahman Rashid Hassan Khatab (Qar'us) et al. v. Judea and Samaria Area Military Commander et al.*

16. Eli Ilan and Cesar Yeudkin, *The Seam Zone Barrier in the Taybeh Far'un Sector—Expert Opinion*, filed in HCJ 3771/02, *a-Ras Village Council et 32 al. v. Judea and Samaria Area Military Commander Yitzhak Eitan et al.*

17. HCJ 3325/02, *Abd al-Rahman Rashid Hassan Khatab (Qar'us) et al. v. Judea and Samaria Area Military Commander et al.* (unreported) (decision dated April 25, 2002).

18. HCJ 3325/02, *Abd al-Rahman Rashid Hassan Khatab (Qar'us) et al. v. Judea and Samaria Area Military Commander et al.*, TakSC 2000 (2): 1200 (judgment dated May 9, 2002). A similar judgment was given in HCJ 3771/02, *a-Ras Village Council et 32 al. v. Judea and Samaria Area Military Commander Yitzhak Eitan et al.*, TakSC 2002 (2): 876 (judgment dated May 9, 2002).

19. HCJ 11344/03, *Faez Salim et al. v. IDF Commander in the Judea and Samaria Area*, TakSC 2009 (3): 4349 (judgment dated September 9, 2009).

20. Government of Israel Resolution No. 2077, June 23, 2002.

21. This case was concluded with no judgment on the merits, after the justices clarified during the hearing that the petition should be withdrawn. The petitioners agreed, reserving the right to file a specific objection asking to change the route of certain segments of the fence—HCJ 7783, 7784/02 *Sharim and al-Hadi v. IDF Commander in the West Bank* (unreported) (judgment dated November 17, 2002).

22. State response in HCJ 7784/02, para. 3.

23. Convention (IV) Respecting the Laws and Customs of War on Land and its annex: Regulations Concerning the Laws and Customs of War on Land. The Hague, October 18, 1907, Regulation 23(g).

24. State response in HCJ 7784/02, paras. 3 and 19. Italics added.

25. HCJ 8172/02, *Ibtisam Muhammad Ibrahim v. IDF Commander in the West Bank*, TakSC 2002 (4): 1078 (2002), p. 1080.

26. Arieli and Sfard, *The Wall of Folly*, p. 44.

27. The full title is Special Rapporteur on the situation of human rights in the Palestinian territories occupied since 1967.

28. Following a reform in this institution, the name of the commission was changed in 2006 to the Human Rights Council.

29. E/CN.4/2004/6 of September 8, 2003.

30. General Assembly resolution ES-10/13 of October 21, 2003.

31. "Report of the Secretary-General prepared pursuant to General Assembly resolution ES-10/13" (November 24, 2003), A/ES-10/248: "In keeping with the request of the General Assembly in paragraph 1 of resolution ES-10/13, I have concluded that Israel is not in compliance with the Assembly's demand that it 'stop and reverse the construction of the wall in the Occupied Palestinian Territory,'" https://unispal.un .org/DPA/DPR/unispal.nsf/0/A5A017029C05606B85256DEC00626057 (accessed September 27, 2016).

32. UN General Assembly resolution of December 8, 2003, A/Res/ES-10/14.

33. HCJ 639/04, *Association for Civil Rights in Israel v. IDF Commander in the Judea and Samaria Area and Head of the Civil Administration* (Petition for Order Nisi), January 19, 2004.

34. HCJ 7957/04, *Zaharan Yunis Muhammad Mara'abe v. Prime Minister of Israel*, TakSC 2005 (3): 3333 (May 15, 2005), p. 3367. English translation of judgment available on the website of the Israeli Judicial Authority, http://elyon1.court.gov.il/files _eng/04/570/079/A14/04079570.a14.pdf (accessed September 27, 2016).

35. Muhammad Dahleh interview with the author, March 21, 2016, and e-mail correspondence, September 11, 2016.

36. Muhammad Dahleh interview with the author, March 21, 2016.

37. HCJ 2056/04, *Beit Sourik Village Council v. Government of Israel*, IsrSC 58 (5): 807 (judgment dated June 30, 2004), p. 828. English translation of the judgment available on the website of the Israeli Judicial Authority, http://elyon1.court.gov.il/files _eng/04/560/020/a28/04020560.a28.pdf (accessed September 27, 2016).

38. Ibid., para. 32, the court referred to Arts. 23 (g) and 52 of The Hague Regulations and Art. 53 of the Fourth Geneva Convention.

39. Ibid., para. 60.

40. Ibid., para. 61.

41. Ibid.

42. Ibid., para. 86.

43. Arieli and Sfard, *The Wall of Folly*, p. 106.

44. Aluf Benn and Yuval Yoaz, "Mazuz and Mofaz Scold Fence Administration Head for Criticizing High Court," *Haaretz*, July 2, 2004. See also Yinon Kadri and Amir Bouhbout, "Top Fence Administration Official Scolded," *NRG*, July 1, 2004.

45. "Supplying Security," *Yedioth Ahronoth*, July 1, 2004.

46. Ibid.

47. "Legal Consequences of the Construction of a Wall in the Occupied Palestinian Territory" (Advisory Opinion of July 9, 2004), *ICJ Reports* 2004, p. 136, para. 120.

48. Ibid., para. 121.

49. Ibid., paras. 137–39.

50. Ibid., para. 9 of the opinion of Judge Buergenthal.

51. HCJ 7957/04, *Zaharan Yunis Muhammad Mara'abe v. Prime Minister of Israel*, petition, para. 37.

52. Ibid., paras. 101–109.

53. Ibid., para. 7.

54. Ibid., TakSC 2005 (3): 3333 (May 15, 2005), p. 3367. English translation of judgment available on the website of the Israeli Judicial Authority, http://elyon1.court .gov.il/files_eng/04/570/079/A14/04079570.a14.pdf, pp. 13–14 (accessed September 27, 2016).

55. HCJ 10714/06, *Yassin Yunis Muhammad Mara'abe et al. v. Government of Israel et al.*, and HCJ 10309/06, *Alfei Menashe Local Council v. Government of Israel et al.*, TakSC 2007 (3): 3434.

56. HCJ 2732/05, *Head of 'Azzun Village Council v. Government of Israel et al.*, Response on behalf of the Respondents, June 30, 2005, para. 17. English translation available on the website of HaMoked, http://www.hamoked.org/files/2015/6449_eng.pdf (accessed September 27, 2016).

57. Ibid., para. 17.

58. Ibid., Supplementary Response on behalf of the Respondents, February 19, 2006, para. 12.

59. HCJ 2732/05, *Head of 'Azzun Village Council v. Government of Israel et al.*, TakSC 2006 (2): 3672 (June 15, 2006).

60. The parliamentary question and the response are posted on the website of MK Dov Hanin, http://www.dovblog.org/dov/336.html (accessed September 27, 2016) (Hebrew).

61. Akiva Eldar, "Tirza Ignoring Order to Stop Acting for State on Fence," *Haaretz*, January 15, 2007, http://www.haaretz.com/tirza-ignoring-order-to-stop-acting-for -state-on-fence-1.210118 (accessed September 27, 2016).

62. Yuval Yoaz, Associated Press, "Justice Minister: West Bank Fence Is Israel's Future Border," *Haaretz*, December 1, 2005, http://www.haaretz.com/news/justice-minister -west-bank-fence-is-israel-s-future-border-1.175645 (accessed September 27, 2016).

63. Arieli and Sfard, *The Wall of Folly*, chapter 11.
64. Haytham al-Khatib, *Children of Palestine* (London: Palestine in Print, 2015); Haytham al-Khatib, *Occupied Palestine Through My Lens* (London: Palestine in Print, 2015); and Rahmah Abu Hamdah, *Roots Run Deep: Life in Occupied West Bank* (self-published, 2013). Both photographers are village residents turned photojournalists during the years of struggle waged by the village.
65. The Canadian developers are Green Park and Green Mount. The Israeli company is Heftsiba.
66. We discovered that during the 1990s, the Civil Administration declared a large amount of land as state land as part of a sting. What Bil'in residents were not told was that the background was a false claim that the land had been purchased by a settler body. This is a known method in which settlers tell the Civil Administration they had purchased land, which they ask to be declared state land in order to avoid exposing the purchase. The Civil Administration complies and then allocates the land to the purported purchaser. All of this is done without checking if there was, in fact, a genuine purchase deal. We tried to have the state land declaration retracted in a petition I filed on behalf of the Bil'in village council, but the HCJ dismissed it due to laches and the inability to get to the bottom of the matter after so many years. HCJ 3998/06, *Ahmad Issa Abdallah Yassin et al. v. IDF Commander in the West Bank*, TakSc 2006 (4): 1282 (2006).
67. HCJ 143/06, *Peace Now et al. v. Minister of Education et al.*, TakSC 2007 (3): 3333.
68. Akiva Eldar, "Hundreds of Housing Units Illegally Built Near Bil'in," *Haaretz*, December 15, 2005.
69. HCJ 143/06, decision dated January 12, 2006.
70. HCJ 1526/07, *Bil'in Village Council Head et al. v. Civil Administration Head et al.*, TakSC 2007 (3): 3333.
71. HCJ 8414/05, *Ahmad Issa Abdallah Yassin, Bil'in Village Council Chairman v. The Government of Israel*, TakSC 2007 (3): 3557, September 4, 2007. Translation available on the website of the Israeli Judicial Authority, http://elyon1.court.gov.il/files_eng/05/140/084/n25/05084140.n25.pdf (accessed September 9, 2016).
72. Ibid., emphasis added.
73. "Bil'in Beats IDF," *Ma'ariv*, September 23, 2007.
74. HCJ 8414/05, decisions dated August 3, 2008, and December 15, 2008. See also Shmuel Mittleman, "Defense Minister Defies Bil'in Judgment," *Ma'ariv*, August 4, 2009; Tomer Zarchin, "Beinisch Blasts Gov't for Not Moving Fence Around Bil'in," *Haaretz*, December 16, 2008, http://www.haaretz.com/beinisch-blasts-gov-t-for-not-moving-fence-around-bil-in-1.259590 (accessed September 27, 2016).
75. My office fought at length, on behalf of the family and with the help of Yesh Din, to bring those responsible for killing the Abu Rahmah siblings to justice. The military refused to investigate Jawaher's death, and a High Court petition on this matter was dismissed. A lengthy fight in Bassem's case forced the military to open an investigation, which confirmed that the shooting had been against regulations, but no one was prosecuted after the investigation failed to turn up a suspect.
76. The judgment in ACRI's case on the route near Ni'lin was another success. HCJ 2577/04, *Khawaja et al. v. Prime Minister et al.* (reported in Nevo) (July 19, 2007). The court struck down one segment and ordered it replaced with a route that includes less village land on the "Israeli" side of the fence.
77. B'Tselem website, *The Separation Barrier*, http://www.btselem.org/separation_barrier/map (accessed September 27, 2016).

78. Figures on the website of Shaul Arieli, http://www.shaularieli.com/site/index.asp ?depart_id=77951&lat=en (accessed September 27, 2016). Figures as of 2012. See also UN Office for the Coordination of Humanitarian Affairs, *The Humanitarian Impact of the Barrier*, July 2013.

79. B'Tselem website.

80. OCHA, *The Humanitarian Impact of the Barrier*.

81. HaMoked, *The Permit Regime: Human Rights Violations in West Bank Areas Known as the Seam Zone*, March 2013, pp. 15–19.

82. HCJ 9961/03, *HaMoked: Center for the Defense of the Individual v. Government of Israel*, Amended petition for Order Nisi, April 6, 2006. English translation available on the website of HaMoked, http://www.hamoked.org/items/6653_eng.pdf (accessed September 28, 2016).

83. International Convention on the Suppression and Punishment of the Crime of Apartheid, November 30, 1973, Art. 2 (II).

84. Rome Statute of the International Criminal Court, Arts. 7 (1) (h) together with 7 (2) (g).

85. HCJ 9961/03, *HaMoked: Center for the Defense of the Individual v. Government of Israel*, Amended petition, para. 138.

86. HCJ 639/04.

87. Ibid., pp. 19–22.

88. HCJ 9961/03 639/04, Response on behalf of the State, 13, 2006, paras. 83–84. English translation available on the website of HaMoked, http://www.hamoked.org/files /2010/6655_eng.pdf (accessed September 28, 2016).

89. HCJ 9961/03, *HaMoked: Center for the Defense of the Individual v. Government of Israel*, TakSC 2011 (2): 94, April 5, 2011. English translation available on the website of HaMoked, http://www.hamoked.org/files/2013/114260_eng.pdf (accessed September 28, 2016).

90. Ibid., p. 112.

91. Ibid., p. 121.

92. HCJ 9961/03, HaMoked's response to updating notices issued by the state, November 1, 2011. English translation available on the website of HaMoked, http://www .hamoked.org/items/6659_eng.pdf (accessed September 28, 2016).

6: UNAUTHORIZED OUTPOSTS

1. Government of Israel Resolution 360, November 2, 1992, Sec. B.

2. Art. XXXI (7) of the Israeli-Palestinian Interim Agreement on the West Bank and the Gaza Strip (signed in Washington, D.C., September 28, 1995) stipulates that a prohibition on either party initiating or taking "any step that will change the status of the West Bank and the Gaza Strip pending the outcome of the permanent status negotiations"; the road map for peace in the Middle East (April 30, 2003), states Israel undertakes to freeze all settlement activity (including natural growth); and in the Annapolis Conference of November 2007, Prime Minister Ehud Olmert repeated the commitment to the road map.

3. *One Violation Leads to Another: Israeli Settlement Building on Private Palestinian Property* (Peace Now, October 2006). According to the report, and an update from March 2007, more than 30 percent of the land on which settlements are built is privately owned Palestinian land.

4. Talia Sasson, *Al pi tehom* (Jerusalem: Keter Books, 2016), pp. 30–32 (Hebrew).

5. Talia Sasson, *Opinion Concerning Unauthorized Outposts*, submitted to Prime Minister Ariel Sharon in March 2005.

6. Thirtieth Government of Israel Resolution 3376, March 13, 2005.

7. The first petition was filed by Adv. Gaby Lasky, HCJ 8287/98, *Mossi Raz et al. v. Minister of Defense et al.* (judgment dated December 2, 1999) (unreported). The second petition was filed by me and Avigdor Feldman, HCJ 6431/02, *Yoav Hass et al. v. Government of Israel et al.* (judgment dated December 29, 2002) (unreported).

8. HCJ 6357/05, *Peace Now et al. v. Minister of Defense et al.*, TakSC 2006 (1): 917 (January 18, 2006).

9. HCJ 9051/05, *Peace Now et al. v. Minister of Defense et al.* (filed September 22, 2005).

10. HCJ 3008/06, *Peace Now et al. v. Minister of Defense et al.* (filed April 5, 2006).

11. B'Tselem, *Ofra: An Unauthorized Outpost*, December 2008.

12. See Ofra settlement website, http://www.ofra.org.il/inner/15/sub (accessed November 1, 2016) (Hebrew).

13. B'Tselem *Ofra: An Unauthorized Outpost*, pp. 20–22.

14. HCJ 5023/08, *Sa'id Zahdi Muhammad Shehadeh et al. v. Minister of Defense et al.* (filed June 4, 2008).

15. Yair Ettinger, "Ofra Rabbi Allows Settlers to Build on Shabbat to Beat Court," *Haaretz*, June 12, 2008, http://www.haaretz.com/ofra-rabbi-allows-settlers-to-build-on-shabbat-to-beat-court-1.247680 (accessed November 1, 2016); Roi Sharon, "Ofra: Building on Shabbat to Put Facts on the Ground," *NRG*, June 12, 2008.

16. The Sharon government asked the Defense Ministry to collect data on the status of land and the planning status of all Israeli settlements in the West Bank. Brigadier General Baruch Spiegel was tasked with the mission. In 2009, the database he established was leaked to *Haaretz*. See Uri Blau, "Secret Israeli Database Reveals Full Extent of Illegal Settlement," *Haaretz*, January 1, 2009, http://www.haaretz.com/secret-israeli-database-reveals-full-extent-of-illegal-settlement-1.266936 (accessed November 1, 2016).

17. This also allowed the state to mislead the court without the petitioners being able to refute its arguments, as they lacked the necessary information—as demonstrated in David Kretzmer and Gershom Gorenberg, "Politics, Law, and the Judicial Process: The Case of the High Court of Justice and the Territories," *Mishpat uMimshal* 17 (5775), 1 (Hebrew).

18. The thesis behind Israel's brainchild of "state land declarations" is that the question of who holds the rights to unregistered land hangs on the rules set in Ottoman law, which still applies in the West Bank. According to this law, if certain conditions are fulfilled, any rights to the land expire and return to the sultan, i.e., the regime. Israel has exploited these rules, based on a controversial interpretation of them, to declare close to a million dunams of West Bank land as "state land," transforming it from land considered to be privately owned to public land.

19. Struggles against construction on Palestinian land: Silwad and Ein Yabrud (Amona I, the nine homes); Burqa and Deir Dobwan (Migron); Jabal Artis (Ulpana neighborhood, Beit El North); Silwad and Ein Yabrud (Amona II—the entire outpost); Ein Yabrud (nine structures in Ofra); Dura al-Qara' (two structures in Beit El West); al-Khadr (seventeen structures on Patriarch Road); Immatin (Gilad Farm); Ni'lin (emergency complex in Modi'in Illit); and al-Jib (synagogue in Giv'at Ze'ev). Denial of access and agricultural invasion: Qadum (Kedumim); Silwad (Ofra); Jaba' (Adam); Bil'in (Modi'in Illit); Burqa (Homesh); Beit Furiq (Itamar); Yasuf (Tapuah Ma'arav); Deir Nidham (Halamish); and Sinjil (Giv'at HaRoeh). For a summary of

Yesh Din's proceedings, see "Land Takeover Practices in the West Bank: Summary of Legal Proceedings Which Yesh Din Assisted, 2006–2016," Yesh Din (September 2016).

20. Burqa (Migron); Silwad and Ein Yabrud (Amona II); Jabal Artis (Beit El North); Ein Yabrud (Ofra); Dura al-Qara' (Beit El West); Qadum (Kedumim), and al-Khadr (seventeen structures on Patriarch Road).

21. HCJ 8887/06, *Yussef Moussa Abd'l Rasek Al-Nabouth et al. v. the Minister of Defense et al.*, Takdin Elyon 2011 (3): 2331 (February 8, 2011) (Hebrew).

22. HCJ 9499/08, *Miryam Hassan Abd'l Kareem Hammad et al. v. the Minister of Defense et al.*, Takdin Elyon 2014 (4) 12708 (December 25, 2014).

23. HCJ 9060/08, *Abd'l Janni Yassin Khaled Abdalla et al. v. the Minister of Defense et al.* (ruling of September 21, 2011, unpublished).

24. HCJ 8887/06, ibid., n. 21 (decisions of March 25, 2012, and August 29, 2012).

25. HCJ 9669/10, *Abd'l Rakhman Ahmed Abd'l Rakhman Kassem v. the Minister of Defense*, Takdin Elyon 2014 (3): 10086 (September 8, 2014).

26. HCJ 9060/08 (decision of May 9, 2012).

27. Nine homes in Amona; two apartment buildings in Beit El West; one structure on Patriarch Road; three structures in Gilad Farm; entire complex of emergency facilities in Modi'in Illit; structure used as synagogue in Giv'at Ze'ev.

28. Fence removal: Silwad and Ein Yabrud (Ofra); Jaba' (Geva Binyamin). Removal of invasion and securing access: Qadum (Kedumim); Bil'in (Modi'in Illit); Burqa (Homesh); Beit Furiq (Itamar and its outposts); Yasuf (Tapuah Ma'arav); Deir Nidham (Halamish); and Sinjil (HaRoeh).

29. HCJ 5023/08, *Said Zahdi Muhammed Shehade et al. v. the Minister of Defense et al.*, Takdin Elyon 2015 (1): 6399 (February 8, 2015).

30. HCJ 7891/07, *Peace Now Movement—Sha'al Educational Projects v. the Minister of Defense et al.*, Supplementary Affidavit on behalf of the State of November 10, 2011.

31. HCJ 4457/09, *Muhammed Ahmed Yassin Menna v. the Minister of Defense et al.* (judgment of July 27, 2011, published in Nevo.co.il).

32. HCJ 2295/09, *Mustaffa Ahmed Muhammed Khalil Phadiyya, Head of A-Sawyya Village Council v. the Minister of Defense et al.* (judgment of July 31, 2013, published in Nevo.co.il).

33. According to Peace Now's settlement watch team, six new outposts were established during this time; one of them is the new site for the evacuated outpost of Migron. For a full list of the outposts, see http://peacenow.org.il/outposts (accessed November 22, 2016).

34. See, e.g., HCJ 2817/08, *Munnir Hussein Hassan Moussa v. the Minister of Defense et al.* (judgment of April 29, 2008, published in Nevo.co.il); HCJ 1486/12, *Azzat Assad Rashid Tzuan v. the Minister of Defense et al.* (judgment of April 22, 2014, published in Nevo.co.il).

35. Chaim Levinson, "Israel to Give Evacuated Beit El Settlers Four More Public Buildings," *Haaretz*, February 19, 2014, http://www.haaretz.com/israel-news/.premium -1.575014 (accessed November 1, 2016).

36. Peace Now also tried to impede illegal construction on public land in several cases in which new neighborhoods were established without state or planning authorities' approval. In each of the four petitions Peace Now filed on this issue (construction in the settlements of Kiryat Netafim, Halamish, Shvut Rachel, and Shilo), the outcome was the mobilization of the Netanyahu government for the

retroactive approval of the construction. The case of Shvut Rachel concerned twenty housing units. The government approved the advancement of plans for six hundred units. The only price paid by the settlers was a certain delay in construction. In one case, the council sent Peace Now flowers as a thank-you for helping push building plans that had been awaiting government-level approval for years. As a result, illegal construction on public land and the establishment of entire neighborhoods without permits continues to this day, with a clear message from the Netanyahu government to the settlers: you'll build illegally and we'll retroactively approve.

37. Ziv Stahl, "From Occupation to Annexation: The Silent Adoption of the Levy Report on Retroactive Authorization of Illegal Construction in the West Bank," Yesh Din (February 2016).

38. *Under the Radar: Israel's Silent Policy of Transforming Illegal Outposts into Official Settlements*, Yesh Din (March 2015); *Netanyahu Established 20 New Settlements for Tens of Thousands of Settlers*, Peace Now, 2015. Since publication of these reports several additional outposts were approved.

39. Hezki Baruch, "Levin: Government Won't Survive Amona Evacuation," *Arutz Sheva*, June 13, 2016 (Hebrew).

40. Barak Ravid and Chaim Levinson, "Netanyahu Warns Cabinet: Outpost Legalization Bill Could Lead to International Probe Against Israeli Officials," *Haaretz*, November 28, 2016, http://www.haaretz.com/israel-news/.premium-1.755837 (accessed April 11, 2017).

41. The worst clash between Netanyahu and President Obama revolved around the agreement that was taking shape between world powers, led by the United States, and Iran to stop Iran's nuclear program. Netanyahu thought the agreement was not restrictive enough and in March 2015, in an unusual move, spoke before both houses of Congress in an attempt to thwart Obama's policy. Netanyahu failed and the agreement was signed.

42. Security Council decisions made according to Chapter VII of the Charter of the United Nations are binding and the council has enforcement powers. Decisions made under Chapter VI of the charter do not come with enforcement powers and there is a dispute over whether they are legally binding. The International Court of Justice ruled, in its advisory opinion on Namibia, that Chapter VI decisions are also binding; see *Legal Consequences for States of the Continued Presence of South Africa in Namibia (South West Africa) Notwithstanding Security Council Resolution 276 (1970)*, Advisory Opinion of June 21, 1971, para. 113.

43. Jonathan Lis and Barak Ravid, "Netanyahu Congratulates Trump Victory as Israeli Ministers Hail 'End of Two-State Solution,'" *Haaretz*, November 9, 2016, http://www.haaretz.com/israel-news/1.752088 (accessed April 11, 2017).

44. Yotam Berger and Nir Hasson, "For Israel's Right, Trump's Election Heralds Settlement Construction Surge," *Haaretz*, November 13, 2016, http://www.haaretz.com/israel-news/.premium-1.752589 (accessed April 11, 2017).

45. In an op-ed I wrote for *Haaretz* at the time Mandelblit approved the use of "abandoned" plots for the benefit of Amona residents, I said, "Lately, behind the scenes of the Amona affair, he has sacrificed the public's interest, seriously undermined fundamental tenets of the rule of law, and completely subjugated the law and the state's legal counsel to the wishes of the boss and to serving a colonial ideology of dispossession." Michael Sfard, "Let's Talk About Mandelblit," *Haaretz*, December 18, 2017 (Hebrew).

46. Order Regarding Abandoned Property (Private Property) (Judea and Samaria) (No. 58), 5727–1967.

47. Even Plia Albek, who was the director of the State Attorney's Office's civilian department and famously supported the settler project (and developed the system of state land declarations to allocate land for settlement construction and expansion), maintained that abandoned land could not be used to build Israeli settlements. Plia Albek, "Land in Judea and Samaria," lecture given at Beit HaPraklit in Tel Aviv, May 28, 1985.

48. Determined in a memo by Senior Attorney General Assistant Gil Limon, November 28, 2016.

49. HCJ 9949/08, *Hamad et al. v. Minister of Defense et al.* (decision dated November 14, 2016), TakSC 2016 (4): 4861.

50. UN Security Council Resolution 2334 (2016), passed pursuant to Chapter VI of the Charter of the UN during its 7853rd session (December 23, 2016).

51. Order No. 1777 Regarding Approval of Construction and Waiver of Permit for Temporary Housing Sites with Regional Significance (Temporary Order) (Judea and Samaria), 5777–2016.

52. Uncredited, "Amona Live Updates: After Years of Delay, Israel Evacuates Illegal West Bank Outpost," *Haaretz*, February 2, 2017, http://www.haaretz.com/israel-news/LIVE-1.768926 (accessed April 11, 2017).

53. HCJ 794/17, *Ziada et al. v. IDF Commander in the West Bank et al.*, TakSC 2017 (1): 5618 (February 1, 2017).

54. A study conducted by Peace Now estimates that the Regularization Law would result in the confiscation of eleven thousand dunams of privately owned Palestinian land: "The Grand Land Robbery: Another Step Toward Annexation," *Peace Now* (November 2016). The law also instructs the confiscation of Palestinian farmland that had been invaded by settlers. According to one estimate, there are some twenty-seven thousand dunams of such land: Dror Etkes, "Israeli Settler Agriculture as a Means of Land Takeover in the West Bank," *Naboth's Vineyard* (October 2013), p. 73.

7: SECURITY AND THE PICCOLO

1. See, e.g., International Covenant on Civil and Political Rights, 1966, Art. 9.

2. International Covenant on Civil and Political Rights, 1966, Art. 4 (a).

3. Convention (IV) Relative to the Protection of Civilian Persons in Time of War. Geneva, August 12, 1949 (Fourth Geneva Convention), Art. 78.

4. Jean S. Pictet, ed., *Commentary: The Fourth Geneva Convention Relative to the Protection of Civilian Persons in Time of War* (Geneva: ICRC, 1958), pp. 367–68.

5. Upon the occupation, the power to issue administrative detention orders was established in the Order Regarding Security Provisions (Judea and Samaria) (No. 378), 5730–1970. The order has been updated several times, and currently, administrative detention in the West Bank is performed by virtue of Arts. 284–94 of the Order Regarding Security Provisions [Consolidated Version] (Judea and Samaria) (No. 1651), 5770–2009.

6. Order No. 1651, Art. 272.

7. Administrative detention powers in the areas under Israeli law were previously stipulated in the Mandatory Defense (Emergency) Regulations 1945, Arts. 108, 111, and 112. In 1979 an Israeli law was enacted: Emergency Powers (Detention) Law 5739–1979.

8. Order No. 1651, Art. 280.

9. Figures from B'Tselem website, http://www.btselem.org/administrative_detention /statistics. See also Tamar Peleg-Sryck, "The Mysteries of Administrative Detention," in A. Baker and A. Mater, eds., *Threat: Palestinian Political Prisoners in Israel* (New York: Pluto Press, 2011), p. 124.

10. Tamar Peleg-Sryck, interview with the author, July 1, 2015.

11. The Israeli system puts an emphasis on the courts as active critics. A different system, employed in the United Kingdom, for instance, relies on the appointment of "special advocates" with security clearance for the detainees, in addition to their defense counsel. This special advocate may review the classified material but cannot share its contents with the detainee. He or she may also receive information from the detainee that enjoys client-attorney privilege. This allows the lawyer to get a fuller picture of the allegations and to make arguments, in camera, with the client absent, that an "ordinary" defense lawyer would not know to make. This system has also come under fire for driving a wedge between client and counsel and for the fact that so long as the detainee knows not what the allegations are, he or she cannot give even the special advocate information relevant to his or her defense.

12. HCJ 11006/04, *Khadri v. IDF Commander in Judea and Samaria*, para. 6 (2004).

13. HCJ 9441/07, *Agbar v. IDF Commander in Judea and Samaria*, para. 8 (2007).

14. Peleg-Sryck, "The Mysteries of Administrative Detention," p. 133.

15. Ibid., p. 130.

16. HaMoked and B'Tselem, *Without Trial: Administrative Detention of Palestinians by Israel and the Interment of Unlawful Combatants Law*, 2009, pp. 20–22.

17. "An administrative detention order issued against a person is a rare measure utilized by the competent authority. It is located outside the ordinary legal system, which stipulates the prerequisites for an arrest. Administrative detention violates personal liberty. Such harm is justified by law only in special, exceptional conditions, which necessitate use of the aforesaid extreme and unusual measure. . . . When using administrative detention orders, proportionality must always be adhered to." ADA 8607/04, *Fahima v. State of Israel*, IsrSC 59 (3): 258, 262 (Justice Procaccia); "Administrative detention is a difficult default, and must remain so," HCJ 94417/07, *Muhammad Musbah Ta'ah Ajbar v. IDF Commander in the Judea and Samaria Area*, TakSC 2007 (4): 5234 (2007). See also HCJ 3239/02, *Iyad Ashak Mahmoud Mar'ab v. IDF Commander*, TakSC 2003 (1): 937 (February 5, 2003); HCJ 2320/98, *Abd al-Fatah Mahmoud al-M'almala et al. v. IDF Commander et al.*, TakSC 98 (2): 571 (July 19, 1998); HCJ 3267/12, *Thair Aziz Mahmoud Halahleh v. Military Commander of the Judea and Samaria Area*, TakSC 2012 (2): 2239 (2012).

18. HCJ 6843/93, *Ahmad Suleiman Musa Katmash v. IDF Commander*, TakSC 94 (2): 2084 (April 18, 1994).

19. HCJ 2320/98, p. 581.

20. Dan Yakir interview with the author, June 25, 2015.

21. Shiri Krebs, "Lifting the Veil of Secrecy: Judicial Review of Administrative Detentions in the Israeli Supreme Court," *Vanderbilt Journal of Transnational Law* 45, no. 3 (May 2012): 639.

22. HCJ 907/90, *Taysir Mustafa Shehadeh Zeid v. IDF Commander*, TakSC 90 (2): 187 (1990). Interestingly, in at least two cases, the High Court accepted petitions filed by the military commander and reversed rare decisions by military judges to release

detainees. See HCJ 6845/05, *IDF Commander in the Judea and Samaria Area v. Judge of the Military Court of Appeals for the Judea and Samaria Area and Gaza Strip et al.*, TakSC 2005 (3): 1442 (2005); HCJ 1389/07, *IDF Commander in the Judea and Samaria Area v. Military Court of Appeals et al.*, TakSC 2007 (1): 2821 (2007).

23. Tamar Peleg-Sryck, interview with the author, July 1, 2015.

24. See, e.g., HCJ 6843/93, *Ahmad Suleiman Musa Katmash v. IDF Commander*, TakSC 94 (2): 2084 (1994), p. 2085.

25. HCJ 1389/07, para. 5.

26. See, e.g., HCJ 1546/06, *Ghazawi v. IDF Commander in the West Bank*, TakSC 2006 (1): 3413 (2006), p. 3415.

27. See, for instance, in HCJ 3267/12, *Thair Aziz Mahmoud Halahleh v. Military Commander of the Judea and Samaria Area*, TakSC 2012 (2): 2239 (2012). The material against the petitioners, members of Islamic Jihad, indicated that "a major part" of one petitioner's role was "transferring money." The other had connections in the Gaza Strip and abroad, "mainly with regards to funds."

28. Jacky Khoury, "Prison Hunger Strikes Proliferate Following Khader Adnan," *Haaretz*, April 4, 2012 (Hebrew).

29. *Hunger Strikes by Palestinian Prisoners in Israeli Prisons*, Physicians for Human Rights–Israel (January 2013), pp. 9, 13 (Hebrew).

30. See, e.g., HCJ 5580/15, 5575/15, *a-Din Alan v. ISA et al.*, TakSC 2015 (3): 7508 (2015); HCJ 7027/16, *Malek Qadi v. Military Commander*, TakSC 2016 (3): 10642 (2016); HCJ 6878/16, *Mahmoud Ahmad Khalil Balboul v. Chief Military Prosecutor*, TakSC 2016 (3): 10222 (2016).

31. HCJ 5580/15, opinion of Justice Elyakim Rubinstein, para. F.

32. HCJ 779/88, *Mahmoud Abd al-Hadi Muhsin al-Fasfous v. Minister of Defense*, IsrSC 43 (3): 576 (1989).

33. Ibid.

34. Memorandum from Mr. Yaakov Avnun to Director General and Deputy Director General of the Ministry of Foreign Affairs, *Summary of Visit to Office of Military Governor of Gaza*, June 13, 1967. The Conflict Records' Digital Repository (Akevot Institute), Document 1000576.

35. Defense (Emergency) Regulations 1945 Regulation (hereinafter: Regulation 119).

36. These demolition orders were revoked when it turned out that there had been a delay in implementing the order, that the house slated for demolition did not belong to the family of the assailant or that the assailant had not lived there, and when the family member's role in the attack was indirect. HCJ 7040/15, *Hamed v. Military Commander of the West Bank*, reported in Nevo (November 12, 2015), opinion of President Naor, paras. 45–46; HCJ 1125/16, *Hamed Mar'i et al. v. Military Commander of the West Bank*, reported in Nevo (March 31, 2016). Unofficial translation available on the HaMoked website, http://www.hamoked.org/files/2015/HCJ%20 6754_15_judgment.pdf (accessed November 4, 2016); HCJ 1336/16, *Atrash et al. v. GOC Home Front Command*, reported in Nevo (April 3, 2016). Unofficial translation available on the HaMoked website, http://www.hamoked.org/files/2016/1336_16 _eng.pdf (accessed August 11, 2017).

37. *Timeline—Punitive House Demolitions*, HaMoked: Center for the Defense of the Individual, http://www.hamoked.org/timeline.aspx?pageID=timelinehousedemo litions (accessed November 10, 2016).

38. Ibid.

39. Art. 46 of the Regulations annexed to The Hague Convention (IV) Concerning the Laws and Customs of War on Land (hereinafter: The Hague Regulations) prohib-

its interference with private property; Art. 56 of the Fourth Geneva Convention prohibits the destruction of private property belonging to residents of an occupied territory.

40. Regulation 23(7) of The Hague Regulations stipulates that the destruction or seizure of enemy property is prohibited "unless such destruction or seizure be imperatively demanded by the necessities of war."

41. The law does permit demolition of unlawful construction pursuant to planning and construction law, but this is a complex issue that has no bearing on the matter at hand.

42. HCJ 434/79, *Nuzhat Taher Ahmad Sahweil v. Commander of the Area*, IsrSC 34 (1): 464 (1979).

43. Art. 33 of the Fourth Geneva Convention stipulates, "No protected person may be punished for an offense he or she has not personally committed. Collective penalties and likewise all measures of intimidation or of terrorism are prohibited. Pillage is prohibited. Reprisals against protected persons and their property are prohibited." Art. 50 of The Hague Regulations also prohibits collective punishment, stating, "No general penalty, pecuniary or otherwise, shall be inflicted upon the population on account of the acts of individuals for which they cannot be regarded as jointly and severally responsible."

44. Article 46 of the regulations.

45. Art. 43 of The Hague Regulations concludes with the provision that the occupier must respect "unless absolutely prevented, the laws in force in the country."

46. HCJ 897/86, *Ramzi Hana Jaber v. GOC Central Command et al.*, IsrSC 41 (2): 522 (1987).

47. Guy Harpaz, "Being Unfaithful to One's Own Principles: The Israeli Supreme Court and House Demolitions in the Occupied Palestinian Territories," *Israel Law Review* 47, no. 3 (November 2014): 425.

48. HCJ 6026/94, *Nazal et al. v. IDF Commander in the Judea and Samaria Area*, IsrSC 48 (5): 338 (1994).

49. One jurist who wrote about the subject called this recursion the "Rolling Error." Eitan Diamond, "The Sins of the Son and the Rolling Error," *Hearot Psika* 51 (January 2016): 43, https://www.colman.ac.il/sites/default/files/diamond.pdf (accessed November 25, 2016) (Hebrew).

50. Art. 43 of Regulation 119 qualifies the duty to respect local law with the words "unless absolutely prevented" from the occupier to do so. Moreover, Regulation 119 *permits* house demolitions—it does not *necessitate* them. When normative provisions prohibit the use of discretionary powers, discretion clearly obliges that they not be used.

51. HCJ 2418/97, *Abu Fara v. Major General Uzi Dayan*, TakSC 1997 (2): 3504 (1997), quoted and acceded to by numerous justices. See, e.g., President Naor in HCJ 9353/08, *Hisham Abu Dheim et al. v. GOC Home Front Command*, TakSC 2009 (1): 85 (2009), para. 7; Justice Melcer in HCJ 1633/16, *A v. Military Commander of the West Bank*, TakSC 2016 (2): 9461 (2016), para. 31.

52. HCJ 5359, 4772/91, *Hizran v. IDF Commander in the Judea and Samaria Area*, IsrSC 46 (2): 150 (1992); HCJ 2722/92, *al-ʿImrin v. Military Commander of the Gaza Strip*, IsrSC 46 (3): 693 (1992); HCJ 6026/94 *Nazal v. IDF Commander in the Judea and Samaria Area*, IsrSC 48 (5): 338 (1994); HCJ 2006/97, *Ghneimat v. GOC Central Command*, IsrSC 51 (2): 651 (1997).

53. HCJ 1730/96, *Adel Salem Abed Rabo Sabih v. Major General Ilan Biran*, IsrSC 50 (1): 353 (March 19, 1996). Unofficial translation available on the HaMoked website,

http://www.hamoked.org/files/2010/4930_eng.pdf (accessed November 10, 2016). In this judgment, Justice Cheshin explained the reason why he had strayed from his objection to house demolitions as follows: "Even as the trumpets of war sound, the rule of the law shall make its voice heard. But, let us admit a truth: in such places its sound is like that of the piccolo, clear and pure, but drowned out in the din" (para. 10 of his opinion).

54. See, e.g., Justice Turkel in HCJ 6288/03, *Sa'adeh v. GOC Home Front Command*, IsrSC 58 (2): 289, p. 294 (2003); Justice Elyakim Rubinstein in HCJ 8091/14, *HaMoked: Center for the Defense of the Individual et al. v. Minister of Defense et al.* (unreported). Unofficial translation available on the HaMoked website, http://www.hamoked.org/files/2014/1159007_eng.pdf (accessed November 4, 2016), para. 16.

55. HCJ 9353/08, *Hisham Abu Dheim et al. v. GOC Home Front Command*, TakSC 2009 (1): 85 (2009), p. 91. Unofficial translation available on the HaMoked website, http://www.hamoked.org/items/110991_eng.pdf (accessed November 4, 2016). My emphasis.

56. In the early days of the First Intifada, for instance, Israel demolished the homes of members of the "shock committees" set up in the Occupied Territories and accused of beating Israeli collaborators or violent public disturbances. See HCJ 610/89, *Ibrahim Muhammad Saleh Bahri v. IDF Commander*, IsrSC 44 (1): 92 (1989); HCJ 723/89, *Hassan Shehadeh Salem Abu Daqa v. IDF Commander*, TakSC 89 (3): 147 (1989).

57. See HCJ 2722/92, *al-'Imrin v. Military Commander of the Gaza Strip*, IsrSC 46 (3): 693, para. 15.

58. Interview with the author, November 10, 2015.

59. HCJ 7733/04 *Mahmud Ali Nasser et al. v. the IDF commander of the West Bank*, reported in Nevo (June 20, 2005). For more on the IDF committee, see footnote on page 396.

60. HCJ 4597/14, *'Awawdeh et al. v. West Bank Military Commander*, reported in Nevo (July 1, 2014), para. 15. Unofficial translation available on the HaMoked website, http://www.hamoked.org/images/1158437_eng.pdf (accessed November 4, 2016).

61. Ibid., para. 19. See further examples, "the power is an administrative power and its use is meant to deter, and in so doing, maintain public order." HCJ 798/89, *Mahmoud Hussein Mahmoud Shukri v. Minister of Defense*, TakSC 90 (1): 75 (January 10, 1990). See also, e.g., HCJ 6026/94, *Nazal v. IDF Commander in the Judea and Samaria Area*, IsrSC 48 (5): 338 (November 17, 1994), p. 348; HCJ 2418/97, *Abu Fara v. Major General Uzi Dayan*, IsrSC 51 (1): 226, para. 3; HCJ 8091/14 (HaMoked), para. 17 of the opinion of Justice Rubinstein and the many references therein.

62. HCJ 434/79.

63. Together with my office associates at the time, lawyers Roni Pelli and Noa Amrami.

64. English translation of the petition available on the HaMoked website, http://www.hamoked.org/files/2014/1159000_eng.pdf (accessed November 10, 2016).

65. Yuval Shani, Mordechai Kremnitzer, Orna Ben Naftali, and Guy Harpaz. Opinion available on HaMoked's website, http://www.hamoked.org/Document.aspx?dID=Documents2512 (accessed November 25, 2016).

66. HCJ 5290/14, *Qawasmeh et al. v. Military Commander of the West Bank Area*, TakSC 2014 (3): 6620 (2014). Unofficial translation available on the HaMoked website, http://www.hamoked.org/files/2014/1158616_eng.pdf (accessed November 4, 2016).

67. HCJ 8091/14, *HaMoked: Center for the Defense of the Individual et al. v. Minister of Defense et al.*, reported in Nevo (December 31, 2014). Unofficial translation available on the HaMoked website, http://www.hamoked.org/files/2014/1159007_eng.pdf (accessed November 4, 2016); HCJ 4597/14 and HCJ 5290/14; Justice Rubinstein, para. 16; remarks of Justice Hayut in the opening paragraphs of her opinion.

68. Ibid., opinion of Justice Hayut.

69. Michael Sfard, "The Curse of the HCJ: Personal Responsibility for Collective Punishment," *Mivzeky He'Arot Psika* 15 (January 2016).

70. HCJFH 360/15, *HaMoked et al. v. Minister of Defense et al.*, reported in Nevo (November 12, 2015). Unofficial translation available on the HaMoked website, http://www.hamoked.org/files/2015/1159125_eng.pdf (accessed November 12, 2016); Justice Shoham in HCJ 7220/15, *'Aliwa et al. v. Commander of IDF Forces in the West Bank* (reported in Nevo, December 1, 2015). Unofficial translation available on the HaMoked website, http://www.hamoked.org/files/2015/1159935_eng .pdf (accessed November 12, 2016); Justice Zylbertal in HCJ 8150/15, *Abu Jamal et al. v. GOC Home Front Command*, reported in Nevo (December 22, 2015), para. 17. Unofficial translation available on the HaMoked website, http://www.hamoked .org/files/2015/1160003_eng.pdf (accessed November 4, 2016); Justice Barak-Erez in HCJ 8567/15, *Halabi et al. v. Commander of IDF Forces in the West Bank*, reported in Nevo (December 28, 2015), para. 1 of her judgment. Unofficial translation available on the HaMoked website, http://www.hamoked.org/files/2015/1159919_eng .pdf (accessed November 4, 2016); and Justice Vogelman in HCJ 5839/15, *Sidr v. IDF Commander of the West Bank*, reported in Nevo (October 15, 2015), para. 6 of his opinion. Unofficial translation available on the HaMoked website, http://www .hamoked.org/files/2015/5839_15.pdf (accessed November 4, 2016).

71. A stark example of this is the reasoning for applying discriminatory norms given by South African justices who presided during, apartheid. For an interesting study on the subject, see David Dyzenhaus, *Judging the Judges, Judging Ourselves: Truth, Reconciliation and the Apartheid Legal Order* (Oxford: Hart Publishing, 1998); Robert M. Cover, *Justice Accused: Antislavery and the Judicial Process* (New Haven, CT: Yale University Press, 1975).

72. HCJ 8091/14, paras. 4 and 21 of the opinion of Justice Sohlberg.

73. HCJFH 360/15.

74. HCJ 5839/15, opinion of Justice Vogelman, para. 6.

75. HCJ 7220/15, *'Aliwa et al. v. Commander of IDF Forces in the West Bank*, para. 17 reported in Nevo (2015), para. 3 of the judgment of Justice Mazuz. Unofficial translation available on the HaMoked website, http://www.hamoked.org/files/2015 /1159935_eng.pdf (accessed November 4, 2016).

76. HCJ 8150/15, *Abu Jamal et al. v. GOC Home Front Command.*

77. HCJFH 360/15; HCJFH 2624/16, *Masudi et al. v. Commander of IDF Forces in the West Bank* (decision March 31, 2016). Unofficial translation available on the HaMoked website, http://www.hamoked.org/files/2016/1160399_eng.pdf (accessed November 4, 2016); HCJ 2828/16, *Abu Zeid et al. v. Commander of the Military Forces in the West Bank et al.* (decision May 2, 2016). Unofficial translation available on the HaMoked website, http://www.hamoked.org/files/2016 /1160463_eng.pdf (accessed November 4, 2016). According to the law, the panel itself may decide to add members, but this power is rarely used and it is only available after deliberations begin, not ahead of time (Sec. 26 (2) of the Court Law [incorporated version] 5734–1984). An attempt to use this power also failed, HCJ 1336/16, *Atrash et al. v. GOC Home Front Command* (decision March 29, 2016).

78. "MK Moti Yogev: Supreme Court Justice Uzi Vogelman Has Sided with the Enemy," *Ynet*, October 22, 2015 (Hebrew).

79. "Following Online Attacks, Supreme Court Justice Vogelman Gets Security Detail," *Haaretz*, October 25, 2015 (Hebrew).

80. With the exception of one case from 1993, in which the High Court revoked a demolition order, replacing it with partial demolition, HCJ 5510/92, *Turqman v. Minister of Defense.*

81. In a shooting attack on June 29, Malachi Rosenberg was murdered and three others were injured.

82. HCJ 7040/15, *Hamed v. Military Commander of the West Bank*, reported in Nevo (November 12, 2015).

83. HCJ 6745/15, *Abu Hashiyeh et al. v. Military Commander of the West Bank*, reported in Nevo (December 1, 2015). Unofficial translation available on the HaMoked website, http://www.hamoked.org/files/2015/HCJ%206754_15_judgment.pdf (accessed November 4, 2016).

84. HCJ 1125/16, *Hamed Mar'I et al. v. Military Commander of the West Bank*, reported in Nevo (March 31, 2016). Unofficial translation available on the HaMoked website, http://www.hamoked.org/files/2015/HCJ%206754_15_judgment.pdf (accessed November 4, 2016).

85. HCJ 1336/16, *Atrash et al. v. GOC Home Front Command*, reported in Nevo (April 3, 2016). Unofficial translation available on the HaMoked website, http://www.hamoked.org/files/2016/1336_16_eng.pdf (accessed August 11, 2017).

86. HCJ 1638/16, *Muna Sayah v. IDF Commander*, reported in Nevo (September 27, 2016).

87. Dissents given in HCJ 5844/15, *Hashlamun* (Vogelman), HCJ 7220/15, *'Aliwa* (Mauz), HCJ 8150/15, *Abu Jamal* (Mazuz); HCJ 1014/16, *Skafi* (Zylbertal); HCJ 1630/16, *Masudi* (Mazuz); HCJ 1938/16, *Abu a-Rob*, HCJ 1999/16, *Nassar*, HCJ 2002/16, *Kamil* (Joubran); HCJ 1721/16, *Dwayat* (Vogelman), HCJ 1629/16, *'Amer* (Baron).

88. HaMoked website, http://www.hamoked.org/Document.aspx?dID=Updates1783 (accessed November 4, 2016).

89. Interview with the author on June 25, 2015.

90. "Cobra Helicopter Liquidates Top Tanzeem Member," *Globes*, November 11, 2000 (Hebrew).

91. "Barak: Anyone Who Hurts Us Gets Hurt," *Ynet*, November 11, 2000, http://www.ynet.co.il/articles/0,7340,L-244129,00.html (accessed November 4, 2016) (Hebrew). The IDF spokesperson issued the following release the day after the incident: "During an operation initiated by the IDF in the area of the village of Beit Sahur this morning, an air force helicopter fired missiles toward the vehicle of a senior operative of Fatah-Tanzeem. The pilots reported exact hit on the target. The operative was killed and his lieutenant, who was with him, was injured . . . the Fatah operative is Hussein Abayat, resident of Bethlehem, suspected of planning and executing multiple shooting attacks against security forces, the neighborhood of Gilo and Rachel's Tomb."

92. Fatalities before Operation "Cast Lead," B'Tselem website, http://www.btselem.org/statistics/fatalities/before-cast-lead/by-date-of-event (accessed November 4, 2016).

93. These defenses are stipulated in Israeli law in sections 34 (j) and 34 (k) of the Penal Code 5737–1977. Though self-defense and necessity do apply to protecting property as well, international law stipulates that a threat to life is acceptable only when attempting to deflect a threat to life. See "Basic Principles on the Use of Force and Firearms by Law Enforcement Officials" (adopted by the Eighth UN Congress on the Prevention of Crime and the Treatment of Offenders, Havana, Cuba, August 27 to September 7, 1990), Art. 9.

94. CrimA 4765/98, *Nidal abu Saadeh v. State of Israel*, TakSC 99 (1): 1380 (1999).

95. Renata Capella and Michael Sfard, "The Assassination Policy of the State of Israel" (Public Committee Against Torture in Israel and Law: Palestinian Society for the Protection of Human Rights and the Environment, 2002).

96. Convention (IV) Respecting the Laws and Customs of War on Land and its annex: Regulations Concerning the Laws and Customs of War on Land. The Hague, October 18, 1907, Regulation 1; Art. 13, shared by the First and Second Geneva Conventions; Art. 4 of the Third Geneva Convention. The definition of civilian is negative (anyone who is not a combatant); and Art. 50 (1) of the First Additional Protocol to the Geneva Conventions.

97. The names of these resistance organizations speak to their self-perception as military organizations, the Defense (the Haganah), the National Military Organization (known as Etzel or the Irgun), and Freedom Fighters of Israel (known as Lehi).

98. Additional Protocol (I) to the Geneva Conventions (June 8, 1977), Art. 51 (3).

99. The official commentary of the ICRC on this article determines this. Y. Sandoz, C. Swinarski, and B. Zimmermann, eds., *Commentary on the Additional Protocols* (The Hague: Martinus Nijhoff, 1987), pp. 618–19.

100. HCJ 769/02, *Public Committee Against Torture in Israel et al. v. Government of Israel* (petition filed January 24, 2002).

101. HCJ 5872/01, *MK Muhammad Barakeh v. Prime Minister et al.*, IsrSC 56 (3): 1.

102. HCJ 769/02, *Public Committee Against Torture in Israel et al. v. Government of Israel*, Supplementary Summations on Behalf of the State (January 26, 2004), p. 1 (Hebrew).

103. "Salah Shehadeh Killed with 15 Other Civilians," *Ynet*, July 23, 2000, http://www.ynet.co.il/articles/0,7340,L-2015833,00.html (accessed November 4, 2016) (Hebrew).

104. The commander of the Israel Air Force at the time, Major General Dan Halutz, spoke about Shehadeh's killing in an interview to *Haaretz*. Halutz said he slept very well at night, and when asked how a pilot feels when he drops a bomb that may kill children, he replied, "A slight bump on the aircraft when the bomb is released. It goes away after one second. That's it." (Vered Levy Barzilay, "The High and Mighty," *Haaretz* weekend supplement, August 24, 2002.) An English version of the story is available online, though it does not contain the statement about the bump on the aircraft: http://www.haaretz.com/the-high-and-the-mighty-1.36291 (accessed November 4, 2016). After the incident and the remarks made by the commander of the air force, Feldman and I litigated a case meant to prevent Halutz's appointment first as deputy chief of staff, then as chief of staff (HCJ 5757/04, *Yoav Hass et 30 al. v. Military Advocate General et al.*, reported in Nevo). We also litigated a case demanding a criminal investigation of the incident (HCJ 8794/03, *Yoav Hass et al. v. Military Advocate General*, reported in Nevo). The first petition was dismissed after Halutz clarified his statements in writing, and the court criticized them. The second petition was dismissed given the state's consent to have former security officials conduct a noncriminal inquiry, to which the petitioners objected. Halutz was ultimately appointed chief of staff, and the inquiry that was conducted concluded strangely that the serious outcome of the assassination that was carried out in the heart of a residential neighborhood was a result of lack of intelligence regarding the presence of civilians in Shehadeh's vicinity. No legal action was taken against anyone involved in the assassination.

105. Motion for interim order was dismissed several times, HCJ 769/02, decisions August 19, 2002; September 22, 2002; and July 8, 2003 (unreported).

106. Though Deputy President Theodor Orr initially dismissed the request to join (HCJ 769/02, *Public Committee Against Torture in Israel et al. v. Government of Israel*,

IsrSC 57 (6) 285 [decision September 3, 2003]), but in the judgment the court ultimately decided to let them join.

107. HCJ 769/02, *Public Committee Against Torture in Israel et al. v. Government of Israel*,
IsrSC 62 (1): 5070. English translation available on the High Court website, http://
elyon1.court.gov.il/files_eng/02/690/007/a34/02007690.a34.pdf.

108. Ibid., paras. 27–28.

109. Ibid., para. 61.

110. On the definition of combatants and civilians, see note 96.

111. HCJ 769/02, paras. 35–37.

112. "[A] civilian who has joined a terrorist organization which has become his 'home,'
and in the framework of his role in that organization he commits a chain of hostilities, with short periods of rest between them, loses his immunity from attack
'for such time' as he is committing the chain of acts. Indeed, regarding such a civilian, the rest between hostilities is nothing other than preparation for the next hostility" (ibid., para. 39).

113. Ibid., para. 40.

114. Ibid., opinion of Justice Rivlin, para. 2.

115. Ibid., opinion of President Barak, para. 40.

116. Ibid., para. 64.

117. http://www.btselem.org/statistics/fatalities/after-cast-lead/by-date-of-event
(accessed November 4, 2016).

CONCLUSION: SANDING THE SLOPE

1. Jules Lobel, *Success Without Victory: Lost Legal Battles and the Long Road to Justice
in America* (New York: New York University Press, 2003).

2. Ibid., p. 7.

3. *Brown v. Board of Education of Topeka*, 347 U.S. 483 (1954).

4. For information about the history of the case, see, e.g., Michael Klarman, *Brown v.
Board of Education and the Civil Rights Movement* (New York: Oxford University
Press, 2007), p. 55.

5. *Obergefell v. Hodges*, 576 U.S. (2015).

6. Klarman, *Brown v. Board of Education and the Civil Rights Movement*, chapter 7
(pp. 149–74); see also Yuval Elbashan, *The Lawyers of the Oppressed: The Law as a
Tool for Social Change* (Tel Aviv: Yedioth Ahronoth and Sifrei Hemed, 2014),
pp. 69–75 (Hebrew).

7. Ibid. This is Gerald Rosenberg's main thesis in his important book, Gerald N.
Rosenberg, *The Hollow Hope: Can Courts Bring About Social Change?*, 2nd ed.
(Chicago: University of Chicago Press, 2008).

8. Klarman, *Brown v. Board of Education and the Civil Rights Movement*, chapter 7,
presents a complex position whereby *Brown* did cause a strong backlash and radi-
calization in the southern states but, on the other hand, galvanized the antisegre-
gation camp and played a critical role on the way to the Civil Rights Act that
prohibited it (pp. 212, 221).

9. See Professor Kretzmer's analysis of the nature of courts that adjudicate in external conflict: Kretzmer, *The Occupation of Justice*, p. 191.

10. Ibid., pp. 189–91.

11. One example is the petitions filed by HaMoked: Center for the Defense of the Individual on behalf of Palestinians who are denied travel abroad from the West Bank.

In certain years, 75 percent of the petitions ended without a hearing, after the authorities retracted the travel ban. Research undertaken by ACRI in 2008 regarding the outcomes of its occupation court cases between 1985 and 2004 showed that 45 percent of the cases ended in a settlement, or with the opposing party backing down: Mark Wisman, *ACRI's Work in the Occupied Territories: Research and Evaluation* (litigation), 2008 (Hebrew). Particularly high numbers were observed in a study of actions brought by ACRI and HaMoked from 1989 to 1995: 69 percent and 89 percent of the petitions filed by the organizations, respectively, culminated with relief without a judgment (though, in this particular study, not all ACRI cases considered were related to the OPT): Yoav Dotan and Menachem Hofnung, "Interest Groups in the Israeli High Court of Justice: Measuring Success in Litigation and in Out-of-Court Settlements," *Law and Policy* 23, no. 1 (January 2001): 18.

12. Michael Sfard, "The Price of Internal Legal Opposition to Human Rights Abuses," *Journal of Human Rights* 1, no. 1 (March 2009): 37.

13. ACRI's research, which supported the conclusion that legal proceedings have a mitigating effect on policy, also went up only to 2004; see Wisman, *ACRI's Work in the Occupied Territories.*

14. For a similar conclusion, see Jessica Montell, *Learning from What Works: Strategic Analysis of the Achievements of the Israel-Palestine Human Rights Community* (Swedish International Development Cooperation Agency, 2015), p. 20.

15. HCJ 4481/91, *Bargil v. Government of Israel* (Judgment o August 25, 1993), IsrLR 158 (official English translation), p. 5.

16. South African Supreme Court justices Smalberger, Howie, Marais, Scott submission to the truth and reconciliation commission, p. 9; quoted in Dyzenhaus, *Judging the Judges, Judging Ourselves*, p. 58.

17. For a similar analysis that the court's willingness to intervene in security matters is inversely proportional to the risk that there would be a link (real or perceived) between its ruling and the materialization of the security risk the state cites as grounds for the legality of its action, see Kretzmer, *The Occupation of Justice.*

18. For the United States, see Lobel, *Success Without Victory*, pp. 264–69, and the introduction, pp. 1–9; for South Africa, see Richard Abel's enthralling research about the legal fight against apartheid from the late 1970s to the early 1990s: Richard Abel, *Politics by Other Means: Law in the Struggle Against Apartheid, 1980–1994* (New York: Routledge, 1995), p. 549: "The legal battles described in this book did not win the war by themselves. But they empowered the masses while offering some protection from state retaliation. They strengthened the commitment of the anti-apartheid movement to legality . . . they forged one of the few bonds across racial lines."

19. In her study, Jessica Montell asserts that in Israel, litigation contributed to every achievement made by the human rights community with respect to policies used in the OPT: Montell, *Learning from What Works*, p. 20.

20. *Sunday Tribune*, March 27, 1983.

21. Raymond Wacks, "Judges and Injustice," *South African Law Journal* 101 (1984): 266.

22. John Dugard, "Should Judges Resign? A Reply to Professor Wacks," *South African Law Journal* 101 (1984): 286.

23. Dugard, in ibid., quoting an article by Raja Shehadeh, founder of Palestinian human rights NGO Al-Haq: Raja Shehadeh, *The West Bank and the Rule of Law* (New York: International Commission of Jurists, 1980), p. 45.

24. Wacks, "Judges and Injustice," pp. 282–83.
25. Wisman, *ACRI's Work in the Occupied Territories*; Montell, *Learning from What Works.* It is worth noting that these studies considered extended periods (each covered two decades) but did not examine whether there is a trend toward increased or decreased chances of obtaining remedy over time.
26. Some prominent examples include: The dismissal of the petition regarding the constitutionality of the "Nakba Law," which imposed sanctions on entities that mark Israel's Independence Day as the day of the Palestinian catastrophe—a law that mainly impinges on the political freedom of Israel's Palestinian citizens (HCJ 3429/11, *Haifa Orthodox High School Alumni et al. v. Minister of Finance and the Knesset*, TakSC 2012 [1]: 245) (the petition was dismissed based on the "ripeness" doctrine and on the grounds that the issue has not generated a sufficient factual basis to be ready for judicial resolution); the dismissal of a petition to repeal a law that allowed admission boards in small communities in the Negev and Galilee regions to reject applicants for residency because they were deemed not to fit the community "socially" or "culturally"—which was considered a tool for screening out minority groups, primarily Arabs (HCJ 2311/11, 2504/11, *Uri Sabah et al. v. Knesset et al.*, TakDin 2014 [3] 11844—this petition was also dismissed on the grounds that it was not "ripe" for ruling); the dismissal of a petition against a law that imposed administrative sanctions on parties that publicly call for an economic, cultural, or academic boycott, including on the settlements, and instituted this as an actionable tort (HCJ 5239/11, 5392/11, 5549/11, 2072/12, *Uri Avneri et al. v. Knesset et al.*, TakSC 2015 [2]: 1920) (the law was declared to be constitutional, while omitting the section that allowed for compensation without proof of damage, which had been struck down).
27. "Address and Reply on the Presentation of a Testimonial to S. P. Chase by the Colored People of Cincinnati," reprinted in Paul Finkelman, ed., *Fugitive Slaves and American Courts*, vol. 1 (New York: Garland, 1988), p. 252.

ACKNOWLEDGMENTS

This book could not have been written without the help of many people.

First, I would like to thank all those who agreed to be interviewed and share their memories and insights with me: attorneys Muhammed Dahleh, Elias Khoury, Felicia Langer, Tamar Peleg-Sryck, Andre Rosenthal, Raja Shehadeh, Leah Tzemel, and Dan Yakir, as well as Hannah Friedman.

A special thank you to my mentor and friend Avigdor Feldman, whom I interviewed for this book but in fact have been interviewing constantly for years.

I am grateful for the help I received from attorneys Yehudit Karp, Joshua Shoffman, Sliman Shahin, and Michael Ben-Yair; Professor David Kretzmer; Brigadier General Ilan Paz, Ret, and Yoar Rosenberg, who helped me with research.

Friends and colleagues who agreed to read parts of the manuscript gave useful and enriching comments. Thanks to Professor Orna Ben-Naftali, Dr. Ron Dudai, Professor Guy Harpaz, attorney Shlomy Zachary, Lior Yavne, Dr. Limor Yehuda, Professor Jules Lobel, architect Alon Cohen-Lifshitz, Hagit Ofran, Dr. Amir Paz-Fuchs, and attorney Neta Patrick.

My faithful first readers, my spouse, Nirith, and my father, Leon, accompanied the writing process daily; their critical reading sharpened and improved the book.

My thanks also extend to my exquisite translator, Maya Johnston, who not only masterfully translated my words but was also a wonderful reader, the kind that every author aspires to have; to Shai Efrati, who patiently and creatively drew the maps; to the staff of the Open Society Fellowship program, particularly Stephen Hubbell, who granted the resources and supportive environment for research and writing; and to the team at Metropolitan Books, especially my editor, Riva Hocherman, whose deep insights, sensitive and clear thinking, and delicate Sisyphean weeding of my text brought it to a level it would never have reached without her. I thank fate (and Stephen Hubbell) every day for introducing me to Riva.

I am also grateful to each and every member of my office staff through-out the years, all wonderful people filled with a sense of mission—I have had the privilege of teaching them and the pleasure of learning from them. To the office team who kept the flame burning while I was away, busy with this project, my special thanks: attorneys Emily Schaeffer Omer-Man, Michal Pasovsky, Moria Shlomot, Sofia Brodsky, Karin Torn-Hibler, and our office manager, Yuval Yekutiel.

Finally, thank you to my sister, Emi, whose friendship is one of my greatest assets.

INDEX

Page numbers in *italics* refer to maps.

ABOUT THE AUTHOR

Michael Sfard is one of Israel's leading human rights lawyers. A former conscientious objector, he received the Emil Grunzweig Human Rights Award and an Open Society Fellowship. His writing on human rights has appeared in *The New York Times*, *Haaretz*, *The Independent*, and *Foreign Policy*. He lives in Tel Aviv.